# Small Business Management

## An Entrepreneur's Guide to Success

SECOND EDITION

# Small Business Management

## An Entrepreneur's Guide to Success

SECOND EDITION

William L. Megginson
UNIVERSITY OF GEORGIA

Mary Jane Byrd
UNIVERSITY OF MOBILE

Charles R. Scott, Jr.
UNIVERSITY OF ALABAMA

Leon C. Megginson
UNIVERSITY OF MOBILE

Irwin
McGraw-Hill

Boston, Massachusetts   Burr Ridge, Illinios   Dubuque, Iowa
Madison, Wisconsin   New York, New York   San Francisco, California   St. Louis, Missouri

*Dedicated to our spouses—*

*Peggy, Jerry, Addie, and Joclaire*

**Irwin/McGraw-Hill**

*A Division of The* ***McGraw-Hill*** *Companies*



**Irwin Book Team**
Publisher: *Rob Zwettler*
Executive editor: *Craig S. Beytien*
Editorial assistant: *Kimberly Kanakes*
Marketing manager: *Michael Campbell*
Project supervisor: *Lynne Basler*
Production supervisor: *Pat Frederickson*
Coordinator, Graphics and Desktop Services: *Keri Johnson*
Assistant manager, desktop services: *Jon Christopher*
Compositor: *Carlisle Communications, Ltd.*
Typeface: *10/12 Palatino*
Printer: *Times Mirror Higher Education Group, Inc. Print Group*

**Library of Congress Cataloging-in-Publication Data**

Small business management : an entrepreneur's guide to success /
William L. Megginson . . . [et al.]. — 2nd ed.
p. cm.
Includes index.
ISBN 0-256-21893-5
1. Small business—Management. 2. Small business—Management—
Case studies. I. Megginson, William L.
HD62.7.S5943 1997
658.02'2—dc20 96–7836

*Printed in the United States of America*
3 4 5 6 7 8 9 0 WCB 3 2 1 0 9 8 7

# PREFACE

This is an exciting and stimulating time to be involved in small business—either as an owner or as a student interested in becoming one. Events since the publication of the first edition of *Small Business Management: An Entrepreneur's Guide to Success* have drastically changed the environment in which entrepreneurs and small business owners operate.

While operating any business—small *or* large—is now more complex and challenging, it also provides a more creative, interesting, and rewarding experience. Current events indicate that the last few years of this Twentieth Century will present even more stimulating, challenging, and rewarding—but frustrating—opportunities to those millions of intrepid men and women who own and/or manage these essential enterprises.

But success will require commitment, desire, knowledge, and hard work on your part—plus a certain amount of luck!

## To the Student

This Second Edition of *Small Business Management: An Entrepreneur's Guide to Success*—like the First Edition—takes a practical, down-to-earth approach to planning, organizing, and managing a small business. While based on current research, theory, and practice, the material is presented from a "how-to" perspective, with many practical examples and applications from the business world. In fact, all four authors have had meaningful experience in the "real world" as an owner, manager, or employee of a small business.

The material explores the role of small business and its growing importance. It also discusses the reasons for and against owning such firms and stresses up-to-date thinking in preparing, starting, organizing, and operating a small business. It explains how to achieve optimum benefits from the limited resources available to small firms and how to plan for growth and succession.

### Organization of the Book

Part I, The Challenge of Owning and Managing a Small Business, explains the important role of small business, the characteristics of entrepreneurs and small business owners, reasons why you should or should not own a small business, some current opportunities and challenges in small business, and the legal forms you can choose for your business.

Part II, Planning for and Organizing a Business, discusses how to become the owner of a small business, how to do strategic and operational planning, the growing opportunities in franchising, how to prepare and present a winning business plan—along with a Sample Business Plan, and obtaining the right financing for your business.

Part III, Marketing Goods and Services, discusses how to develop marketing strategies for producing a product; selling and distributing it; and doing global marketing, marketing research, and other related activities.

Part IV, Organizing and Managing the Business, explains the important role played by human resources in a business. It also discusses how to recruit, select, train, and compensate adequate and competent human resources. Students are encouraged to learn how to communicate with, motivate, and maintain favorable relationships with employees—and their union—when one is involved.

Part V, Operating the Business, deals with such operating factors as locating and laying out facilities, purchasing and maintaining inventory, and assuring quality control.

Part VI, Financial Planning and Control, explains how to plan for profit; how to budget and control operations; and how to deal with taxes, estate planning, and record keeping. Finally, much new information is provided concerning the use of computer technology and management information systems to do these things more effectively.

Part VII, Providing Present and Future Security for the Business, tells how to use insurance and crime prevention for better risk management; how to deal with laws, social responsibility, and business ethics; and how to plan for the future—including more on tax and estate planning.

## Aids to Learning

Each chapter begins with relevant, thought-provoking quotations, along with numbered Learning Objectives that set the stage for what should be learned from the chapter. These are then coordinated with the chapter summary. A Profile, which describes how an actual business or business owner operates, is related to the subject of the chapter.

The text—written for the TV and computer generation—provides many interesting visuals such as photos, tables, figures, charts, checklists, and cartoons, along with real-life examples that illustrate the concepts being discussed. Each chapter also includes at least one box entitled "Using Technology to Succeed," which explains how to use related technology to improve operations. Important words or phrases that are defined in the chapter are boldfaced in the text for easy recognition and then defined in the margin.

End-of-chapter features are a summary—called "What You Should Have Learned"—which is coordinated with the numbered Learning Objectives to help you review the text material; questions to test mastery of the chapter; one or two cases for you to analyze; a short case to show how to apply the material learned; and an activity to stimulate your creative processes—and hopefully—prove interesting to you.

We hope this material will attract—and/or expand—your interest in small business. We also hope you will identify with the individuals profiled in the text and cases and through them and their experiences learn to be a better owner or manager of a small firm.

## To the Instructor

You, the instructor, will find this second edition of *Small Business Management: An Entrepreneur's Guide to Success* easy and interesting to teach from. One reason for that statement is because there are so many interesting features to the text.

The strengths of this text include simple, clear, and concise conversational writing style, numerous visuals, and the use of examples to reinforce the basic concepts being presented. The prevailing topics of interest to small business owners, such as diversity, global issues, improving and expanding quality, franchising, computer operations—including the Internet and its "mind-boggling" implications for business, as well as society—taxes and government regulations, estate planning, ethics and social responsibility, preparing and presenting a meaningful business plan, risk management, and—of course—how to plan for and make a profit, have been included in sufficient depth to be meaningful to you and your students. We have included Learning Objectives, a Profile, and at least one box on Using Technology to Succeed in each chapter, along with a summary of what you should have learned, questions, and at least one "real-world" case. Some chapters have appendixes to help explain or expand on the text material.

Each chapter begins with philosophical, thought-provoking quotations to pique students' interest in the main thoughts being presented in the chapter. These quotes are followed by numbered behavioral Learning Objectives that prepare readers for what they should learn from the chapter. These objectives are then coordinated with the chapter summary, called What You Should Have Learned. The learning objectives are followed by a Profile, which is a close-up view of a small business and its owner(s) or manager(s). For the most part, the Profiles feature actual business situations and events in small firms. This Profile provides the tone for the chapter and focuses students' attention on the main thoughts being presented as they read the balance of the material.

Each chapter contains many types of visuals, including photographs, figures, tables, and—where appropriate—cartoons. Examples, illustrations, and real-life vignettes are set off from the body of the text in a different font to help students see how the material they are learning has applied to actual small business situations. The most important words and/or phrases defined in the text are boldfaced for easy recognition and the definitions are then repeated in the margin. Endnotes are used to give authority to, and cite the sources of, the material used so that readers can get further information if desired. They are grouped at the end of the book, however, to prevent "clutter" on the text page.

Several end-of-chapter features should aid learning. For example, chapter summaries, called "What You Should Have Learned," are coordinated with the numbered Learning Objectives to provide a basis for better review of the material. Short-answer and discussion-type review questions can be used for student assignments, class discussion, or quizzes. Finally, a case, application, and activity are provided to help students analyze the text material from the point of view of real-world situations.

## Important Current Issues Facing Small Business People

We have included topics about which small business owners and managers tend to be concerned. These include taxes and their payment, business laws, social responsibility, and managerial ethics. Also, topics such as marketing, particularly global marketing; developing and presenting a business plans; and use of computer technology have been included.

Next, the discussions of location and purchasing, with an orientation toward retailing and services, is included. The expanding roles of small businesses, franchising, diverse groups, and sources of financing are covered from a practical, applications-oriented point of view. Finally, the functional areas are covered from a small business perspective. These features make this an excellent, up-to-date teaching tool, relevant to today's changing environments.

An innovative feature is the *Workbook for Developing a Successful Business Plan,* which provides a hands-on guide for use in developing an actual business plan. This is in addition to the Sample Business Plan, which is an appendix to Chapter 8. In addition, each text comes with its own CD—ROM *Multimedia MBA,* from Compact Publishing, Inc. This should help you learn from other people's mistakes and develop a winning business strategy—in an enjoyable multimedia format.

## Acknowledgments

Our thanks go to those who contributed suggestions, cases, profiles, and examples to the text. Our recognition is shown by the sources at the end of each case and Profile. Thanks are also due for the many contributions made by teachers, entrepreneurs, managers, professional people, and members of the North American Case Research Association.

Our special thanks go to Dr. Walter H. Hollingsworth, of the University of Mobile, and to Dr. Charles E. Scott, Loyola College in Maryland, for their expert contributions to the computer technology and management information systems areas.

We also appreciate the research and writing contributions of Jay and Ragan Megginson. In addition, Janet Wharton made significant and serious contributions with her end-of-chapter games and puzzles.

Comments and contributions from colleagues around the country and the following reviewers were most helpful.

Paul J. Londrigan, *Charles Mott Community College*
Barry Ashmen, *Bucks County Community College*
William Motz, *Lansing Community College*
Kathy Daruty, *Los Angeles Pierce College*

We'd also like to thank the following colleagues for their response to the survey we sent out:

Mainuddin Afza, Bloomsburg University
Sol Ahriarah, SUNY at Buffalo
Robert Alclair, Providence College
Susan Alvey, Endicott College
John Anderson, Saginaw Valley State College
J. Richard Anderson, Stonehill College
Robert Anservitz, Mercer College
Peter Antuniou, Maric College-Vista Campus
Joe Anway, Longview Community College
Charles Armstrong, Kansas City Community College
Barry Ashman, Burtis County Community College
Chandler Atkins, Adirondack Community College
Ed Atzenhofer, Clark State College
Michael Avery, Stetson University
Marsha Bagley, Iowa Wesleyan
L. G. Bailey, San Antonio College

Richard Baker, Mohave Community College
Lee Baldwin, University of Mary Hardin–Baylor
Richard E. Bawin, Cedarville College
Josephine Bazan, Holyoke Community College
Amy Beattie, Champlain College
Herb Beadles, Otero Junior College
Robert Beaudry, Hesser College
Ismael Betancourt, York College–City College of New York
Richard Bevan, Kodiak College
Bonnie Bolinger, Ivy Tech State College
Alfred Bourassa, Community College of Vermont
Ernest Bourgeois, Castleton State College
Dan Bowen, Dalton College
Charles Bowles, Regis University at Colorado Springs
Kevin Boyd, Kansas Wesleyan University
James Boyle, Glendale College
Martin Bressler, Thomas College
John Britton, Salve Regina University
Harvey Bronstein, Oakland Community College
Charles Brown, Tennessee Temple University
Del Brown, Norfolk University
Randall Brown, California State–Stanislaus
Shannon Brown, University of Mobile
William Bullard, University of Hawaii
Albert Bundons, Johnson Community College
Kersaw Burbank, Eastern College
Lyvonne Burlson, Rollins College–Brevard Campus
Carroll Burrell, San Jancinto College–Central
Nancy Burton, SUNY–Cobleskill
John Buss, LeMoyne–Owen College
Shirley Callard–Miramar College
Douglas Campbell, Norwalk Tech Community College
Elizabeth Camerson, Alma College
David Carter, Abilene Christian University
Janet Caruso, Briarcliffe College
Rickey Casey, University of the Ozarks
Chan Sup Chang, Lander University
Bonnie Chavez, Santa Barbara City College
Michael Cicero, Highline Community College
Susan Clinton, Cameron University
Gary Cloutier, Keene State
Gloria Cockerell, Collin County
Paul Cohn, Castleton State
Joe Coley, Defiance College
Ron Cooke, Rider University
Rachna Condos, American River College
Sherry Cook, Life College
Bobbie Corbett, Northern Virginia Community College
William Corsover, Barry University
William Crandall, College of San Mateo
Derek Crews, Anderson Broaddus College
Bruce Cudney, Middlesex Community College
Steve Czarsty, Mary Washington College
Bruce Davis, Weber State University
Joseph Davis, Florida Community College at Jacksonville
Aaron Dean, Ambassador University
Patti DeRosa, Lorain County Community College
Judy Dietert, Southwest Texas State University
Victor DiMatteo, Richard Stockton College
R. Dollinger, Kankakee Area Career Center
Harry Domicone, California Lutheran University
Bonnie Ann Dowd, Palomar College
Robert Dowling, California State University–Dominguez Hills
H. Leroy Drew, Central Maine Tech

Joann Duffy, Sam Houston State University
James Dumville, Chowan College
Marguerite Ehlen, Nassau Community College
Dennis Elbert, University of North Carolina
Clifton Elliot, Williamsburg Tech College
Darcy English, Yakima Valley Community College
W. D. English, University of Mary Hardin-Baylor
Daryl Erdman, University of St. Thomas
Charles Erickson, Carroll College
Susan Everett, Clark State Community College
Ken Faklert, Utah Valley State College
Gregory Fallon, Montanta State University-Northern
N. Paul Fenton, Barry University
Lloyd Fernald, University of Central Florida
Todd Finkle, University of North Carolina at Charlotte
Ed Fitzpatrick, Finger Lakes Community College
Charles Flaherty, University of Minnesota
Tim Folta, University of Kentucky
Nancy Ford, Oklahoma Baptist University
Deborah Freedman, Purdue-North Central
Leatrice Freer, Pittsburgh Community College
Olene Fuller, San Jacinto College–North
Diane Garsomble, University of Wisconsin at Superior
Demetrius Giovas, SWI–El Paso
Steven Goldberg, University of New Haven
James Goss, West Valley College
Cecil Green, Riverside Community College
Patricia Greene, Rutgers University
W. Bill Greenwood, Shepherd College
Glenn Grothous, Merrimac Community College
Jim Gwinn, Caldwell College
Mark Halsey, Eastern College
William Hartley, SUNY-Fredonia
Bernard Hasson, Camar College–Port Arthur
Ron Heiser, Kishwaukee College
William Hemphill, Harding University
Florence Henning, Trumbull Business College
Gary Hensel, Northwestern Business College
Harvey Herslip, Minot State University
Norm Heydoer, Southwestern Florida College of Business
Neil Hilkert, Deleware Valley College
Jay Hollowell, Commonwealth College
Lorene Holmes, Jarvis Christian College
Sandra Honig, Wichita State University
Stephen Horner, Bethany College
James Hovendick, San Jacinto College
Fred Hughes, Faulkner University
Rodney Hurley, Hillsborough Community College
Jamaluddin Hussain, Purdue University–Calumet
Uldis Inveiss, Carroll College
Alan Jackson, Bellevue University
Rolm Jessup, San Jose State University
Jack Johnson, Consumines River College
Lance Johnson, Southeastern Tech
Wyman Johnson, Chaska High School
Jeanne Johnston, Olean Business Institute
Martin Jonas, Berkshire Community College

J. Preston Jones, Nova Southeastern University
James Jones, Del Mar College
Stephen Jones, Michigan Christian College
Richard Judd, University of Illinois at Springfield
Megan Kalina, University of Wisconsin at River Falls
Harriet Kandelman, Barat College
Paul Keaton, University of Wisconsin at Lacrosse
Jim Keefe, Denver Institute of Technology
Michael Kelsey, Northwest Tech
Bruce Kemelgor, University of Louisville
Joseph Kenary, Johns Hopkins
Jim Kennedy, Angencina College
Vern Kinderknecht, Garden City Community College
A. Dale King, Lenoir-Rhyne College
John Kohls, Gonzaga University
Frank Koniges, San Diego Mesa College
Alfred Konuwa, Butte College
David Krueger, Oklahoma City University
Darwin Krumrey, Kirkwood Community College
Kathy Kuecker, National College
Howard Lacey, Concordia University at Austin
Kenneth Lacho, University of New Orleans
Patricia Laidler, Massasoit Community College
Robert Lawes, University of Honolulu–Chaminade
George Lee, Kamiakin College
Richard Lewandowski, University of Akron
Thomas Lloyd, Westmoreland County Community College
Gina Lord, Cosumnes River College
Richard Lowery, Bowie State
Don Lucy, Ursuline College
Norman McElvany, University of Vermont
Jug McKeever, Stevens State Tech
Charles McKinney, Whitworth College
Richard Maglian, Quincy University
Jimmy Manning, Valdustos Technical University
Joseph Manno, Montgomery College
Larry Martin, Iowa Central Community College
Bob Matthews, Oakton Community College
Charles Matthews, University of Cincinnati
Bruce Mathcowitz, Buffalo Lake College–Hector
Michael Matukonis, SUNY-Oneonta
Denise Mazur, Detroit College of Business–Warren
James McDermott, Mount Ida College
Kim Milbrandt, University of Sioux Falls
Thomas Milligan, St. Phillip's College
Monica Montoya, Santa Fe Community College
Robin Moore, Judson College
Robert Morgan, Southeast Community College-Lincoln
J. L Morgan, Mississippi State University
Peter Moutsatson, Montcalm Community College
Celeste Mulvena, Wilmington College
David Murphy, Madisonville Community College
Cal Muth, Florida Institute of Technology
David Nakamaejo, Kapiolani Community College
Robert Nelson, University of Illinois
Janet Nichols, University College, Northeast
Joan Nichols, Emporia State
Loretta Nitschke, Milligan College
Randy Nochols, Harris-Stowe State
Ralph Norico, Lynn University
Peit Nwobodo, Indiana University-East

Martha Ocampo, San Joaquin Delta College
Tony Oretga, California State–Bakersfield
Robert Pacheco, Massapit Community College
George Padgett, Mission High School
Alan Pankratz, Santa Fe Community College
Don Parks, Southwestern University
Linda Parry, University of Minnesota–Duluth
Rob Payne, Shawnee State University
Vince Pennisi, Hudson Valley Community College
Stanley Peters, Southeast Community College
David Peterson, Iowa Lakes Community College
Greg Powell, Southern Utah University
Laura Prosser, National College
Jill Purdy, University of Washington
Richard Randall, Nassau Community College
George Rauth, New Jersey Institute of Technology
Mitchell Redio, Monroe Community College
Craig Reese, St. Thomas University
Gary Reiman, City College of San Francisco
Wallace Ritter, Fullerton College
Elizabeth Robinson, West Liberty State
Edward Rogaff, Baruch College
Bob Roller, Kennesaw State
David Roos, Allen County Community College
F. Rotundo, New York University
William Sackett, Itasca Community College
Joseph Salamone, SUNY-AB
Ehsan Salek, Virginia Wesleyan
Rick Saucier, East Maine Technical College
Jack Schoenfelder, IUY Tech State College
Robert Schutter, Marian College
R. Scully, Barry University
John Setnicky, Xavier University of Louisiana
Michael Sheidy, Northwest Community College
John Shepherd, Gardner Edgerton High School
Alan Siegel, Franklin Institute of Boston
Bruce Siemsen, Colby Community College
Roger Smalley, Southern Illinois University
Sheridan Smith, Southwestern Community College
Thomas Stoll, Ohio State University-ATI
Nancy Storhbusch, Southwestern Wisconsin Technical College
Larry Strain, Lehigh University
Randy Stuart, Hawaii Pacific University
James Swenson, Moorehead State University
Jack Synold, Wausau East
Assad Tavakoli, Fayetteville State
Russel Taylor, College of New Rochelle
Sherrie Taylor, Texas Women's University
Harold Tepool, Vincennes University
Kimberly Thomasson, Kentucky College of Business
Michael Thompson, Delta State University
Thomas Thompson, University of Maryland
Kay Tracy, Gettysburg College
Scott Traxler, Averett College
Craig Tunwall, SUNY Institue of Technology–Utica
A.H. Turley, Ricks College
James Voss, Penn State–Behren
Gloria Walker, Florida Community College
Lee Wallace, Sul Ross University–Rio Grande College
Jeffrey Walls, Indiana Institute of Technology

Darlene Ward, Charlotte High School
William Ward, Sigmund Weis School of Business
Fred Ware, Valdosta University
Steven Warren, Rutgers University
Charles Washington, University of North Carolina
Amanda Watlington, Terra Community College
Randi Waxman, Columbia University College
Jim Wells, DBCC–Main Campus
Dianne Welsh, East Washington University
Ron Weston, Contra Costa College
Mark Weyman, Barry University
Ronald Wharton, University of Minnesota–Duluth
Kathy White, JEL/North Central
Robert Whitehorne, College of William and Mary
David Wiley, Anne Arundel Community College
Dennis Williams, Pennsylvania College of Technology
James Wilson, UT Pan Am
Bob Wiseman, Chabot Community College
Gary Wishniewsky, California State University–Hayward
Joette Wisnieski, Indiana University of Pennsylvania
Tom Wortham, Golden Gate University
Robert Wyatt, Unia University
Raymond Zagorski, University of Naska-Kenai-Peninsula College

It pleases us greatly to give a resounding vote of thanks and praise to our spouses, Peggy Megginson, Jerry Byrd, Addie Scott, and Joclaire Megginson. Their support, suggestions, and patience have lightened our task. In addition, Joclaire Megginson was of tremendous assistance with her computer, phone, printer, and Internet searches. She was the intermediary who took the authors' ideas and converted them into more usable form for Suzanne S. Barnhill's drafting of the final text, which was sent to Irwin.

We have no adequate way of expressing our sincere appreciation to Suzanne, except to say this text would not have been possible without her help in editing, correcting, revising, typing, and proofreading. Her final drafts sent to Irwin were the best we have seen in our years of publishing. In addition, her suggestion—and in some cases drafting—of additional text material was very helpful. Her contributions have been of inestimable value in making the production of this book possible.

Also, thanks go to J. B. Locke, who coordinated the logistics involved in copying and shipping the material to Irwin and acquiring and processing permissions from publishers and people featured in the Profiles and Cases. Also, we thank Jonathan Austin, Heather Bedgood, Holly Paul, Shannon Wynn, Jennifer Garris, and Heather Steward for the assistance they gave us in preparing the text materials, obtaining permissions, and providing other meaningful assistance.

Donna Counselman made a great contribution with her preparation of the Sample Business Plan—with the help of Andrea Bryant. She also did considerable research in the library and elsewhere in order to update the material, as well as to work with Gayle M. Ross in preparing the *Instructor's Manual.*

Gayle made a tremendous contribution by preparing the excellent *Instructor's Manual.* It should materially assist teachers in presenting the text material.

We would also like to thank our supportive colleagues and friends at Richard D. Irwin, Inc.—Michael Campbell, Marketing Manager; Lynne

Basler, Project Editor; Kerry Johnson, Photo Researcher; Bethany Stubbe, Graphics Supervisor; Pat Frederickson, Project Supervisor; Jon Christopher, Pre-Press Buyer; Kimberly Kanakes, Editorial Assistant, who has helped us so very much; and especially Craig Beytien, Executive Editor—for their assistance in helping us produce this Second Edition.

Finally, we would like to thank the following people from the University of Mobile: Dr. Mike Magnoli, President; Dr. Audrey Eubanks, Vice-President for Academic Affairs; and Dr. Anne Lowery, Interim Dean of the School of Business. The J. L. Bedsole Foundation also gave generous support. Without it, we could not have completed this important work.

If we can be of assistance to you in developing your course, please contact any one of us.

**William L. Megginson**
**Mary Jane Byrd**
**Charles R. Scott**
**Leon C. Megginson**

# CONTENTS IN BRIEF

# TABLE OF CONTENTS

# Small Business Management

## An Entrepreneur's Guide to Success

SECOND EDITION

CHAPTER 1

# The Dynamic Role of Small Business

*There are nice problems to have and not so nice problems to have. Right now, [small] business owners tend to have the nice kind of problems.*—William Dennis, senior research fellow at the National Federation of Independent Business's NFIB Foundation

*Small businesses may still fail in prodigious numbers, but the small business owner is clearly a winner—an American folk hero, a source of jobs and growth, a role model, a cultural icon. . . . The entrepreneur has been transformed . . . into a courageous taker of risks.*—Bernard Wysocki, Jr., small business editor, *The Wall Street Journal*

## LEARNING OBJECTIVES

After studying the material in this chapter, you will be able to:

1. Explain why now is an interesting time to study small business.
2. Define the term *small business.*
3. List the unique contributions of small businesses.
4. Describe some current problems small businesses face.
5. Describe some current trends challenging small businesses.

*P R O F I L E*

## FOOD FROM THE 'HOOD: LEARNING THE MORAL AND ETHICAL RESPONSIBILITIES OF BUSINESS

Jaynell Grayson, a junior at Crenshaw High School in Los Angeles, rides three different buses from her grandfather's house in Watts to her new company, Food From the 'Hood, housed in the high school. The company, founded by Grayson and 38 other inner-city teenagers, launched its first product, a bottled salad dressing, in 1993.

The company got its seed (start-up) money from a grant provided by Rebuild LA, the city's riot recovery agency. The company later received help from marketing consultant Norris Bernstein, who read in the newspaper that the kids were unsure how to market their product. Grayson's group first attempted to distribute the dressing by appealing to the Lucky Supermarket where Grayson worked after school. Bernstein then volunteered to teach them the basics of distribution. He also introduced them to key contacts in the packaged goods and supermarket industries.

D

Nearly every supermarket in Southern California has agreed to stock the salad dressing, thanks to the philanthropic nature of the store managers. Obtaining shelf space for the product cleared one major hurdle any new food item must overcome, but now the product will have to stand on its own to win sales and vital market share.

The product has been doing well and seems to stand a good chance of succeeding. An executive at California's largest grocer, which carries the dressing chainwide, says, "We see lots of companies trying to develop new products that don't do half the research that these high school kids did. They've done all the work necessary to introduce a product to the marketplace and develop it into a good business."

What has Food from the 'Hood done with its profits? The student entrepreneurs have followed the examples of those who helped them by donating a quarter of the profits to the needy and putting the rest into a college scholarship fund for the student owners.

*Source:* Adapted from Williams G. Nickels, James M. McHugh, and Susan M. McHugh, *Understanding Business,* 4th ed. (Burr Ridge, IL: Richard D. Irwin, 1996), p. 115.

You have probably never heard of Jaynell Grayson or her company. Neither had we until we started revising the first edition of our popular book about entrepreneurs and small business owners. But you *have* heard of companies such as Wal-Mart, Sears, McDonald's, Dell Computer, Intel, and Microsoft. All of them were started as small businesses by then-unknown entrepreneurs such as Sam Walton, Richard Sears, Michael Dell, Andrew Groves, Ray Kroc, and Bill Gates. By capitalizing on their imagination, initiative, courage, dedication, hard work, and—often—luck, they turned an idea into a small, struggling business that became a large successful one. In fact, Bill Gates is now known as "the richest person in America," worth $13.4 billion.[1]

Now it is your turn to see if you can start (or restart) your career as an entrepreneur—by converting an idea into a small business. According to Joseph Nebesky, who has served as an adviser to the U.S. Agency for International Development, the Small Business Administration, and the National Council on the Aging, these small firms "are the backbone of the American economy, [since they] create two of every three jobs, produce 40 percent of the gross national product [GNP], and invent more than half of the nation's technological innovations."[2] During the last decade, small businesses created 63.6 percent of all new American jobs and accounted for 43 percent of GNP.[3]

## It's an Interesting Time to be Studying Small Business

As you can see, this is an interesting, challenging, and rewarding time to be studying small business, for owning and operating such a firm is one of the best ways to fulfill the "great American dream." Many Americans believe this is one of the best paths to riches in the United States.[4] Apparently this is true, for a study by the U.S. Trust found that nearly 40 percent of the top 1 percent of the wealthiest Americans* got there by building a small business. Table 1–1 shows how they made their money. Every year, around three-quarters of a million Americans turn this dream of owning a business into a reality. And most of these dreams become true success stories.

Q

> For example, a straw poll of those attending a Pasadena, California, IBM Users Group meeting found that a quarter of them had already started part-time small businesses, and another half were "ready to take the plunge."[5]

As an indication of this popularity, a report to the 1995 White House Conference on Small Business concluded that there were about 9 million self-employed Americans. It also estimated that the number would exceed 11.5 million by the year 2005.[6]

The following are some reasons for the increased interest in small business:

- The number of small businesses is growing rapidly.
- Small firms generate most new employment.

---

*Those individuals earning $200,000 or more a year, or with $3 million or more in assets.

**Table 1–1** Success Ladder

| How successful business owners made their money | |
|---|---|
| Real estate | 15% |
| Building/machinery | 14% |
| Produce/perishables | 10% |
| Oil and gas | 10% |
| Auto sales/repairs | 10% |
| Groceries/restaurants | 8% |
| Insurance | 5% |
| Retail | 5% |
| Consulting | 5% |
| Other professional services | 4% |
| Technology | 4% |
| Wholesale | 3% |
| Other | 3% |

*Source:* U.S. Trust, as reported in Daniel Kadlec, "Small Business: No Small Potatoes," *USA Today*, November 1, 1994, p. 3B. Copyright 1989, USA TODAY. Reprinted with permission.

- The public favors small business.
- There is increasing interest in small business entrepreneurship at high schools and colleges.
- There is a growing trend toward self-employment.
- Small business is attractive to people of all ages.

## The Number of Small Businesses Is Growing Rapidly

G

The development of small business in the United States is truly an amazing story. As an economic power, U.S. small businesses rank third in the world, behind only the U.S. economy as a whole and the Japanese economy.[7] If small business is this important, how many small firms are there in the United States? While the estimates vary greatly, the U.S. Small Business Administration (SBA) estimates that there are about 20 million small companies, which is the figure we will use throughout this text.[8]

More important than the number of small businesses, though, is the fact that the number of such firms is growing by about 750,000 each year. For example, Dun & Bradstreet Corp. estimated that in 1994 incorporations (not counting proprietorships and partnerships) rose 5 percent—to a record 741,657.[9] Growth was particularly strong in the South Atlantic states as well as California and Massachusetts. Also significant is the fact that about nine new firms are organized for every one that fails.

Several years ago, someone erroneously claimed that "four out of five small businesses fail in their first five years of operation."[10] But, a recent Dun & Bradstreet census of 250,000 businesses found that "almost 70 percent of all firms that started in 1985 were still around."[11]

In an earlier study of 814,000 businesses started in 1977 and 1978, Bruce A. Kirchoff of the New Jersey Institute of Technology found that over half survived more than eight years. While 18 percent failed—they did not have assets to cover their liabilities—28 percent closed voluntarily. Of the others, 28 percent were operated by their original owners, and 26 percent had new owners. He concluded that "entrepreneurs aren't stupid. They look around and realize their chances of success are far better than those proclaimed by the 'experts.' "[12]

Not only has there been an increase in the number of small businesses, but there has also been a recent rapid rise in employment by them. For example, according to the National Federation of Independent Business (NFIB), 15 percent of small companies planned to increase employment in the latter half of 1995, and 25 percent reported having difficulty filling current positions.[13]

## Small Firms Generate Most New Employment

As shown above, small businesses contribute greatly to employment, especially in the creation of *new jobs.* According to R. Wendell Moore, an official of the SBA, businesses with fewer than 500 employees, representing slightly over half of all private employment, produce the most new jobs.[14] From 1987 to 1992, according to a Cognetics Inc. study, "Firms with fewer than 100 employees added a net of 5,864,000 jobs, of which 85 percent paid average or better wages." During the same period, large firms lost a net 2,320,000 jobs, and 96 percent of them were high paying.[15] The growth was found in all job sectors, not just the "hot" areas, such as high tech.

Also, while profits of the Forbes 500 rose 14 percent in 1993, and revenues rose 3.5 percent, *their employment declined 1 percent to 20.2 million.*[16] And, as you can see in Figure 1–1, 41 percent of smaller firms added to their staff, while only 20 percent of the larger ones did. Finally, employment at the Fortune 500 companies declined by more than 1 million over the last five years.[17]

Recent Bureau of Labor Statistics figures indicate that around 71 percent of future employment in the fastest-growing industries (such as medical care, business services, and the environment) will likely come from small businesses—and these are areas where small firms are quite competitive.

Robert L. Bartley, editor of *The Wall Street Journal,* calls the last decade the heyday of "an expanding, entrepreneurial economy."[18] Some new names that

**Figure 1–1** Small Companies Lead in New Hires

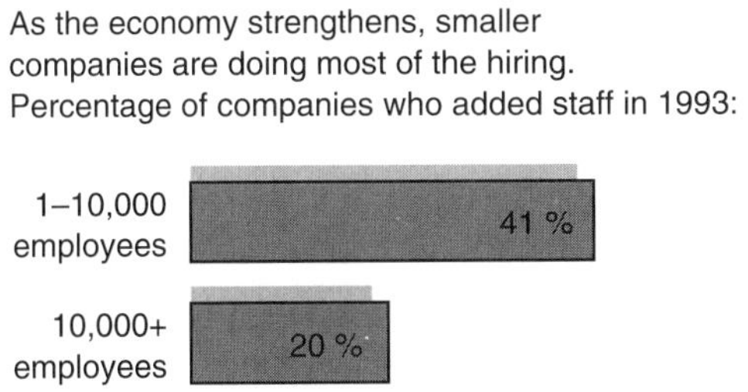


*Source:* Olsten Survey, as reported in *USA Today,* April 29, 1994, p. 1B. Copyright 1994, USA TODAY. Reprinted with permission.

exploded on the business landscape during that time were Microsoft, Lotus, Apple, Sun MicroSystems, Liz Claiborne, and McCaw Cellular.

Finally, small businesses are a particularly good source of jobs for older workers. According to a study for the SBA, businesses with fewer than 25 employees *account for more than two-thirds of new hiring of workers age 65 and over.*[19] **D**

## The Public Favors Small Business

Generally, small business owners and managers believe in the free enterprise system, with its emphasis on individual freedom, risk taking, initiative, thrift, frugality, and hard work. In fact, a Gallup survey of 600 adults for the Center for Entrepreneurial Leadership in Kansas City, Missouri, found that half of the respondents expressed an interest in owning a small business.[20] Also, the public evidently believes that small business should continue to be healthy and flourish, for a survey by Comprehensive Accounting Corporation found that, while 77 percent of those surveyed knew of the high failure rate of small firms, 53 percent of them would still have liked to own one to fulfill the great American dream.[21]

Another indication of interest in small business and entrepreneurship is the large number of magazines aimed at that market. These include older ones, such as *Black Enterprise, Entrepreneur, Inc.,* and *Hispanic Business,* and many new ones. Some of these journals are targeted for specific markets. *Family Business* targets family-owned businesses; *Entrepreneurial Woman* aims at female business owners; and *Your Company,* sent free by American Express to the million or more holders of its small-business corporate card, targets small firms. Other journals include *Journal of Small Business Management, Small Business Journal, New Business Opportunities,* and *Business Week Newsletter for Family-Owned Businesses.* **D**

## Interest Increasing at High Schools and Colleges

Another indication of the growing favor of small business is its acceptance as part of the mission of many high schools and colleges, where entrepreneurship and small business management are now academically respected disciplines. Virtually unheard of 20 years ago, courses in entrepreneurship were offered at 417 colleges in 1992.[22]

This trend is evident not only at small schools, as the following example illustrates.

> Most of the 1974 graduates of the Harvard Business School headed for medium-sized to large employers. But by 1992, more than a third of a 115-person sample had been fired or laid off, and 62 percent were working for small firms.[23]

The considerable interest at colleges and universities is also shown by the formation of many student organizations to encourage entrepreneurship. For example, the Association of Collegiate Entrepreneurs (ACE), founded in 1983 at Wichita State University, now has hundreds of chapters throughout the world. Other organizations include the University Entrepreneurial Association (UEA) and Students in Free Enterprise (SIFE). The following photo shows members of SIFE chapter after winning an award for a service project.

Photo courtesy of M. Jane Byrd.

Community colleges, especially, are now offering courses for small business owners. One study found that 90 percent of community colleges offer such courses, while 75 percent of public community colleges also provide training courses. This activity is one of the fastest-growing areas in the community college field. Many colleges and universities are now offering specialized business courses, such as programs in family business, franchising, and international operations, as well as job fairs and career days.

Finally, many students are now starting businesses to finance their own education.

> For example, Mark Frank went to Washington University at St. Louis to study accounting and finance. He noticed that many students bought items such as computers, VCRs, and microwave ovens at the beginning of the year and then had to cart them home during summer break. He started renting the basement of his house on campus to provide storage space for other students. With his profits, he bought microwave ovens and other conveniences which he also rented to students. After two years, he had earned an $18,000 profit from his basement operations.[24]

*"It's going to be a tough job market this year."*

*Source:* Reprinted from *The Wall Street Journal,* September 26, 1995, by permission of Cartoon Features Syndicate.

According to a long-running survey by the Higher Education Research Institute at the University of California at Los Angeles, America's students are still attracted to the entrepreneurial life. As shown in Figure 1–2, 41 percent of college freshmen in 1994 said succeeding in their own business was essential or very important to them. While this figure was less than the 52 percent in 1985, it was still at about the same level as in the 1970s.

Not only college and university students but also students in lower-level schools are interested in small business and entrepreneurship—as you saw in

**Figure 1–2** Tomorrow's Entrepreneurs—Share of College Freshmen Who Say Succeeding in Their Own Business Is Essential or Very Important

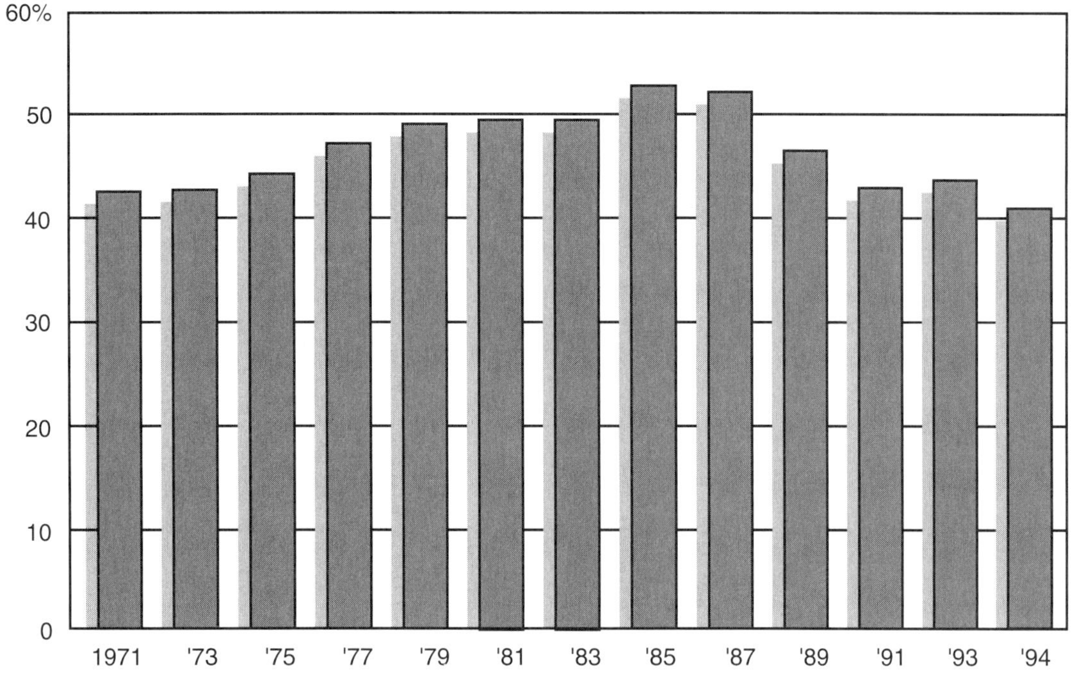


*Source:* Correspondence and communication with personnel at the Higher Education Research Institute at UCLA.

the opening profile. Nearly 70 percent of high school students are interested in launching their own business, according to the previously mentioned Gallup survey.[25] One of the reasons given by the students was distrust of government and big business.

> For instance, one student was quoted as saying, "If you work for yourself, you reap more benefits than you would if you worked underneath someone." This student planned to open a computer graphics business of her own and not rely on a big company for her pay.[26]

## Trend Toward Self-Employment

The growth rate for self-employment is greater than the growth rate of the general work force. Small business grew rapidly from the mid-1980s to the mid-1990s as investors became more willing to assume the risk of starting or revitalizing small businesses. Many of these were middle-aged executives from large corporations who were eager to put their management skills to work in reviving smaller companies in aging industries.

Q

This trend is still alive, for among 2 million new businesses formed in 1993 that Dun & Bradstreet evaluated, 20 percent were one- and two-person operations. Also, the new small business people were better educated, and their companies were more sophisticated than those of previous generations. These new firms are increasingly providing consulting services to other businesses.[27]

## Small Business Is Attractive to All Ages

Entrepreneurship knows no age limits! From the very young to the very old, people are starting new businesses at a rapid rate. Particularly heartening is the large number of young people who are entrepreneurs. In 1994, the U.S. Bureau of Labor Statistics found 272,000 young people age 20 to 24 were self-employed—up 10 percent in only one year. Another study at Babson College indicated that nearly 10 percent of Americans between the ages of 25 and 34 were trying to start their own business.[28] See Figure 1–3 for the percentage of various age groups who are trying to start their own business.

Age is not a requirement for success in starting small businesses, as the following examples show.

Photo courtesy of M. Jane Byrd.

Megan Crump is a good example of a young entrepreneur. She is seven years old and has found an exciting way to make money. After a successful evening of trick-or-treating, Megan took all her candy to school and sold it to her schoolmates for a handsome profit of $3 the first day and $1 the second day. She later held a yard sale where, among other things, she sold her sister's used bicycle for $9. Megan is our future and her resourcefulness should continue to stimulate our economy well into the 21st century.[29]

Howard Stubbs is known as "Mr. Hot Dog" in the South Bronx, an area known for its drug dealers, rubble-strewn lots, and burned-out buildings. As a 15-year-old student at Jane Addams Vocational High School, Stubbs borrowed $800 from friends and relatives to buy an umbrella-topped hot dog cart. Two years later, he grossed $10,000! He bought hot dogs—with all the trimmings—for 33 cents and sold them for $1; soda costs 20 cents and sells for 75 cents. Stubbs worked at his stand on weekends, school holidays, and during the summer; he also sold candy at school and gave haircuts to his friends—for $5.[30]

D

Older people are also involved in forming new companies as small businesses offer the most opportunities and flexibility to retirees.

**Figure 1–3** Starting Out

**Percentage of Americans who are trying to start a business, by age group**

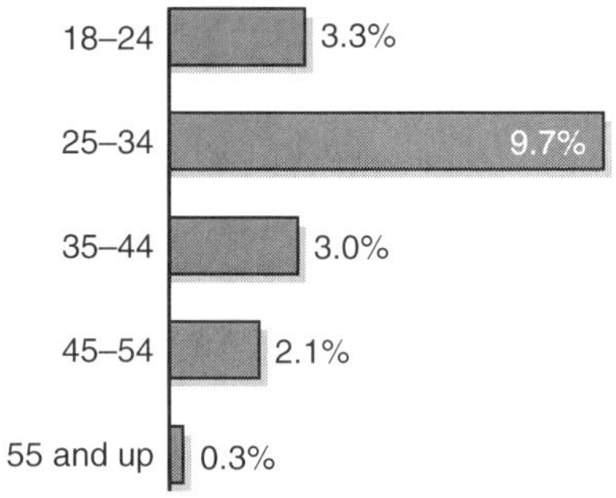


*Source:* Study by Paul Reynolds, Babson College, as reported in Stephanie N. Mehta, "Young Entrepreneurs Turn Age to Advantage," *The Wall Street Journal,* September 1, 1995, p. B1. Reprinted with Permission of THE WALL STREET JOURNAL, © 1995 Dow Jones & Company, Inc. All Rights Reserved Worldwide.

> For example, after devoting nearly 30 years to the law—rising to partner in charge of the London office of Rogers & Wills—Joni Nelson quit in 1991 at age 53 to turn her love of gardening into a new career. Chelsea American Flower Shows, her new company, organizes flower shows around the country. She says of her new career, "I'm a capitalist at heart. I want to work until I'm 80."[31]

New Challenger Index data show that among those who have become entrepreneurs, the percentage over age 40 has risen from an average of 63.5 in 1992 to 87.5 in 1993.[32] Also, many groups, such as the American Association of Retired Persons (AARP), colleges, and private consultants now offer classes—and, more importantly, support groups—specifically for retirement-aged potential and actual entrepreneurs.[33] Also, 40 percent of those who form new businesses each year already have some management experience, and one-fourth of them have managed or owned a business before.

A word of caution is needed at this point. If you start a business, you can't just "turn it off and on" like a light switch; that is, you can't take time off whenever you want to. If your business is to succeed, you can't shut down for holidays or vacations or when things aren't going well.

## Defining Small Business—No Easy Task

Now that we've seen how much interest there is in small business, what *is* a small business? There is no simple definition, but let's look at some definitions that are frequently used.

### What Is Small?

What is a small business? At first, this question appears easy to answer. Many places of business that you patronize—such as independent neighborhood grocery stores, fast-food restaurants, hair stylists, dry cleaners, video or

**Table 1–2** Classification of Businesses by Size, According to SBA

| | |
|---|---|
| Under 20 employees | Very small |
| 20–99 | Small |
| 100–499 | Medium |
| 500 or more | Large |

*Source:* Small Business Administration.

record shops, and the veterinarian—are examples of small businesses. However, even with 8,500 employees, American Motors was once considered a small business: the SBA deemed it eligible for a small business loan. Why? Because American Motors *was* small compared to its giant competitors—General Motors, Ford, and Chrysler. Chrysler bought the smaller company in 1987.

Q

Qualitative factors are also important in describing small businesses. The Committee for Economic Development says that *a small business has at least two of the following features:*[34]

- Management is independent, since the manager usually owns the business.
- Capital is supplied and ownership is held by an individual or a few individuals.
- The area of operations is primarily local, although the market isn't necessarily local.
- The business is small in comparison with the larger competitors in its industry.

Perhaps the best definition of small business is the one used by Congress in the Small Business Act of 1953, which states that *a small business is one that is independently owned and operated and is not dominant in its field of operation.*[35] We'll use that definition in this text, unless otherwise indicated.

As will be shown in Chapter 9, the SBA, for loan purposes, uses different size criteria by industries. In general, however, it uses the size classification shown in Table 1–2.

## Distinguishing between Small Business and Entrepreneurial Ventures

We also need to distinguish between small businesses and entrepreneurial ventures. In fact, the rapidity of the rate of growth has been shown to be one useful way to distinguish between small business owners and entrepreneurs.[36]

A **small business** is independently owned and operated, is not dominant in its field, and doesn't engage in new or innovative practices.

A **small business** (or mom-and-pop operation) is any business that is independently owned and operated, is not dominant in its field, and does not engage in many new or innovative practices. It may never grow large, and the owners may not want it to, as they usually prefer a more relaxed and less aggressive approach to running the business. In other words, they manage the business in a normal way, expecting normal sales, profits, and growth.

On the other hand, an **entrepreneurial venture** is one in which the principal objectives of the entrepreneur are profitability and growth. Thus, the business is characterized by innovative strategic practices and/or products. The entrepreneurs and their financial backers are usually seeking rapid growth, immediate—and high—profits, and a quick sellout with—possibly—large capital gains.

In an **entrepreneurial venture,** the principal objectives of the owner are profitability and growth.

It is not always easy to distinguish between a small business owner and an entrepreneur, for the distinction hinges on their intentions. In general, a **small business owner** establishes a business for the principal purpose of furthering personal goals, which *may* include making a profit. Thus, the owner may perceive the business as being an extension of his or her personality, which is interwoven with family needs and desires.

A **small business owner** establishes a business primarily to further personal goals, including making a profit.

On the other hand, the **entrepreneur** starts and manages a business for many reasons, including achievement, profit, and growth. Such a person is characterized principally by innovative behavior and will employ strategic management practices in the business, as the following example indicates.

The goals of an **entrepreneur** include growth, achieved through innovation and strategic management

> Court L. Hague (or "Corky," as he is known), age 47, has a driving compulsion: He loves to start new businesses. While most entrepreneurs start one, two, or three enterprises in their lifetime, so far he has founded—or acquired with the intent to expand—28 companies.
>
> In the early 1970s, after one year teaching algebra and earning a degree in accounting from the University of Texas, he started his "acquisition binge." By the mid-1980s, he was simultaneously running 12 companies.
>
> He selected most of his companies by leafing through the Yellow Pages to find "solid businesses that could benefit from splashier ads." He has owned a sign business, an air conditioner factory, a dry-wall supplier, travel agencies, bike stores, pawnshops, and software companies—just to mention a few.
>
> He bases his success on three guiding principles: (1) get good people, (2) stick to what you know best, and (3) watch the business like a hawk.[37]

Of course, the owner's intentions sometimes change, and what started out as a small business may become an entrepreneurial venture, as the following example shows.

> Texas Long Distance, a small Dallas business, was started by Bill Wiese, 65, a retired executive; his wife, Chleo; his son Roger; and his nephew John. The company began by using long-distance lines leased from discounters (such as Sprint) and secondhand switching equipment to find the cheapest route for each call. Bill Wiese said the initial objective of Texas Long Distance was to have a good time and—it was hoped—make some money at it.
>
> But the business became an entrepreneurial venture in 1989 when it evolved into a full-service long-distance company with new switching equipment, more lines, and over 800 customers. With offices in Austin and Houston, as well as Dallas, the firm employed 25 to 26 people, including Scott Wiese, another of Bill's sons. Its name was changed to Digital Network Inc., to reflect its new mission.[38]

Q

**Figure 1–4** Percent Distribution of Business Establishments and Employees by Size of Employer

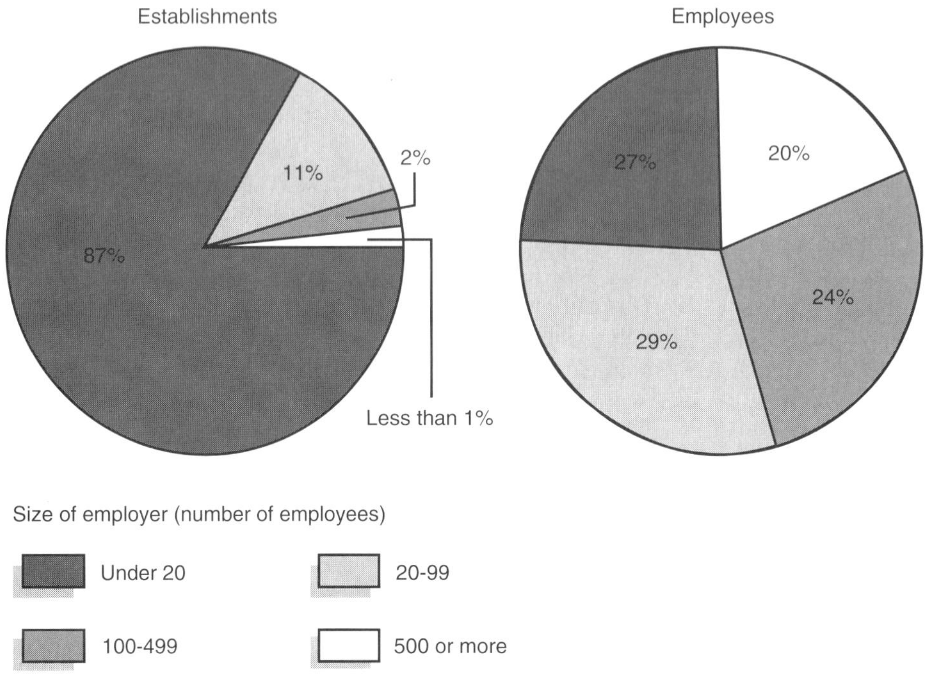


*Source:* U.S. Bureau of the Census, *Statistical Abstract of the United States, 1994,* 114th ed. (Washington, DC: U.S. Government Printing Office, 1994), Table 845, p. 546.

## Size, Sales, and Employment

The Internal Revenue Service classifies 96 percent of American businesses as small.* Yet small businesses generate only 12 percent of the total receipts each year, while the 4 percent of firms that are classified as large generate 88 percent of all revenues.[39]

Still, as has been shown, one of the greatest advantages of small businesses is their ability to create new jobs. Figure 1–4 shows that small businesses† account for 50 percent of employees in all U.S. businesses.

As you can see from Figure 1–5, small firms are more prevalent in agriculture, contract construction, and wholesale and retail trade, where they provide over 90 percent of all employment. Yet they generate the largest number of actual jobs in services (22,205,000 employees), retail trade (18,994,000), and manufacturing (11,790,000). These figures show how important small firms are in generating employment opportunities.

*The definition of small is based on the amount of annual revenue—$1 million or less.
†Those having fewer than 500 employees.

**Figure 1–5** Percent Distribution of Employees in Large and Small Firms in Selected Industries

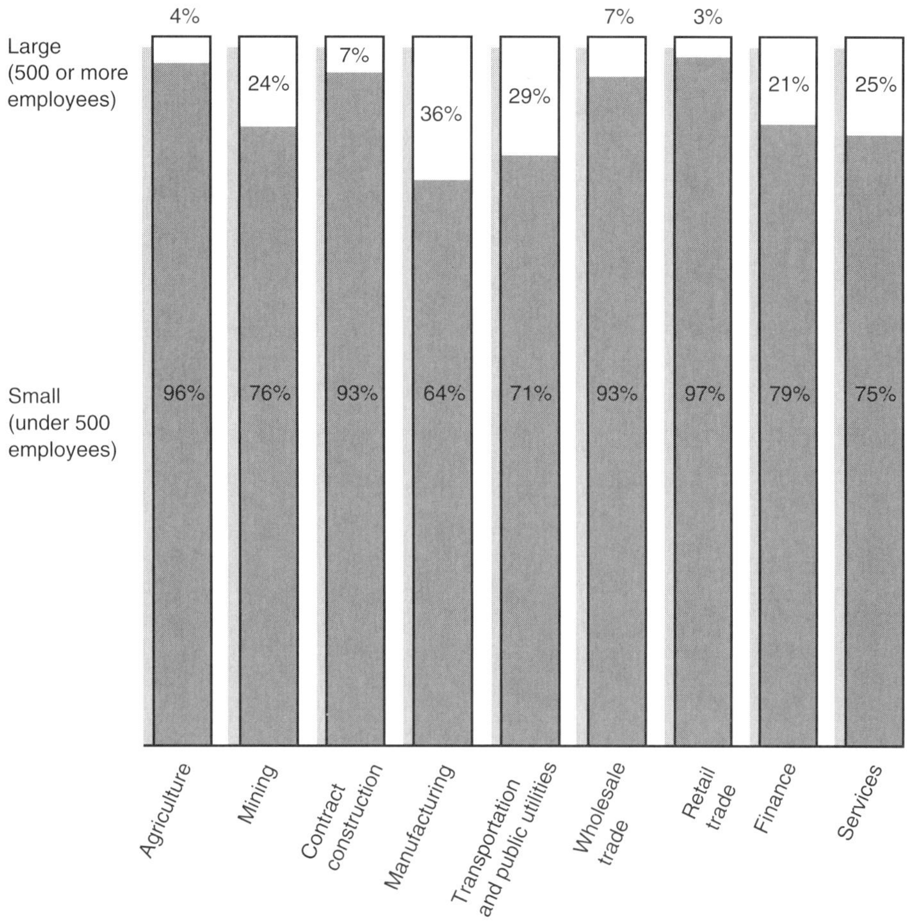


*Source:* U.S. Bureau of the Census, *Statistical Abstract of the United States, 1994,* 114th ed. (Washington, DC: U.S. Government Printing Office, 1994), Table 845, p. 546.

## Some Unique Contributions of Small Businesses

As indicated throughout this chapter, small firms differ from their larger competitors. Let's look at some major contributions made by small businesses that set them apart from larger firms.

Smaller firms tend to:

- Encourage innovation and flexibility.
- Maintain close relationships with customers and the community.
- Keep larger firms competitive.
- Provide employees with comprehensive learning experiences.

- Develop risk takers.
- Generate new employment.

## Encourage Innovation and Flexibility

Q

Smaller businesses are often sources of new ideas, materials, processes, and services that larger firms may be unable or reluctant to provide. In small businesses, experiments can be conducted, innovations initiated, and new operations started or expanded. As mentioned earlier, over half of today's technological developments originated in small business. This trend is especially true in the computer field, where initial developments have been carried on in small companies.

> For example, it is no coincidence that IBM didn't produce the first electronic computer, as it already owned 97 percent of the then-popular punched-card equipment, which the computer would tend to make obsolete. Instead, the Univac was conceived and produced by a small firm formed by John Mauchly and J. Presper Eckert. However, while they were design experts, they lacked production and marketing skills, so they sold out to Remington Rand, which controlled the remaining 3 percent of the punched-card business. So the first giant computers at organizations such as the U.S. Census Bureau and General Electric's Appliance Park plant in Kentucky in January 1954 were Univacs. Nonetheless, IBM's marketing expertise overcame Remington's production expertise, and IBM soon dominated the computer industry.

## Maintain Close Relationships with Customers and Community

Q

Small businesses tend to be in close touch with their communities and customers. They can do a more individualized job than big firms can, thereby attracting customers on the basis of specialty products, quality, and personal services rather than solely on the basis of price. While competitive prices and a reputation for honesty are important, an atmosphere of friendliness makes people feel good about patronizing the business and encourages them to continue shopping there.

## Keep Larger Firms Competitive

Smaller companies have become a controlling factor in the American economy by keeping the bigger concerns on their toes. With the introduction of new products and services, small businesses encourage competition—if not in price, at least in design and efficiency, as happened in California's Silicon Valley, where the personal computer was developed.

## Provide Employees with Comprehensive Learning Experiences

A small business provides employees with a variety of learning experiences not open to individuals holding more specialized jobs in larger companies. Along with performing a greater variety of functions, small business employees also have more freedom to make decisions, which can lend zest and interest to employees' work experience. So small businesses train people to become better leaders and managers and to develop their talents and energies more effectively.

### Develop Risk Takers

Small businesses provide one of the basic American freedoms—risk taking, with its consequent rewards and punishments. Small business owners have relative freedom to enter or leave a business at will, to start small and grow big, to expand or contract, and to succeed or fail, which is the basis of our free enterprise system. Yet founding a business in an uncertain environment is risky, so much planning and study must be done before start-up.

### Generate New Employment

As repeatedly emphasized throughout this chapter, small businesses generate employment by creating job opportunities. Small firms also serve as a training ground for employees, who, because of their more comprehensive learning experience, their emphasis on risk taking, and their exposure to innovation and flexibility, become valued employees of larger companies.

## Some Problems Facing Small Businesses

Just as small companies make unique contributions, there are special problems that affect them more than larger businesses. These problems can result in limited profitability and growth, the decision to voluntarily close the business, or financial failure.

A survey by the NFIB in 1994 found that the most important problems facing small business owners were (1) taxes, (2) regulation and red tape, (3) insurance costs, (4) weak sales, (5) competition from large companies, and (6) finding good workers. Figure 1–6 shows how these problems rank in severity.

With these pressing problems, you would think small businesses would be short lived. But as shown earlier, small firms don't fail as often as people think. Instead, *the vast majority of businesses that close do so for voluntary*

**Figure 1–6** Big Woes for Small Businesses

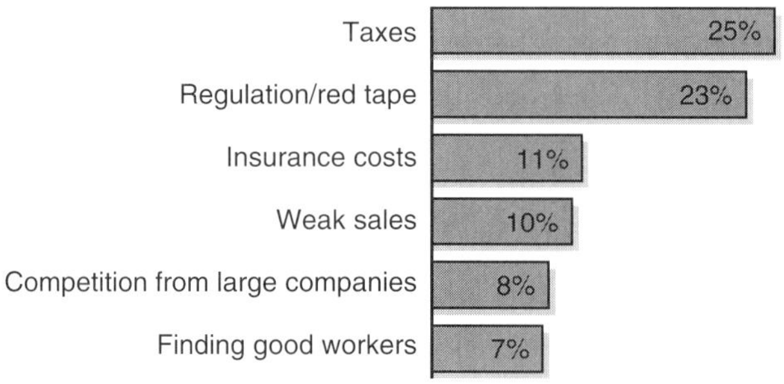


*Source:* National Federation of Independent Business, as reported in *USA Today,* June 10, 1994, p. 1B. Copyright 1994, USA TODAY. Reprinted with permission.

*reasons,* such as the desire to enter a more profitable business, legal changes, and disenchantment, or a family's decision to leave the business after the owner's death.

Why do new businesses fail? A Minota Corporation survey of 703 businesses with fewer than 500 employees found that the main reasons are (1) lack of capital (48 percent), (2) no business knowledge (23 percent), (3) poor management (19 percent), (4) inadequate planning (15 percent), and (5) inexperience (15 percent).[40]

It can be concluded from these two surveys that the primary problems facing small business owners are: (1) *inadequate financing,* (2) *inadequate management,* and (3) *burdensome government regulations and paperwork.* These will be discussed in detail in later chapters.

## Current Trends Challenging Entrepreneurs and Small Business Owners

Small firms are now experiencing fundamental changes in the ways business is conducted and people are being employed. If they are to overcome the problems just discussed, they must be prepared to recognize and cope with some current trends that will challenge their best performance. The most important of these are: (1) a more diverse work force, (2) empowerment and team performance, (3) exploding technology, (4) occupational and industry shifts, and (5) global challenges.

### A More Diverse Work Force

**Diversity** in the work force is achieved by employing more members of minority groups, women and older workers.

D

Entrepreneurs and owners of small firms must develop more effective human relation skills if they are to successfully deal with the growing **diversity** in the work force. For example, while nearly half of the work force in 1975 was white males, they will compose only about 12 percent of *all net new hires* by the year 2005. White males' share of the work force is expected to fall to about 29 percent by that year, while the share of workers categorized as African-American, Hispanic, and Asian, Native American, and other is expected to rise significantly. So the future work force will look more nearly like that shown on the right in Figure 1–7 than like its 1990 composition, shown on the left.

While women are entering the work force at about the same rate as men, the men, who have been in the work force longer, are retiring at a faster rate. Thus, like racial and ethnic minorities, women will assume an even greater role in entrepreneurship and small business.

People in the work force are also aging, along with the rest of the population. For example, about 40 percent of the workers in 1990 were between 35 and 54 years old. By the year 2005, this age group will increase to about 50 percent. At the other end of the spectrum, as women have fewer children, there will be fewer young workers than at present, causing a further imbalance in the work force.

Thus, tomorrow's entrepreneurs must be particularly sensitive to the need for, and the ability to provide, more effective employment for a diverse group of employees.

**Figure 1–7** Distribution of the Labor Force by Race and Heritage

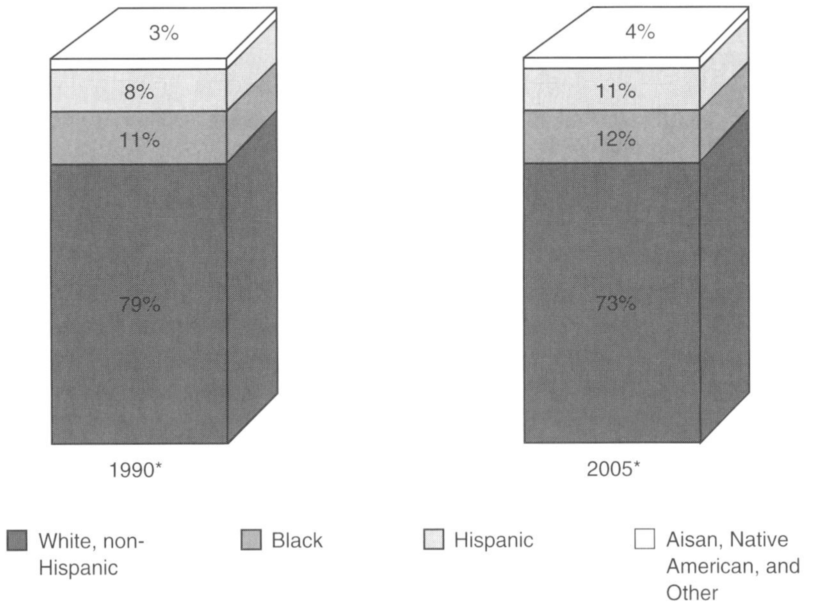


*Estimated; does not add to 100 percent because of rounding.

*Source:* "Tomorrow's Jobs," from the *Occupational Outlook Handbook*, 1992–93 edition (Washington, DC: U.S. Department of Labor, Bureau of Labor Statistics), p. 3.

## Empowerment and Team Performance

**Empowerment** is giving employees experiences and responsibilities that equip them to function more effectively on their own.

As small businesses seek **empowerment** for their employees by equipping them to function more effectively on their own, owners and managers will increasingly be using work teams. Small firms, as well as large, are increasingly organizing teams or cells that recommend changes intended to make better things happen or to make things run more smoothly. These teams are not an end in themselves but a means to an end, which is better performance than team members would achieve working on their own. Thus, the owner-manager becomes a leader who facilitates activities by presenting ideas in a group setting, by running different kinds of meetings, and by sharing skills knowingly, willingly, and freely, while letting the employees make many decisions that the owner formerly made. Thus, managers will let subordinates learn by making decisions, stepping in to take control only when it becomes necessary.

Q

> For example, Sam Walton was applying such concepts as flat organizations, empowerment, and gain-sharing long before anyone gave them these names. Thus, in the 1950s, he was sharing information and profits with his employees.[41]

## Exploding Technology

Few jobs in small firms are unaffected by improvements in communication and computer technology. Thus, small business management is being drastically changed as automated robotics are introduced in the production

## USING TECHNOLOGY TO SUCCEED

### Dillard Focuses on Computer Technology

An example of exploding technology is the system used by Dillard Department Stores, which has a near-fanatical focus on computer technology. Questions such as "Are Estée Lauder cosmetics selling as fast as anticipated in Santa Fe?" or "How much business is each store doing as of 11 o'clock each day?" can be answered in seconds with Dillard's state-of-the-art information system. Its Quick Response program orders basic items, such as Christian Dior lingerie, from the vendor each week—electronically, without human intervention—on the basis of the previous day's and week's sales.

Another example, is Wal-Mart Stores, Inc., which informed its suppliers in 1990 that it was adopting electronic data interchange, and if the suppliers wanted to continue selling merchandise to Wal-Mart, they would have to adopt it also.

*Sources:* Based on Lynda Radosevich, "EDI Spreads Across Different Business Lines," *Computerworld,* October 18, 1993, pp. 69–73; "Dillard Stores' Profit in April Quarter Was Flat, Disappointing Some Analysts," *The Wall Street Journal,* May 12, 1994, p. B4; and Jon Van, "Laptop Leads Cast of Office Offerings, but Bosses Must Filter What's Needed from What's New," *Chicago Tribune,* March 17, 1991, pp. 20–27.

Q

departments, marketing people are using computer-aided promotional and sales activities, and accounting departments are using improved computer skills.

The primary effect of exploding technology on small companies will be in improving the selection and training of workers and overcoming their own resistance to change. Therefore, owners and managers must keep up to date themselves on the latest technologies so they can effectively train their people, as you can see from the nearby Using Technology to Succeed.

### Occupational and Industry Shifts

Q

The many mentioned technological advancements, such as automation, computers, robotics, and communication, along with changing markets resulting from cultural changes, have caused drastic shifts in occupations and industries. First, there is a declining emphasis on the traditional "smokestack" industries, with a concurrent shift toward more people-related activities, such as health care services, banking, financial services, retail trade, transportation, and computer services, which are exceptionally well suited to small businesses.

**Reinvention** is the fundamental redesign of a business, often resulting in reduction in size and markets.

**Reengineering** is the redesign of operations from scratch.

**Downsizing (Rightsizing)** is reducing the number of employees and increasing efficiency.

Among these shifts, **reinvention,** particularly including a reduction in the size and markets for businesses, has led to fewer job opportunities for those who are less well trained and educated. At the same time, many of the larger companies have **reengineered** their activities, which has involved wiping the slate clean as far as current operations are concerned and asking: "If we blew this place up and started over, what would we do differently? What should we eliminate? What can we do that would make things easier for our customers?" These and similar activities have essentially resulted in **downsizing** (sometimes call **rightsizing**) whereby the number of people an organization employs is reduced as it strives to become leaner and meaner by reducing human resources and consolidating departments and work groups.

Q

For example, some of the best known companies, such as Bell Atlantic, American Express, Eastman Kodak, Taco Bell, General Motors, IBM, and Sears have been reinvented, reengineered, and/or downsized. The result has been the disappearance of 23,000 managerial jobs each month.[42] This movement is giving people more responsibility for making more decisions and not acting like automatons, but they must work harder and are under more pressure. A survey of a dozen big employers showed that two-thirds of their workers were stretched so thin that they could not take advantage of flexible work schedules, personal leave, or other benefits, as "they're just hoping to retain what they've got."[43] *These shifts help smaller firms as many highly skilled workers and managers are joining the ranks of small business owners and managers.*

## Global Challenges

G

The trend in business is to become more active in global activities, and those interested in small business management need to understand at least what the problem is and what results are. In essence, we are in an age of global competition that is essentially a one-world market. Consequently, *we estimate that up to one-half of all today's college graduates will work in some type of global activities in the future.*

In 1991, international sales by U.S. multinationals were 20 percent of all corporate revenues, and exports of services are growing even faster than product exports. For example, service exports grew in 1992 at an average rate of 12.6 percent, almost double the 6.7 percent increase in merchandise exports.[44]

One result of this global challenge is the large number of large and small U.S. businesses that are foreign owned. And these foreign-owned companies tend to have different management styles than their original American owners. This means small business owners and managers must learn to adjust and adapt to cultural differences and find ways to adapt to nontraditional styles. While foreign ownership may lead to differing management styles, the American consumers may not realize the change.

For example, few Americans know or care that consumer products for sale with RCA and GE brand names are owned by a French company, Thompson SA. Magnavox and Sylvania are owned by Philips Electronics of the Netherlands; and Quasar is made by Japan's Matsushita Electric Industries. And, as Figure 1–8 indicates, it really doesn't make that much difference.

**Figure 1–8**

'Next up, we need to decide which is best for the deficit: Buying a Toyota made in Tennessee, or a Dodge made in Tokyo.'

Reprinted by permission, Tribune Media Services.

## WHAT YOU SHOULD HAVE LEARNED

**1.** This is a challenging and rewarding time to be studying small business because the field is so popular and is expected to continue growing in employment and productivity. The public attitude toward small business is favorable, and self-employment is so popular that around three-quarters of a million people—young and old—start their own businesses each year.

**2.** Defining *small business* is difficult because the definition of smallness varies widely. In general, a small business is independently owned and operated and is not dominant in its field of operation. It is difficult to draw a clear distinction between a *small business* and an *entrepreneurial venture*, as the distinction depends on the intentions of the owners. If they start a small business and want it to stay small, it is a small business. If, on the other hand, they start small but plan to grow big, it is an entrepreneurial venture. Although around 96 percent of U.S. businesses are small, they generate only 12 percent of the total receipts each year, while firms with fewer than 500 employees account for 80 percent of existing jobs.

**3.** Small firms differ from larger ones in many ways, but their unique contributions include *(a)* flexibility and room for innovation, *(b)* the ability to maintain close relationships with customers and the community, *(c)* the competition they provide, which forces larger companies to remain competitive, *(d)* the opportunity they give employees to gain experience in many areas, *(e)* the challenge and freedom they offer to risk takers, and *(f)* the employment opportunities they generate.

**4.** Some problems that plague small companies more than larger ones—and limit their development—are *(a)* inadequate financing, *(b)* inadequate management (especially as the firm grows), and *(c)* burdensome government regulation and paperwork.

**5.** Some current trends challenging small businesses are *(a)* a more diverse work force, *(b)* empowerment and team performance, *(c)* exploding technology, *(d)* occupational and industry shifts, and *(e)* a move to global operations.

## QUESTIONS FOR DISCUSSION

1. Do you agree that this is an interesting time to be studying small business? Why are you doing so?
2. All of us have personal experiences with small business—as an owner, employee, friend, or relative of an owner, or in other relationships. Explain one or more such experience(s) you have recently had.
3. What comes to your mind when you think of a small business? How does your concept differ from the definition given in this chapter?
4. Distinguish between a small business and an entrepreneurial venture. If you were to start your own business, which would you wish it to be? Why?

5. How do you explain the growing interest young people have in small business? Relate this to your personal small business experience.
6. What are the unique contributions of small businesses? Give examples of each from your own experience owning or working in a small business or from small businesses that you patronize.
7. What are some problems facing small businesses? Again, give examples from your experience.
8. Name and explain some current trends challenging small businesses.

## CASE 1

### SUE THINKS OF GOING INTO BUSINESS

Sue Ley had been a truck driver for a local oil company for about four years. Before that, she had worked as a forklift truck operator in the same company. In a recent interview, she said, "I was getting fed up with this type of work. I like working with people and thought I'd like to get into selling. One day a friend in personnel, when I indicated interest in getting into marketing, called my attention to the company's education program, which pays tuition for employees taking college courses. So I applied for it and was accepted."

Sue, whom the interviewers found to be a woman of above-average intelligence, personality, and drive, enrolled in the marketing program at the local university. She completed her marketing coursework and graduated in three years with a business administration degree. She had continued driving the truck while working on her degree.

When she approached her employer about the possibility of transferring to the marketing department, she was told it would be four or five years before there would be an opening for her.

A short time later, Sue's uncle suggested she go into business for herself. The uncle, who had taken over Sue's grandfather's steel oil drum cleaning business about 200 miles away, advised her that she could make around $100,000 per year ($300,000 by the third year) if she started and ran a business of this sort. He offered to help her form a business and get it started.

Sue, who had been married and had two grown children, said, "I could not see any future with the oil company in marketing, and I did not want to drive trucks the rest of my life. I had saved $25,000 that I could put into the business. Why not?"

### QUESTIONS

1. What do you see as Sue's alternatives?
2. What are Sue's qualifications for going into business for herself?

3. What are Sue's deficiencies?
4. What do you think of Sue's uncle's profit predictions?
5. What do you recommend that Sue do?

*Source:* Prepared by William M. Spain, Service Corps of Retired Executives (SCORE), and Charles R. Scott, University of Alabama.

## APPLICATION 1–1

John was recently laid off from his job with a leading computer manufacturer. He decided to use his expertise and contacts to open his own business. After some discussion, he and his brother-in-law Jim opened a small business, which they named J&J Computers.

Shortly after opening, they saw slow growth in sales. They were able to penetrate the market because of their low expenses and John's contacts in the computer field. They had two other full-time employees along with four part-time workers.

Eventually, John and Jim want to increase the size of their operations.

### QUESTIONS

1. Does J&J Computers fit the definition of a small business? Why?
2. Is this a small business or an entrepreneurial venture?
3. To what extent is John's background in the computer field of help in this business?

# ACTIVITY 1–1

*Directions:* Use information learned in this chapter to unjumble the following terms. Then unjumble the circled letters to solve the puzzle.

1. T N N E L A R I E E R U R P E   E T R V E N U

2. P N E E R U T E R R E N

3. M L A S L   S I U S S B N E

4. L S A M L   U S E N B S I S   E W N R O

1. Entrepreneurial Venture 2. Entrepreneur 3. Small Business 4. Small Business Owner Solution: Start Small

CHAPTER

# 2

# Why Own or Manage a Small Business?

*Entrepreneurship isn't an event, it's a career. True entrepreneurs do it over and over again whether they succeed or fail.*—Charles W. Hofer, professor of management, University of Georgia

*Guts, brains, and determination—key ingredients of the American entrepreneurial spirit—[have] sustained this nation through good times and bad, and launched it on an economic journey unlike any ever witnessed in history.*—John Sloan, Jr., president and CEO, National Federation of Independent Business

## LEARNING OBJECTIVES

After studying the material in this chapter, you will be able to:

1. Explain why people start small businesses.
2. Describe the characteristics of successful small business owners.
3. Assess how qualified you are to be a small business owner.
4. Explain the requirements for success in small business.

# PROFILE

## JUDY JONES' TRY J. ADVERTISING AGENCY

Photo courtesy of Judy Jones.

Judith Anne Jones' advertising agency, Try J. Advertising, of Carlsbad, California, sells service. It specializes in automobile dealerships such as Toyota Carlsbad and Lexus Carlsbad. When asked what started her in business, Jones gave the following answer:

> I was attracted to creative writing by my father, Scott W. Erwin, who was an announcer, copywriter, advertising manager, and manager of a radio station in Baton Rouge, Louisiana. My mother's career, library work, also influenced my career, as her dedication to her field set an example to me and gave me the opportunity to go to college. I studied advertising in the School of Journalism at Louisiana State University, including taking extra courses during summers to achieve a certificate of specialization in public relations.
>
> After graduating in 1976, I became a field reporter for the *Louisiana Contractor Magazine,* which led to my first pair of work boots and hard hat. After three years, I transferred to the *San Diego Contractor Magazine.* My stay there was brief, as I had to sell ads in Los Angeles two weeks out of every month. Its smog and crowded freeways energized me to start my own business in Carlsbad.
>
> After being marketing director for Wendy's Old-Fashioned Hamburgers' San Diego County Region, I joined the Ad Group, an advertising agency, as the account executive for one of its main accounts, the San Diego Toyota Dealers' Advertising Association. One of the dealers appreciated my work so much he offered me a position at his store, Toyota Carlsbad, from which I started my own ad agency in 1981.

Try J. Advertising, Inc., was incorporated with Judy Jones as president and equal shareholder with Louis V. Jones, president of Toyota Carlsbad. The two later married, and Judy bought out his interest. In addition to Ms. Jones, the agency's staff consists of two full-time account executives; a computer technician, who develops graphic cuts; and a bookkeeper who works as an independent contractor.

Jones and her people (1) provide for clients' printing needs by acting as their agent; (2) prepare items such as business cards, letterheads, and stationery; (3) prepare and distribute newsletters to clients' employees and customers; (4) write and print direct-mail pieces; (5) produce training videos; (6) write and produce radio, newspaper, and television ads; and (7) plan special events, such as grand openings and new model introductions.

*Source:* Correspondence and communication with Judith Anne Jones.

Now that you've seen the dynamic role played by small business, it's time to see what is needed to succeed in owning such a business. Also, it's time for you to determine whether you have the qualities needed to succeed in a small business.

## Why People Start Small Businesses

Owning a small business provides an excellent opportunity to satisfy personal objectives while achieving the firm's business objectives. Probably in no other occupation or profession is this as true. But there are almost as many different reasons for starting small businesses as there are small business owners. Those reasons can be summarized as (1) to satisfy personal objectives and (2) to achieve business objectives.

### To Satisfy Personal Objectives

Small business owners have the potential to fulfill many personal goals. In fact, owning a small business tends to satisfy most of our work goals. According to a survey by Padgett Business Services USA, Inc., the best things about owning a small business are independence, control, and satisfaction. Figure 2–1 shows how these rank, as well as the worst part of owning a business.

> A National Bureau of Economic Research study found that in Great Britain, 46 percent of the self-employed were "very satisfied," versus 29 percent of those working for others. In the United States, the numbers were 63 percent versus 47 percent.[1]

The objectives of owners of small businesses differ from those of managers of larger firms. Managers of large companies tend to seek security, place, power, prestige, high income, and benefits. By contrast, the primary objectives of small business owners are to:

- Achieve independence.
- Obtain additional income.

**Figure 2–1** Best and Worst of Business

What small business* owners say are the best and worst things about owning a business.

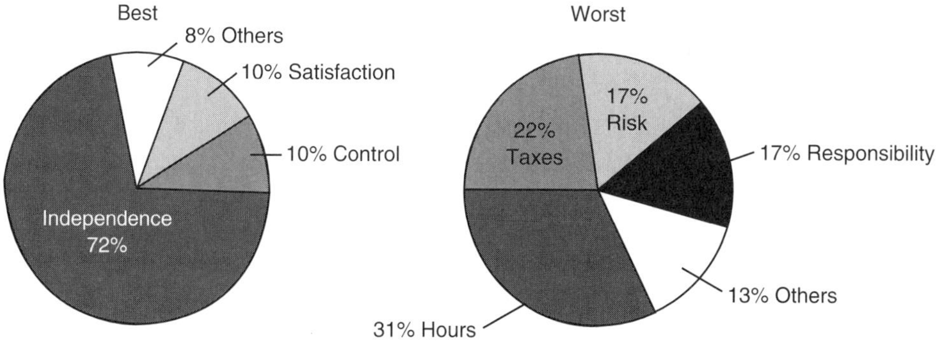


*Fewer than 20 employees.

*Source:* Padgett Business Services USA, Inc., survey, as reported in *USA Today*, June 13, 1995, p. 1B. Copyright 1995, USA TODAY. Reprinted with permission.

- Help their families.
- Provide products not available elsewhere.

In summary, the personal objectives of small business owners tend to be achievement oriented, as opposed to those of managers of large firms, who tend to be power and prestige oriented. How these personal objectives are achieved depends on the knowledge, skills, and personal traits these owners bring to the business.

For example, Bob and Susan Shallow operate a hot air balloon ride business within a 250-mile radius of their home base. Susan gave up a career in real estate so she could devote full time to running the enterprise, called Gulf View Balloon Company. Gulf View's revenue comes from balloon rides, sales, and services. Susan explained their success by saying, "We really love balloons and ballooning. It's something Bob and I can do together, and ballooning is something people can do with their families."[2]

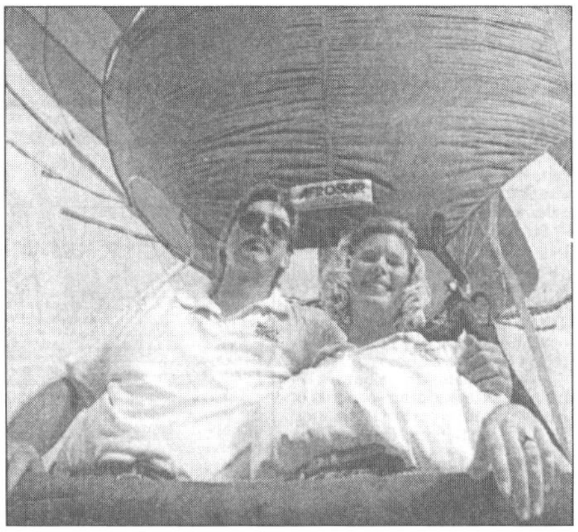

Photo by G. M. Andrews, *Mobile* (Alabama) *Press.*

## *To Achieve Independence*

While all the above objectives may lead someone to own a small business, the owner's primary motive is usually independence (see Figure 2–1), that is, freedom from interference or control by superiors. Small business owners tend to want autonomy to exercise their initiative and ambition; this freedom often results in innovations and leads to greater flexibility, which is one of the virtues of small businesses. People who operate small firms know they are running a risk when they strike out on their own, but they hope to realize their goal of independence. In essence, owning your own business provides a feeling of satisfaction that may be missing if you work for someone else. As you can see from Figure 2–2, this is the choice the prospective entrepreneur must make.

## *To Obtain Additional Income*

Many people start a business to obtain needed income. This need varies with different people. For example, a retired person may want to earn just enough to supplement Social Security payments and possibly provide a few luxuries; that person may be content with a business that provides a small supplement to retirement income, as the following example illustrates.

Margaret Williamson began sewing when she was 10. She learned much from her mother and from home economics classes in high school. In the mid-1930s, she was employed by a government works program, the WPA, and later she sewed for her family, making all her daughter's school clothes.

**D**

**Figure 2–2** Which Road to Take?

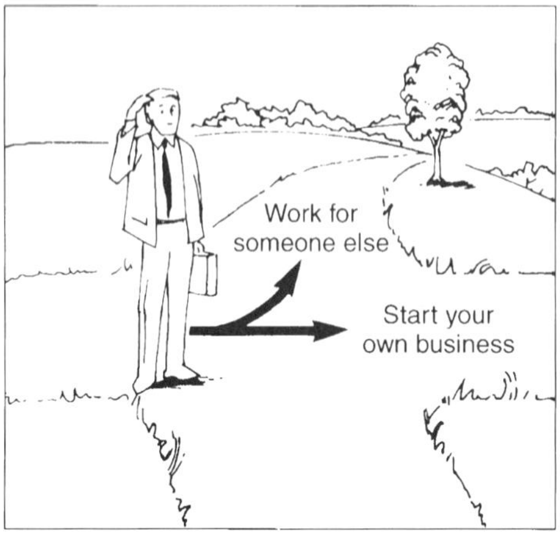


In the 1960s, Mrs. Williamson began making and selling handicrafts to boost her Social Security income. The Alabama Cooperative Extension Service advised her on marketing her crafts, with instructions on how to participate in craft shows and how to make effective displays. This training gave her the opportunity to participate in many local craft shows and school bazaars, and she has displayed items in local beauty shops and schools.

Photo courtesy of Barbara Smith, University of Mobile.

On the other hand, owning a business can provide the opportunity to make a great deal of money and to take advantage of certain tax benefits.* In fact, you are 10 times more likely to become a millionaire by owning your own business than by working for someone else.[3] Yet not all small business owners and managers make a lot of money.

At times, a person may start a small business after being unable to find employment elsewhere or being discharged from a larger firm. And professional athletes, whose bodies are a wasting asset and who must retire early, often find a second career in small businesses they have formed. For example, Roger Staubach, former quarterback for the Dallas Cowboys, is the owner of a multimillion-dollar real estate business.[4]

### *To Help Their Families*

Small business owners are probably motivated as much by personal and family considerations as by the desire for profit. Students may return home to operate the family business so their parents can retire or take life easier. They may take over the firm on the death of a parent or form a business to help their family financially.

*You should consult your lawyers and tax accountants, though, to make sure you stay on the right side of tax laws, which have been modified to remove many of these benefits!

## USING TECHNOLOGY TO SUCCEED

### Using a Video Screen to Aid Surgery!

Dr. Mark C. Komorowski uses an instrument called the Agee Carpal Tunnel Release System to repair cases of painful carpal tunnel syndrome. Dr. Komorowski's instrument looks something like a power drill with a camera, light, and retractable blade. The instrument reverses the incision and therefore leaves the palm intact, which reduces recovery time from six weeks to two weeks. The surgeon can see inside the wrist on a video screen and complete the procedure in 10 to 12 minutes.

*Source:* Jenni Laidman, "New Tool Reduces Carpal Tunnel Recovery Time," *Mobile* (Alabama) *Register,* August 28, 1994, p. 16-E.

G Q

> For example, a few years ago, Rebiya Kader secretly made and sold children's clothes to supplement her husband's income, which was insufficient to feed their six children. At the time, private enterprise was illegal in China, where she lived. In addition, the Muslim culture to which she belonged looked down on women working outside the home. But she persisted, and today she manages a $10.4 million organization and is the richest woman in Xinjiang.[5]

### *To Provide Products Not Available Elsewhere*

Q

The saying "Necessity is the mother of invention" applies to the beginning of many firms. In fact, most American economic development has resulted from innovations born in small firms. Relative to the number of people employed, small firms produce two-and-a-half times as many new ideas and products as large firms.[6] (See Using Technology to Succeed.) The first air conditioner, airplane, automobile, instant camera, jet engine, helicopter, office copier, heart pacemaker, foam fire extinguisher, quick-frozen foods, sliced and wrapped bread, vacuum tube, zipper, and safety razor—not to mention the first giant computer, as well as many other breakthroughs—either resulted from the creativity found in small companies or led to the creation of a new business.

> For example, Lloyd Mandel recognized a need for more economical funerals. As most funeral homes began to offer more services such as expensive seals and elaborate services, he identified a growing need for basic rituals. Mandel opened such a "funeral store" in a Skokie, Illinois, mall six years ago.
>
> He was so successful that he was bought out by the huge Service Corp International. He is now a regional vice president who does research and similar ventures for Service Corp.[7]

## To Achieve Business Objectives

One of the most important functions the business owner must perform is setting **objectives**, which are the ends toward which all the activities of the company will be aimed. Essentially, objectives determine the character of the firm, for they give the business its direction and provide standards by which to measure individual performance.

**Objectives** are the goals toward which the activities of the business are directed.

Among the objectives that are important to a business are:

- Service
- Profit
- Social
- Growth

These objectives tend to be interrelated. For example, the service objective must be achieved to attain the profit objective. Yet profits must be made if the business is to continue to reach its social and service objectives. Growth depends on attaining both profit *and* social objectives, which are not necessarily incompatible.

### *Service Objective*

In general, the objective of a business is to serve customers by producing and selling goods or services (or the satisfactions associated with them) at a cost that will ensure a fair price to the consumer and adequate profits for the owners. Thus, a person who aspires to operate a small business *must set service as the primary objective—but seek profit as a natural consequence*. The pragmatic test for a small firm is this: If the firm ceases to give service, it will go out of business; if profits do not result, the owners will cease operations.

### *Profit Objective*

The **profit motive** is expecting to make a profit as the reward for taking the risk of starting and running the business.

We expect a private business to receive a profit from its operations because profit is acceptable in a free-enterprise economy and is considered to be in the public interest. Simply stated, the **profit motive** is entering a business to make a profit, which is the reward for taking risks. Profits are needed to create new jobs, acquire new facilities, and develop new products. Profits are not self-generating, however; they result from satisfying the customer's demand for a product. Goods or services must be produced at a low enough cost to permit the firm to make a profit while charging customers a price they are willing and able to pay.

Profits, then, are the reward for accepting business risks and performing an economic service. They are needed to assure the continuity of a business.

### *Social Objective*

**Social objectives** are goals regarding assisting groups in the community and protecting the environment.

As discussed further in Chapter 23, successful small businesses must have **social objectives**, which means helping all groups in the community, including customers, employees, suppliers, the government, and the community itself. Even small firms have a social responsibility. Owners occupy a trusteeship position and should act to protect the interests of all parties as well as to make a profit. Profit and social objectives are not necessarily incompatible.

Another important social contribution of the small organization is the opportunity to provide employees with a sense of belonging, identity, and esprit de corps.

### *Growth Objective*

Owners of small firms should be concerned with growth and should select a growth objective, which will depend on answers to questions such as the following:

- Will I be satisfied for my business to remain small?
- Do I want it to grow and challenge larger firms?
- Do I seek relative stability or mere survival?
- Do I seek a profit that is only "satisfactory," considering my effort and investment, or do I seek to maximize profits?

### Need to Mesh Objectives

Personal and business objectives can be integrated in small business. A survey of 97 small owner-managed firms in the San Antonio area revealed a close connection between profitability, customer satisfaction, manager satisfaction, and nonfinancial rewards.[8] It also indicated increased chances of success when the objectives of the business—service at a profit—are meshed with the owner's personal objectives. The results of the study indicate that small firms can achieve both personal and business objectives.

> For example, as shown in Chapter 1, a national Gallup survey of 602 high school students in Kansas City, Missouri, indicated that 70 percent wanted to open their own independent businesses. The reason they gave was that "they don't trust government, and they don't trust big business."[9]

D

## Characteristics of Successful Small Business Owners

The abilities and personal characteristics of the owner(s) exert a powerful influence on the success of a small company. Also, the methods and procedures adopted in such a firm should be designed not only to offset any personal deficiencies the owner may have but also to build on his or her strengths.

What characterizes owners of successful small companies? A set of characteristics for small business entrepreneurs developed by Victor Kiam (found in the case at the end of the chapter) includes willingness to make sacrifices, decisiveness, self-confidence, ability to recognize and capitalize on opportunities, and confidence in the venture.

Another set of characteristics was suggested by a new study by the U.S. Trust Company of mostly longtime small business owners. Nearly half of those studied were from poor or lower-middle-class families. On the average, they had started their careers with a part-time job, such as a paper route, at age 10. They were working full time by 18, and by 29 they owned their own businesses. While 6 percent had dropped out of high school, 23 percent had earned a high school diploma, another 27 percent had some college, 29 percent had finished college, and 17 percent had completed professional or graduate school. *Three out of four had financed their own college education by working.* At the time of the survey, they were working 60 hours per week and taking only two weeks' vacation each year.[10]

By and large, small business owners are well educated. A 1995 Padgett Business Services survey of business owners with fewer than 20 employees found that 97 percent of them had at least a high school education. Half had at least a college education. (See Figure 2–3 for more details.)

**Figure 2–3** Education Level of Small Business Owners*

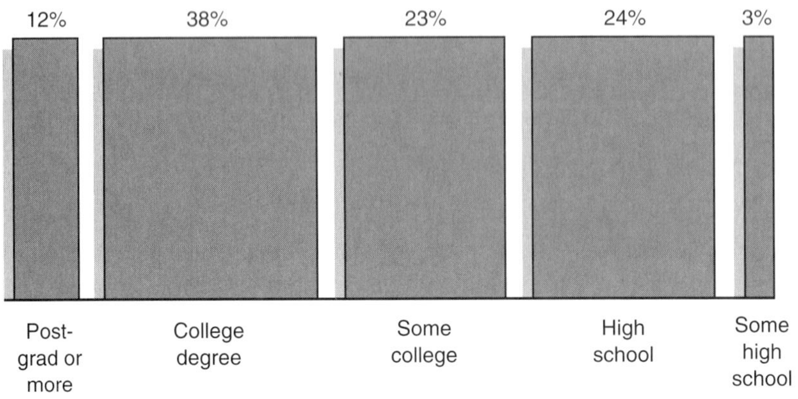


*Those that employ fewer than 20 people.
*Source:* Padgett Business Services USA, Inc., survey, as reported in *USA Today,* September 25, 1995, p. 1B. Copyright 1995, USA TODAY. Reprinted with permission.

From these and many other sources, we conclude that the characteristics of successful owners of small businesses are that they:

- Desire independence.
- Have a strong sense of initiative.
- Are motivated by personal and family considerations.
- Expect quick and concrete results.
- Are able to react quickly.
- Are dedicated to their business.
- Enter business as much by chance as by design.

## Desire Independence

As shown earlier in the chapter, those people who start small businesses seek independence and want to be free of outside control. They enjoy the freedom that comes from "doing their own thing" and making their own decisions—for better or for worse.

## Have a Strong Sense of Initiative

Owners of small businesses have a strong sense of initiative that gives them a desire to use their ideas, abilities, and aspirations to the greatest degree possible.[11] They are able to conceive, plan, and carry to a successful conclusion ideas for a new product. This is not always true in a larger organization.

Another aspect of initiative usually seen in small business owners is their willingness to work long, hard hours to reach their goals. They tend to be capable, ambitious, persevering individuals.

## Are Motivated by Personal and Family Considerations

As shown earlier, small business owners are often motivated as much by personal and family considerations as by the profit motive. They start and operate their businesses to help their parents, children, and other family members. It's interesting to note that 34 percent of all families of small business owners "always" have dinner at home together, and another 34 percent do so "frequently."[12] The flexibility afforded small business owners is a great advantage in planning family activities such as this.

As will be discussed in Chapter 24, there now seems to be a trend toward children helping their parents—financially and otherwise—to start small firms. This trend builds on the past practice of parents helping their children, as the following classic example shows.

D

> John H. Johnson, one of the nation's leading black entrepreneurs, founded Johnson Publishing Company, which owns *Ebony* and *Jet* magazines, radio stations, and a cosmetic firm. When asked what was the key to his success, Johnson answered, "My mother . . . made so many sacrifices. . . . She even let me mortgage her furniture [for $600] . . . to start my business . . . I couldn't let her down."[13] Now he's one of the nation's 400 richest individuals, and his daughter, Linda Johnson Rice, heads the company. She says, "I was exposed to the company at an early age. While other kids played after school, I'd come work in my dad's office."[14]

Another interesting trend is the shift toward more couples doing business together, as several of our previous examples have shown. According to the SBA's Office of Advocacy, this will be the fastest-growing category of new businesses during the 1990s. The number of such firms nearly doubled during the 1980s.[15]

> A good example are Lalla Shanna Brutoco and her husband Rinaldo, co-owners of a San Francisco gift shop and mail-order firm. The couple opened The Red Rose Collection, Inc., in their garage in 1986 as a proprietorship. By 1993, it had incorporated and earned $16 million in profits. It was listed on the *Inc.* 500 list as one of the top 100 fastest-growing privately held businesses in the San Francisco Bay area.
>
> Rinaldo is chairman of the board, CEO, president, and chief operating officer and is considered "the brains of the business aspects." Lalla Shanna, with the title of Vice-President/Merchandising and Creative Director, is responsible for merchandise selection and the creative display of the merchandise in the catalogs.[16]

## Expect Quick and Concrete Results

Small business owners expect quick and concrete results from their investment of time and capital. Instead of engaging in the long-range planning that is common in large businesses, they seek a quick return on their capital. And they become impatient and discouraged when these results are slow in coming.

## Are Able to React Quickly

Small businesses have an advantage over larger firms in that they can react more quickly to changes occurring both inside and outside the company. For example, one characteristic of a small business is its vulnerability to technological and environmental changes. Because the business is small, such changes have a great effect on its operations and profitability. A small business owner must therefore have the ability to react quickly.

Q

> In 1980, Mary Ann Liebert left her post as vice president of marketing for the publisher Marcal Dekker, Inc., to get in on the ground floor of the fledgling genetic engineering industry. She launched her company, Lieberts, in a corner of her apartment and was soon publishing *Genetic Engineering News*, a trade journal, and the *Journal of Interferon Research*, a research publication.
>
> When she asked her husband to sell one of his collection of cars to help pay for a new kitchen, he said he didn't know its value. She responded, "There's no auto investment publication for collectors?" When he said no, she said, "There will be one tomorrow." And there was.[17]

### Are Dedicated to Their Business

Small business owners tend to be fiercely dedicated to their company. With so much of their time, energy, money, and emotions invested in it, they want to ensure that nothing harms their "baby." Consequently, they have a zeal, devotion, and ardor often missing in managers of big companies.

### Enter Business as Much by Chance as by Design

An interesting characteristic of many small business owners is that they get into business as much by chance as by design. These are the owners who quite frequently ask for assistance in the form of management training and development. This type of individual differs sharply from those who attend college with the ambition to become professional managers and who gear their programs toward that end.

> For example, 17-year-old Levi Strauss emigrated from Bavaria to America in 1847. After peddling clothing and household items from door to door in New York for three years, he sailed by clipper ship to California with a load of denim to make tents for gold miners. There was little demand for tents but great demand for durable working clothes, so the ever-adaptable Strauss had a tailor make the unsold cloth into waist-high overalls, called them "Levi's," and was in business.[18]

## Doing an Introspective Personal Analysis

Now that you have seen some characteristics of successful small business owners, do you think you have enough of those characteristics to be successful? The following personal evaluation will help you decide this important question. No one of these items is more important than any other; rather, you need to determine whether the combination of qualities you have will help you succeed as a small business owner.

## Analyzing Your Values

To manage your firm effectively, you need a set of basic principles to serve as guidelines for managerial decision making. The more important questions you need to ask are the following: What are your true motives? What real objectives do you seek? What relative weights do you give to service, profit, and social responsibilities? What type of interpersonal relations do you want to establish with employees and customers?

Everyone has a philosophy, whether conscious or unconscious, and that philosophy depends on personal values—that is, a conviction of what is right or wrong, desirable or undesirable. Your personal philosophy will more than likely become your management philosophy. Your business objectives and resulting policies and procedures will be based on that philosophy. In the business world, the greatest esteem seems to be granted to those people viewed as builders—that is, the ones who create a product and a company to produce it.

## Analyzing Your Mental Abilities

Next, you should analyze your mental abilities to determine the type of business that will satisfy your objectives. Ask questions such as these: Can I see my choice of a business in its entirety—physically and economically? Can I see things logically, objectively, and in perspective? Can I generate ideas about new methods and products? Can I interpret and translate ideas into realistic activities? Can I accurately interpret the feelings, wants, and needs of others?

Remember, *you don't have to have all these abilities to be a successful small business owner*. But an analysis of them can help you understand what you can do if you try. It helps determine how you can move toward succeeding in business.

## Analyzing Your Attitudes

Another way to determine whether you should become a small business owner is to analyze your attitudes. Ask questions such as these: Am I willing to accept responsibility? Am I mentally and emotionally stable? Am I committed to the idea of operating a small business? Am I willing to take risks? Can I tolerate irregular hours? Am I self-disciplined? Self-confident? Let us again emphasize that you will not—and need not—have all the necessary attitudes, but you should be able to develop as many of them as feasible.

If your answer to the questions in this section was yes, or if you feel that you can make it yes in the near future, you may have the qualities that would make an entrepreneurial venture a satisfying and rewarding activity. The self-test in Figure 2–4 should help you decide whether you have these qualities.

In addition, Jerry White, director of the Caruth Institute of Owner-Managed Business at Southern Methodist University, thinks you should have stamina, self-motivation, and self-confidence, and be a calculated risk taker.[19]

**Figure 2–4** Test Your Potential as an Entrepreneur

Do you have what it takes to be a success in your own business? Below is a list of 20 personality traits. Consider each carefully—and then score yourself by placing a check under the appropriate number with 0 being the lowest and 7 being the highest. Tally your score and find out what kind of entrepreneur you would make, using the key below.

| | 0 | 1 | 2 | 3 | 4 | 5 | 6 | 7 |
|---|---|---|---|---|---|---|---|---|
| I have the ability to communicate. | ___ | ___ | ___ | ___ | ___ | ___ | ___ | ___ |
| I have the ability to motivate others. | ___ | ___ | ___ | ___ | ___ | ___ | ___ | ___ |
| I have the ability to organize. | ___ | ___ | ___ | ___ | ___ | ___ | ___ | ___ |
| I can accept responsibility. | ___ | ___ | ___ | ___ | ___ | ___ | ___ | ___ |
| I can easily adapt to change. | ___ | ___ | ___ | ___ | ___ | ___ | ___ | ___ |
| I have decision-making capability. | ___ | ___ | ___ | ___ | ___ | ___ | ___ | ___ |
| I have drive and energy. | ___ | ___ | ___ | ___ | ___ | ___ | ___ | ___ |
| I am in good health. | ___ | ___ | ___ | ___ | ___ | ___ | ___ | ___ |
| I have good human relations skills. | ___ | ___ | ___ | ___ | ___ | ___ | ___ | ___ |
| I have initiative. | ___ | ___ | ___ | ___ | ___ | ___ | ___ | ___ |
| I am interested in people. | ___ | ___ | ___ | ___ | ___ | ___ | ___ | ___ |
| I have good judgment. | ___ | ___ | ___ | ___ | ___ | ___ | ___ | ___ |
| I am open-minded and receptive to new ideas. | ___ | ___ | ___ | ___ | ___ | ___ | ___ | ___ |
| I have planning ability. | ___ | ___ | ___ | ___ | ___ | ___ | ___ | ___ |
| I am persistent. | ___ | ___ | ___ | ___ | ___ | ___ | ___ | ___ |
| I am resourceful. | ___ | ___ | ___ | ___ | ___ | ___ | ___ | ___ |
| I am self-confident. | ___ | ___ | ___ | ___ | ___ | ___ | ___ | ___ |
| I am a self-starter. | ___ | ___ | ___ | ___ | ___ | ___ | ___ | ___ |
| I am a good listener. | ___ | ___ | ___ | ___ | ___ | ___ | ___ | ___ |
| I am willing to be a risk taker. | ___ | ___ | ___ | ___ | ___ | ___ | ___ | ___ |

Key:

| | |
|---|---|
| 110–140 | Very strong |
| 85–109 | Strong |
| 55–84 | Fair |
| 54 or below | Weak |

Prepared by Sherron Boone and Lisa Aplin of the University of Mobile.

## What Leads to Success in Managing a Small Business?

Although it is difficult to determine precisely what leads to success in managing a small business, the following are some important factors:

- Serving an adequate and well-defined market for the product.
- Acquiring sufficient capital.
- Recruiting and using human resources effectively.
- Obtaining and using accurate information.

- Coping with government regulations effectively.
- Having expertise in the field on the part of both the owner and the employees.
- Managing time effectively.

## Serving an Adequate and Well-Defined Market

As shown in Part II of this book, there must be an adequate demand for your product. One of the greatest assets you can have is the ability to detect a market for something before others do and then devise a way of satisfying the market. A company providing venture capital to small business entrepreneurs found that 90 percent of the 2 million U.S. millionaires owned their own firms. The primary reason for this was that larger firms rejected the new—and often superior—ideas of employees, who then went out and started their own companies.[20]

> In 1961, Ross Perot suggested to IBM, his employer, that they emphasize software rather than hardware. After being turned down by top management the second time, Perot left his lucrative job and founded EDS, a data processing firm. He later sold it to GM for several million dollars.

It also helps if you can find a market that is not being satisfied and design a unique product for it, as happened in the following example.

> When Ann and Michael Moore were in the Peace Corps in West Africa, they noticed how peaceful the native children were. The mothers carried their children in pouches on their chest or back, held in place by straps over the shoulders and tied around the waist. The mother could go about her work with her hands free, and the child was comforted by the closeness of its mother. The Moores started making the same kind of cloth pouch when they returned home. Over $4.5 million worth of Snuglis had been sold worldwide when they sold Snugli, Inc., to the Huffy Corporation in 1985.[21]

Photo courtesy of Snugli, Inc.

## Acquiring Sufficient Capital

As shown in Chapter 1, a major problem for small business owners is obtaining sufficient capital, at a reasonable price, to acquire the resources needed to start and operate a business. Owners who become successful have been able to obtain needed funds, either from their own resources or from others. They are willing to delay satisfying the desire for profit or dividends now, in the long-run interest of the business.

Although lack of investment capital is a problem for small firms, even worse is a shortage of working capital. In fact, probably *the biggest crisis for a small business is a lack of cash,* as will be discussed in Chapter 19.

## Recruiting and Using Human Resources Effectively

The effective recruitment and use of human resources are especially important to owners of small businesses, who have a closer and more personal association with their employees than do managers of larger businesses. Workers in a small firm can be a good source of information and ideas, and their productivity should increase if you allow them to share ideas with you, especially if you recognize and reward their contributions.

## Obtaining and Using Accurate Information

You need to stay informed of financial and marketing conditions affecting your business. You must analyze and evaluate information and develop plans to maintain or improve your position. The "information explosion" of the 1980s has not been accompanied by an increased ability to interpret and use all the data available. Instead, information's increased complexity sometimes overwhelms small business owners. There are limits to the amount and types of information owners can absorb and use in their operations.

## Coping with Government Regulations

As discussed in Chapters 1 and 23, the days when small businesses were exempt from governmental regulation in areas such as equal employment opportunity, occupational safety and health, and environmental protection have passed. Instead, the cost in time and money to comply with the regulations is of major concern to small business owners, whose responses are varied and often negative (see Figure 2–5). Not only must small business owners be able to handle red tape effectively, but it is especially important that they become involved in governmental activities.

What can small business owners do about government regulation? Possible responses include the following:

- Learn as much as possible about the regulations, especially if they can be helpful to you. You will find throughout this text descriptions of many laws, regulations, and agencies, including the SBA, available to help smaller firms.
- Challenge detrimental or harmful laws, either alone—perhaps appearing before a legislative small business committee—or by joining organizations such as the National Federation of Independent Business.
- Become involved in the legal–political system, either by electing representatives who will help change the laws or by running for office yourself.
- Find a better legal environment, if possible, even if it means moving to a different city, county, or state.
- Learn to live with the laws and regulations.

## Having Expertise in the Field

If you are to succeed in a business of your own, ambition, desire, drive, capital, judgment, and a competitive spirit are not enough. In addition, you'll

**Figure 2–5** Coping with Government Regulation

*Source:* © 1995 King Features Syndicate, Inc. World rights reserved.

need technical and managerial know-how and expertise to perform the activities necessary to run the business. Some types of business, such as general retail establishments, may need only general skills. But the more technical and complex the business is, the greater the need for specialized skills, which can be acquired only through education, training, and experience, as the following example shows.

Q

> In 1989, Honeybee Robotics won a $1.5 million contract to operate a joint venture with Ford Aerospace to produce the "hands" for a robot that Martin Marietta was to build for NASA. The robot was the most sophisticated space robot ever planned.
>
> While Honeybee was too small to get one of the major contracts with NASA on its own, it had the specialized expertise to design and build sophisticated computer-driven robot systems, particularly robotic arms and effectors, or "hands." Honeybee had made such camera-guided robot arms to pick up vials from conveyor belts and place them symmetrically in rows, accurate to within 1/1,000 of an inch. This technical expertise and experience was the reason Honeybee got the contract, according to the company's president.[22]

## Managing Time Effectively

The effective use of time is especially important to small business owners because of the many and varied duties that only they can perform. While managers of large firms can delegate activities to others, freeing time for other uses, small business owners are limited in their ability, or willingness, to do so. They often prefer to do things themselves rather than delegate authority to others. Another problem is the long hours worked by new business owners. Over half (53 percent) of such owners spend 60 hours or more per week working at their business, according to a study by the National Federation of Independent Business.[23] And over three-fourths of them spend 50 or more hours per week on the job.

Where do these long hours go? A survey of people who had owned their businesses between three and four-and-a-half years found that most of their time is devoted to selling and production.[24] Dealing with employees and suppliers, keeping records, and arranging financial matters are also great consumers of time.

While there is no magic formula for effective time management, the following are some specific methods for saving your time:

- Organizing the work, including delegating to subordinates as many duties as feasible.
- Selecting a competent person to sort out unimportant mail, screen incoming calls, and keep a schedule of appointments and activities.
- Using electronic equipment for letters and memos.
- Adhering to appointment and business conference times.
- Preparing an agenda for meetings, confining discussion to the items on the agenda, and making follow-up assignments to specific subordinates.

## WHAT YOU SHOULD HAVE LEARNED

**1.** People start businesses for many personal and business reasons. While income is an important consideration, the primary personal reason is to achieve independence. The need to exercise initiative and creativity leads entrepreneurs to take the risk involved in striking out on their own. Many small business owners are also motivated by family considerations, such as taking over a family business to permit parents to retire or starting a family business to have more time with their families. Also, some people start businesses chiefly to provide a product or service not readily available elsewhere. Finally, some entrepreneurs start businesses to achieve business objectives such as providing services to their customers; making a profit; providing social benefits to society; and growing into large, profitable organizations.

**2.** The characteristics most typical of the more successful business owners are that they *(a)* desire independence, *(b)* have a strong sense of enterprise, *(c)* tend to be motivated by personal and family considerations, *(d)* expect quick and concrete results, *(e)* are able to react quickly to change, *(f)* are dedicated to their business, and *(g)* often enter business as much by chance as by design.

**3.** If you are interested in becoming an entrepreneur, you should carefully examine your values, mental abilities, and attitudes to see if you have the characteristics required for success. Your ability to think logically, generate new ideas, translate these ideas into a useful product, do effective planning, and relate to the feelings and needs of customers and employees is also important. Your success in any business depends on your level of aspiration, willingness to accept responsibility, ability to handle setbacks and disappointments, commitment to the business, willingness to take risks, ability to live with an irregular schedule, self-discipline, and self-confidence.

**4.** The most prevalent factors leading to success in managing a small business are *(a)* serving an adequate and well-defined market, *(b)* acquiring sufficient capital, *(c)* recruiting and using human resources effectively, *(d)* obtaining and using accurate information, *(e)* coping effectively with government regulations, *(f)* having expertise in one's chosen field, and *(g)* managing time effectively. In essence, it is sticking to the basics that leads to success rather than using gimmicks or catering to fads.

## QUESTIONS FOR DISCUSSION

1. Discuss the four personal objectives that people seek when starting a new business.
2. Explain the four business objectives small business owners try to achieve.
3. Explain the interrelationship between the *service* and *profit* objectives.
4. Are the social objectives really that important to small business owners? Explain your answer.
5. What are some characteristics found in successful small business owners? Evaluate the importance of each of these.
6. How did you make out with the self-test in Figure 2–4? Do you think the results accurately reflect your potential? Explain.
7. What factors lead to success in owning a small business?

# CASE 2

## VICTOR K. KIAM II—HOW TO SUCCEED AS AN ENTREPRENEUR

Photo courtesy of Remington Products, Inc.

In a famous TV commercial, Victor Kiam says, "I was a dedicated blade shaver until my wife bought me this Remington Microscreen shaver . . . I was so impressed with it, I bought the company." Whether or not that was the reason for his purchase of Remington Products, Inc., Kiam did pick up the firm from Sperry Corporation in 1979 for a "mere" $25 million, most of which was provided by Sperry and various banks. Since then, sales have increased manyfold. Market share has more than doubled, and profits have skyrocketed. Since 1988, Kiam has been the majority owner of the New England Patriots.

Kiam's success has been based on the guiding principles he has followed since 1935, when he became an entrepreneur at the age of eight. That summer, when people stepped off the streetcar named *Desire* near where he lived in New Orleans, they looked as if they would drop if they didn't have something cold to drink. Victor's grandfather staked him $5 to buy 100 bottles of Coca-Cola to sell to the suffering passengers. The young entrepreneur set his price at 10 cents, a 100 percent markup, expecting to make a substantial profit. Sales zoomed, and his supply of drinks was soon sold out. He and his grandfather were both shocked when Victor learned he had only $4 to show for his efforts. Since this new venture was launched during the Depression, most customers couldn't pay the 10 cents; being softhearted, Victor couldn't turn them away. While this business was a financial disaster, it did build much goodwill for him and taught him some valuable business lessons.

After acquiring an M.B.A. degree from Harvard in 1951 and after 18 years of selling foundation garments for Playtex and toothpaste for Lever Brothers, Kiam bought an interest in the Benrus Corporation, where he sold watches and jewelry for another 11 years. These 29 years of experience, not to mention his years as CEO at Remington, demonstrate that he fits the profile of a successful entrepreneur—a profile Kiam developed in his best-selling book *Going for It! How to Succeed as an Entrepreneur*.

In the book, Kiam says a person has "the right stuff" if he or she can answer the following questions affirmatively:

- Am I willing to sacrifice?
- Am I decisive?

- Do I have self-confidence?
- Can I recognize an opportunity when it presents itself and capitalize on it?
- Do I have confidence in my proposed venture?
- Am I willing to lead by example?

In his book *Live to Win*, Kiam explains how you can figure your "Personal Balance Sheet" and your "Intangible Balance Sheet."

During 1994, Remington continued to transform itself from a brand synonymous with electric razors by entering the small innovative electronic appliance field. With a $30 million campaign of TV advertising and infomercials, it introduced the Soundmate Personal Safety Siren.

By 1995, Remington was reviewing acquisition proposals from a number of companies.

## QUESTIONS

1. What business and personal needs might Victor Kiam have been attempting to satisfy when he decided to risk millions on Remington Products, Inc.?
2. How, and to what degree, has Kiam's background and personal business experience helped him build Remington Products into the profitable company that it is?
3. Consider some of the risks and obstacles Kiam had taken and overcome in 1979 just before he bought Remington Products. Would you have been willing to take a multimillion-dollar chance? Why or why not?
4. Assume that you are now CEO of Remington Products, a multimillion-dollar company. What would you do to increase the company's market share, profitability, and competitive advantage?
5. What personal and entrepreneurial qualities might Kiam possess that have helped him achieve his success? Which of these would you classify as the most important?

*Sources:* Based on Victor Kiam, *Going for It! How to Succeed as an Entrepreneur* (New York: William Morrow, 1986) and *Live to Win* (New York: Harper & Row, 1989); "Remington Considers Acquisition Proposals," *The Wall Street Journal,* March 8, 1995, p. C17; and correspondence with Remington Products.

## *APPLICATION 2–1*

Robert had been working as a textile engineer for the past 20 years when he decided to open his own textile mill. Acting on that decision, he bought one of the textile mills that had been operating in the red. In a short time, he managed to turn the business around, and his mill became one of the most successful in the nation.

## QUESTIONS

1. What were Robert's reasons for opening or buying his own business?
2. Did his background help him succeed? If so, how?

## ACTIVITY 2–1

*Directions:* Use information learned in this chapter to unjumble the following terms. Then unjumble the circled letters to solve the puzzle.

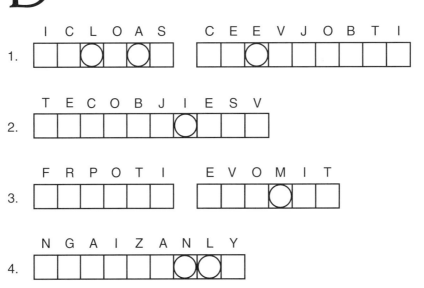

1. I C L O A S    C E E V J O B T I
2. T E C O B J I E S V
3. F R P O T I    E V O M I T
4. N G A I Z A N L Y

1. Social Objective 2. Objectives 3. Profit Motive 4. Analyzing Solution: All Mine

CHAPTER 3

# Opportunities and Challenges in Small Business

*Success is going from failure to failure without loss of enthusiasm.*—Sir Winston Churchill

*The role of small and midsized firms . . . has never been more important to America's future.*
—Tom Peters, co-author of *In Search of Excellence*

## LEARNING OBJECTIVES

After studying the material in this chapter, you will be able to:

1. Discuss some currently promising opportunities for small business.
2. Present some practical ideas for small business opportunities.
3. Explain some growing opportunities in small business for women and ethnic groups.
4. Discuss some areas of concern for small business owners, especially the problem of poorly planned growth, and the prospect for failure.

*P R O F I L E*

## SHANGHAI RESTAURANT

G

Mai Gu (upper right) and one of her daughters with two of her favorite customers. Photo courtesy of Leon C. Megginson

Mai and Bob Gu are a perfect example of the adage, "Hard work pays off." Married for eight years, the couple has gone from working in other people's restaurants to owning and operating Shanghai Restaurant, a successful small restaurant they opened in Mobile, Alabama, in 1988. Their first establishment was a modest operation, serving only takeout Chinese and South Vietnamese cuisine. Mai was the sole cook for the business, coming in at 9 A.M. and working until at least 10 at night, except on Sundays. (With success, she now works from 8 A.M. until 11 P.M.)

Business was very good, so the couple decided to expand operations. They moved to a larger building where they were able to include dining space and table service. Since their opening day there, the Gus say, business has been steady.

Bob and Mai also opened a small Oriental market adjacent to the restaurant. It offered everything from special Oriental teas and spices to hand-carved clocks. According to Mai, the market didn't attract much business on its own, but occasionally drew a curious restaurant customer.

The couple used personal experience in the restaurant industry and a sharp business sense to successfully launch their own enterprise. They had both held various jobs in restaurants long before they met in early 1988. Mai has always loved to cook, so she used her culinary skills to find work in Oriental restaurants, first in Los Angeles and then in Mobile.

In 1972, Mai divorced her South Vietnamese husband in order to "find my fortune in America." She knew she wanted to cook, so she looked for work in the restaurant field. Not satisfied with the job prospects that Los Angeles offered, she moved to Mobile in 1975. For several years, she worked in the kitchen of a successful Hunan restaurant. Although working behind the scenes, she was learning all she could about the operations. Then Bob Gu, who had moved to Mobile from China, entered the picture. It wasn't long before the two were married and had started their own business.

Bob was the planner; Mai was the implementer. Bob took care of the "paper" end of the business, managed the books and ordered supplies and equipment, while Mai ran things in the kitchen and on the restaurant floor. Greeting customers with genuine graciousness when they enter the front door, cooking Oriental dishes with an expertise that comes only from years of hands-on culinary experience, and taking time to chat with the regulars, Mai and Bob are the perfect hosts. It is quite obvious that they enjoy what they are doing.

Although they own a house in Mobile, Bob and Mai live in an apartment above the Oriental market to save money. They supplement their income by renting their house to carefully screened tenants. According to them, the benefits of having additional funds for restaurant and market supplies outweigh the inconveniences of living above their business.

Employees of the restaurant, from the cooks in the kitchen to the waitresses, are family members lending a hand to make the operation a success. Mai seems especially proud of the fact that all her children work for her in one capacity or another. This family involvement adds another dimension to the dining experience for the customer; when you see the same friendly faces each time you visit a restaurant, it eventually feels as if you were eating a meal at home.

Hoping to attract new customers, Mai and Bob obtained a liquor license for the restaurant. They also advertised in the local newspaper and the local Chinese Business Directory in an effort to increase revenues.

Their enterprise, hard work, and dedication have paid off. In 1994, Mai visited her family in Vietnam to show them she had "found her fortune." Shortly thereafter her mother died.

In November 1995, the couple expanded the Oriental market into a new operation, which they named the International Market, located several blocks from the restaurant on another busy thoroughfare. It features Chinese and Spanish food imported from China and Latin America. In addition, they cater to the local market by stocking Mardi Gras items such as beads, toys, masks, balloons, and related decorations. Their customers include wholesalers, retailers, and the general public.

Continuing their successful division of work at the restaurant, Mai manages the restaurant while Bob manages the Market.

*Source:* Prepared by Ragan Workman Megginson, formerly of Alabama Radio Network.

In Chapter 1, we described the dynamic and expanding role of small business, and in Chapter 2, we explained why you might want to own and manage such a business. In this chapter, as the Profile indicates, we discuss some opportunities available in small business, suggest areas for innovation by small business, explain some growing opportunities for women and ethnic groups, and discuss some areas of concern for small business owners, especially the problem of poorly planned growth and the possibility of failure.

## Where Are the Opportunities?

You can explore the opportunities to become a small business owner in many ways. First, study industry groupings or categories to see what types of small businesses are growing, especially those that are providing new employment. Second, study the factors affecting the future of industries and businesses. Third, study some innovative ideas that entrepreneurs are turning into successful businesses. From all this information, you can see where opportunities exist for a new business.

## What Are the Fastest-Growing Industries?

According to the Bureau of Labor Statistics, no industry is growing faster than services, and this trend is expected to continue at least into the 21st century. This trend is evident in both the number of new businesses being created and, as Figure 3–1 shows, the number of new jobs being created. Most of the growing industries are dominated by small private companies. According to the SBA's Office of Advocacy, only construction and personnel/supply services tend to be dominated by larger businesses.

In a study of 290 industries, Naula Beck & Associates found that the top job-creating industry from 1990 to 1995 was the temporary personnel industry. This expansion in jobs resulted from the "downsizing," "rightsizing" of major companies during the past decade. Also, according to Ms. Beck, 5 of the top 20 job-creating industries were health care related. Together, private hospitals, home health care, nursing facilities, and doctors' offices of all types produced roughly 1.5 million new jobs from 1990 to 1995. Employment in home health care more than doubled.[1]

These figures tend to be confirmed by the SBA. It found that small businesses provide over half of all jobs. Figure 3–2 shows in which industries job growth occurred in 1994.

We may have led you to believe that small businesses are being formed primarily by daring young entrepreneurs who use their college degrees to turn brilliant ideas into glamorous high-tech firms. But these firms are only the most visible ones. Instead, most small firms are just that: small, limited in scope, and involving long hours of hard work to perform everyday activities needed by the general public.

**Figure 3–1** Where the New Jobs Will Be

**These industries are expected to produce the most new jobs by the year 2000.**

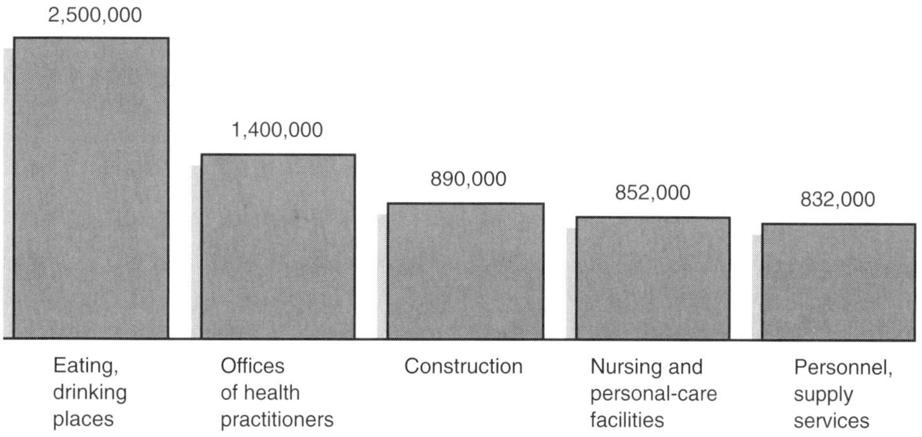


*Source:* U.S. Department of Labor, Bureau of Labor Statistics.

**Figure 3–2** Small Business Job Growth

**Small businesses provide 55% of all jobs. 1994's fastest-growing small business industries:**

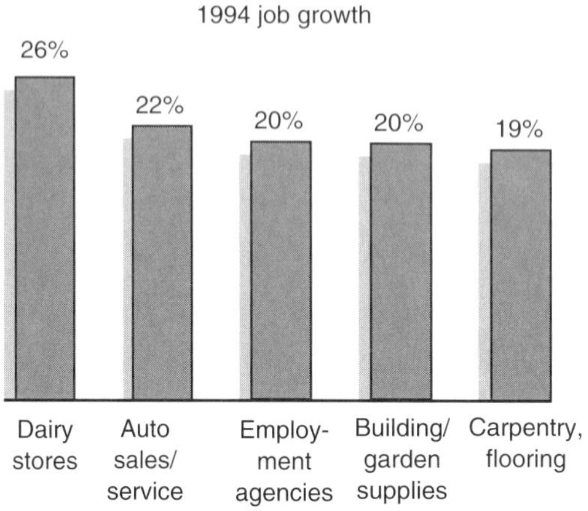


*Source:* Small Business Administration, as reported in *USA Today*, June 20, 1995, p. 1B. Copyright 1995, USA TODAY. Reprinted with permission.

## Factors Affecting the Future of an Industry or a Business

Q

Many changes are now occurring that will affect the future of an industry or business (see Using Technology to Succeed), and small business owners should study them intently to adjust to them. These changes can cause slow-growing industries to speed up or fast-growing ones to slow down. For instance, the previously mentioned Beck study found that the more professional technicians or other "knowledge workers" an industry has, the greater the chance that it will create new jobs. The study defined such **high-knowledge industries** as those in which 40 percent or more of workers are high-knowledge workers.[2]

**High-knowledge industries** are those in which 40 percent or more of human resources are professionals, technicians, or other "knowledge workers."

Another important reality to consider is that a change that provides an opportunity for one industry or business may pose a threat to others. For example, aging of the population may increase the need for retirement facilities but hurt industries supplying baby needs.

Figure 3–3 shows some selected examples of factors that affect various industries and businesses. These factors will be discussed more fully in Chapters 5, 6, and 8.

## Some Practical Ideas for Small Businesses

As shown in Chapter 1, entrepreneurs tend to be innovative and to develop new ideas. Some innovative ideas currently being developed should lead to the big businesses of tomorrow. These new types of business provide opportunities for those wanting to become small business owners.

Q

One way to determine future trends is to see which small businesses are growing most rapidly. *American Business Information* used a unique approach to determine the business categories that had grown the most rapidly. It surveyed Yellow Pages listings and found which categories showed an

## USING TECHNOLOGY TO SUCCEED

### Technology Lets Taxis Trade Cash for Credit

For years, taxicab companies have been trying to find a way to accept credit cards. The drawback has been to find a feasible way to see if cards have been stolen or if the owner has overused the credit limit. Also, cabdrivers have been reluctant to fork over part of their fee to credit card companies, instead of accepting the cash customers are in the habit of paying.

All that is now changing, as taxis are finally going plastic! In late 1992, over 600 of New York City's 12,000 cabs were equipped with machines connected to their meters that read the magnetic strip on American Express cards. The cabdriver punches in tips and tolls, and a receipt, in duplicate, pops out. The driver still must check against a list of lost or stolen cards, but that is expected to change soon. By the end of 1993, cab companies will be able to obtain credit card authorization by sending a signal to the dispatcher, who electronically checks the card number and then notifies the driver if everything is OK.

MasterCard International plans to test the system in Montreal and other major cities by 1994. It will also experiment with pizza deliverers, plumbers, and other workers on wheels to get them to use the system.

One drawback is that most of the 171,000 cabs in the United States are driven by independent contractors who are reluctant to pay the usual 3 to 5 percent of the amount charged as a discount fee to the credit card companies. However, this is changing, as drivers say people who use cards generally leave fatter tips that more than offset the discount fee.

*Source:* Dell Jones, "Technology Lets Taxis Trade Cash for Credit," *USA Today,* November 1992, p. 6B. 

increase. Figure 3–4 shows the fastest-growing business categories for 1995. In addition to those, the power of personal computers has made possible many new home-based businesses. As shown in Chapter 2, computers can be used to produce goods and services and to manage other types of business on your own.

**Figure 3–3** Examples of Factors Affecting Industry and Business Trends

1. *Economics*—gross national product (GNP), interest rates, inflation rates, stages of the business cycle, employment levels, size and characteristics of business firms and not-for-profit organizations, and opportunities in foreign markets.
2. *Technology*—artificial intelligence, thinking machines, laser beams, new energy sources, amount of spending for research and development, and issuance of patents and their protection.
3. *Lifestyle*—career expectations, consumer activism, health concerns, desire to upgrade education and climb the socioeconomic ladder, and need for psychological services.
4. *Political-legal*—antitrust regulations, environmental protection laws, foreign trade regulations, tax changes, immigration laws, child-care legislation, and the attitude of governments and society toward the particular type of industry and business.
5. *Demographics*—population growth rate, age and regional shifts, ethnic moves and life expectancy, number and distribution of firms within the industry, and size and character of markets.

**Figure 3–4** Business Booms: Top 10 Growing Business Categories

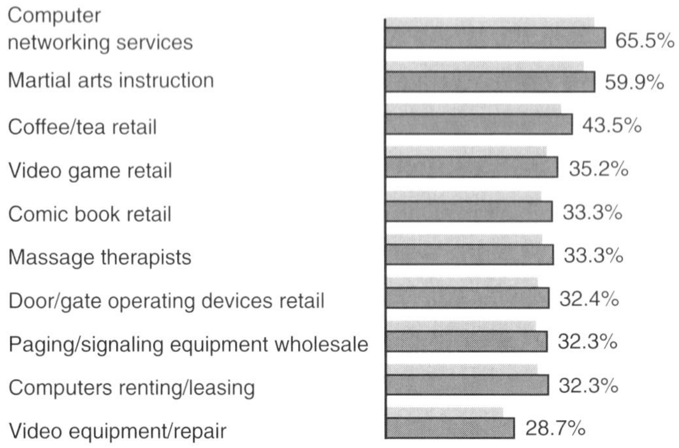


*Source:* American Business Information, Spring 1995. Reprinted from KIWANIS Magazine. Copyright 1995 by Kiwanis International.

David Gumpert, author of *How to **Really** Create a Successful Business Plan*, looked at emerging trends and problems, talked to those in the know, and came up with the following ventures that seemed to be headed for success in the 1990s:[3]

- Catering.
- Computer and office machine repair.
- Day care.
- Educational services and products.
- Career counseling.
- Financial planning.
- Home health care.
- Printing, copying, and mailing.
- Marketing, promotion, and public relations.
- Senior fitness and recreation.
- Specialized delivery services.

For example, Cuisine Express provides fast, effective delivery of meals from seven gourmet restaurants in Maryland to customers in the Bethesda, Chevy Chase, Glen Echo, and Somerset areas. Customers choose the restaurant and meal they desire and place an order with Cuisine Express's operator. The operator orders the meal from the restaurant, and a driver picks it up, delivers it, and collects payment by Visa, MasterCard, or personal check.

## Growing Opportunities for Women and Diverse Ethnic Groups in Small Businesses

D

Starting a small business provides an excellent chance for women and members of diverse ethnic groups to gain economic freedom. The opportunities for women, African-Americans, Hispanics, Asians, and Native Americans are escalating in number and frequency, as will be shown by several examples in this chapter.

## Increasing Opportunities for Women

The 1980s has been called the "decade of women entrepreneurs."[4] In fact, the last two decades can be called that, for women are starting new businesses at twice the rate of men.[5] The number of self-employed women has grown from 1.2 million in 1969[6] to 7.7 million in 1995 according to Catalyst, a women's research group.[7] This was a jump of 43 percent in just the past three years.[8] Still, only 6 percent of all U.S. women were self-employed, as compared to 19 percent of Koreans and 12 percent of Russians.[9]

According to the U.S. Census Bureau, women's share of total nonfarm businesses—excluding large female-owned corporations—reached 34.1 percent in 1995,[10] as compared to only 5 percent in 1972.[11] They founded 70 percent of all new firms in 1991 and are expected to own half the nation's small businesses by the year 2000.[12] Companies owned by women generated nearly $1.4 trillion in sales and employed 15.5 million people in the United States—as compared to *only 11.5 million employed worldwide* by the Fortune 500 firms.[13]

Most women entrepreneurs are still concentrated in the more traditional areas, such as public relations, retailing, marketing, data processing, business services, and human resources. However, according to the National Foundation for Women Business Owners, the change in women-owned businesses is occurring faster in the nontraditional industries such as manufacturing, transportation, communications, finance/real estate and construction, as shown in Table 3–1. The number of women-owned proprietorships in those industries increased from 2.78 million in 1980 to 5.96 million in 1990—a 114 percent increase.[14] As the following example illustrates, the federal government is helping this trend to grow.

Reprinted from *The Wall Street Journal* by permission of Cartoon Features Syndicate.

> Federal law specifies that 5 percent of all U.S. procurement contracts should go to businesses owned by women. In 1993, women had received U.S. contracts worth $179.1 million for their businesses; however, this accounted for only 1.8 percent of the total.[15]

**Table 3–1** Women-Owned Business Growth

Women-owned businesses are expanding into industries dominated by men.

| Growth in companies owned by women vs. all in that field, 1991–94: | Women-owned | All firms |
|---|---|---|
| Manufacturing | +13% | -2% |
| Transport communications | +18% | +5% |
| Construction | +19% | -1% |
| Finance/real estate | +21% | +14% |

*Source:* The National Foundation for Women Business Owners, as reported in *USA Today*, April 26, 1995, p. 1B. Copyright 1995, *USA TODAY*. Reprinted with permission.

An earlier poll of National Association of Women Business Owners members found that these owners are not the mythical women who inherited the family, or their spouse's, business. Instead, 90 percent of them either started the business for themselves, bought a business, or bought a franchise—primarily to prove that they could succeed, to earn more money, or to control their work schedule. The surveyed women entrepreneurs were highly educated—only 5 percent of those responding had a high school education or less—and over half (57 percent) worked over 50 hours per week.[16]

Opportunities for women entrepreneurs are growing all across the nation, as are the organizations to help women found their own businesses. These include the National Women's Business Council; the Women's Economic Development Corporation in Minneapolis, Minnesota; the Women's Business Development Center in Chicago; the Midwest Women's Business Owners Development Joint Ventures in Detroit; and the American Women's Economic Development Corporation (AWED) in New York. Also, Young Women's Christian Association groups around the country have been helping for years.

In 1995, Dr. Laura Tyson, chairwoman of the National Economic Council, set up a high-level task force to plan ways to help women start and expand their own businesses. The group, which includes representatives from each of the major federal agencies, will work closely with the National Women's Business Council.[17] There are also many private groups providing assistance.

G

An example is Olga Mapula, a former teacher, educational consultant, marketing and promotions manager for a radio station, and field representative for the Social Security Administration. Ten years ago, she opened the Communications Group, a consulting firm in El Paso, Texas. She has a special interest in working along the Mexican-American border, as the people there are "in need of economic, social, and community resources."[18]

Globally speaking, women are rapidly advancing by becoming entrepreneurs. As the economic status of women is expanding worldwide, we are learning that many women are discovering talents for running businesses. The United Nations Development Program encourages women in developing nations to launch small businesses. G

> For instance, Kamala Lamechhane recently opened a restaurant in a mountainous tourist area one hour from Katmandu, Nepal. With a beautiful panoramic view and a steady flow of customers, she earns $40 to $60 a week. She uses that to supplement her family's farm income.[19] G

Yet there are many problems still facing women entrepreneurs, including getting a loan, dealing with male employees and clients, getting moral support in the industry, and dealing with female employees and clients. To overcome some of these problems, the Women's Business Ownership Act, passed in late 1988, extended antidiscrimination laws to include commercial and personal credit for women.[20]

## Increasing Opportunities for Diverse Ethnic Groups

Small business ownership also provides growing opportunities for many ethnic groups. Small business has traditionally owed a great deal to immigrants, who have been responsible for much of the surge in new firms. A flood of immigrants poured into the United States around the turn of the century, and many of our great companies were started by newcomers. D

Now, the situation is quite similar, as 8.7 million people moved to the United States in the 1980s.[21] Nearly half of these were from Mexico, the Caribbean, and Central and South America; and over a third were from Asia. These promising entrepreneurs, with their bilingual skills, family ties, and knowledge of how things are done in other countries, can contribute—especially to the growing Asian and Latin American markets. But the influence of immigrants is also felt at home. For example, the computer industry today is highly dependent on microprocessor chips made by Intel, which was founded by Andrew Grove, a refugee from Hungary. When he came to the United States in 1957 at age 20, he had only the clothes on his back and $20.[22]

The U.S. economy is increasingly feeling the impact of ethnic entrepreneurs as big corporations step up efforts to market their wares to minority-owned businesses. Industry has learned the importance of communications; they are finding that minority business communities, with their linguistic and cultural complexities, aren't easy to navigate. New and more sophisticated ways of selling to target markets result from these findings.

> For example, Pacific Telesis Group opened a unit in San Francisco for Vietnamese customers. They can order phone services in Vietnamese, and Pacific Telesis can send out Vietnamese-speaking sales representatives or mail bilingual information to Vietnamese-American business owners.[23] G

According to the National Minority Suppliers Council, there are estimated to be 1.5 million minority-owned businesses in the United States.[24] That number is more than double the 741,640 minority businesses in 1982. D

The annual revenue of these 1.5 million firms is estimated as high as $100 billion, compared to $34.4 billion in 1982.

While the expansion of minority businesses is quite desirable and beneficial to the U.S. culture and economy, there are at least two problems. First, according to William Dennis, an economist with the National Federation of Independent Business, "the primary impediment to entrepreneurship for ethnic groups on the low end of the scale is a lack of community role models."[25]

A second problem is the possibility of increased tensions arising from ethnic diversity in business. This tendency is particularly troublesome in very small firms where workers are crowded, as the following example shows.

D Q

> Emma Colquitt is president and co-owner of Cardiac Concepts Inc., a Texas outpatient lab specializing in providing cardiovascular tests. Most of her 11 employees are women and minority members, representing half a dozen religious faiths. She fears that the ethnic and religious diversity may seriously harm production.
>
> Three members of the small group work in the office. One of them, a Roman Catholic Hispanic woman, complained that another woman, who was black and a Jehovah's Witness, had "listened sympathetically as a customer 'bashed' Catholicism."[26]
>
> Ms. Colquitt did what many small business owners are now doing to ease tensions: she hired a consultant to conduct a workshop on how to get along.

The National Minority Suppliers Council estimates that by the year 2000 minorities could account for 34 percent of the U.S. population, up from the present 25 percent. According to Joan Parrot-Fonseca, director of the Minority Business Development Agency, "A strong minority business community benefits America as a whole."[27]

### *Opportunities for Blacks*

There are many good opportunities for African-Americans in small business since small firms hire about 10.5 times as many blacks as do large firms. According to the Commerce Department's Minority Business Development Agency, the number of black-owned businesses grew rapidly from 1987 to 1992—from 424,165 to 620,192. This was a 46 percent increase, as compared to a 26 percent increase for all businesses.[28]

D

According to *Black Enterprise* magazine, sales and employment at the nation's largest black-owned companies far outpaced those of their majority-owned competitors from 1992 to 1993.[29] The rate of increase of these black-owned firms stood at 50 percent above its level at the start of the 1990s. Figure 3–5 shows the rate of increase in revenue and sales for these firms from 1992 to 1993.

According to Barbara Lindsey, founder of the Los Angeles Black Enterprise Expo, while African-Americans make up 12 percent of the U.S. population, they account for only 3 percent of its business owners.[30] And most black-owned businesses are small. While they account for 3 percent of all U.S. companies, they employ only 1.1 percent of U.S. workers. In fact, 87 percent of black-owned companies consist of only the owner.

**Figure 3–5** Black-Owned Businesses Boom

**The United States' largest black-owned businesses and top 100 auto dealers topped $10 billion in revenue for the first time in 1993. How they've grown, 1992 to 1993:**

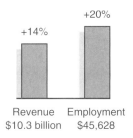

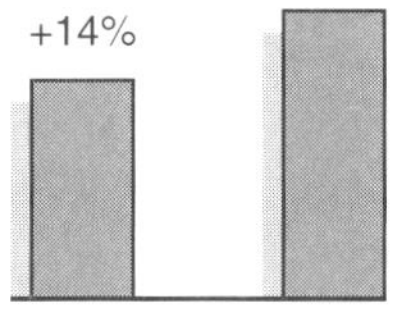


*Source: Black Enterprise,* as reported in *USA Today,* May 11, 1994, p. 1B. Copyright 1994, USA TODAY. Reprinted with permission.

The role of black entrepreneurs is rapidly changing. Once engaged primarily in mom-and-pop businesses such as barbershops, cleaners, and grocery stores, they are now moving into such fields as electronics, advertising, real estate development, insurance, health care, computers, and automobile dealerships.

> For example, Carolyn Colby, founder of Colby Care Nurses, Inc., provides health care services to clients in predominantly black and Hispanic areas. "Because we're a black-owned company, we can cover areas that other companies cannot and will not cover," she says. Many black entrepreneurs like Ms. Colby are fulfilling social needs as well as making a profit.[31]

D

Black entrepreneurs are now organizing for empowerment in order to reach success.[32] For instance, there is "The Network," an informal, but powerful, system of contacts and relationships that is helping drive economic growth in the black business community. It draws in successful people, from entrepreneurs to business executives to entertainers.

Some of its members are Earvin "Magic" Johnson, basketball star and co-owner of Pepsi-Cola of Washington, D.C.; Oprah Winfrey, TV personality and owner of Harpo Productions; J. Bruce Llewelyn, owner of Queen City Broadcasting, Philadelphia Coca-Cola Bottling, and Garden State Cable; and Earl Graves, owner of *Black Enterprise* magazine and co-owner of Pepsi-Cola of Washington.[33] Ron Brown, U.S. Commerce Secretary, was a member before his tragic death in early 1996.

Big companies are also helping blacks start small businesses. They do it through creating joint ventures, lending their personnel to help start—or advise—the business, providing low-cost facilities, and providing an assured market, as the following example illustrates.

> As part of its minority supplier program, McDonald's asked George Johnson and David Moore to start a business making croutons for the new line of salads it planned to introduce. Johnson and Moore, managers at a brewing company, had never run a business, knew nothing about baking, and had only one client—McDonald's. They invested $100,000

each and, with such an assured market, persuaded a Chicago bank to lend them $1.6 million. Also, a McDonald's bun and English muffin supplier bought a Chicago pork-processing plant and leased it back to their company, Quality Croutons, Inc. Sales for the first year exceeded $4 million, including sales to McDonald's, United Airlines, Kraft Foods, and Pizza Hut.[34]

### *Opportunities for Hispanics*

D

Hispanics are also forming small businesses at a record rate. During the mid- to late 1980s, this growth was nearly five times as great as that for all U.S. firms, including minority firms.

Hispanic businesses are booming particularly in the food area. This field was previously dominated by mom-and-pop grocers, but supermarkets are now invading the field because of the Hispanic view of shopping as a social event. Also, the national appetite for Hispanic food is rapidly growing.

G

For instance, in 1993, Rafael Rubio won the SBA's award for "California's Entrepreneurial Success." Now Rubio's Home of the Fish Taco, as he named his company, owns and runs 17 restaurants in the San Diego–Orange County area. Rubio is going national and hopes to be operating in all major metropolitan areas by the year 2000.[35]

The Hispanic market represents one of the fastest-growing groups of customers in the country. According to the U.S. Census Bureau, the Hispanic population grew 53 percent from 1980 to 1990, over five times the overall U.S. growth rate.[36] Hispanic entrepreneurs are trying to capitalize on this growth, especially in the high-tech field, as the following example illustrates.

Q

In 1994, *Hispanic Business* magazine recognized Mevatec Corporation as the fastest-growing Hispanic-owned high-technology company in the country. Mevatec also made the *Inc.* 500 list as the 43rd-fastest-growing U.S. small business. This growth occurred under the leadership of Nancy Archuleta, Mevatec's president for the past 10 years.[37]

Another rapidly growing area of Hispanic small business is radio. From 1990 to 1993, the number of Hispanic-owned stations increased 21 percent, from 322 to 390.[38]

### *Opportunities for Asians*

G

From 1980 to 1990, the U.S. Census Bureau found that the total Asian and Pacific Islander population in the United States increased from about 3,500,000 to around 7,274,000, a 108 percent growth.[39] The greatest increase was among the Chinese (104 percent), Filipinos (82 percent), Japanese (21 percent), Asian Indians (126 percent), Koreans (126 percent), and Vietnamese (135 percent).

D

This flood of immigrants has resulted in a wave of small mom-and-pop businesses; according to the Census Bureau, there are now 57 Asian-owned firms per 1,000 Asians, compared to 21 Hispanic-owned firms per 1,000 Hispanics and 15 black-owned ones per 1,000 African-Americans.[40] Koreans have the highest rate of self-employment of any ethnic or racial group.[41]

These immigrants are also helping to ensure the future growth of knowledge industries in the country. For instance, one-third of our engineers and computer chip designers are foreign born. And Asians constitute over 20 percent of students at our elite universities.[42]

A key factor in Asians' success is their tradition of self-employment. Also, they are motivated to open their own businesses because language and cultural barriers prevent them from obtaining ordinary wage or salary jobs. Hence Asians go into business for themselves, even if it means setting up a street stand or opening a store in a poor, run-down neighborhood. Also, as shown in Figure 3–6 and in the following example, Asian immigrants receive considerable support from cultural networks when they try to set up a small business.

> Dae Song, 36, arrived in Baltimore from Korea with $400, which he soon lost. Unable to speak or understand English and not knowing what to do, he moved in with an aunt and started working in the family's dry-cleaning business in a Washington suburb. After learning the business, he opened his own shop with help from a Korean support group. Each of the 30 members of the group contributed $1,000 to Dae Song as a loan. Eventually, each of them will have access to the full $30,000 to finance his own business.[43]

Cultural factors alone do not explain the outstanding success of Asian entrepreneurs. Instead, a study of small businesses in California—the state with the highest concentration of Asian businesses—found several important differences between businesses owned by Asians and those owned by non-Asians. While only 69 percent of non-Asians had a business plan when they started their company, 84 percent of Asians did. Also, Asians were more prone to use personal computers and to use outside attorneys and accountants to assist them. According to a spokesman for Pacific Bell Directory, which sponsored the study, Asian businesspeople are prospering not because they are Asians but because they understand the key ingredients of running a successful business.[44]

**Figure 3–6** Asians Benefit from Networking

**Recently arrived Asian immigrants establishing U.S. business enterprises gain support from cultural networks.**

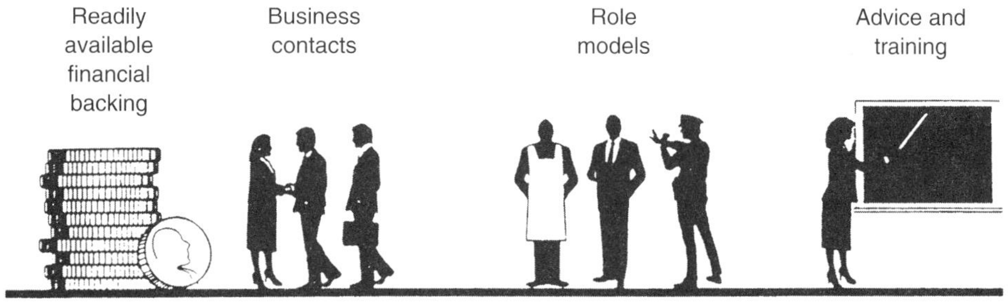


*Source:* U.S. Department of Commerce, as reported in Robert Lewis, "Asian Immigrants Find Large Profits in Small Stores," *Mobile* (Alabama) *Press Register,* March 5, 1989, p. G-1. Adapted with permission of Newhouse Graphics.

*Opportunities for Native Americans*

D Because of their earlier harsh treatment and banishment to reservations, opportunities for Native Americans have not been favorable. For example, according to the U.S. Bureau of Indian Affairs, the unemployment rate for the nation's 2 million Indians in 1993 was 35 percent.[45] Average annual household incomes were less than $7,000. Now, however, several development groups are trying to change this pattern.

G

> For example, there are about 40 funds in the United States modeled after that of the Grameen Bank of Bangladesh, a pioneer in small-scale group lending.[46]
>
> One of the most prominent of these is the Lakota Fund, which was established eight years ago on the Pine Ridge Indian Reservation in Kyle, South Dakota. Located near the site of the Wounded Knee attack by U.S. troops in the late 1800s, it serves members of the Reservation's Oglala Sioux tribe. During its first six years of operation, it lent over $428,000 to 200 individuals.
>
> Among these is Carol Puckett, owner of the Kyle Cafe. From April to August 1993, she and three employees sold about $6,000 worth of hamburgers, chicken, and tacos each month. She is well on her way to paying off the Lakota Fund loan she used to start the cafe.[47]

## Areas of Concern for Small Business Owners

So far, we have indicated that opportunities abound for anyone with a good idea, the courage to take a chance and try something new, and some money to invest. That's what small business is all about. But, as shown in Chapter 1, the success of smaller firms tends to be limited by factors such as inadequate management, shortages of capital, government regulation and paperwork, and lack of proper record keeping. Two other concerns are (1) poorly planned growth that is too slow or too fast and (2) the danger of failure.

### Poorly Planned Growth

Poorly planned growth appears to be a built-in obstacle facing many small businesses. For example, if the owners are incapable, inefficient, or lacking in initiative, their businesses may flounder and eventually fail. If the owners are only mediocre, their businesses remain small. However, if the owners are efficient and capable and their organizations succeed and grow, they risk losing the very things they seek from their companies.

For instance, as small businesses succeed, their owners may begin to feel trapped. Instead of feeling on top of the world, they feel like prisoners of long hours and hard work. Todd Logan, who owned and operated a publishing and trade show company, cites five core symptoms that entrepreneurs must understand and change if they are to overcome this problem.

- Despair over the loss of closeness in important personal relationships.
- Unshakable anxiety despite accomplishments.
- Anger toward others.

- Frustration that the lack of significant current progress is preventing forward movement.
- The paradox itself: You own your own business, yet you don't enjoy it.[48]

### *Loss of Independence or Control*

With growth, owners must please more people, including employees, customers, and the public. There are also new problems, such as hiring and rewarding managers and supervising other people—exercising the very authority they may resent in others.

Many otherwise creative entrepreneurs are poor managers. They can generate ideas and found the business but are unable to manage it on a day-to-day basis. If the firm becomes large enough to require outside capital for future success and growth, the owner may lose control over the company, as the following example shows.

> Two design geniuses, Steven Jobs, 21, and Steve Wozniak, 19, founded Apple Computer in 1976 with capital obtained by selling Jobs's Volkswagen microbus and Wozniak's Hewlett-Packard scientific calculator. They managed its growth until 1980, when they sold stock in it to the public. Although Jobs and Wozniak were worth $165 million and $88 million, respectively, they could not manage the day-to-day operations, so they hired John Sculley away from PepsiCo to manage the floundering firm.
>
> But both men were unhappy when Apple grew so big that they lost control. In 1985, after a dispute with Sculley, Wozniak sold his Apple stock and founded another company, Cloud 9. And when Jobs was ousted as chairman by the directors representing the outside stockholders, he sold all but one share of his stock and also formed a new company, NeXT, Inc.

Q

### *Typical Growth Pattern*

Historically, the ownership and management of small businesses have tended to follow a growth pattern similar to that shown in Figure 3–7. During stage 1, owners manage the business and do all the work. In stage 2, the owners still manage their companies but hire employees to help with routine and/or management activities. In stage 3, the owners hire managers to run the firms. Thus, the business takes on the form, the characteristics, and many of the problems of a big business.

The length of service of professional managers (as opposed to owner-managers) in small businesses tends to be relatively short; they move from one company to another as they progress upward in rank and earnings. Often, owners must give managers a financial interest in the business to hold them.

## Threat of Failure

As shown in Chapter 1, the threat of failure and discontinuance is a reality for many small businesses. A **discontinuance** is a voluntary decision to quit. A discontinuance may result from any of several factors, including health,

A **discontinuance** is a voluntary decision to terminate a business.

**Figure 3–7** Stages in the Development of a Small Business

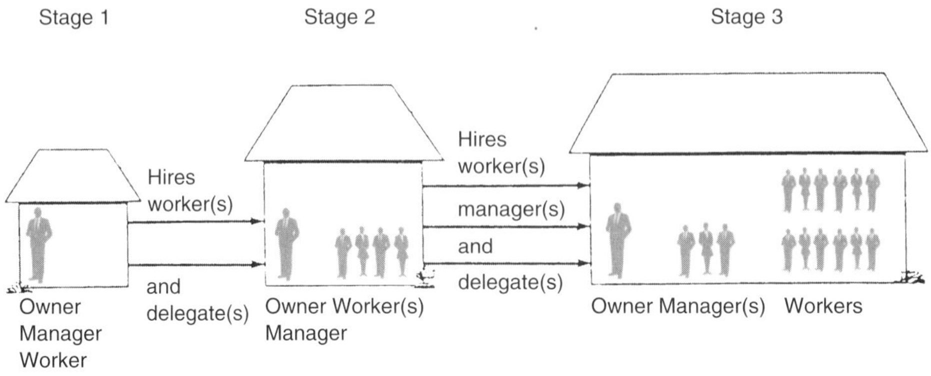


A **failure** results from inability to succeed in running a business.

**Formal failures** are failures ending in court with loss to creditors.

In **personal (informal) failures,** the owner who cannot succeed voluntarily terminates the business.

changes in family situation, and the apparent advantages of working for someone else.

A **failure** results from inability to make a go of the business; things just don't work out as planned. There are two types of failure: (1) **formal failures**, which end up in court with some kind of loss to the creditors, and (2) **personal (informal) failures**, where the owner cannot make it financially and so voluntarily calls it quits. Personal failures are far more numerous than formal ones. People put their money, time, and effort into a business only to see losses wipe out the investment. Creditors usually do not suffer, as the owners tend to absorb the losses. The owners are the ones who pack up, close the door, and say, "That's it!"

## WHAT YOU SHOULD HAVE LEARNED

**1.** There are many opportunities for prospective small business owners, especially in business and professional services, high-tech manufacturing, bars and restaurants, and other services. The best opportunities are in small firms, limited in scope, that involve long, hard hours working to satisfy basic human needs.

**2.** Some practical suggestions for future small firms are specialized shopping, desktop publishing, helping organizations computerize their activities, applications of fax machines, utilization review firms to help employers reduce their health care costs, and specialized delivery services.

**3.** Opportunities in small business abound for women and diverse ethnic groups. Women are starting new businesses at a rapid rate. They now own one-third and are expected to own half of all small firms by the year 2000. Women owning small firms tend to be well educated, capable, and committed owners.

While black entrepreneurs are progressing in small business, their firms tend to be smaller and less profitable than other firms. The Hispanic market is growing fast and expects to provide many opportunities in the future, especially in mom-and-pop food stores. Cultural networks, along with shrewd business practices—such as having a business plan, hiring professional consultants, and using computers—are aiding the flood of Asian entrepreneurs. Native Americans so far are not enjoying many of the benefits of entrepreneurship, but many groups are now trying to assist them.

**4.** Unplanned growth and failure are of particular concern to small business owners. While poorly planned growth can be a real problem, failure to grow can mean the death of a business.

Another problem is failure and/or discontinuance. Some businesses discontinue for health, family, or other personal reasons, while others fail. Although relatively few of these are formal failures, personal failures resulting from unprofitability or general discouragement can be just as devastating for small business owners.

## QUESTIONS FOR DISCUSSION

1. Name the fastest-growing small businesses, as indicated by the number of jobs. Explain their growth.
2. As far as new firms are concerned, what are the fastest-growing industries during the 1990s?
3. Name some practical ideas for small businesses during the 1990s.
4. Evaluate the opportunities in small business for women, African-Americans, Hispanics, Asians, and Native Americans.
5. How does success cause problems for some small businesses? Can you give examples from your experience or suggest ways to avoid the problems of growth?

## *CASE 3*

## SHERRI HILL—DRESSING THE WORLD'S MOST BEAUTIFUL WOMEN

Sherri Hill believes in taking advantage of opportunities when they knock! Opportunity knocked for her in 1985, when a contestant in the Miss Oklahoma pageant bought a dress from Sherri's family-run shop in Norman, Oklahoma.

Wanting to "watch our dress," she and her partners attended the pageant. She was disturbed during the show to see another contestant wearing the same design as theirs. While their client was understanding about the duplication, the partners were upset.

Vonda Vass (left) and Sherri Hill show gowns worn by Miss USA contestants. Photo by Jay Ferchaud, © 1989, *Mobile* (Alabama) *Press Register.* 

Seeing the problem caused by more than one contestant's wearing the same design, Sherri decided to capitalize on the situation by custom-designing and selling dresses on a registration basis. When a customer buys a "Temptations by Sherri Hill" dress costing anywhere from $1,500 to $6,000, the design is registered to that person on a computer system so no other contestant can purchase the same dress.

Soon after her dresses were seen by the Miss Oklahoma and Miss USA pageant directors, she became the exclusive designer of gowns for the Miss Universe, Miss USA, and Miss Teen USA winners. At the 1988 Miss America contest, 48 women wore her gowns—which were all of different design! At the 1989 Miss USA pageant, seven finalists were gowned by Ms. Hill, as was Courtney Gibbs, the 1988 Miss USA, who was also present.

As you can see, what was an embarrassing moment at the time proved to be the knock that opened the door to a successful enterprise.

*Source:* Cathy Jumper, "Oklahoma Woman Designer of Gowns for Beauty Pageants," *Mobile* (Alabama) *Register,* February 28, 1989, pp. 1-B, 3-B.

## QUESTIONS

Q

1. Discuss the way Ms. Hill capitalized on her embarrassing moment.
2. What qualities did she apparently have that led to her success?
3. If you were Ms. Hill, what would you do now?

## *APPLICATION 3–1*

Anna was a homemaker who had been out of work since the birth of her first child. While the child was still small, she decided to open a child care center to care for the children of other families in the neighborhood.

Anna had been socially active in the community, and her good relationships stood her in good stead. Her child care business soon started to boom. As the word spread, more and more working women in the area began to leave their children with Anna. Before long, her house became too small to accommodate the large number of children that were being brought to her.

It was not long before operating conditions began to deteriorate. Without her realizing what was happening, Anna's reputation for good-quality service was damaged. Parents started taking their children elsewhere.

## QUESTIONS

1. Is child care a good business to go into?
2. What were Anna's qualifications for the business?
3. Why did her business deteriorate so badly?
4. What could she have done to prevent the failure?

## ACTIVITY 3–1

*Directions:* Use information learned in this chapter to unjumble the following terms. Then unjumble the circled letters to solve the puzzle.

1. M A R F O L    L U I A F S E R
2. R E U F I A L
3. N L R E P O S A    M I R N L O F A    U A I R L S E F
4. O T N N S D I U C A C E N I

1. Formal Failures 2. Failure 3. Personal Informal Failures 4. Discontinuance Solution: Life

CHAPTER

# 4

# Legal Forms of Ownership

*Good order is the foundation of all good things.*—Edmund Burke

*To me, going public [incorporating] would be like selling my soul.*—Carlton Cadwell, manufacturer

## LEARNING OBJECTIVES

After studying the material in this chapter, you will be able to:

1. Name the legal forms of ownership a small business can have.
2. Explain the reasons for and against forming a proprietorship.
3. Explain the reasons for and against forming a partnership.
4. Explain the reasons for and against forming a corporation.
5. Discuss some other legal forms a business can take.

*P R O F I L E*

## JAN WEILER—SHOWING TOURISTS THE SITES

Photo courtesy of Joni Kincade Plomp

Many people in the United States, if they think of Alabama at all, think of it as landlocked. Even many Alabamians are surprised to discover that their state offers many miles of beautiful sugar-sand beaches that rival those anywhere else on the Gulf Coast. But tourists have begun to discover Alabama's "Pleasure Island," and "snowbirds"—long-term winter visitors from states farther north, especially in the Midwest—return year after year to the beachfront communities of Gulf Shores and Orange Beach as well as elsewhere in Alabama's Baldwin County.

Needless to say, a flourishing tourist trade has developed. One of the major attractions is Riviera Centre, a giant outlet mall near the beach. But one person had the vision to see that the area had more to offer than "sand and Riviera Centre." Jan Weiler, owner/operator of Landmark Tours, Inc., provides small-group excursions to show visitors and residents alike some of the lesser-known features of Baldwin County, paying special attention to historic sites such as Blakeley, site of the last major battle of the Civil War. With a 15-passenger van that's custom designed with safety features and a sound system, she offers more than a dozen guided tours of Mobile Bay's Eastern Shore, Gulf Shores, and Orange Beach. The tours include historic homes and churches, artists at work, barnyard visits for children, walking tours of natural preservation areas, and downtown shopping tours. Weiler also provides "step-on" service for tour groups traveling in larger chartered buses and can develop custom tours for conventioners and their spouses.

Weiler's background for this business might seem unlikely, but each of her previous careers and jobs helped prepare her for this one. After raising "three nifty kids" in the Cedar Falls/Waterloo area of Iowa, she joined a brokerage firm, attended its "Registered Representative Securities School," and became one of the first few women stockbrokers in Iowa. Later she joined her second husband's farmland realty firm. In 1987 they left the world of real estate and began to travel. They spotted a "salty old trawler" in Fort Myers, Florida, bought it and named it *Equal,* then cruised thousands of miles along the East Coast and through inland waterways until they discovered the Eastern Shore town of Fairhope, Alabama, about 30 miles from the Gulf. They "fell in love (doesn't everyone?)" with the area, sold the trawler, and settled there permanently in 1990.

Weiler knew she wanted to start a business, but while she figured out what kind of business was needed she worked at Burris Farm Market in Loxley. From talking with the customers who came to buy produce, she realized that even long-time residents were unaware of some of the treasures their county had to offer. So she began to do research for a tour service.

In addition to the market research that must be done by anyone thinking of starting a business, Weiler had to gather material for her tour commentaries. She got this information by interviewing the locals, through exhaustive trips to local libraries, and from newspaper articles. She says there were no shortcuts in this process, and she purposely went slowly to guarantee a quality product.

She had to move cautiously to avoid stepping on toes, too, since established tour services regarded her proposed business as a threat. She started business as a sole proprietorship in Fairhope on April 1, 1994, offering a variety of tours with the slogan "Let's go 'site' seeing!" After a year of success in Fairhope, she felt ready to expand her business to Gulf Shores. Her Fairhope operation had required only a city business license, but securing a franchise to operate in Gulf Shores took months and 17 pages of detailed information because she had to deal separately with state, county, and municipal government agencies. When she was finally cleared for takeoff in Gulf Shores, in July 1995, she reorganized as an S corporation. Ironically, although she can operate in either Fairhope or Gulf Shores, she can't carry people between the two cities, as that would put her in competition with the common carriers.

What makes Weiler so successful in her business? Tour-goers might cite her curiosity about local history, geography, and people, coupled with her enthusiasm for sharing her knowledge with others. She herself mentions "long-term goals, patience, and—above all—quality." It also helps that she knows what she wants to do and where she wants to go, can make decisions quickly, can reason both logically and intuitively, and instinctively knows what is the best thing to do in tough situations.

What does she find the most exciting thing about her career as a tour guide? "It has to be the people!" she says. "It's just a lot of fun."

*Source:* Prepared by Suzanne S. Barnhill from discussions with Jan Weiler and from Joni Kincade Plomp, "Tours Agency Shares the Sights as Well as Facts," *Baldwin Press Register,* December 25, 1995, p. 3.

## Selecting the Right Legal Form

Going into business for yourself and being your own boss is a dream that can become either a pleasant reality or a nightmare. Though it may be satisfying to give the orders, run the show, and receive the income, other factors must be considered when choosing the legal form to use. Income tax considerations, the amount of free time available, responsibility for others, and family wishes—as well as the amount of available funds—must also be considered in choosing a proprietorship, partnership, corporation, or other legal form for the business.

## Factors to Consider

When choosing the proper legal form for your business, you should ask several basic questions. For example, to what extent is your family able to endure the physical, psychological, and emotional strains associated with running the business? Second, how easy is it to start, operate, and transfer to others your interest in the company? Third, to what extent are you and your family willing to accept the financial risks involved, including being responsible for not only your own losses and debts but also those of other people? Finally, how much information about yourself, your family, and your economic status are you willing to make public? For example, if you choose the corporate form, information about the business—including profits and/or losses—may have to be made public knowledge.

The choice of legal form does not have to be final. The usual progression is to start as a proprietorship or partnership and then move into a corporation.

## Relative Importance of Each Form

As you can see from Figure 4–1, the proprietorship is by far the most popular form of business in the United States. Around 74 percent of all businesses are proprietorships, while only 18 percent are corporations, and 8 percent are

**Figure 4–1** Relative Position of U.S. Proprietorships, Partnerships, and Corporations

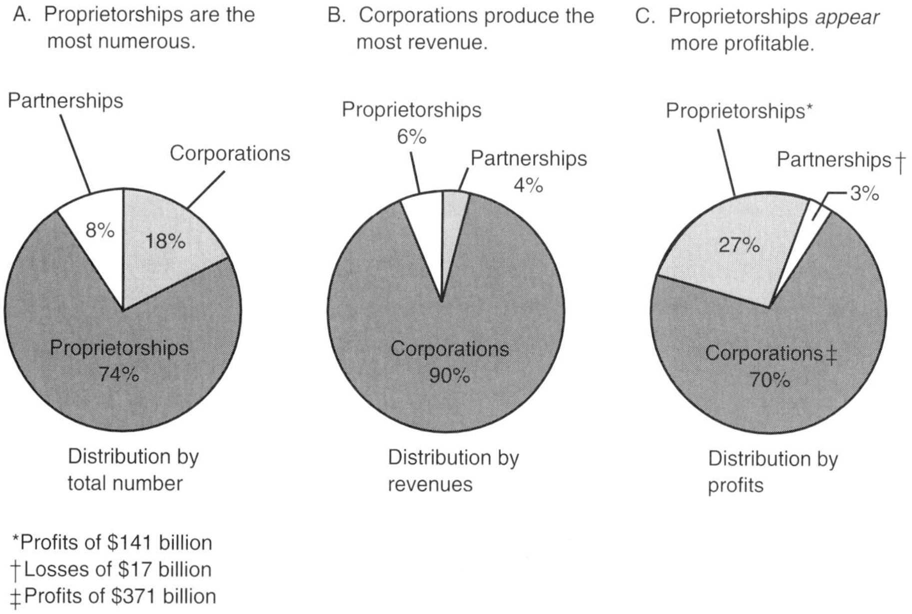


*Source:* U.S. Department of Commerce, *Statistical Abstract of the United States, 1994* (Washington, DC: U.S. Government Printing Office, 1994), Table 883, p. 539.

**Table 4–1** Comparison of Proprietorships, Partnerships, and Corporations in Selected Industries

| Industry | Percentage of firms in the industry | | | Percentage of industry's business receipts | | |
|---|---|---|---|---|---|---|
| | Proprietorships | Partnerships | Corporations | Proprietorships | Partnerships | Corporations |
| Services | 85 | 3 | 12 | 22 | 14 | 64 |
| Trade | 69 | 5 | 26 | 7 | 3 | 90 |
| Construction | 79 | 3 | 18 | 15 | 5 | 80 |
| Finance, insurance, real estate | 48 | 30 | 22 | 2 | 6 | 92 |
| Manufacturing | 54 | 4 | 42 | 1 | 2 | 97 |

*Source: Statistical Abstract of the United States, 1994* (Washington, DC: U.S. Government Printing Office, 1994), computed from Tables 882 and 883, p. 539.

partnerships. Notice in Table 4–1 that the proprietorship is most popular in all industries. Finance, insurance, and real estate use the partnership more frequently than do the other industries.

While the proprietorship is the most popular form, it accounts for only a small share of total revenues. As Figure 4–1 shows, proprietorships generate only around 6 percent of all revenues, while corporations account for 90 percent, and partnerships provide around 4 percent.

Table 4–1 shows that corporations dominate the business receipts in all areas. However, proprietorships account for significant revenues in services and construction.

Figure 4–1 shows that proprietorships appear to be the most profitable form; they received 27 percent of profits on only 6 percent of revenues. Partnerships accounted for 4 percent of revenues and 3 percent of profits. Corporations received only 70 percent of the profits on 90 percent of the sales. These numbers should be interpreted with caution, however, since proprietorship "profits" include net financial return to owners. In a corporation, much of that return would be included in wage and salary expense and deducted from profit.

## Why Form a Proprietorship?

A **proprietorship** is a business that is owned by one person.

A **proprietorship** is a business that is owned by one person. It is the oldest and most prevalent form of ownership, as well as the least expensive to start. Most small business owners prefer the proprietorship because it is simple to enter, operate, and terminate and provides for relative freedom of action and control—as shown in Figure 4–2. Finally, the proprietorship has a favorable tax status. As will be shown in Chapter 20, it is taxed at the owner's personal income tax rate. In these respects, you may find it an attractive form to use, as millions of proprietors now do.

**Figure 4–2** Weighing the Advantages and Disadvantages of a Proprietorship

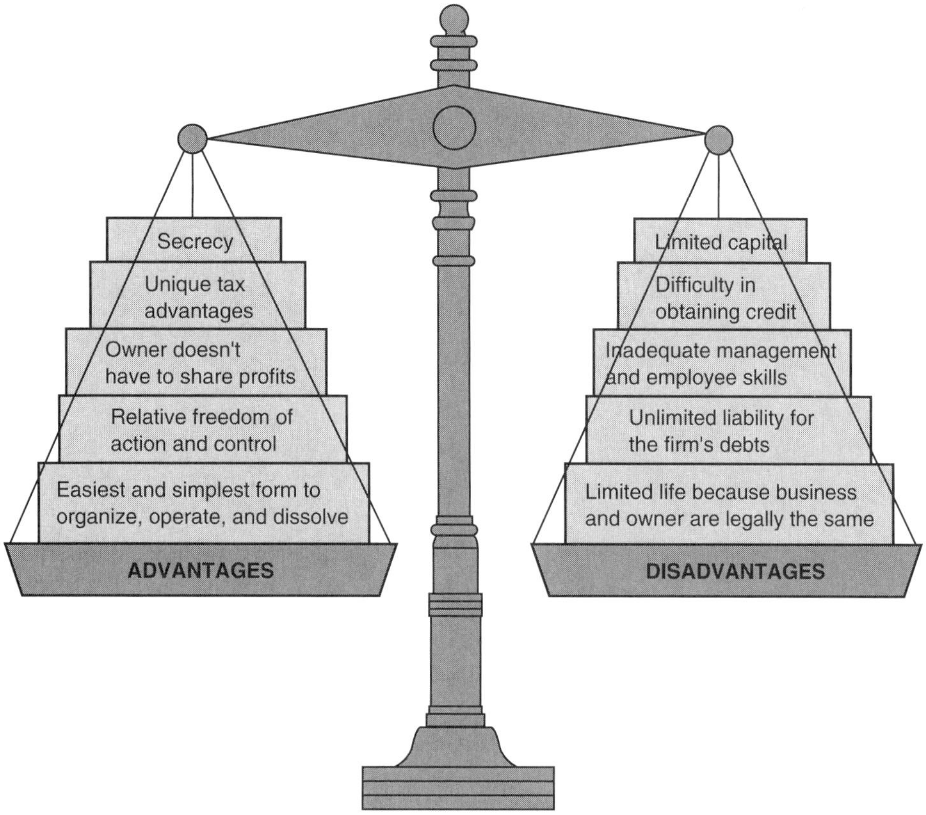


> Notice in Case 4–2 at the end of the chapter how easy it was for Henry Kloss to begin operating as a proprietor while a student at the Massachusetts Institute of Technology. All he had to do was find a place to produce and sell his cabinets. He probably did not even have to pay taxes. Also, he was independent, with no co-owners to cause him problems.

Figure 4–2 also shows some negative factors that should be considered. First, from a legal point of view, the business and its owner are one and the same and cannot be separated. Consequently, the business legally ends with the proprietor's death, and some legal action must be taken to restart it. Second, if the business does not have enough funds to pay its obligations, the owner must use personal assets to pay them. Figure 4–2 summarizes the major advantages and disadvantages of owning a proprietorship.

## Why Form a Partnership?

A **partnership** is a business owned by two or more persons who have unlimited liability for its debts and obligations.

A **partnership** is a voluntary association of two or more persons to carry on as co-owners of a business for profit. As shown in Figure 4–3, the partnership is similar to the proprietorship but is more difficult to form, operate, and terminate. As with the proprietorship, profits are taxed only once—on each

**Figure 4–3** Weighing the Advantages and Disadvantages of a Partnership

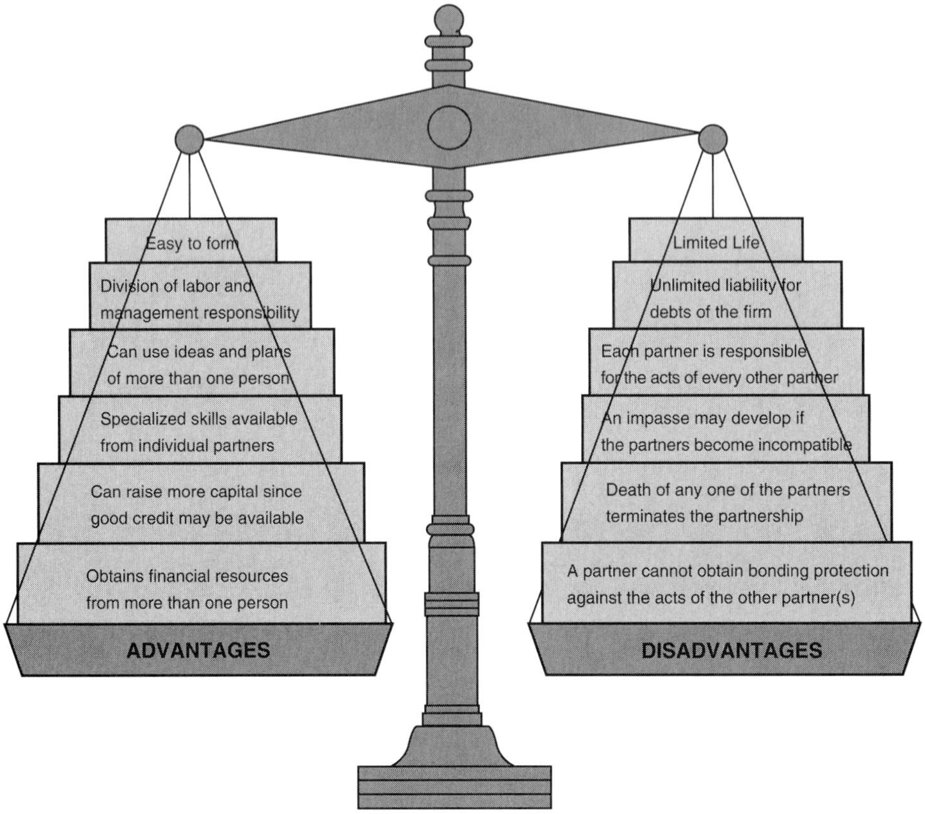
Easy to form
Division of labor and management responsibility
Can use ideas and plans of more than one person
Specialized skills available from individual partners
Can raise more capital since good credit may be available
Obtains financial resources from more than one person
ADVANTAGES
Limited Life
Unlimited liability for debts of the firm
Each partner is responsible for the acts of every other partner
An impasse may develop if the partners become incompatible
Death of any one of the partners terminates the partnership
A partner cannot obtain bonding protection against the acts of the other partner(s)
DISADVANTAGES

partner's share of the income—not twice, as in the corporation. Partnerships, however, are generally more effective than proprietorships in raising funds and in obtaining better ideas, management, and credit. Mel Farr is an example of this type of arrangement.

**D**

Mel Farr was All-American when he played football for the UCLA Bruins from 1963 to 1967. The number one draft choice of the Detroit Lions in 1967, he was named the NFL's "Rookie of the Year." After being on the All Pro Team in 1967 and 1972, he retired from the NFL in 1974 because of extensive injuries.

Farr started preparing for his post-football career early. He worked in Ford's Dealer Development Division, played football, and in 1971 earned his college degree from the University of Detroit. After retiring from the NFL, he remained with Ford to help set up its training program for minority dealers.

In 1975, Farr and a partner bought a bankrupt Ford dealership in Oak Park, Michigan. By 1978 Farr was able to buy out his partner. He then came up with a brilliant and successful marketing coup for his dealership. For years he starred in a series of TV ads, dressed in a crimson cape and asking viewers to "See Mel Farr, Superstar, for a Farr better deal!" They did! He became the youngest honoree in the "Top 100 Black Businesses in America" when it was first published by *Black Enterprise* magazine in 1978. In 1978 he was cited by President Carter for outstanding achievements in business, and he has received numerous other awards and recognitions.

Farr was inducted into the prestigious UCLA Sports Hall of Fame in 1988 and in 1992 headed the Ford-Lincoln-Mercury Dealers Association.[1]

Photo courtesy of Mel Farr Enterprises.

Figure 4–3 also shows that the partnership has many drawbacks. For example, the death of any one of the partners legally terminates the business, and legal action is needed to revive it. This disadvantage may be overcome, however, by an agreement among the partners stating that the remaining partner(s) will purchase the interest of the deceased partner. Further, the partnership itself usually carries insurance to cover this contingency.

## How a Partnership Operates

Each partner is responsible for the acts of all the other partners. Thus, all partners—except in a limited partnership (see next section)—are liable for all the debts of the firm; even the personal property of each partner can be used to satisfy the debts of the partnership. Nor can a partner obtain bonding protection against the acts of the other partner(s). Therefore, each partner is bound by the actions of the other partners, as the following example illustrates.

*"Doctor, our business partnership is so shaky, we don't even talk shop during the TV commercials!"*

Edward Nickles, a 37-year-old Bostonian, was delighted when his small accounting firm, Pannell Kerr Forster, made him a partner. But his joy was short-lived; after the firm paid $1 million of a $5 million legal settlement, his annual income plummeted from $145,000 to $65,000. Later, the firm dropped its partnership structure and reorganized itself into six separate professional corporations in five states.[2]

An impasse can easily develop if the partners can't agree on basic issues. Consequently, the business may become inoperative (or even dissolve).

Q

This is what happened at Acoustic Research, as described in Case 4–2 at end of chapter. When there was a disagreement over day-to-day operations, Kloss and the others pulled out and sold their interest, but one partner stayed in.

## Types of Partnerships

In a **general partnership,** each partner actively participates as an equal in managing the business and being liable for the acts of other partners.

In a **limited partnership,** one or more general partners conduct the business, while one or more limited partners contribute capital but do not participate in management and are not held liable for debts of the general partners.

Partnerships may be general or limited. In a **general partnership,** each partner is known to the public and held liable for the acts of the other partners. In a **limited partnership,** there are one or more general partners and one or more limited partners, whose identity is not generally known. The firm is managed by the general partners, who have unlimited personal liability for the partnership's debt. The personal liability of the limited partners is limited to the amount of capital they have contributed. Limited partners may be employees of the company but may not participate in its management.

Limited partnerships were quite popular during the rapid business expansion of the 1980s. But their popularity has diminished during the 1990s, as many of the highly speculative deals have soured.

For example, in 1995 a federal judge in New York granted preliminary approval of a $110 million settlement against Prudential Securities, a subsidiary of Prudential Insurance Company, for selling "highly speculative partnerships to investors in the 1980s."[3] Including other investor claims against the company for "soured partnerships," Prudential will likely pay out over $1.5 billion in legal claims and costs resulting from various partnerships it sold to investors during the 1980s.

## Rights of Partners

If there is no agreement to the contrary, each general partner has an equal voice in running the business. While each of the partners may make decisions pertaining to the operations of the business, the consent of all partners is required to make fundamental changes in the structure itself. The partners' share of the profits is presumed to be their only compensation; in the absence of any agreement otherwise, profits and losses are distributed equally.

**Articles of copartnership** are drawn up during the preoperating period to show rights, duties, and responsibilities of each partner.

Ordinarily, the rights, duties, and responsibilities of the partners are detailed in the **articles of copartnership.** These should be agreed on during the preoperating period and should spell out the authority, duties, and responsibilities of each partner. (See Using Technology to Succeed for software that can be used for this purpose.)

A partnership is required to file Form 1065 with the IRS for information purposes. The IRS can, and sometimes does, challenge the status of a partnership and may attempt to tax it as a separate legal entity.

# Why Form a Corporation?

In one of the earliest decisions of the U.S. Supreme Court, a corporation was defined as "an artificial being, invisible, intangible, and existing only in

## USING TECHNOLOGY TO SUCCEED

### How to Form a Limited Partnership

Software is now available with programs to help organize small businesses. One type in particular is available through the Attorneys' Computer Network, Inc. One program is *The Limited Partnerships Library.* By answering relevant multiple-choice, yes/no, and fill-in-the-blank questions, the user can develop the necessary limited partnership agreements, certificates, and various other provisions or options. The options include deferred capital contributions, loans from partners, and reporting requirements.

Other programs offered are *The Shareholders Agreements Library, The Corporate Kits Library,* and many others. Information regarding these programs may be obtained from Attorneys' Computer Network, Inc.; 415 Marlboro Road; Kennet Square, PA 19348. Phone (215) 347-1500.

*Source:* Jim H. Fernandez, J.D., University of Mobile, Mobile, Alabama.

contemplation of the law." In other words, a **corporation** is a legal entity whose life exists at the pleasure of the courts. The traditional form of the corporation is called a **C corporation.**

A **corporation** is a business formed and owned by a group of people, called stockholders, given special rights, privileges, and limited liabilities by law.

The **C corporation** is a regular corporation that provides the protection of limited liability for shareholders, but its earnings are taxed at both the corporate and shareholder levels.

The formation of a corporation is more formal and complex than that of the other legal forms of business. The minimum number of persons required as stockholders varies with individual state laws, but it usually ranges from three to five. The procedure for formation is usually legally defined and requires the services of an attorney. Incorporation fees are normally based on the corporation's amount of capital.

The corporate form offers several advantages, as shown in Figure 4–4. Since the corporation is separate and distinct from the owners as individuals, the death of one stockholder does not affect its life. Also, each owner's liability for the firm's debts is limited to the amount invested, so personal property can't be taken to pay the debts of the business (with certain limited restrictions, such as loan guarantees, nonpayment of taxes, and malfeasance). Finally, since the owners are not required to help run the firm's operations, large amounts of capital can be raised relatively easily.

Notice in Case 4–2 that Henry Kloss decided to incorporate when he needed more capital but wanted to restrict his liability and reduce the chances of disruption from partners. This made it easier for him to sell his interest to Singer and to raise money from friends when he organized Kloss Video.

The many disadvantages of the corporation, also shown in Figure 4–4, might keep you from choosing it for your business. The main problem is double taxation, as the corporation pays taxes on its profit, and then individual owners pay taxes on their dividends. (As will be shown later, this is one reason for using an S corporation.) Also, the area of operations is limited by the corporation's charter, and the process of incorporation is complex and costly.

**Figure 4–4** Weighing the Advantages and Disadvantages of a Corporation

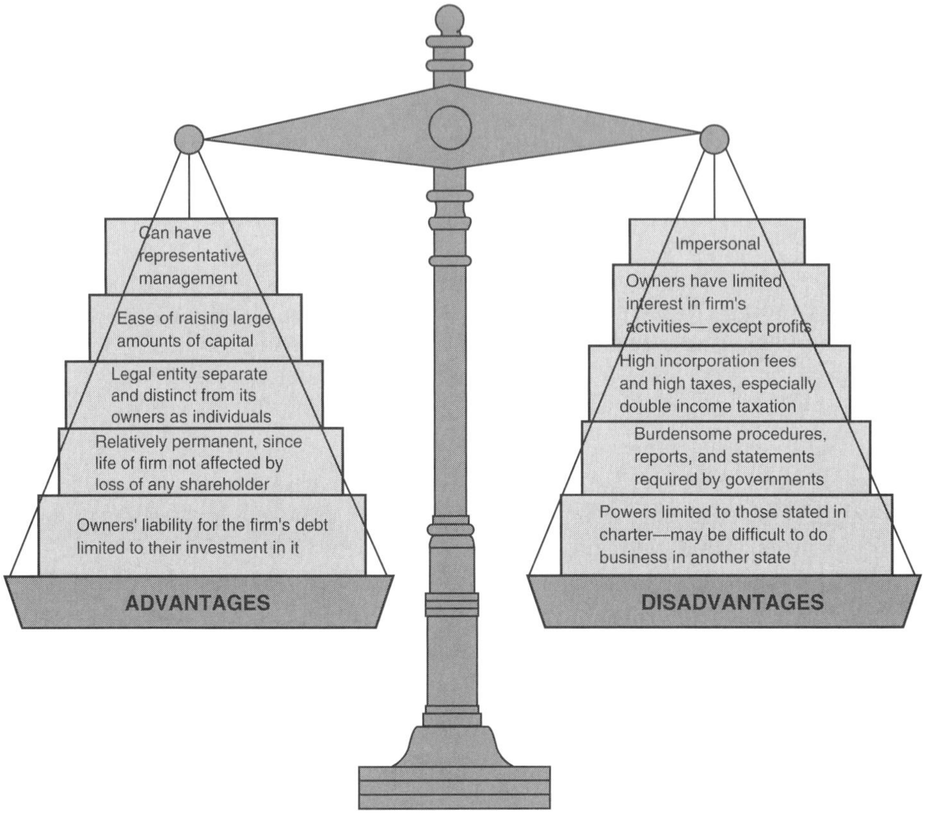


## How to Form a Corporation

**Articles of incorporation** are the instrument by which a corporation is formed under the corporation laws of a given state.

A **corporate charter** states what the business can do and provides other organizational and financial information.

To form a corporation, **articles of incorporation** must be prepared and filed with the state in exchange for a **corporate charter,** which states what the business can do and provides other information. Also, the procedures, reports, and statements required for operation of a corporation are cumbersome, and because the owners' powers are limited to those stated in the charter, it may be difficult for the corporation to do business in another state.

Because the legal requirements for incorporating vary from state to state, it might be advantageous to incorporate in a state favorable to business, such as Delaware. Delaware's incorporation requirements are so lenient that, despite its small size, it charters more corporations than any other state. Texas, however, has fewer filing requirements and simpler forms than any other state.

One danger in any business is that one of the owners will leave and start a competing business. Even if trade secrets are not stolen, the new competitor will have acquired business knowledge at the corporation's expense. It may not be possible to prevent such defections, but incorporators can make provisions during the incorporation process for recovering damages for any loss the firm suffers.

One way is to include a **buy–sell agreement** in the articles of incorporation. This arrangement details the terms by which stockholders can buy out each other's interest. Also, if the success of the venture is dependent on key people, insurance should be carried on them. This type of insurance protects the resources of the firm in the event of the loss of these people (see Chapter 22).

A **buy–sell agreement** explains how stockholders can buy out each other's interest.

Adequate bond and insurance coverage should be maintained against losses that result from the acts of employees and others.

## How a Corporation Is Governed

The initial incorporators usually operate the corporation after it is formed. But they are assisted by other stockholders, directors, officers, and executives.

### *Stockholders*

The stockholders are the corporation's owners. In a small company, one or a few people may own most of the stock and therefore be able to control it. In a large corporation, however, holders of as little as 10 percent may be able to control the company. Often, the founders have the controlling interest and can pick the people to be on the board of directors.

### *Board of Directors*

The board of directors represents the stockholders in managing the company. Board members can help set goals and plan marketing, production, and financing strategies. However, some owners prefer to run the company alone, without someone "looking over their shoulder."

There are many sources of effective outside directors, such as experienced businesspeople, investors, bankers, and professionals such as attorneys, CPAs, or business consultants. It is becoming difficult, however, to obtain competent outsiders to serve on boards—especially of small companies—because liability suits may be filed against them by disgruntled stockholders, employees, customers, or other interested parties.[4]

### *Corporate Officers*

While their titles and duties vary, corporate officers usually include the chairman, president, secretary, and treasurer. Within limits set by stockholders and the board, these officers direct the day-to-day operations of the business. As the business grows, others are often added to constitute an executive committee, which performs this function.

## The S Corporation

Corporations with 35 or fewer stockholders and no corporate shareholders or incorporated subsidiaries can, under certain circumstances, reduce the burden of taxes by forming an S corporation (formerly called a *Subchapter*

An **S corporation** is a special type of corporation that is exempt from multiple taxation and excessive paperwork.

*S corporation*). The **S corporation** eliminates multiple taxation of income and the attendant paperwork, as well as certain other taxes. For example, regular corporations must deduct Social Security taxes on income paid to owners employed by the firm, as well as pay the employer's share of the taxes. But if an owner receives an outside salary above the maximum from which such taxes are deducted, the S corporation neither deducts nor pays Social Security taxes on the owner's income.

If the income from corporate operations is distributed to the stockholders of an S corporation, they pay taxes on it at their individual rates. While the payment process is similar to that of a partnership, the corporation must file a special federal income tax return.

There are, however, significant costs to electing S corporation status. These corporations can issue only one class of stock—common. This may limit equity financing in some cases, because other forms of stock, which can't be issued by the S corporation, are preferred by many venture capitalists. Another disadvantage is that all shareholders must be individuals, estates, or some type of personal trust. Therefore, no other corporation or partnership may invest in the company. Finally, tax rules for S corporations are very tough and confusing, as the following example shows.

> In 1990, Dallas-based Hartfield & Co., a wholesale distributor of industrial valves, reorganized as an S corporation. While savings in taxes more than justified the switch, George Boles, Hartfield's chief financial officer, had to cope with "one of the murkiest and most volatile aspects of the tax code."[5] According to him, "The Subchapter S rules have got to be some of the toughest in the land."

In 1995, there were about 1.9 million companies organized as S corporations.[6]

## Other Forms of Business

Other legal forms can be used by a small business owner. The most popular of these are the limited-liability company (LLC), the trust, the cooperative, and the joint venture.

### The Limited-Liability Company (LLC)

The **limited-liability company (LLC)** combines the advantages of a corporation, such as liability protection, with the benefits of a partnership, such as tax advantages.

Since 1977, a rapidly growing number of states have authorized the formation of **limited-liability companies (LLCs)** to help entrepreneurs gain the benefit of limited liability provided by the corporation without its double taxation.[7] By 1995, 46 states and the District of Columbia recognized LLCs.[8]

The LLC is attractive to many small business owners, for without some shield from personal liability, an owner can be held personally liable for the company's debts, which is a major deterrent to prospective proprietors and partners. Like a partnership, an LLC distributes profits and losses directly to owners and investors, who must report them on their personal income tax return. But, like a corporation, it shields their assets from liability claims.

> Because of worries about environmental problems and the liabilities associated with them, clients of F. B. Kubic, a Wichita, Kansas, accounting

firm, used an LLC for an oil and gas venture. They needed the limited-liability protection because of potential lawsuits arising from environmental problems.[9]

In July 1994, KPMG Peat Marwick announced its intention to reorganize its U.K. operations from partnership status to a limited-liability corporation. The reasons for the change include the fact that professional liability insurance coverage had become almost unavailable.[10]

G

Because of its newness and the fact that some states still do not recognize LLCs, you may run into difficulty if you operate in one of these states. Also, the Securities and Exchange Commission (SEC) has joined the states to ensure that LLCs are not used to avoid U.S. securities laws.[11]

## The Trust

A trust is designed to overcome some of the disadvantages of the general partnership; it provides continuity of life as well as ease of transferring ownership. It also provides certain tax advantages.

A **trust** differs from a corporation in that it is established for a specific time period or until certain designated events occur. The trust, which receives specific assets from the person(s) establishing it, is administered by a trustee or a board of trustees. The trust covenant defines the purpose of the trust, names the beneficiary or beneficiaries, and establishes a formula for distributing the trust's income and assets.

A **trust** is established for a specific time period to hold and distribute assets for the benefit of others.

## The Cooperative

A **cooperative** is a business composed of independent producers, wholesalers, retailers, or consumers that acts collectively to buy or sell for its clients. Usually the cooperative's net profit is returned to the patrons at the end of each year, resulting in no profits and no taxes to it. To receive the advantages of a cooperative, a business must meet certain requirements of federal and state governments. The cooperative form of business is usually associated with farm products—purchasing, selling, and financing farm equipment and materials, and/or processing and marketing farm products.

A **cooperative** is a business owned by and operated for the benefit of patrons using its services.

Q

Delta Pride Catfish Inc. of Indianola, Mississippi, the farm-raised catfish capital of the United States, is such a cooperative. Catfish farming, the nation's largest aquaculture industry, is done primarily by small farmers who don't have the expertise or resources to do their own marketing. So they join cooperatives

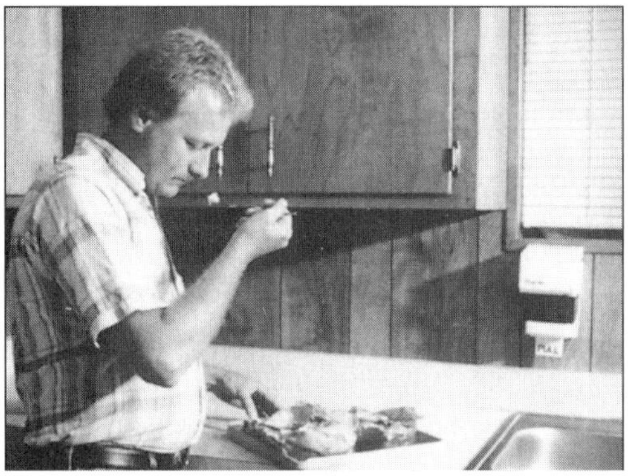

Photo courtesy of Walter Harrison, Jr., Delta Pride Catfish, Inc.

that provide aggressive marketing and financing. Delta Pride, the largest U.S. processor of fresh fish, is a farmer-owned cooperative with nearly 200 members, each of whom receives one share of stock for each acre of land in production. Delta Pride's members own 64,000 acres of catfish ponds.[12]

## The Joint Venture

A **joint venture** is a form of temporary partnership whereby two or more firms join in a single endeavor to make a profit.

Working relationships between noncompeting companies are quite popular these days and may become even more so in the future. The usual arrangement is a **joint venture,** which is a form of temporary partnership whereby two or more firms join in a single endeavor to make a profit. For example, two or more investors may combine their finances, buy a piece of land, develop it, and sell it. At that time, the joint venture is dissolved.

Many small businesses are using their research and development capabilities to form joint ventures with larger companies that provide them with marketing and financial clout, as well as other expertise.

According to Toby Walters, research manager for the Joint Venture Database, corporate partnering arrangements are increasing. He says, "It's more common in high-tech industries, companies involved with the information superhighway, and the communications companies."[13] Those who are interested in finding a corporate partner to form a joint venture are advised to contact the executive director of the trade association representing the industry they are targeting.

Joint ventures are becoming quite popular in global operations. This trend is especially noticeable in China and Vietnam,[14] as well as Russia, since those areas are trying to attract U.S. capital. As you can see from Case 4–1 at the end of the chapter, as well as the following example, they appear to have succeeded.

G

For example, six Russian joint ventures involving Western partners received tax breaks on oil exports in late 1994. While five of the partners were relatively well-known companies, the sixth was Aminex PLC, a small firm registered in Dublin, Ireland, but operating from the United Kingdom. It exported 380,000 barrels of Russian crude to the West from the Komi Republic during December 1995.[15]

In summary, in an endeavor where neither party can achieve its purpose alone, a joint venture becomes a viable option. Usually, income derived from a joint venture is taxed as if the organization were a partnership.

## How to Evaluate the Legal Form of Organization

A small business may change its legal form many times during its life. There are many and varied factors that influence these decisions. Figure 4–5 provides a checklist that owners of small firms should consider using when making this type of decision.

**Figure 4–5** Checklist for Evaluating Legal Forms of Organization

- Under what legal form of organization is the firm now operating?
- What are the major risks to which the firm is subjected?
- Does the legal form of organization give the proper protection against these risks?
- Does the firm supplement its legal form of protection with public liability insurance?
- Is unlimited liability a serious potential problem?
- Has the present form limited financial needs in any way?
- What is the relative incidence of the firm's major risks?
- Are there tax advantages available by changing the legal form of organization?
- Have you considered the management advantages of alternative legal forms?
- Are you aware of the features of a Subchapter S corporation? Would they be beneficial?
- Is the company using all the advantages of the present legal form of organization?

*Source:* Verona Beguin, ed., *Small Business Institute Student Consultant's Manual* (Washington, DC: U.S. Small Business Administration, 1992), Appendix F5.

## WHAT YOU SHOULD HAVE LEARNED

**1.** Although your choice of legal form is important, it is not final, for many businesses progress from one form to another. While most small businesses are proprietorships, they generate only a small proportion of business revenues; yet they seem to be quite profitable. Most other U.S. businesses are corporations and partnerships. Corporations account for most of the revenues and profits.

**2.** A proprietorship is a business owned by one person. It is simple to organize, operate, and dissolve and gives the proprietor much freedom. The owner gets all the profits (if any), is not required to share information with anyone, and has some unique tax advantages. Since the business is legally inseparable from its owner, it ends when he or she dies. The owner is personally liable for all the debts of the business and may find it hard to raise money or get credit.

**3.** A partnership is jointly owned by two or more people and is automatically dissolved by the death of any partner. The partners share its profits, its management, and its liabilities. The partnership can combine the resources of several people but can also be difficult to manage if the partners disagree. Moreover, except for limited partners, all partners bear responsibility for the actions of the other partners, and bonding protection against such actions is not available.

**4.** A corporation is a legal entity separate from its owners. Because owners aren't personally responsible for its liabilities, the corporate form makes it possible to raise large amounts of capital, provides representative management, and assures the continuity of the business regardless of what happens to individual owners. Its main disadvantages are double taxation, the expense and paperwork of incorporation, and the limitations of its charter, which may make it difficult to operate in another state.

Stockholders have the right to make decisions submitted to them for a vote but may be dominated by a majority of the owners. The board of directors, which is elected by the stockholders, is responsible for running the company, but day-to-day operations are directed by company management.

For simple businesses, with 35 or fewer shareholders and no corporate shareholders or incorporated subsidiaries, the S corporation offers relief from multiple taxation and some of the burdensome paperwork.

**5.** Other forms of business include limited-liability companies (LLCs), trusts, cooperatives, and joint ventures.

## QUESTIONS FOR DISCUSSION

1. What are some basic questions to ask when deciding on the legal form to choose for a small business?
2. Define *proprietorship, partnership, corporation, trust, cooperative,* and *joint venture.*
3. What are some advantages and disadvantages of a proprietorship?
4. What are some advantages and disadvantages of a partnership?
5. What are some advantages and disadvantages of a corporation?
6. Distinguish between a general partnership and a limited partnership.
7. Distinguish between a C corporation, an S corporation, and a limited-liability company (LLC).

## *CASE 4–1*

### SIBERIAN JOINT VENTURE

G

White Nights Joint Enterprise is a combination of U.S. oil companies and Siberian oil fields. The name refers to the long Siberian summer nights and also plays on "white knights," an allusion to the U.S. investors. The arrangement is simple and involves incremental sharing of excess oil recovered from three oil fields. "Excess oil" is defined as all production in excess of the 25-year projection by the Russian producers.

When the joint venture was organized, it was the first of its kind in the entire Russian oil industry. The Russian partner is Varegan Oil and Gas, a state-owned company that receives all the oil included in the 25-year projections, plus half of the additional oil and 10 percent royalties on the rest in exchange for the use of its oil fields. The U.S. partners, Anglo-Suisse and Philbro Energy Production, receive the remaining 40 percent of the excess production.

The U.S. companies were invited to help the Russian industry, which needed money, equipment, and technology not available in Siberia. In time, it was discovered that, although there was a shortage in parts and technology, it was the Russian technique and experience that allowed the drilling process to become efficient.

## QUESTIONS

1. What kind of combination is described in the above case?
2. What are the advantages for the U.S. partners? The Russians?
3. Who wins? Explain.

*Source:* Adapted from J. Taylor Buckley, "Joint Venture Boosts Siberian Oil Flow," *USA Today,* March 12, 1992, p. 7B. 

# CASE 4–2

## HENRY E. KLOSS—PROPRIETOR, PARTNER, AND CORPORATE OWNER

As an undergraduate at Massachusetts Institute of Technology, Henry E. Kloss first ventured into business by designing, making, and selling cabinets for stereos. He did this to pay his way through school.

After military service, Kloss returned to Cambridge, where his skills as a cabinetmaker, combined with his interest in electronics and sound, led him to Edgar Villchur, who had an idea for an acoustic suspension system. They formed a partnership, Acoustic Research, in 1954 and pioneered the production of acoustic suspension speakers, which made all other types of loudspeakers obsolete. Half the company stock went to Kloss and two other investors, while the other half went to Villchur. Disagreement over day-to-day management eventually required a separation, so Kloss and the two top managers left. They sold their interest for about $56,000 and formed KLH Corporation to produce low-cost, full-range speakers. Later, they expanded their product base by adding items such as the Dolby® noise reduction system. Their sales doubled from $2 to $4 million in the year after they were the first to use transistors in a consumer product—a portable stereo.

In 1964, KLH was sold to Singer for $4 million, of which Kloss received $1.2 million in stock. (Unfortunately for him, Singer stock was the second-biggest loser on the New York Stock Exchange the next year.) Over three

Photo courtesy of Henry E. Kloss.

years, however, he had sold most of his stock on the open market. Kloss ran KLH for Singer until 1967; but when Singer chose not to enter the TV market, Kloss left and sold the rest of his stock to Singer for $400,000.

Kloss then spent two years developing a working model of a large-screen TV set—called Videobeam—in the basement of his home. By then he was out of money, so he founded Advent Corporation to produce projection TVs and high-quality, low-priced speakers as well as the Videobeams. Advent had constant financial problems due to its low prices for its high-quality speakers and TV sets. By 1975, its bankers forced Advent to raise new capital, which resulted in Kloss's being demoted from president to chief scientist—and then leaving the country.

Kloss spent the next two years perfecting a low-cost method of manufacturing the tubes for his large-screen TV. In 1979, he founded Kloss Video with $400,000 of his own money and $400,000 from private sources. Kloss became president and treasurer of the company. Its two-piece, large-screen projection set, the Novabeam—which sold for about $3,000—had sharper and brighter images than those of its competitors. Because of insufficient public interest in big-screen TV, Kloss Video reentered the speaker market. Kloss Video's stock declined after reaching its top price in 1983, when Kloss's 60 percent share was worth about $15 million.

By 1987, Kloss Video was interested in emphasizing consumer sales, so the directors asked Kloss to search for a new president from outside the company. Instead, they chose one of their own for the position and appointed Kloss as head of research and development.

Kloss left to start a new company, Cambridge SoundWorks, in nearby Newton, Massachusetts. Its total capital was a $250,000 no-equity loan from Dr. Henry Morgan, who had been associated with Kloss for several years. Its Ensemble Speaker System comprised four separate units: two woofers and two tweeters. The speakers were known for "quality and affordability."

Kloss continues to be an innovative entrepreneur.

*Source:* Correspondence with Henry Kloss and Kloss Video; and various other sources, such as Kloss Video 10-K filings and proxy statements; Hans Fantel, "Henry Kloss's Mail-Order Speakers," *The New York Times*, February 19, 1989, p. H32; and Alan Deutschman, "How to Invest in a Startup Business," *Fortune*, Fall 1989, pp. 115–22.

## QUESTIONS

1. What caused Henry Kloss's partnership, Acoustic Research, to fall apart? Explain.

2. What inherent problem(s) do you see in having a 50-50 percent ownership (and management) of a company, as was the case in Acoustic Research? Explain.
3. Kloss started and has been involved with four corporations. How might he have avoided the problems he eventually had with his first three corporations? Would you classify Kloss as a success? Why or why not?
4. Assume that you have been hired by Kloss's newest corporation, Cambridge SoundWorks, as a consultant. Your job is to keep Kloss from repeating past mistakes and help him avoid making new ones. What advice and counsel would you give?
5. Putting aside financial considerations, speculate as to which form of business ownership was most rewarding to Kloss.

## APPLICATION 4–1

### DB BIKES

David recently opened a small bike shop after completing a course in small business management at a local community college. The business started flourishing, and, to gain more capital, David asked Becky to join him in the venture. They formed DB Bikes, and both had an equal share in the business, as well as sharing equal liability.

Soon they realized they could not manage the business alone, as they didn't have enough funds to meet the growing customer demand. So they decided to incorporate and sell shares to the public. The business is now called DB Bikes, Inc.

### QUESTIONS

1. What form of business was DB Bikes when David owned it alone?
2. What kind of business did it become when Becky joined the business?
3. What kind of partnership did David and Becky have? Explain the difference between this and other kinds of partnerships.
4. What kind of business did it become when they sold shares?

# APPLICATION 4–2

## JO FRANCES'S DILEMMA

Jo Frances, after retiring from teaching, formed a business she called "The Little Schoolhouse on the Farm." Her main activity was tutoring children with learning disabilities. The business has been operating for five years with a full complement of students, who come individually after regular school hours.

Ann, a cousin of Jo Frances, recently widowed, came to live near her. Since Ann had training that Jo Frances needed for her business, she started working for Jo Frances, earning an hourly wage. Although this arrangement seemed satisfactory for the time being, Jo Frances was not sure how well it would work in the long run. Because Ann was teaching some of Jo Frances's students, there was a certain amount of competition, and Jo Frances wondered if it might not be a good idea to redefine their relationship by forming a partnership, a corporation, or some other type of arrangement.

### QUESTIONS

1. What would you recommend to Jo Frances?
2. Why?

# ACTIVITY 4–1

*Directions:* Use information learned from this chapter to "link the labyrinth."

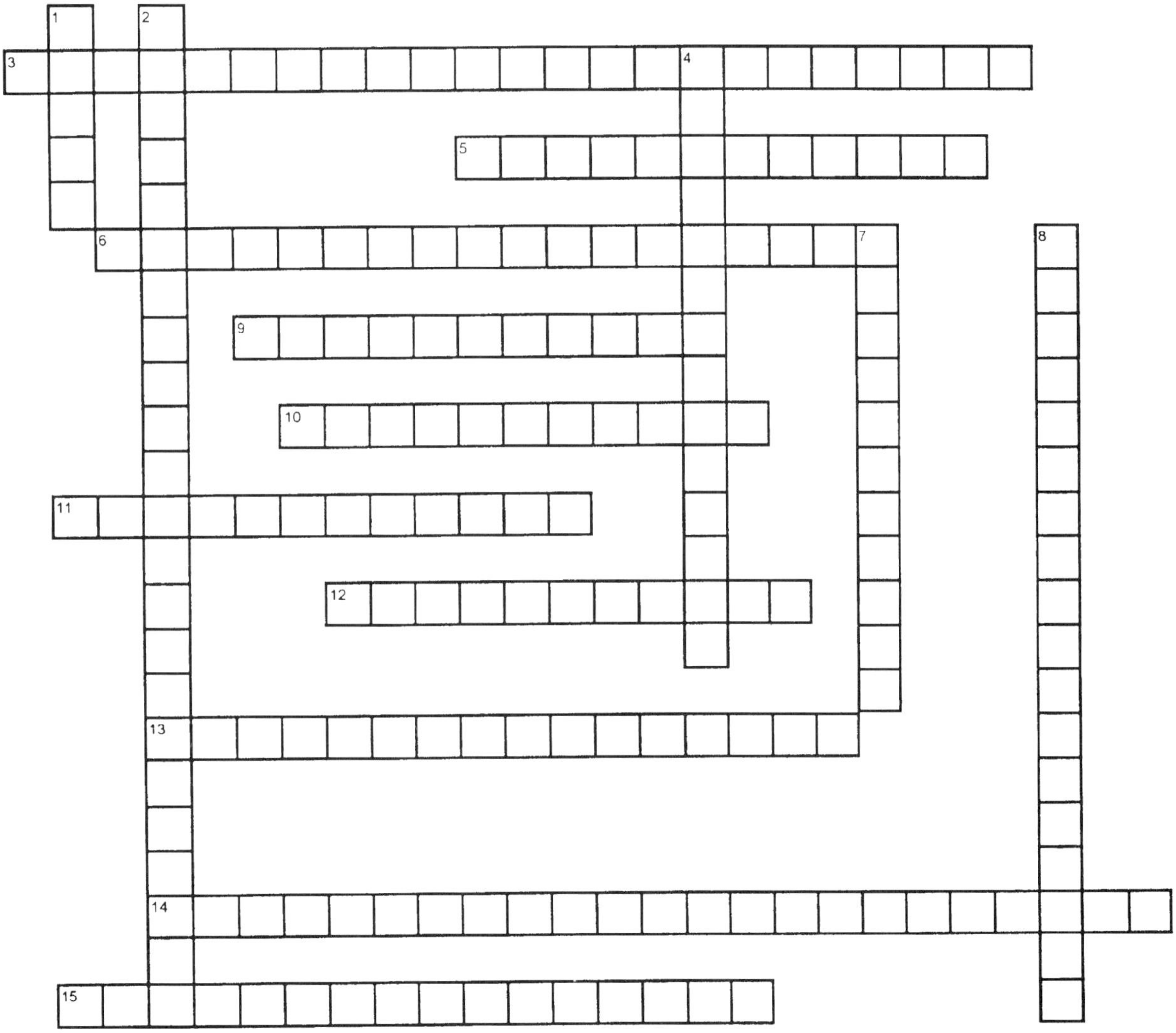

ACROSS

3 Instrument

5 Exempt from multiple taxation and excessive paperwork

6 Equal participation in management and liability

9 For the benefit of patrons

10 Earnings are taxed at corporate and shareholder levels

11 Temporary partnership

12 Formed and owned by stockholders

13 Provides organizational and financial information

14 Show rights, duties, and responsibilities of each partner

15 Explains how stockholders can buy each other's interest

DOWN

1 Hold and distribute assets for the benefit of others

2 Combines advantages of corporation with benefits of a partnership

4 Business owned by one person

7 Two or more owners with unlimited liability

8 Partners contribute capital, but are liable for what?

ACROSS 3 Articles of incorporation 5 S corporation 6 General partnership 9 Cooperative 10 C corporation 11 Joint venture 12 Corporation 13 Corporate charter 14 Articles of copartnerships 15 Buy sell agreement
DOWN 1 Trust 2 Limited liability company 4 Proprietorship 7 Partnership 8 Limited partnership

CHAPTER

# 5

# How to Become the Owner of a Small Business

*Living below your means is never a mistake, and that is even more true with a start-up business.*—Robert Caldwell

*There is no such thing as growth industries. There are only companies organized and operated to create and capitalize on growth opportunities.*—Theodore Levitt

## LEARNING OBJECTIVES

After studying the material in this chapter, you will be able to:

1. Explain how to go into business for yourself.
2. Describe the steps involved in the procedure recommended for going into business.
3. Describe how to search for and identify a product needed by the public—that is, how to find your niche.
4. Describe how to study the market you are entering, including sources of information.
5. Decide whether to start a new business, buy an existing one, or buy a franchise.

# PROFILE

## ON TIME AND WITHIN BUDGET

When Herman J. Russell, founder and chairman of the highly successful Atlanta-based H. J. Russell & Company, thinks of his entrepreneurial achievements, he thanks his father, who owned a small subcontracting business. Using lessons learned from his father as his key to success, Russell turned a small brick and mortar business he formed in 1956 into a diversified construction and engineering company that is one of the largest black-owned businesses in the United States, with sales of $150 million in 1993. Russell became the first black member of the Atlanta Chamber of Commerce in 1962 and became its president in 1981.

Photo courtesy of H. J. Russell & Co.

Russell learned from his father the trade of plastering and the value of saving. While still in junior high, he bought a small plot of land from the City of Atlanta for $125. During his senior year in high school, he started building a duplex on his property and finished it during his first summer break from Alabama's Tuskegee Institute.

On graduation from Tuskegee, he converted his part-time building activities into H. J. Russell Plastering Company. After earning an excellent reputation Russell moved into building apartment complexes.

Russell has been involved in numerous joint-venture projects with many other contractors, including the Georgia-Pacific headquarters building in Atlanta, many other office buildings and apartment complexes throughout the Southeast, four underground stations for Atlanta's rapid rail system, the Martin Luther King Community Center, the underground people mover at Atlanta's Hartsfield International Airport, and many projects for the 1996 Olympics.

Russell says his extensive knowledge of the construction industry—which he learned the hard way, from the ground up—has been a vital factor in his success. Another important key to success is his consistent dependability. He is well known for completing high-pressure projects on time and—probably more importantly—within budget.

Russell expressed his business philosophy in these words: "I've always believed in a philosophy of controlled growth. There is no quick fix to success; it requires lots of hard work and sacrifice."

*Source:* Based on information in Donald C. Mosley, Paul R. Pietri, and Leon C. Megginson, *Management: Leadership in Action,* 5th ed. (New York: HarperCollins College Publishers, 1996), p. 94; and correspondence with H. J. Russell & Company.

**Figure 5–1** How a Business Is Formed and Operates

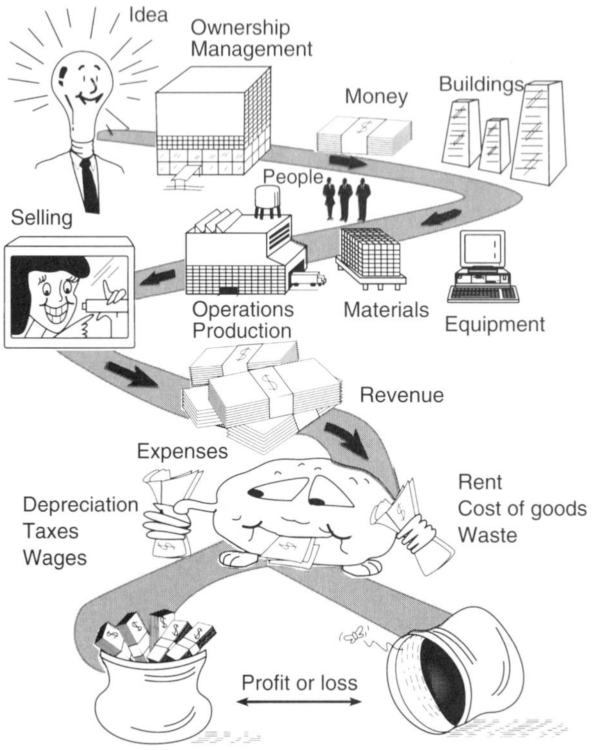


As you can see from the Profile, many opportunities exist for enterprising people to go into business for themselves. As shown in Figure 5–1, the process begins when you have an idea for a new product,* such as an innovative computer game. Then you decide on the ownership and management of the business and obtain resources—in the form of people, buildings and equipment, materials and supplies, and the money to finance them. You then begin producing and selling the product to obtain revenues to pay expenses and provide you with a profit, so you can repeat the cycle.

While the concept is simple, the actual process is not as easy as it may appear from the figure. In fact, the actual process of choosing a business to enter is quite complex, as will be shown in this and the following chapters.

## How to Go into Business for Yourself

Chapter 2 cites many reasons for starting a small business, and Chapter 3 describes available opportunities. Those who decide to take the important step of starting their own business must do extensive planning in order to increase their chances of success. Now we would like to explain how to actually go into business—if that is what you would like to do.[1]

---

*Technically, a product can be either a physical good or a service. To prevent repetition, we will use the term *product* to mean both.

## USING TECHNOLOGY TO SUCCEED

### Computerized Start-Ups

If you think multimedia is just for fun and games, let Irwin New Media change your thinking. Irwin, the leading publisher of business books for students and professionals, and SoftKey International, publisher of the award-winning *Time Almanac* CD-ROM series, have recently released a complete, interactive CD-ROM business resource that focuses on corporate and small organizations.

The first Irwin ProMBA™ product—*Multimedia MBA: Small Business Edition*—was published in 1994. It was named "one of the 100 Best CD-ROMs of 1994" by *CD-ROM World* magazine. The program deals with such topics as accounting, promotion and advertising, entrepreneurship, human resource management, business law, and retailing.

Another program, *How to Write a Business Plan,* developed by the American Institute of Small Business, provides practical information on how to create a business plan. It offers tips on sales forecasting, marketing and competitive analyses, and projected balance sheets, cash flow data, and profit and loss statements. It can be used with Apple's Macintosh as well as IBM-compatibles. (Note: For further information on creating a business plan, call 1-800-328-2906.)

## How to Start a Business

Once the decision is made to go into business, proper planning becomes essential. While there is no one tried-and-true procedure that will work for everyone, you should at least follow some logical, well-thought-out procedure.[2] The above Using Technology to Succeed suggests some shortcuts available if you have a computer.

"Dad, now that I've got my MBA, I'll pay you back by giving you a job in my new company—which you promised to finance."

## Steps in Starting a Business

If you *really want to start a new business,* how do you do it? We've tried to compress all the details into the following eight steps:

1. Search for and identify a needed product.
2. Study the market for the product, using as many sources of information as feasible.
3. Decide whether to start a new business, buy an existing one, or buy a franchise.
4. Make strategic plans, including setting your mission, strategic objectives, and strategies.

5. Make operational plans, including setting policies, budgets, standards, procedures, and methods and planning the many aspects of producing and marketing the product.
6. Make financial plans, including estimating income and expenses, estimating initial investment, and locating sources of funds.
7. Develop these plans into a detailed business plan.
8. Implement the plan.

The first three of these steps are covered in this chapter. Steps 4, 5, and 6 are discussed in Chapter 6, and steps 7 and 8 are covered in Chapter 8. Implementing the business plan is also covered throughout the text.

## Identifying a Needed Product, or Finding Your Niche

Many business owners fail because they see the glamour of some businesses—and the apparent ease with which they are run—and think, "I know I can make a lot of money if I start my own business." While a few do succeed without adequate preparation, the majority fail. Although proper planning does not ensure success, it does improve the chances of succeeding.

Planning starts with searching for a product to sell. According to William A. Sahlman, who teaches entrepreneurial finance at Harvard, "Being bright-eyed and bushy-tailed isn't necessarily a barometer of success. If people succeed, it's because they really understand an industry and perceive some need or service that no one else has seen."[3] So first find your product!

The list of possible products is almost unlimited, considering the variety of goods and services offered by the nearly 21 million U.S. businesses now in existence. What types of businesses are available? Not all the fields are open, but there is very likely a potential new business; you just have to find it. The best place to start searching is to find your appropriate market niche. This process is called **niche marketing**, which is the process of finding a small—but profitable—demand for something, then producing a custom-made product for that market. The following is a classic example of niche marketing for the student market.

**Niche marketing** is the process of finding a small—but profitable—demand for something and producing a custom-made product for that market.

Photo courtesy of David Carter.

In 1958, Clifton Hillegass was given the rights to course outlines for 16 of Shakespeare's plays. Since he was working as a buyer and seller of college texts, he hesitated to produce and sell these outlines because of possible conflict of interest. Still, he believed there was a market niche, so he borrowed $4,000 from a bank and started printing copies of what he called "Cliffs Notes." His wife used a portable typewriter to write some 1,000 letters to college bookstores. Orders poured in, and Cliffs Notes, Inc., now has an 80 percent market share. In 1989, Hillegass turned down a $70 million offer for his business.[4]

Another area where niche marketing was used is producing specialty products for microwave oven users.

> For example, certain brands of paper towels are marketed specifically for microwave use. But Abbey Fleck, watching her father run out of paper towels while microwaving bacon, had a brainstorm for a microwave bacon rack. After experimenting for two years, Abbey and her father settled on a bacon hanger design. In conjunction with Armour Foods, Abbey and her father have sold over 72,000 "Makin' Bacon" utensils for $6.99 each.[5]

D

Some of the most successful small firms find a "niche within a niche" and never deviate from it, as shown by the Profile of H. J. Russell.

## How to Decide on a Product

How can the right product be found? Most new businesses were at one time uncommon or innovative, such as selling front pouches for parents to carry children in, selling or renting videotapes, and selling computer software. Talking to large companies may help you identify opportunities that can be handled better by a small business. Newspapers are filled with advertisements for "business opportunities"—businesses for sale, new products for sale by their inventors, and other opportunities to become one's own boss. Bear in mind, though, that *these ideas are not always feasible, so proceed with caution.*

Don't forget to look to the past for a "new" product. Consumer tastes run in cycles, so it may be time to reintroduce an old product.

> For example, the magazine *Victoria* is devoted to Victorian-style decorating; and old-fashioned clothes for children—at thoroughly modern yuppie prices—are sold in trendy stores and catalogs.
>
> "High Tea"—old-fashioned English tea, scones, French pastries, and fruit trifle—is served daily at the Oak Bay Beach Hotel in Victoria in a picturesque lounge overlooking a bay.

G

Hobbies, recreation, and working at home require study, training, and practice that can lead to products of new design or characteristics. In addition, the subject of needed products and services often comes up in social conversation. Bankers, consultants, salespeople, and anyone else can be good sources of ideas. But it takes observation, study, vision, and luck to recognize the appropriate product for your business. Or sometimes it takes only a phone call, as the following example illustrates.

> Maggie and Gary Myers made a lot of long-distance calls in 1994 while Gary was working for a geological consulting company in east Texas and Maggie was working at South Baldwin (County, Alabama) Hospital. In one conversation, Gary learned that Maggie had to travel an hour either east or west to find a satisfactory selection of uniforms. This suggested a market niche for a business that would reunite them.
>
> Now, after much research, and with the aid of a member of **SCORE (Service Corps of Retired Executives)**, they are the proud owners of Specialty Uniforms, opened in January 1995. They specialize in hospital and restaurant uniforms and special-order hard-to-find items.[6]

**SCORE (Service Corps of Retired Executives)** is a group of retired—but active—managers from all walks of life who help people develop their business ideas.

G

Photo courtesy of C. E. Sims, *Baldwin* (County, Alabama) *Press Register.*

Both Maggie and Gary had previous managerial experience—Maggie, especially, as she had been an executive assistant to both the governor and lieutenant governor of the Virgin Islands. She had also worked in management for General Dynamics in San Diego and for the executive vice president of Remington Products—across the hall from Victor Kiam II, the nationally known entrepreneur (see Case 2).

The search for and identification of a product require innovative and original thinking, including putting the ideas together in an organized form. For example, if the chosen product is now being provided by competitors, what change is necessary for you to compete successfully or avoid competition? Can an original approach be used in serving the public? Not always!

For example, things looked good for Steven Freeman, age 29. He was soon to marry, get his MBA from the Wharton School, and revolutionize Manhattan's real estate market: He would use a computer database to match buyers and sellers. But after working for 18 months and investing $30,000 of his family's money, he quit; not enough people were willing to pay for the service to make it profitable.[7]

Looking into the future requires extensive reading and contacts with a wide variety of people. Constant questioning of changes that are occurring and critical analysis of products and services being received provide ideas. Innovation is alive and well and will continue its surge ahead. Each new idea spawns other ideas for new businesses.

## Choosing the Business to Enter

In choosing the business to enter, first eliminate the least attractive ideas from consideration and then concentrate on selecting the most desirable one. It is important to eliminate ideas that will not provide the challenges, opportunities, and rewards—financial and personal—that you are seeking. Be rather ruthless in asking, "What's in it for me?" as well as, "What can I do to be of service to others?" Questions like those in Figure 5–2 will be helpful. Also, concentrate on the thing(s) you would like to do—and can do—not on what someone else wants for you.

For example, Dairl M. Johnson found his niche when he started a business as a result of hurting his back. After 20 years of back pain, his physician sent him to a Relax a Back retail store. Johnson was so pleased with the success of the products the store offered—office chairs, beds, car seats, and portable seats providing postural support—that he quit his job with

**Figure 5–2** Questions to Ask to Help Eliminate Possible Businesses

- How much capital is required to enter and compete successfully in this business?
- How long will it take to recoup my investment?
- How long will it take to reach an acceptable level of income?
- How will I live until that time?
- What degree of risk is involved? Am I willing to take that risk?
- Can I make it on my own, or will I need the help of my family or others?
- How much work is involved in getting the business going? In running it? Am I willing to put out that much effort?
- Do I want to acquire a franchise from an established company, or do I want to start from scratch and go it on my own?
- What is the potential of this type of business? What are my chances of achieving that potential?
- Is sufficient information available to permit reaching a meaningful decision? If so, what are the sources of information?
- Is it something I would enjoy?

IBM and started a chain of Relax a Back franchise stores. He expected sales of $3 million by the end of 1995 and $10 million by 1997. His success, says Johnson, was "a natural chain of events."[8]

After eliminating the unattractive ideas, get down to the serious business of selecting the business to which you plan to devote your energy and resources. One way of doing this is to talk to friends, various small business owners, relatives, financial advisers, or lawyers to find out what kinds of products are needed but not available. Try to get them to identify not only existing types of businesses but also new kinds. Then consider the market for the kinds of products and businesses they have suggested.

Several self-help groups of entrepreneurs in various parts of the country can be called on at this stage, as well as later stages. These groups help potential entrepreneurs find their niche and then assist them in surviving start-up, operating, and even personal problems. SCORE members can also be important sources of information. There are now about 388 SCORE chapters located in the United States and its territories. SCORE has a budget of about $3.5 million and 11 paid staff members in the Washington, D.C., office. Last year, SCORE provided advice to more than 175,000 current and prospective business owners and conducted 3,900 workshops.[9]

Although, as shown in Figure 5–3, women business owners seek outside advice more often than men do, it is a good idea for all prospective business owners to get help and advice from as many people as possible. Joseph Nebesky, who has served as adviser to many agencies, including the SBA and the National Council on Aging, offers the following suggested sources for advice, in addition to those already mentioned:[10] D

- Small Business Administration
- The National Council on Aging (NCOA) Q

**Figure 5–3** Seeking Advice

**Women business owners consult with other people more than men do. Proportion of entrepreneurs—men and women—frequently seeking advice from:**

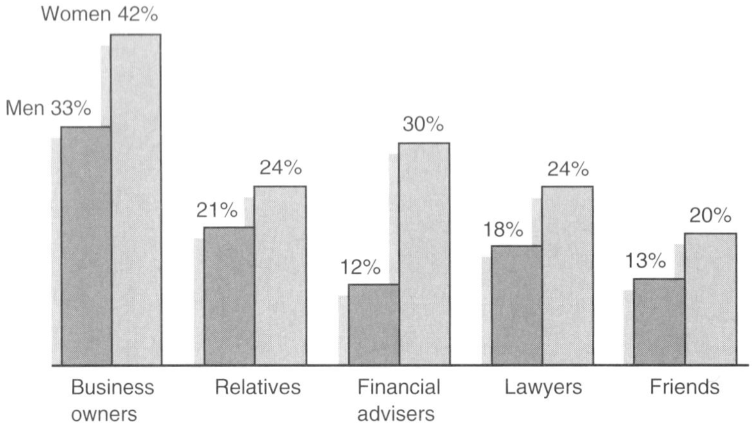


*Source:* National Foundation for Women Business Owners, as reported in "Entrepreneurs and the Gender Gap," *U.S. News & World Report,* August 1, 1994, p. 13. Copyright, August 1, 1994, U.S. NEWS & WORLD REPORT.

- State Economic Development Agencies
- Chambers of Commerce
- *Directory of Trade Associations in the United States*
- U.S. Department of Commerce (Office of International Trade)
- Local colleges
- Public libraries

When obtaining advice from outsiders, though, remember it is your resources that are at stake when the commitment is made, so the ultimate decision must be yours. *Don't let someone talk you into something you are uncomfortable with.*

After discussing the need for the product with other people, select the business that seems best for you. To be more methodical and objective in your evaluation, you might prepare a checklist similar to the one in Figure 5–4. It is used by a consultant with the MIT Enterprise Forum to help people

**Figure 5–4** Business Selection Survey Checklist

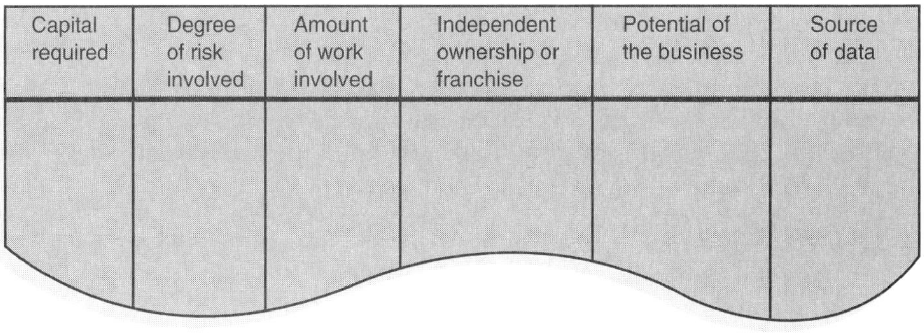
Capital required
Degree of risk involved
Amount of work involved
Independent ownership or franchise
Potential of the business
Source of data

decide what business to enter. You could use these criteria to help you decide whether suggestions you've received are appropriate for you. If not, make other lists until you find an idea that matches your ability, training, experience, personality, and interests.

Initially you may want to make more than one choice and leave yourself some options. Remember to consider your personal attributes and objectives in order to best utilize your capabilities. Let your mind—not your emotions—govern your decisions.

## Studying the Market for the Product

After selecting the product and business, look at the market potential for each one. If a market does not exist—or cannot be developed—don't pursue the project any further. On the other hand, there may be a market in a particular location or a segment of the population that needs your product.

Small businesses usually select one segment of the population for their customers, or choose one product niche, since they do not have sufficient resources to cover the whole market. Also, small businesses cannot include as large a variety of products in their efforts as large businesses can. Hence, a small business must concentrate its efforts on the customers it can serve effectively.

### Methods of Obtaining Information about the Market

There are many ways to identify a market, and all can be generally classified as marketing research. As will be discussed in Chapter 12, **market research** consists of gathering, recording, classifying, analyzing, and interpreting data related to the marketing of goods and services. Formal research programs can be very valuable in giving direction, but they can also be expensive. Computers are helping to increase the amount of information gathered while reducing the cost.

**Market research** is the systematic gathering, recording, and analyzing of data related to the marketing of goods and service.

Another means of collecting data is a search of existing literature. The first places to look in a library are the "technical section" and the "government documents section." You should examine Census Bureau data on subjects such as population, business, and housing.

The SBA also can be a helpful source of data, as can the research divisions of chambers of commerce, colleges, and trade associations, as well as local business leaders, bankers, and congressional representatives. Talking with others, even potential competitors, can yield useful information.

The U.S. Department of Commerce is another good source of information, as its district offices have well-stocked libraries of census data. The department publishes many useful books on planning and organizing small businesses.

### Method Used to Study the Market

There are four things you need to do when estimating your sales and market share. First, determine the size of the industry and market segment you want to enter. Second, estimate your competition and figure out its market share. Third, determine how you stack up against the competition. Finally, estimate your own sales volume.

### *Estimating the Size of the Market*

Before launching a business, you should find out, by asking the following questions, whether the market for it is large enough to accommodate a newcomer:

- How large is the industry?
- Where is the market for the company, and how large is it?
- Are sales to be made to a selected age group, and, if so, how large is that group?
- What are the size and distribution of income within the population?
- Is the sales volume for this kind of business growing, remaining stable, or declining?
- What are the number and size of competitors?
- What is the success rate for competing businesses?
- What are the technical aspects (state of the art) of the industry?

### *Estimating the Competition*

In studying the market area, the number of similar businesses that have gone out of business or merged with a competitor should be determined. A high number of these activities usually signals market weakness. Analysis of competitors' activities may also indicate how effectively a new company can compete. Is the market large enough for another firm? What features—such as lower price, better product, or more promotion—will attract business? Can these features be developed for the new firm?

Determine the kinds of technology being applied by other firms in the industry. For example, do other machine shops use hand tools, or do they have state-of-the-art equipment, including robots? The level of technology is significant in determining operating costs.

G

Normally, the biggest worry for small businesses is their large national or global competitors. But the natural advantage goes to the "excellent" company—large *or* small. Small businesses need to know and understand their competitors and operate from strengths, not weaknesses. They should strive for low overhead, use no-frills assets, and look for a better real estate deal. Small, growing companies should stay out of the path of focused market leaders and deliver unprecedented value to the chosen customers in their market niche.[11]

### *Estimating Your Share of the Market*

By now, you should be able to arrive at a ballpark figure for your sales volume and share of the market. First, determine the geographic boundaries of the market area and estimate how much of your product might be purchased. Finally, make an educated guess as to what part of this market you might attract as your share.

## Deciding Whether to Start a New Business, Buy an Existing One, or Buy a Franchise

By now, you have probably decided what type of industry you want to enter and have done an economic feasibility study of that industry and the potential business. The next step is to decide whether to start a new business

**Figure 5–5** Which Road to Take?

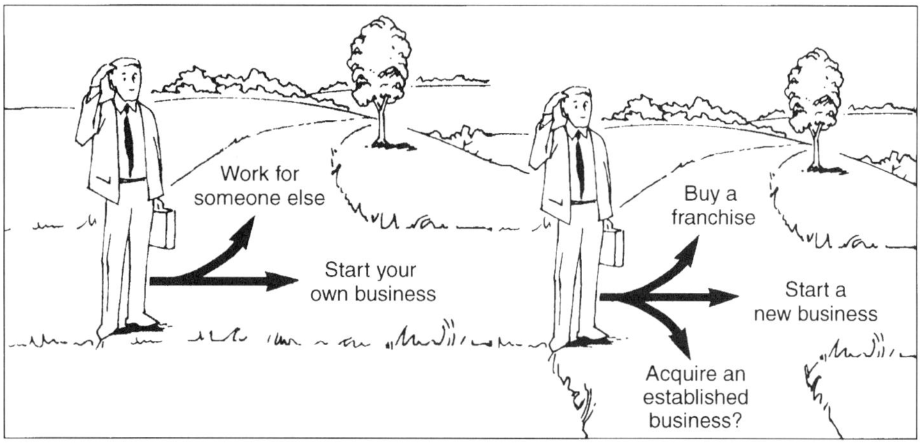


from scratch, buy an established business, or buy a franchise. As shown in Figure 5–5, many prospective business owners find themselves in a quandary over which direction to take. The material in this section may be helpful in making the choice more effectively.

## To Start a New Business?

Most successful small business owners start their own business because they want others to recognize that the success is all theirs. Often, the idea selected is new, and the businesses for sale at the time do not fit the desired mold. Also, the facilities needed should be new so the latest ideas, processes, and procedures can be used. Size of company, fresh inventory, new personnel, and new location can be chosen to fit the new venture.

All this is exciting and—when successful—satisfying. But the venture is also challenging because everything about it is new, it demands new ideas, and it must overcome difficulties. Moreover, because everything is newer, a larger investment may be required.

### *Reasons for Starting a New Business*

Some reasons for starting a new business lie in the owner's freedom to:

- Define the nature of the business.
- Create the preferred type of physical facilities.
- Obtain fresh inventory.
- Have a free hand in selecting and developing personnel.
- Select the competitive environment, to a certain extent.
- Take advantage of the latest technology, equipment, materials, and tools to cover a void in acceptable products available.

For example, Kathy Kolbe raised such a fuss about the lack of stimulating educational materials in her children's schools that she was appointed to head a committee to develop a program for gifted children. Finding no such materials, she wrote and produced her own. She offered these

> materials to several publishers, but they rejected her offer, considering the market too small to be profitable. So she took $500 from her savings and launched a firm called Resources for the Gifted. She wrote catalogs and sent them to around 3,500 schools and parents. Her first few years were tough, but after six years, she was grossing $3.5 million a year.[12]

### *Reasons for Not Starting a New Business*

Some reasons for not starting a new business are:

- Problems in finding the right business.
- Problems associated with assembling the resources, including the location, building, equipment, materials, and work force.
- Lack of an established product line.
- Production problems associated with starting a new business.
- Lack of an established market and channels of distribution.
- Problems in establishing basic management systems and controls.
- The risk of failure is higher in small business start-ups than in acquiring a franchise or even buying an existing business.

## To Buy an Existing Business?

Buying a business can mean different things to different people. It may mean acquiring the total ownership of an entire business, or it may mean acquiring only a firm's assets, its name, or certain parts of it. Keep this point in mind as you study the following material. Also remember that many entrepreneurs find that taking over an existing business isn't always a "piece of cake."

### *Reasons for Buying an Existing Business*

Some reasons for buying an established business are:

- Personnel are already working.
- The facilities are already available.
- A product is already being produced for an existing market.
- The location may be desirable.
- Relationships have been established with banks and trade creditors.
- Revenues and profits are being generated, and goodwill exists.

> For example, when the owner of the Speedy Bicycle Shop suddenly decided to sell the business, Don Albright, the manager, arranged to buy it. He alerted all the customers who had Christmas layaways to come and collect their purchases before the owner closed the shop.
>
> This gained Don a lot of goodwill when he reopened the shop as his own. Although he had to come up with a lot of capital to purchase new inventory, he already had the experience of managing the shop.

### *Reasons for Not Buying an Existing Business*

Some reasons for not buying an ongoing business are:

- The physical facilities may be old or obsolete.
- The employees may have a poor production record or attitude.

- The accounts receivable may be past due or uncollectible.
- The location may be bad.
- The financial condition and relations with financial institutions may be poor.
- The inventory may be obsolete or of poor quality.

For example, a group of investors considered buying a coal mine in West Virginia. Because the market for coal was favorable, they thought they had a good deal. However, they found the local coal was of such poor quality that the market would not accept the firm's product. The group decided not to invest.

## *To Buy or Not to Buy*

Even if there are several businesses to choose from, the evaluation finally comes down to one business that must be thoroughly evaluated before the final decision is made. The steps in this procedure can be compared to these involved in launching a space shuttle. The countdown involves several weeks of intense preparation before the crew climbs into the cabin. Then comes the final countdown. Until the last few seconds, the flight (mission) can be aborted, but from that point on, "all systems are go."

Photo courtesy of National Aeronautics and Space Administration.

The same tends to be true when buying an established business. Up to a given point, the buyer can change the decision to buy. Beyond that point, the decision is final.

*A word of caution is needed here.* Past success or failure is not sufficient foundation for a decision of whether or not to buy a given business. Instead, you must make a thorough analysis of its present condition and an appraisal of what the business might do in the future. The following are some important questions to be asked when making the decision to buy an ongoing business.

1. **Why is the business available for purchase?** This question should help establish the validity of the owner's stated reason for selling the business. Some reasons provide a challenging opportunity, as this example shows.

Robert Sinclair dropped out of college in his senior year for financial reasons. After working several years for a building supply firm, he went to work as manager of the metal door division for a partnership engaged in diversified construction of commercial buildings. Because the partners were so busy with their other activities, Bob was left to run the division by himself. Finally, he offered to buy the division from the partners, and they accepted.

2. **What are the intentions of the present owners?** After selling a business, former owners are free to do what they wish unless restricted by contract. What has been said before the sale and what happens afterward may not be the same. Some questions needing answers are: Will the present owner remain in competition? Does he or she want to retire or leave the area? What is the present owner's physical—and financial—health?

For example, Ron Sikorsky spotted the following in the newspaper one Sunday: "For reasons of health, owner willing to sacrifice successful, profitable sandwich shop, priced for immediate sale." Ron dashed over to the Submariner. The place was full, and business was great. (All the owner's friends just happened to need a sandwich that day.) Following some haggling, Ron and the owner shook hands, and Ron wrote a check for $10,000 of his savings.

A month later, Ron found out the hard way that the business had been ready to fold when he took the bait. The former owner's friends were gone, and business was terrible, but the former owner's (financial) health was miraculously improved!

3. **Are environmental factors changing?** The demand for a firm's product may rise or fall, or the niche may change, because of such factors as changes in population characteristics, neighborhood, consumer habits, zoning, traffic patterns, environment, tax law, or technology. The following examples illustrate this point.

Dr. Greham Bayne of San Diego discovered that 82 percent of emergencies don't require an ambulance ride or emergency room services. To fill the gap for those who did need some type of medical assistance, he started Call Doctor. Dr. Bayne treats non-life-threatening medical emergencies by sending a fully equipped ambulance to people's homes.[13]

Similarly, Denise Lores, owner of Professional Health Care Services in Fairhope, Alabama, saw a market niche in transporting bedridden or wheelchair-bound patients between home, hospitals, and nursing homes. Her Specialized Transportation Services provides a fully equipped ambulance for nonemergency transportation.

4. **Are physical facilities suitable for present and future operations?** To be suitable, facilities must be properly planned and laid out, effectively maintained, and up-to-date.

5. **Is the business operating efficiently?** A prospective buyer should know whether a business will need to be "whipped into shape" after purchase. Are the personnel effective? Is waste excessive or under control? Is the quality of the product satisfactory, and is the inventory at the proper level and up-to-date? The following two actual situations are examples of waste and obsolescence.

*An example of waste:* A potential buyer of a carpet mill noticed the mill's employees were slicing off one to three inches on each side of the carpets as they were being produced. In the follow-up analysis, he found that if the machines were properly set, the mill could save $10,000 per day.

*An example of inventory obsolescence:* The owner of a hardware store decided to sell his business. A prospective buyer found 200 horse collars among the antiquated stock.

6. **What is the financial condition of the firm?** It is important to know whether the firm is a good financial risk. This can be determined by checking variables such as the validity of financial statements, the cash position, the cash flow through the business, various financial ratios, the amount and terms of debt, and the adequacy of cost data.

7. **How much investment is needed?** Remember the investment includes not only the purchase price of the existing firm but also capital needed for renovations, improvements, and start-up activities.

8. **What is the estimated return on investment?** This estimate should be realistic and not based on wishful thinking. It should include potential losses as well as potential gains.

9. **Is the price right?** One important factor that should always be considered is the price asked for the firm. Sometimes, a successful ongoing business can be bought at a fraction of its value. But while you may be lucky enough to get such a bargain, be wary of pitfalls. For example, a retailer may offer to sell a business for "the current price of assets—less liabilities." But the accounts receivable may be a year or more in arrears, while the inventory consists of unsalable goods.

10. **Do you have the necessary managerial ability?** Some people have a special talent for acquiring ongoing businesses that are in economic difficulty and turning them around. If you have—or can develop—this special talent, the ability is valuable to society and profitable to you, the new entrepreneur.

For example, an experienced small businessman sold his business and searched for another business to get involved in. His interests included managerial challenge, economic growth, and profit. After looking at several possibilities, he acquired a small company that manufactured a top-quality airport service vehicle. The company needed additional capital and more effective management. The new owner was able to bring these two ingredients into the company and make it a success.

## To Buy a Franchise?

As you will see in Chapter 7, franchising is expanding rapidly and appears to be very successful. Yet franchisers have failed, and some franchisees have suffered severe losses. So the decision to buy a **franchise** is a serious one.

A **franchise** is an agreement whereby an independent businessperson is given exclusive rights to sell a specified good or service.

### *Reasons for Buying a Franchise*

Franchise agreements normally spell out what both the franchiser and franchisee are responsible for and must do. Each party usually desires the success of the other. The franchiser brings proven and successful methods of operation and business images to aid the franchisee.

If you decide to become a business owner, you can obtain guidance from experienced people by obtaining a franchise. Franchises are available in a wide range of endeavors, so you may be able to find one that combines your talents and desires, as the following example shows.

> David and Tamara Kennedy, of Sausalito, California, once made their living skippering and being a chef aboard yachts around the world. But they were drawn to an ad by a nautical bookstore franchise—Armchair Sailor Bookstore—seeking to expand nationally. "Must have a love of the sea and know how to sail," it said. "While we won't become millionaires," they confessed after buying a franchise, "we love what we're doing and are doing something we know about. It's been a learning experience for both of us."[14]

Another reason for buying a franchise is that it probably has many of the requirements for success. The market niche has been identified, and sales activities are in place. Also, the business may already be located, managed, and running. The questions to ask about franchises are: How much help do I need? Can a franchise help me enough to more than cover the costs of the franchise?

Most potential small business owners do not have the competencies or resources to get started successfully. But the franchiser can provide supplemental help through its experience and concentrated study of the field. These talents come from both successes and failures in the past. A study of the services listed in the contract, in relation to your needs, shows the value to you.

### *Reasons for Not Buying a Franchise*

A franchise is not a guarantee of success. The costs may outweigh the benefits from its purchase. Including expenses such as the initial investments and fees, as well as royalty payments, a franchise can be costly. Also, it may not fit the owner's desires or direction, or it may not give the franchisee enough independence. Also, overpriced, poorly run, uninteresting, and white elephant franchises are potentially disastrous, as the following example illustrates.

> A man put up $2,000 as a guaranteed investment for candy machines after the franchiser promised to find good locations for the machines. These failed to materialize, however, because all the desirable locations were already in use. The franchiser disappeared, and the man lost his $2,000.

Even under the best of conditions, franchisers tend to hold an advantage, as shown in Table 5–1. Usually, this relates to operating standards, supply and material purchase agreements, and agreements relating to the repurchase of the franchise. Also, there are constraints as to the size of the territory and the specific location. Moreover, you sometimes have no choice about the layout and decor. However, careful study of franchisers' past records and contract offerings can lead to selection of a potentially successful franchise operation.

**Table 5-1** How Franchising Benefits Both Franchisee and Franchiser

| Selected benefits to the franchisee | Selected benefits to the franchiser |
|---|---|
| 1. Brand recognition | 1. Faster expansion and penetration |
| 2. Management training and/or assistance | 2. Franchisee motivation |
| 3. Economies of large-scale buying | 3. Franchisee attention to detail |
| 4. Financial assistance | 4. Lower operating costs |
| 5. Share in local or national promotion | |

## WHAT YOU SHOULD HAVE LEARNED

**1.** The first thing to do in becoming a small business owner is to decide whether it is what you *really want to do*. Then, proper planning becomes essential to chart your new venture. The time of starting your new business is also important.

**2.** Although there is no set procedure for starting a business, there are steps that can be taken to help ensure success. They are *(a)* search for a needed product; *(b)* study the market for the product; *(c)* decide whether to start a new business, buy an existing one, or buy a franchise; *(d)* make strategic plans, including setting a mission, objectives, and strategies; *(e)* make operational plans, including setting up policies, budgets, procedures, and plans for operating the business; *(f)* make financial plans, including estimating income, expenses, and initial investment, and locating sources of funds; *(g)* prepare a business plan; and *(h)* implement the plan. The first three steps were discussed in this chapter.

**3.** The product to sell can be found by *(a)* reading books, papers, and other information; *(b)* having social and business conversations with friends, support groups, businesspeople, and others; and *(c)* using checklists, questioning people, and doing marketing research.

**4.** Studying the market for the problem involves estimating *(a)* the size of the market, *(b)* the competition and its share of the market, and *(c)* your own share of the market.

**5.** Next, you should decide whether to *(a)* start a new business, *(b)* buy an existing one, or *(c)* buy a franchise. There are compelling arguments for and against each of these alternatives. Starting a new business means it is your own, but the process is time-consuming and quite risky.

When you buy an existing business, you acquire established markets, facilities, and employees. But you must be sure when you buy that all aspects of the business are in good shape and that you are not inheriting someone else's problems.

Buying a franchise may help bring success in a hurry, since it provides successful management and operating procedures to guide the business. But you must be able to succeed on your own, for a franchise does not ensure success. Also, the cost may be high, or the franchiser may not perform satisfactorily.

## QUESTIONS FOR DISCUSSION

1. Is planning really as important in starting a business as the authors say? Defend your answer.
2. What are some important factors to consider in choosing the type of business to enter?
3. How can you identify a business you would like to own? What characteristics do you have that would help make that business successful?
4. How do you determine the market for a product? Your share of that market?
5. What kinds of answers to the questions in Figure 5–2 would lead you to eliminate a business from consideration?
6. What are some characteristics you should consider in studying the potential market for a proposed business?
7. What are some reasons for and against starting a new business?
8. What are some reasons for and against buying an existing business?
9. What are some reasons for and against buying a franchise?

## CASE 5

### TIM LEWIS FILLS A NICHE

Photo courtesy of *The Tuscaloosa* (Alabama) *News.*

Tim Lewis owns T. A. Lewis and Associates in Birmingham, Alabama, a consulting firm that designs telephone, data, and video systems. In this information age, Lewis's success might seem inevitable, but it is based on experience, hard work, and finding a market niche.

The Lewis story began in his hometown of Tuscaloosa, about 35 miles southwest of Birmingham, where Lewis gained both business and technical skills. While in high school he worked as a salesman at a local shoe store. In addition, he served as business manager for the James Brown Singers, a local community choir.

After earning an electrical engineering degree from the University of Alabama, Lewis became an account manager and sales trainer for TMC, a new and growing long-distance phone company. When he went to places such as Rust Engineering in Birmingham to sell it long-distance service, executives would ask him many questions and seek his advice. The buyers wanted his opinion on what kind of fax machines, voice-mail systems, and copy machines to buy. They wanted some knowledgeable person to give them fair and unbiased answers. He would offer suggestions, and most of the time his advice turned out to be right, so they kept asking him.

At that point, it occurred to Lewis that a market niche might exist that no one was filling. When he studied the market, he learned that it was very difficult for small to medium-sized firms to get objective information on products. Most "consultants" were representatives of particular manufacturers; if clients weren't interested in buying the products they were selling, they weren't interested in giving advice.

After about 18 months of research, Lewis prepared a comprehensive business plan. Then, with the help of the Birmingham Business Assistance Network (an incubator organization for small businesses), he took the plunge and ventured out on his own. The contacts he had made while working with TMC provided a springboard. When he left TMC, he had accounts at seven Birmingham-area hospitals, and the business he got from them spread. That's why a third of his customers are in the health care industry.

He now has 18 full-time employees and is planning to expand by adding a training facility.

Lewis continues to live in Tuscaloosa and drives 90 minutes to and from his facility in Birmingham. Of this commuting time, he says, "I've got a cellular phone and a beeper, so I can work on the way up and work on the way back."

*Source:* Gilbert Nicholson, "Filling a Niche," *The Tuscaloosa* (Alabama) *News,* October 22, 1995, p. 1E.

## QUESTIONS

1. What do you think of Lewis's method of finding an unfilled niche?
2. What expansion possibilities are there for him in this expanding technological age?
3. What suggestions would you make to him as to where to live? Explain.

## APPLICATION 5–1

Kim recently graduated from a small liberal arts university and is now looking for a job. Because of a sluggish economy, her efforts have been fruitless. She has decided to start her own small business by opening a restaurant.

Kim lives in a small town with no major shopping centers and no national franchises. She decided to open a drive-in or fast-food store in the town. Her grandfather provided the funding for the project and gave her what little advice he could.

After only three months in business, Kim realized that her business was going broke. She wanted to sell the business but could not find a buyer.

## QUESTIONS

1. What mistake(s) did Kim make?
2. Do you think if Kim had done market research she would have opened a franchise instead of an independent operation? Why?
3. Why do you think she is unable to sell her business?

## ACTIVITY 5–1

*Directions:* Use information learned in this chapter to unjumble the following terms. Then unjumble the circled letters to solve the puzzle

1 O C S E R

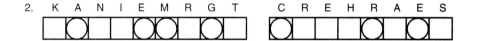

2. K A N I E M R G T C R E H R A E S

1. SCORE 2. Marketing Research Solution: Can Create

# CHAPTER 6

# Doing Strategic and Operational Planning

*Businesses don't plan to fail, they just fail to plan.*—Old business adage

*After you have made up your mind just what you are going to do, it is a good time to do it.* —Josh Billings

## LEARNING OBJECTIVES

After studying the material in this chapter, you will be able to:

1. Tell why planning is so important—yet so neglected—in small businesses.
2. Distinguish between the two basic types of planning.
3. Explain the role of strategic planning, and give some examples.
4. Explain the role of operational planning, and give some examples of what is involved.
5. Explain the role of financial planning, and give some examples of it.

## P R O F I L E

# ZEINER FUNERAL HOMES

Photo courtesy of Reuben Feuerborn

Reuben Feuerborn is a third-generation funeral home director/embalmer/mortician. If you ask him why he chose this particular career, he will tell you that he has "always liked the service these businesses provide to families in periods of their greatest need." While his family owns a funeral home, Mr. Feuerborn was not affiliated with his family's business at the time of this case. Instead, Mr. Feuerborn was employed by Zeiner Funeral Homes, a sole proprietorship located in the Midwest.

Zeiner Funeral Homes began in 1912 in Marion, Kansas, as the Thompson Funeral Home. In 1969, it was sold to Gerald Harp, who operated the business until 1986. Mr. Harp then sold it to Ty Zeiner, the present owner.

Mr. Zeiner next purchased the Hillsboro Memorial Chapel in Hillsboro, Kansas, in 1989. Further expansion took place in 1991, with the addition of the Florence Funeral Home in Florence, Kansas. After the last expansion, Mr. Zeiner changed the name of the Florence Funeral Home to Zeiner Funeral Home and continued to operate it as a branch of the Marion operation.

Pre-need burial policies, which are prefunded funeral plans, were sold at all three locations. About 90 percent of Zeiner's business, however, is providing needed services at the time of death, no prearrangements having been made.

Regulatory compliance is always an issue in any business, and funeral homes are no exception. In addition to all zoning, business license, and other state and local requirements, funeral home premises are regularly inspected by OSHA and the State Board of Mortuary Arts. Also, the board inspects prefunded policies; Kansas state law requires that the funds received from each policy be placed in a separate account, which is periodically audited. The board also regulates the renewal of professional licensing for funeral directors, funeral establishments, morticians, and embalmers. In turn, the Federal Trade Commission (FTC) requires all funeral homes to provide a "general price list," an itemized list of all available services along with the price for each service. A copy of this list must be provided to anyone upon request or before any funeral arrangements are made.

When asked about ethical issues in the profession, Mr. Feuerborn said, "Nearly every issue we have to deal with is an ethical one that some unscrupulous undertaker has violated at some time or other in the past. However, there are no questionable issues if you treat the members of every family as if they were your own."

According to the National Association of Funeral Directors, the average cost for a funeral in 1995 was $4,500—in addition to an approximate $3,500 burial fee. If cremation is chosen, an additional charge of "a few hundred dollars" is added to the other costs.

Gordon Bigelow, executive director of the American Board of Funeral Service Education in Brunswick, Maine, tracks statistics for the 42 U.S. colleges that offer degrees in mortuary science. The 1995 enrollment figures indicated that more than 3,150 students were studying in this field, an increase of 2,200 from the 1991 enrollment. It's also interesting to note that 36 percent of the students were female, up 9 percent from 10 years earlier. Bigelow did not know why enrollment was increasing, but believed that it was probably because there were more job openings than there were professionals to fill them.

*Source:* Conversations and correspondence with Reuben Feuerborn; Jane Meredith Adams, "Mortuary Schools Getting Record Number of Students," *Mobile* (Alabama) *Register*, October 8, 1995, p. 10-A; and Maggie Jackson, "Death's Sting," ibid., pp. 1-F and 2-F.

The Profile illustrates some of the problems and steps involved in planning, organizing, and developing a new business. The first three of those steps were discussed in Chapter 5, and steps 7 and 8 will be covered in Chapter 8. Steps 4, 5, and 6 are explained in detail in this chapter.

## The Role of Planning

**Planning** is the process of setting objectives and determining actions to reach them.

To become an effective business owner-manager, *you must look ahead.* In selecting the business to enter, as discussed in Chapter 5, you are doing just that—planning for the future. As shown in Figure 6–1, planning should be the first step in performing a series of managerial functions because it sets the future course of action for all aspects of the business. **Planning**, which is the process of setting objectives and devising actions to achieve those objectives, answers such questions as these: What business am I in? What finances do I need? What is my sales strategy? Where can I find needed personnel? How much profit can I expect?

### Why Small Businesses *Need to* Plan

Planning is one of the most difficult activities you must do. Yet it is essential that you do it because, before taking action, you must know where you are going and how to get there. Outsiders who invest or lend money need to know your chances of success. Plans provide courses of action, information to others, bases for change, and a means of delegating work. In summary, well-developed plans can (1) interest moneyed people in investing in your business, (2) guide the owner and managers in operating the business, (3) give direction to and motivate employees, and (4) provide an environment to attract customers and prospective employees.

**Figure 6–1** How Planning Relates to Other Managerial Functions

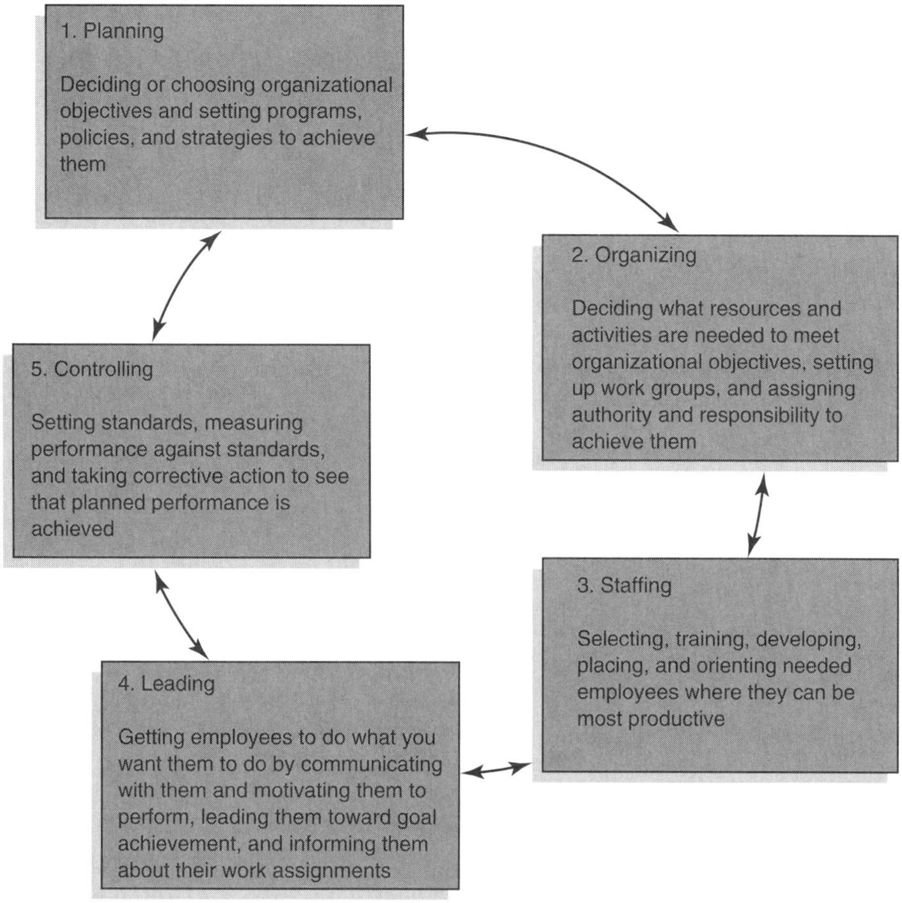


## Why Small Businesses *Neglect* Planning

Although planning is so important, it is one of the most difficult managerial activities to perform. Therefore, small businesspeople, preoccupied with day-to-day operations, often neglect planning. However, they should remember that, while predicting the future is *risky,* doing no planning can be *disastrous.*

Many small business owners neglect planning, because (1) day-to-day activities leave them little or no time for planning, (2) they fear the problems and weaknesses planning may reveal, (3) they lack knowledge of how to plan, and (4) they feel that future changes cannot be planned for.

Planning requires original thinking, takes time, and is difficult to do, but it does help one prepare to take advantage of promising opportunities and cope with unexpected problems.

## Types of Planning

As shown in Table 6–1, planning is usually divided according to the nature of the planning and the time frame. These criteria set the level in the

**Table 6–1** Some of the Most Important Types of Plans and Planning Functions

| Types of plans and planning functions | Examples |
|---|---|
| **Strategic planning:** | |
| *Mission:* The long-term direction of the business. | To provide financial security at low cost. |
| *Objectives:* Shorter-term ends to help achieve the mission. | |
| For total firm. | Earn a 20% return on investment in 1997. |
| For functional area. | Increase penetration of market by 25% by 1998. |
| *Strategies:* Means to achieve an end, or courses of action needed to achieve objectives. | |
| For total firm. | Establish control procedures to control costs by 1997. |
| For functional area. | Use 1 percent of sales to improve and expand service. |
| **Operational planning:** | |
| *Policies:* Guides to action that provide consistency in decision making, particularly in repetitive situations. | *Personnel policy:* Promote from within, giving preference to promotions for present employees. |
| *Methods and procedures:* Prescribed manner of accomplishing desired output. | *Employee selection procedure:* Complete application form, test, interview, investigate, select. |
| *Budgets and standards:* Plans for future activities using measures for control. | *Cash budget:* For planning use of money. |

**Strategic planning** provides comprehensive long-term direction to help a business accomplish its mission.

**Operational planning** sets policies, procedures, and standards for achieving objectives.

organization where the planning is usually done and the amount of research required to do it.

The first type, which is long-range, high-level planning, is called **strategic planning**. It consists of (1) setting the company's mission and establishing the objectives that need to be attained to accomplish it and (2) determining strategies, which are the methods used to achieve those objectives.

**Operational planning** is needed to carry out the strategic plans and operate the business. It sets policies, methods, procedures, and budgets.

## The Role of Strategic Planning

**Strategic management** concerns the health and survival of an organization.

As **strategic management** concerns the health and survival of any organization, the pressure for change is greater in small businesses than in their larger rivals.[1] Strategic planning is perhaps the most important type of planning done by owners and managers of small businesses, for it provides the major, comprehensive, long-term plan that determines the nature of the business. Historically, however, studies have shown that only about a third of small firms use long-range strategic planning.[2]

Table 6-1 shows that strategic planning consists of two parts: the firm's mission and objectives, and its strategies. The following are some examples of strategic planning:

- Selecting the type of business to enter.
- Formulating the mission of the company.
- Deciding whether to start a new business, buy an existing one, or buy a franchise.
- Choosing the product or service to sell.
- Deciding on the market niche to exploit.
- Choosing the type of organization to use.
- Determining financial needs.
- Selecting the location for the business

> For example, a recent study by three CPAs indicated the significance of location to small businesses. They studied which small firms in their areas were succeeding and which were failing.
>
> Jacqueline L. Babicky's consulting group found that the types of business doing well in the Portland, Oregon, area were those that had taken steps to differentiate themselves and/or their products from others in the mainstream. Larry Field's firm found a growing number of small high-tech businesses were moving into the Phoenix, Arizona, region to provide secondary parts to larger manufacturers.
>
> On the other hand, C. Norman Pricher and his staff found that one type of business in Orlando, Florida, was not doing well. They learned that indoor foliage, the region's biggest industry concentration, was doing poorly.[3]

## Mission and Objectives

The **mission** is the long-range vision of what the business is trying to become. It is concerned with broad concepts such as the firm's image, with the basic services the firm plans to perform (e.g., "entertainment" instead of just "movies"), and with long-term financial success. Once set, missions are rarely revised.

A business's **mission** is its long-term vision of what it is trying to become.

A clear definition of your mission enables you to design *results-oriented objectives and strategies.* Sometimes the mission also requires organization reengineering, as described in the following example.

> One of the largest third-party administrators for small business group life and health insurance, Plan Services Inc., did just that. In 1990, it reengineered not only its business but its information systems organizations as well. It completed a business strategic plan and then formed a group to work on technological developments.
>
> The group's first step was to develop an information strategic plan, which provided the roadmap needed to ensure that the company's mission was achieved. The group's technical strategy was to downsize to lower costs and increase the company's customer-focused client-server environment. Intelligent workstations, graphical user interfaces, and various productivity tools were used.[4]

**Objectives** are the goals that give shorter-term direction to the business and serve as benchmarks for measuring performance. Examples of objectives might include: "To increase total sales by 8 percent a year" and "To introduce

**Objectives** are the purposes, goals, and desired results for the business and its parts.

**Table 6–2** Example of How Objectives Can Be Set

| Firm's objectives | 1997 | 1998 | 1999 | 2000 |
|---|---|---|---|---|
| Total net profit (income) after taxes | $_____ | $_____ | $_____ | $_____ |
| Return on investment (ROI) (net income after taxes/total assets) | _____ | _____ | _____ | _____ |
| Return on equity (ROE) (net income after taxes/equity) | _____ | _____ | _____ | _____ |
| Total sales volume (units) | _____ | _____ | _____ | _____ |
| Total sales volume ($) | _____ | _____ | _____ | _____ |
| Return on sales (ROS) (net income after taxes/sales) | _____ | _____ | _____ | _____ |
| To attain a ____ percent share of market by the end of 1998. | | | | |
| To have a ____ percent debt-to-equity ratio in the capital structure initially, declining to ____ percent debt-equity at the end of 1999. | | | | |
| To develop a new product by the end of the year 2000. | | | | |

within the next two years a new product aimed at the middle-class consumer." Objectives are more specific than missions and are revised more frequently. Table 6–2 illustrates how objectives can be set. Choosing the mission and objectives for a small business involves two important considerations: the business's external environment and the internal resources that give it a competitive edge.

### *The External Environment*

Many consultants and other advisers are pushing small companies to give more emphasis to their external environments. In a study of 100 companies, the Futures Group, of Glastonbury, Connecticut, found that "managers who spend more time evaluating external factors such as their competitors, the U.S. market climate, and emerging technology can better manage and forecast business than those who focus on internal factors.[5] This practice was found to improve their strategic plans.

Other external environmental factors to consider include clients, the economy, and many other influences. Changes caused by the introduction of videotapes, computer hardware and software, lasers, and population aging, for example, have been a blessing to some companies and a death warrant to others. The expanding communication and transportation systems require that even the smallest companies keep abreast of a constantly widening range of events.

> For example, as major airlines continue to withdraw jet service from regional areas that are unprofitable, smaller regional carriers are presented with a great opportunity. Small regional commuter services should identify areas of need and plan to close the gap. Analysts at the Federal Aviation Administration (FAA) estimate that 10.5 percent of airline pas-

sengers used regional services in 1994. They also forecast steady increase into the 21st century.[6]

## *Internal Resources and Competitive Edge*

The internal resources found in small businesses include those listed below. Also, to be competitive, the resources must include the characteristics listed.

1. **Human resources** include both management and nonmanagement people and include key operating employees such as production supervisors, sales personnel, financial analysts, and engineers. To keep the company competitive, these people must be motivated, imaginative, qualified, and dedicated.

**Human resources** are the personnel that make up the business's work force.

2. **Physical resources** include buildings, tools and equipment, and service and distribution facilities. For the company to be competitive, these resources must be strategically located, be productive, be low in operating costs, be effective distributors, and make the proper product.

**Physical resources** are the buildings, tools and equipment, and service and distribution facilities that are needed to carry on the business.

3. **Financial resources** include cash flow, debt capacity, and equity available to run the business. To make the company competitive, company finances must be adequate to maintain current levels of activities and to take advantage of future opportunities. Many accountants suggest that aspiring entrepreneurs get their financial house in order before starting. This includes setting aside funds for taxes and Social Security and as a cushion against financial reversals.[7] This advice is echoed in Figure 6–2, which stresses the importance of having "good financing ready" before starting a small business.

**Financial resources** include the cash flow, debt capacity, and equity available to finance operations.

If a small firm has exceptionally good resources and they are effectively used, it can have a **competitive edge** over its competitors. Therefore, a proper evaluation of available resources may permit you to focus on your customers and provide them with a little something extra, which gives you a competitive edge.

A **competitive edge** is a particular characteristic that makes a firm more attractive to customers than its competitors.

**Figure 6–2** Advice for Entrepreneurs

**What small business owners say is the most important advice for starting a business:**

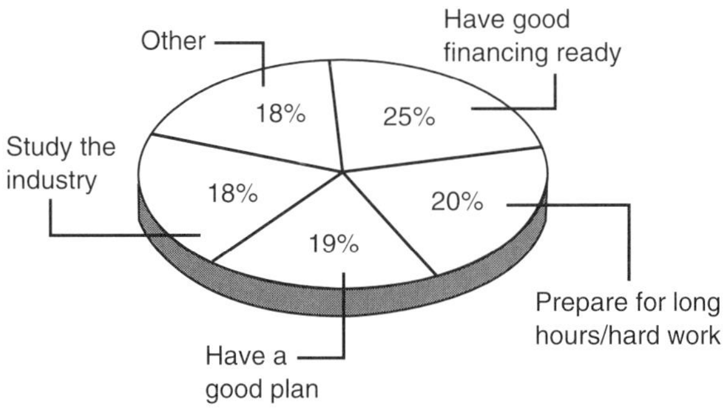


*Source:* Padgett Business Services, as reported in *USA Today,* October 23, 1995, p. 1B. Copyright 1995, USA TODAY. Reprinted with permission.

D

A classic example of this type of competitiveness is provided by a Portland, Oregon, restaurant called Old Wives' Tales. It has incorporated a 130-square-foot play area for children into the dining room, thus redefining the eating-out experience for parents. This consumer focus did require sacrifices, as the playroom takes up the space of 20 revenue-generating seats. Also, there is less turnover; customers stay longer because their children are happy. But the practice has produced a loyal base of customers who drive there from all over Portland.[8]

As you can see from this example, a small business must align its mission, objectives, and resources with its environment if it is to be effective. The proper evaluation of its competitive edge can make a small firm's planning more realistic and lead to greater profitability.

## Strategies

**Strategies** are the means by which a business achieves its objectives and fulfills its mission.

**Strategies** are the means by which the mission and objectives sought by a small business can be achieved. A basic question in setting strategies is: How should the business be managed to achieve its objectives and fulfill its mission? To be most effective, strategies should give a business a competitive advantage in the marketplace (see Using Technology to Succeed). They should combine the activities such as marketing, production or operations, research and development, finance, and personnel in order to use the firm's resources most effectively.

Figure 6–3 shows how a strategy can be set up to fulfill the mission of a small business. Notice that John Smith will provide certain services and policy coverage to clients so they will have maximum personal financial security at the lowest possible cost.

**Management by objectives (MBO)** is a management technique for defining goals for subordinates through agreement between them and their supervisors.

**Management by objectives (MBO)** is one method for attaining established goals. Many companies have found MBO programs helpful in aligning the employees' goals with the firm's objectives. MBO emphasizes goal orientation, with employees setting objectives for themselves. Their manag-

**Figure 6–3**

**Mission/Strategy of John Smith**
**General Agent**
**Tulsa, Oklahoma**

*Mission:* To provide the maximum amount of personal financial security at the lowest possible cost while maintaining the highest quality of individualized service.

*Objective:* To serve the financial needs of businesses, individuals, and their families in the Tulsa area through guaranteed income to meet loss from death or disability, through these services and policy coverages.

- Estate tax planning
- Qualified pension and profit sharing
- Group life and health
- Ordinary life
- Business interruption

## USING TECHNOLOGY TO SUCCEED

Financial resources—especially cash flow—can seriously affect the success of small businesses. Mark Knauff was pleasantly surprised to discover how easy it was for him to install a debit system at his company, Pink Guitar, Inc., in Centerville, Virginia.

Before adding this system to his business, he noticed that many customers who left his store to use a nearby automated teller machine (ATM) changed their minds and did not return to make a purchase. Because Knauff already had equipment in use for charging purchases to various credit cards, his bank was able to do some reprogramming and add some equipment and in a few hours Knauff was all set up to accept debit cards. The cost? Less than $200.

There are now more than 200 million ATM cards in the United States, and approximately 22 percent of merchants accept them. More than 26 percent of others were planning to offer this form of payment to their customers within the next 18 months.

Advantages for the vendor are twofold: It saves money and is faster and cleaner than taking checks or cash. Also, it tends to give merchants a competitive edge over their competitors.

*Source:* Bob Weinstein, "Getting Carded," *Entrepreneur,* September 1995, pp. 76, 78.

ers meet with them to discuss, change, and/or reach agreement on those objectives, how they can be accomplished, and how they relate to achieving the firm's overall objectives. Q

A well-designed MBO program provides each employee with appropriate feedback on results compared with the planned objectives. Employees are expected to overcome obstacles that stand in the way of achieving those objectives. Near the end of a designated period, employees prepare reports for review and discussion with their supervisor.

### How Reengineering Affects Strategic Planning

During the early days of reengineering, many experts thought it was only for large companies. Now, though, many people in the field think small businesses need to rethink and redesign the way their organization operates. Thus, while top management must be involved, lower levels of managers and workers seem to be more involved in integrating their company's vision, mission, objectives, and strategies into their strategic planning.[9] Q

## THE ROLE OF OPERATIONAL PLANNING

Why do so many small businesses fail? Probably the underlying reason in most cases is lack of proper operational planning. Such planning is vital because it helps potential entrepreneurs avoid costly blunders, saves time, and results in a more polished final product. Three types of planning will improve a small business owner's chances of success: (1) operational planning before starting the business; (2) a business plan to attract investors, financiers, and prospective employees; and (3) continuous planning and control after the business starts operating.

As shown in Chapter 5 (Figure 5–1), the business process involves (1) providing the business with the proper financial, physical, and human resources; (2) converting them through some form of operations into goods or services; and (3) distributing them to other processors, assemblers, wholesalers, retailers, or the final consumer. Businesses can be set up to perform any one or more of the parts of this process.

## Setting Up Policies, Methods, Procedures, and Budgets

As you can see from Table 6–1, operational planning starts with setting policies, methods and procedures, and budgets, which together form the basis for the other part of operational planning.

**Policies** are general statements that serve as guides to managerial decision making and supervisory activities.

**Methods** and **procedures** provide standing instructions to employees on how to perform their jobs.

**Budgets** are detailed plans, expressed in monetary terms, of the results expected from officially recognized programs.

**Policies** guide action. They exist so that managers can delegate work and employees will make decisions based on the thinking and wishes of the business owner. **Methods** and **procedures** provide employees with standing instructions for performing their jobs. They comprise detailed explanations of how to do the work properly, and in what order it should be done. **Budgets** set the requirements needed to follow the strategies and accomplish the objectives. For example, a cash budget shows the amount and times of cash income and outgo. It helps the manager determine when and how much to borrow.

## Planning to Operate the Business

The second part of operational planning—planning to operate the business—includes:

1. Choosing your location.
2. Planning operations and physical facilities.
3. Developing sources of supply for goods and materials.
4. Planning your human resource requirements.
5. Setting up the legal and organizational structure.
6. Determining your approach to the market.
7. Establishing an efficient records system.
8. Setting up a time schedule.

### *Choosing a Location*

The type of business influences most of your location decisions, as they relate to access to customers, suppliers, employees, utilities, and transportation, as well as compliance with zoning regulations and other laws. The mission of the business is also a basic consideration in seeking the right location. As will be shown in Chapter 16, each type of firm has its own factors to consider and gives priority to those that most affect the business.

### *Planning Operations and Physical Facilities*

A firm's ability to sell its product is based on its ability to produce that good or service, as well as on its market potential. Good selection and efficient arrangement of physical facilities, then, are important. Too much capacity increases costs, which can reduce the company's competitive position; too little capacity reduces the availability of goods and causes loss of sales. Therefore, a proper balance between production and sales volume is needed. Planning starts with the estimate of sales and the operations needed to produce the product(s). Using these estimates, the machines and personnel needed for the demand can be determined.

Another important decision is whether to buy facilities or lease them. Any such choice between purchase and lease is based on differences in initial investment cost, operating performance and expense, and tax considerations. A photocopier is an example of an item that should probably be leased rather than purchased. Because of rapid improvements—and the need for prompt and proper maintenance—leased copiers will probably give more dependable service than purchased ones. Chapter 16 provides more details on locating and laying out facilities.

### *Developing Sources of Supply for Goods and Materials*

The largest expense for companies selling products usually is purchasing materials, supplies, and/or goods; this cost is often more than 50 percent of the cost of products sold. Therefore, the ability to purchase these at favorable prices can lead to profitability—or vice versa. Lowest-cost materials do not necessarily mean inferior quality, and small firms should take every opportunity to reduce costs. But small businesses usually find it difficult to compete with large ones on the basis of price alone. Instead, they can more successfully compete on the basis of better quality, service, delivery, and so forth. The business must be sure to have sources of supply that meet its standards in all ways, including competitive prices. This topic is covered in greater detail in Chapter 17.

### *Planning Human Resource Requirements*

**Human resource planning** can be one of the most frustrating tasks facing small businesses, as they are not big enough to hire the specialized people needed. You therefore need to estimate how much time you will spend in the business, for the less time you can devote to the business, the more important it will be to have capable employees. And these employees must be able to work with less supervision than in larger firms. Some important questions to ask yourself are: How many workers are needed? Where will they be obtained? How much must I pay them? These and similar questions are discussed in Chapters 13, 14, and 15.

**Human resource planning** is the process of converting the business's plans and programs into an effective work force.

### *Setting Up the Legal and Organizational Structure*

Your organization structure must be developed taking into consideration the legal and administrative aspects of the business. Both legal and administrative structures offer several options, so you must select the structure that best serves your needs. Many small business owners, especially if they have started as sole proprietors, may have difficulty envisioning a management structure beyond that shown in Figure 6–4, but retaining too much authority is one of the best ways to kill your small business.

The legal form of a business, as discussed in Chapter 4, may be a proprietorship, partnership, corporation (C corporation or S Corporation), limited-liability company (LLC), trust, cooperative, or joint venture. The firm's administrative structure should be based on factors such as (1) the strategic plan, including the business mission and objectives; (2) the owner's personal and business objectives; (3) the plans, programs, policies, and practices that will achieve those objectives; and (4) the authority and responsibility relationships that will accomplish the mission or purpose of the firm. These aspects of organization are discussed in greater detail in Chapter 15.

**Figure 6–4**

"As you see, we have a highly centralized organization."

*Source:* Reprinted from Donald C. Mosley, Paul H. Pietri, and Leon C. Megginson, *Management: Leadership in Action,* 5th ed. (New York: Harper CollinsCollege Publishers, 1996), p. 274. Reprinted with permission.

## *Determining Approach to Market*

The volume of sales and income of a small firm depend on its marketing strategies and activities. If a study of the environment determines that there is a sufficiently large market for the firm's product(s), plans must be made to capture enough of that market to be successful. Even if your company's service is the best, you must tell potential customers about it. Many methods of marketing are in use; the ones used must be chosen for the particular business.

> For example, a number of years ago, a man living in New England conceived of a rubber, instead of metal, dustpan. He had a dozen samples of the new product custom-made in a variety of colors and headed to Boston to hawk his wares in Filene's and Jordan Marsh. Neither seemed interested in the dustpan.
>
> Still, because he was sure that homemakers would buy his product, he decided to test-market the dustpan by calling on them. Pulling into a residential street, he parked his car and set out to ring doorbells. Just 45 minutes later, he returned to his car with only two pans left.
>
> Convinced that his idea was good, Earl Tupper developed a company—Tupperware—to market the product directly to consumers.

Once a target market is chosen, you must provide for sales promotion and distribution to it. The product to be offered should again be studied carefully to determine answers to the following questions: What qualities make it special to the customer? Are there unique or distinct features to emphasize, such as ease of installation or low maintenance? Should the company use newspaper advertising or mailings to publicize the product? These and other marketing questions are discussed in more detail in Chapters 10, 11, and 12.

### *Establishing an Efficient Records System*

Even in a small business, simple records and information systems must be used. But they must be designed to help you control your business by keeping track of activities and obligations and also to collect certain types of information demanded by outside organizations such as government agencies. For example, you must maintain records of such data as (1) the date each employee is hired, the number of hours each one works, and the wages and benefits paid; (2) inventories, accounts receivable, and accounts payable; (3) taxes paid and owed; and (4) units of each product sold.

Accounting systems must be designed to keep track of your finances. Incoming revenues and outgoing expenses are processed into accounts that record changing values of assets, liabilities, and equity. The system for planning and controlling the finances can be based on a budget system that sets goals against which actual results can be compared.

The system of records for employees has expanded greatly during recent years as government and legal controls have increased. Efforts to match skills to jobs and promote the proper person require records of factors such as experience, performance, education, and training. Records of accidents help identify unsafe practices.

Many other records are needed to help make the small business operate successfully. Management information systems, covered in Chapter 21, should be selected and designed to aid management in this respect.[10]

### *Setting Up a Time Schedule*

Once you decide to go ahead with the formation of the business, you should establish a time schedule to provide an orderly and coordinated program. The schedule should probably include the prior planning steps. Many of these steps can be and often are performed simultaneously. A SCORE representative can provide valuable assistance.

## The Role of Financial Planning

**Financial planning** can be quite simple or very complex, as shown in Chapters 9, 18, and 19 but it should involve at least the following:

1. Estimating income and expenses.
2. Estimating initial investment required.
3. Locating sources of funds.

**Financial planning** involves determining what funds are needed, where they can be obtained, and how they can be controlled.

### Estimating Income and Expenses

The steps described so far set the stage for determining the profit (or loss) from operating your new business. Income from sales (also called *revenue*) can be estimated by studying the market, and expenses (also called *costs*) can

**Net profit** is the amount of revenue (sales) over and above the total amount of expenses (costs) of doing business.

**Variable expenses** change in relation to volume of output: When output is low, the expenses are low, and when output is high, expenses rise.

be calculated from past experience and other sources, such as knowledgeable people, a library, or a trade association. After all costs have been estimated, they can be totaled and subtracted from the estimated sales income to obtain the expected **net profit** (or loss), as shown in the worksheet for Dover Enterprises* in Figure 6–5. When making your estimates, remember two key points. First, these expense and income (or loss) estimates are usually for only the first year of operations. However, if you also make an income analysis for an expected typical year in the future as well as for the first year, the exercise can provide valuable information for planning purposes.

Second, while total expenses do move up and down with sales volume, they do not vary as much. Some expenses, such as materials, which rise in direct proportion to increases in sales volume and drop as sales volume drops, are called **variable expenses**. Other expenses, such as depreciation on

*An actual company, but the name is disguised at the owner's request.

**Figure 6–5**

**DOVER ENTERPRISES**
**Worksheet for Estimated Annual Income, Expenses, and Profit (Loss)***

| | Units sold | | | | | |
|---|---|---|---|---|---|---|
| | 10,000 | | 20,000 | | 30,000 | |
| Income | | | | | | |
| Sales income ($5/unit) | | $ 50,000 | | $100,000 | | $150,000 |
| Cost of goods sold: | | | | | | |
| Production cost ($1.62/unit) | $16,200 | | $32,400 | | $48,600 | |
| Shipping boxes and labels ($0.04/unit) | 400 | | 800 | | 1,200 | |
| Depreciation (mold) | 2,500 | | 2,500 | | 2,500 | |
| Total production expenses | | 19,100 | | 35,700 | | 52,300 |
| Gross profit | | 30,900 | | 64,300 | | 97,700 |
| Other operating expenses | | | | | | |
| Salaries | 30,000 | | 30,000 | | 30,000 | |
| Telephone | 3,000 | | 3,500 | | 4,000 | |
| Rent | 2,100 | | 2,100 | | 2,100 | |
| Insurance | 400 | | 400 | | 400 | |
| Office expense | 1,000 | | 1,100 | | 1,200 | |
| Sales promotion | 7,000 | | 8,000 | | 9,000 | |
| Freight | 1,000 | | 2,000 | | 3,000 | |
| Travel | 4,000 | | 4,000 | | 4,000 | |
| Taxes and licenses | 4,000 | | 4,000 | | 4,000 | |
| Miscellaneous | 1,000 | | 2,000 | | 3,000 | |
| Total operating expenses | | 53,500 | | 57,100 | | 60,700 |
| Net profit (loss) | | ($22,600) | | $ 7,200 | | $ 37,000 |

*Projections for three levels of sales.

buildings, which do not vary in value as sales volume rises or falls, are called **fixed expenses**. Also, there are some expenses, such as supervision, that combine variable and fixed costs.

**Fixed expenses** do not vary with output, but remain the same.

Changes in sales volume drastically affect the amount of net profit: As sales volume rises (say from 10,000 to 20,000 units), losses are reduced and profits may rise; as sales volume drops (say from 20,000 to 10,000), profits drop and losses may occur. An in-depth discussion of profit planning, including break-even analysis, may be found in Chapters 18 and 19.

*Don't forget to also prepare a personal budget!* As Robert Caldwell, a New York financial planner, emphasizes, "Living below your means is never a mistake, and that is even more true with a start-up business."[11] Therefore, you—and your family—must have enough income to live on during the time you are moving from being an employee to being an employer. If your standard of living drops too drastically, it will probably be devastating to your family. So, in addition to determining the expected income and expenses of the business, also estimate your continuing needs, and where you will get the resources to satisfy them.

## Estimating Initial Investment

You will need money and/or credit to start your business. You must pay for items such as buildings, equipment, materials, personnel, inventory, machines, business forms, and sales promotion at the outset before income from sales starts providing the means to pay these expenses from internal sources. Credit may be extended to help sell the products, but this only adds to operating expenses.

The worksheet in Figure 6–6 provides a logical method of calculating the initial cash needs of a new business such as Dover Enterprises. The figures in column 1 are estimates that have already been made for the income statement for the first year. The amount of cash needed is some multiple of each of the values in column 1, as shown in column 3. The total of these multiple values is an estimate of the money needed to start the business and is shown in column 2. This sum can be considerable:

> Coopers & Lybrand, for example, discovered that founders of 328 fast-growing businesses risked an average of $82,300 to start their companies.[12] Figure 6–7 shows where their money came from.

Note that the cash needed to start the business—shown in column 2—represents the delay between paying money out for expenses and receiving it back as revenue. The item called *starting inventory* is an illustration of buying goods in one period and selling them in another. But inventories of goods and supplies—in the form of purchases and recurring inventories—continue to exist for the life of the business. Therefore, funds obtained from investments in the business or from loans must continue for its life unless they are paid off.

Because cash does not produce revenue, it should not sit idle but should be used to earn income. The amount of cash a business needs, and has, will vary during the year, since most businesses have busy and slack periods. To keep the investment and borrowing low, **cash flow** projections must be made. The worksheet in Chapter 19 (Figure 19–1) is a form that can be used to make such projections, which can be compared with what actually happens.

**Cash flow** is the amount of cash available at a given time to pay expenses.

Figure 6–6

**DOVER ENTERPRISES**
**Estimated Monthly Expenses and Starting Costs**
**December 1, 19__**

| Item | (1) Estimate of monthly expenses based on sales of $100,000 per year | (2) Estimate of how much cash you need to start your business (see column 3) | (3) What to put in (2) (Multipliers are typical for one kind of business. You must decide how many months to allow for in your business.) |
|---|---|---|---|
| | **Estimated monthly expenses** | | |
| Salary of owner-manager | $2,500 | $5,000 | 2 times column 1 |
| All other salaries and wages | — | — | 3 times column 1 |
| Rent | 175 | 525 | 3 times column 1 |
| Travel | | 1,000 | As required |
| Advertising | 700 | 2,100 | 3 times column 1 |
| Delivery expense | 100 | 300 | 3 times column 1 |
| Supplies | 100 | 300 | 3 times column 1 |
| Recurring inventory and purchases | — | — | Check with suppliers for estimate |
| Telephone and telegraph | 300 | 900 | 3 times column 1 |
| Other utilities | — | — | 3 times column 1 |
| Insurance | | 400 | Payment required by insurance company |
| Taxes, including Social Security | 325 | 1,300 | 4 times column 1 |
| Interest | — | — | 3 times column 1 |
| Maintenance | — | — | 3 times column 1 |
| Legal and other professional fees | — | — | 3 times column 1 |
| Miscellaneous | 200 | 600 | 3 times column 1 |

You might contact your nearest SBA office to get information to help you estimate your start-up costs. Also, various financial firms and certified public accountants have computed some helpful standard figures.

## Locating Sources of Funds

Once the amount of funds needed is known, you must find sources for those funds. The many sources from which to obtain funds to start and operate a business boil down to two: the owner and others. These two sources are discussed in detail in Chapter 9, so only the highlights are discussed here.

**Figure 6–6** *(concluded)*

**Starting costs you have to pay only once**

| | | |
|---|---|---|
| Fixtures and equipment: | | |
| Telephone, $203; mold, $11,280; computer, $750 | $12,233 | Enter total from separate list |
| Decorating and remodeling | — | Talk it over with a contrator |
| Installation of fixtures and equipment | — | Talk to suppliers from whom you wish to buy these |
| Starting inventory | 5,000 | Suppliers will probably help you estimate this |
| Deposits with public utilities | — | Find out from utilities companies |
| Legal and other professional fees | — | Lawyer, accountant, and so on |
| Licenses and permits | (Part of taxes above) | Find out from city offices what you have to have |
| Advertising and promotion for opening | (Part of advertising above) | Estimate what you'll use |
| Accounts receivable | 1,200 | What you need to buy more stock until credit customers pay |
| Cash | 1,000 | For unexpected expenses or losses, special purchases, etc. |
| Other | | Make a separate list and enter total |
| Total estimated cash you need to start with | $31,858 | Add up all the numbers in column 2 |

*Source:* This basic worksheet is based on *Checklist for Going into Business,* Management Aides No. 2.016 (Washington, DC: Small Business Administration), p. 4.

**Figure 6–7** Dig Deep to Open Business—Founders of 328 fast-growing businesses risked on average $82,300 to start their companies.

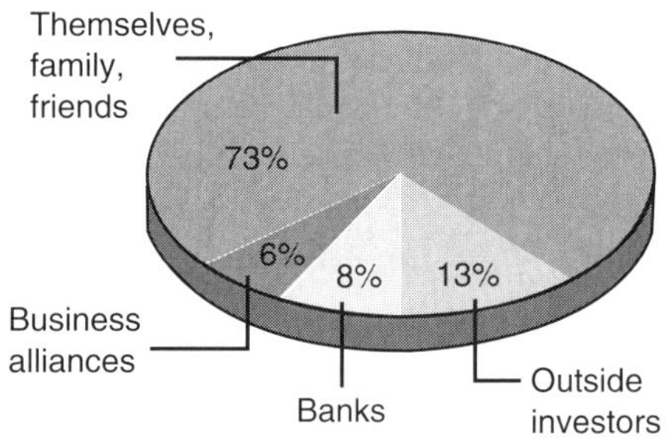


*Source:* Coopers & Lybrand, as reported in *USA Today,* August 26, 1994, p. 1B. Copyright 1994, USA TODAY. Reprinted with permission.

Before approaching a funding source, decide how much money you and others will put into the business and how much should come from other sources.

> For example, Don Dover started Dover Enterprises with his own money and investments from three relatives. All investors owned the company and made up its board of directors. Don, as president, also managed it on a day-to-day basis.

## *Using Your Own Funds*

Some small business owners prefer to invest only their personal funds and not borrow to start or operate a business. Others believe they should use little of their own money and instead make as much profit as possible by using their interest in the business as security when obtaining funds from others. Normally, owners control a company; they take the risks of failure but also make the decisions. To maintain control, you must continue to invest more personal funds than all the other investors combined. Moreover, you can maintain control only so long as lenders do not become worried about the safety of their money.

## *Using Funds from Others*

There are several sources of outside funds. These can be generally divided into *equity investors,* who actually become part owners of the business, and *lenders,* who provide money for a limited time at a fixed rate of interest. Both run the risk of losing their money if the business fails, but this gamble is offset for investors by the possibility of large returns if the business is successful. Since the rate of return for lenders is fixed, some security is usually given to offset their risk.

You may be able to find investors interested in a venture opportunity. Such people might be found among relatives, friends, attorneys, bankers, or securities dealers.

You will also find that many people who are not willing to assume the risks of ownership are willing to lend money to a business. They include private individuals, private financial institutions, merchandise and equipment vendors, and government agencies. There are many outright grants available from government agencies to start new businesses, especially for women and ethnic groups.

D

> For example, in November 1995 the National Minority Business Council started a program in New York to help minority entrepreneurs raise money and attract customers. The council assigned some of its top officials to serve as mentors to other selected members. The mentors were to work for six months with their protégés to spruce up their businesses and business plans. They were also to introduce the members to potential financiers and customers.[13]

G

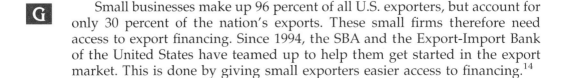

Small businesses make up 96 percent of all U.S. exporters, but account for only 30 percent of the nation's exports. These small firms therefore need access to export financing. Since 1994, the SBA and the Export-Import Bank of the United States have teamed up to help them get started in the export market. This is done by giving small exporters easier access to financing.[14]

## WHAT YOU SHOULD HAVE LEARNED

**1.** Planning, one of the key managerial functions, is usually done first, since everything else depends on it. While planning establishes directions and goals for any business, it is especially difficult in small firms, where management is often fully engaged in day-to-day operation and "can't see the forest for the trees." Some barriers to planning in small firms are the fear of learning things you would rather not know, the unpredictability of plans, the uncertainty of plans, and especially the lack of adequate time to plan.

**2.** Strategic planning—from which other plans are derived—determines the very nature of the business. Next comes operational planning, which sets policies, methods and procedures, budgets and standards, and other operating plans.

**3.** Strategic planning includes the company's mission, which tells what type of business you are in. Once the mission is determined, a company can establish its objectives, which set the goals it hopes to reach and provide a way of keeping score on its performance. Strategies provide the means to reach objectives.

**4.** Operational planning, which includes policies, budgets, standards, procedures, and methods, *forms the basis for preparing the business plan.* It involves planning the overall operations of the business, including *(a)* choosing its location, *(b)* planning operations and physical facilities, *(c)* developing supply sources for goods and materials, *(d)* planning personnel requirements, *(e)* setting up the legal and organizational structure, *(f)* determining the approach to the market, *(g)* establishing an efficient records system, and *(h)* setting up a time schedule.

**5.** Financial planning involves estimating income and expenses, estimating investment required, and locating sources of funds. Income and expenses should be estimated to ensure that the proposed business will be feasible. Estimates should be based on the firm's first year of operation, as well as a typical "good" year, since investors may be willing to assume some risk of loss at the beginning to achieve greater gains later. Also, estimates should be made of personal needs during the transition period. These projections permit the prospective new owner to estimate the initial investment needed. Finally, sources of funds must be determined. The two sources are the business owner(s) and others, either private individuals or lending institutions.

## QUESTIONS FOR DISCUSSION

1. Explain why planning is so badly needed by small businesses. Why is it so often neglected?
2. Explain the two overall categories of planning. What are the essential differences between the two?
3. Explain the two components of strategic planning.
4. Discuss the factors to be considered in formulating a business's mission.

5. Explain each of the following: policies, methods and procedures, budgets, and standards.
6. In planning to operate the business, what are the factors that must be planned for? Explain each.
7. What is involved in financial planning?
8. What are the two sources of funds for a small business? Explain each.
9. Why is funding for diverse ethnic groups so important?

## *CASE 6*

## ARTWATCHES—TURNING A COLLEGE THESIS INTO A $4 MILLION BUSINESS

Geoff Walsh is living proof that not all businesses start with a furrowed brow. Instead, entrepreneurship came easily to him. At age 10, he ran a lemonade stand; at 23, he owned a $4 million-a-year business—ArtWatches.

ArtWatches, selling wristwatches whose faces are reproductions of paintings by Degas, Picasso, Renoir, and van Gogh, was conceived in 1988, when Walsh was an undergraduate at the University of Pennsylvania's Wharton School of Business. He and his roommate took advantage of the craze for Dan Quayle watches when the vice presidential nominee was a popular target for the press. After the roommate sold "several hundred" Quayle timepieces, Walsh, seeing that watches with reproductions had a bright future, wrote a business plan for ArtWatches as his undergraduate thesis.

After studying copyright law and searching museums for licensing agreements, he obtained the rights to reproduce eight Impressionist works on watches. He started the business in November 1989.

One problem he encountered was in obtaining suppliers and setting up distributors, as there were only about a dozen businesses in the world that controlled the manufacturing side of the industry. Walsh was fortunate to get one of the premier Hong Kong companies to help him, assembling the watches' Japanese components with straps made by a Philadelphia company.

His timing was good—and bad. The good news was that demand for watches doubled from 1980 to 1989. The bad news was that the 1990s recession made mincemeat of the $17 million sales estimate in his business plan. Then, in early 1990, Bulova Corporation introduced its Classic Moments line of reproduction paintings, including four that Walsh was also producing.

Walsh countered by changing his market from the upper middle class, who bought the Bulova watch, to mall shoppers—the 18- to 40-year-old suburbanites, who could afford the $45 to $50 price of ArtWatches.

ArtWatches are sold in retail stores, boutiques, museum shops, catalog stores, and department stores and on the QVC Home Shopping Network.

Also, through a promotional deal with Toshiba, everyone in Japan who buys one of its big-screen TVs gets a free ArtWatch.

*Source:* Abstracted from Michelle Osborn, "An Entrepreneur Who's Worth Watching," *USA Today,* April 18, 1991, p. 4B. Copyright 1991, USA TODAY. Reprinted with permission.

## QUESTIONS

1. Which type(s) of planning did Walsh use? Explain.
2. What does this case show about the need for planning?
3. How do you explain Walsh's success?
4. What does the case show about the need for a business plan?

# APPLICATION 6–1

Martin, a marketing major at State University, recently did a market survey for one of his classes. The results convinced him that detailing for automobiles would be a good business to enter. But he knew that to start such a business he needed considerable funds. His personal funds—and those of his family—were not enough to start the new business.

He had found a desirable location for his business, and his fellow students could work with him, But he still lacked the necessary funds. As a student, he would work part time, but that would not provide the needed funds.

## QUESTIONS

1. What does Martin need to do now?
2. What are other possible sources of funds for him?
3. Do you think his absence from the business while in class would affect his business? What could he do to cope with this problem?

# ACTIVITY 6–1

*Directions:* Use information from this chapter to solve the "strategic squares."

**ACROSS**

1 Makes a firm more attractive

3 Converting plans into an effective work force

5 Standing instructions

8 Equity to finance operations

11 Change in relation to volume of output

13 Black and white

14 Determine action to reach objectives

16 Guides to supervisory activities

17 Small

19 Make up the work force

20 Do not vary with output

21 Long-term direction

**DOWN**

2 Set standards for achieving objectives

4 Equipment needed to carry on business

6 Means by which a business fulfills its mission

7 Cash available at a given time to pay expenses

9 How funds can be controlled

10 Revenue above expenses

12 Desired results for the business

13 Detailed monetary plans

15 Long-term mission

18 Management technique

ACROSS 1 Competitive edge 3 Personnel planning 5 Methods 8 Financial resources 11 Variable expenses 13 BW 14 Planning 16 Policies 17 SM 19 Human resources 20 Fixed expenses 21 Strategic planning DOWN 2 Corporation planning 4 Physical resources 6 Strategies 7 Cash flow 9 Financial planning 10 Net profit 12 Objectives 13 Budgets 15 Mission 18 MBO

CHAPTER 7

# Growing Opportunities in Franchising

*Buying a franchise is probably the quickest, easiest, and most successful way of becoming an entrepreneur.*—Colonel Harlan Sanders, founder of Kentucky Fried Chicken

*Franchising is so extensive and diverse that it's no longer just a way of doing business, it's becoming a way of life.*—Andrew Kostecka, franchising specialist for the U.S. Department of Commerce's International Trade Association

## LEARNING OBJECTIVES

After studying the material in this chapter, you will be able to:

1. Discuss the extent of franchising.
2. Define franchising, and describe the two most popular types of franchises.
3. Tell why franchising is growing so rapidly.
4. Explain how to evaluate opportunities in franchising.
5. Discuss the future of franchising, especially in international operations.

# PROFILE

## LA-VAN HAWKINS AND RAYMOND O'NEAL—URBAN ENTREPRENEURS

When you think of hamburgers, the words that come to mind are more likely to be "pickles, ketchup, and mustard" than "economic empowerment." It may sound odd at first—burgers helping to build neighborhoods—but that's what one man is determined to accomplish.

Photo courtesy of Craig Beytien

La-Van Hawkins, president and chief executive officer of Inner City Foods Incorporated, is one of America's most successful, but extraordinary, entrepreneurs. His story demonstrates both the potential and the importance of entrepreneurship to the continued success of American business, especially minority entrepreneurship.

Hawkins grew up in one of Chicago's poorest and most dangerous areas, the Cabrini Green housing project. His first job was sweeping floors at a local McDonald's. He concluded early in his career that many businesses would not locate in mostly African-American urban neighborhoods. Unlike others, however, he saw that reality as an opportunity, not only for his own benefit but also as a way to provide employment and income for people in those communities.

What sets Hawkins and his Inner City Foods Incorporated apart from other businesses that avoid poor, mostly black urban neighborhoods, is that Hawkins seeks them out. Consequently, he now owns over 30 Checkers restaurant franchises in the inner-city areas of Atlanta, Baltimore, and Philadelphia. All provide jobs and income to communities that are usually considered too great a risk by national chains and fast-food outlets.

In 1994, Hawkins' restaurants generated sales of $50 million, and he has recently been given a seat on the board of directors of the Checkers Corporation. His growing fast-food empire is providing a fast track into the business world for hundreds of African-American men and women.

Hawkins expects to open 100 more inner-city restaurants in the next three years, in places like Harlem and Bedford-Stuyvesant in New York. His unique and successful business strategies are drawing the attention of urban business and political leaders around the country to La-Van Hawkins.

*Source:* Adapted from William G. Nickels, James M. McHugh, and Susan M. McHugh, *Understanding Business,* 4th ed. (Burr Ridge: Richard D. Irwin, 1996), p. 27.



D

This Profile illustrates the many exciting opportunities in one of the fastest-growing and most important segments of U.S. business: franchising. This attractive alternative to starting a new business has helped tens of thousands of entrepreneurs achieve their dream of owning a business of their own. In Chapter 5, we discussed the reasons to buy—and not to buy—a franchise. In this chapter, however, we present a more detailed look at franchising's role.

## Extent of Franchising

The U.S. Department of Commerce estimated that there were 543,000 franchised outlets in the United States in 1991 and their sales totaled $758 billion. As you can see from Figure 7–1, franchise sales more than doubled in the last decade, and the number of establishments grew by 23 percent. According to Arthur Karp, chairman of the International Franchise Associa-

**Figure 7–1** Franchising Shows Steady Growth

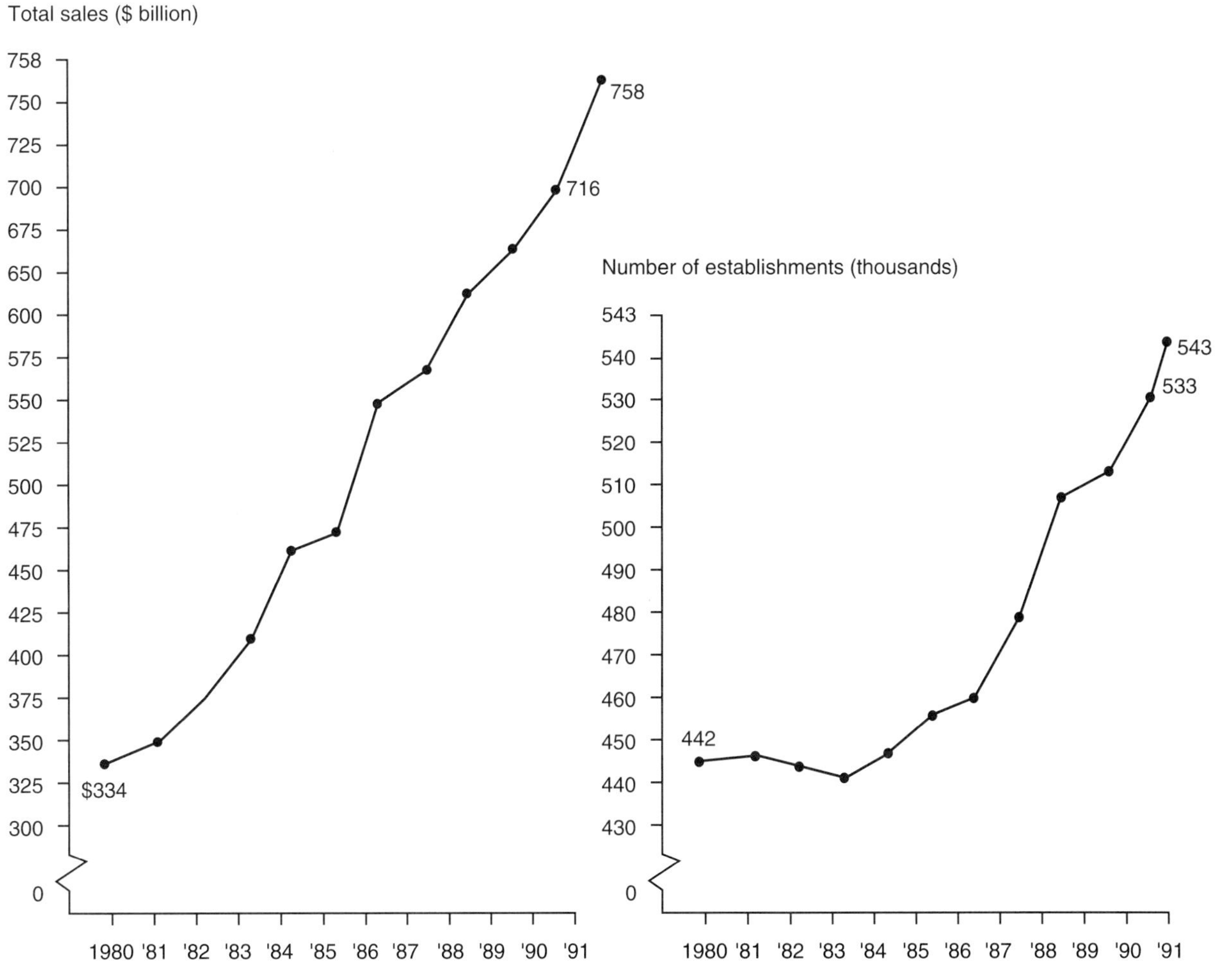


*Source:* Based on data from *Franchising in the Economy* (Washington, DC: U.S. Department of Commerce, various years); and U.S. Bureau of the Census, *Statistical Abstract of the United States, 1994* (Washington, DC: Government Printing Office, 1994), Table 1291, p. 790.

**Figure 7–2** Franchising Accounts for Nearly 41 Percent of Retail Sales

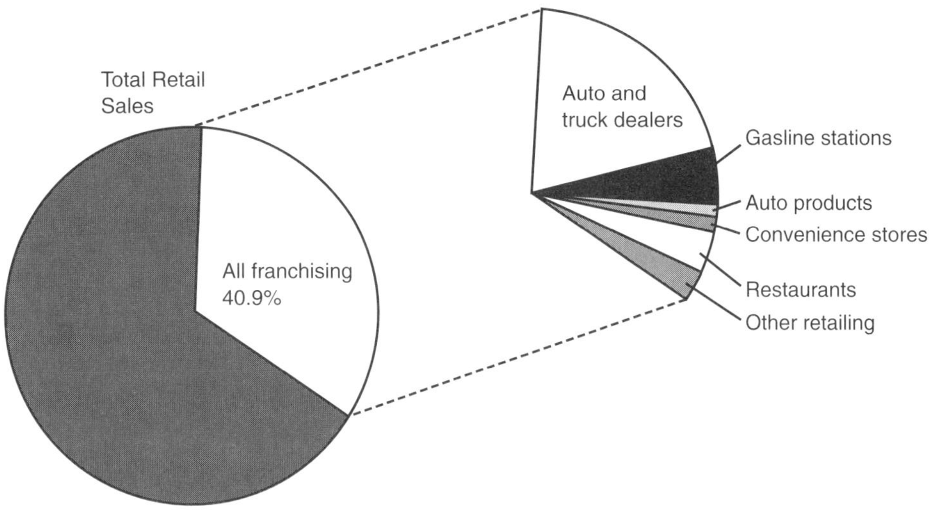


*Source:* International Franchise Association, as reported in *USA Today*, November 19, 1995, p. 8B. Copyright 1995, USA TODAY. Reprinted with permission.

tion (IFA), U.S. franchises create around 300,000 *new jobs* each year, as each new franchise creates 8 to 10 new jobs, and a new franchise opens about every 17 minutes.[1] Franchising also provides direct employment for some 10 million people, including many younger and older workers who otherwise would be unable to find jobs.

According to the International Franchise Association (IFA), franchising is strong in retailing, especially auto and truck dealers, gasoline stations, and restaurants. As Figure 7–2 shows, franchises accounted for around 41 percent of retail sales in 1995, and it is estimated that 87 percent of all franchising receipts come from retailing.[2] Karp estimated that retail sales from franchising would exceed the trillion-dollar mark by 1994 and account for over 50 percent of total retail sales by the year 2000.[3]

## What Is Franchising?

We will define franchising by describing the process and parties involved, and then discuss the two most popular types of franchises. These are (1) product and trademark franchising and (2) business format franchising.

### Definition

**Franchising** is a marketing system based on a legal arrangement that permits one party—the franchisee—to conduct business as an individual owner while abiding by the terms and conditions set by the second party—the franchiser.

The **franchise** is the agreement granting the right to do business and specifying the terms and conditions under which the business will be conducted. The **franchiser** is the company that owns the franchise's name and distinctive elements (such as signs, symbols, and patents) and that

**Franchising** is a marketing system whereby an individual owner conducts business according to the terms and conditions set by the franchiser.

A **franchise** is an agreement whereby an independent businessperson is given exclusive rights to sell a specified good or service.

The **franchiser** owns the franchise's name and distinctive elements and licenses others to sell its products.

**Figure 7–3** Types of Franchising Systems

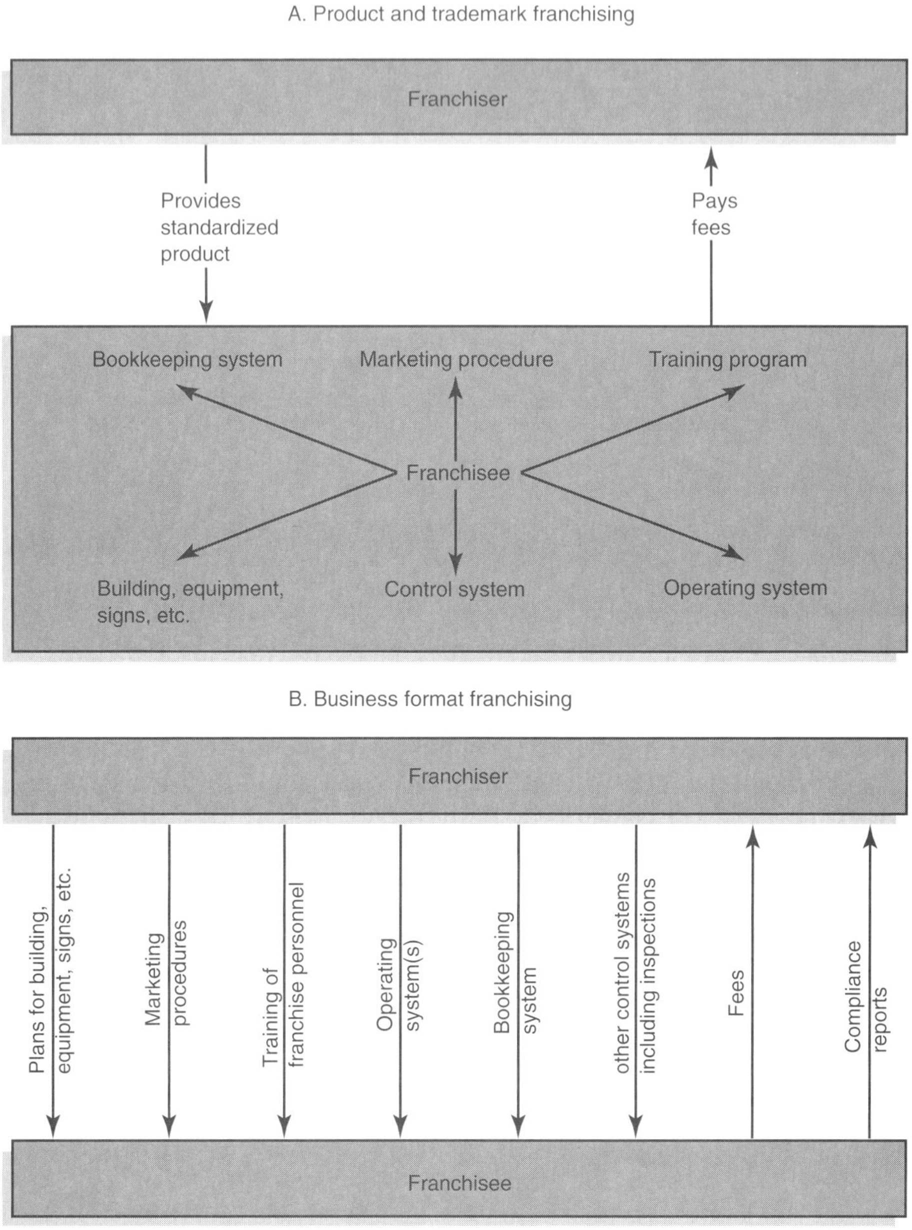


The **franchisee** is an independent businessperson who agrees to sell the product according to the franchiser's requirements.

grants others the right to sell its product. The **franchisee** is usually an independent local businessperson who agrees with the franchise owner to operate the business on a local or regional basis. While the franchisee is given the right to market the franchiser's designated goods or services, that marketing must be done according to the terms of the licensing agreement. The contract specifies what the franchisee can and cannot do and prescribes certain penalties for noncompliance.

While many franchising opportunities exist, they do not automatically spell success. Instead, caution is called for in dealing with franchisers who promise a guaranteed return on your investment, for contracts with these elusive or vanished companies often prove worthless.

### Types of Franchising Systems

As shown in Figure 7–3, there are at least two types of franchising systems. They are (1) product and trademark franchising and (2) business format franchising.

**Product and trademark franchising** is an arrangement under which the franchisee is granted the right to sell a widely recognized product or brand. Most such franchisees concentrate on handling one franchiser's product line and identify their business with that firm. Familiar examples include automobile and truck dealerships, gasoline service stations, and soft-drink bottlers. The franchiser exercises very little control over the franchisee's operations; what control there is has to do with maintaining the integrity of the product, not with the franchisee's business operations.

**Product and trademark franchising** grants the franchisee the right to sell a widely recognized product or brand.

**Business format franchising** is a relationship in which the franchisee is granted the right to use an entire marketing system, along with ongoing assistance and guidance from the franchiser. In 1991, there were about 410,000 business format franchises operating in the United States, with sales of $232 billion.[4] The industry groups with the largest volume of sales in this type of franchising are restaurants, retailing (nonfood), hotels and motels, business aids and services, automotive products and services, and convenience stores.

**Business format franchising** grants a franchisee the right to market the product and trademark and to use a complete operating system.

> When Ray Kroc set up McDonald's as a franchiser (see the case at the end of this chapter), he controlled the trade name (McDonald's), symbol (golden arches), and operating systems. In turn, he permitted franchisees to use them under controlled conditions—for a fee. Kroc also controlled all aspects of quality that characterized the successful operations of the original drive-in.

## Why Franchising Is Growing in Importance

If you think of all the franchises you've been involved with during the past week, you can see why they're growing in importance.

### Recent Rapid Growth

Franchising has been one of the fastest-growing areas of U.S. business during the past decade or so. The number of franchise establishments increased over 436 percent during the last two decades,[5] and this trend is expected to continue through the 1990s. Business format franchising has accounted for most of this growth.

Earlier, product and trademark franchising dominated the franchise field, but its role has declined rapidly during the past two decades as business format franchising has skyrocketed.

**Figure 7–4** Dwindling Dealerships, Dwindling Profits

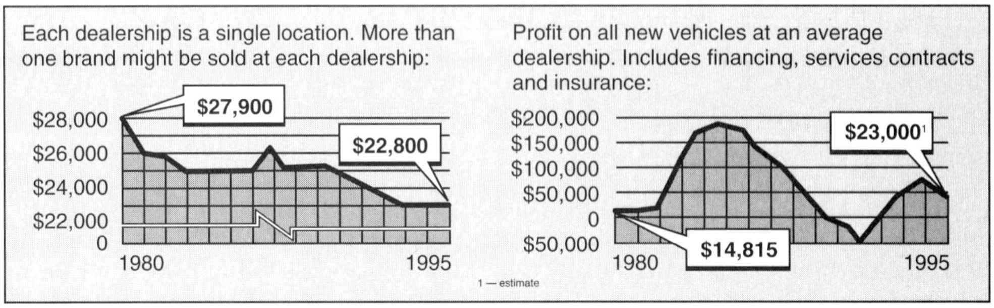


*Source:* NADA industry analysis, as reported in *USA Today*, December 13, 1995, p. 1B. Copyright 1995, USA TODAY. Reprinted with permission.

For example, a revolution is occurring in the business of selling cars, and not all dealers will survive. Investment bankers and venture capitalists are rapidly moving into the car business. They threaten to do to "mom-and-pop" car dealers what Wal-Mart did to the corner drugstore. In fact, more than half a million car shoppers have turned to Wal-Mart's warehouse club—Sam's Club—for reference to its dealer network since 1991. And AutoByTel helped broker more than 25,000 car purchases on the Internet in just 10 months in 1995. It was bracing for a five-fold increase in 1996.[6] Figure 7–4 shows what's happening to the number of dealerships and their sales.

## Causes of Rapid Growth

There are many reasons franchising, especially business format franchising, has become so popular. First, a franchiser has already identified a consumer need and created a product to meet that need, as well as a convenient and economical method of marketing it. For example, in single-parent or dual-career homes, few people want to spend precious time preparing meals, so they head for a fast-food outlet such as Wendy's. Reluctance to make dental or doctor's appointments far in advance—with a good chance of spending hours in the waiting room—has led to franchising of walk-in health care services, such as LensCrafters and United Surgical Centers. Increasing leisure time has resulted in franchising of recreational and exercise activities, such as Jazzercise. In other words, franchises have emerged to cater to many consumer and business needs that were not being recognized or satisfied elsewhere.

Second, as Colonel Sanders said in the opening quotation, one of the best ways to succeed in small business is to buy an established franchise, because the failure rate is much lower than for small independent businesses, according to SBA estimates.[7]

A third reason for franchising's popularity is that franchisees have the support of established management systems for bookkeeping, marketing, operations, and control. And these systems give franchisees the benefit of business experience without their having to acquire it for themselves.

A major drawback to franchising, though, is the voluminous paperwork needed to provide disclosure documents to potential franchisees. These statements, required by the Federal Trade Commission (FTC), provide background and financial position information about the franchiser and the franchise offering.

## How to Tell Whether a Franchise Is Right for You

While franchising opportunities abound, intensive study and evaluation are needed before you enter into such an arrangement. When you buy a franchise, you're relying not only on your own business expertise and experience but also on the franchiser's business ideas, skills, capital, and ethics.

> Two highly publicized failures illustrate this point. Minnie Pearl Chicken failed because the franchiser lacked adequate capital to service the franchisees, and Wild Bill Hamburgers was a "franchising fraud that fleeced millions of dollars from more than 100 investors." Another failure was Conway Twitty's "Twittyburgers."[8]

While nothing is guaranteed to protect you in buying a franchise, you can reduce your risks by taking the actions discussed in this section. See Figure 7–5 for specific questions to ask when checking out a potential franchise.

### Look at the Opportunities

In investigating franchises, learn which ones are growing the fastest so as to get in on growth possibilities. You can do this by studying such sources as *Entrepreneur* magazine's annual listing of the best performers and the U.S. Commerce Department's *Franchise Opportunities Handbook,* published annually. Also, your local SBA office or SCORE chapter, schools with small business development centers, chambers of commerce, and libraries can be of great help.

### See What the Franchise Can Do for You

At this point, you should decide whether you're willing to give up some of your independence by buying a franchise. While you may cherish your freedom to operate as you choose, you might prefer to receive the management training and assistance provided by the franchiser. For entrepreneurs with little business experience, the assistance they can get from the franchiser justifies some sacrifice of their independence.

When you buy a franchise, you'll pay up front to buy a building or rent space, renovate a store or office, lease or buy equipment, buy inventory, and receive other facilities. Then you'll pay the franchiser a one-time franchise fee and regular royalty fees. For these fees and costs—ranging from around 3 to 7 percent—you can expect the kind of help shown in Figure 7–6. Those considering buying a franchise should ask themselves if they are willing to pay these fees, accept the franchiser's regulations, and give up a certain amount of their independence.

**Figure 7–5** How to Check Out a Franchise

Q

**The franchise**

1. Does your lawyer approve of the franchise contract being considered?
2. Does the franchise call on you to take any steps that your lawyer considers unwise or illegal?
3. Does the franchise agreement provide you an exclusive territory for the length of the franchise, or can the franchiser sell a second or third franchise in the territory?
4. Is the franchiser connected in any way with any other franchise handling similar merchandise or services?
5. If the answer to Question 4 is yes, what is your protection against the second franchiser?
6. Under what circumstances and at what cost can you terminate the franchise contract if you decide to cancel it?
7. If you sell your franchise, will you be compensated for goodwill?

**The franchiser**

8. How many years has the franchiser been operating?
9. Has it a reputation among local franchisees for honesty and fair dealing?
10. Has the franchiser shown you any certified figures indicating net profit of one or more franchisees that you have personally checked?
11. Will the franchiser assist with:
    *a.* A management training program?
    *b.* An employee training program?
    *c.* A public relations program?
    *d.* Capital?
    *e.* Credit?
    *f.* Merchandising ideas?
12. Will the franchiser help find a good location for the new business?
13. Is the franchiser adequately financed to implement its stated plan of financial assistance and expansion?
14. Does the franchiser have an experienced management team trained in depth?
15. Exactly what can the franchiser do for you that you can't do for yourself?
16. Has the franchiser investigated you carefully enough to be sure of your qualifications?
17. Does your state have a law regulating the sales of franchises, and has the franchiser complied with that law?

**The franchisee**

18. How much equity capital will you need to purchase the franchise and operate it until it reaches the break-even point? Where are you going to obtain it?
19. Are you prepared to give up some independence to secure the advantages offered by the franchise?
20. Do you really believe you have the qualifications to succeed as a franchisee?
21. Are you ready to spend much or all of your remaining business life with this franchise company?

**The market**

22. Have you determined that an adequate market exists in your territory for the good or service at the prices you will have to charge for it?
23. Is the population in the territory expected to increase, remain the same, or decrease over the next five years?
24. Will the good or service be in greater, about the same, or less demand five years from now than it is today?
25. What is the competition in the territory for the good or service:
    *a.* From nonfranchised firms?
    *b.* From franchised firms?

*Source: Franchising Opportunities Handbook* (Washington, DC: U.S. Department of Commerce, January 1988), pp. xxxii–xxxiv.

**Figure 7–6** Services Provided by Competent Franchisers

- Start-up assistance, such as market information, site location, building and equipment design and purchase, and financial advice.
- A proven and successful system for operating the business.
- A standardized accounting and cost control system for business records. These records are audited periodically by the franchiser's staff. In many instances, standard monthly operating statements are required. The franchiser develops a set of standard performance figures based on composite figures of reporting franchisees and returns a comparative analysis to the franchisee as a managerial aid.
- In some instances, financial assistance to cover land, building, equipment, inventory, and working capital needs.
- Assistance in the purchase of the site and the construction of a standardized structure with a design identified with the franchise.
- A training program to help prepare employees to operate and manage the unit. (The more successful franchisers have their own special training schools, such as McDonald's Hamburger University and the Holiday Inn University.)
- A well-planned and well-implemented national or regional advertising program to establish and maintain a uniform image.
- A set of customer service standards created by the franchiser and its professional staff, who make regular inspection visits to assure compliance by the franchisee.
- Sensitivity and responsiveness to changing market opportunities.
- The advantage of discounts for buying in large quantities.

## Investigate the Franchise

You should investigate the franchiser and the franchise business as thoroughly as possible. First, be sure to look at more than one franchise and investigate similar franchises in the same line of business. Review the brief descriptions of franchises in the Commerce Department's *Franchise Opportunities Handbook,* and consult other guides and literature available from your library or the other sources mentioned above.

## Study the Franchise Offering Circular

The Federal Trade Commission requires that a franchise give prospective franchisees a formal agreement and a franchise offering circular at least 10 days before the contract is executed or before any money is paid.[9] This **prospectus** or **disclosure statement** should provide background on the franchiser and its financial position; the financial requirements for a franchisee; and the restrictions, protections, and estimated earnings of the franchise.

A **prospectus** or **disclosure statement** provides background and financial information about the franchiser and the franchise offering.

## Check with Existing Franchisees

Contact several of the franchise owners listed in the disclosure statement and ask about their franchising experiences. Preferably, seek those who have been in the business for several years. They should be able to give the best advice about what to expect in the first year of operation—typically the period during which the success or failure of a new franchise is determined, as the following example illustrates.

> "I'd always wanted to go into business by myself," said Susan McKay, owner of the first Handle With Care packaging store franchise in Florida. She took the plunge after doing a lot of research, planning, "soul searching," and investigating other franchises. Also, as part of her research, she requested disclosure documents and then talked with current franchisees. She warns, "If you have any questions at all, have someone familiar with franchising look at it. Do all your research first!"[10]

## Obtain Professional Advice

The legal requirements of franchising are such that both franchiser and franchisee should "work with a franchise attorney from day one."[11] The potential franchisee especially should obtain professional assistance in reviewing and evaluating any franchise under consideration. The financial statements will reveal to a professional accountant, banker, or financial analyst whether the franchiser's financial condition is sound or whether there is a risk that it will be unable to meet its financial and other obligations. It's also important to check to see whether you'll be required to stock items that you don't need or can't sell, or whether the contract can be terminated for insufficient reason, as the following example shows.

> Toni Cironi had a franchise with White Sewing Machine Company to sell its White brand machine as well as its Elna brand. Last year, Cironi sold $15,000 of the White brand and $60,000 of the Elna brand. White's national sales manager tried to get him to sell more Whites. Cironi couldn't do so, because a nearby dress shop was buying them for $97 and selling them for $149, while he paid $140 and sold them for $200. White canceled his franchise.[12]

Legal advice is the most important professional assistance you need before investing in a franchise. A lawyer can advise you about your legal rights and obligations in relation to the franchise agreement and may be able to suggest important changes in it that will protect your interest better. A lawyer should also tell you of any laws that may affect the franchise, especially taxation and personal liability aspects.

## Know Your Legal and Ethical Rights

G

The International Franchise Association (IFA), the only U.S. international trade association serving franchisers in more than 50 countries, has a code of ethics that covers a franchiser's obligations to its franchisees. Each member company pledges to comply with all applicable laws and to make sure its disclosure statements are complete, accurate, and not misleading. Furthermore, it pledges that all important matters affecting its franchise will be contained in written agreements and that it will accept only those franchisees who appear to possess the qualifications needed to conduct the franchise successfully. The franchiser agrees to base the franchisee's compensation on the sale of the product, not on the recruitment of new franchisees.

In considering the franchisee's rights, what happens if the franchiser attempts to buy back the franchise when it becomes very profitable? Should the franchisee be required to sell, as happened in the following example?

> One of the latest contract provisions of Subway's tight control of franchisees is so restrictive that the SBA has intervened. In an unusual action, the SBA refused to guarantee loans to buyers who sign what has become the standard contract offered by Doctor's Associates Inc., Subway's franchiser. The offending provision, apparently unprecedented in the contracts of other large franchisers, gave Doctor's the right to repurchase franchises "at any time." It also made it easier to oust "difficult" or "underperforming" franchisees. Critics say it "drastically undermines franchisees' ownership rights."
>
> Doctor's has since agreed to amend the provision, but only for those who seek SBA assistance.[13]

Other problem areas for franchisees include (1) the high price of supplies that must be bought from the franchiser,[14] (2) inadequate servicing,[15] (3) slashing technical support and services,[16] and (4) fraud, as illustrated by the following example.

G D

> When Marc Wojcik trained as a Salsa's Gourmet Mexican Restaurant franchisee in 1993, he saw a rosy future. But it turned out that Mr. Wojcik had stumbled into a web of allegedly fraudulent franchise systems.
>
> According to the Federal Trade Commission (FTC), the four franchise promoters and the eight companies they controlled—including the franchiser of Salsa's—used fraudulent sales techniques, understating franchisees' start-up costs and promising to refund fees if promised earnings didn't materialize. Instead, they delivered little or nothing that they had promised some 400 U.S. franchisees. Wojcik said he lost $150,000 on his Salsa's franchise in St. Petersburg Beach, Florida.[17]

In October 1994, Congress passed a law requiring the SBA to provide clients with information on the risks and benefits of franchising. However, the agency has been slow complying with it.[18]

## The Future of Franchising

The future of franchising is indeed bright, and the number and variety of U.S. franchises are expected to continue to grow. As indicated earlier, franchises now account for nearly 41 percent of all retail trade, and the Commerce Department expects this figure to increase to one-half by the year 2000.

### Expected Areas of Growth

The industries that especially lend themselves to franchising are restaurants; motels; convenience stores; electronics; and automotive parts, accessories, and servicing. Not all franchises in these categories are of a quality worthy of selection, nor are these categories the only ones worthy of consideration; but they do appear to be good growth areas.

**Figure 7–7** Fast-Food Tastes by Gender

**Males/females who eat at fast-food restaurants serving:**

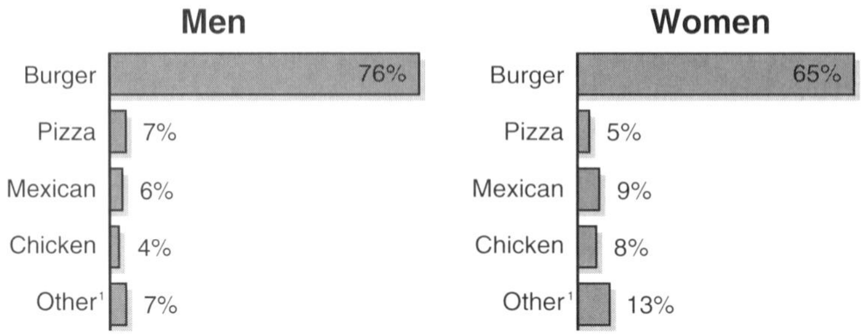


[1]Led by seafood, salad, deli, and Chinese

*Source:* Maritz Marketing Research, Inc., as reported in *USA Today,* October 5, 1995, p. 1D. Copyright 1995, USA TODAY. Reprinted with permission.

## *Restaurants*

The success of restaurants, especially those offering fast foods, is related to many variables, including demographic factors such as the high percentage of young adults and singles in the population and the increasing number of women working outside the home. The changing gender distribution will affect demand at various fast-food outlets. Figure 7–7 shows how women and men differ in their fast-food tastes.

Other factors that seem to have had a positive influence on success are product appeal to a growing segment of the market, fast service, a sanitary environment, and buildings and signs that are easily recognizable. You may think of restaurant franchises such as McDonald's, Burger King, Wendy's, and other fast-food outlets, but, as shown in Figure 7–8, franchising is also becoming dominant in the traditional restaurant market as well. "Chains such as Applebee's, Chili's, The Olive Garden, and Outback Steakhouse are now creating their own revolution in full-service dining." Earlier successful chains such as Howard Johnson's and Big Boy were deposed by McDonald's, but the new restaurant franchises, aiming at a narrow market niche, are posing a serious threat to established independent restaurants.[19]

**Figure 7–8** Gobbling Up Business

**Chains now dominate the fast-food industry and are soon expected to control sales in full-service restaurants.**

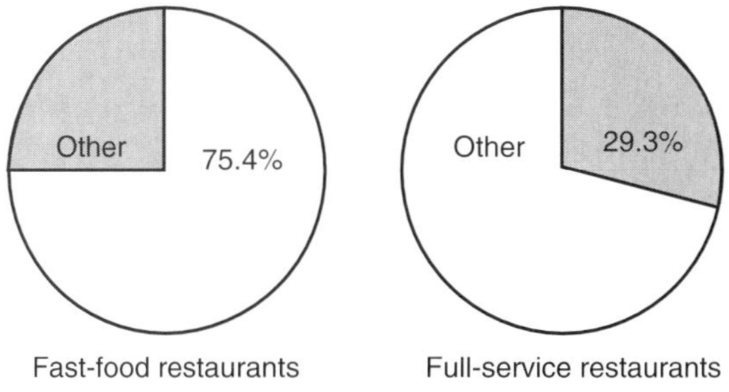


*Source:* Basic data from Technomic Inc., as reported in *U.S. News & World Report,* November 28, 1994, p. 83. Copyright November 28, 1994, US News & World Report.

## USING TECHNOLOGY TO SUCCEED

"We know all about you" could be the theme of many businesses, including franchises. By asking questions—and often promising free samples, coupons, or other products as an incentive—numerous companies have found out many interesting facts about us and our lifestyles.

For example, Burger King has amassed a database of around 5 million children between the ages of two and eight. They are members of the Burger King Kids Club. The franchise ties in with companies such as Disney and others that target children as clients. Burger King then shares this information with its franchisees, who can target the youngsters "by everything from age to name to ZIP code."

*Source:* "Large Corporations Know Your Profile," *USA Today*, December 19, 1995, p. 4B. Copyright, 1995, USA TODAY. Reprinted with permission.

### *Motels*

The motel industry has experienced explosive growth since the interstate highway system began in 1956 and the growing affluence and mobility of Americans created a market for quality motels. The industry has grown from mom-and-pop units (with an often questionable image) to one dominated by large corporate empires. These corporations not only sell franchises to independent businesspeople but also operate some of the most profitable units themselves. Best Western is considered to have the largest number of establishments.

### *Convenience Stores*

While the term *convenience store* is usually associated with food outlets, it can cover other types of specialty shops. Some examples of these franchises are Jitney-Jungle, the Bread Basket, T-Shirts Plus, and Health Mart.

### *Electronics*

With the rapid growth in electronic fields such as music, video, TV, and computers, franchising has naturally followed. Radio Shack has long been a franchise, and its computers are standard equipment for school and business applications. Some other well-known franchises are Circuit City, Babbage's, American Software, and Muzak. (See Using Technology to Succeed for an interesting application of electronics.)

### *Automotive Parts, Accessories, and Servicing*

Automotive franchises have been around for a long time as retail outlets for parts and accessories. Some of the units have been affiliated with nationally known tire manufacturers such as General Tire. A comparatively recent entry into the automotive franchise field is the specialty service shop. Some examples are shops specializing in muffler and shock absorber repairs and parts, such as Midas International; shops providing technical assistance and specialized parts for "customizing" vans; and diagnostic centers with sophisticated computerized electronic equipment. Also, the number of automotive service franchises, such as Precision Tune and Jiffy Lube, has been growing as gasoline stations shift from full service to self-service, and many of these franchises use former service station facilities. According to the president of Valvoline Instant Oil Change Co., "It was the decline of the neighborhood service station that gave rise to our business. . . . Many of the original sites used for our centers were such stations."[20]

## Other Areas of Expected Development

A growing number of small business owners are finding that they do not have the expertise, the resources, or the time to package and ship their wares. This trend has led to the expansion of franchises to address these needs for local outlets. In addition to packaging and shipping, these franchises offer other services, such as private mailbox rentals, faxing, photocopying, and quick printing.

> One such franchise is Pak Mail of America Inc. Its activities solve the need of small companies for effective service while keeping costs low.[21]

Changing demographics are also creating a need for new franchises. There have been many franchises for health care and fitness. Now there is a need to merge these activities, as there are more single parents and less physical activity on the streets and playgrounds. The following example shows what can be done in this area.

G

> In 1979, W. Berry Fowler started a one-person tutoring service—Sylvan Reading Achievement Center—in Portland, Oregon. After growing into a profitable franchiser, with 67 units in operation, Fowler sold his business for over $3.5 million and retired at age 41.
>
> Five years later, Fowler abandoned leisure to found the Little Gym International Inc. franchise in Kirkland, Washington. There were 76 franchises in operation by 1994, and Fowler planned to have a master U.S. licensee develop 185 Little Gym units in Japan by 1997.[22]

Another trend is toward mergers of franchises in related fields. These mergers result in stronger and more powerful franchises.

**Synergy** is the concept that two or more people, working together in a coordinated way, can accomplish more than the sum of their independent efforts.

**Combination franchising (multiformat franchising, dual branding, complementary branding)** big-name franchise operations offer both companies' products under the same roof.

> One example of this trend was when four profitable multi-unit franchisees of Pennzoil Company's Jiffy Lube International merged to form Heartland Automotive Services Inc. Located in Omaha, Nebraska, Heartland had 66 outlets in 1995.[23]

There is a growing emphasis on **synergy** among U.S. small businesses as they try to *reengineer* and *rightsize* themselves. One way they are doing this is by combining noncompeting franchises into one location. This latest rage in franchising goes by many names, such as **combination franchising, multiformat franchising, dual branding,** and **complementary branding.**[24] The concept, however, is the same by any name: Big-name franchise operations team up with each other to offer both companies' products under the same roof. Figure 7–9 lists some of the many franchisers using the dual brand concept. Notice that the products carried under this arrangement tend not to be directly competitive.

**Figure 7–9** Teaming Up

*Franchisers currently using the dual-brand concept include:*

- Arby's/Sbarro
- Baskin-Robbins/Dunkin' Donuts

- Blimpie/I Can't Believe It's Yogurt/Java Coast Coffee
- Carl's Jr./Green Burrito
- Carl's Jr./Long John Silver's
- Denny's/Baskin-Robbins
- El Pollo Loco/Foster's Freeze
- KFC/Taco Bell
- Rally's Hamburgers/Green Burrito
- Taco Bell/T. J. Cinnamons

*Some of the big-name fast-food franchisers now found in convenience stores:*

- Blimpie
- Burger King
- McDonald's
- Subway
- Taco Bell

*Source:* Lynn Beresford, "Seeing Double," *Entrepreneur,* October 1995, p. 166–67. Reprinted with permission from *Entrepreneur Magazine,* October 1995.

Two other interesting developments are (1) catering to home-based small businesses and (2) moving into nontraditional sites. According to Francorp, a consulting firm that maintains a database on 3,400 franchisers, the number offering home-based formats rose from 91 at the end of 1993 to 138 in July 1994.[25]

G

An example of the second trend is Dryclean USA Inc., a unit of Johnson Group Cleaners PLC in Bootle, England, which in 1994 opened a unit inside an Amoco Corporation gas station in Miami. And in New York, Tess Becker, a franchisee of Gymboree Corporation, wants to put a Gymboree play facility inside Yankee Stadium.[26]

Perhaps the most ambitious scheme, however, is McDonald's plan to launch the world's first airborne fast-food restaurant. Swissair's Crossair unit and Hotelplan, a Swiss tour operator, plan to turn one of Crossair's jetliners into a flying McDonald's, with Golden Arches colors, decor, and garb. Dubbed "the ketchup flight" and geared to attract families, the experiment will follow up on McDonald's success in serving its fare on European trains and ferries, as well as supplying Happy Meals for youngsters on United flights.[27]

## Global Franchising

G

The success achieved by some U.S. franchises has resulted in growing global interest and opportunity. For example, Figure 7–10 shows that nearly 400 U.S.-based franchise companies were operating over 35,000 overseas outlets in 1990, and that number is rapidly increasing. For example, the IFA found in a 1992 survey that the number of such outlets increased tenfold from 1971 to

**Figure 7–10** Global Franchising

Franchising Companies: 374
Number of franchising outlets: 35,046

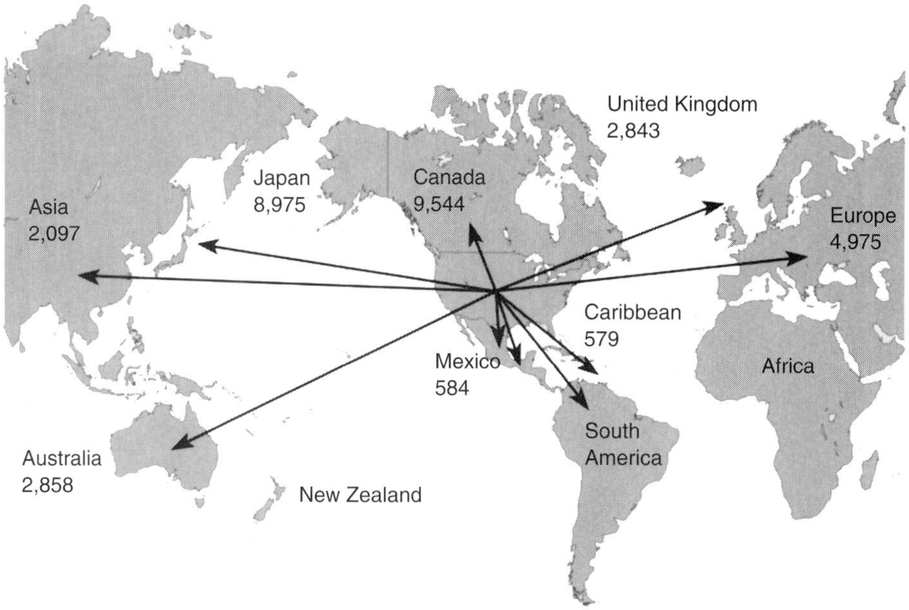


*Source:* U.S. Department of Commerce, Bureau of Industrial Economics, *Franchising in the Economy, 1988–90* (Washington, DC: Government Printing Office, 1990), p. 99.

1988.[28] Another survey found that an estimated 20 percent of U.S. franchisers operate internationally by means of company units, master licenses, individual franchises, or joint ventures.[29]

Franchises also help the U.S. balance of trade. For example, in 1994, franchising accounted for $458 million in exports but only $10 million in imports, and the favorable gap is widening each year. Germany, Canada, Japan, the United Kingdom, and Mexico are our biggest sources of export revenue.[30]

Global operations also help the franchisers. For example, McDonald's revenues from foreign sales topped 50 percent of the total, and that figure is expected to be 60 percent by the end of this decade.[31] McDonald's is obviously committed to global expansion: it is opening two foreign stores for every new U.S. outlet.

> Another global operator is KFC International (formerly Kentucky Fried Chicken), which has more than 3,600 restaurants outside the United States. They are located on six continents and produce annual sales of over $2 billion. Although it owns more than 1,000 units, KFC's global units are operated primarily through franchise and joint-venture arrangements. In these arrangements, KFC holds an equity stake in the operations, from which it earns a percentage of profits.
>
> Through a joint venture with Mitsubishi, more than 800 KFC restaurants operate in Japan, more than in any other country outside the United States. Even in Japan, half a world away from the Colonel's roots, the company's menu, sign, and packaging are nearly identical to those found in U.S. restaurants. As you can see from the photo of KFC's Hiroshima restaurant, the name and image of Colonel Sanders are easily recognizable and transcend language barriers.[32]

Photo courtesy of KFC International.

U.S. franchisers have been especially successful in Eastern Europe. Many U.S. law firms specializing in franchising are already setting up branches abroad, such as East Europe Law Ltd., in Budapest, Hungary.

Fast-food franchises have been particularly successful abroad. Because the fast-food industry isn't as well developed in other countries, U.S. franchises have a great opportunity to be leaders in many markets. For example, franchises such as McDonald's, Pizza Hut, and Pepsi are flourishing in Eastern European countries. Pepsi advertises on Russian TV—in Russian.[33]

Expansion into other countries is not always smooth, however, and problems can develop easily. For instance, when McDonald's offered its non-kosher Quarter Pounder in its first unit in Jerusalem, Orthodox Jewish protesters surrounded the store. Still, the store, which opened in May 1995, did a brisk business.[34] On the other hand, when it opens stores in India, where Hindus regard cows as sacred, McDonald's will substitute veggie burgers for its traditional "all-beef patties."[35]

McDonald's also made news when city officials demanded that it vacate its central Beijing site—on which the franchise held a 20-year lease. After the case drew international condemnation, the central government intervened. McDonald's was considering a new, smaller design.[36]

Burger King is also facing problems with its European, African, and Middle East franchises. Many franchisees say they need more guidance and support—as well as lower prices for franchiser-approved paper goods and food supplies from Burger King.[37]

But there is also good news. Chick-Fil-A, the Atlanta-based franchiser, is expected soon to announce plans to open franchises in Africa. Within the next couple of years, the company plans to open 54 restaurants scattered over 10 countries in the southern end of the continent.[38]

According to Joseph R. Lunsford, chairman of Franchise Concepts, Inc., an Atlanta-based management company for four franchise chains, Africa is an attractive market for franchises. He said the relatively untapped continent "is one of the more lucrative markets . . . for master licensees and franchisees."[39]

Growing franchise industries also include maid and personal services; home improvements; business aids and services (such as accounting, collections, and personnel services); automobile products and services; weight-control centers; hair salons and services; and private postal services.

> For example, the California-based Mail Boxes Etc.® franchise, with 1,600 franchisees, was recently granted an exception to the Mexican constitution's ban on private postal services. Each MailBoxes unit in Mexico pays $1,000 to register as an official post office. In 1995, MailBoxes tried to expand its operations into the Dallas/Fort Worth airport.[40]

While franchising offers many opportunities overseas, it still isn't as popular in other countries as it is here. For example, franchising accounts for only 10 percent of retail sales in England and 11 percent in France, as opposed to 34 percent in the United States.[41]

## Minority Ownership of Franchises

D

Minority ownership of franchises has made steady progress over the years, especially in automobile and truck dealerships. According to a study of 366 franchise chains in 60 businesses, about 10 percent of franchises are operated by minorities.[42]

While the major barriers continue to be lack of financing and expertise, minority ownership is now growing, as shown in the opening Profile. According to Shingler-Hollis Investment Group, a small business development/franchise consultant, the minority community is insisting on getting more information from franchisers.[43] The result is that franchise executives and government agencies are increasingly alerting potential franchisees to franchise opportunities, including financing, training, and support activities.

Some of the larger fast-food chains have programs to target aid to minority buyers, as the following examples illustrate.

> Shoney's Inc., which franchises Shoney's, Lee's Famous Recipe Country Chicken, and Captain D's Seafood, defers a big chunk of the initial franchise fee and slashes initial royalties for minority owners. KFC reduces liquidity requirements by over one-half and guarantees loans made by local banks to minority operators of its restaurants.

G

The primary group that implements federal policies benefiting minority entrepreneurship is the Minority Business Development Agency (MBDA). Among its many other activities, it operates the **Minority Vendor Profile System,** a computerized database listing minority firms. The system is designed to match minority entrepreneurs with available marketing opportunities.

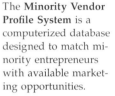

The **Minority Vendor Profile System** is a computerized database designed to match minority entrepreneurs with available marketing opportunities.

You have probably heard comments about so many new jobs during the past two decades being just "burger flippers."[44] There may be a grain of truth to such statements, but fast-food franchises provide excellent opportunities for upward mobility for new, inexperienced workers. This mobility is particularly impressive for immigrants and minorities.[45] Dennis Perdomo, the Hispanic manager of a Pizza Hut in South Central Los Angeles, explained this mobility by saying, "We teach people team building, time management, basic math [and] even how to assimilate." The following examples illustrate the opportunities franchises can offer.[46]

D

> In 1965, Ed Rensi, McDonald's current president and CEO, started at $0.85 an hour in Columbus, Ohio.
>
> At Pizza Hut, 40 percent of the managers at its 6,000 company-owned stores started as part-time crew members. Every one of them is now a salaried employee with health insurance. Some 54 percent of Pizza Hut's assistant managers also started as crew members. They also have health insurance.

The reason franchise operations are so desirable as a training ground was explained by Herman Cain, president of Godfather's Pizza. He said, "The people . . . our industry is able to hire are not as educated . . . experienced . . . and skilled as other people. There are very few other people who *would* hire and train them."

## Turning Your Dream into a Reality

We've presented much information to help you decide whether or not you want to go into franchising. You've also been told how to investigate whether a franchise is right for you or not. Figure 7–11 provides a step-by-step review of what is required for you to become a franchisee. It also estimates the time required for each of the steps. While all these steps may not be required, and the time spans are not universal, the information is a good overview of the activities required by many franchisers and the time it takes to do each of them.

**Figure 7–11** What's Needed to Become a Franchise Owner

Step-by-step review of what needs to be done and how long it will take to turn the dream of owning your own business into the reality of opening day.

| Phase | 1<br>Decide to become a franchisee | 2<br>Make decision and invest<br>$ _____ | 3<br>Real estate | 4<br>Construction | 5<br>Equipment and inventory |
|---|---|---|---|---|---|
| Action items | Investigate and select your franchise | Decide, buy, sign contract; pay $ _____ | Look for proper store site:<br>*a.* Storefront type<br>*b.* Build to specs, freestanding | Conform to franchise contract:<br>*a.* Leasehold improvements<br>*b.* Construct building per drawings | Order and install all equipment; order opening inventory—goods |
| Time span | 3 months to 2 years | 3 months | 2 to 12 months | 3 to 11 months | 1 to 3 months |

| Phase | 6<br>Hiring | 7<br>Training | 8<br>Pre-opening final check | 9<br>Opening and operations | 10<br>Contract term |
|---|---|---|---|---|---|
| Action items | Hire manager or assistant manager; hire crew; fill out state and federal forms | Get your training in franchiser's school; learn procedures and methods | Construction; punch list; permits; bank accounts; marketing plan; inventory | First soft opening; later grand opening<br>Employee daily work schedule<br>Daily sales reports<br>Cash register tapes, money<br>Deposit cash in bank nightly<br>Insurance accuracy<br>Pay royalty and advertising fees | Work and manage your own franchise |
| Time span | 2 to 6 weeks | 2 weeks to 2 months | 1 day to 2 weeks | Select a Friday, Saturday, or Sunday | |

*Source:* Ralph J. Weiger, "Franchise Investigation Time Span," *Franchising World,* March/April 1989, p. 18. Copyright International Franchise Association, Washington, DC.

## WHAT YOU SHOULD HAVE LEARNED

**1.** Franchising sales have more than doubled in the last decade, and the number of establishments is also increasing. Franchising is strongest in retailing, accounting for about 41 percent of retail sales and 87 percent of all franchising receipts. It's expected to increase to 50 percent by the year 2000.

**2.** Franchising is a marketing system that permits the franchisee to conduct business as an individual owner under the terms and conditions set by the franchiser. The two most common franchising systems are *(a)* product and trademark franchising and *(b)* business format franchising. In the first, franchisees acquire the right to sell the franchiser's product and use its trademark, but they are relatively free to use their own operating methods. In the second, the franchiser determines virtually every aspect of the franchisee's operations, including management policies, accounting methods, reporting forms, designs, and furnishings. The number of product and trademark franchises has declined, particularly in auto dealerships and gasoline service stations.

**3.** Business format franchising has increased steadily because it provides a ready market and management system, and the failure rate is lower than for independent businesses.

**4.** Franchising is a good way for someone to enter business. But you should carefully research the industry and investigate the particular franchise to determine whether the assistance provided by the franchiser is worth the sacrifice of independence. You should study the franchise offering circular, check with existing franchisees, and obtain professional advice to understand your rights and obligations. Franchisers who belong to the International Franchise Association (IFA) subscribe to a code of ethics that provides protection to their franchisees.

**5.** The future of franchising looks good, especially for restaurants; motels; convenience stores; electronics; automotive parts, accessories, and servicing; packaging and shipping; health care and fitness; combination franchising; and catering to home-based small businesses. International franchising is one of the fastest-growing areas of franchising. Minority ownership of franchises is also growing, and special efforts are being made to encourage minority franchising.

## QUESTIONS FOR DISCUSSION

1. What distinguishes a franchise from an independent small business?
2. What are the two most important forms of franchising? Describe each.
3. Describe why franchising is growing in importance.
4. How can you decide whether a franchise is right for you? Explain.
5. Why is the number of product and trademark franchises declining?
6. What are some expected areas of growth for franchising in the future?
7. Why is franchising growing internationally?
8. What is happening to opportunities in franchising for minorities?

# CASE 6

## RAY KROC—FATHER OF FRANCHISING

Photo courtesy of McDonald's Corporation.

Ray Kroc, himself a billionaire, probably made more people millionaires in less time than anyone else in history. And he did it after he was 52 years old and in poor health. Now his "brainchild"—McDonald's—has over 13,000 stores in 65 countries, with over $19 billion in systemwide sales.

Kroc, a high school dropout, sold everything from paper cups in Chicago to real estate in Florida before he wound up selling electric milkshake mixers in the early 1950s. At that time, a hamburger and a shake took about 15 to 30 minutes to prepare at any of the thousands of small, independent drive-ins scattered across the country.

In 1954, Kroc received an order from a drive-in in San Bernardino, California, for eight machines that could make five milkshakes at a time. His curiosity led him to visit Richard and Maurice McDonald to see why they needed to make 40 shakes at a time. He found people lining up at a window, ordering, and leaving in about 30 seconds with bags of hamburgers, fries, and shakes—all for under a dollar. He thought the assembly-line operation, based on clean, instant service with a family atmosphere, was the most amazing merchandising operation he'd ever seen. Kroc persuaded the brothers to let him set up a complete franchising operation, including finding operators and locations, building drive-ins, and ensuring that they maintained the McDonalds' high standards. He left with a contract to franchise McDonald's worldwide and pay the brothers 0.5 percent of restaurant sales.

Kroc opened his first drive-in under this arrangement in Des Plaines, Illinois, in 1955. By 1961, there were 323 of the golden-arches stores, and the McDonalds wanted to retire. Kroc bought their rights for $2.7 million. At the time, sales were $54 million and earnings were around $175,000. Also, the company had some company-owned restaurants. When he died in 1984, at age 81, Kroc was a billionaire. And his franchisees were doing quite well, too. Average store sales were over $1 million and there were before-tax profit margins of 15 to 20 percent.

Kroc did for the fast-food industry what Henry Ford had done for the automobile industry. He was truly the "Father of Franchising."

*Sources:* Based on correspondence with McDonald's Corporation, Oak Brook, Illinois; as well as various published sources, such as annual reports.

## QUESTIONS

1. Identify and discuss several reasons for the success of the McDonald's franchising operation.
2. What type of franchising system is a McDonald's franchise? Explain.
3. Despite its phenomenal success, speculate as to why one might not want to invest in a McDonald's franchise.
4. You have decided to become a franchise owner. What are some factors you must consider before you enter into a franchise arrangement with McDonald's?
5. Based on its past successes, while considering current and future competition, speculate as to the future of the McDonald's chain. Consider opportunities for growth.

# *APPLICATION 7–1*

Muhammad is a foreign student from Pakistan who has been studying in the United States for the past five years. He is so impressed with Pizza Hut's pizza that he wants to open a franchise in his home country.

He does his market research and decides the project is feasible. Muhammad then approaches the franchiser for an agreement. He plans to offer a spicy pizza to accommodate the tastes of the local population.

## QUESTIONS

1. What do you think are Muhammad's chances of success?
2. What must he do to succeed?
3. What do you think is the future of global franchising?

## ACTIVITY 7–1

*Directions:* Use information from this chapter to solve the puzzle below.

ACROSS

3 See 2 Down

5 Owns name of 4 down

7 Grants franchisee the right to sell recognized product

8 Sells according to franchiser's requirements

9 Marketing system

10 Grants franchisee the right to trademark

DOWN

1 Matches minority entrepreneur with marketing opportunities

2 Background about the franchiser

4 Exclusive right to sell specified good

6 See 7 Across

ACROSS 3 Disclosure statement 5 Franchiser 7 Product franchising 8 Franchisee 9 Franchising 10 Business format franchising DOWN 1 Minority Vendor Profile System 2 Prospectus statement 4 Franchise 6 Trademark franchising

CHAPTER

# 8

# Preparing and Presenting the Business Plan

*A completed business plan is a guide that illustrates where you are, where you are going, and how to get there.*—Charles J. Bodenstab

*A business plan may tell you by the time you're done that this isn't a profitable business. If you go into the business without a path to walk down, without some sort of guidelines, you're in real trouble.*—Geoff Walsh

## LEARNING OBJECTIVES

After studying the material in this chapter, you will be able to:

1. Tell why a business plan is needed and what purpose it should serve.
2. Explain how to approach the preparation of the business plan.
3. List the components of a business plan.
4. Suggest ways to write and present the plan.
5. Prepare a sample business plan.

# *P R O F I L E*

## SAM AND TERESA DAVIS DO THEIR HOMEWORK BEFORE LAUNCH

Photo by Shawn Scully, *The Tuscaloosa* (Alabama) *News*, May 7, 1995, p. E1.

When Sam and Teresa Davis decided it was time for a career change, they opted to start their own business rather than work for someone else. After considering the options, Sam, who had 18 years of marketing and managing experience with a large regional department store, and Teresa, who was a veteran teacher, chose to open a school supply store in Northport, Alabama, near the University of Alabama in Tuscaloosa. Knowing that many small businesses fail because of poor planning, the Davises chose to start their venture the right way—by doing extensive strategic and operational planning.

One of the first steps the Davises took early in their endeavor was to seek the services of the University of Alabama's Small Business Development Center. Sam cites the Center's *Small Business Handbook* as an invaluable asset that answered questions concerning such important details as taxes, business licenses, zoning problems, and advertising.

Before getting in over their heads, the Davises knew they had to do extensive research and write a comprehensive business plan. This step would not only assist their fund-raising efforts but also serve as a blueprint for the process of making their dream a reality. The key word, according to Sam, was research. "The biggest problem was gathering the facts to write a detailed business plan."

The Davises did their homework well. First, they made numerous trips to school supply stores in surrounding cities, such as Montgomery, Birmingham, and Huntsville. They also took their idea directly to their potential clients—teachers and school administrators. Finally, after carefully assembling the needed information, they wrote a detailed business plan.

One thing the Davises learned from their research was that there was little or no diversity among school supply stores. To avoid being just another run-of-the-mill school supply store—and risk market saturation—they needed to find a unique twist, something to set their store apart from the others. They found their niche by adding a work area that includes a letter and shape cutter, a laminator, and a copier to produce transparencies.

This unique idea proved to be the solution to one of the most difficult problems new businesses face—getting customers in the door. "Sometimes we have as many as six university students at a time working on some school project here," Teresa says. Others using the center include junior and senior high students working on science and social studies projects, as well as church workers. Through their research, the Davises also discovered that the growing home schooling trend had been virtually ignored by other supply stores; this opened a new market for their products. The Davises cite this as another key factor in their success.

As a result of their painstaking research and creative ideas, the Davises' store, Learning Experiences, has been tremendously successful. Now, as they advise potential entrepreneurs, the Davises emphasize two points about formulating a good business plan and running an effective business: (1) entrepreneurs *must* have firsthand knowledge of the product or service they plan to offer, and (2) they must create a distinctive niche by making the business unique in some fashion.

*Source:* Various, but especially Gilbert Nicholson, "By the Book . . . Entrepreneurs Do Homework Before Launch," *The Tuscaloosa* (Alabama) *News*, May 7, 1995, p. E1.

As the Davises discovered, a new business results from the prospective owner's having both a good idea for producing and selling a product and the ability to carry out the idea. This truth was confirmed in a survey of the 665 fastest-growing private companies in which 88 percent "succeeded by taking an ordinary idea and pulling it off exceptionally well."[1] Yet other things—such as buildings and machines, human resources, materials and supplies, and finances—are also needed. These needs are developed from the strategic, operational, and financial planning described in Chapter 6. And all that planning needs to be formalized into a **business plan**, which is a tool for attracting the other components of the business formation package—the people and the money. A well-developed and well-presented business plan can provide small business owners with a much greater chance of success—and reduce their chances of failing.

A **business plan** sets forth the firm's objectives, steps for achieving them, and its financial requirements.

D

For example, 16-year-old David M. Lance blames the demise of his small newsletter business on a business plan that stressed market share rather than profitability. America's leading teenage automotive editor and publisher was forced out of business just months after he finally learned to drive the cars he had been writing about for years.[2]

## Purposes of the Business Plan

The business plan could be the most useful and important document you, as an entrepreneur, ever put together. When you are up to your ears in the details of starting the business, the plan keeps your thinking on target, keeps your creativity on track, and concentrates your power on reaching your goal.

The plan can be a useful money-raising tool to attract venture capital for those entrepreneurs who are willing to dilute control of their company. Although few owners use a plan to attract venture funds, many more use a formal business plan to obtain loans from lending agencies.

For example, when Steven and Barbara Chappell were ready to start their Our Hero Restaurant franchise, they did not have enough savings to pay the rent and other expenses. So they drew up a 20-page plan—including blueprints, personal data, itemized lists of requirements for materials and supplies, and statistics from the Our Hero franchiser—and presented it to four banks. Since all of them offered to lend the required funds, the Chappells negotiated with the bank that offered the best terms.[3]

*"Dad, have you come to a decision on my comprehensive business plan for my allowance?"*

Copyright 1993 by J. Nebesky.

But an effective plan does more than just help convince prospective investors that the new business is sound. It provides a detailed blueprint for the activities needed to finance the business, develop the product, market it, and otherwise manage the new business. Business plans are also used for planning the continuing operations of a firm, as the following example illustrates.

Ava DeMarco, a 32-year-old graphics designer, and Robert Brandegee, a 28-year-old who favors torn blue jeans and bandannas as work attire, founded their Pittsburgh-based Little Earth Productions to help with recycling. Their research convinced them, though, that their business should cater to two powerful market trends—environmental protection *and* style. Therefore, the accessories they produce and sell—which include notebooks, backpacks, and belts—are not *only environmentally friendly* but also *hip*. Made entirely from recycled materials such as license plates, auto seat belts, soda cans, and bottle caps, these products are commendably "green," but they are also very stylish and attractive.

Used with permission of Little Earth Productions. Photo courtesy of David Aschkenas.

According to DeMarco, "The trouble with most eco-clothing is it's dull." Brandegee agrees that fashion is the main draw for the increase in their sales from $500,000 in 1994 to $1.9 million in 1995. Using recycled materials gives them a competitive edge.[4]

Because an effective business plan helps determine the feasibility of an idea, it should include a detailed analysis of factors such as the following:

- The proposed product.
- The expected market for it.
- The strengths and weaknesses of the industry.
- Planned marketing policies, such as price, promotion, and distribution.
- Operations or production methods and facilities.
- Financial aspects, including expected income, expenses, profits (or losses), investment needed, and expected cash flow.

In addition, a properly developed, well-written business plan should answer questions such as the following:

- Is the business formation package complete?
- Would it be attractive to potential investors?
- Does the proposed business have a reasonable chance for success at the start?
- Does it have any long-run competitive advantages to the owner? To investors? To employees?
- Can the product be produced efficiently?
- Can it be marketed effectively?
- Can the production and marketing of the product be economically financed?
- Can the new company's business functions—operations, distribution, finance, and human resources—be properly managed?
- Are the needed employees available?

In summary, a properly developed and written plan provides more than mere facts. It serves as (1) an effective communication tool to convey ideas, research findings, and proposed plans to others, especially financiers; (2) the basis for managing the new venture; and (3) a measuring device by which to gauge progress and evaluate needed changes. Developing and writing a business plan takes much time, effort, and money, but the results can make the difference between the company's success and failure. The following Using Technology to Succeed shows you how to access the experience of others with your CD-ROM drive.

With implementation of the North American Free Trade Agreement (NAFTA), many small and medium-sized Mexican companies are beginning to appreciate the need for business planning. Previously, the majority of such firms did not recognize the need to improve the quality of their product, invest in state-of-the-art technology, or develop innovative marketing plans. Now, however, those that want to compete with larger companies are beginning to stress product quality, update their technology, and design effective business plans.[5]

## USING TECHNOLOGY TO SUCCEED
### Entrepreneurs on CD-ROM

Business plan software can quite capably help you consider the necessary issues for starting a business, and it lets you draw on the experience of others as you chart your own course. However, if you have a CD-ROM drive, you have access to some programs that are less task oriented and more lively. These programs let you listen to the advice of entrepreneurs who've built successful businesses, and they offer guidance beyond what you might find with a traditional business plan program.

*How to Really Start Your Own Business,* from ZELOS Digital Learning and *Inc.* magazine, is a multimedia version of *Inc.*'s book and video with the same title and similar content. It uses audio clips and a presentation-style format to impart the wisdom of founders of organizations such as Pizza Hut and David's Cookies.

*Multimedia MBA,* from Compact Publishing, Inc., takes a much broader approach, covering a variety of management, financial, legal, and marketing information. If you want the opportunity to learn from other people's mistakes and to develop a winning business strategy in an enjoyable multimedia format, you should consider these titles.

For information on *How to Really Start Your Own Business,* contact ZELOS Digital Learning, 110 Pacific Avenue, Suite 219, San Francisco, CA 94111; (800) 345-6777.

For information on *Multimedia MBA,* contact Compact Publishing, Inc., 5141 MacArthur Boulevard, Washington, DC 20016; (800) 227-5609.

*Source:* Adapted with permission from the article, "Business Planning Made Easy" from various sources, including *Office Systems95,* June 1995, p. 74.

## Preparing the Plan

When developing a business plan, you should consider the firm's background, origins, philosophy, mission, and objectives, as well as the means of fulfilling that mission and attaining those objectives.[6] A sound approach is to: (1) determine where the business is, by recognizing its current status; (2) decide where you would like to be, by clarifying your philosophy about doing business, developing the firm's mission, and setting objectives; and (3) determine how to get to where you want to be, by identifying the best strategies for accomplishing the business's objectives.

Figure 8–1 shows one approach to preparing a business plan. It is the one we recommend for those who are serious about succeeding in small business ownership.

### Who Should Prepare the Plan?

If the prospective owner is the only one involved in the business, he or she should prepare the plan, with the advice and counsel of competent advisers. But if the business is to be organized and run by more than one person, it should be a team effort. You might encourage each manager to prepare a part of the plan. We also recommend having other key employees help in the planning stage, which will improve communication and motivation.

There are several software packages available to assist one in planning and preparing the business plan. Ideally, such a system should include

Q

**Figure 8–1** How to Prepare a Business Plan

- Survey consumer demands for your product(s) and decide how to satisfy those demands.
- Ask questions that cover everything from the firm's target market to its competitive position.
- Establish a long-range strategic plan for the entire business.
- Develop short-term, detailed plans for all those involved with the business, including the owner(s), managers, and employees.
- Plan for every part of the venture, including operations, marketing, general and administrative functions, and distribution.
- Prepare a plan that uses staff time sparingly.

several key characteristics. To begin with, it should be user-friendly and have plenty of examples to help you. Spreadsheet-like templates for individual data input and automated integration between the modules or sections are also needed. The *Irwin ProMBA™—Multimedia MBA: Small Business Edition*—(which came with the purchase of this textbook—see Using Technology to Succeed in Chapter 5 for more details) contains all the templates and analysis tools you will need to prepare your plan. The *ProMBA,* however, will only help you to organize and prepare data. You must then formalize your plan.

### Developing Action Steps

You can collect needed information from the steps discussed in Chapters 5 and 6, as well as from business associates and from legal, management, and financial consultants. Discussions with people both inside and outside the business are useful in gathering and evaluating this information.

The focus of the plan should be on future developments for the business, with steps set up to deal with specific aspects, such as product development, marketing, production or operations, finance, and management. Realistic, measurable objectives should be set, and the plan's steps should be delegated, monitored, and reported regularly.

Questions such as the following are useful in developing action steps: Who will be responsible for each course of action? What is the time frame for achieving each objective? What are the barriers to achieving the objectives? How can those barriers be overcome? Have the necessary controls been considered?

## Components of the Plan

Because the business plan is such an important document, it should be arranged logically and presented clearly to save the reader time and effort, as well as to ensure understanding. While the information that should be included tends to be standardized, the format to be used is not. (Figure 8–2 presents a typical format.)

**Figure 8–2** Typical Business Plan Format

1. Cover sheet
   - Business name, address, and phone number
   - Principals
   - Date
2. Executive summary
   - Abstract—mission statement
   - Objectives
   - Description of products or services
   - Marketing plan
   - Financial budget
3. Table of contents
4. History
   - Background of principals, or company origins
   - History of products or services
   - Organization structure
   - Company history in brief
5. Description of the business
6. Definition of the market
   - Target market/area
   - Market analysis
   - Competitor analysis
   - Industry analysis
7. Description of products or services
   - What is to be developed or produced
   - Status of research and development
   - Status of patents, trademarks, copyrights
8. Management structure
   - Who will enact plan
   - Organizational chart
   - Communication flowchart
   - Employee policies
9. Objectives and goals
   - Profit plan
   - Marketing plans
   - Manufacturing plans
   - Quality control plans
   - Financial plans
10. Financial data
    - Pro forma income statements (three years)
    - Pro forma cash flow analyses (first year, by months)
    - Pro forma balance sheets (three years)
    - Cost-volume-profit analyses where appropriate
11. Appendixes
    - Narrative history of firm in detail
    - Résumés of key employees
    - Major environmental assumptions
    - Brochures describing products
    - Letters of recommendation or endorsement
    - Historical financial data (at least three years)
    - Details of:
      *a.* Products and services
      *b.* Research and development
      *c.* Marketing
      *d.* Manufacturing
      *e.* Administration
      *f.* Finance

Regardless of the specific format chosen, any plan should include at least the following elements:

1. Cover sheet.
2. Executive summary.
3. Table of contents.
4. History of the (proposed) business.

5. Description of the business.
6. Definition of the market.
7. Description of the product(s).
8. Management structure.
9. Objectives and goals.
10. Financial data.
11. Appendixes.

## Cover Sheet

The cover sheet presents identifying information, such as the business name, address, and phone number. Also, readers should know at once who the principals are.

## Executive Summary

The **executive summary** is a brief overview of the most important information in a business plan.

The **executive summary** of your plan must be a real "grabber"; it must motivate the reader to go on to the other sections. Moreover, it must convey a sense of plausibility, credibility, and integrity. Your plan may be one of many evaluated by representatives of lending institutions. They tend to evaluate the worth of the plan on the basis of this summary; if it generates sufficient interest, the remainder of the document may be assigned to other persons for review. The executive summary outlines the entire business plan, its major objectives, how these objectives will be accomplished, and the expected results. Therefore, it is sometimes first sent to potential investors to see if they have any interest in the venture; if so, the entire plan will then be sent to them.

Remember, *the executive summary is just that—a summary—so keep it short!* It may be difficult to get so much information on one or two pages, but try to do so. Also, even though the summary is the initial component of the plan, *it should be written only after the rest of the plan has been developed.*

Figure 8–3 presents a sample outline of the executive summary required of all individuals and firms seeking equity capital from the Venture Capital Exchange of the University of Tulsa. We recommend that your summary also contain sections on the ownership and legal form of the business.

## Table of Contents

Because the table of contents provides an overview of what's in the plan, it should be written concisely, in outline form, using alphabetical and numerical headings and subheads.

## History of the (Proposed) Business

Background information on the person(s) organizing the business, as well as a description of that person's contributions, should be discussed at this point. Explanations of how the idea for the product or firm originated and what has been done to develop the idea should also be included. If the owner or owners have been in business before, that should be discussed, and any failures should be explained.

**Figure 8–3** Sample Outline of an Executive Summary

A. Company
   1. Who and what it is
   2. Status of project/firm
   3. Key goals and objectives
B. Product/service
   1. What it is
   2. How it works
   3. What it is for
   4. Proprietary advantages
C. Market
   1. Prospective customers
   2. How many there are
   3. Market growth rate
   4. Competition (list three to six competitors by name and describe)
   5. Industry trends
   6. How the firm will compete
   7. Estimated market share
      *a.* In one year
      *b.* In five years
D. Operations
   1. How product/service will be manufactured/provided
   2. Facilities/equipment
   3. Special processes
   4. Labor skills needed
E. Channels of distribution: how product/service will get to end users
F. Management team
   1. Who will do what
   2. Their qualifications
   3. Availability
G. Sources and application of funds
   1. Present needs
   2. Future needs

One-page profit and loss statement showing annual totals for first three years, including detailed costs of goods sold and overhead (general and administrative) breakdowns.

*Source:* Entrepreneur Application Profile used by Venture Capital Exchange, Enterprise Development Center, The University of Tulsa, Tulsa, Oklahoma.

## Description of the Business

It is now time for you to describe your business! More information is needed than just a statement of what the firm does—or plans to do—and a listing of its functions, products, or services. This definition should tell what customer needs the business intends to meet. In writing this component, it might be helpful to distinguish between how you perceive the business and what potential customers might think of it. Think about questions such as these:

### From the *Owner's* Perspective:

What do you think will sell?
What is your largest line of inventory?
Where is your greatest profit made?

### From the *Customer's* Perspective:

What do you think they need or want to buy?
What is the best-selling item?
On what product or service is most personnel time spent?

Ask yourself whether the answers to these questions are closely aligned and compatible or divergent. If they are divergent, the business may be in trouble. If they are compatible—or can be made compatible—there is a good chance of success, as the following example illustrates.

> The sales manager of an FM radio station evaluated the results of efforts to sell advertising and found that advertising customers obtained 45 percent or more of their business volume from the black community. Yet that group made up only a small portion of the station's listening audience, and the station had never attracted the desired volume of advertising. A shift to black disc jockeys and a program format attuned to the black community produced a substantial increase in advertising revenues.

## Definition of the Market

While the definition of the market is one of the most important—and most difficult—parts of the plan to develop, it should at least indicate the target of your marketing efforts, as well as the trading area served. It must answer questions such as these: Who buys what and why? What are your customers like? Does the competition have any weaknesses you can exploit?

## Description of the Product(s)

This section should describe the firm's existing or planned product(s). The status of all research done and developments under way should be described, along with discussions of any legal aspects, such as patents, copyrights, trademarks, pending lawsuits, and legal claims against the firm. Are any government approvals or clearances needed? Catalog sheets, blueprints, photographs, and other visuals—if available—are helpful and should be included.

## Management Structure

This is the place to describe your management structure, especially the expertise of your management team. Explain how its members will help carry out the plan. You could also discuss employee policies and procedures. To repeat: It is important to demonstrate the proven ability and dedication of the owner and staff.

## Objectives and Goals

This part outlines what your business plans to accomplish, as well as how and when it will be done and who will do it. Sales forecasts as well as production, service, quality assurance, and financial plans should be discussed. Other items of interest to potential investors include pricing and anticipated profits, advertising and promotion strategies and budgets, a description of how the product(s) will be distributed and sold, and which categories of customers will be targeted for initial heavy sales effort, and which ones for later sales efforts.

## Financial Data

One important purpose of the business plan is to indicate the expected financial results from operations. The plan should show prospective investors or lenders why they should provide funds, when they can expect a return, and what the expected rate of return on their money is. At this point in the new business's development, assumptions—or educated guesses—concerning many issues may have to be made. For example, assumptions must be made about expected revenues, competitors' actions, and future market conditions. Assumptions, while necessary, should be designated as such, and financial projections should be realistically based on how increased personnel, expanded facilities, or equipment needs will affect the projections. The budgetary process to be used is an important part of the business plan. And prices should reflect actual cost figures, as the following example illustrates.

> In a college town, a restaurant owner who was in financial difficulty sought aid from the SBA. The first question asked by the SCORE volunteer assigned as a consultant was: "What's the most popular item on your menu?" The owner replied, "Our $6.25 steak dinner." The consultant asked for a scale and a raw steak. He showed the restaurant owner that the raw steak alone cost $5.10. Obviously, the reason for the steak dinner's popularity was the markup of less than 23 percent on the cost of the steak alone. It was also the underlying cause of the business's financial troubles.

### Appendixes

Other components needed in the plan are the firm's organizational structure, including organization charts. This part should include résumés of the officers, directors, key personnel, and any outside board members. If any of these have any special expertise that increases the chances of success, this should be mentioned. Historical financial information, with relevant documents, should also be included. Brochures, news items, letters of recommendation or endorsements, photographs, and similar items should be included as well.

## Presenting the Plan

We know a SCORE adviser who tells his clients, "Investors decide during the first five minutes of studying the executive summary whether to reject a proposal or consider it further." Therefore, *presenting the business plan is almost as important as preparing it*. All the work is in vain if potential investors aren't interested in it. Presentation involves both writing the plan and presenting it to the targeted audience.

> This point was strongly reinforced by Joseph Mancuso, author of a leading book on how to prepare and present business plans. The director of the Center for Entrepreneurial Management in New York asserts that "a good business plan takes a minimum of five months to write, but you've got to convince your readers in five minutes not to throw [it] away."[7]

Q

### Writing the Plan

John G. Burch, a writer on entrepreneurship, makes the following suggestions for writing an effective plan:[8]

- *Be honest*, not only by avoiding outright lies, but also by revealing what you actually feel about the significant and relevant aspects of the plan.

- *Use the third person,* not the first person ("I" or "we"). This practice forces you to think clearly and logically from the other person's perspective.
- *Use transitional words,* such as *but, still,* and *therefore,* and *active, dynamic verbs* as a means of leading the reader from one thought to another.
- *Avoid redundancies,* such as "*future* plans," since repetition adds nothing to the presentation.
- *Use short, simple words,* where feasible, so the plan will be easy to understand and follow.
- *Use visuals,* such as tables, charts, photos, and computer graphics to present your ideas effectively.

The plan should be prepared in an 8½-by-11-inch format, typed, and photocopied, with copies for outsiders attractively bound. Most business plans can—and should—be presented effectively in 25 to 30 pages—or less. Of course, the plan should be grammatically correct, so have someone proofread it before you present it.

The plan should be reviewed by people outside the firm, such as accounting and business consultants, other businesspeople, and attorneys, before it is sent to potential investors or lenders. Other helpful reviewers might include a professional writer, editor, or English teacher.

When pertinent, the cover and title page should indicate that the information is proprietary and confidential. However, there is always the chance that this practice might offend a potential investor.

## The Written/Oral Presentation

In an oral presentation, you should present the plan in person to investors or lenders. Presenting your plan involves creative skills on your part to give the impression that you have (or plan to have) a profitable and stable business, and that its chances of continuing that way are good. Your listeners will be looking very carefully at *you,* to see what kind of person *you* are, for *you are the business*—and vice versa. Both written and oral presentations should be very positive and quite upbeat.

The plan should be delivered from the listener's perspective, not yours. Both oral and written presentations should demonstrate that you have a marketable product and that the business has a feasible plan for aggressively marketing it—at a profit. You should provide visual aids for key segments of the plan and be prepared for specific questions concerning the following:

- The adequacy of the research and development behind the product.
- The validity of the market research.
- Your understanding of the business.
- Financial projections and why they will work.
- Relative priority of the objectives.
- Your ability to "make it happen."

The amount of detail in the market data and financial projections will vary according to the plan's purpose. If it is to raise equity or debt financing, more detail is needed; if it's to improve operations and motivate employees, less detail is needed.

You must remember that you are probably the best expert on your product or service and may have only one brief opportunity to present your plan. Jeffrey Adduci, president of Regional Investment Bankers Association (RIBA), tells of five traps entrepreneurs must avoid while presenting their business plan to potential investors:[9]

- *Failure to state the obvious.* State the facts and be brutally honest about what you want.
- *Unwillingness to rehearse.* Off-the-cuff presentations lead to disaster.
- *Poor or no use of visual aids.* Slides are most effective.
- *Poor Q&A performance.* You're the expert—be one!
- *Failure to follow up.* After the presentation, use a mailing or other form of communication to keep your project in the minds of potential investors. It's important to remember that they will soon forget you if they're not reminded from time to time.

Even the best-prepared plan, though, may not be accepted by potential investors.

> In 1946, J. Presper Eckert, Jr., one of the inventors of the ENIAC®, the first digital computer, fired off a business plan to IBM, hoping it would yield an investment to produce and distribute the UNIVAC®, the first giant electronic computer. IBM President Thomas J. Watson, Sr., after careful review, responded that it was the company's opinion that the world would ultimately need only about 5 or 10 computers, and Eckert's machine was therefore of no interest to IBM.

## Implementing the Plan

Now you are ready to take the plunge! It is time to get a charter, obtain facilities and supplies, hire and train people, and start operating. Using the capital structure plan and the sources of funds you have developed, obtain the funds and put them in a checking account ready for use. Obtain the services of an attorney to help acquire the charter (if the business is to be incorporated), obtain occupational licenses and permits, and take care of other legal requirements.

Once the funds, charter, and permits are in hand, refer to the timetable and start negotiating contracts; purchasing equipment, materials, and supplies; selecting, hiring, and training employees; establishing a marketing program; setting the legal structure in place; and developing an information system to maintain the records needed to run the business.

You are now a small business owner! You are operating your own business, you have all the risks, and you hope to receive the benefits and rewards of being on your own. Be ready for unforeseen problems, however, that may occur during the start-up period.

## Sample Business Plan

A sample business plan is presented as an appendix at the end of this chapter. It is a proposal for a new college bookstore. Notice that it closely follows the form presented in Figure 8–2.

## WHAT YOU SHOULD HAVE LEARNED

**1.** A business plan is important for obtaining funds and as a blueprint for operating success. The research and analysis required to write an effective plan help you focus on the company's goals, markets, expected performance, and problems that might be encountered. The plan keeps you from jumping into an enterprise without adequate thought and planning, and then serves as a yardstick against which to measure performance.

**2.** The owner is the best person to prepare the plan, but key personnel should also help with the preparation. They can best define its mission, philosophy, and objectives; and, determine how it should be organized and operated. Professionals and businesspeople should be consulted for information and advice about specific aspects of the business.

**3.** The plan should include at least the following: *(a)* cover sheet, *(b)* executive summary, *(c)* table of contents, *(d)* history of the (proposed) business, *(e)* description of the business, *(f)* definition of the market, *(g)* description of the product(s), *(h)* management structure, *(i)* objectives and goals, *(j)* financial data, and *(k)* appendixes. When used to raise funds, detailed financial projections of expected sales, profits, and rates of return should be emphasized.

**4.** The plan should be honest, logical, interesting, thorough, and easy to understand. It should be reviewed by outsiders qualified to judge its content and/or style before it is presented to potential investors. The plan should be presented from the listener's point of view, using a marketing approach. The important point is to create the impression of a profitable and stable business run by capable and responsible people.

**5.** From discussions in this and the two previous chapters, you should be able to prepare an effective business plan.

## QUESTIONS FOR DISCUSSION

1. What is the purpose of a business plan? Explain.
2. How can a business plan be useful even to a prospective business owner who does not need outside capital?
3. What should the business plan include?
4. Do you think the preparation of a business plan is as important as the authors claim? Explain.
5. Who should prepare the plan? Why? Why should the writer get help from outside professionals and businesspeople?
6. How should a business plan be written and presented?

# CASE 8

## USING COMPUTER SOFTWARE TO PREPARE A BUSINESS PLAN

Can a floppy disk substitute for the years at a graduate school of business? Probably not! But a number of software producers have developed programs to help guide unskilled entrepreneurs through business planning, calculating the cash value of a business, preparing business plans, and so forth. These programs help people with no experience, or those from specialized fields, start a new business where knowledge from many areas is needed.

Some of the programs are little more than electronic form letters with spaces for the entrepreneur to complete to impress outside capital sources. Others are complete systems that not only ask questions but also give meaningful advice based on the knowledge and beliefs of management experts. For example, Business Resource Software, Inc., a Texas company, has a program called *Business Insight,* which costs $495. According to Randy Ziegenhorn, an Illinois wholesale seed dealer, it provided him an insight into better marketing strategies. He said he sold more oats in one month than he had in the previous two years. The program did what his college English literature degree and experience as a farmer could not do—helped him do "strategic business thinking."

Value Express's $195 program is designed specifically to calculate the cash value of a business.

The American Institute of Small Business has a program called *How to Write a Business Plan,* with accompanying instructions and examples.

*Entrepreneur* magazine has a good plan called *Developing a Successful Business Plan,* which operates on IBM-PCs or compatibles.

In essence, what the programs do is ask questions about the business that the user must answer. This provides a logical approach to business planning.

*Source:* Adapted from William M. Bulkeley, "With New Planning Software, Entrepreneurs Act Like M.B.A.s," *The Wall Street Journal,* June 2, 1992, pp. B1, B4, and other sources. 

## QUESTIONS

1. To what extent do you think these programs are a substitute for business experience and knowledge? Explain.
2. How would you use one of these programs if you were starting a new business?
3. What do you see as the primary use of these programs in the future?

## APPLICATION 8–1

Heather and Sue have been working with a bridal shop for almost seven years, altering dresses and tuxedos. They are quite fast and efficient at their current jobs and are well respected by their employer for their talent.

Heather has been a seamstress for 25 years. Before that, she was an assistant manager for another dress rental company. Sue has been sewing for the last 14 years. She started out by making quilts that she sold at craft fairs, but later decided she didn't want to travel that much any more.

Many of their customers ask them if they do personal jobs in addition to their job at the bridal shop. Heather and Sue have always wanted to start their own business. They work well together and have become friends over the years. If they were to start their own business, Heather says they could work out of her home because both of her children have grown up and moved away.

### QUESTIONS

1. Do Sue and Heather have a marketable business or service?
2. What types of preparation are needed if they are to start their own business?
3. What types of budgeting needs will Sue and Heather have?

## ACTIVITY 8–1

*Directions:* Using information learned in this chapter, unscramble the two terms below. Then unscramble the circled letters for some not-so-small advice.

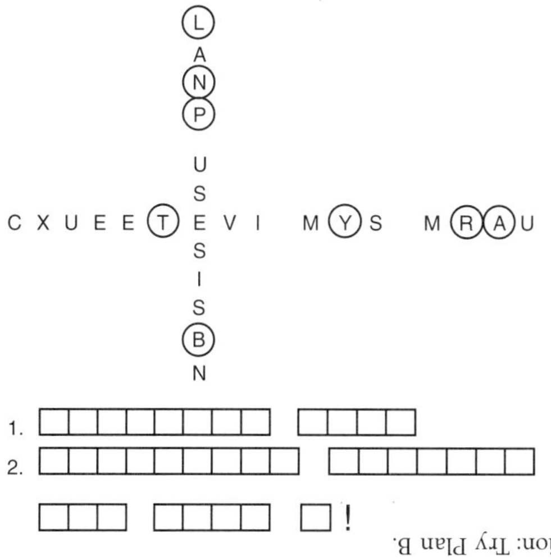


1. Business plan 2. Executive summary Solution: Try Plan B.

# APPENDIX

## A Sample Business Plan: Bookshelf, Inc*

## Executive Summary

### The Company

Bookshelf, Inc., a college bookstore, will provide students, faculty, and other people at the University of Mobile with an alternative place to purchase their books and supplies. The company will offer a full line of textbooks and other supplies associated with an academic setting.

### Marketing Strategy

Bookshelf, Inc., will serve University of Mobile students and faculty. The company will advertise its buyback and pricing policies in flyers and ads in the school paper before its opening to attract customers. The company also plans to offer a 50 percent buyback for books being used in 1995 fall and 1996 spring semesters before the store opens in August 1996.

### Operations

Bookshelf, Inc., will be managed by the four principals: Andrea Bryant, Donna Counselman, Chuck Parmer, and Nathan Patterson. Retail services will be provided by the principals on a rotating basis.

### The Management Team

The four principals are working toward various degrees in the field of business at the University of Mobile and each owns 25 percent of the proposed business. Chuck Parmer will hold the office of president; Donna Counselman, vice president; Nathan Patterson, treasurer; and Andrea Bryant, secretary.

The goal of the management team is to: (1) operate the business at a marginal profit for the first year, (2) grow with the university, and (3) eventually expand to serve other private schools and universities in the area.

The four principals each hold full-time jobs, but have flexible schedules. This allows each principal to work at the store 20 hours a week. Each principal plans to work for the company full time in the future, either at the present location or at another location serving other colleges or universities.

### Financial Considerations

As shown in Exhibit 1, the projected profit for the first year is $36,122. This figure is expected to increase considerably in future years.

---

*Prepared by Andrea Bryant, Donna J. Counselman, Chuck Parmer, and Nathan Patterson of the University of Mobile.

**Exhibit 1** Bookshelf, Inc.'s, Projected Income Statement, 1996–1997

| | |
|---|---|
| **Sales** | **$245,000** |
| Cost of goods sold | 128,386 |
| Gross profit | 116,614 |
| Controllable expenses: | |
| Salaries | 48,000 |
| Advertising | 2,868 |
| Legal / accounting | 600 |
| Office supplies | 1,200 |
| Telephone | 1,200 |
| Utilities | 1,500 |
| Miscellaneous | 469 |
| Fixed expenses: | |
| Insurance | 1,944 |
| Rent | 8,100 |
| Tax /license | 150 |
| Interest | 14,461 |
| Total expenses | 80,492 |
| Net profit | $ 36,122 |

## Table of Contents



### Source of Funds

The principals were able to secure a $300,000 loan from a private individual, which when combined with the owners' cash of $40,000 gives Bookshelf, Inc., working capital of $340,000. The loan was provided by one of the principals' grandparents who wishes to remain unidentified; the amount of the loan represents slightly over 88 percent of total working capital.

## I. History and Background of the Business

Bookshelf, Inc., will be a corporation run by Andrea Bryant, Donna Counselman, Chuck Parmer, and Nathan Patterson. The four principals are all students at the University of Mobile working toward various master's and bachelor's degrees.

The idea to open a college bookstore came from the principals' unhappiness with the current system. A competing bookstore holds a contract with the university to provide textbooks and supplies to all students, faculty, and other personnel. The principals feel that the competing bookstore's prices are too high and buyback prices too low, and some general business practices are unpopular.

The revenue gained from operations will not be the primary source of income for the principals. Each of them will hold another job, but be responsible for various duties including counter sales, stocking shelves, and controlling inventory, advertising, and performing any other activities that are required by the corporation.

## II. Definition of the Business

The mission of Bookshelf, Inc., is to provide students, faculty, and other personnel at the University of Mobile with an alternative bookstore that sells textbooks at the lowest practical price, while maintaining quality services for its customers. The corporation's pricing and buyback policies, combined with its quality service and products, should result in satisfactory profits.

## III. Definition of the Market

Bookshelf, Inc., will serve the students and faculty at the University of Mobile. The store will be located in the Saraland Loop Shopping Center, which is readily accessible to customers both on and off campus.

### A. Customers

The corporation expects to serve roughly 630 students and faculty during its first semester of operations. This number is approximately 30 percent of the school's student, faculty, and staff population. The principals expect the number of customers to rise each successive semester due to competitive prices, its buyback policy, good service, and the growth of the university.

### B. Competition

The Bookshelf has only one competitor, which is—at present—the only supplier of texts and materials to students and faculty. Along with textbooks, the other competing bookstore sells notebooks, pens, pencils, backpacks, clothing with the school's emblem and logo, and other items relating to academic studies.

### 1. Competitor's Strengths

1. Facility is located on campus, so it is quite convenient to daytime students and staff.
2. The competing bookstore currently holds a contract with the university to provide texts and other supplies.
3. The competing bookstore offers credit vouchers that can be obtained through the university's Business Office. This practice allows students to charge books and supplies to their school account.
4. The store at the university is not the primary source of income to the business, as it operates another larger store in another area of the university community.
5. The competing bookstore has experience in selling college textbooks and supplies.
6. The competing bookstore has an inventory of used textbooks.
7. The competing bookstore is already established with book publishers.

### 2. Competitor's Weaknesses

1. Most students at the university do not live on campus.
2. The competing bookstore's hours of operation during most of the semester are inconvenient.
3. The facility is small; the store has only two checkout counters, and the area can become crowded quite easily.
4. Many students are unhappy with pricing and buyback policies.
5. The competing bookstore does not carry enough used textbooks, which can be attributed to its buyback practices.
6. The competition does not have enough employees to serve its customers adequately at the beginning of each semester.
7. The competitor occasionally experiences stockouts in many required freshman and sophomore courses.

## C. Growth Strategy

After consulting University of Mobile officials, the principals found that there are nearly 2,000 students enrolled in some type of course or program. School officials expect the number to increase by 8 percent, or 160 students, during the next year. The summer sessions are expected to grow by 10 percent each year.

The principals expect to garner 30 percent of new and returning students in the fall of 1996. They feel that their market share will grow in proportion to increased enrollment, roughly 8 to 18 percent.

Bookshelf, Inc., will be located in a shopping center that will be growing. The shopping center is currently comprised of Delchamps, the Wright Cut, Godfather's, and a Mobile Press Register regional office. However, within the next year, the YMCA, a new drugstore, and an auto parts distributor will be joining the shopping center. With the addition of the YMCA to the shopping center, the Bookshelf will be able to attract even more people.

Cummings & White-Spunner, our property management representatives, have also left us the option of expanding our facilities—as needed. If we feel that it would be beneficial to expand operations, management will allow us to expand by increasing our space into the adjoining facility.

### D. Marketing Strategy

The strategic marketing plan for Bookshelf, Inc., includes: the naming of the store, the buyback policy, the pricing policy, advertising, and product line.

The naming of the store was done by distributing flyers in many of the university's classes, which allowed students to vote for their favorite name. The flyers were then collected, votes tallied, and the name Bookshelf, Inc., selected by the principals.

The buyback policy includes purchasing used books from students at one-half of the original price. This policy will also be an essential part of the initial start-up cost, for we must continually increase the inventory of used textbooks. To attract students, and to get the bookstore known, Bookshelf will buy students' used textbooks that they bought from the competitor for one-half of the price they paid for them during the previous year.

To remain competitive, Bookshelf, Inc., will mark up new textbooks 40 percent, and used textbooks 25 percent. All other merchandise will have a markup of 30 percent. This policy will allow the company to make a profit, while offering customers the best prices available.

Advertising for the company will consist of flyers, ads in the University of Mobile newspaper—*The Communicator*—and word of mouth. Advertising will be aimed at raising customer awareness before the store opens, as well as increasing the number of customers each semester after it opens.

The product line consists of new and used textbooks, notebooks, pens, pencils, and a few related accessories. The company plans to expand its product line in the future to include other academic supplies and University of Mobile memorabilia such as backpacks, T-shirts, hats, cups, mugs, and car tags.

## IV. Description of Products

Bookshelf, Inc., will sell textbooks for most classes being offered by the University of Mobile. After operations are under way, it will carry books for all classes. The store will also carry notebooks, tablets, pens, pencils, backpacks, and other academically related products.

## V. Management Structure

The corporate structure will consist of a president, vice president, treasurer, and secretary. Principals will maintain their current jobs, while hoping to parlay the business into a chain of stores serving colleges and universities around the southeastern section of the United States.

## VI. Objectives and Goals

The goals and objectives of Bookshelf, Inc., are derived from the concept of offering both quality and service at a fair price. The company plans to increase market share continuously. This will be done through aggressive advertising on campus and innovative policies, such as buying back used textbooks for 50 percent of the purchase price.

The Bookshelf, Inc., also plans to expand operations to other colleges and universities within the next 10 years. The company plans to target students in those areas around college and university bookstores that have little or no competition. The company also intends to sponsor activities, clubs, and various events at schools it is affiliated with.

## VII. Financial Data

A. Cash Flow Projections, August 1996–July 1997

**1996**

| | Startup | August | September | October | November | December |
|---|---|---|---|---|---|---|
| **Beginning cash** | | $286,705 | $385,270 | $378,038 | $370,806 | $362,371 |
| **Receipts:** | | | | | | |
| Cash sales | | 108,000 | 1,000 | 1,000 | 1,000 | 1,000 |
| Loan | 300,000 | | | | | |
| Owner's cash | 40,000 | | | | | |
| **Total receipts** | $340,000 | $394,705 | $386,270 | $379,038 | 371,806 | 363,371 |
| **Expenditures:** | | | | | | |
| Rent | | 675 | 675 | 675 | 675 | 675 |
| Purchases | 48,145 | | | | | |
| Salaries | | 4,000 | 4,000 | 4,000 | 4,000 | 4,000 |
| Advertising | | 717 | | | 717 | |
| Legal/accounting | | 50 | 50 | 50 | 50 | 50 |
| Office expenses | | 100 | 100 | 100 | 100 | 100 |
| Utility | | 125 | 125 | 125 | 125 | 125 |
| Telephone | | 100 | 100 | 100 | 100 | 100 |
| Insurance | | 486 | | | 486 | |
| Tax & license | 150 | | | | | |
| Interest/loan | | 1,250 | 1,242 | 1,234 | 1,226 | 1,218 |
| Principal/loan | | 1,932 | 1,940 | 1,948 | 1,956 | 1,964 |
| Miscellaneous | | | | | | |
| Subtotal | 48,295 | 9,435 | 8,232 | 8,232 | 9,435 | 8,232 |
| Capital purchases | 5,000 | | | | | |
| **Total Expenditures** | 53,295 | 9,435 | 8,232 | 8,232 | 9,435 | 8,232 |
| **Ending cash** | $286,705 | $385,270 | $378,038 | $370,806 | $362,371 | $355,139 |

## Cash Flow Projections (*continued*)

**1997**

| | January | February | March | April | May | June | July |
|---|---|---|---|---|---|---|---|
| **Beginning cash** | $355,139 | $406,763 | $398,328 | 391,096 | 383,864 | 350,333 | 349,101 |
| **Receipts:** | | | | | | | |
| Cash sales | 108,000 | 1,000 | 1,000 | 1,000 | 8,000 | 7,000 | 7,000 |
| Loan | | | | | | | |
| Owner's cash | | | | | | | |
| **Total receipts** | 463,139 | 407,763 | 399,328 | 392,096 | 391,864 | 357,333 | 356,101 |
| **Expenditures:** | | | | | | | |
| Rent | 675 | 675 | 675 | 675 | 675 | 675 | 675 |
| Purchases | 48,145 | | | | 32,097 | | |
| Salaries | 4,000 | 4,000 | 4,000 | 4,000 | 4,000 | 4,000 | 4,000 |
| Advertsing | | 717 | | | 717 | | |
| Legal/accounting | 50 | 50 | 50 | 50 | 50 | 50 | 50 |
| Office expenses | 100 | 100 | 100 | 100 | 100 | 100 | 100 |
| Utility | 125 | 125 | 125 | 125 | 125 | 125 | 125 |
| Telephone | 100 | 100 | 100 | 100 | 100 | 100 | 100 |
| Insurance | | 486 | | | 486 | | |
| Tax & license | | | | | | | |
| Interest/loan | 1,209 | 1,201 | 1,193 | 1,185 | 1,176 | 1,168 | 1,160 |
| Principal/loan | 1,973 | 1,981 | 1,989 | 1,997 | 2,006 | 2,014 | 2,022 |
| Miscellaneous | | | | | | | |
| Subtotal | 56,377 | 9,435 | 8,232 | 8,232 | 41,532 | 8,232 | 8,232 |
| Capital purchases | | | | | | | |
| **Total expenditures** | 56,377 | 9,435 | 8,232 | 8,232 | 41,532 | 8,232 | 8,232 |
| **Ending cash** | $406,762 | $398,328 | $391,096 | $383,864 | $350,332 | $349,101 | $347,869 |

B. Pro-Forma Balance Sheet Projection

| | |
|---|---|
| Assets: | |
| Cash | $347,869 |
| Inventory | 48,145 |
| Equipment | 2,500 |
| Total assets | $398,514 |
| Liabilities/owners' equity | |
| Liabilities: | |
| Loan | 274,247 |
| Accounts payable | 48,145 |
| Total liabilities | 322,392 |
| Owners' equity: | |
| Paid-in capital | 40,000 |
| Retained earnings | 36,122 |
| Total owners' equity | 76,122 |
| Total liabilities and owners' equity | $398,514 |

C. Comparative Ratios, as of end of July 1997

| | |
|---|---|
| Current ratio | 1.24 |
| Debt-to-equity | 8.93 |
| Net profit margin | 0.14 |
| Return on stockholders' equity | 2.34 |

The ratios shown above indicate financial strength for a new company. Bookshelf, Inc., needs to work on decreasing its debt-to-equity ratio, which should be taken care of in the near future.

## VIII. Appendixes

Exhibit 2. Location of Facility
Exhibit 3. Layout of Facility
Exhibit 4. Demographics of the Area
Exhibit 5. Loan Payment Schedule

**Exhibit 2** Location of Facility

**Exhibit 3** Layout of Facility

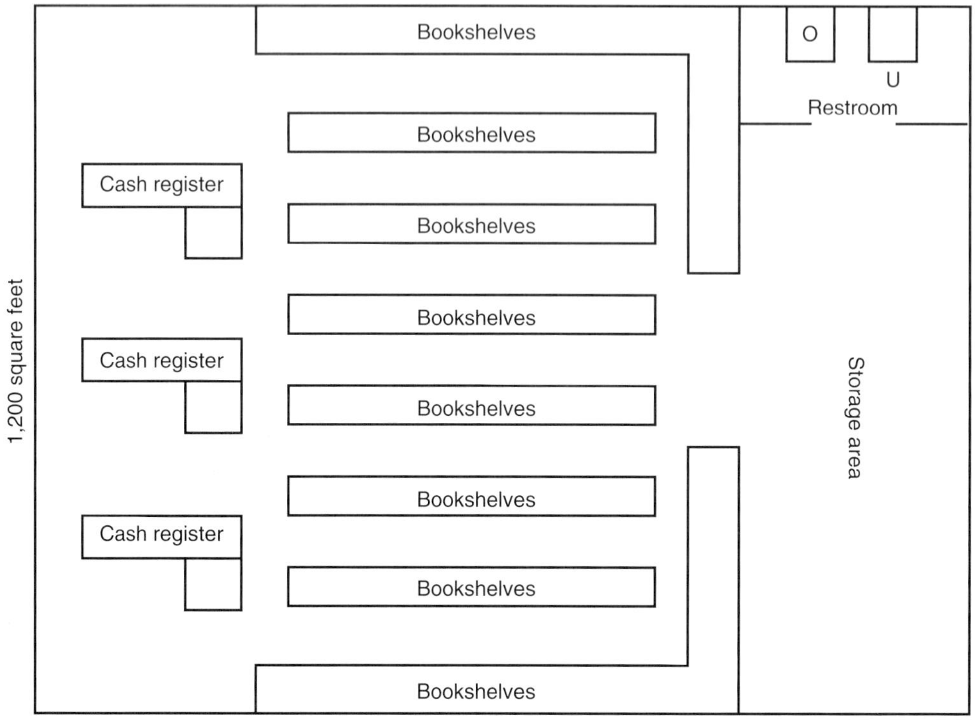

**Exhibit 4** Demographics of the Area

Saraland Shopping Center | Site: 1063
Saraland, AL | Coord:30:47.60 88:04.50

| Description | 1.0 mile radius | 3.0 mile radius | 5.0 mile radius |
|---|---|---|---|
| Population | | | |
| 1995 projection | 2,110 | 21,276 | 67,460 |
| 1990 estimate | 2,068 | 21,342 | 68,236 |
| 1980 census | 1,956 | 21,305 | 69,678 |
| 1970 census | 1,595 | 20,535 | 71,022 |
| Growth 70–80 | 22.65% | 3.75% | -1.89% |
| Households | | | |
| 1995 projection | 847 | 8,445 | 24,238 |
| 1990 estimate | 798 | 8,174 | 23,611 |
| 1980 census | 691 | 7,511 | 22,085 |
| 1970 census | 469 | 6,091 | 19,857 |
| Growth 70–80 | 47.28% | 23.32% | 11.22% |
| Population by race & Spanish origin | 1,956 | 21,305 | 69,678 |
| White | 98.43% | 90.23% | 45.95% |
| Black | 0.80% | 9.05% | 53.55% |
| American Indian | 0.31% | 0.39% | 0.27% |
| Asian & Pacific Islander | 0.28% | 0.16% | 0.10% |
| Other races | 0.18% | 0.16% | 0.13% |
| Spanish origin—new category | 0.56% | 0.70% | 0.95% |
| Occupied units | 691 | 7,511 | 22,085 |
| Owner occupied | 72.04% | 70.93% | 62.46% |
| Renter occupied | 27.96% | 29.07% | 37.54% |
| 1980 persons per household | 2.83 | 2.83 | 3.14 |
| Year round units at address | 724 | 7,913 | 23,683 |
| Single units | 79.90% | 85.50% | 86.13% |
| 2 to 9 units | 4.13% | 5.80% | 8.33% |
| 10+ units | 9.62% | 4.65% | 2.21% |
| Mobile home or trailer | 6.35% | 4.05% | 3.33% |
| Single/multiple unit ratio | 5.81 | 8.18 | 8.17 |
| 1990 estimated households by income | 798 | 8,174 | 23,611 |
| $75,000 or more | 1.88% | 1.39% | 1.10% |
| $50,000 to $74,999 | 7.93% | 6.86% | 5.49% |
| $35,000 to $49,999 | 21.03% | 17.79% | 12.99% |
| $25,000 to $34,999 | 18.02% | 17.40% | 13.92% |
| $15,000 to $24,999 | 20.42% | 19.84% | 18.04% |
| $7,500 to $14,999 | 16.94% | 17.82% | 20.31% |
| Under $7,500 | 13.77% | 18.90% | 28.15% |
| 1990 estimated average hh income | $27,764 | $25,268 | $21,196 |
| 1990 estimated median hh income | $25,144 | $21,651 | $17,086 |
| 1990 estimated per capita income | $10,787 | $9,709 | $7,360 |
| Households by type | 690 | 7,508 | 22,083 |

**Exhibit 4** *(continued)*

| Saraland Shopping Center<br>Saraland, AL<br><br>Description | 1.0 mile radius | Coord:30:47.60<br>3.0 mile radius | Site: 1063<br>88:04.50<br>5.0 mile radius |
|---|---|---|---|
| Single male | 6.84% | 5.69% | 7.12% |
| Single female | 8.69% | 12.12% | 11.28% |
| Married couple | 71.84% | 68.45% | 56.27% |
| Other family—male head | 2.34% | 2.21% | 3.26% |
| Other family—female head | 8.68% | 10.09% | 20.45% |
| Nonfamily—male head | 1.03% | 0.96% | 0.96% |
| Nonfamily—female head | 0.59% | 0.48% | 0.66% |
| Households with children 0–18 | 325 | 3,312 | 11,296 |
| Married couple family | 82.69% | 82.21% | 65.20% |
| Other family—male head | 3.68% | 2.67% | 3.60% |
| Other family—female head | 13.39% | 14.77% | 30.81% |
| Nonfamily | 0.24% | 0.34% | 0.39% |
| 1980 owner occupied property values | 429 | 4,734 | 11,928 |
| Under $25,000 | 15.94% | 25.46% | 41.43% |
| $25,000 to $39,999 | 38.05% | 38.13% | 30.94% |
| $40,000 to $49,999 | 29.25% | 19.35% | 13.75% |
| $50,000 to $79,999 | 14.87% | 14.96% | 12.14% |
| $80,000 to $99,999 | 0.92% | 1.42% | 1.16% |
| $100,000 to $149,000 | 0.47% | 0.51% | 0.43% |
| $150,000 to $199,999 | 0.08% | 0.05% | 0.05% |
| $200,000+ | 0.42% | 0.12% | 0.11% |
| 1980 median property value | $38,586 | $34,896 | $29,839 |
| Population by urban vs rural | 1,956 | 21,305 | 69,678 |
| Urban | 100.00% | 95.01% | 94.82% |
| Rural | 0.00% | 4.99% | 5.18% |
| Population enrolled in school | 459 | 5,008 | 19,749 |
| Nursery school | 1.41% | 2.23% | 2.74% |
| Kindergarten & elementary (1–8) | 65.56% | 66.20% | 62.17% |
| High school (9–12) | 24.51% | 23.85% | 24.56% |
| College | 8.53% | 7.72% | 9.50% |
| Population 25+ by education level | 1,092 | 12,242 | 35,610 |
| Elementary (0–8) | 17.53% | 21.63% | 27.67% |
| Some high school (9–11) | 20.66% | 23.36% | 24.56% |
| High school graduate (12) | 46.50% | 39.36% | 33.26% |
| Some college (13–15) | 10.57% | 10.26% | 9.92% |
| College graduate (16+) | 4.73% | 5.39% | 4.59% |
| 1990 population by sex | 2,068 | 21,342 | 68,236 |
| Male | 49.10% | 48.48% | 47.61% |
| Female | 50.90% | 51.52% | 52.39% |
| 1990 population by age | 2,068 | 21,342 | 68,236 |
| Under 5 years | 6.51% | 6.73% | 8.60% |
| 5 to 9 years | 8.10% | 7.91% | 10.09% |

**Exhibit 4** *(continued)*

| Saraland Shopping Center<br>Saraland, AL<br>Description | 1.0 mile radius | Site: Coord:30:47.60<br>3.0 mile radius | 1063<br>88:04.50<br>5.0 mile radius |
|---|---|---|---|
| 10 to 14 years | 7.16% | 7.31% | 8.93% |
| 15 to 19 years | 6.66% | 6.88% | 7.56% |
| 20 to 24 years | 8.49% | 7.76% | 7.28% |
| 25 to 29 years | 7.52% | 7.52% | 8.25% |
| 30 to 34 years | 9.16% | 8.91% | 9.13% |
| 35 to 44 years | 15.60% | 14.43% | 13.43% |
| 45 to 54 years | 10.99% | 10.08% | 8.43% |
| 55 to 59 years | 4.40% | 4.32% | 3.51% |
| 60 to 64 years | 4.35% | 4.54% | 3.75% |
| 65 to 74 years | 7.39% | 8.50% | 6.66% |
| 75+ years | 3.67% | 5.11% | 4.38% |
| 1990 median age | 33.10 | 33.70 | 29.67 |
| 1990 average age | 34.99 | 35.92 | 32.53 |
| 1990 female population by age | 1,053 | 10,996 | 35,752 |
| Under 5 years | 6.13% | 6.23% | 7.95% |
| 5 to 9 years | 7.78% | 7.41% | 9.49% |
| 10 to 14 years | 7.42% | 6.97% | 8.36% |
| 15 to 19 years | 6.48% | 6.64% | 7.24% |
| 20 to 24 years | 8.15% | 7.64% | 7.42% |
| 25 to 29 years | 7.38% | 7.37% | 8.06% |
| 30 to 34 years | 8.65% | 8.26% | 8.79% |
| 35 to 44 years | 15.24% | 14.13% | 13.58% |
| 45 to 54 years | 11.49% | 10.27% | 8.75% |
| 55 to 59 years | 4.24% | 4.54% | 3.66% |
| 60 to 64 years | 4.40% | 4.56% | 3.89% |
| 65 to 74 years | 8.43% | 9.59% | 7.43% |
| 75+ years | 4.20% | 6.39% | 5.37% |
| 1990 female median age | 34.04 | 35.54 | 31.19 |
| 1990 female average age | 35.90 | 37.44 | 33.98 |
| Total retail store items ($ 000) | 8,702 | 81,799 | 191,173 |
| Restaurant ($ 000) | 1,489 | 13,406 | 27,996 |
| Footwear ($ 000) | 218 | 2,129 | 4,831 |
| Home furnishings ($ 000) | 606 | 5,748 | 13,796 |
| Home improvements ($ 000) | 363 | 3,941 | 9,079 |
| Jewelry ($ 000) | 231 | 1,969 | 5,634 |
| Sporting goods ($ 000) | 118 | 1,053 | 2,523 |
| Toys ($ 000) | 83 | 829 | 2,117 |
| Apparel ($ 000) | 840 | 7,669 | 21,074 |
| Grocery/drug items ($ 000) | 4,754 | 45,055 | 104,123 |
| 1990 population (est) | 2,068 | 174 | 68,236 |
| 1990 households (est) | 798 | 8,174 | 23,611 |

*Source:* CREST/KHA/KSA/MRI/NPD/USDL

**Exhibit 5** Loan Payment Schedule

| Date | Payment number | Payment amount | Principal | Interest | Principal balance |
|---|---|---|---|---|---|
| Opening Balance | | | | | $300,000 |
| 8/30/96 | 1 | 3,182 | 1,932 | 1,250 | 298,068 |
| 9/30/96 | 2 | 3,182 | 1,940 | 1,242 | 296,128 |
| 10/31/96 | 3 | 3,182 | 1,948 | 1,234 | 294,180 |
| 11/30/96 | 4 | 3,182 | 1,956 | 1,226 | 292,224 |
| 12/31/96 | 5 | 3,182 | 1,964 | 1,218 | 290,259 |
| 1/31/97 | 6 | 3,182 | 1,973 | 1,209 | 288,287 |
| 2/28/97 | 7 | 3,182 | 1,981 | 1,201 | 286,306 |
| 3/31/97 | 8 | 3,182 | 1,989 | 1,193 | 284,317 |
| 4/30/97 | 9 | 3,182 | 1,997 | 1,185 | 282,320 |
| 5/31/97 | 10 | 3,182 | 2,006 | 1,176 | 280,314 |
| 6/30/97 | 11 | 3,182 | 2,014 | 1,168 | 278,300 |
| 7/31/97 | 12 | 3,182 | 2,022 | 1,160 | 276,278 |
| 8/31/97 | 13 | 3,182 | 2,031 | 1,151 | 274,247 |
| 9/30/97 | 14 | 3,182 | 2,039 | 1,143 | 272,208 |
| 10/31/97 | 15 | 3,182 | 2,048 | 1,134 | 270,160 |
| 11/30/97 | 16 | 3,182 | 2,056 | 1,126 | 268,103 |
| 12/31/97 | 17 | 3,182 | 2,065 | 1,117 | 266,039 |
| 1/31/98 | 18 | 3,182 | 2,073 | 1,108 | 263,965 |
| 2/28/98 | 19 | 3,182 | 2,082 | 1,100 | 261,883 |
| 3/31/98 | 20 | 3,182 | 2,091 | 1,091 | 259,792 |
| 4/30/98 | 21 | 3,182 | 2,100 | 1,082 | 257,693 |
| 5/31/98 | 22 | 3,182 | 2,108 | 1,074 | 255,584 |
| 6/30/98 | 23 | 3,182 | 2,117 | 1,065 | 253,467 |
| 7/31/98 | 24 | 3,182 | 2,126 | 1,056 | 251,342 |
| 8/31/98 | 25 | 3,182 | 2,135 | 1,047 | 249,207 |
| 9/30/98 | 26 | 3,182 | 2,144 | 1,038 | 247,063 |
| 10/31/98 | 27 | 3,182 | 2,153 | 1,029 | 244,911 |
| 11/30/98 | 28 | 3,182 | 2,162 | 1,020 | 242,749 |
| 12/31/98 | 29 | 3,182 | 2,171 | 1,011 | 240,579 |
| 1/31/99 | 30 | 3,182 | 2,180 | 1,002 | 238,399 |
| 2/28/99 | 31 | 3,182 | 2,189 | 993 | 236,210 |
| 3/31/99 | 32 | 3,182 | 2,198 | 984 | 234,013 |
| 4/30/99 | 33 | 3,182 | 2,207 | 975 | 231,806 |
| 5/31/99 | 34 | 3,182 | 2,216 | 966 | 229,590 |
| 6/30/99 | 35 | 3,182 | 2,225 | 957 | 227,364 |
| 7/31/99 | 36 | 3,182 | 2,235 | 947 | 225,130 |
| 8/31/99 | 37 | 3,182 | 2,244 | 938 | 222,886 |
| 9/30/99 | 38 | 3,182 | 2,253 | 929 | 220,632 |
| 10/31/99 | 39 | 3,182 | 2,263 | 919 | 218,370 |
| 11/30/99 | 40 | 3,182 | 2,272 | 910 | 216,098 |
| 12/31/99 | 41 | 3,182 | 2,282 | 900 | 213,816 |

**Exhibit 5** *(continued)*

| Date | Payment number | Payment amount | Principal | Interest | Principal balance |
|---|---|---|---|---|---|
| 1/31/00 | 42 | 3,182 | 2,291 | 891 | 211,525 |
| 2/29/00 | 43 | 3,182 | 2,301 | 881 | 209,224 |
| 3/31/00 | 44 | 3,182 | 2,310 | 872 | 206,914 |
| 4/30/00 | 45 | 3,182 | 2,320 | 862 | 204,594 |
| 5/31/00 | 46 | 3,182 | 2,329 | 852 | 202,265 |
| 6/30/00 | 47 | 3,182 | 2,339 | 843 | 199,926 |
| 7/31/00 | 48 | 3,182 | 2,349 | 833 | 197,577 |
| 8/31/00 | 49 | 3,182 | 2,359 | 823 | 195,218 |
| 9/30/00 | 50 | 3,182 | 2,369 | 813 | 192,850 |
| 10/31/00 | 51 | 3,182 | 2,378 | 804 | 190,471 |
| 11/30/00 | 52 | 3,182 | 2,388 | 794 | 188,083 |
| 12/31/00 | 53 | 3,182 | 2,398 | 784 | 185,684 |
| 1/31/01 | 54 | 3,182 | 2,408 | 774 | 183,276 |
| 2/28/01 | 55 | 3,182 | 2,418 | 764 | 180,858 |
| 3/31/01 | 56 | 3,182 | 2,428 | 754 | 178,429 |
| 4/30/01 | 57 | 3,182 | 2,439 | 743 | 175,991 |
| 5/31/01 | 58 | 3,182 | 2,449 | 733 | 173,542 |
| 6/30/01 | 59 | 3,182 | 2,459 | 723 | 171,083 |
| 7/31/01 | 60 | 3,182 | 2,469 | 713 | 168,614 |
| 8/31/01 | 61 | 3,182 | 2,479 | 703 | 166,135 |
| 9/30/01 | 62 | 3,182 | 2,490 | 692 | 163,645 |
| 10/31/01 | 63 | 3,182 | 2,500 | 682 | 161,145 |
| 11/30/01 | 64 | 3,182 | 2,511 | 671 | 158,634 |
| 12/31/01 | 65 | 3,182 | 2,521 | 661 | 156,113 |
| 1/31/02 | 66 | 3,182 | 2,532 | 650 | 153,582 |
| 2/28/02 | 67 | 3,182 | 2,542 | 640 | 151,040 |
| 3/31/02 | 68 | 3,182 | 2,553 | 629 | 148,487 |
| 4/30/02 | 69 | 3,182 | 2,563 | 619 | 145,924 |
| 5/31/02 | 70 | 3,182 | 2,574 | 608 | 143,350 |
| 6/30/02 | 71 | 3,182 | 2,585 | 597 | 140,765 |
| 7/31/02 | 72 | 3,182 | 2,595 | 587 | 138,170 |
| 8/31/02 | 73 | 3,182 | 2,606 | 576 | 135,564 |
| 9/30/02 | 74 | 3,182 | 2,617 | 565 | 132,947 |
| 10/31/02 | 75 | 3,182 | 2,628 | 554 | 130,319 |
| 11/30/02 | 76 | 3,182 | 2,639 | 543 | 127,680 |
| 12/31/02 | 77 | 3,182 | 2,650 | 532 | 125,030 |
| 1/31/03 | 78 | 3,182 | 2,661 | 521 | 122,369 |
| 2/28/03 | 79 | 3,182 | 2,672 | 510 | 119,696 |
| 3/31/03 | 80 | 3,182 | 2,683 | 499 | 117,013 |
| 4/30/03 | 81 | 3,182 | 2,694 | 488 | 114,319 |
| 5/31/03 | 82 | 3,182 | 2,706 | 476 | 111,613 |
| 6/30/03 | 83 | 3,182 | 2,717 | 465 | 108,896 |
| 7/31/03 | 84 | 3,182 | 2,728 | 454 | 106,168 |
| 8/31/03 | 85 | 3,182 | 2,740 | 442 | 103,428 |

**Exhibit 5** *(continued)*

| Date | Payment number | Payment amount | Principal | Interest | Principal balance |
|---|---|---|---|---|---|
| 9/30/03 | 86 | 3,182 | 2,751 | 431 | 100,677 |
| 10/31/03 | 87 | 3,182 | 2,762 | 419 | 97,915 |
| 11/30/03 | 88 | 3,182 | 2,774 | 408 | 95,141 |
| 12/31/03 | 89 | 3,182 | 2,786 | 396 | 92,355 |
| 1/31/04 | 90 | 3,182 | 2,797 | 385 | 89,558 |
| 2/29/04 | 91 | 3,182 | 2,809 | 373 | 86,749 |
| 3/31/04 | 92 | 3,182 | 2,821 | 361 | 83,929 |
| 4/30/04 | 93 | 3,182 | 2,832 | 350 | 81,097 |
| 5/31/04 | 94 | 3,182 | 2,844 | 338 | 78,253 |
| 6/30/04 | 95 | 3,182 | 2,856 | 326 | 75,397 |
| 7/31/04 | 96 | 3,182 | 2,868 | 314 | 72,529 |
| 8/31/04 | 97 | 3,182 | 2,880 | 302 | 69,649 |
| 9/30/04 | 98 | 3,182 | 2,892 | 290 | 66,757 |
| 10/31/04 | 99 | 3,182 | 2,904 | 278 | 63,853 |
| 11/30/04 | 100 | 3,182 | 2,916 | 266 | 60,938 |
| 12/31/04 | 101 | 3,182 | 2,928 | 254 | 58,010 |
| 1/31/05 | 102 | 3,182 | 2,940 | 242 | 55,069 |
| 2/28/05 | 103 | 3,182 | 2,953 | 229 | 52,117 |
| 3/31/05 | 104 | 3,182 | 2,965 | 217 | 49,152 |
| 4/30/05 | 105 | 3,182 | 2,977 | 205 | 46,175 |
| 5/31/05 | 106 | 3,182 | 2,990 | 192 | 43,185 |
| 6/30/05 | 107 | 3,182 | 3,002 | 180 | 40,183 |
| 7/31/05 | 108 | 3,182 | 3,015 | 167 | 37,169 |
| 8/31/05 | 109 | 3,182 | 3,027 | 155 | 34,141 |
| 9/30/05 | 110 | 3,182 | 3,040 | 142 | 31,102 |
| 10/31/05 | 111 | 3,182 | 3,052 | 130 | 28,049 |
| 11/30/05 | 112 | 3,182 | 3,065 | 117 | 24,984 |
| 12/31/05 | 113 | 3,182 | 3,078 | 104 | 21,906 |
| 1/31/06 | 114 | 3,182 | 3,091 | 91 | 18,816 |
| 2/28/06 | 115 | 3,182 | 3,104 | 78 | 15,712 |
| 3/31/06 | 116 | 3,182 | 3,117 | 65 | 12,596 |
| 4/30/06 | 117 | 3,182 | 3,129 | 52 | 9,466 |
| 5/31/06 | 118 | 3,182 | 3,143 | 39 | 6,324 |
| 6/30/06 | 119 | 3,182 | 3,156 | 26 | 3,168 |
| 7/31/06 | 120 | 3,181 | 3,168 | 13 | 0 |
| Grand Total | | $381,836 | $300,000 | $81,836 | $ 0 |

## Sources of Information

Information on property and demographics provided by Cummings & White-Spunner. All other information generated by the authors of the plan.

CHAPTER

9

# Obtaining the Right Financing for Your Business

*Money is the seed of money.*—Jean-Jacques Rousseau

*Many of the financial problems plaguing small businesses are avoidable, provided entrepreneurs analyze their own funding needs objectively and with sufficient lead time to act decisively.*
—Small Business Administration

## LEARNING OBJECTIVES

After studying the material in this chapter, you will be able to:

1. Explain the importance of proper financing for a small business.
2. Tell how to estimate financial needs, and explain some principles to follow in obtaining financing.
3. Explain why equity and debt financing are used, and describe the role each plays in the capital structure of a small firm.
4. Distinguish the types of equity and debt securities.
5. Describe some sources of equity financing.
6. Describe some sources of debt financing.
7. Explain what a lender looks for in a borrower.
8. Discuss some problems faced by minority entrepreneurs in obtaining financing.

# P R O F I L E

## ROY MORGAN—PIONEER IN AIR MEDICAL TRANSPORT SERVICES

Photo courtesy of Air Methods Corporation.

Roy Morgan, president of Air Methods Corporation of Englewood, Colorado, was a pioneer in providing rapid air medical transport services. After helping to develop the first hospital helipad in Salt Lake City, at Holy Cross Hospital, he brought in the first patient by helicopter, flying him in on the skids of a Bell 47, which was the method used during the Korean War.

Later, after seeing three seriously burned firefighters waiting for primitive medical attention, he saw the critical need to provide rapid medical response for people working in remote areas. After approaching several Colorado hospitals, Roy interested St. Mary's Hospital in Grand Junction in the project. But first he had to have a helicopter.

Roy and his wife, Dorothy, and friends Austin Clark and Ralph Mulford scraped together enough money to form a corporation and make the down payment on a helicopter. Roy and Dorothy took out a second mortgage on their house; sold a camper, a pickup truck, and stock in Western Airlines; and used their savings account to get the funds. Their friends made similar sacrifices. Air Methods had a Texas company convert the helicopter to provide a medical interior and then started the contract with St. Mary's Hospital AIR LIFE in August 1980.

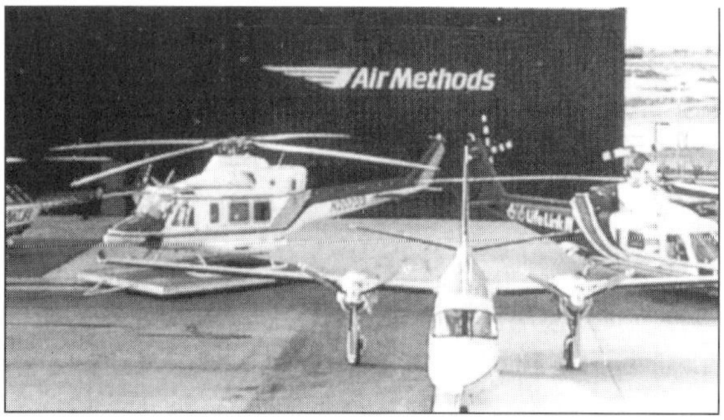


Photo courtesy of Air Methods Corporation.

By 1985, Air Methods had started new programs in Greeley, Colorado; Denver, Colorado; Texarkana, Arkansas; Minneapolis/St. Paul, Minnesota; and Bend, Oregon. To add another new program with the University of Utah Hospital in Salt Lake City, Air Methods shareholders expanded to include David and Cheryl Ritchie and Dennis and David Beggrow.

In November 1991, Air Methods merged with Cell Technology and became a publicly held corporation. According to Morgan and current chairman and CEO Terry Schreier, "Obtaining access to capital is one big benefit to becoming a public company." By selling shares in 1992, the company raised $7.2 million to help lower debts and increase working capital.

The new arrangement was so successful that by the end of 1992 Air Methods was serving 43 hospitals in 13 states. It had 25 helicopters and five airplanes (all of them medically equipped), 250 employees, and revenues of $18.5 million.

Not surprisingly, success bred competition. By late 1994, there were 217 helicopter ambulance services operating throughout the United States.

Air Methods has managed to remain competitive, however, partly through the judicious use of appropriate financing. In 1995, Air Methods had 19 long-term operating contracts for emergency medical programs in 14 states. The latest addition was with the newly created Texas Airlife in San Antonio, representing the Baptist Memorial Hospital System and the University Hospital System. Its fleet had expanded to 30 helicopters and 12 airplanes. The average cost of a flight to a hospital is $2,600, which is a small part of the average $160,000 hospital bill.

*Source:* Written by Gayle M. Ross from communication and correspondence with Air Methods Corporation. Other sources include Eugene Carlson, "Airborne Medical-Service Firms See Soaring Growth," *The Wall Street Journal*, July 14, 1992, p. B2; Gene G. Marcial, "A Medical Play Gains Altitude," *Business Week*, November 22, 1993, p. 124; Lisa Scott, "Air Ambulances, Hospitals Renegotiate," *Modern Healthcare*, May 30, 1994, p. 32; and Lee Reeder, "Air Methods Announces New Service," *AirMed*, September/October 1994, p. 32.

The Profile shows the importance of a truth that has been shown repeatedly in this text: *Sufficient capital is essential not only for small business start-ups but also for their continued operation.* One main reason for the high failure rate of small businesses is inadequate or improper financing. Too often, insufficient attention has been paid to planning for financial needs, leaving the new business open to sudden but predictable financial crises. Even firms that are sound financially can be destroyed by financial problems, for one difficulty most commonly experienced by rapidly growing firms is that they are unable to finance the investment needed to support sales growth.

## Estimating Financial Needs

The degree of uncertainty surrounding a small firm's long-term financial needs primarily depends on whether the business is already operating or is just starting, as mentioned in the Profile. If a business has an operating history, its future needs can be estimated with relative accuracy, even with substantial growth.

Even for an existing business, however, an in-depth analysis of its *permanent* financial requirements can be valuable. It may show the current method of financing the business to be unsound or unnecessarily risky. As a general rule, small businesses' long-lived assets, such as buildings and other facilities, should be financed with long-term loans, while short-lived assets, such as inventory or accounts receivable, should be financed with short-term loans.

## Principles to Follow

A new business, or a major expansion of an existing business, should be evaluated with great care, paying particular attention to its capital requirements. For example, the firm's **fixed assets** should be financed with equity funds, or with debt funds having a maturity approximately equal to the productive life of the asset.

**Fixed assets** are those that are of a relatively permanent nature and are necessary for the functioning of the business.

No business, however, can be financed entirely with debt funding, nor would such a capitalization be desirable—even if creditors were willing to lend all the funds required. Such a capital structure would be extremely risky, both for the creditors and for the business. This is especially true of **working capital,** which includes the current assets, less current liabilities, that a firm uses to produce goods and services and to finance the extension of credit to customers. These assets include items such as cash, accounts receivable, and inventories. Management of working capital is always a central concern for managers of small firms because they are often undercapitalized and overdependent on uninterrupted cash receipts to pay for recurring expenses. Therefore, small business managers must accurately estimate their working capital needs in advance and obtain sufficient financial resources to cover these needs, plus a buffer for unexpected emergencies.

**Working capital** is current assets, less current liabilities, that a firm uses to produce goods and services, and to finance the extension of credit to customers.

## Using Cash Budgets

An important tool small business managers can use to project working capital needs is a **cash budget.** Such a budget estimates what the out-of-pocket expenses will be during the next year to produce a product(s) for sale and when revenues from these sales are to be collected. In most businesses, sales are not constant over the year, so revenues vary a great deal from one period to another, while the costs of producing them tend to be relatively constant. For example, most retailers have their greatest sales period from Thanksgiving to Christmas. Yet, if they extend their own credit, payments are not received until the following January or February—or even later. Also, small producers may have produced the goods during the previous summer and had to bear the out-of-pocket costs of production for up to six months before actually receiving cash payments.

**Cash budgets** project working capital needs by estimating what out-of-pocket expenses will be incurred and when revenues from these sales are to be collected.

In general, therefore, when sales are made on credit, *the firm must carry the costs of production itself for an extended period.* A cash budget can help the manager predict when these financing needs will be the greatest and plan the firm's funding accordingly. An accurate assessment of seasonal financing needs is especially important if commercial bank loans are used, since bankers usually require a borrower to be free of bank debt at least once a year.

# Reasons for Using Equity and Debt Financing

While **equity** is the owner's share of the firm's assets, the nature of this claim depends on the legal form of ownership. For proprietorships and partnerships, the claim on the assets of the firm is that they are the same as the owner's personal assets. Equity financing in a corporation is evidenced by shares of either common or preferred **stock.**

**Equity** is an owner's share of the assets of a company. In a corporation, it is represented by shares of common or preferred stock.

**Stock** represents ownership in a corporation.

**Common stockholders** are the owners of a corporation, with claim to a share of its profits and the right to vote on certain corporate decisions.

**Preferred stockholders** are owners with a superior claim to a share of the firm's profits, but they often have no voting rights.

**Debt financing** comes from lenders, who will be repaid at a specified interest rate within a specified time span.

**Common stockholders** are the real owners of a corporation, and their financial claim is to the profit left after all other claims against the business have been met. Because they almost always retain the right to vote for company directors and/or on other important issues, common stockholders exercise effective control over the management of the firm.

**Preferred stockholders,** on the other hand, have a claim to the firm's profits that must be paid before any dividends can be distributed to the common stockholders; but they often pay for this superior claim by giving up their voting rights.

The other kind of capital, or funding, that a firm uses is called **debt financing,** which comes from lenders, who will be repaid at a specified interest rate within an agreed-on time span. The lenders' income does not vary with the success of the business, while the stockholders' does.

As discussed in Chapter 4, capital can also be raised by using a limited partnership, which combines the benefits of both debt and equity financing.

## Role of Equity Financing

The role of equity financing is to serve as a buffer that protects creditors from loss in case of financial difficulty. In the event of default on a contractual obligation (such as an interest payment), creditors have a legally enforceable claim on the assets of the firm. It takes preference over claims of the common and preferred stockholders. From an investor's point of view, common stock investments should have a higher financial return than debt investments because equity securities are riskier.

## Role of Debt Financing

With debt financing, principal and interest payments are legally enforceable claims against the business. Therefore, they entail substantial risk for the firm (or for the entrepreneur if the debt is guaranteed by personal wealth). Despite the risks involved, however, small firms use debt financing for several reasons. First, the cost of interest paid on debt capital is usually lower than the cost of outside equity, and interest payments are tax-deductible expenses. Second, an entrepreneur may be able to raise more total capital with debt funding than from equity sources alone. Finally, since debt payments are fixed costs, any remaining profits belong solely to the owners. This last strategy, employing a fixed charge to increase the residual return to common stockholders, is referred to as employing **financial leverage.**

**Financial leverage** is using fixed-charge financing, usually debt, to fund a business's operations.

A **lease** is a contract that permits use of someone else's property for a specified time period.

One type of debt financing that is becoming more popular is leasing facilities and equipment from someone outside the business instead of buying them. A **lease** is a contract that permits you to use someone else's property, such as real estate, equipment, or other facilities, for a specified time period. While a lease is not usually classified as debt, it is in many respects financially very similar.

From the small business owner's point of view, the benefits of a lease are that (1) the payments are tax deductible, and (2) it may be possible for the business to lease equipment when it would be unable to secure debt financing to purchase it. A growing number of small firms are signing up for the extra services leasing can provide.

For example, Ryder Commercial Leasing & Services frees a small company of the paperwork of buying and operating vehicles. It handles the equipment, drivers, routing, and warehousing of trucks—that is, it performs the entire distribution function.[1]

## Types of Debt and Equity Securities

Small companies use many types of securities, some of which are described below. This listing is incomplete but sufficient to illustrate the variety of financial sources that is a hallmark of the American financial system. Potential small business owners should remember that if they have a viable project, financing can be obtained from some source!

### Equity Securities

To start operating, all firms must have some equity capital. In corporations, **common stock,** which represents the owners' interest, usually consists of many identical shares, each of which gives the holder one vote in all corporate elections. (See Figure 9–1 for an example of a share of stock in a new small business.) Common stockholders have no enforceable claim to dividends, and the liquidity of the investment will depend largely on whether there is a public market for the firm's stock.

**Common stock,** representing the owners' interest, usually consists of many identical shares, each of which gives the holder one vote in all corporate elections.

**Figure 9–1** A Share of Stock in a Small Business

NUMBER 8

SHARES

INCORPORATED UNDER THE LAWS OF THE STATE OF ALABAMA

Bloomin' Lollipops, Inc.

The Corporation is authorized to issue 1,500 Shares—Par Value $1 Each

This Certifies that SPECIMEN is the owner of fully paid and non-assessable Shares of the above Corporation transferable only on the books of the Corporation by the holder hereof in person or by duly authorized Attorney upon surrender of this Certificate properly endorsed.

In Witness Whereof, the said Corporation has caused this Certificate to be signed by its duly authorized officers and to be sealed with the Seal of the Corporation.

Dated ____________

SECRETARY PRESIDENT

EXCELSIOR-LEGAL, INC. P.O. BOX 889 NORCROSS, GA. 30091

*Source:* Courtesy of Dot and Jiggs Martin of Bloomin' Lollipops, Inc.

## USING TECHNOLOGY TO SUCCEED

### Stock Trading on the Run

Do you want to buy a hot stock, but are not near a telephone, or you don't want to talk to your broker? Now you can use Mobile Trader. The cellular-phone-sized device uses a wireless modem and attaches to any laptop, notebook, or desktop computer. Windows-based software enables users to buy or sell stocks, bonds, stock options, futures, and mutual funds.

To conduct transactions, all you do is use a mouse to click the appropriate transaction on Windows. The order is then sent via wireless signal directly to a stock exchange. A confirmation is sent back to you all in seconds. Trades are secure, since transmissions are scrambled. You can also access up-to-date stock quotes and financial news and send E-mail and faxes. Ram Mobile Data, a venture of Ram Broadcasting and BellSouth, provide the infrastructure to send wireless signals from Mobile Trader.

Mobile Trader can be used anywhere you can take a portable computer—even on airplanes. At present, investors must have accounts with Geldermann Securities or Bernard Richards Securities, small New York-based brokerages.

*Source:* Donna Rosato, "Device Allows Stock Trading on the Run," *USA Today*, October 19, 1994, p. 2B. Copyright 1994, USA Today. Reprinted with permission.

**Preferred stock** has a fixed par value and a fixed dividend payment, expressed as a percentage of par value.

A corporation may also issue **preferred stock,** with a fixed par value (the value assigned in the corporation's charter, usually $100 per share). It entitles the holder to a fixed dividend payment, usually expressed as a percentage of par value, such as 8 percent (equal to $8 per year). This dividend is not automatic; it must be declared by the firm's board of directors before it can be paid. Nor is it a legally enforceable claim against the business. However, no dividends can be paid to the common stockholders until preferred stock dividends have been paid. Moreover, preferred dividends that have been missed typically cumulate and must be paid in full before payments can be made to common stockholders. Preferred stock usually conveys no voting rights to its holder.

The 1990s have been the decade of the stockholder in the United States. At the end of 1995, there were around 50 million U.S. stockholders.[2] As you can see from the Using Technology to Succeed, it is getting easier than ever to buy stocks.

A new and emerging kind of equity financing is the Small Company Offering Registration (SCOR). SCOR is a uniform registration, permitted in most states, that lets a company raise up to $1 million by selling common stock directly to the public. The price per share must be at least $5. SCOR offerings are important to small businesses because they cut through antiquated legal barriers and facilitate buying and selling small business investments. If state laws permit SCOR, companies can trade their common stock on NASDAQ's electronic OTC bulletin board.[3]

## Debt Securities

Debt securities are usually in the form of bonds or loans. In general, publicly issued debt (such as bonds or commercial paper) is more commonly used by larger firms, whereas small companies rely more on private loans from financial institutions such as commercial banks, insurance companies, or finance companies.

A distinction is usually made among **short-term securities** (those with maturities of one year or less), **intermediate-term securities** (those with maturities of one to five years), and **long-term securities** (those with maturities of more than five years). As we will discuss more thoroughly in the next section, commercial banks prefer to make short- and intermediate-term loans; other financial institutions, such as insurance companies, prefer to make long-term loans.

**Short-term securities** mature in one year or less.

**Intermediate-term securities** mature in one to five years.

**Long-term securities** mature after five years or longer.

If a small business manager negotiates a loan from a bank or other single lender, the amount of the loan is simply the amount borrowed. However, if securities are sold to the public or are privately placed with several lenders, most companies will issue the debt in the form of **bonds.** These have a standard denomination, method of interest payment, and method of principal repayment.

A **bond** is a debt security with a standard denomination, method of interest payment, and method of principal repayment.

Long-term debt secured by real estate property is a **mortgage loan,** whereas a **chattel mortgage loan** is debt backed by some physical asset other than land, such as machinery, transportation equipment, or inventory. Furthermore, many of the "unsecured" loans that banks extend to small businesses require personal guarantees by the manager or directors of the firm. Such loans are implicitly secured by the personal assets of these individuals.

A **mortgage loan** is long-term debt that is secured by real property.

A **chattel mortgage loan** is debt backed by some physical asset other than land, such as machinery, equipment, or inventory.

## Sources of Equity Financing

Obtaining sufficient equity funding is a constant challenge for most small businesses, particularly for proprietorships and partnerships. The only way to increase the equity of these two types of firms is either to retain earnings or to accept outsiders as co-owners. For corporations, the choices may be more varied. Some of the more frequently used sources of equity funding are discussed here.

### Self

People who start a small business must invest a substantial amount of their own funds in it before seeking outside funding. Outside investors want to see some of the owner's own money committed to the business as some assurance that she or he will not simply give up operating the business and walk away from it. Many owners also prefer using their own funds because they feel uncomfortable risking other people's money or because they do not want to share control of the firm.

> Dr. Richard Meyer, an Albuquerque, New Mexico, consultant, found that entrepreneurs can commonly finance as much as $100,000 of start-up costs with the help of family and friends. However, he found in the latest National Census of Early-Stage Capital Financing that the gap in financing still unfilled is the gap between $100,000 and $1 million.[4]

### Small Business Investment Companies (SBICs)

**Small business investment companies (SBICs)** are private firms licensed and regulated by the SBA to make "venture" or "risk" investments to small firms. SBICs supply equity capital and extend unsecured loans to small

**Small business investment companies (SBICs)** are private firms licensed and regulated by the SBA to make "venture" investments in small firms.

enterprises that meet their investment criteria. Because they are privately capitalized themselves (although backed by the SBA), SBICs are intended to be profit-making institutions, so they tend not to make very small investments.

SBICs finance small firms by making straight loans and by making equity-type investments that give the SBIC actual or potential ownership of the small firm's equity securities. SBICs also provide management assistance to the businesses they help finance.

SBICs prefer to make loans to small firms rather than equity investments, so we will discuss them further under the heading "Sources of Debt Financing" later in this chapter.

## Venture Capitalists

Entrepreneurs often complain that it is "lonely at the top." If so, a venture capitalist can serve as a form of security blanket when needed. Traditionally, venture capital firms have been partnerships composed of wealthy individuals who make equity investments in small firms with opportunities for fast growth, such as Federal Express, Apple Computer, and Nike. In general, they have preferred to back fast-growth industries (usually high-tech ones), since the ultimate payoff from backing a successful new business with a new high-tech product can be astronomical.

*"I run a small investment firm. Unfortunately, it used to be a large investment firm!"*



Venture capitalists *are not a good source of funding for new businesses—especially the mom-and-pop variety.* At least that seems to be suggested by the fact that more than two-thirds of all venture capital goes to expand existing businesses rather than to start new ones. Also, the number of firms offering venture capital declined 12 percent from 1990 to 1995.[5]

> Initial public offerings (IPOs) of small companies backed by venture capitalists have had a tough sell in recent years. The $4.1 billion raised in 1994 was only 60 percent of the record set in 1993. This was mainly due to a group of less mature companies that had a disappointing year of revenues. By the end of 1995, however, it was clear that "private equity funding" would probably reach record levels by early 1996.[6]

A new generation of small venture capitalists is jumping in to fill the gap left by the departure of the traditional financiers. These new firms are returning to the more traditional relationship with small businesses: They are acting as business incubators and hands-on advisers.[7] See Table 9–1 for a listing of some of these new firms.

Foreign stock exchanges are also sources of venture capital. They tend to have easier regulations for listing, require less paperwork, and have lower legal and administrative costs, as the following example shows.

**Table 9–1** The New Generation

| Firm | Location | Fund size ($ millions) | Industry focus |
|---|---|---|---|
| Benchmark Capital | Menlo Park, California | $85 | Information technology |
| Hummer Windblad Venture Partners | Emeryville, California | 60 | Software |
| CW Group, Inc. | New York | 58 | Health care; medical products and services |
| Onset Enterprise Associates | Palo Alto, California | 51.5 | Technology |
| Ampersand Ventures | Wellesley, Massachusetts | 44 | Chemicals and materials |
| Inroads Management Partners, LP | Evanston, Illinois | 42 | General |
| Geocapital Partners | Fort Lee, New Jersey | 40 | Information processing |
| Medical Innovation Partners | Minneapolis, Minnesota | 35.1 | Medical products and services |
| Three Arch Management, LP | Menlo Park, California | 27.5 | Life-science and medical-device companies |
| MedVenture Partners II, LLC | Orinda, California | 20 | Health care and software |

*Source: Private Equity Analyst*, as reported in *The Wall Street Journal*, July 13, p. B1. Reprinted with permission of THE WALL STREET JOURNAL, © 1989 Dow Jones & Company, Inc. All Rights Reserved Worldwide.

G

The Vancouver (Canada) Stock Exchange (VSE) is a popular source of venture capital for many small U.S. firms. The VSE specializes in natural resource exploration companies and small new technology firms, such as Neti Technologies Inc., an Ann Arbor, Michigan, software firm, and Sellectek (now operating as Global-Pacific Minerals, Inc.), a Menlo Park, California, software distributor. Sellectek used the VSE to raise $1.5 million.

As of January 29, 1990, with its Vancouver Computerized Trading System (VCT), the VSE became the first North American stock exchange to fully convert from the traditional "outcry market" to a fully automated trade execution system (Figure 9–2). Now, all trading occurs in the offices of member brokerage firms.

The VSE has a two-tier system that recognizes the stages of development of companies as they grow and mature. Its rules and regulations are designed to (1) provide a niche for venture companies and (2) maintain the integrity of the marketplace. Also, by using the VSE—rather than making deals with private U.S. venture capitalists—entrepreneurs can keep greater control of their businesses. The VSE has a proven record of performance, as shown by its third-place standing (after the Toronto and New York exchanges) in trading volume among North American stock exchanges.

One entrepreneur, Kim O. Jones, raised about $2.5 million by listing his company on the VSE. Also, in 1994, software developer Forecross Corporation of San Francisco chose the VSE to underwrite its initial public offering of 1.7 million shares and was looking to make some key deals with Canadian banks to gain a foothold in that country.

For more information, the VSE may be reached at (604) 689-3334.[8]

**Figure 9–2** Vancouver Computerized Trading System (VCT)

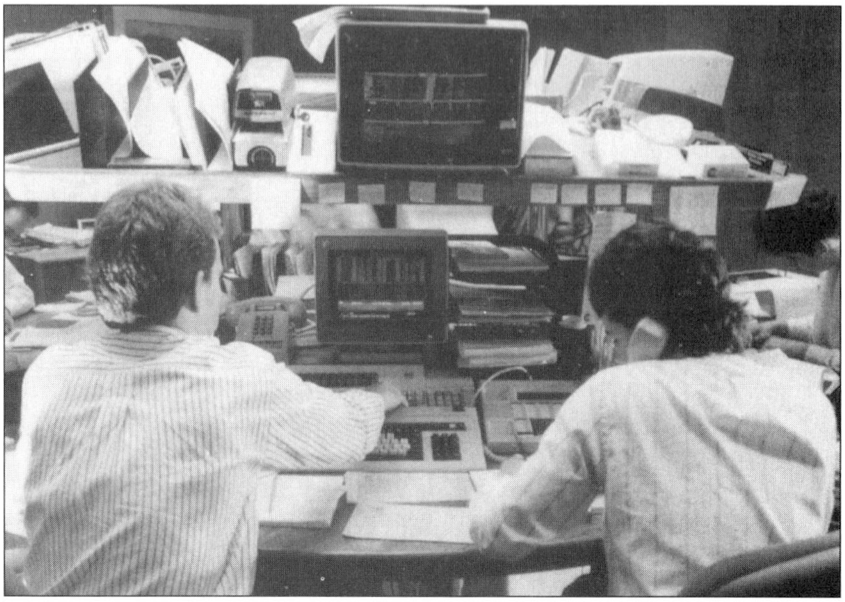

Photo courtesy of Vancouver Stock Exchange.

Many venture capitalists rely more heavily on the executive summary of a business plan (see Chapter 8) than on the plan itself in making investment decisions. So many long and complex plans are presented to them that they need a quick way to evaluate proposals in order to quickly discard those they do not want to consider further. The percentage of business plans accepted by venture capitalists for investment purposes is very low.

The Center for Entrepreneurial Leadership, launched in Kansas City in 1992, is trying to change this. In 1995, it launched a Fellows Program to help venture capitalists and entrepreneurs understand each other's needs.[9]

You should be aware when approaching either a venture capitalist or an SBIC for possible funding that neither will view your business the same way you do. While you may be content to remain relatively small in order to retain personal control, this is the last thing a professional investor will want. An SBIC or a venture capitalist will invest in a firm with the expectation of ultimately selling the company either to the investing public (through an initial public stock offering) or to a larger company. This potential conflict of goals can be very damaging to the new business owner unless the differences are explicitly addressed before external financing is accepted.

## Angel Capitalists

**Angel capitalists** are wealthy local businesspeople and other investors who may be external sources of equity funding.

Entrepreneurs have always tapped financial patrons, such as friends, relatives, and wealthy individuals, for beginning capital. These **angel capitalists** or **business angels** are a diverse group of high-net-worth individuals who will invest part of their assets in high-risk, high-return entrepreneurial ventures.[10] The University of New Hampshire's Center for Venture Research estimated that as many as 90 percent of small businesses are started with the financial help of friends and relatives.[11] It has also been estimated that angel capitalists provide up to four times as much total investment capital for small businesses as do the professional venture capital firms.

> The New York City Police Pension Fund is an example of an angel capitalist. A few years ago, it set aside $50 million to lend to small businesses. These loans were to be guaranteed by the SBA.[12]

## Other Sources

In some cases, small business entrepreneurs may be able to acquire financial assistance from business incubators, employee stock ownership plans, their own customers, bartering, and others.

### *Business Incubators.*

A big movement now encouraging the financing and development of small businesses is business incubators. **Business incubators** are usually old buildings, such as factories or warehouses, that have been renovated, subdivided, and rented to new companies by entrepreneurs, corporations, universities, governments, or groups such as chambers of commerce. Their purpose is to shelter young enterprises, offer moral support, and provide support services, including low overhead, until the enterprises are ready to go out on their own. The number of such incubators in the United States and Canada grew from a handful in 1980 to 530 in 1995, of which 30 were targeted for businesses owned by minorities and women.[13]

**Business incubators** are old buildings that have been renovated, subdivided, and rented to new companies by groups desiring to assist young enterprises until they are healthy enough to go out on their own.

D

> A classic example of an incubator is Chicago's Fulton-Carroll Center, housed in a 100-year-old former factory. The Center, founded in 1980, provides management assistance, low rent, shared services, and cooperation with other entrepreneurs. Three-fourths of the employees come from within a three-mile radius, and most are minorities. By 1992, the Fulton-Carroll Center had helped develop 177 new businesses and create 1,500 jobs, 80 percent of them going to local black and Hispanic residents.[14] June Lavelle was its first director.

Photo courtesy of June Lavelle

Some other successful incubators are:[15]

- The Technology Enterprise Center, started in Richland, Washington, in 1994.
- Rensselaer Polytechnic Institute's incubator in Troy, New York, which offers unfinished space to new tenants.

- Southland Development, Inc., in Chicago, which cuts costs by using apprentices at local craft unions and community colleges to do carpentry and construction.
- Kansas City's Center for Business Innovation, which uses local graduate students to assist incubator tenants in areas such as accounting and law.

## *Employee Stock Ownership Plans (ESOPs)*

**Employee stock ownership plans (ESOPs)** allow small businesses to reap tax advantages and cash flow advantages by selling stock shares to workers.

For existing small businesses, another source of financing is **employee stock ownership plans (ESOPs),** to be discussed in Chapter 14. The company reaps tax advantages and cash flow advantages from selling shares to workers. The plan also makes employees think like owners, tending to make them more productive.

## *Your Customers*

Your customers are another source of financing. It happens often, and in many ways. For example, mail-order vendors, especially those who use TV commercials, require the customer to pay when ordering; they then have that money for operations, while the customer waits several weeks for delivery of the goods. Also, it is customary for artisans and contractors to require a substantial down payment before beginning to produce the product.

> For example, Diane Allen, a portrait artist, requires a down payment of one-third of the total price before she will begin a portrait. This money not only assures that the contract will be honored but also can be used to buy supplies and cover other expenses.

An innovative new source of start-up financing for high-tech entrepreneurs has become available in recent years. This involves obtaining capital from an established potential client.

## *Bartering*

**Bartering** consists of two companies exchanging items of roughly equal value.

G

**Bartering** is an increasingly popular method of financing small businesses. In its simplest form, bartering consists of two companies swapping items of roughly equal value. But as this age-old business practice has become more popular—partly because of the competitive global business environment—bartering has become more creative. Now business owners trade everything from employee perquisites to corporate airfare with barter credits.

Bartering lends itself to many uses, such as (1) business travel, (2) debt collection, (3) closing a sale, (4) employee perks and bonuses, and (5) a line of credit. As bartering has become more popular—and complex—corporate barter networks, or regional trade exchanges, have developed to provide the needed exchange mechanism.

In 1994, networks of around 1,000 companies provided and received products and services through an intermediary. In 1993, North American firms traded more than $6 billion worth of goods and services, according to the International Reciprocal Trade Association.[16] (See the case at the end of the chapter for more details.)

## Sources of Debt Financing

Although the more entrepreneurial small businesses may aggressively seek the kinds of equity funding we have been discussing, most small businesses are more likely to use debt financing. This is true at least in part because there are more sources for such financing, several of which are described here.

### Trade Credit

**Trade credit** refers to purchases of inventory, equipment, and/or supplies on an open account in accordance with customary terms for retail and wholesale trade. In general, trade credit is one of the most important sources of debt financing for small business because it arises spontaneously in the normal course of operating the business. Firms seeking new and expanded wholesale and retail markets for goods have the option of using **consignment selling.** Small auto, major appliance, and farm equipment dealers consider consignments a form of trade credit because payments to suppliers are made only when the products are sold rather than when they are received in stock.

**Trade credit** is extended by vendors on purchases of inventory, equipment, and/or supplies.

With **consignment selling,** payments to suppliers are made only when the products are sold, rather than when they are received in stock.

### Commercial and Other Financial Institutions

Traditional financial institutions may provide the small business owner with borrowed funds. The proportion of funds such institutions make available ranges from 25 to 60 percent of the value of the total assets. Usually, the cost of such financing is higher than that of other alternatives, but such funds may be the most accessible.

#### *Commercial Banks*

A few years ago, an exhaustive study found that 90 percent of small and midsized businesses identified their local bank as their primary financial institution for banking and other financial services. While commercial banks are still a good source for small borrowers who have funds of their own and proven successful financial experience, rarely will they make conventional loans to a start-up business. Although banks realize that these small firms are a strong market, with strong demand, they also know they don't provide the return sought by banks. In other words, "small business loans are . . . regarded as expensive to service and marginally profitable."[17]

However, "[the belief that] lending to small business doesn't pay is a mistaken one," says Robert Barney, chief economic adviser to the U.S. Small Business Administration.[18] Data that banks must submit to their regulatory agencies indicate that at two groups of banks—those with assets of less than $100 million and those with assets between $100 million and $300 million—those that are friendly to small businesses had a higher return on assets. The banking institutions charge a higher rate of interest to small companies to offset the greater risk, and the result is a greater return. Additionally, some financial institutions specializing in small business loans become more knowledgeable and therefore more efficient.

The tendency for banks to service only existing accounts for small firms was emphasized by Charles Freeman, CEO of a New York financial services company that specializes in commercial loans backed by the U.S. Small

Business Administration. "Banks are looking to expand credit, but they are mostly expanding existing credit lines, not opening new ones."[19] The lack of the collateral required to secure the debt causes many problems for small firms.

For example, Hydrokinetic Designs Inc. was recently offered a contract to test-market 10,000 shower heads. It could not take advantage of the offer, however, because it could not afford to stock the units. Hydrokinetic was twice refused bank loans because it lacked sufficient fixed assets, such as plant or equipment, to pledge as collateral—although it had $450,000 of inventory and receivables. Instead of producing the units in-house, Hydrokinetic outsources the production process to a contract manufacturer.[20]

**Microloans** are loans for less than $100,000 for which the borrower applies directly to the bank rather than through the SBA, which eliminates most of the paperwork.

**Microloans,** which are loans for $100,000 or less, are a popular product for small business financing. The loans eliminate much of the paperwork borrowers are required to submit. Instead of submitting separate applications and documentation to both the bank and the SBA, the small business applies directly to a participating bank. The SBA guarantees only 50 percent of the loan, not 90 percent as for other loans. But the simplicity and reduced paperwork of microloans have made them attractive. In fact, the number of participating banks rose from 18 to 362 from mid-February to mid-June 1995.[21]

A **line of credit** permits a business to borrow up to a set amount without red tape.

If your business is successful, you may want to open a **line of credit** with your bank. This is an arrangement whereby the bank permits an ongoing business to borrow up to a set amount—say $50,000—at any time during the year without further red tape. The business writes checks against its account, and the bank honors them up to the maximum amount.

Usually, except for firms with an exceptionally high credit rating, the business is required to pay up all unsecured debts for a short period—say 10 to 15 days—each year to prove its creditworthiness. This is usually done when the firm's cash level is at its highest in order not to inconvenience the borrower too much.

A well-prepared business plan, as described in Chapter 8, should help lower a firm's interest rate and possibly even extend the term of the loan. Even then, however, you may find it more advantageous to finance the business with a personal loan.

### *Insurance Companies*

Insurance companies may be a good source of funds for a small firm, especially real estate ventures. The business owner can go directly to the company or contact its agent or a mortgage banker. While insurance companies have traditionally engaged in debt financing, they have more recently demanded that they be permitted to buy an equity share in the business as part of the total package.

## Small Business Administration (SBA)

One primary purpose of the SBA is to help small firms find financing, including those having trouble securing conventional financing, especially at reasonable rates. Many small firms need term loans of up to 25 years, but most lenders limit their lending to short-term loans.

The SBA helps these small firms in several ways, including offering guarantees on loans made by private lenders and offering direct specialized financing.[22] As indicated earlier, it also provides some venture capital through SBICs. The SBA-licensed SBICs also include some **specialized SBICs** (called **SSBICs**) to assist socially or economically disadvantaged enterprises, which, in turn, provide future capital through equity-purchased long-term loans or loan guarantees. Much attention is currently being given to SBICs by Congress and the President.

D

**Specialized small business investment companies (SSBICs)** assist social and economically disadvantaged businesses with venture capital.

## *Guaranteed Loans*

The SBA guarantees 30 to 40 percent of all long-term loans to small businesses under its 7(a) program. The loans can be used to (1) purchase land, buildings, or equipment; (2) provide working capital; (3) refinance existing debt; or (4) provide seasonal lines of credit. To qualify, a business must be unable to obtain private financing on reasonable terms but must have a good chance of success. Also, the borrower must meet the size standards shown in Table 9–2.

The SBA guarantees up to 90 percent of a loan made by a lender for up to $155,000, and 85 percent of the balance, up to $750,000. The lender checks with the SBA before formal application for "ballpark" feasibility of the proposed project. The loan terms are usually 5 to 7 years for working capital and up to 25 years for real estate or equipment. The interest rate is set at 2.25 to 2.75 percent over the lowest prime rate.

**Table 9–2** Eligibility for SBA-Guaranteed Business Loans by Industry Type

| Type of industry | Restrictions |
|---|---|
| Manufacturing | Maximum number of employees may range from 500 to 1,500, depending on the industry in which the applicant is primarily engaged. |
| Wholesaling | Maximum number of employees not to exceed 500. |
| Services | Annual receipts not exceeding $3.5 million to $17.5 million, depending on the industry in which the applicant is primarily engaged. |
| Retailing | Annual sales or receipts not exceeding $3.5 million to $17.5 million, depending on the industry. |
| Agriculture | Annual receipts not exceeding $1.5 million to $3.5 million, depending on the industry. |

*Source:* Executive Office of the President, Office of Management and Budget, *1995 Catalog of Federal Domestic Assistance* (Washington, DC: U.S. General Services Administration, June 1995), p. 652.

The applicant must provide the lender with (1) the purpose of the loan; (2) history of the business; (3) financial statements for three years (balance sheet and income statements) for existing businesses; (4) amount of applicant's investment in the business; (5) personal résumés; (6) projections of income, expenses, and cash flow; and (7) signed *personal* financial statements.

The lender then forwards the application directly to SBA officers. The SBA looks for (1) management ability and experience in the field; (2) at least a simple, but feasible, business plan; (3) an adequate investment (generally 20 to 30 percent of equity by the entrepreneur); and (4) ability to repay the loan from projected income.

### *Specialized Financing*

The SBA also makes specialized loans to handicapped persons, disabled and Vietnam-era veterans, small general contractors, and disaster victims. For example, the SBA's CAPLines Program operates four specialized loan and line of credit programs. These are:[23]

- Seasonal line: designed to assist businesses during their peak seasons.
- Contract line: used to finance labor and materials for performing contracts.
- Builders line: used to finance labor and materials for small general contractors and builders.
- Standard asset-based line of credit: used to assist businesses to meet credit qualifications for long-term credit.

## Small Business Investment Companies (SBICs)

In addition to indirect equity financing, as previously discussed, SBICs also make qualified SBA loans. The SBA matches each dollar an SBIC puts into a loan. Loans are usually made for a period of 5 to 10 years. An SBIC may stipulate that it be given a certain portion of stock purchase warrants or stock options, or it may make a combination of a loan and a stock purchase. The latter combination has been preferred.

Recent changes in SBICs have created a surge in their popularity. They are no longer limited to the sale of debentures but are now permitted to sell securities similar to preferred stock. One must remember, however, that SBA funds are federal government monies and may dry up as attitudes in Washington change.[24]

## Economic Development Administration (EDA)

The Economic Development Administration (EDA) makes a variety of direct loans to industries located in economically depressed communities or in communities that are declared regional economic growth centers. This financial assistance usually starts where the SBA authority ends, at $750,000.

The direct loans made by the EDA may be used for fixed assets or working capital. In addition, the EDA may extend guarantees on loans to private borrowers from private lending institutions, as well as guarantees of rental payments on fixed assets.

## U.S. Department of Agriculture (USDA)

The U.S. Department of Agriculture (USDA) has also started investing in small business. With its novel programs to develop nonfood, nonfeed uses of farm products, the department has spent millions of dollars on large and small businesses to induce them to come up with innovative products.

> One example was an enterprising 11-year-old in Mankato, Minnesota, who developed a product—which felt like wood and looked like granite—from shredded newspapers, blended with glue in her mother's blender (which didn't survive the experiment). A local group of investors, which was looking for a "**green product**" to commercialize, adopted the girl's idea. But financing was a problem, so the USDA offered a $1 million loan if the company could raise the same amount, which it easily did.
>
> According to Scott Taylor, vice president of Phenix Composites Inc., "The stamp of approval from a prestigious body like the USDA helped us raise $4.5 million." The company began full-scale production on May 16, 1994.[25]

D Q

A **green product** is an environmentally friendly product offered for sale commercially.

## What Lenders Look For

What do lenders look for when considering a loan to a small business? In essence the basics apply today as they did in the past. First, if the loan is for a new business, the lender wants to see if you can live within the income of the business. Given your expected revenues and expenses, will you be able to repay the loan? How much collateral can you put up to insure the lender against your inability to repay?

Second, if the money is for an existing business, the lender will look at its track record. If there are problems, you will be expected to explain what's going to happen to make a difference in the future. Do you have a new business plan? Are you going to buy new equipment or technology? Is there a new marketing plan?

To a large extent, your ability to attract money will depend on the lender's perception of your character as well as your ability to return the money. First, *income* is important. Second, the lender will also look at your *stability*, to see how long you've lived in a given residence or neighborhood, as well as how long you've worked at a particular job or run a business.

In summary, your request for financing will almost certainly be checked by some major credit company, using computerized reference services. Therefore, knowing that your credit record will be checked immediately by the computer, you should ask for a credit printout (which can be obtained free or for a few dollars) before you apply for funds. This will give you an opportunity to correct any errors or misunderstandings in your credit record.

Figure 9–3 provides some steps to use in developing a better relationship with investors, along with some questions the investor should ask you. Remember, while lenders should have an interest in how financially sound your business is, *they should not have a voice in managing it.* If you permit them to, they in reality become partners and must share responsibility for any failures.

**Figure 9–3** How to Improve the Entrepreneur-Investor Relationship

There are at least five steps you should take in order to assure a good working relationship with the investor:

1. Establish the range of funds you will need.
2. Identify the investor's skills and abilities that could help advance your venture.
3. Find an investor with interests and personality traits similar to yours.
4. Find a long-term investor, not one who wants to "make a quick buck" and get out.
5. Find an investor with more to offer you than just money, so that you may avoid having to hire outside consultants.

There are certain things the investor should find out about you:

1. Can you and the investor work together as a team?
2. Do you appear to be flexible and willing to accept new management if the project is highly successful?
3. Are you truly committed to this endeavor, and are you willing to expend the energy and resources to make it a success?
4. Can you accept constructive criticism, feedback, and assistance?
5. Do you have definite, fixed, realistic goals, and where do you plan to be in, say, one year? Five years? Ten years?

*Source:* International Reciprocal Trade Association, as reported in *The Wall Street Journal,* November 26, 1990. Reprinted with permission of THE WALL STREET JOURNAL, © 1990 Dow Jones & Company, Inc. All Rights Reserved Worldwide.

## Problems with Minority Financing

D

As indicated earlier (Chapters 3 and 6), minority-owned small businesses have particular problems financing their operations. The SBA's so-called Section 8(a) program did channel $4.4 billion in U.S. contracts to minority-owned firms in 1994[26]—and $19 billion in the previous seven years[27]—but much of it was invested in businesses located in predominantly white neighborhoods.

> For example, an Associated Press computer analysis of "minority set-aside" contracts between 1987 and 1993 is shown in Figure 9–4. Notice that 83.7 percent of the funds and 78.9 percent of the contracts went to businesses located in predominantly white neighborhoods, and 74.8 percent of all minority-owned businesses were in such neighborhoods.

It was particularly difficult for black women to obtain financing. There were, however, exceptions. The following example shows what one black female entrepreneur was able to do—with the help of the SBA.

D

> After working for 13 years in various departments at Hughes Aircraft Corporation, Ella Williams, believing in herself, decided to form a small business. With the help of the SBA's Section 8(a), she took out a 21 per-

**Figure 9–4** Minority Contracts Awarded to Minority-Owned Business between 1987 and 1993

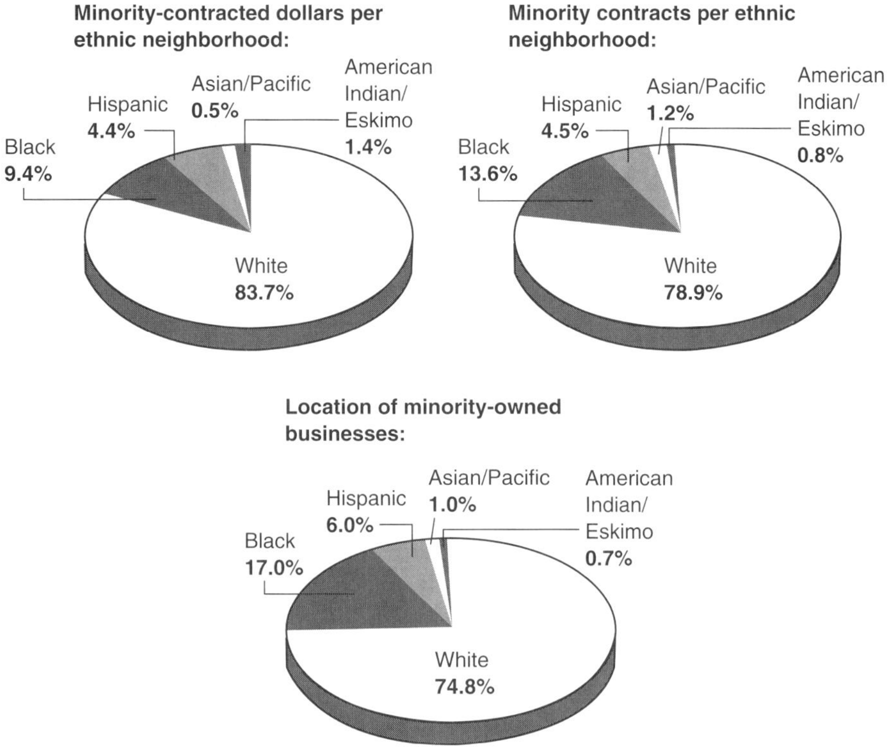


Note: Numbers do not add up to 100 percent due to rounding

*Source:* Associated Press article published in the *Mobile* (Alabama) *Press Register,* April 11, 1994, p. 5-B. Adapted with permission.

cent second mortgage on her house and founded Aegir Systems to provide engineering services to the aircraft industry. Williams' baking skills helped her succeed, as she'd ply clients with home-cooked muffins.

She struggled for three years—often collecting and selling aluminum cans to support herself and her two children. It took time to convince white-male–dominated firms that a black-woman–owned company could deliver, but she eventually did.

In 1993, Northrop named Aegir its "Small Business Supplier of the Year." Ella Williams is now a millionaire.[28]

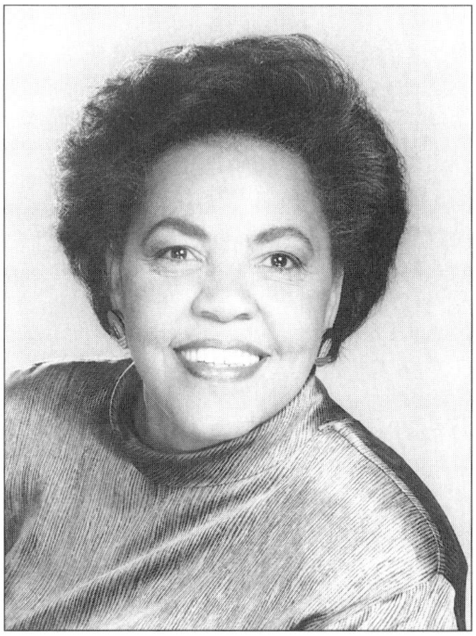

Photo courtesy of Ella Williams of Aegir Systems.

# WHAT YOU SHOULD HAVE LEARNED

**1.** Providing for financial needs is crucial to the success of a small business, which may be undercapitalized and living hand to mouth. Sufficient short- and long-term financing is needed to provide for fluctuations in sales or an unexpected business slump.

**2.** For a start-up venture, the assets of a business should be financed with equity or with debt funds having a maturity about equal to the productive life of the asset. A useful tool for estimating financial needs is the cash budget, which projects the amounts and timing of expenses and revenue for the year.

**3.** The two major sources of funds are equity and debt financing. Equity financing never has to be repaid and provides an interest in the business, including a share of the profits and a voice in decision making. Debt financing, which must be repaid whether the company is profitable or not, is less expensive than equity financing, since interest payments are tax deductible, and it does not require as high a rate of return.

**4.** The most frequently used types of equity securities are common and preferred stock. Common stock conveys voting rights but has no enforceable claim to dividends. Preferred stock entitles the shareholder to a fixed rate of dividend whenever profits are sufficient, but preferred stockholders usually have no voting rights. Debt securities include short-, intermediate-, and long-term loans and bonds. Loans made by a lender in standard denominations are called bonds. Long-term debt secured by real property is a mortgage loan, whereas a chattel mortgage loan is backed by some other physical asset. A lease can also be a form of debt financing.

**5.** Sources of equity financing include funds from the owner, family and friends, small business investment companies (SBICs), venture capitalists, angel capitalists, business incubators, employees, customers, and bartering.

**6.** Sources of debt financing include trade credit, commercial and other financial institutions—including commercial banks and insurance companies—the SBA, SBICs, the U.S. Department of Agriculture, and the Economic Development Administration (EDA). The SBA finances business ventures through guaranteed loans, direct loans, and participating loans.

**7.** When deciding whether or not to finance a small business, lenders look for factors such as ability to repay the debt, the owner's and the business's financial and business track record, and the owner's income, stability, and debt management.

**8.** Minorities have considerable trouble getting their businesses financed. Black women, particularly, have difficulty. Even when outside financing is available, much of it goes to black-owned businesses located in predominantly white neighborhoods.

## QUESTIONS FOR DISCUSSION

1. Discuss the basic rules to follow in financing a business venture.
2. Why should small business managers assess working capital needs in advance?
3. What are some reasons small business entrepreneurs use equity financing? Debt financing?
4. What are the factors that determine the classification of debt securities?
5. List and discuss the primary sources of equity financing.
6. List and discuss the primary sources of debt financing.
7. Compare equity financing to debt financing.
8. Evaluate the role of the SBA in providing operating and venture capital.
9. How would you propose improving the financing of minority-owned businesses?

## *CASE 9*

### SHORT OF CASH? TRY BARTERING

Often, the greatest obstacle to success for a small business is inadequate financial resources. Lack of dependable funding results in the closing of thousands of small businesses each year. Some owners of cash-strapped small businesses are taking matters into their own hands by using innovative methods to conserve cash. One such method is bartering.

Bartering, perhaps the oldest form of trade, involves swapping—rather than purchasing—everything from automobiles to health services. It is a creative way to increase sales, move surplus inventory, and utilize excess capacity. Some small firms have even used bartering as a way to collect bad debts, as well as a source of financing.

It works like this: A barter company acts as an intermediary for companies desiring to swap products and services. To become a member of the barter exchange, a company pays a fee averaging about $500 and a 10 percent transaction fee. Once a member, the firm can accumulate "barter" or "trade dollars" in return for offering products and services on the exchange. A firm can then use the trade dollars to purchase goods or services offered by any other member of the exchange.

For example, Andriana Furs Inc., which sells fur coats, has bartered about $100,000 in furs. According to owner Sohrab Tebyanian, "I can get what I want without paying cash for it." Tebyanian has used his trade dollars to purchase advertising spots on local TV and radio stations and to acquire new computers and phones for his offices.

The Chicago White Sox baseball team has also used bartering. It bartered thousands of dollars worth of game tickets to pay the company that washed windows in the Comiskey Park skyboxes, as well as to pay for printing and floral arrangements for the opening day.

The barter system is particularly popular with airlines and hotels because of the excess capacity that is normal for them. With a little extra effort, these companies can offer seats and rooms that probably would have gone unused anyway. Therefore, almost every major airline and hotel company, including the Ritz-Carlton and Marriott chains, uses the system.

According to the International Reciprocal Trade Association of Alexandria, Virginia, businesses enter the barter system by signing up with a barter network or broker. Many of the over 400 such services in the United States are listed under "Barter and Trade Exchanges" in the Yellow Pages. The largest of these exchanges, such as ITEX Corporation of Portland, Oregon, have more than 20,000 businesses as members.

Long seen as an underground business method, bartering became a popular financing method in 1982, when the Internal Revenue Service recognized it as legitimate trade. The only requirement was that "barter" or "trade dollars" be treated as "real dollars" for tax purposes. Users of barter pay cash for tips and sales taxes.

However, bartering is not a cure-all for cash-poor companies. Depending on the exchange, a business may be limited in its choice of products or services. Also, it may be dangerous if firms don't fully understand the cash cost of a trade dollar. Taxes must still be paid on all sales—just as if cash had been used—and the tax bill can often be a shock!

Bartering is still unfamiliar territory to many firms, but as small businesses face financial difficulties, bartering will continue to gain popularity.

*Source:* Adapted from various sources, including Mark Robichaux and Michael Selz, "Small Firms, Short on Cash, Turn to Barter," *The Wall Street Journal,* November 26, 1990, p. B1; Hal Lancaster, "Pay for Things the Old-Fashioned Way: Barter," *The Wall Street Journal,* February 28, 1995, p. B1; and Bob Ortega, "Swap the Sweat of Your Brow for a Suite Right on the Beach," *The Wall Street Journal,* June 16, 1995, p. B1.

## QUESTIONS

1. Identify and discuss some advantages and disadvantages of the barter system.
2. How might bartering be used as a source of funding for a small business?
3. Would bartering work in all types of businesses? Speculate as to which type of firm might use bartering. Which one might not?
4. You have started the business you always dreamed of having. Describe how you would personally use bartering in your firm.

# APPLICATION 9–1

J&J Computers was started several years ago. When it started growing a few years back, its owners needed more money to expand their business and meet the growing demands of their customers. In an effort to raise more capital, the owners approached the area bank and took out a loan.

They soon realized, however, that they needed more money because their business was growing at a much faster pace than originally predicted. The owners decided to go public and sold an issue of common stock. They were thereby able to raise enough capital to continue operating and were able to meet the demands of their customers—and creditors.

## QUESTIONS

1. When J&J Computers took out a loan from the bank, what kind of financing was it?
2. Why do you think they preferred to take a loan first?
3. What kind of financing is it when you sell stock?
4. Who are the stockholders and what are their rights?

# ACTIVITY 9–1

**D***irections:* In the puzzle below, find the following terms from this chapter: angel capitalists, bond, business incubators, chattel mortgage loan, cash budget, common stockholders, consignment selling, debt financing, equity, ESOPs, fixed assets, intermediate-term securities, financial leverage, lease, line of credit, long term securities, mortgage loan, preferred stock, preferred stockholders, SBICs, short-term securities, stock, trade credit, working capital.

| | | | | | | | | | | | | | | | | | | | | |
|---|---|---|---|---|---|---|---|---|---|---|---|---|---|---|---|---|---|---|---|---|
| T | R | A | B | I | Z | S | I | N | T | P | R | E | W | X | W | O | R | H | O | C |
| C | F | I | X | N | V | A | P | T | A | B | D | E | O | B | N | C | A | S | M | O |
| A | F | O | R | T | S | H | R | O | D | I | U | O | R | F | A | N | G | G | H | N |
| P | R | E | F | E | R | R | E | D | S | T | O | C | K | H | O | L | D | E | R | S |
| J | S | S | I | R | K | S | F | E | N | E | Y | T | I | U | Q | E | L | Q | U | I |
| W | T | E | R | M | A | T | E | B | Y | O | U | I | N | E | O | P | R | S | T | G |
| L | I | Z | A | E | M | E | R | T | F | T | B | O | G | G | S | H | N | I | W | N |
| P | D | C | L | D | U | L | R | F | T | S | P | T | C | A | L | S | A | N | H | M |
| S | E | H | T | I | A | B | E | I | D | T | C | I | A | R | I | E | O | A | A | E |
| R | R | X | I | A | D | U | D | N | E | S | R | D | P | E | N | I | L | O | R | N |
| O | C | B | N | T | S | S | S | A | Y | I | C | E | I | V | O | T | E | L | T | T |
| T | F | U | S | E | R | Q | T | N | P | L | O | R | T | E | Q | I | G | E | O | S |
| A | O | C | S | T | T | U | O | C | A | A | M | C | A | L | W | R | A | G | N | E |
| B | E | N | E | E | O | I | C | I | U | T | E | E | L | L | E | U | G | A | M | L |
| U | N | S | N | R | D | C | K | N | F | I | G | D | X | A | C | C | T | G | O | L |
| C | I | T | F | M | K | L | K | G | E | P | N | A | C | I | A | E | R | T | R | I |
| N | L | E | L | S | O | W | V | R | I | A | A | R | J | C | G | S | O | R | T | N |
| I | V | S | R | E | D | L | O | H | K | C | O | T | S | N | O | M | M | O | C | G |
| S | T | S | S | C | C | R | E | D | L | L | H | W | B | A | D | R | L | M | T | E |
| S | E | A | H | U | S | E | E | M | O | E | G | O | E | N | R | E | E | C | T | M |
| E | B | D | O | R | J | C | S | N | K | G | N | Q | A | I | T | T | T | P | A | P |
| N | Z | E | R | I | B | N | I | N | G | N | I | D | S | F | Y | G | T | I | H | L |
| I | X | X | Z | T | A | O | L | B | J | A | F | B | E | A | R | N | A | O | C | O |
| S | E | I | T | I | R | U | C | E | S | M | R | E | T | T | R | O | H | S | J | Y |
| U | C | F | V | E | K | R | N | I | L | L | O | T | S | E | S | L | C | U | M | E |
| B | N | R | M | S | T | E | G | D | U | B | H | S | A | C | G | I | S | N | O | C |

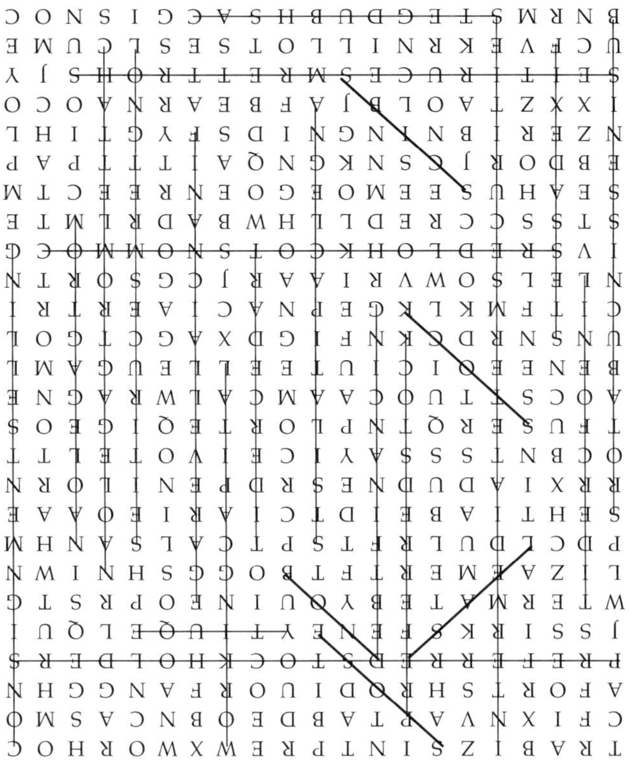

CHAPTER 10

# Developing Marketing Strategies

*We don't focus enough attention on adequate product differentiation, much less on distribution channels, service organizations, or the reputation of vendors. We tend to forget that those things tremendously influence what someone buys.*—William H. Davidow, venture capitalist and author of *Marketing High Technology*

## LEARNING OBJECTIVES

After studying the material in this chapter, you will be able to:

1. Describe the marketing concept, and explain how it can be used by a small business.
2. Explain how to develop and implement a marketing strategy.
3. Explain how the product life cycle affects marketing strategies.
4. Explain how packaging affects marketing.
5. Describe how prices are set and administered.
6. Show how marketing services differs from marketing goods.

# PROFILE

## BYRD SURVEYING: MARKETING A SERVICE

Photo courtesy of M. Jane Byrd.

Byrd Surveying is a small land surveying corporation established in 1974 that employs between 20 and 25 people. Its primary business is subdivision development and boun- dary surveys, but the firm also does mortgage loan surveys, percolation tests, and construction layout work.

Gerald Byrd, the president and CEO, is licensed in Alabama, Florida, and Mississippi. As in any professional service organization, ethics is a main concern, and many forms of advertising are not considered ethical for this industry. Opportunities for marketing the services are few because professional associations are used to get the word out about the business and its services.

Byrd belongs to the Mortgage Bankers Association and is the director of the local chapter. He is also "Council Director Emeritus" of the Homebuilders Association and is active in the Realtors Association.

Byrd is active in the Alabama Society of Professional Land Surveyors, of which he is the local chapter treasurer, a state director, and a member of the Professional Standards Committee. In addition, he serves as a technical adviser for the Alabama Board of Registration for Professional Engineers and Land Surveyors. As a result of his work with various planning and zoning groups, such as the Mobile City Planning Commission, Byrd has been appointed county surveyor.

Such professional memberships can mean many extra hours of service and hard work. Because his membership is a marketing tool, however, Byrd is always an active and working member, serving on the various boards and attending all meetings and organizational functions. These associations hold many charitable activities, from fishing rodeos to actual construction of buildings and homes. Active members provide services, supplies, and labor for many causes.

To maintain an image of friendly professionalism, Byrd also personally delivers many of his finished jobs. This is a follow-up prospecting function. During this visit to the client, questions can be answered and new projects brainstormed. Pricing, timing, and criteria may also be discussed one-to-one at this time of personal contact. It is also very important that all phone calls and "drop-ins" be treated with courtesy and respect. "Let's not forget the Q quality of the finished product," Byrd says. His business creed is: "A satisfied client is a continuing client."

Despite all the hours necessary to own and manage a small business, Byrd still finds time to pursue his favorite hobby—flying!

*Source:* Prepared by W. Jay Megginson from conversations with Gerald Byrd, his associates, and fellow professionals.

This Profile illustrates an important aspect of the marketing function—marketing a service. It also gives an overview of marketing, including the importance of the marketing concept, product development, and customer service. This chapter is about those and other marketing strategies.

Companies with a reputation for superior marketing tend to share some basic strategies for successful marketing. These include:[1]

- Moving quickly to satisfy customer needs.
- Using pricing to differentiate the product/service.
- Paying attention to packaging.
- Building customer loyalty.
- Offering samples and demonstrations.
- Educating customers.

## The Marketing Concept

The **marketing concept** involves giving special consideration to the needs, desires, and wishes of present and prospective customers.

The **marketing concept** helps a business focus its efforts on satisfying customer needs in such a way as to make a satisfactory profit. The concept comprises three basic elements: a customer orientation, a goal orientation, and the systems approach. This concept is based on the truth that the survival of a small business depends on providing service. With such a customer orientation, small firms will try to identify the group of people or firms most likely to buy their product (the target market) and to produce goods or services that will meet the needs of that market. Being consumer oriented often involves exploring consumer needs and then trying to satisfy them, as the following example shows.

> Janet Forti and June Negrycz recognized that both GapKids and BabyGap ignore a significant market—parents who want to dress their children in something other than T-shirts and denim. To fill that neglected niche, the pair opened Olivia and Sam, a children's specialty store, in the gentrified Cobble Hill neighborhood of Brooklyn, New York. The shop has prospered from the first day.[2]

In focusing on customer orientation, however, the small firm must not lose sight of its own goals. Goals in profit-seeking firms typically center on financial criteria such as profit, return on investment, or market share.

In a **system** all parts of the business work in unison.

The third component of the marketing concept is the systems approach. In a **system** all parts of the business work together. Thus, consumer needs are identified, and internal procedures are set up to ensure that the right goods and services are produced, distributed, and sold to meet those needs.

## Determining Customers' Needs

Your understanding of customers' needs starts with the realization that when people buy something, they purchase satisfaction as well as goods or services. Consumers do not simply choose a toothpaste, for example. Instead, some want a decay preventive, some seek pleasant taste, others desire tooth brighteners, and still others will accept any formula at a bargain price. Thus, understanding customers' needs means being aware of the timing of the purchase, what customers like and dislike, or what "turns them on."

> For example, the owner of a ladies' dress shop in a small town has a good business. Many of her customers live as far as 50 miles away. She knows her customers by name, understands their needs, and buys with them as individuals in mind. When she goes to market, she thinks, "This style is perfect for Mrs. Adams," or "Jane would love this." Then she calls Mrs. Adams or Jane when that style comes in.

## Meeting Customers' Needs

The marketing concept should guide the attitudes of the firm's salespeople, who should be encouraged to build personal relationships with customers. For example, one retail salesperson, to build a following, writes to 20 customers every day, describing new stock that should appeal to the specific customer.

Small firms should also do little favors for customers. Although people may be uncomfortable with big favors that they cannot repay, small acts of thoughtfulness make them feel that the business cares about them. Customers want a business to be helpful, and outstanding service will often generate good word-of-mouth advertising.

> For example, Avon Products Inc. insists it can sell clothes successfully by offering customers not only convenience but also low catalog shopping prices. In addition, the company offers the services of a personal shopper. Avon has about 440,000 salespeople in the United States, who have developed an extensive network of intimate relationships with customers.[3]

Keeping customers satisfied is more difficult than it seems, because it involves all aspects of the business. Customer satisfaction involves not just employees and customers but other factors as well, such as store design and upkeep, method of employee payment, and methods for providing feedback to and from customers. Unfortunately, as Yankelovich Partners found in a recent survey, the majority of consumers feel they are not being served properly. Figure 10–1 shows how consumers react to this problem.

## Implementing the Marketing Concept

In implementing the marketing concept, you should use the systems approach. As mentioned above, all parts of the business must be coordinated and marketing policies must be understood by all personnel to avoid problems such as that in the following example.

**Figure 10–1** Consumers Talking Back

Eight-five percent of consumers say they must look out for themselves in the marketplace. Many are seeking product information and giving feedback after buying. Those who have:

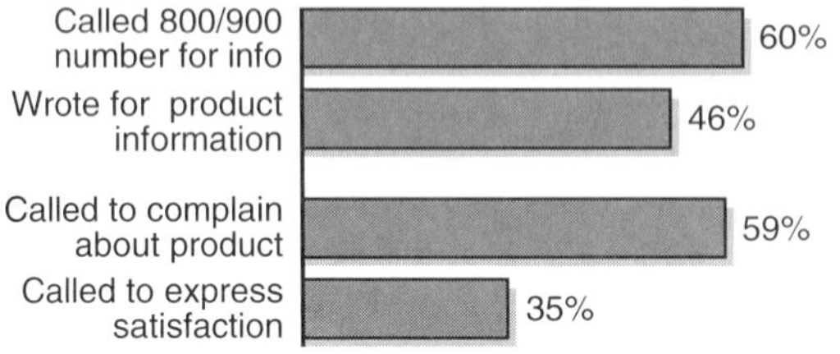


*Source:* Yankelovich Partners for *USA Weekend* magazine, as reported in *USA Today,* October 19, 1995, p. 1B. Copyright 1995, USA TODAY. Reprinted with permission.

> A store sent its customers a flyer urging them to use its credit plan. Yet one customer received the flyer in the same mail with a harsh letter threatening repossession of earlier purchases if the customer's account wasn't paid within 24 hours.

*"It's table 44 on his cellular phone. He wants a waiter."*

*Source:* Reprinted from *The Wall Street Journal*; permission Cartoon Features Syndicate

You should try to apply the marketing concept by using one or more of the following ideas.

### *Be Conscious of Image*

You should evaluate the business frequently to see what kind of image it projects—from the customers' point of view. You should ask: Can my customers find what they want, when they want it, and where they want it, at a competitive price?

### *Practice Consumerism*

**Consumerism** involves prodding businesses to improve the quality of their products and to expand consumer knowledge.

The major concerns of the consumer movement during the last three decades have been the rights of consumers to buy safe products, to be informed, to be able to choose, and to be heard. **Consumerism** recognizes that consumers are at a disadvantage and works to force businesses to be responsive in giving them a square deal. You can practice consumerism by doing such things as performing product tests, making clear the terms of sales and warranties, and being truthful in advertising.

### *Look for Danger Signals*

There are many danger signals that can indicate when the marketing concept is not being followed. Your business is in trouble if, over time, it exhibits one or more of the signs listed in Table 10–1. An uninterested employee—or manager—turns customers off, as the following example shows.

**Table 10–1** Danger Signals Indicating Marketing Problems

| Indicator | Indication |
|---|---|
| Sales | Down from previous period |
| Customers | Walking out without buying |
| | No longer visiting store |
| | Returning more merchandise |
| | Expressing more complaints |
| Employees and salespeople | Being slow to greet customers |
| | Being indifferent to or delaying customer |
| | Not urging added or upgraded sales |
| | Having poor personal appearance |
| | Lacking knowledge of store |
| | Making more errors |
| | (Good ones) leaving the company |
| Store image | Of greed through unreasonable prices |
| | Inappropriate for market area |
| | Unclear, sending mixed signals |

Thomas Shoemaker was hunting for some Con-Tact paper in a Peoples Drug store in Washington, D.C. He finally gave up the search and was walking out when he saw a man with a Peoples ID badge adjusting some stock on a shelf. When Shoemaker asked him if the store carried Con-Tact paper, the man replied, "I don't know. I don't work here. I'm the manager."[4]

## Seeking a Competitive Edge

There is a close relationship between key success factors and the competitive edge that a small business should seek. Some of these factors, based on industry analysis, were discussed in Chapter 6. Your **competitive edge** is something that customers want and only you can supply, which gives you an advantage over your competitors. Some factors that might provide such an advantage are quality, reliability, integrity, and service, as well as lower prices. In some industries, such as electronics or toys, novelty and innovation provide the most important competitive edge; in many small businesses, however it can be something as simple as courtesy, friendliness, and helpfulness.

A **competitive edge** is a particular characteristic that makes one firm more attractive to customers than its competitors.

# Developing a Marketing Strategy

As a small business owner, you should develop a marketing strategy early in your business operations. Such a strategy consists of (1) setting objectives, (2) choosing target market(s), and (3) developing an effective marketing mix.

## USING TECHNOLOGY TO SUCCEED

### Generation PC

If your marketing campaign is limited to glossy catalogs or storefront window displays, we suggest you read further. According to a 1995 study conducted by Forester Research Inc. of Cambridge, Massachusetts, there's a new generation of technically advanced PC users on the way who will expect more from businesses.

Just who are they? Well, they're the growing number of youth who are dumping traditional toys in favor of computers. Today's children have an unprecedented aptitude for new technology, according to the study, which found that 13.7 million U.S. children have access to home PCs—and this number is expected to grow to 30.4 million by the year 2000.

What does this mean for you? As more and more children are exposed to the PC, it will change the way companies sell products and promote themselves. In the near future, companies will need high-quality interactive experiences to draw in customers. They'll also need to hire employees with a high-tech bent. And you'd better sit up and take notice *now:* The study concludes that companies have only three to five years to prepare for this new brand of consumer.

*Source:* Reprinted with permission from *Entrepreneur Magazine,* October 1995.

## Setting Objectives

Marketing objectives should be tied in with your competitive edge. For example, an image of higher quality than competitors' products at comparable prices may be an objective. To achieve this objective and still make planned profits requires aligning all operations, including the added costs of improved quality, adequate capital, and so forth. Objectives must consider customers' needs as well as the survival of the business. To attain objectives, a target market must be identified and served.

## Choosing Target Markets

A **target market** is the part of the total market toward which promotional efforts are concentrated.

The **target market** of a business should be the customers most likely to buy or use its product(s). Only when a clear, precise target market has been identified can an effective marketing mix be developed, as shown in Using Technology to Succeed.

### *Use Market Segmentation*

**Market segmentation** is identifying and evaluating various layers of a market.

To define a target market requires **market segmentation**, which is identifying and evaluating various layers of a market. Effective market segmentation requires the following steps:

1. Identify the characteristics of two or more segments of the total market. Then, distinguish among the customers in each segment on the basis of such factors as their age, sex, buying patterns, or income level. For example, adults desire a table-service restaurant more than do teenagers and young children, who generally prefer a fast-food format.
2. Determine whether any of those market segments is large enough and has sufficient buying power to generate profit for your business.

3. Align your marketing effort to reach that segment of the market profitably.

> For example, Ryka Inc., a 25-employee firm in Weymouth, Massachusetts, was able to take a segment of the $4 billion-a-year athletic shoe market away from giants such as Nike, Reebok, and L.A. Gear by concentrating on athletic shoes for women.[5]

## *Shifting Target Markets*

Choosing and maintaining a target market is becoming more difficult because of changing consumer characteristics. Therefore, small business owners should study the environment for shifts in such factors as population patterns, age groups, and income levels, as well as regional patterns of consumption.

*Population, Age, and Income Shifts.* The underlying market factor determining consumer demand is the number and type of people with the purchasing power to buy a given product. In general, the U.S. population is shifting from the East and North to the West and South. Other important population factors are household size and formations, education, and the number of married couples, singles, single-parent families, unmarried couples, and children. According to the U.S. Census Bureau, the average size of U.S. households declined from 3.5 in 1940 to 2.7 in 1987 and is expected to be only 2.5 by the year 2000.[6] D

Age groups also change. The average age of Americans has been rising and is expected to continue to rise in the foreseeable future. As you can see from Figure 10–2, the percentage of young people and young adults is declining, while the 35-and-over group—especially the 45-to-64-year-old group—is increasing rapidly. As people in each age group differ in their consumption patterns, different marketing strategies are needed.

> For example, the demographic group that is eligible for senior citizen discounts is exploding. The travel industry has recognized this shift and offers special discounts of 10 to 30 percent on airline, car rental, and hotel costs to those 50 years and older. There are now more than 75 million Americans who qualify.[7] D

The 50-plus market is expected to grow more than 50 percent in the next 30 years, according to the U.S. Bureau of the Census. Figure 10–3 illustrates how the explosion is expected to occur.

The most dramatic population shifts now occurring are the aging of the baby boomers and the need to use and conserve the skills and work ethic of older workers. According to one authority, the aging of the "boomers" coincided with a change in their work ethic. On entering their 40s, they took stock of their lives and decided they wanted "a lifestyle at least as good as their predecessors'."[8] Members of this group are looking for more personal fulfillment, including more time with family and friends—and more time alone. This trend may cause a change in their spending habits.

The second trend—the need to use and conserve the skills of older workers—is forcing employers to find productive ways to use those who want to keep on working. During the coming decade, employers will have to

**Figure 10–2** Selling to Older Consumers

The growing ranks of older consumers and a decline in the size of the youth market are leading companies to redesign products and sales appeals to capture the increasingly influential senior citizen and aging baby boomer markets.

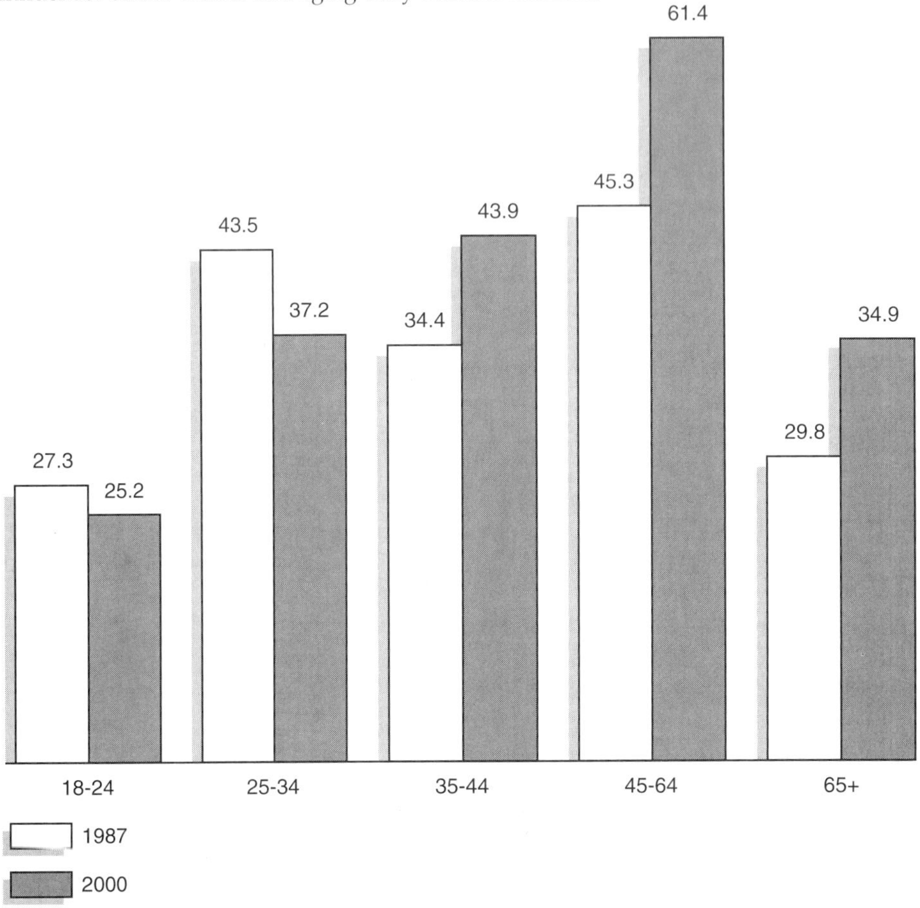


*Estimated.
*Source:* U.S. Census Bureau data, as reported in a Newhouse News Agency graphic, *Mobile* (Alabama) *Press Register,* March 5, 1989, p. 1-D. Mobile Press Register, © 1989. All rights reserved. Reprinted with permission.

choose from an aging work force, as shown in Figure 10–2, since there'll be a crunch for younger workers with both basic and technical skills. In fact, *the number of 18-to-35-year-olds will actually decline,* which will require redesigning jobs; rehiring retirees as consultants, advisers, or temporaries; using phased-in retirement programs; and aggressively recruiting older workers.

One of the most important sources of consumer purchasing power is personal income. By the year 2000, the household income of those earning over $35,000 should increase to 43 percent of the total, while that of those earning $15,000 to $35,000 should drop to 33 percent. These estimates are partly explained by the large increases in the number of two-income married couples as a percentage of all married couples. Purchases also vary considerably by region and state, and these variations affect your marketing plans.

**Figure 10–3** Senior Spenders—U.S. population age 50 and over, in millions

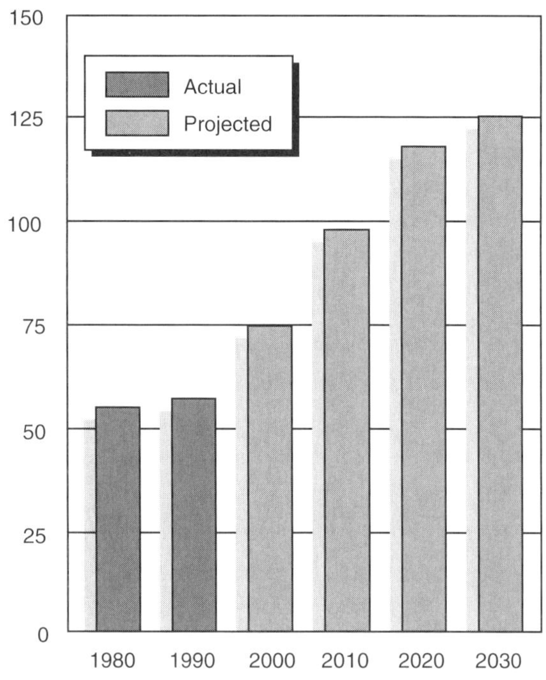


*Source:* U.S. Bureau of the Census, as reported in *The Wall Street Journal,* August 30, 1993, p. B2. Reprinted by permission of *The Wall Street Journal* © 1993 Dow Jones & Company, Inc. All Rights Reserved Worldwide.

*Regional Differences in Purchases.* Purchasing habits and patterns also vary by region. These variations are significant, for where people live is one of the best clues as to what they buy.

> For example, automakers tailor cars to specific regions to exploit regional differences in taste. In the Northeast, which has crowded freeways, drivers are concerned about safety. But in wide-open, less-crowded states such as Wyoming and Nebraska, car owners want to be sure that parts and service will be available. Texas drivers like lots of power and acceleration, while Californians look for dependability and passenger comfort.[9]

In the mid-1990s, demographic forces were dramatically changing the nation's geographic economic balance. In addition to the flood of immigrants into New York, Florida, California, and the Southwest, there was an internal mass migration. People were drawn from California and the Northern states to the Southern and Southwestern states. These latter states are experiencing an economic boom.[10] D

## Developing an Effective Marketing Mix

A **marketing mix** consists of controllable variables that the firm combines to satisfy the target market. Those variables are the Four Ps: product, place, promotion, and price. The right *product* for the target market must be developed. *Place* refers to the channels of distribution. *Promotion* refers to any method that communicates to the target market. The right *price* should be set to attract customers and make a profit.

A **marketing mix** is the proper blending of the basic elements of product, price, promotion, and place into an integrated marketing program.

## THE PRODUCT LIFE CYCLE

You may find that your most effective strategy is to concentrate on a narrow product line, develop a highly specialized product or service, or provide a product-service "package" containing an unusual amount of service. In setting strategy, competitors' products, prices, and services should be carefully analyzed. This is not easy to do because of the large number of new products introduced each year; for example, there were 17,000 new products introduced in the United States in 1992.[11]

### Stages of the Product Life Cycle

Products are much like living organisms: They are brought into the world, they live, and they die. When a new product is successfully introduced into the firm's market mix, it grows; when it loses appeal, it is discontinued. A new product may have a striking effect on the life cycle of other products as well.

> Phonograph records are a good illustration of the product life cycle. Although 78 RPM records coexisted with the 45s, they gave way to the long-playing vinyl 33s. Then the compact disc (CD) began to dominate the market, threatening all records, even the 45s, which had maintained their hold on jukeboxes. Jukeboxes that play CDs offer vastly superior quality, along with lower maintenance costs. By the early 1990s, although a few audiophiles still maintained that CDs were "cold" and "lifeless— and could not match vinyl LPs in richness of tone, CDs had almost entirely supplanted vinyl records, though they continued to coexist with the cheaper cassette tapes. In 1995, although CDs themselves seemed secure, CD *players* were threatened by new technologies. Most CD-ROM players also play audio discs, and digital video disc (DVD) players that can also play CDs look likely to be the next wave.

The **product life cycle** consists of four stages: introduction, growth, maturity, and decline.

As shown in Figure 10–4, the **product life cycle** has four major stages: introduction, growth, maturity, and decline. As a product moves through its cycle, the strategies relating to competition, promotion, distribution, pricing, and market information should be evaluated and possibly changed. You can use the life-cycle concept to time the introduction and improvement of profitable products and the dropping or recycling of unprofitable ones.

#### *Introduction Stage*

The introduction stage begins when a product first appears on the market. Prices are usually high, sales are low, and profits are negative because of high development, promotion, and distribution costs. In this stage, it is vital to communicate the product's features, uses, and advantages to potential buyers. Only a few new products—such as telephones, microwave ovens, and home computers—epresent major innovations. More often, a "new" product is an old one in a new form. Many products never get beyond the introduction stage because of insufficient or poor marketing research, design or production problems, or errors in timing the product's introduction.

**Figure 10–4** Sales and Profits during the Product Life Cycle*

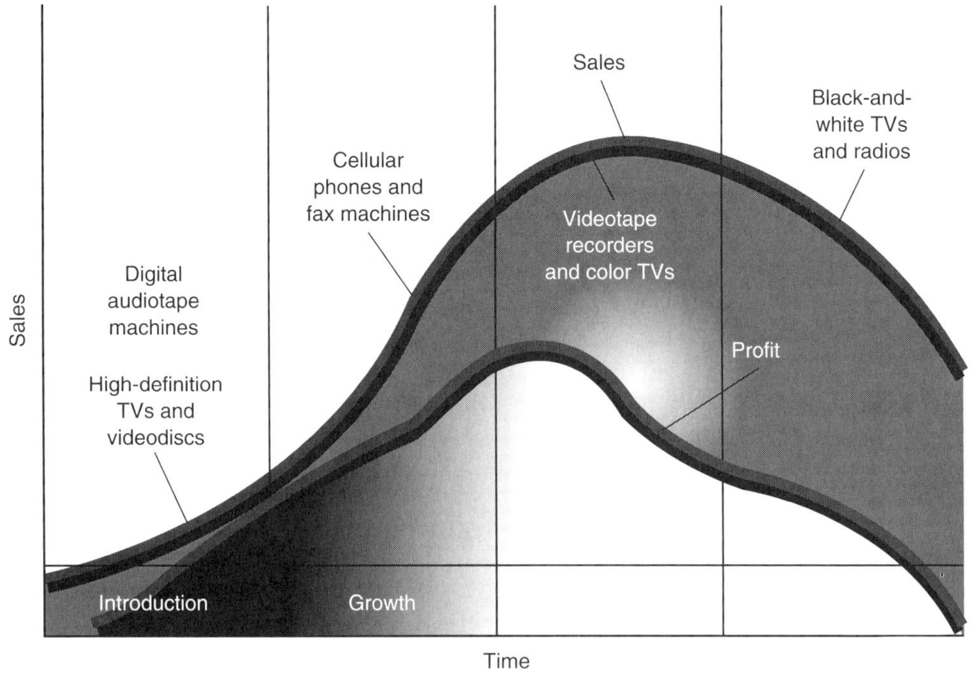


*Note that profit levels start to fall *before* sales reach their peak. When profits and sales start to decline, it's time to come out with a new product or remodel the old one to maintain interest and profits.
*Source:* William G. Nickels, James M. McHugh, and Susan M. McHugh, *Understanding Business*, 4th ed. (Burr Ridge, IL: Irwin, 1996), p. 449. Reprinted with permission.

## *Growth Stage*

During the growth stage, sales rise rapidly and profits peak. As competitors enter the market, they attempt to develop the best product design. During this stage, marketing strategy typically encourages strong brand loyalty. The product's benefits are identified and emphasized to develop a competitive niche.

## *Maturity Stage*

Competition becomes more aggressive during the maturity stage, with declining prices and profits. Promotion costs climb; competitors cut prices to attract business; new firms enter, further increasing competition; and weaker competitors are squeezed out. Those that remain make fresh promotional and distribution efforts.

## *Decline Stage*

Sales fall rapidly during the decline stage, especially if a new technology or a social trend is involved. Management considers pruning items from the product line to eliminate unprofitable ones. Promotion efforts may be cut and plans may be made to phase out the product.

For example, the Swanson TV Dinner, developed in 1955, had food to be cooked in an oven on an aluminum tray and eaten while watching TV. It flourished at the height of television's Golden Age but has now been relegated to the Smithsonian Institution for possible display at the National Museum of American History. As VCRs have facilitated "time shifting" of dinner-hour TV programs, the TV dinner has been replaced as a convenience food by microwavable meals that can be "nuked" in just a few minutes.[12]

### Need for a Wide Product Mix

The life-cycle concept indicates that many, if not most, products will eventually become unprofitable. Hence, small firms should investigate and evaluate market opportunities to launch new products or extend the life of existing ones. You should have a composite of life-cycle patterns, with various products in the mix at different life-cycle stages; as one product declines, other products are in the introduction, growth, or maturity stages. Some fads may last only a few weeks or months (consider the craze for Barbie dolls during the 1995 Christmas season), while other products (refrigerators, for example) may be essentially unchanged for years.

## Packaging

Packaging, because it both protects and promotes the product, is important both to you as well as to your customers. Packaging can make a product more convenient to use or store and can reduce spoiling or damage. Good packaging makes products easier to identify, promotes the brand at the store, and influences customers in making buying decisions.

G

Many top-selling global brands have a common thread—*and it's not money.* Products such as Coca-Cola, Campbell's soup, and Colgate toothpaste all have one very important thing in common—*they're all packaged in red!* Others with red logos or names are Kellogg's, Post, Nabisco, Dole, Del Monte, Lipton, Dentyne, and many other best sellers. Packaging experts and color psychologists say that a product's color and consumer buying preferences are closely linked. Red is considered to be warm and bright.[13]

A better box, wrapper, can, or bottle can help create a "new" product or market. For example, a small manufacturer introduced a liquid hand soap in a pump container, and it was an instant success. Sometimes, a new package improves a product by making it easier to use, such as motor oil sold in reclosable plastic containers. Packaging can also improve product safety, as when drugs and food are sold in child-proof bottles and tamper-resistant packages. Sometimes variations in packaging are a last resort when everything else has been tried.

In the summer of 1993, PepsiCo faced discouragingly slow growth in sales. The growing popularity of alternative beverages, such as iced teas, fruit-flavored drinks, and carbonated waters, had made inroads into the traditional cola market. So the company, having already tinkered with the contents of Pepsi—cutting calories, removing caffeine, changing the

Photo courtesy of PepsiCo.

color—began to focus on new boxes, bottles, and cans. As a result, shoppers in Pittsburgh could buy the Cube, a cardboard container holding 24 cans of Pepsi. Other areas were test markets for Pepsi Jr., a 12-ounce resealable bottle; Pepsi Mini, a compact 8-ounce can; and the Big Slam, a one-liter bottle.

Packaging has become increasingly important in a crowded market, says Michael Bellas, president of Beverage Marketing Group, a New York consulting firm. "Packaging now communicates something to the consumer. It could be value, purity, or quality," he says. "Before, you had a 12-ounce can, and that was it."

Indeed, packaging has been responsible for some of the largest increases in sales in the soft-drink industry. Now taken for granted, the six-pack and two-liter bottle are comparatively recent innovations.[14]

There now seems to be a reversal in recent packaging trends. Formerly, customers seemed to prefer recyclable packaging material—and lots of it. But *Packaging Digest,* a trade magazine, found that nearly 90 percent of surveyed consumers said no more packaging should be used than is necessary to protect the product. Ease of opening and reclosing the package ranked high with consumers.[15]

Photo by Philip Saltonstall; used by permission of *Forbes.*

Packaging was the problem Ted Taylor, of Fresh International Corporation in Salinas, California, had to overcome to achieve his dream of getting prepared fresh salads to consumers without going through the commodity produce markets. He wanted to bag a serving of salad that would stay fresh for weeks—without wilting and becoming discolored.

He solved his problem by developing (and patenting) his own bag, which slowed the rate at which the greens decompose. After his death in 1991, his sons, Bruce and Steve, carried on his marketing innovations—although Steve was skeptical at first. Now, Fresh International's "Fresh Express" prepackaged salad has 40 percent of the packaged-salads business.[16]

## How to Price Your Product

Pricing can make the difference between success and failure for any business, but it is especially crucial for small businesses. Dr. Anne B. Lowery, a marketing scholar, has concluded that owners of small businesses may not be able to consider all the many and complex economic variables involved in price setting. She has summarized demand, supply, and other variables into four categories, which she calls "the four Cs of pricing."[17] They are:

- Customer
- Company
- Competition
- Constraints

The first two categories are internal and therefore largely within the control of the owner or manager. The last two are generally considered external to the business and therefore largely beyond the control of the small business.

In considering these four categories, there are three practical aspects of pricing that you must consider. First, regardless of the desirability of the product, the price must be such that customers are willing—and able—to pay it.

Second, you must set your price to maintain or expand your market share and/or profit. If the new product is successful, competitors will introduce either a better product or a cheaper one.

Third, if you want to make a profit on the new product, the price must be sufficiently greater than cost to cover development, introduction, and operating costs.

### Establishing Pricing Policies

As shown in Table 10–2, there's a large variety of pricing policies you can adopt, but the first three deserve particular attention: product life cycle, meet the competition, and cost-oriented pricing.

#### *Effect of Product Life Cycle*

A **skimming price** is one set relatively high initially in order to rapidly skim off the "cream" of profits.

A **penetration price** is one set relatively low to secure market acceptance.

Notice the role played by the product life cycle, as discussed earlier. When you introduce a new product, you have two alternatives: (1) to set a **skimming price**, which will be high enough to obtain the "cream" of the target market before competitors enter, or (2) to set a **penetration price**, which will be low enough to obtain an adequate and sustainable market. Small producers sometimes use a combination approach, setting a realistic price but making an initial purchase more attractive by issuing discount coupons.

#### *Meeting the Competition*

You can also set prices by meeting the competition, that is, following the pricing practices of competitors. But this practice can lead to severe losses if cost and volume of sales aren't taken into account. Small firms with an attractive, possibly unique product should not be afraid to charge what the product is worth, considering not only what it costs to provide the product but also what the market will bear.

**Table 10–2** Potential Pricing Policies for a Small Business

| Policy area | Description |
|---|---|
| Product life cycle: | |
| Skimming price | Aimed at obtaining the "cream" of the target market at a high price before dealing with other market segments. |
| Penetration price | Intended to try to sell to the entire market at a low price. |
| Meet the competition | Below the market price. |
| | At the competitors' price level. |
| | Above the market price. |
| Cost-oriented pricing | Costs are accumulated for each unit of product, and a markup is added to obtain a base price. |
| Price flexibility: | |
| One price | Offering the same price to all customers who purchase goods under the same conditions and in the same quantities. |
| Flexible price | Offering the same products and quantities to different customers at different prices. |
| Suggested retail price | Manufacturers often print a suggested price on the product or invoice or in their catalog. |
| List prices | Published prices that remain the same for a long time. |
| Prestige pricing | Setting of high prices used, say, by fur retailers. |
| Leader pricing | Certain products are chosen for their promotional value and are priced low to entice customers into retail stores. |
| Bait pricing | An item is priced extremely low by a dealer, but the salesperson points out the disadvantages of the item and switches customers to items of higher quality and price. (This practice is illegal.) |
| Odd pricing | Prices end in certain numbers, usually odd, such as $0.95—e.g., $7.95, $8.95. |
| Psychological pricing | Certain prices for some products are psychologically appealing; there can be a range of prices that customers perceive as being equal to each other. |
| Price lining | Policy of setting a few price levels for given lines of merchandise—e.g., ties at three levels: $8, $16, and $25. |
| Demand-oriented pricing | Potential customer demand is recognized, and prospective revenues are considered in pricing. |

## *Cost-Oriented Pricing*

Cost-oriented pricing is basic to all pricing policies. Total costs provide a floor below which prices should not be permitted to go, especially for long periods. Cost-oriented pricing involves adding a markup to the cost of the item.

### *Markup*

**Markup** is the amount added to the product's cost to determine the selling price.

**Markup** is the amount added to the cost of the product to determine the selling price. Usually, the amount of the markup is determined by the type of product sold, the amount of service performed by the retailer, how rapidly the product sells, and the amount of planned profit. Markup may be expressed in terms of dollars and/or cents, or as a percentage.

The way to figure markup percentage on cost is:

$$\text{Markup as percentage of cost} = \frac{\text{Dollar amount of markup}}{\text{Cost of the item}}$$

For example, assume a retailer is pricing a new product that costs \$6. The selling price is set at \$9. Therefore, the total amount of markup is \$3: selling price (\$9) less cost (\$6) equals markup (\$3). The markup percentage, then, is:

$$\text{Markup percentage (cost)} = \frac{\$3}{\$6} = 50 \text{ percent}$$

### *Discounts and Allowances*

A **discount** is a reduction from the list price given to customers as an inducement to buy more of a product.

**Allowances** are given to customers for accepting quality or quantity reductions.

Sellers often use discounts and allowances to increase sales. **Discounts,** which are reductions from a product's normal list price, are given to customers as an inducement to buy the item. **Allowances** are given to customers for accepting less of something or as an adjustment for variations in quality. Some of the more popular discounts and allowances are shown in Table 10–3.

## How Prices Are Set by Small Businesses

Prices are set differently by small service firms, retailers, wholesalers, producers, and building contractors. Some of the more popular methods are described here.

### *By Service Firms*

Service firms either charge the "going rate" (that is, the usual rate for a given job) or they may set prices according to those prevalent in their industry. They try to set a price based on the cost of labor and materials used to provide the service, as well as direct charges, such as transportation costs, and a profit margin. Many firms charge customers an hourly rate, based on the time required to perform the services, plus any travel expenses. Others incorporate the labor, materials, and transportation costs into an hourly rate, or a rate based on some other variable.

### *By Retailers*

A **customary price** is what customers expect to pay because of custom, tradition, or social habits.

Different types of products are priced differently. Staple convenience goods, such as candy, gum, newspapers, and magazines, usually have customary prices or use the manufacturer's suggested retail price. **Customary prices** are the prices customers expect to pay as a result of custom, tradition, or social habits.

**Table 10–3** Discounts and Allowances Provided by Small Businesses

| Reduction | Description |
|---|---|
| Cash discounts | Given as a reduction in price to buyers who pay their bill within a specified time period (e.g., 2/10, net 30 days). |
| Functional or trade discounts | List price reductions given to channel members for performance of their functions. |
| Quantity discounts | Reduction in the unit price granted for buying in certain quantities. |
| Noncumulative | Apply to individual shipments or orders only. |
| Cumulative | Apply to purchases over a given period (e.g., a year). |
| Seasonal discounts | Induce buyers to stock earlier than immediate demand would dictate. |
| Promotional allowances | Provided by manufacturers and wholesalers to retailers for promotion (e.g., point-of-purchase display materials, per case discounts, and cooperative advertisements). |
| Trade-ins | Allowance provided to customer by retailer in the purchase of, say, a major electric appliance. |
| Push money or prize money | Allowances provided retailers by manufacturers or wholesalers to be given to salespersons for aggressively selling particular products. |

> For example, Hershey Chocolate Company sold candy bars for 5 cents in 1940. As cocoa and sugar became scarce and more expensive because of World War II, the price didn't rise for a while. Instead, the size of the bars was cut in half by the end of 1942.

G

Some discount and food stores discount prepriced items such as candy, gum, magazines, a set percentage—say 10 or even 20 percent. Food World discounts all prepriced items 10 percent, and Wal-Mart discounts greeting cards 20 percent and sewing patterns nearly 50 percent.

Fashion goods, by contrast, have high markups but are drastically marked down if they do not sell well. High markups are also used on novelty, specialty, and seasonal goods. When the novelty wears off, or the selling season ends, the price goes down.

> Early-bird shoppers after holidays expect to find markdowns up to 50 or even 75 percent on Christmas wraps and toys or on Easter candy and stuffed rabbits. Customers also expect discounts on novelty items marketed as "stocking stuffers," holiday party clothes, and extravagantly priced items intended as gifts.

**Unit pricing** is listing the product's price in terms of some unit, such as a pound, pint, or yard.

Most grocery stores use **unit pricing** for products such as meats, produce, and deli items, charging so much per ounce or pound for each item. Information about unit prices of other items facilitates comparison shopping by customers.

Although influenced by competitors', vendors', and customary prices, retailers still must determine their own prices for the products they sell. The retailer's selling price should cover the cost of goods, selling and other operating costs, and a profit margin. In some cases, however, a store might use **loss leaders**, or items sold below cost, to attract customers who may also buy more profitable items.

A **loss leader** is an item priced at or below cost to attract customers into the store to buy more profitable items.

### *By Wholesalers*

Wholesalers' prices are usually based on a markup set for each product line. Since wholesalers purchase in large quantities and cannot always immediately pass along price increases, price drops can cause heavy losses. Therefore, they may sometimes quote different prices to different buyers for the same products.

### *By Producers*

While meeting competitors' prices is common among small producers, many set their prices relative to the cost of production, using a break-even analysis. As shown in Chapter 18, their costs include purchasing, inventory, production, distribution, selling, and administrative costs, as well as a profit margin. Those figures are totaled to arrive at a final price.

### *By Building Contractors*

**Cost-plus pricing** is basing the price on the basis of all costs, plus a markup for profit.

Most building contractors use **cost-plus pricing**. They start with the cost of the land; add expected construction costs for items such as labor, materials, and supplies; add overhead costs; add financing and closing costs and legal fees; and add the real estate broker's fee. They then total the costs and add on a markup for profit. Figure 10–5 shows how this formula would apply to a $100,000 house being constructed in a big-city suburb.

## Other Aspects of Pricing

Product, delivery, service, and fulfillment of psychological needs make up the total package that the customer buys. A price should be consistent with the image the business wants to project. Since customers often equate the quality of unknown products with their prices, raising prices may actually increase sales.

However, the reverse might also be true: Selling at a low price might lead customers to think the product is of low quality. Sometimes, "cheap" can be too cheap, especially when compared to nationally advertised products.

In summary, small business owners commonly make two errors in setting prices for their products. First, they charge less than larger businesses and consider themselves price leaders. Because of their relatively small sales, costs per unit tend to be higher for a smaller business than for a larger one. Therefore, *small firms generally should not attempt to be price leaders.*

Second, many firms offering services performed personally by the owner undercharge during the early period of operation. The owner mistakenly

**Figure 10–5** Pricing a $100,000 House

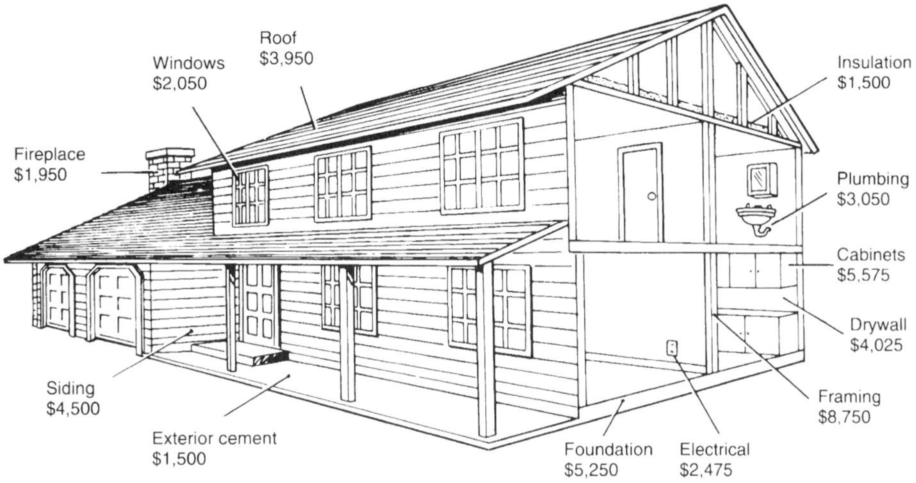


*Source:* Data from Carol Nanninga, "Constructing a Price," *Journal-American,* June 24, 1984, p. G1, as adapted by Louis E. Boone and David L. Kurtz, *Contemporary Marketing,* 5th ed. (New York: Dryden Press, 1986), p. 478. Reproduced with the permission of the *Journal-American.*

believes prices can be raised later as more customers are secured. However, it is easier to lower prices than to raise them, and raising them usually creates customer dissatisfaction.

## Strategy for Marketing Services

Because the service sector of our economy is so important and has certain unique features, we will cover strategies for marketing services separately from marketing goods.

### Nature of Service Businesses

There are two categories of services: personal and business. **Personal services** include activities such as financial services, transportation, health and beauty, lodging, advising and counseling, amusement, plumbing, maid services, real estate, and insurance. **Business services** may include some of these, plus others that are strictly business oriented, such as advertising agencies, market research firms, economic counselors, certified public accountants (CPAs), and personal service agents, as the following example illustrates.

**Personal services** are performed by a business for consumers.

**Business services** are provided to another business or professional.

> ProServ Inc., a Washington-based sports marketing firm, performs various services for professional athletes, such as representing them in salary talks with management, negotiating the contract, handling the player's investment and legal needs, and lining up product endorsements.[18]

Personal services can be performed by individuals or by automated equipment. Two examples of the latter are automatic car washes and computer time-sharing bureaus.

There are many opportunities in service industries because the demand for services is expected to grow faster than for most other types of businesses. Some reasons for increased spending on services include rising discretionary income, services as status symbols, more women working outside the home (and earning more), and a shorter workweek and more leisure time.

On the other hand, service businesses have severe competition, not only from other firms but also from potential customers who perform the services themselves and from manufacturers of do-it-yourself products.

## How Services Differ

Since service firms must be chosen on the basis of their perceived reputation, a good image is of utmost importance. There are few objective standards for measuring the quality of services, so they are often judged subjectively. Not only is a service usually complete before a buyer can evaluate its quality, but also defective services cannot be returned.

Services cannot be stored in inventory, especially by firms providing amusements, transportation services, and room accommodations. Special features or extra thoughtfulness that create a memorable experience will encourage repeat business in service firms.

G

Photo by David Rae Morris. Copyright 1995, USA TODAY. Reprinted with permission.

An excellent example of how special features can create a memorable experience that customers enjoy is the revival of "afternoon tea." Many modern hotels in Canada and the United States now follow this British tradition. The sales pitch for this tradition "in these hurry-up times is its relaxing quality," says Mort Hochstein, columnist for *Nation's Restaurant News.* The accompanying photo shows tea being served in Windsor Court Hotel's Le Salon, with a harpist playing and tea servers in lace-trimmed Victorian-style blouses and long skirts.[19]

The level of customer contact required to provide the service also varies. That is, the longer a customer remains in the service system, the greater the interaction between the server and customer. Generally, economies of scale are more difficult to achieve in high-contact services than in low-contact ones. For example, a beauty salon is a high-contact system, with the receptionist, shampoo person, and stylist all interacting with the customer. On the other hand, an automated car wash may have little contact with a customer.

## Developing Service Marketing Strategies

Strategies for marketing services differ according to the level of customer contact. For example, in low-contact services the business doesn't have to be located near the customer. But a high-contact service, such as a plumbing firm, must be close enough to quickly meet the customer's needs. Quality control in high-contact services consists basically of doing a good job and maintaining an image and good public relations. Thus, if employees have a poor attitude, the firm may lose customers. Sometimes a company can gain a competitive edge by turning a low-contact service into a high-contact one, departing from the service approach taken by competitors.

> For example, Mobil Corporation, suffering major losses in its gasoline retailing business, conducted extensive research that identified five types of gasoline buyers. Of these, only one type, representing only 20 percent of the total, based their buying decision solely on price. Moreover, some of the other types, such as the Road Warriors (higher-income, middle-aged men who drive 25,000 to 50,000 miles a year) and the True Blues (men and women with moderate to high incomes who are loyal to a brand and sometimes to a particular station) were more likely to buy premium gasoline and tended to spend much more not only on gas but also on convenience store items than the Price Shoppers.
>
> As a result, at Mobil, the focus is no longer on price competition. "The theory now," says a Mobil executive, "is to blow the customer away with product quality and service." The new strategy, dubbed Friendly Serve, has already proved to be a money maker, raising revenue as much as 25 percent at some of the stations experimenting with the concept. Just cleaning up the facilities and making them safer by increasing the light sparked sales gains of 2 to 5 percent, while adding helpful attendants pushed sales up another 15 to 20 percent.
>
> Adding services has allowed Mobil to raise pump prices. An extra two cents a gallon across the board translates into an additional $118 million a year and will not deter the shoppers Mobil is now trying to attract. "Most people don't worry about several cents," says an oil industry analyst. "They'd rather not have the pump nozzle greasy." Perhaps the most promising amenity, though, is uniformed attendants scurrying around looking for ways to help customers. One Orlando station manager sums it up: "We're going out there talking to our customers; we want them to feel like they're somebody."[20]

### *Primacy of the Marketing Concept*

The marketing concept is more important for service businesses than for other types of businesses, since customers often can perform the service themselves. The business must demonstrate why it is to the customer's advantage to let the service firm do the job.

### *Pricing Services*

The price for a service should reflect the quality, degree of expertise and specialization, and value of its performance to the buyer. As shown earlier, a high price tends to connote quality in the mind of the customer, so lower prices and price reductions may even have a negative effect on sales, particularly in people-based businesses.

The pricing of services in small firms often depends on value provided rather than on cost. Customers will pay whatever they think the service is worth, so pricing depends on what the market will bear. Pricing decisions often consider labor, materials, and transportation costs, as the following example illustrates.

Mobile Press Register photograph © 1989. All rights reserved.

Lynn Brown's Mini-Maid franchise team takes from 30 to 90 minutes to make beds, scour sinks, clean glass doors, sweep and mop or wax floors, vacuum carpets, clean bathrooms, polish furniture, load the dishwasher, wipe cabinets, shine counters, change bed linens, remove garbage, freshen the air, and do general pickup.

Brown furnishes all the cleaning supplies needed, as well as the labor. Depending on the size of the house, her prices range from approximately $25 to $50. Also, in estimating the price—which Brown does on the phone for new customers—she considers the frequency with which customers use her services. The more often they use Mini-Maid, the better their rate.

Brown has a small office in her home with a 24-hour-a-day answering service, but most of her workweek is spent in her minivan. Her biggest expenses are payroll, telephone, transportation, advertising, her answering service, and cleaning supplies. Brown says her success results from doing specific activities, in a specific way, for a specific price—which, as she says, is the Mini-Maid way.[21]

## *Promoting Services*

Word-of-mouth advertising, personal selling, and publicity are usually used by small firms to promote their business. Often, the message will have a consistent theme, which is related to the uniqueness of the service, key personnel, or the benefits gained by satisfied customers. Small service firms typically include the Yellow Pages, direct mail, and local newspapers. Specialty advertising, such as calendars with the firm's name, may be considered. Referrals, which ask satisfied customers to recommend the service to friends, can be quite effective. Belonging to professional and civic organizations and sponsoring public events are also important in building a firm's revenues and profitability, as the Profile for this chapter illustrates.

## Implementing Your Marketing Strategy

Now that you have developed your marketing strategy, how do you implement it? Implementation involves two stages: the introductory stage and the growth stage.

### The Introductory Stage

When introducing a new product, you should (1) analyze present and future market situations, (2) fit the product to the market, and (3) evaluate your company's resources.

#### *Analyze Market Situations*

This step determines the opportunities that lie in present and future market situations, as well as problems and adverse environmental trends that will affect your company. Because market size and growth are vital, potential growth rate should be forecast as accurately as possible.

#### *Fit Product to Market*

You should design your products to fit the market and then find other markets that fit those products. A market niche too small to interest large companies may be available.

> For example, a small firm manufacturing truck springs found that its product was a standard item produced by larger firms that could benefit from economies of scale. Because price competition was so severe, management decided to specialize in springs for swimming pool diving boards. This change in product strategy proved to be highly profitable.

#### *Evaluate Company Resources*

Your company's strengths, as well as its limitations, should be determined at each stage of the marketing process. Financial, cost, competitive, and timing pressures must be viewed realistically, and successes and failures need to be understood and regarded as important learning experiences.

### The Growth Stage

Once you begin to grow, you can adopt one of three strategies: (1) expand products to reach new classes of customers, (2) increase penetration in the existing target market, or (3) make no marketing innovations but try instead to hold your present market share by product design and manufacturing innovations.

#### *Expand Products to Reach New Markets*

To reach new markets, you may add related products within the present product line, add products unrelated to the present line, find new applications in new markets for the firm's product, or add customized products,

**Diversification** involves adding products that are unrelated to the present product line.

perhaps upgrading from low-quality to medium- or high-quality goods. This is **diversification**, or product line expansion, which tends to increase profits; contribute to long-range growth; stabilize production, employment, and payrolls; fill out a product line; and lower administrative overhead cost per unit.

G

> The fast-food industry, for example, is furiously competitive in the "comfort food" segment. Comfort food is food that tastes like home cooking. One chain—Boston Chicken—is renaming its operations "Boston Market" and adding turkey, ham, and meat loaf to its menu in most of its 565 stores. Boston Market projected that an additional 325 stores would open in 1995, and 3,000 would open internationally within the next 10 years.[22]

The major pitfall of diversification is that the firm may not have the resources to compete effectively. But the advantages seem to outweigh the pitfalls in most cases.

### *Increase Penetration of Present Market*

You may want to increase the sales of existing products to existing customers. If so, you might reduce the number and variety of products and models to produce substantial operating economies.

### *Make No Marketing Innovations*

The strategy of retaining current marketing practices without trying to innovate may suit your company if its strength lies in its technical competence. It is often advisable for retail store owners to follow this strategy.

Over the long term, a firm may follow one strategy for several years with the intent to change after certain marketing goals have been reached. But the change should occur if progress is desired.

## WHAT YOU SHOULD HAVE LEARNED

**1.** You use the marketing concept when you focus your efforts on satisfying customers' needs—at a profit. Consumer needs and market opportunities should be identified, and the target market(s) most likely to buy their products should be determined. You should seek a competitive edge that sets your firm apart from, and gives it an advantage over, competitors.

**2.** A marketing strategy involves setting marketing objectives and selecting target market(s) based on market segmentation. It means knowing consumers' needs, attitudes, and buying behavior, as well as studying population patterns, age groups, income levels, and regional patterns. Finally, the marketing mix, which consists of the controllable variables, product, place, promotion, and price, should weigh heavily in decision making.

The marketing strategies you can adopt are to expand products to reach new classes of customers, increase penetration in the existing target market, or make no marketing innovation but copy new marketing techniques instead.

**3.** A product life cycle has four major stages: introduction, growth, maturity, and decline. Strategies related to competition, promotion, distribution, and prices differ depending on the product's stage of the cycle.

**4.** Packaging both protects and promotes the product. It not only makes products more convenient and reduces spoiling or damage, but also makes products easier to identify, promotes the brand, and makes the purchase decision easier.

**5.** Pricing objectives should be set in order to achieve your firm's overall objectives. The "best" selling price should be cost and market oriented. Some pricing concerns for small businesses are product life cycle, meeting the competition, and cost orientation. Most small businesses use cost-oriented pricing methods, using markups, discounts, and allowances. Different types of small firms use varying pricing practices.

**6.** The marketing of services differs from the marketing of goods. There are few objective standards for measuring service quality, but quality should be emphasized. Also, price competition in standardized services is quite severe, output of service firms is difficult to standardize, and services cannot be stored.

## QUESTIONS FOR DISCUSSION

1. What is the marketing concept, and why is it so important to small firms?
2. How are the key success factors for a firm related to its competitive edge?
3. What is market segmentation, and how can it be made more effective?
4. Discuss some characteristics that should be considered in selecting a target market.
5. What controllable variables are combined into a marketing mix to satisfy the target market?
6. What are the major stages of the product life cycle, and how do marketing strategies differ at each stage?
7. In what ways is packaging important to small firms and their customers?
8. What are the three basic aspects that should be considered in pricing products? Explain cost-oriented pricing. What is markup?
9. Explain how service firms, retailers, wholesalers, manufacturers, and building contractors actually set prices.
10. How does the marketing of services differ from the marketing of goods?

# CASE 10

## FINDING A SPECIAL NICHE

As a future small business owner, you may be asking, "Could I start a business and compete with the big boys without getting stomped?" The answer is often a resounding "Yes!" A small firm can often home in on a market niche and take customers away from large businesses. Eastern Connection Inc. (ECI), a small overnight-delivery company, has challenged the overnight-delivery giants, such as Federal Express and UPS, for a piece of the pie. So far, ECI has experienced phenomenal success.

ECI has developed a simple marketing strategy. Instead of going head-to-head with its giant competitors, ECI has developed a regional niche, serving only major East Coast cities. ECI concentrates on high-volume locations and avoids delivering one or two packages to many remote places.

James Berluti, part owner and manager of ECI, employed a classic marketing strategy. Seeing that there was a need for a low-cost, regional overnight-delivery service, he began to plan how to best meet that need. He chose his target market: regional, high-volume locations. Berluti developed an aggressive marketing mix: lower prices than competitors' and guaranteed door-to-door delivery by 9 A.M. With $130,000 he had raised, he opened for business.

Berluti realizes that long-term success is not guaranteed. Multibillion-dollar Federal Express and UPS are quite capable of fighting back. ECI cannot even begin to match the millions of dollars spent on advertising by the "big boys." Nor can it hope to match the sophistication of Federal Express's computerized tracking system. Nevertheless, Berluti remains optimistic about the future. Believing that "people want the most purchasing power for their dollar," Berluti is convinced that in the overnight-delivery game he can provide this better than anybody else.

*Source:* Suzanne Alexander, "Small Firm's Single-Coast Strategy Delivers the Goods. Eastern Connection Finds a Regional Niche in Overnight Mail," *The Wall Street Journal*, March 6, 1991, p. B2. Reprinted by permission of *The Wall Street Journal* © 1991 Dow Jones & Company, Inc. All Rights Reserved Worldwide.

## QUESTIONS

1. Explain the marketing strategy employed by ECI.
2. In your opinion, what key factors are responsible for the success of this small business? Discuss.
3. Imagine that you have been hired as the company's new marketing manager. What recommendations would you make to ECI's manager?
4. Speculate as to whether or not ECI should expand out of its market niche and try to "grab a bigger piece of the pie."
5. Speculate as to this company's chances of long-term survival in this competitive market.

# APPLICATION 10-1

Akim, a high school teacher, wanted to earn some extra money to help provide better for himself, his wife, and their expected baby. After studying the lawn care business in the local area, he decided there was a place for him to operate a part-time business. His niche was cutting and caring for private lawns and doing contract work on common ground in prosperous neighborhoods.

Using his credit cards, Akim bought the equipment he needed. Then he used his home computer and printer to make up business cards and circulars to be distributed in the neighborhoods he had selected as his niche.

Akim priced his service by stating a low figure based on the time he thought it would take to finish the job. Then, based on that experience, he'd set a price to do the yard in the future.

Things went well until summer vacation. Then business improved so much that he couldn't handle it all by himself, but he had difficulty finding capable and dependable help. Also, many of his customers wouldn't pay when billed. Finally, unable to find a quick and reasonable source of repairs for his equipment—which he could ill afford, anyway—he called it quits after two years. He was unable to sell his equipment!

## QUESTIONS

1. What did Akim do right in starting his business?
2. Was there anything he should have done that he didn't do?
3. What marketing concepts apply to a small business of this nature?

# ACTIVITY 10–1

*Directions:* Use the description by each letter in "marketing strategies" to solve the puzzle below.

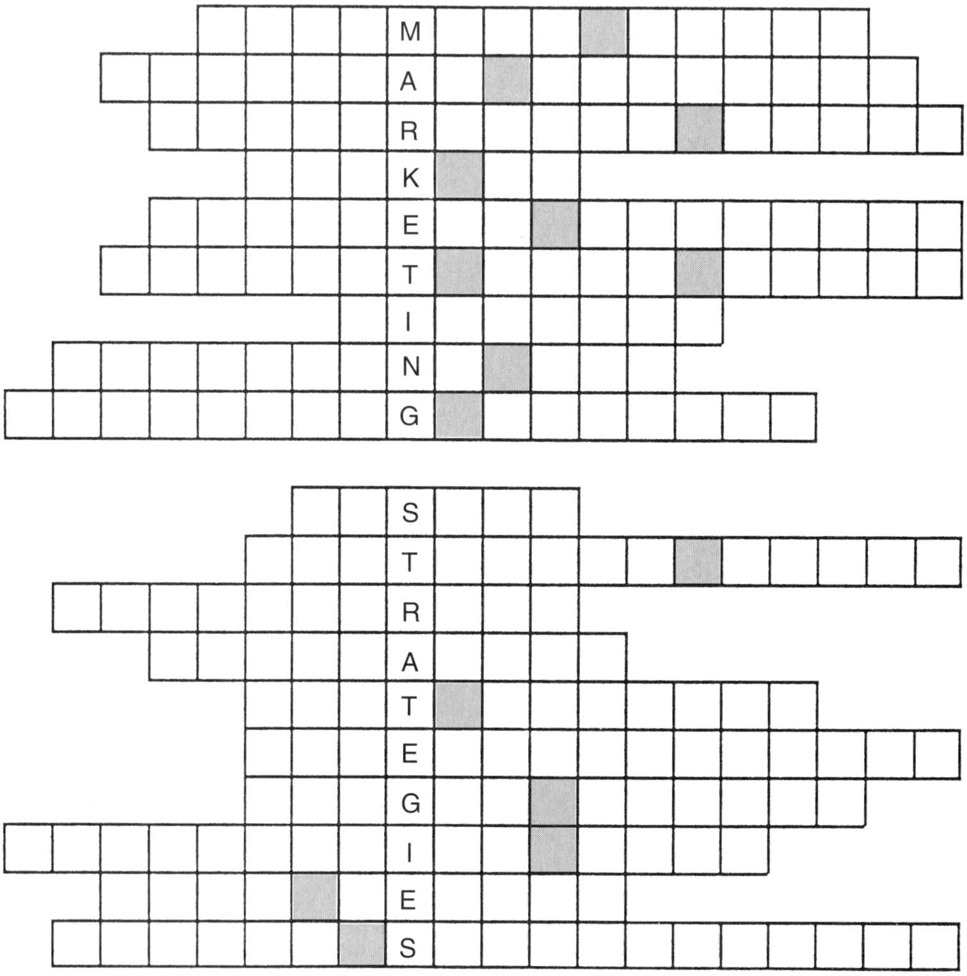

M High price to obtain "cream" of profits

A By business for consumers

R Set low to secure market acceptance

K Added to product's cost to determine selling price

E Provided to another business or professional

T Introduction, growth, maturity, and decline

I Inducement to buy more of a product

N Proper blending of elements into an integrated marketing program

G Give special consideration to present and prospective customer wishes

S All parts of the business work together

T What customers expect to pay

R Prodding businesses to improve product quality and expand consumer kowledge

A Given to customers for accepting quality or quantity reductions

T Listed as pound, pint, or yard

E Adding unrelated products to the present product line

G Where promotional efforts are concentrated

I Characteristic that makes a firm more attrative than its competitors

E Item priced below cost to sell more profitable items

S Identifying and evaluating various layers of a market

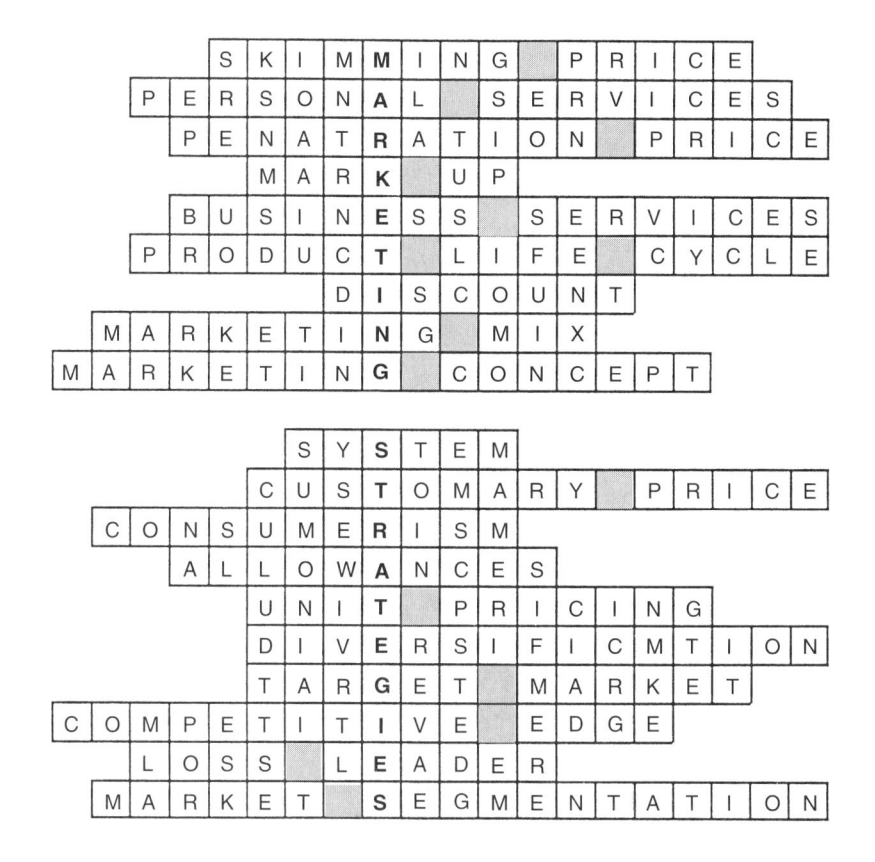

SKIMMING PRICE
PERSONAL SERVICES
PENETRATION PRICE
MARKUP
BUSINESS SERVICES
PRODUCT LIFE CYCLE
DISCOUNT
MARKETING MIX
MARKETING CONCEPT

SYSTEMS
CUSTOMARY PRICE
CONSUMERISM
ALLOWANCES
UNIT PRICING
DIVERSIFICATION
TARGET MARKET
COMPETITIVE EDGE
LOSS LEADER
MARKET SEGMENTATION

CHAPTER

# 11

# Marketing the Product

*Don't sell the steak; sell the "sizzle."*—Dale Carnegie sales slogan

*Sales-management skills are very different from selling skills, and talent in one area does not necessarily indicate talent in the other.*—Jack Falvey, management consultant, speaker, and writer

## LEARNING OBJECTIVES

After studying the material in this chapter, you will be able to:

1. Describe different channels of distribution used for marketing products and discuss factors to consider in choosing an appropriate channel.
2. Describe the functions of intermediaries used in selling a product.
3. Describe the creative selling process used in personal selling.
4. Describe the use of advertising to promote the sale of a product.
5. Explain the role(s) of merchandising, sales promotion, and publicity in a small business.
6. Discuss some opportunities and problems involved in selling to ethnic groups.

# PROFILE

## SPRINGDALE TRAVEL, INC.

In the late 1970s, Murray E. Cape recognized the profitable opportunities represented by the travel industry. Recognizing the imperfection in the marketing niche, he responded on May 22, 1978, by opening Springdale Travel, Inc. Springdale Travel represents all major airlines, tour companies, hotels, and cruise lines—both domestically and globally.

Photo courtesy of M. Jane Byrd

Since then, Springdale Travel, Inc., has grown into three different operational units: Cruise Quarters, which has four full-time and two part-time agents; Vacation World, with three full-time and one part-time agent; and—the heart of the business—Springdale Travel, with 23 full-time agents and 12 supporting services employees. In addition, the agency provides on-site services to five large corporations, with facilities in each of the client's corporate headquarters.

The travel agency accounts for many products and services. Currently, Springdale Travel, Inc., segments its target markets into the cruise market, vacation tours and packages, personal travel, and corporate travel. The product mix is approximately 65 percent corporate and 35 percent leisure travel.

Most of the services provided by the agency are customer requests via the telephone, as all the agents (including Cape) have a small workstation with a computer terminal and telephone. There are 30 incoming Essex system phone lines into the main office, with switching capabilities to Cruise Quarters and Vacation World. The beauty of the Essex system is that the lines can be tagged for specific uses, such as a specific number of lines to ring in, a specific number for calling out, and a specific number that are mixed for both incoming and outgoing calls. This system provides an effective control system for nonessential outgoing phone calls.

Another advantage is automatic call distribution (ACD), which assigns specific blocks of lines to particular agents or groups of agents. For example, certain agents are assigned to handle specific corporate accounts, and the system will ring on their lines first. If a given agent is busy, the call will cycle to any other reservation agent; if all other agents are busy, the system offers the client the option of holding or voice mail. All agents, including the on-site agents, log into the main phone system to receive calls.

Mail, facsimile, and Internet e-mail can also be used by customers to communicate with Springdale Travel. The agents can make and confirm most arrangements at first contact by using sophisticated computerized systems. When it is time to issue the ticket, the company will mail the customer's purchases, deliver them (locally), or hold them for pickup either at the agency or at the point of departure.

In addition to various local zoning and licensing requirements, Springdale Travel, Inc., must deal with many other regulations. Federal and state statutes govern agency relationships. Travel agencies apply to and receive appointment from the Airlines Reporting Corporation (ARC). ARC's purpose is to provide a method of approving authorized agency locations for the sale of transportation, as well as to specify cost-effective procedures for processing records and funds from ticket sales to member airlines. An appointment from ARC is an authorization to act as an agent on the member airline's behalf. Through the *ARC Handbook,* ARC provides a complex and specific agreement to which participating agencies must adhere. It contains many guidelines, including bonding requirements, application procedures for adding branch locations, specific document processing instructions, requirements for ordering and maintaining ticket stock, procedures for billing, and others.

Travel agents have a responsibility to represent the interests of the companies they serve. However, agents must also ensure that their clients receive the value and service they need. So Springdale Travel is a "go-between" representing the interests of both.

Photo courtesy of M. Jane Byrd

Springdale Travel, Cruise Quarters, and Vacation World are located next to one another in a busy shopping mall. Springdale Travel's main location opens onto the exterior of the shopping complex, while the other two maintain attractive storefronts that open directly into the mall near a main entrance. The storefront locations allow ever-changing window displays to attract the leisure traveler into the offices. Displays are frequently modified or changed to highlight the new attractions or "hot" vacation spots. This practice also allows for seasonal and market segmentation. For example, at the time of writing, Vacation World had a window display of the Tower of Terror, a new attraction at Disney's MGM theme park, that created a lot of interest in both adults and children.

All three locations feature entire walls filled with racks of attractive travel brochures and magazines. This arrangement allows the shopper a chance to browse for points of interest—both domestically and globally.

*Source:* Prepared by M. Jane Byrd from conversations and correspondence with Murray Cape, Bob Bender, and Kari Givens.

The Profile illustrates much of the material covered in this chapter. The people at Springdale Travel are creative in their advertising, sales promotion, and personal selling. This chapter deals with those subjects and also covers the channels of distribution to be used, the use of intermediaries for selling your product, other forms of promotion, and the importance of considering ethnic groups in marketing products.

## Choosing a Distribution Channel

One of the first things a small business producer of goods or services must do to promote sales of its product is to choose a distribution channel. A **distribution channel** consists of the various marketing organizations involved in moving the flow of goods and services from producer to user. The distribution channel acts as the pipeline through which a product flows. While the choice of distribution channels is quite important, it is not a simple one because of the many variables involved. Also, the channels for distributing consumer and industrial goods differ.

A **distribution channel** consists of the marketing organizations responsible for the flow of goods or services from the producer to the consumer.

### Distribution Channels for Consumer Goods

Figure 11–1 shows the traditional channels for distributing consumer goods. As you can see, a small business has essentially two choices: (1) to sell directly to the consumer or (2) to sell through one or more intermediaries. This decision is usually made (at least initially) when choosing what type of business to enter. The first channel (direct from producer to consumer) is the most frequently used by small firms, probably because it is the simplest.

As shown in Chapter 10, small firms performing services and selling goods at retail usually deal directly with consumers. Most of our discussion in this chapter will concentrate on the remaining channels, which use intermediaries.

> Louisiana strawberries are an interesting example of using channel 4. Because strawberries are so perishable, they must be sold quickly. So they are picked, placed in refrigerated railroad cars, and shipped before they are sold. As they travel north, agents or brokers contact wholesalers in cities along the line to Chicago. As the berries are sold, the cars carrying them are diverted to the appropriate city, where the wholesaler picks them up and sells them through the remainder of the channel.*

### Distribution Channels for Industrial Goods

Distribution channels for industrial goods are shown in Figure 11–2. Channel 1 (direct from producer to industrial user) is the most frequently used. In general, items produced in large quantities, but sold in relatively small amounts, move through channel 2. Large, bulky items that have relatively few buyers, or whose demand varies, flow through channel 3.

---

*Sometimes they are not sold by the time they reach Chicago, the train's destination, and must be sold at distressed prices or allowed to rot. Then the farmers not only lose the value of their crop but must pay transportation costs as well.

**Figure 11–1** Distribution Channels for Consumer Goods

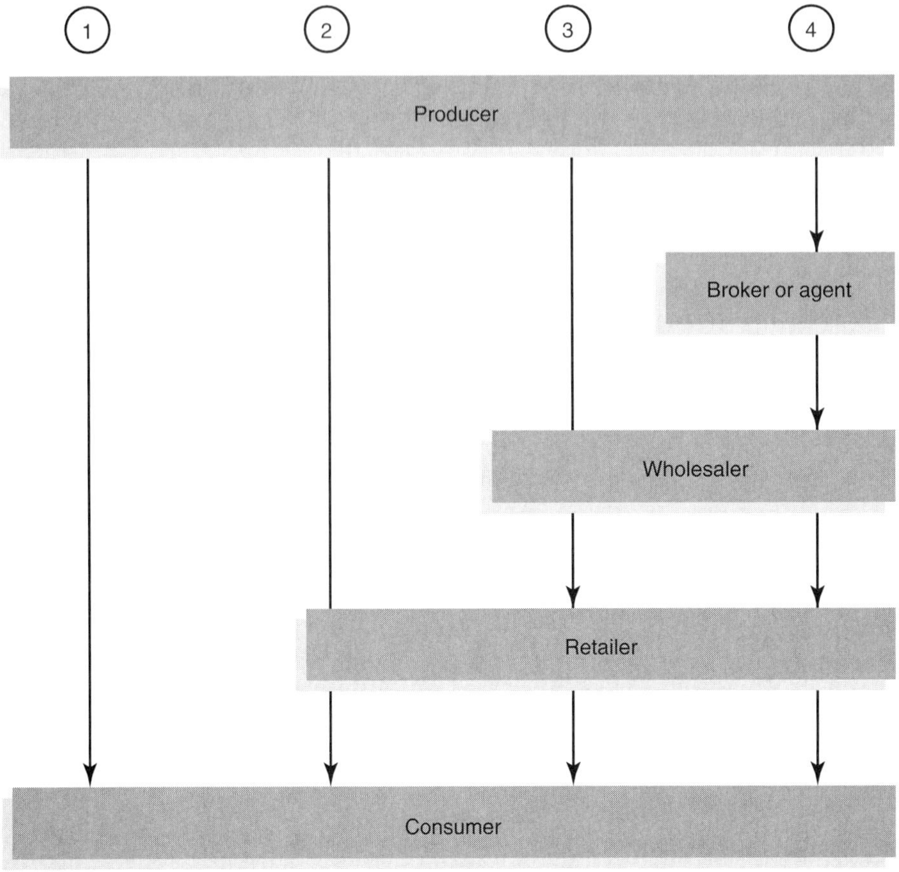


## Factors to Consider in Choosing a Distribution Channel

Small business producers should design their own distribution channels, if feasible, to attain the optimum income. In doing so, they need to seek a *balance between maintaining control over the flow of the product* and *minimizing the cost involved.* The primary factors to consider include the following:

- Geographical markets and consumer types arranged in order of importance.
- Whether the product will be distributed through many outlets, selected outlets, or exclusive distributors.
- Kind and amount of marketing effort the producer intends to exert.
- Need for receiving feedback about the product.
- Adequate incentives to motivate resellers.

New products commonly require distribution channels different from those used for well-established and widely accepted products. Thus, you may introduce a new product using one channel and then switch to another if the product does not sell well. Also, a new channel may be required

**Figure 11–2** Distribution Channels for Industrial Goods

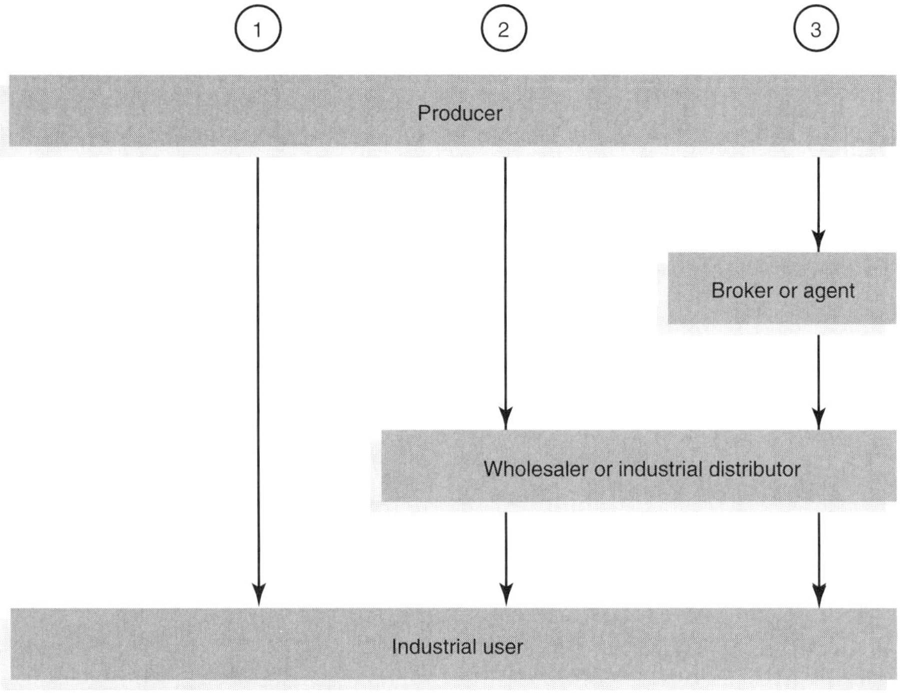


if you seek new markets for your products, as the following example illustrates.

> When Wendell Ward and Percy Hale bought Bellville Potato Chip Company, a small firm in Bellville, Texas, its annual sales were $275,000, but it was losing $12,000 a year. A year later, Ward and Hale made a profit of over $9,000 on sales of $1 million by selling through distributors instead of directly to retailers. The number of their accounts increased from 12 to more than 700.[1]

Finally, multiple distribution channels can create conflicts, and distribution can be hampered unless these conflicts are resolved. This problem should be anticipated and provided for. Choosing the right channel also permits a difference in pricing.

> For example, Hill's Science Diet dog and cat foods are so expensive that they could never compete with other pet foods in grocery stores, so they are sold in pet stores and by veterinarians to people who are evidently willing, on the vet's recommendation, to pay the premium price.

## Selling through Intermediaries

**Intermediaries** are those units or institutions in the channel of distribution that either take title to or negotiate the sale of the product. The usual intermediaries are: (1) brokers, (2) agents, (3) wholesalers, and (4) retailers.

**Intermediaries** are those units or institutions in the channel of distribution that either take title to or negotiate the sale of the product.

## Brokers

**Brokers** bring buyers and sellers of goods together to negotiate purchases or sales.

A **broker**, for a fee, brings the buyer and seller together to negotiate purchases or sales but does not take title to, or possession of, the goods. The broker has only limited authority to set prices and terms of sale. Firms using brokers usually buy and/or sell highly specialized goods and seasonal products not requiring constant distribution, such as strawberries or crude oil. Also, canned goods, frozen-food items, petroleum products, and household specialty products are often distributed through brokers.

## Agents

**Agents** are marketing intermediaries who market a product to others for a fee.

Because brokers operate on a onetime basis to bring buyers and sellers together, a small business that wants a more permanent distribution channel may use an agent to perform the marketing function. These **agents**, who market a product to others for a fee, are variously called *manufacturers' agents, selling agents,* or *sales representatives (reps),* depending on the industry.

## Wholesalers

**Wholesalers** are intermediaries who take title to the goods handled and then sell them to retailers or other intermediaries.

**Wholesalers** take actual physical possession of goods and then market them to retailers, other channel members, or industrial users. They maintain a sales force and provide services such as storage, delivery, credit to the buyer, product servicing, and sales promotion.

## Retailers

**Retailers** sell goods or services directly to the ultimate consumers.

**Retailers** sell goods and services directly to ultimate consumers. They may sell through store outlets, by mail order, or by means of home sales. Included in this category are services rendered in the home, such as installing draperies and repairing appliances.

### *Services Performed by Retailers*

Retailers must essentially determine and satisfy consumer needs. They deal with many customers, each making relatively small purchases. Some major decisions of retailers are what goods and services to offer to customers, what quality of goods and services to provide, whom to buy from and sell to, what type of promotion to use and how much, what price to charge, and what credit policy to follow.

### *Current Trends in Retailing*

The more traditional retail outlets are department stores, mass-merchandising shopping chains, specialty stores, discount stores, factory outlets, supermarkets, and mail-order selling.

**Off-price retailers** are those who buy designer labels and well-known brands of clothing at low prices and sell them at less than typical retail prices.

A newer version of the discount house is **off-price retailers**, such as T. J. Maxx and Hit or Miss. They buy designer labels and well-known brands of clothing at less than wholesale prices and pass the savings along to the customers, using mass-merchandising techniques and providing reduced services.

Another new development is self-service fast-food restaurants. Many of these are now following the gasoline companies' move to cheap, self-help "refueling stops."

**Figure 11–3** Using a "Refueling Stop"

Photo courtesy of the Southland Corporation.

> One such fast-food operation is the Southland Corporation (shown in Figure 11–3). At many of its stores, customers can select the food they want, heat it in a microwave oven, pay the cashier, and either eat the food there or carry it with them. This practice permits the customer to save time by shopping for gas, groceries, and other staples, while eating.

Even supermarkets now use this approach. First came self-service, with the customers selecting their own items, taking them to the checkout counter, and paying the checker-cashier. Now customers in some stores can select, ring up, and pay for their groceries using handheld scanners (see Using Technology to Succeed).

Another innovation is similar to automated teller machines (ATMs), namely, computerized video kiosks in shopping malls that replace salespersons. Many retailers are now installing these devices, which utilize existing technologies, such as computer science, video display, laser disks, voice recognition, and sophisticated graphics.

Shopping from television is another escalating trend. The following example illustrates this relatively new channel of distribution.

> During 1995, the QVC shopping network visited 50 states to find—and sell—offbeat products. During its 50-week "Quest for America's Best," the network sang the praises—and shared in the profits—of 1,000 products made by small-time entrepreneurs. The network sold $53 million worth of merchandise by the end of the Quest. On Saturday, December 16, QVC finished the Quest with a live broadcast featuring Hawaiian cottage industrialists selling seashell candles, tropical cooking sauces, and Kona coffee.

## USING TECHNOLOGY TO SUCCEED

### Honor System Grocery Shopping

Grocery store owners may soon be able to tell whether their customers are honest—or not. A few U.S. retailers have begun testing devices that permit customers to scan their own groceries as they shop, then ring up their own bills.

Symbol Technologies, Inc., which markets the handheld scanning devices used, reported that Finast Supermarkets, based in Maple Heights, Ohio, would be the first user of the technology in the United States, beginning in late 1995. The market's Dutch owner helped develop the technology. Symbol Technologies says a handful of other retailers planned to use the system in early 1996.

In most tests, shoppers entering the store pick up a scanner, which is similar in appearance to a cellular phone. Then each item is scanned as it is dropped into the shopping cart. If the shopper decides not to buy the item, it can be "unscanned." When the shopper has scanned all the desired items, the device prints a final bill, which in some cases can be paid by swiping a credit card through the scanner. Some stores even provide a take-home container that fits into the cart, thereby eliminating the need to unpack and repack items at the end of the line.

Regardless of its technological efficiency, the future of self-scanning depends on the honesty of a store's customers. Thus, retailers agree that the real test is not of the modern equipment but of age-old human nature.

A study of the device in three grocery stores in the Netherlands found that the loss of products from the store shelves through theft or inventory error actually declined with self-scanning. But success in the Netherlands, where people are especially law-abiding, doesn't necessarily forecast what will happen in the rest of the world when the device is in full-scale use.

*Source:* Tara Parker-Pope, "New Devices Add Up Bill, Measure Shoppers' Honesty," *The Wall Street Journal*, June 6, 1995, p. B1. Reprinted with permission of THE WALL STREET JOURNAL, © 1989 Dow Jones & Company, Inc. All Rights Reserved Worldwide.

> The top seller of the year was Donald Hodgskin of Orlando, Florida, who sold 109,559 electrical devices for chasing away mice, rats, and roaches—called Riddex Pest Repellers. Sales of the units were $4.6 million for the year.[2]

Q

Another emerging marketing channel is the Internet (discussed later in the chapter). People are now using it to swap items and information. And some people are using it to sell information, products, and services.

## Selling with Your Own Sales Force

Selling expertise is needed in all business activities. While advertising may entice customers to desire a product, it alone is not usually sufficient to complete a sale. Customers appreciate good selling and dislike poor service. They believe salespersons should show an interest in them and assist them in their buying. Often, when competing businesses carry the same merchandise, the caliber of the salespeople is the principal reason one outsells the other. The following letter, which came from a homemaker in the Washington, D.C., area, illustrates this point.

> I went to the cosmetic counter at Lord & Taylor, intending to get one or—at the most—two items. Instead, the Estée Lauder area sales rep who

> was there gave me such an overwhelming sales pitch that I ended up buying a horrifying amount of stuff. In addition, they signed me up for the free workshop next week, where they will make me over to show what I should be wearing. After trying *three* Lauder counters in *three* different stores *with no satisfaction,* it was nice to have someone take *a personal interest in me.*[3]

## Need for Personal Selling

In self-service operations, the burden of selling merchandise is placed on the producer's packaging and the retailer's display of the merchandise. Some retailers have found that 80 percent of the shoppers who made unplanned purchases bought products because they saw them effectively displayed. Self-service reduces retail costs by having smaller sales salaries and more effective use of store space. However, risks from pilferage and breakage increase.

Some items are packaged differently for self-service. For example, where film is kept behind the counter, the boxes are stacked in bins; but for self-service, the box has a large extra flap with a hole, permitting it to hang on an arm, which increases its visibility and also cuts down on shoplifting. Similarly, the same pens that stand en masse in a bin display in a small office supplies store are packaged in hanging blister packs in drug, grocery, and variety stores.

A quiet revolution is sweeping department store retailing in an effort to counter such factors as apathy, lack of training, and lack of initiative, which have kept salespeople's productivity (and pay) low. Now many retailers are using straight commission, rather than salary or salary plus commission, to pay their salespeople. They hope that the promise of potentially higher pay will motivate existing staff and attract better salespeople (and encourage them to train and develop themselves to be better producers). It seems to be working, as the following example shows.

> John L. Palmerio, a veteran salesman in the men's shoe department at the Manhattan Bloomingdale's store, increased his earnings by 25 percent after switching from a straight hourly scale to a 10 percent commission on sales. Similar experiences are being found at other stores, including the Burdines chain in Florida.[4]

The largest promotional expenditure for small businesses is almost always for personal selling. Effective sales personnel are especially important to small businesses, which have difficulty competing with large ones in such areas as variety, price, and promotion. Personal selling is one activity where small firms, particularly retailers, can compete with larger competitors—and win! But effective selling doesn't just happen. Rather, small business managers must work hard to attain a high level of sales effectiveness. They should be aware of what the selling process involves and of the attributes of effective salespeople.

## Steps in the Creative Selling Process

The creative selling process, as shown in Figure 11–4, may be divided into eight steps. You should inform your people that these steps are needed for effective selling—therefore, they should be known and used.

**Figure 11–4** Steps in the Sales Process

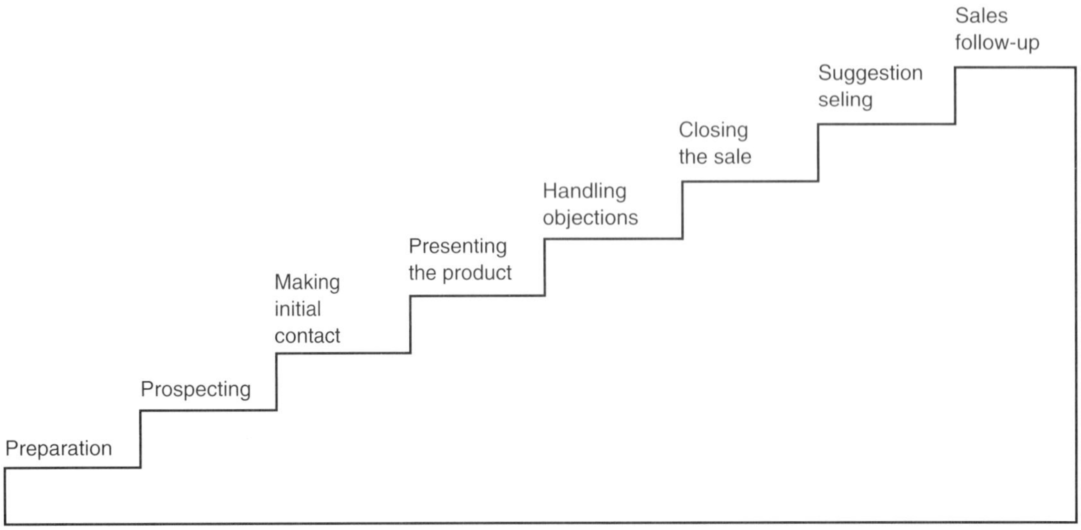


## *Preparation*

Before any customer contact is made, the salesperson should know the company's policies, procedures, and rules; how to operate equipment, such as the cash register; and a great deal about the product, including how and when to use it, its features in comparison with those of other models or brands, and available options (such as color, size, and price).

## *Prospecting*

**Prospecting** is taking the initiative in seeking out customers with a new product.

**Prospecting** consists of taking the initiative in dealing with new and regular customers by going to them with a new product or service idea. An example of new customer prospecting is when a salesperson contacts a prospective bride or new mother and tells her about goods or services that might be appropriate. Regular customer prospecting is effective because a firm's best prospects are its current customers. A salesperson should periodically call regular customers to tell them about products and services, but not so often that they lose the sense of being *special,* or feel they are being badgered.

Prospecting has become much easier with the introduction of address and phone information databases on CD-ROM. Given the 1990 U.S. Supreme Court ruling that phone companies can't copyright directories, a number of software developers have entered the market with CD-ROM-based directories priced so reasonably that many small businesses are beginning to use them to find potential customers. They can gain telemarketing and direct-mail opportunities without using—and paying for—directory assistance calls. Anyone who has a CD-ROM player and needs phone numbers is a potential customer, but CD-ROM databases offer businesses distinct advantages over printed directories because their listings can be sorted and searched not only by geographic area (city, county, state, or ZIP code) but also by industrial classification (for business listings) and in some cases even median home value and length of residence (for residential listings).

A highly rated CD-ROM phone directory is *Select Phone,* made by Pro CD Inc., of Danvers, Massachusetts. Sales at Pro CD doubled in 1994 to about $10 million. Unit sales are growing much faster, since prices of the software are plummeting.[5]

## *Making Initial Contact*

In the initial contact with a customer, the salesperson should begin on a positive note. The salesclerk might ask, "May I help you?" The customer replies, "No, thank you. I'm just looking." This common, automatic greeting shows no creativity on the part of the clerk. Instead, salespeople should treat each customer as an individual, reacting differently to each one. Initial contact also includes acknowledging customers when they enter the sales area, even if they can't be waited on immediately. For example, you could say, "I'll be with you in a moment." When free, you should be sure to say, "Thank you for waiting." These actions will result in fewer customers leaving without being served and produce a higher sales volume.

Whenever possible, serving customers should be given top priority. Nothing is more annoying to a customer than waiting while a clerk straightens stock, counts money, finishes a discussion with another clerk, or continues a phone conversation.

## *Presenting the Product*

In presenting the product to a customer, you should stress its benefits to the buyer. For example, to a customer interested in the fabric and styling of a suit, you could point out how becoming the color is or that the fabric is especially durable or easy to care for. Get the customer involved in the presentation by demonstrating several features of a garment and then have the customer handle it, as shown in Figure 11–5.

At this stage, you should limit the choices the customer has. For example, you could use the "rule of two"—don't show more than two choices at one time. If more than two items are placed before the customer, the chance of a

**Figure 11–5** Presenting the Product

Photo courtesy of Leon C. Megginson

sale lessens, and the possibility of shoplifting increases. For this reason, many stores limit the number of clothing items that may be taken to a dressing room.

Canned sales presentations are generally ineffective, so you should try to find out how much the customer already knows about the product in order to adapt the presentation to the level of the customer's expertise. A sale can be lost both by boring the customer with known facts and by using bewildering technical jargon.

### *Handling Objections*

Objections are a natural part of the selling process. Thus, if the customer presents objections, you should recognize that as a sign of progress, since a customer who doesn't plan to buy will seldom seek more information in this way. In many cases, an objection opens the way for you to do more selling. For example, if the customer says a dress looks out of date, you could answer, "Yes, it does look old-fashioned, but that style is back in fashion." This is more diplomatic than a flat contradiction, such as, "That dress was first shown at the market this season. It's the latest thing."

### *Closing the Sale*

Some closing techniques you can use to help the customer make the buying decision are offering a service ("May we deliver it to you this afternoon?"), giving a choice ("Do you want the five-piece or the eight-piece cooking set?"), or offering an incentive ("If you buy now, you get 10 percent off the already low price.").

### *Suggestion Selling*

You should make a definite suggestion for a possible additional sale. Statements such as "Will that be all?" or "Can I get you anything else?" are not positive suggestions. When a customer buys fabric, you should offer matching thread, buttons, and the appropriate interfacing. A supply of bags is a natural suggestion to a vacuum cleaner buyer. And customers' attention should always be drawn to other items in the product line. Many customers like to receive valid suggestions that keep them from having to come back later for needed accessories.

### *Sales Follow-Up*

Follow-up should be a part of every sale. The close, "Thank you for shopping with us," is a form of sales follow-up if said with enthusiasm and sincerity. The customer leaves on a positive note, and the potential for repeat business increases. Follow-up may also consist of checking on anything that was promised the customer after the sale. If delivery is scheduled for a given day or time, you could check to make sure the promise is met and, if not, notify the customer of the problem.

## Attributes of a Creative Salesperson

Many efforts have been made to identify and isolate those personal characteristics that can predict a knack for selling. So far, however, evidence indicates there is no perfect way to determine who will be successful, for salespeople just do not fit a neat pattern.[6] Still, there are some mental and physical attributes that seem to make some people more effective than others at selling.

Barry J. Farber, author of *State of the Art Selling*[7] and an audio training program of the same name,[8] emphasizes the attributes of a good salesperson by telling salespeople *what not to do.* Figure 11–6 provides his advice.

### *Mental Attributes*

Judgment—often called common sense, maturity, or intelligence—is essential for effective selling. For example, good salespeople don't argue with customers, nor do they criticize the business in front of customers. Tact is also needed. Good salespeople have a positive attitude toward customers, products, services, and the firm.

### *Physical Attributes*

Personal appearance is important for success. For example, a slim salesperson would be more appropriate than a larger person for a health spa. Poor personal hygiene may lead to lost business. An observant manager should watch out for hygiene problems among the staff and, when necessary, counsel offending employees in private.

**Figure 11–6** How to Lose a Sale

1. *Speak more than your potential client.* If you do all the talking, you won't be able to ascertain the needs of the buyer. The most successful sales reps spend 70 to 80 percent of the time listening.
2. *Wing it.* Don't call without first finding out as much as you can about your potential customer. Research the company's size, history, products, and challenges using *Hoover's Handbook, Dun & Bradstreet, Value Line,* or other such resources, which can be found at the library.
3. *Forget to ask questions.* Most people drift off after five or six minutes of a presentation, so be sure to interject questions to keep clients alert and involved. Focus on your buyer's criteria by asking, "What does the next vendor need to do to earn your business? What is your business's biggest challenge? What differentiates your company from your competition?"
4. *Rely on your memory.* You can't afford to miss important points, and nobody's memory is perfect. Ask the customer if it's okay to take notes, and use key points the customer made in a follow-up letter after the sales call. Start it with, "Just to make sure we're on the right track, the following is a list of your key needs . . ."
5. *Go off on tangents.* Instead of expounding on every passing thought, stay focused to make a strong case. Before you start your presentation, give your customers an overview of what you'll be telling them, and highlight key points at the end. Don't forget to follow up.

*Source:* Reprinted from Barry J. Farber, as reported in *AT&T Powersource* 1 (Spring 1995): 20.

## Advertising

**Advertising** informs customers of the availability, desirability, and uses of a product.

**Advertising** informs customers of the availability, desirability, and uses of a product. It also tries to convince customers that the products are superior to those of competitors.

### Types of Advertising

**Product advertising** calls attention to or explains a specific product.

**Institutional advertising** is selling an idea about the company.

Advertising can be either product or institutional. **Product advertising** is self-explanatory; **institutional advertising** is selling an idea about the company. Most advertising by small firms is a combination of the two. Institutional advertising tries to keep the public conscious of the company and its good reputation while also trying to sell specific products, as the following example illustrates.

Photo courtesy of Wendy's International

R. David Thomas, the founder of Wendy's Old Fashioned Hamburgers restaurants, named the business after his daughter, Melinda Lou, nicknamed "Wendy" by her brothers and sisters. In 1989, he began appearing in a series of TV ads built around Wendy. In one ad, he emphasizes quality by saying, "The hamburgers have to be good, or I wouldn't have named the place after my daughter." In another ad, when a voice chides Thomas about his efforts to align a menu board of Wendy's new products, he turns in exasperation and asks, "Wendy, don't you have anything else to do?"

Thomas visits the restaurants and introduces himself with "Hi, I'm Wendy's dad." Market surveys have shown that the consumer identification of Wendy's has jumped about 14 percent, and its nearly 4,000 restaurants increased sales to more than $3 billion in 1992.[9]

### Developing the Advertising Program

To be most effective, an advertising program should be used over an extended time period. The advertising should include preparing customers to accept a new product, suggesting new uses for established products, and calling attention to special sales. Such a program requires four basic decisions: (1) how much money to budget and spend for advertising, (2) what media to use, (3) what to say and how to say it, and (4) what results are expected.

## Setting the Budget

Advertising costs should be controlled by an *advertising budget.* The most popular bases for establishing such a budget are: (1) a percentage of sales or profits, (2) units of sales, (3) objective (task), and (4) executive decision.

With the *percentage of sales or profits* method, advertising costs have a consistent relationship to the firm's sales volume and/or profit level. Thus, as sales/profits go up/down, advertising expenditures go up/down by the same percentage. One disadvantage of using this method is that advertising may be needed most when sales and profits fall. In the short run, cutting advertising expenses might result in small additions to profit; in the long run, it could lead to a deterioration in net income.

Using the *units of sales method,* the firm sets aside a fixed sum for each unit of product to be sold. It is difficult to use this method when advertising many different kinds of products, for sporadic or irregular markets, and for style merchandise. But, as the following example shows, it is useful for specialty goods and in situations where outside factors limit the amount of product available.

> In 1991, with a slump in the ski industry, a weak economy, and much larger rivals hogging market share, Volanti Ski Corporation of Boulder, Colorado, increased its ad budget to more than $1 million. It set aside nearly $200 per pair to advertise and market 4,800 pairs of stainless steel skis retailing for $425 to $525 each. Calls from interested customers increased to over 4,000 from "a handful" in 1990.[10]

While the *objective (task) method* is most accurate, it is also the most difficult and least used method for estimating an advertising budget. Specific objectives are set, such as "to sell 25 percent more of Product X by attracting the business of teenagers." Then the medium that best reaches this target market is chosen, and estimates are made concerning costs.

With the most popular method of all, the *executive decision method,* the marketing manager decides how much to spend. This method's effectiveness depends on the manager's experience and/or intuition.

## Selecting Advertising Media

The most popular advertising media used by small businesses are display ads in newspapers, store signs, direct mail, circulars and handbills, Yellow Pages ads, outdoor signs, radio, television, and the Internet. Probably the best medium for a small business, though, is word-of-mouth advertising from satisfied customers.

### *Some Popular Media Used by Small Firms*

*Display ads* in the local newspaper are effective for most retail and service businesses. *Store signs* are useful in announcing sales or special events and for recruiting personnel. High postage rates are making the use of *direct mail* more expensive. Offset and instant printing have simplified the preparation of small quantities of *circulars* and *handbills;* however, increased printing and distribution costs and the impact of local ordinances are negative features.

*Yellow Pages ads* are effective for special products, services, and repair shops. *Outdoor signs* are useful in announcing the opening or relocation of a business.

*Radio advertising* is helpful for small businesses in thinly populated areas. *Television* has generally been too costly and wasteful for many small firms to use. Now, however, local cable systems and low-power TV stations, broadcasting only 15 to 25 miles, have rates low enough to permit small firms to use them.[11]

**Infomercials** are long—usually, half-hour—TV ads hosted by a hyper "sellevangelist," selling a relatively new product or service.

While not a new advertising medium, the **infomercial** is an effective strategy for a small business in a fast-changing, or young, industry to emphasize its competitive advantages. These "omnipresent half-hour TV ads hosted by hyperthyroid 'sellevangelists,' "[12] can be effective in helping small firms keep growing and enter markets once dominated by giant competitors. However, if they are to be effective in sales, they must be produced professionally, by experts.

> Guthy-Renker, based in Palm Desert, California, is such a professional organization. In 1988, Bill Guthy and Greg Renker, both avid readers of personal success books, decided to make infomercials for a product they truly believed in. So they scraped together $100,000 and bought the rights to Napoleon Hill's book *Think and Grow Rich* and the audiotapes of Hill lecturing. They then hired ex-football great Fran Tarkenton to endorse the product. Next, they bought time on six small-market TV stations and started advertising the get-rich program. The infomercial, which was an instant hit, grossed nearly $10 million by 1988.
>
> The partners had decided earlier to make only high-quality productions and to keep their claims honest. The company ran up an impressive string of successes through the early 1990s selling cosmetics, personal motivation courses, and weight-loss programs. Their gross revenues were expected to top $100 million in 1994.[13]

The Internet *is* a new advertising medium that is exploding in use. As you can see from Figure 11–7, an American International College survey of Forbes 500 CEOs found they expect to generate almost 40 percent of annual sales via this medium within 10 years. But the Internet is also used by small-scale entrepreneurs.

**Figure 11–7** Business on the Internet

CEOs expect to generate almost 40 percent of annual sales via the Internet within 10 years. Percentages who expect their industry will use the Internet to let customers:

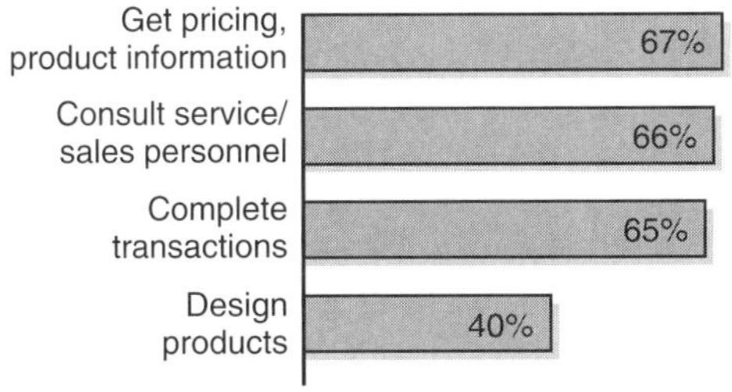


*Source:* American International College survey of Forbes 500 CEOs, as reported in *USA Today,* September 22, 1995, p. 1A. Copyright 1995, USA TODAY. Reprinted with permission.

Instead of blasting out ads to millions of people on the Internet, Dave Asprey, the owner of West American T-shirt Company, occasionally places an e-mail message that only casually refers to the fact that he sells T-shirts.

Why does Asprey hold back? According to him, the Internet is his most important marketing medium. But, as the worldwide network of computer users is famously anticommercial, he fears too frequent use would permanently prejudice Internet users against him and his product. As he explains, "As long as I'm online, business is good, [but] if you exploit it, it's gone."[14]

Photo courtesy of *Entrepreneur Magazine*

## *How to Select the Appropriate Medium*

The medium (or media) you choose will depend on several factors, including the target market, cost, and availability. The media of choice are those that your *target market* pays most attention to, as Figure 11–8 illustrates.

For example, John Alexander's Los Angeles venture, Dreams Come True, Inc., arranges vacations and other events that thrill jaded globetrotters who've "been everywhere and done everything." As the 1990s recession

**Figure 11–8**

*"We may not be attractive to boys yet, but we're certainly attractive to advertisers."*

*Reprinted from* The Wall Street Journal *by permission of Cartoon Features Syndicate*

cut his business by a third, Alexander retargeted his direct mail and promotional activities to people with incomes of over $75,000. His clients dropped from 300 to 100, but the average price of his services increased fivefold, and overall sales and profits increased.[15]

When considering media costs, you must look at both absolute cost and relative cost. *Absolute cost* is the actual expenditure for running an ad. *Relative cost* is the relationship between the actual cost and the number of consumers the message reaches (typically, the cost per 1,000 consumers reached). Finding the lower relative cost should be your objective.

Availability must also be considered, for the local situation will affect the number and kind of media used. Generally, retailers in small communities have fewer options than those in large cities.

## Developing the Message

The ideas or information you want to convey should be translated into words and symbols relevant to the target market. To do so, you must decide what is to be said, how it is to be said, what form it will take, and what its style and design will be.

Skilled employees of the chosen medium can help you develop the ads once you have decided on the central idea. Businesses can also get help from an advertising agency or a graphic arts firm.

## When and How to Use an Advertising Agency

Most small business managers plan their own ad programs, particularly when they consider the rather high costs of retaining the services of an advertising agency. This practice may be false economy, however, because advertising agencies with experienced specialists can help you by: (1) performing preliminary studies and analyses; (2) developing, implementing, and evaluating an advertising plan; and (3) following up on the advertising. Most small agencies tend to specialize in one area. For example, remember from the Profile of Chapter 2 how Try J. Advertising specializes in the automotive field, especially automobile dealerships.

## Measuring the Results of Advertising

**Immediate-response advertising** tries to get customers to buy a product within a short period of time so that response can be easily measured.

Measuring the results of advertising is important. Assume you want to determine whether your advertising is doing the job it was intended to do. You could do so by using some form of immediate-response advertising. **Immediate-response advertising** attempts to entice potential customers to buy a particular product from the business within a short time, such as a day, weekend, or week. The advertising should then be checked for results shortly after its appearance. Some ways of measuring results of these ads are coupons (especially for food and drug items) brought to the store, letters or phone requests referring to the ads, the amount of sales of a particular item, and checks on store traffic. Comparing sales during an offer period to normal sales, tallying mail and phone orders, and switching offers among different media can help determine which medium was more effective.

## Merchandising, Sales Promotion, and Publicity

There are some indications that many businesses are shifting their marketing to other forms of sales promotion.[16] Therefore, merchandising, sales promotion, and publicity are becoming more important in selling a product.

### Merchandising

**Merchandising** is the promotional effort made for a product in retailing firms, especially at the point of purchase. It is the way the product is presented to customers, including items such as window displays, store banners, product label and packaging, and product demonstrations. Window and counter displays are especially effective if they are attractively done and changed frequently. Some manufacturers and wholesalers provide retailers with advice on how to design better store displays and layouts.

**Merchandising** is promoting the sale of a product at the point of purchase.

Some retailers, however, use their own initiative in developing an effective merchandising strategy. the following example shows what one entrepreneur did to merchandise his stores.

Q

> Richard Ost owns three of the smallest drugstores you probably ever saw. Located in one of Philadelphia's "most bombed-out and burned-up" neighborhoods, he was doing $5 million of business a year in 1995, more than twice the rate of average drugstores.
>
> How does he do it? By weaving himself into the fabric of the community. In retail health care, nothing succeeds like sensitivity. So Ost instructs his employees to "be culturally competent." He enforced this idea by labeling prescriptions in Spanish for his Hispanic customers. He loaded into his computer some 1,000 common regimens in Spanish. With a single keystroke, any one of these could be printed in Spanish rather than its English equivalent. Business took off! The program was so popular that he was the first Anglo in the community named "Hispanic Citizen of the Year."
>
> After he bought his second location, an Asian influx hit his business, so he started labeling prescriptions in Vietnamese as well. Soon he was filling over 400 prescriptions a day at just the second location—half in English, 30 percent in Spanish, and 20 percent in Vietnamese.[17]

### Sales Promotion

**Sales promotion,** or activities that try to make other sales efforts (such as advertising) more effective, includes consumer promotions, trade promotions, and sales force promotions. *Consumer promotions* use coupons, discounts, contests, trading stamps, samples, and so forth. *Trade promotions* include advertising specialties, free goods, buying allowances, merchandise allowances, cooperative advertising, and free items given as premiums. *Sales force promotions* consist of benefits, such as contests, bonuses, extra commissions, and sales rallies, that encourage salespeople to increase their selling effectiveness.

**Sales promotion** includes marketing activities (other than advertising and personal selling) that stimulate consumer purchasing and dealer effectiveness.

There are many examples of such promotions. Retailers usually promote the opening of their business. A premium (or bonus item) may be given with the purchase of a product. During out-of-season periods, coupons offering a discount may be given to stimulate sales by attracting new customers. Holidays, store remodeling or expansion, store anniversaries, special purchases, fashion shows, or the presence in the store of a celebrity are other events suitable for promotions.

> In the 1800s, William Wrigley, Jr., left Philadelphia for Chicago to sell soap. He offered baking soda to customers as an incentive to buy soap. Then he tried giving away chewing gum to get people to buy baking soda. Since gum sold best, he concentrated on selling it.
>
> When Wrigley first offered Spearmint in 1893, his marketing message was: "Tell 'em quick and tell 'em often." As a promotional gimmick, he sent a stick of gum to every person listed in the U.S. phone book in 1915.[18]

### Publicity

**Publicity** is information about a business that is published without charge.

**Publicity** can be considered free advertising. When your product, your business, or you as the owner become newsworthy, publicity may result. Many local newspapers are interested in publicizing the opening of a new store or business in their area. Take the initiative by sending a well-written publicity release to a news editor for possible use. Also, information about a new product or employees who perform various community services may be interesting to the editor.

## Considering Ethnic Differences

There are growing opportunities for small businesses to increase the sales of their product to ethnic groups, for they are growing much faster than traditional markets.

D G

However, ethnic groups may require special attention in promoting your product.[19] Language differences are an obvious example, since more than 10 percent of U.S. families speak a language other than English in their home. Some areas have an even higher percentage. For example, about one out of three households in Miami and San Antonio speaks Spanish. You should be careful, however, not to regard all members of an ethnic group as a single target market. Some minority groups seem to be striving for what they perceive as white middle-income standards in material goods. Others disregard these objectives in favor of their traditional values.

The demographics for ethnic groups may vary, too. The median age of most such groups is much lower than that of whites. Since more minorities are in the earlier stages of the family life cycle, they constitute a better market for certain goods, especially durable goods. Separate marketing strategies may be needed for these ethnically or racially defined markets.

The second trend is the growing use of advertising on Hispanic TV stations. The two Spanish-language networks, Telemundo Group Inc. and Univision Inc., attract about 5 percent of the total audience during prime-time television viewing. Univision, founded in 1962, reaches about 85 percent of the nation's 6 million Hispanic households. Telemundo, founded in 1986, reaches about 75 percent.[20] Now, companies such as Domino's Pizza have specialized Hispanic media campaigns for selected areas.[21]

# WHAT YOU SHOULD HAVE LEARNED

**1.** Marketing a product begins with deciding how to get it into the users' hands through a distribution channel. A small business essentially has the choice of selling directly to the customer or selling through intermediaries. In making the choice, you should be guided by the nature of the product, traditional practices in the industry, and the size of the business and of its market.

**2.** The usual intermediaries are brokers, independent agents, wholesalers, and retailers. A broker receives a commission for sales of merchandise without physically handling the goods. Independent agents, such as selling agents and manufacturers' agents (manufacturers' representatives), also represent clients for a commission, but they may do more actual selling than brokers.

Wholesalers take physical possession of the goods they sell and provide storage, delivery, credit to the buyer, product servicing, and sales promotion. Retailers buy goods from manufacturers or wholesalers and sell them to the ultimate consumer. Retailers determine customer needs and satisfy them with choice of location, goods, promotion, prices, and credit policy. The current trends in retailing are toward more self-service, more automation or computerization, and using TV and the Internet.

**3.** Personal selling is required at all levels of the marketing process. All sales personnel should know the steps in the creative selling process, namely, preparation, prospecting, making initial contact, presenting the product, handling objections, closing the sale, suggestion selling, and following up on the sale. A creative salesperson should possess judgment, tact, and a good attitude toward customers, products, services, and the firm.

**4.** Advertising should be continuous and governed by an advertising budget based on *(a)* a percentage of sales or profits, *(b)* a given amount per unit of desired sales, *(c)* the actual amount required to accomplish the sales objective, or *(d)* an executive decision. Advertising media include newspapers, store signs, direct mail, circulars and handbills, Yellow Pages ads, outdoor signs, radio, television, and the Internet. Infomercials are now extensively used to advertise specialty products.

Some factors affecting a company's choice of media are target market, cost, and availability. Using an advertising agency to develop and place advertisements may be desirable. The results of advertising should be measured to determine its effectiveness by some form of immediate-response advertising.

**5.** Merchandising includes window displays, store banners, product labeling and packaging, samples, and product demonstrations. Sales promotion consists of activities that try to make other sales efforts more effective. Publicity, a form of free advertising, may be achieved when a firm or its owner, products, or employees become newsworthy.

**6.** Ethnic groups in the United States may require special attention in the promotion of goods and services, but you should not lump all members of an ethnic group together, since many of them are now adopting the values and tastes of middle America and make up a new and distinct ethnic market.

## QUESTIONS FOR DISCUSSION

1. What are the traditional channels of distribution for consumer goods? Which one is most frequently used? Why?
2. What are three traditional channels of distribution for industrial goods?
3. What factors should be considered in choosing a channel of distribution?
4. Name two types of independent agents. What are the advantages and disadvantages of using them?
5. Why do small businesses use their own sales force? What are some problems involved?
6. Describe the eight steps in the creative selling process.
7. What basic decisions should be made about an advertising program?
8. Distinguish between product and institutional advertising.
9. What are some important functions performed by advertising agencies?
10. What is involved in sales promotion?
11. Describe some opportunities and problems in catering to ethnic differences.

## *CASE 11*

### TAKING YOUR STORE TO YOUR CUSTOMERS

There are several channels that producers can use to get their products to the market. Sometimes these distribution channels may be long and complicated, using several intermediaries between the producer and consumer. However, as Sarah Hammet, owner of Feeling Special Fashions, has shown, it does not have to be that complicated.

Hammet sells clothing specially designed for senior citizens. It is called "adaptive" clothing—dresses and separates for seniors whose mobility and dexterity are restricted. Hammet bypasses the usual intermediaries, such as retail stores, and takes her product directly to the customers. She sells clothing at 50 nursing homes and retirement communities in two states and the District of Columbia.

Four days out of the week, every spring and fall, Hammet and an assistant load half a dozen racks of clothes into the back of a van and hit the road. She conducts fashion shows and offers individual consultations at every facility they visit. This type of personal selling has been effective for Hammet, who thought up the idea in the early 1980s while visiting her elderly father in a Kentucky nursing home. She was appalled by the careless and drab manner in which patients were dressed. Hammet perceived a need and stepped in to fill it.

The clothing she sells is manufactured by Comfort Clothing, Inc., which is located in Canada. The items are stylishly designed and come in various colors and prints. The clothing is different in that armholes are bigger, buttons often hide Velcro® fastenings, and waists are uncinched and come with optional belts. The garments can be stepped into rather than pulled on over the head. They are washable and cost between $40 and $60. Through a combination of creative merchandising and personal selling, Hammet has established a growing business.

## QUESTIONS

1. What type of distribution channels does Feeling Special Fashions use?
2. Should Sarah Hammet consider selling through intermediaries, such as retailers? Discuss the advantages and disadvantages.
3. How would you rate Hammet's selling strategy? Recommend ways she could increase sales.
4. Should Feeling Special Fashions advertise? Discuss the advantages and disadvantages.
5. How do you rate Hammet's chances for success? Why?

# APPLICATION 11–1

J&J Computers (introduced in Application 1–1) grew into a small corporation with huge annual sales. At that point in its growth, the company needed a new sales strategy to meet its customer demands. It had to decide whether to recruit its own sales force or sell its products through other retailers.

The managers decided to sell their products through other retailers and voted down the possibility of opening exclusive outlets. They also voted to increase their advertising budget to give more exposure to their product line.

## QUESTIONS

1. What options did J&J Computers have?
2. Do you think increasing advertising will help promote sales? Why? How?
3. Why do you think management voted down the option of opening exclusive outlets?

## APPLICATION 11–2

Mandy Smith inherited part of her grandfather's farm, on which there was a pecan orchard. Last fall she had an abundance of pecans, so she gathered up several bucketfuls with the help of several of her grandchildren and neighborhood children. She then had them shelled, bagged, and frozen for future baking purposes. However, there were many more pecans still left on the ground.

Hating to see them go to waste, but unable to gather them herself, Smith, at the suggestion of a friend, hired some people from the nearby town and paid them so much per bucket for what they picked up. Smith's friend also suggested that she run an ad in the newspaper telling people that they could come and pick their own pecans for a price much lower than what the local produce stands charged. Her only concern was what to do with the pecans her own workers had picked up.

### QUESTIONS

1. What are some areas of distribution for Smith to consider?
2. How can she find out more about distribution channels?

# ACTIVITY 11-1

*Directions:* Use information from this chapter to solve the "marketing matrix."

ACROSS

1 Selling an idea about a company

5 Bring buyers and sellers together to negotiate sales

7 Intermediaries for a fee

8 Stipulates purchasing and dealer effectiveness

9 Intermediaries who take title

11 Promote sale at point of purchase

12 Sell directly to ultimate consumer

13 Buy designer labels low and sell high

14 Taking initiative with new customers

DOWN

2 Get customer to buy within a short time

3 Marketing organization responsible for the flow of goods or services

4 Calls attention to a specific product

6 Published without charge

10 Informs customer

ACROSS 1 Institutional advertising 5 Brokers 7 Agents 8 Sales pomotion 9 Wholesalers 11 Merchandising 12 Retailers 13 Off price retailers 14 Prospecting DOWN 2 Immediate response advertising 3 Distribution channel 4 Product advertising 6 Publicity 10 Advertising

CHAPTER
12

# Global and Other Marketing Activities

*Time and space cannot be discarded, nor can we ignore the fact that we are citizens of the world.*
—Heywood Broun, author

*Your best customers can sometimes be your best source of information.*—John W. Sample, Miller Business Systems

## LEARNING OBJECTIVES

After studying the material in this chapter, you will be able to:

1. Describe the opportunities available to small businesses in international operations.
2. Discuss the need for marketing research in small businesses and describe how to do it.
3. Explain how physical distribution affects marketing strategy.
4. Discuss some problems involved in granting credit.

*P R O F I L E*

## NOTTOWAY PLANTATION HOME: A FOREIGN-OWNED AMERICAN CASTLE

G

Photo courtesy of Leon C. Megginson

The last half of the 1980s was a time of financial trouble for most Louisiana antebellum homes. Numerous efforts were made to convert historic plantation homes into profitable enterprises—especially as tourist stops.

While many attempts failed, Paul Ramsay, a Sydney, Australia, businessman, succeeded. While he admired the 22 massive Corinthian columns (made of cypress and painted white) that supported the 64 rooms and the more than 53,000 square feet of living space of Nottoway Plantation, he bought it as a revenue-producing investment. Ramsay asked the previous owner, Arline Dease, "What is your occupancy rate? How many tourists are there coming through each year?" Based on Dease's answer, Ramsay paid $4.5 million for the "American Castle" located on the Mississippi River in White Castle, Louisiana, west of New Orleans.

The Italianate and Greek Revival-style mansion was designed in 1849 to be "the largest and finest home in the South, and to be distinguished from all others." Completed in 1859, it was large enough to accommodate John H. Randolph, an extremely wealthy sugar grower, and his wife and 11 children. Living on other parts of the plantation were enough slaves to provide the services needed on a 7,000-acre sugar plantation.

Saved from total destruction during the Civil War by a Northern gunboat officer who was a former guest of the Randolphs, the plantation began to be restored as soon as hostilities ceased. But, as with so many other large plantations, it was hard to survive because of high labor costs.

Arline Dease bought the plantation house, which is surrounded by many old oak and pecan trees, and a small amount of acreage for $870,000 in March 1980. He began an authentic restoration of the property. In addition, he "worked for five long, hard years to build up a thriving tourist business." Five years later, he sold Nottoway to Ramsay for $4.5 million. It was later offered for sale in 1989 for $9 million, but there were no takers.

The plantation has six guest rooms and three elaborate suites in the mansion, plus four rooms in the overseer's cottage. The price of all rooms includes a tour of the mansion, sherry and nuts when guests arrive, a wake-up breakfast of hot sweet-potato muffins, fruit juice, and coffee, as well as a full plantation breakfast in the mansion's first-floor dining room. There is also a beautifully designed and appointed restaurant adjacent to the mansion that specializes in Cajun and Creole cuisine.

The plantation, which is managed by Cindy Hidalgo, expects over 100,000 visitors annually, including tours and overnight guests. According to Hidalgo, the money received from those tourists is at least enough to pay operating expenses and the mortgage debt.

Another Nottoway specialty is candlelight weddings performed in the White Ballroom, followed by a reception in one of the many elaborate rooms of the mansion. Visitors can enjoy swimming, hiking, and sightseeing, including standing on the levee east of the home and watching "that old man river" "it just keeps rolling along."

*Sources:* Various, including information published and provided by Nottoway Plantation Home; *Louisiana Bed & Breakfast,* published by the Louisiana Bed & Breakfast Association; "Romantic Escapes: Plantation Row," a travel program on The Learning Channel, September 25, 1995; and a visit to Nottoway by one of the authors and his wife.

The Profile illustrates an area of growing opportunities, and frustrations, for small firms: global marketing activities. That subject, plus marketing research, physical distribution, and credit management round out our presentation of the marketing activities of small businesses.

## Opportunities for Small Firms in Global Marketing

G

As the opening quotation from Heywood Broun indicates, "we are citizens of the world," whether as individuals or as small business owners. Think of the foreign products you use every day. Do you drive an Audi, Honda, Hyundai, Jaguar, Lexus, Nissan, or Mazda? If so, you're involved in global or international marketing. If the product is one that can be produced, bought, sold, or used almost anywhere in the world, you are engaging in **global marketing**. If, however, the product is one that is exchanged across only a few borders, you are involved in **international trade**.

**Global marketing** involves products that are produced, bought, sold, or used almost anywhere in the world.

**International trade** involves products that are exchanged across only a few borders.

A **multinational corporation** is an organization that does manufacturing and marketing in many countries and is owned and managed by people from many countries.

Both types of marketing are done by **multinational corporations**. A multinational corporation is an organization that does manufacturing and marketing in many countries; it has multinational stock ownership and management. By the time a business reaches this level, it has probably ceased to be a small business.

Look around you and see how many products originated outside the United States. Your coffee, tea, or cola drink? What type of music system do you use? Where was your television set or VCR produced? Look at the remote control to your electronic system and see if it was "Assembled in Mexico" or "Made in Malaysia." If you own a personal computer, chances are good that some of its components were designed, manufactured, or assembled in Japan, South Korea, or Taiwan.

Do you get the point? As students, teachers, consumers, and small business people, we're surrounded by the overwhelming evidence of global

*"Mama, you take the minutes of the meeting...Let's see, New York wants a good recipe for lasagna. What the heck is lasagna?"*

Cartoon by Fred Maes. Copyright by Fred Maes 1996.

and international operations. We estimate that *over half of you will work in some aspect of international activities during your working life.*

This truth not only applies in the United States but is true in Japan, South Africa, and many other countries.

G D

> For example, when NEC Corporation President Dr. Hisashi Kaneko was recently invited to speak at a famous Japanese university, he stated, "I think globalization is [very] important. If we do not open our minds to the challenges and opportunities of working in a global environment, we will never understand the world we live in."[1]
>
> For another example, turn to South Africa. The entrepreneurial adventurers are losing no time taking advantage of the opportunities in places such as Uganda, Malawi, Zimbabwe, and Mozambique. The projects they are working on include everything from trade to huge Western-funded infrastructure construction.[2]

Globalization is a challenge not only to small firms but to large ones as well. Andrew S. Grove, an immigrant who founded and is CEO of Intel Corporation, recently said, "Today's managers [must] adapt to a globalized business world [because] business knows no boundaries." He went on to say, "Every employee, therefore, must compete with every person in the world who is capable of doing the same job."[3]

International marketing has two faces. One is **importing**, which is purchasing and marketing the products of other nations. The other, **exporting**, consists of marketing our products to other nations. We now explore both these facets.

**Importing** involves purchasing and marketing other nations' products.

**Exporting** involves marketing our products to other nations.

## Importing by Small Firms

There are essentially two types of small business importers. First, there are those who engage in actual import activities by importing products and selling them to intermediaries or directly to customers. Second—and much more prevalent—are the millions of small retailers and service businesses that sell international products. Both types are interested in imports for a number of reasons.

**Figure 12–1** Test Your Trade IQ

**Can you go through the day without using something made in China?**

Where is it made?
Check one ✓
USA ☐ ☐ China

| | |
|---|---|
| ☐ ☐ Alarm clocks | ☐ ☐ Sheets and blankets |
| ☐ ☐ Sneakers | ☐ ☐ Vacuum cleaners |
| ☐ ☐ Cordless telephones | ☐ ☐ Miracle Bra |
| ☐ ☐ Christmas ornaments | ☐ ☐ Office machinery |
| ☐ ☐ Aladdin, the action figure | ☐ ☐ *Aladdin*, the video |

*Source:* Ellen Neuborne's visit to a Minneapolis, Minnesota, mall to see what Chinese-made products U.S. consumers use, as reported in *USA Today*, February 24, 1995, p. 1A. Copyright 1995, USA TODAY. Reprinted with permission.

Before reading further, take the test in Figure 12–1. The results will show you how knowledgeable you are about one of our trading partners, China. (See endnote 4 for the researchers' findings.[4])

## *Reasons for Importing*

G

First, imported goods may be the product the company sells to customers or the raw material for the goods it produces. The small company must decide whether to purchase U.S. products, if available, or to import foreign products. If the items are imported, does the company purchase them from a U.S. wholesaler or from firms outside the country?

Photo courtesy of William Waldorf.

Companies from other countries are just as interested in selling to U.S. markets as our producers are in selling to international markets. Thus, imported goods may form the main source of revenue—or competition—for a small business in all stages of buying, producing, and/or selling a product.

Q

Small business owners capitalize on the fact that some Americans have a preference for foreign goods or services. Goods such as English china, Japanese sports cars, Italian leather goods, Oriental carpets, Russian caviar, and French crystal are eagerly sought by American consumers. Also, small U.S. producers should understand that the increasing flow of new and improved products into the country can improve their output or increase their competitive level.

### *Some Problems with Importing*

The benefits of importing must be weighed against the disadvantages. At present, for example, we see foreign goods flooding U.S. markets at the same time that some of our producers are suffering a lack of customers, or even going out of business. This means that foreign-made automobiles, cameras, stereos, TV sets, VCRs, clothing, shoes, calculators, and home computers are being imported in growing numbers. Although manufactured abroad, these imports provide many opportunities for small firms to sell, distribute, and service them. G

While it is probably true that imports generate more jobs than they eliminate, this is small comfort to those small business owners and employees who are adversely affected, as the following example shows.

> Kalart Victor Corporation, the last U.S. maker of 16-millimeter movie projectors, called it quits in 1989, a victim of Japanese competition and the popularity of VCRs. Its projectors had been used in school systems and by government bodies around the world. As these groups switched to VCRs for instructional films, the demand for projectors declined. In 1980, there were five U.S. makers of projectors, with Kalart alone employing 250 people. By 1989, Kalart, the only producer—with fewer than 50 employees—left the market to three Japanese makers.[5]

Another "problem" with imports—if it can be called a problem—is knowing what is "Made in USA" and what is not. Running shoes provide a symbol of how tough it is to figure out what *is* and *is not* made in the United States.

> For example, the New Balance running shoe, often worn by President Clinton and Vice President Gore, is labeled "Made in USA." But, as you can see from Figure 12–2, 29 percent of it is made in China, according to the Made in the USA Foundation. The figure also shows some products that are wholly "home-grown."[6]

## Exporting by Small Firms

Along with the fascination we have with foreign business, there are many misconceptions concerning it, including the following:

1. *Only large firms can export successfully.* Small size is no barrier to international marketing. Today's most likely exporters are not the manufacturing giants, but small companies. According to a 1992 survey by Cognetics Inc., 87 percent of the 51,000 exporters it studied employ fewer than 500 workers.[7]
2. *Payment for goods sold to foreign buyers is uncertain.* Not true, as there are fewer credit losses in international sales than there are domestically.
3. *Overseas markets represent only limited sales opportunities.* On the contrary, around 95 percent of the world's population, and two-thirds of its purchasing power, are outside the United States.

**Figure 12–2** Balancing Act

**New Balance advertises its shoes as "Made in USA." The model 998, sometimes worn by President Clinton and Vice President Gore, has parts from the United States and China.**

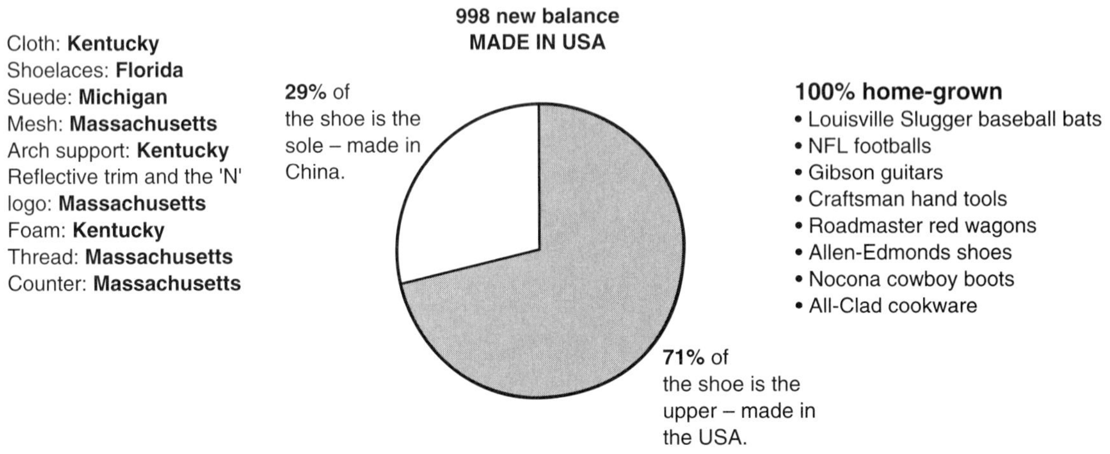


*Source:* Made in the USA Foundation and USA TODAY research, as reported in *USA Today,* July 14, 1995, p. 4B. Copyright 1995, USA TODAY. Reprinted with permission.

4. *Foreign consumers will not buy American products.* Although some goods may not travel or translate well, most American products have a reputation overseas for high quality, style, durability, and many state-of-the-art features. In fact, some products—such as hamburgers, blue jeans, movies, and music albums—are in demand simply because they are American!
5. *Export start-up costs are high.* Not necessarily, since you can begin exporting your products through exporting intermediaries at little real cost to you.

## *Some Opportunities and Risks*

G

Many opportunities are available for small firms interested in international or global operations. However, there are also many risks involved, as you can see from Figure 12–3. In general, the *opportunities* are to expand markets, use excess resources, and increase profits from higher rates of return and possible tax advantages. Exports also help the economic development of our own country. For example, exports account for one-third of the U.S. economy's growth over the past 10 years, and in 1995, we were the world's foremost exporter.[8]

The *risks* derive from the difficulty of getting earnings out of many countries and the changing political, economic, and cultural conditions. Another major problem is the proliferation of tougher standards in the European Community.[9] If this trend continues, it will freeze many of our exporters, particularly small firms, out of the European market.

Among the other problems or risks encountered in global operations is the temptation of entrepreneurs to enter international markets because they see "dollar-dominated opportunities." However, when dealing with currency

**Figure 12–3** Some Opportunities and Risks in International Operations

G

**Opportunities and challenges for small firms:**
Expansion of markets and product diversification
More effective use of labor force and facilities
Lower labor costs in most countries
Availability, and lower cost, of certain desired natural resources
Potential for higher rates of return on investment
Tax advantages
Strong demand for U.S. goods in many countries
Benefits provided to receiving country, such as needed capital, technology, and/or resources

**Problems and risks:**
Possibility of loss of assets and of earnings due to nationalization, war, terrorism, and other disturbances
Rapid change in political systems, often by violent overthrow
Fluctuating foreign exchange rates
High potential for loss, or difficulty or impossibility of retrieving earnings from investment
Unfair competition, particularly from state-subsidized firms
Lower skill levels of many workers in underdeveloped countries
Difficulties in communication and coordination with the home office
Attitudinal, cultural, and language barriers, which may lead to cultural differences and/or misunderstandings

*Source:* Adapted from Donald C. Mosley, Paul H. Pietri, Jr., and Leon C. Megginson, *Management: Leadership in Action*, 5th ed. (New York: HarperCollins, 1996), Table 4.1, p. 116.

exchanges, fast and radical fluctuations are a constant possibility.[10] Also, international business etiquette must be considered. Many books warn Americans of the dire consequences of improper gestures, language, dress, gift giving, and business operations.[11]

> For example, Islamic leaders were very upset about the disposable bags used for McDonald's "Happy Meals" in London. The bags featured the national flags of the 24 competitors in the World Cup competition. Saudi Arabia's flag, however, featured sacred words that should not be crumpled up and thrown away.[12]
>
> Similarly, the number one chewing gum in Singapore (Wrigley's) hit a snag in sales in 1992, when chewing gum was banned in Singapore in order to protect its subways.[13]

Finally, there is a growing problem with copyright and patent violations. This trend is particularly rampant in the electronics and music fields. The Chinese are particularly guilty. Evidently, the Chinese "see nothing wrong with copying or producing any product they have the technology to manufacture."[14]

### *Deciding Whether or Not to Export*

G

If you expect to export, you must be willing to commit the resources necessary to make the effort profitable. Thus, you should make sure you (1) have a product suitable for export, (2) can reliably fill the needs of foreign countries while still satisfying domestic demand, (3) can offer foreign buyers competitive prices and satisfactory credit terms, and (4) are willing to devote the time and skills needed to make export activities a significant part of your business.

The U.S. Department of Commerce has identified 10 countries that have been predicted to be the best partners for potential trading with the United States. They are:[15]

- Argentina
- Brazil
- Greater China (People's Republic of China, Hong Kong, and Taiwan)
- India
- Indonesia
- Mexico
- Poland
- South Africa
- South Korea
- Turkey

These countries are trying to attract trading partners by rebuilding infrastructure and privatizing selected industries. These efforts enhance the countries' attractiveness for small businesses seeking international targets.

According to an Ernst & Young survey of 384 CEOs of small and medium-sized companies, Mexico, Canada, Western Europe, the Pacific Rim, and Latin America represent strong opportunities for growth. Table 12–1 shows the expected growth.

### *Levels of Involvement*

There are at least five levels of involvement in exporting, as shown in Figure 12–4. At level 1, you may not even know you're involved in exporting, since the product is sold to an intermediary, who then sells it to foreign buyers.

At level 2, you actually make a commitment to seek export business. This commitment may be formal or informal, as the following example illustrates:

> Bending Branches Inc. has been shipping hockey sticks across the Canadian border since 1986. It is typical of many small U.S. businesses that enter international operations almost intuitively—without getting advice on exporting or importing from any government or private source of information.

Q

There are many unserved market niches in Canada that welcome U.S. businesses, particularly those that deliver products as ordered, and on time, and cut through the border red tape.[16]

Level 3 is reached when you make a formal agreement with a foreign country to produce and/or distribute your product there.

**Table 12–1** Going Global

**Share of executives of small and midsize companies who said selected foreign markets represented strong opportunity for growth**

| Market | 1994 | 1993 |
|---|---|---|
| Mexico | 33% | 30% |
| Canada | 33 | 34 |
| Western Europe | 31 | 42 |
| Pacific Rim | 27 | 28 |
| Latin America | 13 | 13 |
| Asia | 8 | 13 |
| Eastern Europe* | 7 | 10 |
| Australia | 3 | 3 |
| Middle East | 1 | 4 |

*Includes Commonwealth of Independent States

*Source:* Ernst & Young, as reported in Michael Selz, "Mexico's Appeal to Small Businesses Continues to Grow," *The Wall Street Journal,* October 4, 1994, p. B2. Reprinted by permission of *The Wall Street Journal,* © 1994 Dow Jones & Company, Inc. All Rights Reserved Worldwide.

**Figure 12–4** Five Levels of International Operations

| Degree of product control | Level | | Risk to your company |
|---|---|---|---|
| Great ↑ | 5 | Producing, as well as marketing, your product overseas | Great ↑ |
| | 4 | Beginning to actually market your product overseas by maintaining an office or subsidiary in a foreign country | |
| | 3 | Foreign licensing, involving a formal agreement with a foreign country to produce and/or distribute a product or service | |
| | 2 | Becoming actively involved by making a continuing effort to export | |
| Little | 1 | Doing some exporting on a casual or accidental basis, usually through an intermediary | Little |

*Source:* Adapted from Donald C. Mosley, Paul H. Pietri, Jr., and Leon C. Megginson, *Management: Leadership in Action,* 5th ed. (New York: HarperCollins, 1996), Figure 4.4, p. 120.

G

> For example, Ohio-based Vita-Mix began operating at level 3 in 1991 when it hired an international sales manager. Now, it sells its high-powered blenders to 20 countries, and faxes are coming in from everywhere, including Norway to Venezuela. Exports accounted for 20 percent of the company's $15 million sales in 1992.[17]

At level 4, you begin to maintain a separate sales office or marketing subsidiary in one or more foreign countries. Finally, you begin to engage in foreign production and marketing at level 5. You can do this by (1) setting up your own production and marketing operations in the foreign country, (2) buying an existing firm to do your business, or (3) forming a joint venture, as discussed in Chapter 4.

### *Help with Exporting Is Available*

Despite the barriers facing small firms, help with exporting is available from many sources. This help takes two forms: providing information and guidance and providing financial assistance. The latter is particularly important to small firms because, while they account for 94 percent of all U.S. exporters, they do only 30 percent of the dollar volume of the nation's exports.[18]

Both government and private groups provide practically unlimited information and guidance, including technical expertise. Ten different government agencies and some 200 small business development centers, funded by the SBA, offer export counseling. An SBA pamphlet, *Market Overseas with U.S. Government Help*, provides excellent information on overseas marketing. Other SBA help comes from members of SCORE and ACE, who have many years of practical experience in international trade. Small business institutes also provide export counseling and assistance.

Finally, the U.S. Department of Commerce offers assistance through its International Trade Administration (ITA) and its U.S. and Foreign Commercial Service Agency (USFCSA). The department's computerized market data system has information on nearly 200 nations, and the department has contacts in around 75 countries.[19]

> As an example of how it works, a review of the Commerce Department's "best prospects" list turned up some unexpected markets for small firms. It showed that bicycles were needed in sub-Saharan Africa; the United Kingdom needed candles; Cyprus could not get enough hotel furnishings; fast-food franchises were in short supply in Indonesia; and T-shirts illustrating the Heimlich maneuver were in great demand throughout Western Europe.[20]

Small companies needing export-related electronic data processing services can get help from the Commerce Department's Census Bureau.

You can obtain financial assistance for your export program from the Foreign Credit Insurance Association (FCIA) and the Export-Import Bank of the United States (Eximbank).[21] At Eximbank, access to small business programs is determined by size (as defined by the SBA guidelines discussed in Chapter 9). The bank offers small exporters guarantees for short-term working capital loans; backs fixed-rate, medium-term export loans; and offers no-deductible insurance programs. The SBA also offers direct loan programs for small business exporters, including its Export Working Capital Program (EWCP).[22]

## MARKETING RESEARCH

Q

**Marketing research** is the systematic gathering, recording, and analyzing of data relating to the marketing of goods and services. It is an orderly, objective way of learning about customers or potential customers and their needs and desires. By studying customers' actions and reactions and drawing conclusions from them, you can use marketing research to improve your marketing activities. But bear in mind that marketing research does not solve all problems, as the following examples illustrate.

**Marketing research** is the systematic gathering, recording, and analyzing of data relating to the marketing of goods and services.

> When the Ford Edsel was introduced in 1959, it was the most highly researched car in history, and it had innovations galore. It also had problems—from defective power steering to sticking hoods. The estimated loss was $250 million, or almost $1,117 per car.
>
> And then there was one of IBM's glitches—its PCjr. The late launch, slow microprocessor, and awkward keyboard cost the company $40 million.
>
> Finally, when Coca-Cola introduced "New Coke" to compete with Pepsi's sweeter formula, it provoked a national uproar from diehard loyalists.[23]

Marketing research is helpful at several points in the life of your business. Before starting the business, you can use marketing research to find out whether the location and surrounding population are right for your proposed product. After you open the business, marketing research can help you decide (1) whether to develop new or different products, (2) whether to expand at the original location or open additional locations, and (3) when and where to change emphasis on activities such as channels of distribution and advertising and promotion strategy.

### How Does Marketing Research Fit into Marketing?

Marketing research is part of a company's overall marketing system. By analyzing marketplace data such as attitudinal, demographic, and lifestyle changes, marketing research can help you plan your strategic efforts. The following are some areas where marketing research is effective:

- Identifying customers for the firm's products.
- Determining their needs.
- Evaluating sales potential for both the firm and its industry.
- Selecting the most appropriate channel of distribution.
- Evaluating advertising and promotional effectiveness.

> For example, marketing research techniques are available to correlate data from actual customer purchases, using universal product code scanners in supermarkets and drugstores, with advertising information. The business owner can see how the amount and type of advertising and sales promotion lead to actual purchases.[24]

Q

### How to Do Marketing Research

Marketing research does not have to be fancy or expensive to meet your needs. It deals with people and their constantly changing likes and dislikes,

**Figure 12–5** Plugged In

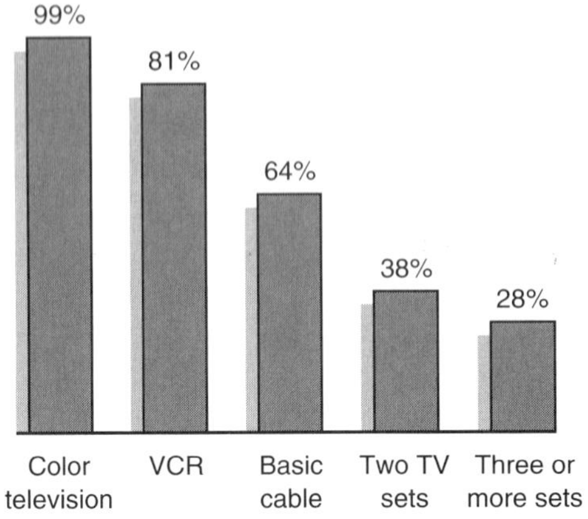


*Source:* Nielsen Media Research, as reported in *USA Today,* August 1, 1995, p. 1D. Copyright 1995, USA TODAY. Reprinted with permission.

which can be affected by many influences. Marketing research tries to find out how things really are (not how you think they are or should be) and what people are really buying or want to buy (not what you want to sell them). Figure 12–5 is an example of research to find out what customers are buying.

In its simplest form, marketing research involves (1) defining the problem and then (2) gathering and evaluating information. Many small business managers unknowingly do some form of marketing research nearly every day. For example, they check returned items to see if there is some pattern. They ask old customers on the street why they have not been in recently. They look at competitors' ads to find out what the competition is selling and at what prices.

> At a university small business seminar, the owner of a wholesaling firm that sold farm equipment and supplies stated that market research was not relevant in a small business. Later, he told the participants he visited dealers to learn their needs for shovels and other items before ordering these items for his stock. Without realizing it, he was doing marketing research.

## *Defining the Problem*

Proper identification of the problem is the most important step in the process, since the right answer to the wrong question is useless. Thus, you should look beyond the symptoms of a problem to get at the real cause. For example, a sales decline is not a *cause* but rather a *symptom* of a marketing problem. In defining the problem, you should look at influences that may have caused it, such as changes in customers' home areas or in their tastes.

## *Gathering and Evaluating Information*

Marketing research can use existing data or generate new information through research. So you must make a subjective judgment and weigh the

## USING TECHNOLOGY TO SUCCEED

### Marketing Research via Television

TV won't be just TV much longer! The "boob tube" has been transformed into a multimedia, interactive communications device. TVs, computers, and telephones have been integrated into systems that will revolutionize the way businesses obtain information.

Businesses that decide to invest in this type of technology will have instant access to virtually unlimited amounts and types of data. An incomprehensible amount of market research information will lie at the fingertips of the organizations that purchase this equipment.

Batten down the hatches: it's time for the rocket ride to the next level of the information age.

*Source:* Kevin Maney, "TVs and PCs to Become Media Centers," *USA Today*, November 19, 1992, p. 1B. Copyright 1992, USA TODAY. Reprinted with permission.

Q

cost of gathering more information against its usefulness. The cost of making a wrong decision should be balanced against the cost of gathering more data to make a better-informed decision, as shown in Using Technology to Succeed.

*Using Existing Information.* You should "think cheap" and stay as close to home as possible when doing marketing research. Looking at your records and files, such as sales records, complaints, and receipts, can show you where customers live or work or how and what they buy, as the following example illustrates.

> The owner of a fabric shop used addresses on checks and cash receipts to pinpoint where her customers lived. She then cross-referenced the addresses with products purchased, which permitted her to check the effectiveness of advertising and sales promotion activities.

Credit records can also yield valuable information about your market, since customers' jobs, income levels, and marital status can be gleaned from them. Employees are a good source of information about customer likes and dislikes because they hear customers' gripes about the firm's products as well as about its competitors. They are also aware of the items customers request that are not stocked. Outside sources of information include publications such as *Survey of Current Business* and *Statistical Abstract of the United States,* trade association reports, chamber of commerce studies, university research publications, trade journals, newspapers, and marketing journals.

*Doing Primary Research.* Primary research can range from simply asking customers or suppliers how they feel about your business to more complex studies such as direct-mail questionnaires, telephone or "on the street" surveys, and test marketing. **Test marketing** simulates the conditions under which a product will eventually be sold. However, even a small market test is costly.

**Test marketing** simulates the conditions under which a product is to be marketed.

Primary research, which includes studies such as surveys, interviews, and questionnaires, should usually be left to experts. You might use this type of research, but take care to ask the right questions and obtain unbiased answers. David Futrell, a consultant with QualPro Inc., offers these tips for developing effective surveys:[25]

- Ask your customers what to ask.
- Be sure the answer will tell you what to do.
- Use a combination of different types of questions.
- Develop a user-friendly design.
- Avoid asking customers to rank lengthy lists of items.
- Address only one issue in each question.

Another type of research involves observing the results of a given action. Sometimes, research methods can be unique, as the following example shows.

> During a three-day promotion, a discount merchandiser gave its customers, free of charge, all the roasted peanuts they could eat while shopping in the store. The merchant encouraged customers to "let the hulls fall where they may" and soon had "litter trails" that provided information on the traffic pattern within the store. Trampled peanut hulls littered the most heavily traveled store aisles and were heaped up in front of merchandise displays of special interest to customers. Thus, the merchant learned how customers acted in the store and what they wanted.

*Using Specialized Research Techniques.* Other techniques include license plate analysis, telephone number analysis, coded coupons, and "tell them Joe sent you" broadcast ads, not to mention just plain people-watching.

In many states, license plates give information about where a car's owner lives—what city or county, for instance. By recording the origin of cars parked at the firm's location, the trade area can be estimated. Similarly, telephone numbers and ZIP codes can tell where people live. This type of data can be found on sales slips, prospect cards, and contest blanks, as well as on personalized checks used for payment.

Coded coupons and "tell them Joe sent you" broadcast ads can be effective, too. The relative effectiveness of your advertising media can be checked by coding coupons and by including in broadcast ads some phrase customers must use to get a discount on a given sale item. If neighborhood newspapers are involved, you can also get some idea of the area from which customers are drawn. Where they read or heard about the discount offered in the ads may also give information about their tastes.

## Using Computerized Databases

Q

A wide variety of information is available at public libraries; many such institutions also offer, for a fee, access to computerized databases, such as Standard & Poor's Daily News and Cumulative News (Corporation Records). By gathering data on selected kinds of companies (such as electronics firms producing home videocassettes) or specific geographic areas (such as firms moving into a particular state or city), you can learn about companies that are expanding operations. Such information may be valuable to small retailers, service businesses, wholesalers, and manufacturers in selecting their target market and marketing strategy.

A variation of computerized databases is now being used by big and small businesses alike—from Federal Express to fast-food franchises to independent cabbies and pharmacists. Computer programs hooked to a phone with Caller ID can create a database that can increase efficiency, enhance security, control inventory, improve marketing, and simplify contacts with customers.

Q

> For instance, if you call your favorite Domino's pizzeria, the person who answers the phone may say something like "Do you want another large deep-dish pepperoni with pineapples and anchovies?" How does the clerk know this much about your tastes? By looking into a convenient high-tech file: a computer that used Caller ID to tell who you are and then called up its records of where you live and what you like.[26]

## Distribution

Because of its many cost-saving potentials, distribution should be important to you. **Distribution** includes the whole range of activities concerned with the effective movement of a product from the production line into the hands of the final customer. To perform the activity effectively, you must make decisions in such important areas as protective packaging, materials handling, inventory control, transportation (internally and externally), order processing, and various aspects of customer service. Because of space limitations, we'll discuss only storing, order processing, and transportation.

**Distribution** involves the effective physical movement of a product from the production line to the final consumer.

### Storing

Until sold or used, goods must be stored by manufacturers, wholesalers, and retailers. While some small manufacturers and wholesalers have their own warehouses, more of them use public warehouses, independently owned facilities that often specialize in handling certain products, such as furniture or refrigerated products. Public warehouses are particularly useful to small firms wanting to place goods close to customers for quick delivery, since the firms then avoid investing in new facilities.

### Order Processing

Effective order processing improves customer satisfaction by reducing slow shipment and incorrectly or incompletely filled orders. It begins the moment a customer places an order with a salesperson. The order goes to the office, often on a standardized order form. After the order is filled, the goods are sent to the customer.

### Transportation

Transportation involves the physical movement of a product from the seller to the purchaser. Since transportation costs are the largest item in distribution, there are many opportunities for savings and improved efficiency. The two most important aspects are choosing the transportation mode to be used and understanding delivery terms. **Transportation modes** are the methods used to take products from one place to another. A small producer has many

**Transportation modes** are the methods used to transfer products from place to place.

**Figure 12–6** Share of Freight Carried by Each Transportation Mode

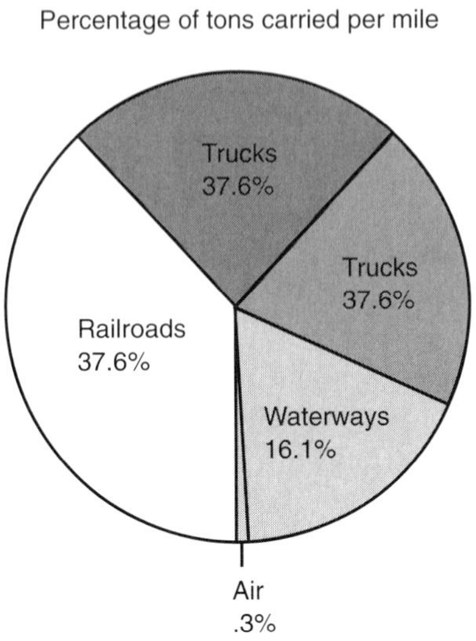


*Source: Railroad Facts,* as reported in *USA Today,* June 25, 1992, p. 3A. Copyright 1992, USA TODAY. Reprinted with permission.

choices of ways to move goods to and from its plant and/or warehouse, and each mode has advantages and disadvantages. Which mode you choose to use will depend on speed, frequency, dependability, points served, capability (which includes capacity, flexibility, and adaptability to handle the product), and cost. The use of containers can also affect the transportation system used. The various modes can be evaluated as to their effectiveness on each of these variables.

Railroads, trucks, pipelines, and waterways are popular means of transporting bulky and heavy materials. Although the modes of transportation are changing, these still tend to be the primary systems used by producers.

As you can see from Figure 12–6, railroads are still important movers of goods. Their primary advantage is the capacity to carry large volumes of goods, fairly quickly, at a low cost. The main disadvantage is that they operate only on fixed routes, often on fixed schedules.

Trucks are playing an increasing part in shipping because of their flexibility and improved highway systems. However, changing traffic and government rules and regulations also affect their use, as the following example shows.

> A Nebraska feed-and-seed store owner spent much time, money, and effort to get the city to rescind a recent ordinance prohibiting tractor-trailers from unloading in front of his store. The extra cost of unloading on the edge of town and transporting sacks of feed and seed to the store would have forced him out of business.

While these modes of transportation are important, the use of air transport is increasing, particularly for items and information that must be delivered in a hurry, as well as for products with a high unit value and low weight and bulk. In such cases, a site near an airport should be considered if the costs are not too high.

The shipment of freight by a combination of truck and rail—called **intermodal shipping**—has reached record levels in recent years. For example, intermodal shipments on Conrail Inc. increased by 20 percent from 1992 to 1993.[27]

**Intermodal shipping** is the use of a combination of truck and rail to ship goods.

Many companies are also using a combination of trucks and air to expedite service. For example, Gateway 2000 and many other mail-order computer vendors use Federal Express. UPS is also used by many small businesses.

## Credit Management

**Credit management** involves (1) deciding how customers will pay for purchases, (2) setting credit policies and practices, and (3) administering credit operations. The objectives of each of these activities are to increase profits, increase customer stability, and protect the firm's investment in accounts receivable, which is often the largest single asset on the firm's balance sheet.

**Credit management** involves setting and administering credit policies and practices.

### Methods of Payment

Customers can pay for purchases in a number of ways, and you must decide early in the life of your business which method(s) to accept. Payment methods include cash, checks, and various kinds of credit. Figure 12–7 shows which method is preferred by adult shoppers.

#### *Cash*

Given a choice, every business owner would probably prefer to make all sales for cash. Record keeping would be easier, and there would be no bad debts. But it is unrealistic to expect buyers to carry cash for every purchase, especially large ones.

**Figure 12–7** Paper or Plastic?

**Adult shoppers who prefer to pay for purchases with:**

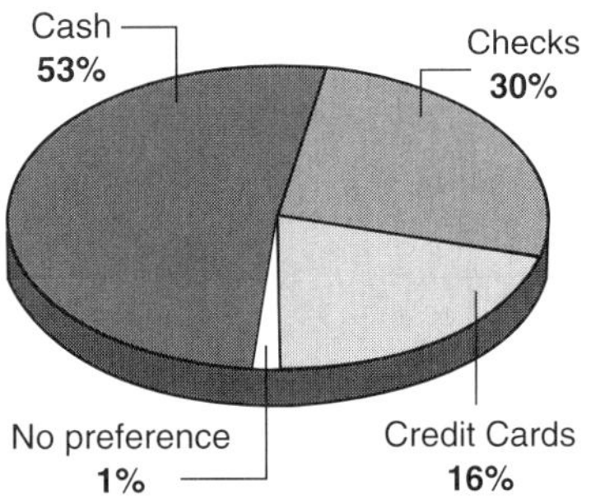


*Source:* Lutheran Brotherhood, as reported in *USA Today,* July 13, 1995, p. 1B. Copyright 1995, USA TODAY. Reprinted with permission.

### *Checks*

Because accepting checks for payment increases sales, most small business owners think the risks involved are worth it. With proper verification procedures, bad-debt losses can be minimized. Checks can be treated the same as cash in record keeping, and they're actually safer to have on hand than cash and easier to deal with in making bank deposits.

### *Credit*

To stimulate sales, various forms of credit may be used, including installment payment plans and credit cards or a business's own credit plan. Granting your own credit allows you to choose your own customers and avoid fees to credit card issuers. Customer accounts can be paid off every month or can be *revolving charge accounts* such as those used by large department stores. For major purchases, you may give the buyer more time to pay before interest is charged or the account is turned over to a finance company. To extend credit even longer, you may offer an *installment payment plan* that gives the buyer up to a year or more to pay for the purchase. Buyers make a down payment, make regular weekly or monthly payments, and pay interest charges on the unpaid balance.

Whenever you extend credit, though, record keeping becomes more complex. Small firms can use manual or computer methods to maintain their charge accounts internally, or they can turn the accounts over to a service firm for handling. Either way, there are costs for billing and collections, as well as bad-debt losses.

Some of these responsibilities and costs can be avoided by accepting bank or corporate *credit cards,* also called *plastic money.* Today's consumers have come to expect most firms of any size to accept the major cards, which are in effect a line of credit granted to the customer by the card issuer, such as Visa, American Express, Discover, MasterCard, and now GE, GM, and AT&T. This may be especially necessary in resort areas or other places where customers are less likely to have large amounts of cash, local checking accounts, or a store charge account.

Although merchants pay a fee to join and a fee on sales, many find it worth the expense; provided they follow required authorization procedures, sellers are guaranteed payment, largely eliminating bad-debt losses. And authorization, once cumbersome, is now almost universally automated through the use of readers that scan the card's magnetic strip, dial the number of a database, get authorization for the charge, and record the sale, all in just a few seconds. These readers are often tied into cash registers or other machines that print a receipt that gives not only the date and amount charged but also the cardholder's name and the merchant's name and address.

As shown by Using Technology to Succeed in Chapter 6, once a business is set up to accept credit cards, it is generally simple to include debit cards as well. *Debit cards* are issued by banks, look like credit cards, and can be scanned in the same way. Instead of a line of credit, however, debit cards represent a plastic check, as the amount of purchase is immediately deducted from the user's checking account. Many banks now offer ATM cards that can be used in this way.

## Setting Credit Policies

While your credit department can contribute to increased sales and profit, several factors should be considered in formulating a credit policy; some are beyond your control. Any credit policy should be flexible enough to accommodate these internal and external factors.

Some credit policies you can use are (1) liberal extension of credit with a liberal collection policy, (2) liberal extension of credit with a strictly enforced collection policy, and (3) strict extension of credit with a collection policy adjusted to individual circumstances. Generally, being liberal in extending credit or in collecting bad debts tends to stimulate sales but increase collection costs and bad-debt losses. Strict policies have the reverse effect. Whatever policy is chosen, you should extend a businesslike attitude toward credit customers.

## Carrying Out Credit Policies

The person managing credit for you should have ready access to the accounts receivable records and be free from interruptions and confusion. Several tools this person can use in performing the function include the accounts receivable ledger or computer printout, invoices and other billing documents, credit files, account lists, credit manuals, reference material, and various automated aids.

## Classifying Credit Risks

You should begin by classifying present and potential customers according to credit risk: good, fair, or weak. These risks can be determined from information in the customer's file, trade reports, financial reports, and previous credit experience.

Good credit risks may be placed on a preferred list for automatic approval within certain dollar limits. Periodic review of these accounts usually suffices. Fair credit risks will require close checking, particularly on large amounts or in case of slow payment. While weak credit risks may be acceptable, they should be closely watched. You can face many problems when you get involved in unwise extension of credit, as the following example illustrates.

> Mr. and Mrs. Neely* invested almost $6,000 of their savings in a venture. They paid $4,000 cash for equipment and set aside the balance to use as working capital.
>
> Sales increased during each of their first 13 months, and all bills were paid. Much capital, however, was tied up in uncollectible accounts receivable. Mr. Neely, who was softhearted, said, "I really don't want to offer credit to anyone, but how can I say that to customers without losing their business?"
>
> After they stopped giving credit, their gross profits dropped by almost one-half. They were so discouraged that they sold the business.

---

*Name disguised at owner's request.

### Investigating Customers' Creditworthiness

A major cause of bad-debt losses is making credit decisions without adequate investigation. Yet prompt delivery of orders is also important. Thus, your credit-checking method should be geared to need and efficiency to improve the sales and delivery of your product. For new accounts, a complete credit application may be desired. Direct credit inquiry can be effective in obtaining the name of the customer's bank and trade references. Many suppliers and banks cooperate in exchanging credit information, but they should be assured that the information obtained will be treated confidentially. Outside sources of valuable credit information include local credit bureaus, which are linked nationally through Associated Credit Bureaus, Inc., and others who provide guidelines and mechanisms for obtaining credit information for almost any area in the United States.

### Establishing Collection Procedures

The collection of unpaid accounts is an important part of credit management. The collection effort should include systematic and regular follow-up, which is vital to establish credibility with the customer concerning credit terms. The follow-up should be timely, which is now feasible since most businesses have computer capacity to show the age of a bill. For example, a statement sent to a customer may indicate that payment was due on a certain date, but that the bill is, say, 30, 60, or 90 days past due.

When an account is past due, prompt contact with the customer, made tactfully and courteously, generally produces results. If this doesn't work, holding customers' orders can be effective. But you should respond rapidly when the customer clears the account so that unnecessary delays in shipping are avoided.

## WHAT YOU SHOULD HAVE LEARNED

**1.** The opportunities in global and international marketing are growing rapidly. All of us—students, teachers, consumers, and large and small businesses—are already involved. Millions of small businesses are importing and selling foreign products. While these imports provide many opportunities for some small firms, they may force some others out of business.

Benefits of exporting are: *(a)* expansion of markets, *(b)* more effective use of resources, particularly personnel, *(c)* potentially higher rates of return on investment, and *(d)* tax advantages. Some problems are *(a)* the difficulty of getting earnings out of the host country, *(b)* unfair competition from state-subsidized firms, *(c)* favorable treatment given to local firms and products, and *(d)* rapidly changing political climates.

Small firms can become involved in international marketing at one of five levels, namely: *(a)* casual, or accidental, exporting; *(b)* active exporting; *(c)* foreign licensing; *(d)* overseas marketing; and *(e)* foreign production and marketing.

Considerable help is available to exporters from the SBA, the U.S. Department of Commerce, chambers of commerce and trade associations, the Export-Import Bank, and the Foreign Credit Insurance Association.

**2.** While relatively few small firms do marketing research, more of them should, because it increases the chance of success and reduces chances of failure. Marketing research does not have to be fancy or expensive. In its simplest form, such research involves defining the problem and gathering and evaluating information. Many small business owners already do market research by checking returned items to see if there is a pattern, correlating consumer addresses with their purchases and payment records, checking to see what types of ads get the best results, and asking customers for suggestions for improving operations. There are many computerized databases for small firms that want to do more formal research.

**3.** Distribution, which is moving the product from the seller to the buyer, includes the vital functions of storing, order processing, and transporting the product.

**4.** Credit management includes deciding on customer payment methods, establishing credit policies, and administering credit operations. A credit policy should be flexible and help increase revenues and profits. Customers should be classified according to their creditworthiness—that is, good, fair, or weak. Credit investigations should be conducted, and the collection of outstanding receivables should be systematic and include regular follow-up. The overall results of the credit functions and collection efficiency should be evaluated to see that they are achieving their objectives.

## QUESTIONS FOR DISCUSSION

1. Do you believe international marketing is as important as stated? Explain.
2. Do you really believe the statement that over half of you will work in some aspect of international activities in your working life? Explain.
3. What are some reasons for importing? What are some problems?
4. How involved are you, as an individual or a small business person, in importing?
5. Name and defend *or* refute the five myths about exporting.
6. List the opportunities available in exporting.
7. Describe some risks and problems involved in exporting.
8. Explain the five levels of involvement in exporting.
9. Why should small firms do marketing research?
10. How does a small firm go about doing marketing research?
11. What is the role of distribution in marketing? Describe three components of distribution discussed in this chapter.
12. What is credit management, and why is it so important to small business? Why is the acceptance of credit cards by small businesses increasing?

# CASE 12–1

## CLARK COPY INTERNATIONAL CORPORATION'S CHINA EXPERIENCE

G

In the early 1980s, China's powerful State Economic Commission launched a major effort to attract small Western enterprises. It was dissatisfied with large firms that sell expensive consumer items such as VCRs that do little to aid China's economy.

This policy helped Clark Copy International Corporation, a small company making plain-paper copiers in a cramped plant in Melrose Park, Illinois, beat out the industry's world leaders to sign a lucrative contract with China. At that time, it had only 14 employees and had earned only $58,000 on $1.5 million of sales for 1982. Clark agreed to sell 1,000 CMC 2000 copiers assembled and ready to use, as well as provide parts and instructions for the Chinese to assemble into another 5,000 machines. Also, Clark would train 1,600 Chinese technicians to manufacture the copiers and other Clark products for domestic and export sales in a new plant in Kweilin in the south of China.

How did Clark do it? According to Clark's founder and president, Otto A. Clark, a Slovak who emigrated to the United States in 1950, "You can't do business in China on a simple buy-and-sell basis, like most multinationals do. Instead, you have to establish a close human relationship and a commitment to stay." That relationship was established with the help of David Yao, Clark's Far East representative, who was born in Shanghai and speaks fluent Chinese. Yao and Clark went to China eight times to negotiate before closing with China's National Bureau of Instrumentation Industries in April 1982. In the mid- to late 1980s, the Chinese attitude toward private enterprise and foreign investments changed, and Clark wasn't permitted to complete the agreement. By 1991, it was out of business.

*Source:* Correspondence with Clark Copy International; the Melrose Park, Illinois, Chamber of Commerce; and others.

## QUESTIONS

1. Evaluate the procedure followed by Otto Clark in his effort to enter global operations.
2. What went wrong? Explain.
3. What—if anything—would you have done differently.

## CASE 12-2

## FULL CIRCLE

St. Petersburg, Florida, entrepreneur Sherry Sacino is so excited about the fast-approaching year 2000 that she plans to celebrate its arrival twice. By crossing the International Date Line from west to east, you can be both the first and the last to celebrate the historic New Year. She is offering a unique way to usher in the new century. For an estimated $5,000, her First Flight company offers participants a chance to ring in the new millennium in Fiji and then do it again 24 hours later in Western Samoa.

*Source:* Adapted from Ingrid Abrahamovich, in *Success*, as reported in *Reader's Digest*, July 1995, p. 70.

### QUESTIONS

1. What is your opinion of this method of exporting U.S. innovation?
2. If you were Sacino, how many such trips would you plan to offer? Why?

## APPLICATION 12-1

## TO OPEN OR NOT TO OPEN?

The following is an actual example of market research done by a prospective restaurant owner who wanted to determine the feasibility of opening a restaurant in a given location.

First, the prospective owner talked to people who worked near the proposed site to see if they would be interested in eating in his restaurant. Then he surveyed the residents in the area to determine their menu preferences, any dissatisfaction with existing restaurants, and the likelihood of their eating at his prospective restaurant.

After that, he had data gathered about competing restaurants and their menus. Then he made a count of customer traffic flow at the competitors' locations, used a Department of Transportation traffic survey, and studied census data concerning demographics at the proposed site.

On the basis of the results of these efforts, he modified the marketing and financial information on his business plan. Later, this information was used in advertising and media planning after the restaurant opened.

## QUESTIONS

1. Evaluate the way the prospective owner did his marketing research.
2. What improvements would you suggest?
3. Is this type of research a valid way of gathering information to use in advertising? Explain.

## ACTIVITY 12–1

*Directions:* Break the code to decipher the key terms from this chapter.

Clue: Z = P

JNPCNPU FSZAUCFKE AU PTZAUCFKE;
X GASZXKR SMYC MYP SXUIPCFKE
UPYPXUGN, CPYC SXUIPCFKE, XKO
GUPOFC SXKXEPSPKC FK AUOPU CA
XYYMUP XOPDMXCP CUXKYZAUCXCFAK
SAOPY XKO OFYCUFLMCFAK AH EAAOY.

WHETHER IMPORTING OR EXPORTING;
A COMPANY MUST USE MARKETING
RESEARCH, TEST MARKETING, AND
CREDIT MANAGEMENT IN ORDER TO
ASSURE ADEQUATE TRANSPORTATION
MODES AND DISTRIBUTION OF GOODS.

CHAPTER 13

# Managing Human Resources and Diversity in Small Firms

*Small businesses must make wooing and keeping employees as high a priority as attracting and retaining customers.*—John L. Ward, Loyola University of Chicago

*Good ideas and good products are "a dime a dozen" but good execution and good management—in a word, good people—are rare.*—Arthur Rock, venture capitalist

## LEARNING OBJECTIVES

After studying the material in this chapter, you will be able to:

1. Explain how small business managers plan personnel needs and develop sources from which to recruit personnel.
2. Name some methods used for recruiting personnel, and describe the steps in the employee selection process.
3. Explain the importance of personnel development, and discuss some development methods.
4. Tell how selection of managers differs from selection of nonmanagerial personnel, and describe some methods of manager development.
5. Discuss the laws that affect personnel recruiting, selection, and development.

# PROFILE

## MARY H. PARTRIDGE AND MICHAEL LEVY: "HIS" AND "HERS" BUSINESSES

Photo courtesy of Michael Levy and Mary H. Partridge

Michael Levy and Mary H. Partridge, a married couple in Austin, Texas, have separate businesses—which they operate out of their home—but share the same office and telephone. He owns and operates Michael Levy & Associates, consultants in training and organization development; she owns and is president of Impact Consulting, consultants in human resource administration and development.

Having separate businesses not only allows them to have their own sense of ownership and direction but also permits them to develop individual client lists and use their particular professional expertise. When they choose, or need, to use each other's specialized abilities, they collaborate. But when they do this, they try to keep clear which one is the practical decision maker for the current project, and the other serves as a creative resource. They find "a comfortable and productive mix."

Their traditional activities include training trainers for both small and large companies. They do this through formal group seminars or by working one-on-one to coach a company's supervisors or other persons responsible for training personnel. They also conduct seminars on training and development for middle managers.

Q

The owners have adjusted their activities to adjust to changing environments. The "downsizing" (or "rightsizing," as many people in the field now call it) of all types and sizes of businesses has led to an emphasis on developing the team after layoffs, transfers, and terminations. The consultants also help the remaining employees adjust to the need to do more and varied work with fewer resources. They refocus the managers' and employees' emphasis on the mission, objectives, and values of the business.

Much of their time is spent on executive coaching, which involves individual consultations with managers to improve their management approach, communication abilities, and leadership style. They also emphasize high-quality performance.

Practicing what they preach, the two consultants avoid hiring staff and incurring burdensome overhead. Instead, they use a network of familiar independent contractors as they are needed to supplement the owners' efforts. Levy and Partridge have developed workable relationships with their own personnel—each other and hired freelancers—and they are able to translate their knowledge and experience to benefit the companies they serve.

*Source:* Correspondence and discussions with Mary H. Partridge and Michael Levy.

The Profile emphasizes the importance of selecting, training, and developing human resources, especially managers. You must have a sufficient supply of adequately trained and motivated employees if you are to succeed as the owner or manager of a small business. In the late 1800s, a young entrepreneur, Andrew Carnegie, expressed this thought when he said, "Take away all our factories, our trade, our avenues of transportation, and our money, but leave our organization, and in four years, I will have reestablished myself." In other words, while physical and financial resources are *important* to any business, large or small, *human resources are vital.* This need was emphasized in an SBA report which concluded that, if small firms are to succeed, they must "boost wages, increase benefits, hire marginal workers, and invest in labor-saving technology."[1]

Thus, being able to identify and hire good employees can mean the difference between having a successful and an unsuccessful business. This process involves (1) planning for, (2) recruiting, (3) selecting, and (4) training and developing employees, all of which are discussed in this chapter.

## Planning for Personnel Needs

D

You can't wait until you need a new employee to think about your personnel needs. Like larger competitors, small businesses must (1) determine personnel needs and (2) develop sources from which to recruit personnel, especially women and diverse ethnic groups. As shown in Chapter 1 and Chapter 3, these groups of workers—and owners—of small businesses are growing much more rapidly than white male workers and business owners. Figure 13–1 dramatically illustrates the shift brought about by government and employers' efforts.

Small businesses find it difficult to carry out these activities, since many are facing absolute labor shortages because of the declining work force, largely brought on by the aging of the U.S. population. According to the U.S. Bureau of the Census, the average age has increased from 26 in 1966 to around 33 in 1990. It is expected to rise to over 37 by the year 2010.[2]

The number of Americans aged 16 to 24 is expected to decrease by more than 7 percent by the year 2000. Because small businesses employ two-thirds of these entry-level workers, they are the first to feel the shortage. In fact, "finding qualified workers" is now one of the top five concerns of small business owners, according to a Dun & Bradstreet survey of 296 such owners.[3] And three-quarters of the 151 affluent Americans responding to a

**Figure 13–1** Growth in Employment of Women and Minorities

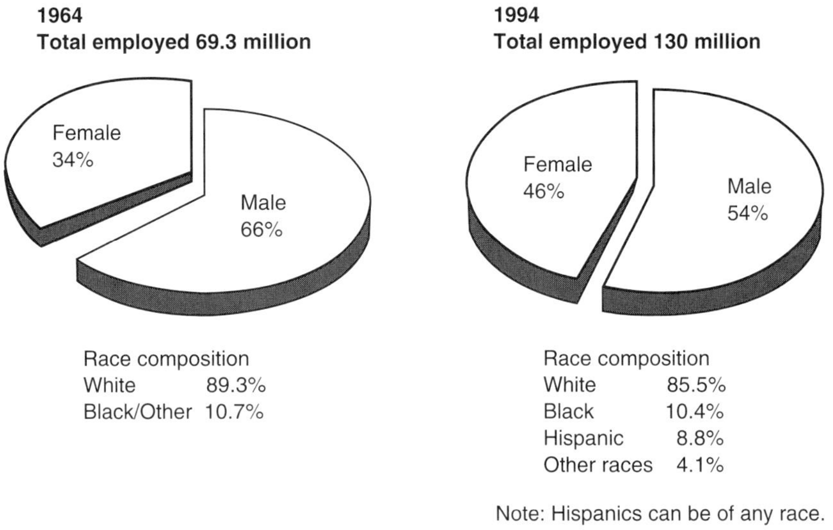


*Source:* Bureau of Labor Statistics, as reported in *USA Today,* May 15, 1995, p. 1B. Copyright 1995, USA TODAY. Reprinted with permission.

U.S. Trust survey said "attracting and keeping skilled workers" was a problem for their privately held companies. ("Government policies" was the greatest threat, cited by 85 percent of the respondents.)[4]

Compounding the problem is the fact that blue-collar jobs are down from 40 percent of the labor force at the end of World War II (1945) to only 25 percent in 1995—and dropping. And because we are in a "postindustrial society," where 80 percent of all jobs require higher-level skills and knowledge, many workers, especially entry-level applicants, lack the education and flexibility needed to transfer from one job to another. And most people now expect to change jobs and careers seven times in their working lives.[5]

This shortage of skilled workers has created a paradox for many small employers. Thousands of prospective employees are being rejected because of inadequate skills. This trend leaves many unhappy employers (because jobs remain unfilled), not to mention frustrated job seekers.

> For example, one construction worker has applied for a job at Lincoln Electric Company three times in the past three years. Although Lincoln currently has about 200 openings it can't fill, this applicant has never made it past the screening interview because of insufficient skills.[6]

This conclusion was confirmed at the 1995 Olsten Forum on Human Resources, held in Melville, New York. Nearly half of a group of surveyed companies were understaffed to some extent. This shortage resulted in increased stress, turnover, and errors, as well as difficulty meeting schedules and providing customer service.[7]

To meet this declining supply of potential employees, many small businesses are changing the way they operate. They are spending more and using new methods to attract more applicants, making their workplaces more attractive, and using employee benefits and other incentives to retain valued employees. Finally, small companies are also stepping up automation and even subcontracting out part of their work to reduce the number of employees needed.[8]

## Determining Types of Employees Needed

**Job specifications** are detailed written statements of work assignments and the qualifications needed to do the job acceptably.

A **job description** lists the duties and responsibilities of a given job.

When business owners want to construct a building, they obtain a set of blueprints and specifications. When they buy merchandise, materials, and supplies, they develop specifications for those items. In the same way, even the smallest businesses should have **job specifications,** which are statements of the mental, physical, and other qualifications required of a person to do the job. Drawing up job specifications begins with a **job description,** which is a list of the job's duties, responsibilities, and working conditions, as well as relationships between it and other jobs in the organization. When the personal qualities, education, training, and experience needed to perform the job are added, the result is a set of job specifications that forms the basis for recruiting and selecting new employees, as shown in Figure 13–2.

Just a word of caution: Job descriptions should be flexible in very small firms to give the owner more freedom in assigning work to available employees, whether the work fits their job description or not.

Don't ask for more than is needed to do the job properly! Ask yourself, "Is a college education really needed, or can a high school graduate do the job?" Or again, "Are three years' experience required, or can an inexperienced person be trained to do the work?" If an inexperienced person can be trained, is there someone to do the training? Increasing education and experience levels raises the starting pay expected, and you may actually be better off training someone to do things your own way.

*"Welcome aboard. You're just what we're looking for. Not too bright, no ambition, and content to stay on the bottom of the ladder and not louse things up!"*

*Source: Savant,* February/March 1988. Cartoon courtesy of J. Nebesky.

## Developing Sources of Personnel

As with purchasing supplies for building and running the business, you need sources from which to seek new workers. Some of these sources are shown in Figure 13–3. Not all of them will be appropriate for all small businesses.

### *Internal Sources*

Filling job openings with present employees rather than going outside the business makes good sense. This method raises morale and improves employees' motivation, since they know they can move up in your firm. It also saves time, effort, and money, since outside recruiting is time-consuming and costly.

Filling jobs from within is also effective because the worker's performance has been observed and evaluated. Further, this method leads to stability. Employees can be upgraded, transferred, or promoted to fill job openings.

**Figure 13–2** Components of a Typical Job Description and Job Specification

- *Identification of job:* Job title, department, code, salary range, supervisor, etc.
- *Job description:*
  *a.* Physical demands of the job and the minimum physical requirements needed to fill it.
  *b.* Working conditions, including psychological conditions such as relationships with others and responsibilities for other people, money, and equipment.
  *c.* Summary of the duties and responsibilities of the job.
  *d.* Days and hours of work.
  *e.* Machines, tools, formulas, and equipment used.
- *Job specifications:*
  *a.* Educational background and knowledge, skills and techniques, and training and experience required to perform the job, as well as special training and development needed.
  *b.* Personal characteristics such as sociability, articulateness, or aggressiveness.

**Figure 13–3** Where to Find Needed Employees

D

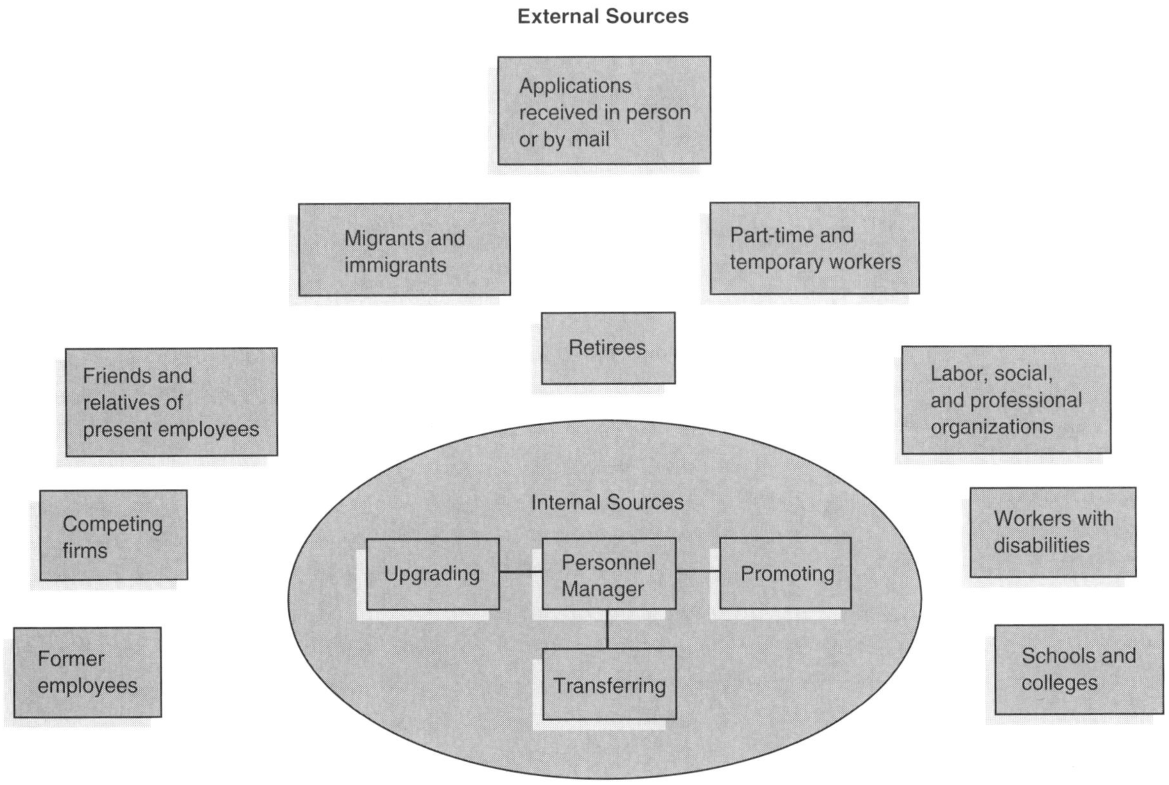

**Upgrading** involves retraining workers so they can do increasingly complex work.

**Upgrading** occurs when an employee who is presently not capable of doing a job that has become more difficult receives training to enable him or her to do the work successfully, as the following example illustrates.

> A small service organization replaced its typewriter with a word processor. The present typist, age 52, had been with the firm for 20 years but didn't know how to use a word processor. Instead of hiring a new operator, management sent the typist to a training program. She mastered word processing in a short time and was soon back at the company using her new skills.

**Transferring** is moving an employee from one job to another, without necessarily changing title or pay.

**Promoting** is moving an employee to a higher position, usually with increased responsibilities, title, and pay.

**Transferring** is moving an employee from one location or department to another, without necessarily changing job title or pay. **Promoting** is moving a person to a higher position, frequently with increased responsibilities, greater status or prestige, a new title, and a higher salary. If the company is family owned, the owners' children can be "promoted" as they become capable of assuming more responsibility. The benefits and complications of hiring family members as employees will be covered in detail in Chapter 24.

### *External Sources*

You may need to use external sources as the business grows, especially to fill lower-level jobs. External sources may also be used to provide new ideas and perspectives and to obtain needed skills when necessary, especially for scientific, technical, and professional positions.

Many small firms keep a list of *former employees* as a potential source of trained workers. If a worker left voluntarily and for good reason, is in good standing, and seeks reemployment, rehiring may be a good idea.

> Diane Allen worked for Bell Stained Glass and Overlay in Mobile, Alabama. When her husband started teaching at a college 40 miles away, she resigned. While hating to lose a good artist, Bell agreed because its business was slow. Later, when Bell moved to a new location and its business increased, Diane was asked to come back, and she agreed.

As will be shown later, *friends and relatives* of present employees may also be a good source of dependable people. But remember, if a friend or relative is hired but doesn't work out and must be terminated, you've lost a friend as well as an employee.

You should make it a habit to keep *applications that come in either through the mail or in person.* Also, in some areas (especially in shopping centers), workers change jobs frequently, so attracting workers from *other businesses*—even competitors—is another good source.

Managers and technical and professional personnel may be found in various *social and professional organizations.* Also, *schools and colleges* can be a good source for skilled personnel and part-time employees. Contrary to popular belief, the occupations expected to grow most during this decade are not in the sophisticated high-tech fields requiring a college education and years of experience. Instead, they will require skills taught in vocational and technical schools—places that train students for a specific career, such as medical assistants, home health care workers, or skilled craft workers.

Other sources of employees are *migrants and immigrants, retirees,* and *workers with disabilities.* Few of us realize the role played by migrant workers in the United States, especially in agriculture. In late 1995, the U.S. Congress was trying to "prevent immigration reform from devastating an important segment of U.S. agriculture—the fruit, vegetable, and nursery growers who depend on seasonal labor . . . to harvest their crops."[9]

*Part-time and temporary workers (temps)* provide scheduling flexibility, as well as a way of reducing hiring (and benefit) costs. No longer is part-time employment only for students seeking summer jobs or homemakers supplementing the family income. Instead, recent college grads, retirees, corporate dropouts (or those pushed out), and others are taking temporary jobs. In fact, research by the National Association of Temporary and Staffing Services (NATSS) shows that older people are increasingly represented in the temporary ranks. A 1994 survey by the organization found that 50 percent of temps were aged 36 to 64, and 2 percent were 65 or over.[10] One group of such workers are those who wish to work less than 40 hours a week. At the 9 out of 10 U.S. companies that use temporaries, "millions of workers have chosen to work as temps in order to suit their lifestyles and workstyles."[11] Thus, they may be hired to work a few hours each day (e.g., as a clerk in a store) or a few days each week (as an industrial engineer or accountant).

> For example, Leonard Grey, part owner of a small Birmingham, Michigan, accounting firm, hired Barbara Fitzpatrick as an accountant for $5,000 less than she was offered by a major accounting firm. Ms. Fitzpatrick, who has a young daughter and works in her husband's business on weekends, didn't want to work 70-hour weeks during tax season. She works four days a week—and up to 55 hours during tax time—and thinks it's worth giving up employee benefits and the higher salary.[12]

The number of temporary workers in the United States has nearly doubled over the last five years (see Figure 13–4). These workers have created one of the largest industries in the nation from the standpoint of number of jobs created. There are currently 5,000 to 6,000 U.S. companies offering temporary help according to a study by NATSS.[13] From 1993 to 1994, the employment of temps increased 21 percent.[14]

**Figure 13–4** A Permanent Increase in Temps

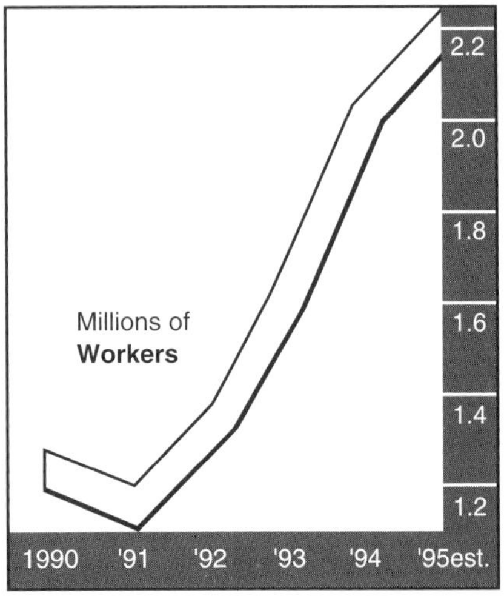


*Source:* National Association of Temporary and Staffing Services, as reported in *Fortune,* October 16, 1995, p. 53. Furtune, © 1995 Time Inc. All Rights Reserved.

Another study by NATSS indicates the nature of temporary employment is changing. As shown in Figure 13–5, industrial and professional jobs are increasing, as opposed to office/clerical, technical, and health care, which decreased.

**Leased manpower** is another source of part-time employees. These workers may work full time for the leasing firm and only part time for the small em-

**Leased manpower** refers to employees obtained from an outside firm that specializes in performing a particular service.

**Figure 13–5** The Changing Face of Temps

**Industry segments employing temporary workers, by percentage of U.S. temporary-help payroll.**

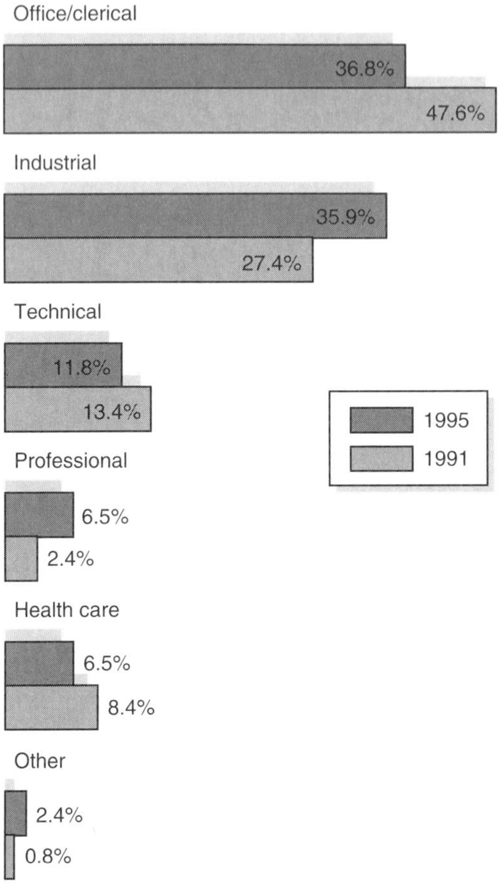


Note: 1995 data are from first quarter.
*Source:* National Association of Temporary and Staffing Services, as reported in Ken Gepfert, "Temps' Changing Roles Mask Their Full Impact," *The Wall Street Journal,* August 2, 1995, p. S1. Reprinted with permission of THE WALL STREET JOURNAL, © 1995 Dow Jones & Company, Inc. All Rights Reserved Worldwide.

ployer. This is an especially useful source of employees for clerical, maintenance, janitorial, and food service tasks.

Leasing saves labor costs for a business, because the employees' health insurance and other benefits are paid by the agency that supplies the needed labor. Also, it permits greater flexibility to cut back on staff when business is slack. This group is fast becoming a permanent part of the American work force.[15] But courts may still extend employer liability to the client company, even though the agreement with the leasing firm states otherwise.[16]

Economic conditions have reshaped our work force in recent years, establishing a smaller "core" of permanent employees surrounded by a flexible border of temporary and part-time workers.

## Recruiting and Selecting Employees

Once the number, types, and sources of employees needed are known, the small business manager starts looking for them. Don't limit applications to people who drop in and ask for a job; instead, go out and recruit.

**Recruitment** is reaching out to attract applicants from which to choose one to fill a job vacancy.

**Networking** is the process of establishing and maintaining contacts with key persons in one's own or another organization as informal development or promotion systems.

### Methods of Recruiting Employees

**Recruitment,** as shown in Figure 13–6, is reaching out to attract a supply of potential employees. It's generally done by advertising or by using employee referrals, temporary help services, **networking,** state and private employ-

**Figure 13–6** Methods Used to Recruit Employees

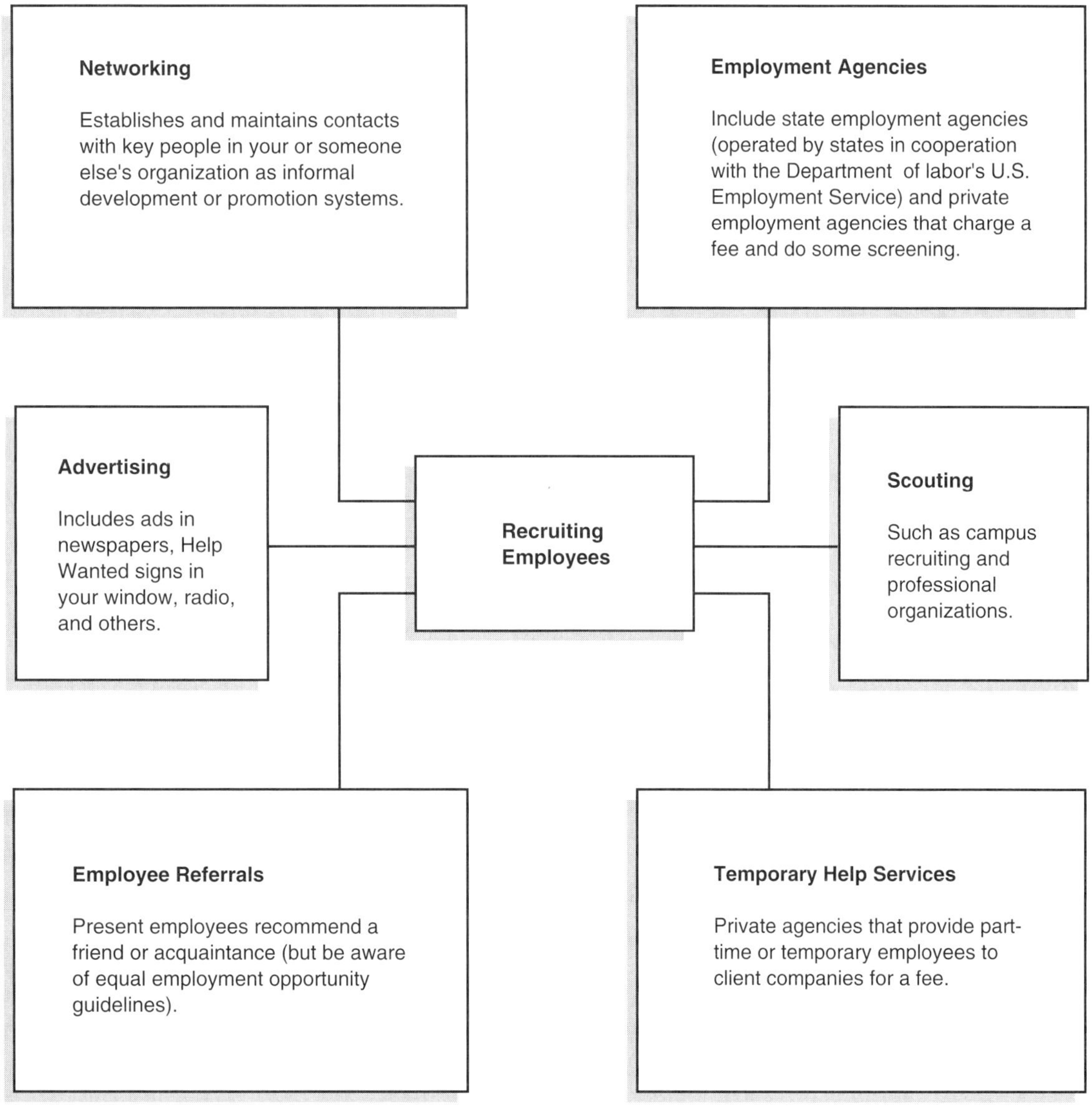
Networking
Establishes and maintains contacts with key people in your or someone else's organization as informal development or promotion systems.
Employment Agencies
Include state employment agencies (operated by states in cooperation with the Department of labor's U.S. Employment Service) and private employment agencies that charge a fee and do some screening.
Advertising
Includes ads in newspapers, Help Wanted signs in your window, radio, and others.
Recruiting Employees
Scouting
Such as campus recruiting and professional organizations.
Employee Referrals
Present employees recommend a friend or acquaintance (but be aware of equal employment opportunity guidelines).
Temporary Help Services
Private agencies that provide part-time or temporary employees to client companies for a fee.

**Figure 13–7** How Companies Recruit

**"Networking" was the fastest-growing method of recruiting workers in 1994–95, with 57% of companies using the method vs. 30% in 1993. Percentage of companies using:**

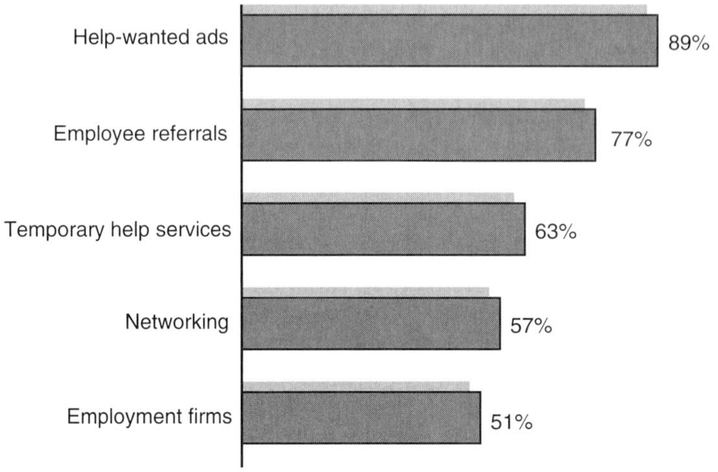


*Source:* 1995 Olsten Forum for Information Management, as reported in *USA Today*, December 13, 1995, p. 1B. Copyright 1995, USA TODAY. Reprinted with permission.

ment agencies, and scouting. Figure 13–7 shows the percentage of companies (large and small) using each method to recruit workers in 1995.

## Method of Selecting the Right Person for the Job

**Selection** involves choosing the applicant who has the qualifications to perform the job.

**Selection** is the process of determining whether an applicant has personal qualities that match the job specifications for a given position. Some of the qualities that working men and women say helped them get ahead are hard work, ability, and high standards.

No potential employee is perfect! So don't expect to find someone with all the qualities you ideally want. Instead, find people who have the qualities you need, and be willing to accept qualities you don't need or want, so long as those qualities don't harm the business. The selection procedure involves (1) gathering information about the applicant, (2) making a job offer, and (3) orienting the new employee.

### *Gathering Information about the Applicant*

Many people applying for a job will not be qualified, so try to find out all you can about what they can—and can't—do. In general, what a person has done in the past best indicates future performance. You should therefore use the most appropriate techniques to help discover a person's past performance and future possibilities.

The amount of information you need to know about an applicant depends on the type of employee being recruited. Figure 13–8 shows some

**Figure 13–8** Techniques for Gathering Information about Potential Employees

| *Techniques used to gather data* | *Characteristics to look for* |
| --- | --- |
| Preliminary screening or interview | Obvious misfit from outward appearance and conduct |
| Biographical inventory from application blank, résumé, etc. | Lacks adequate educational and performance record |
| Testing<br>Intelligence test(s) | Fails to meet minimum standards of mental alertness |
| Aptitude test(s) | Lacks specific capacities for acquiring particular knowledge or skills |
| Proficiency or achievement test(s) | Unable to demonstrate ability to do job |
| Interest test(s) | Lacks significant vocational interest in job |
| Personality test(s) | Lacks the personal characteristics required for job |
| In-depth interview | Lacks necessary innate ability, ambition, or other qualities |
| Verifying biographical data from references | Unfavorable or negative reports on past performance |
| Physical examination | Physically unfit for job |
| Personal judgment | Overall competence and ability to fit into the firm |

*Applicants who are available as potential employees*

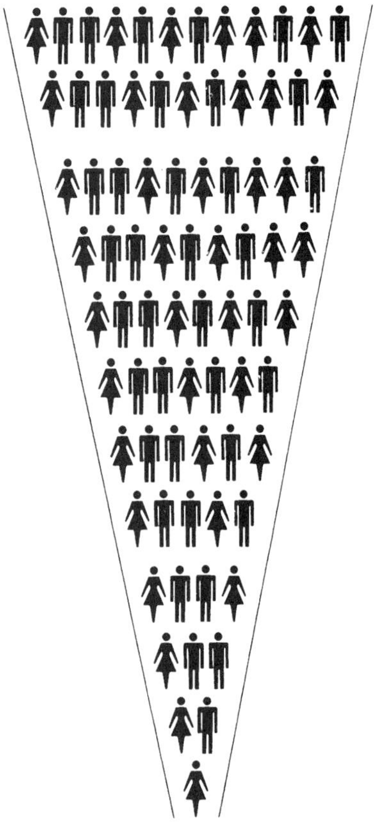

*Source:* Leon C. Megginson, Geralyn M. Franklin, and M. Jane Byrd, *Human Resource Management* (Houston, TX: Dame Publications, 1995), Figure 6–5, p. 154.

selection techniques that are frequently used to gather the information, but not all are needed for every job.

*Using Employee Input.* When selecting human resources, it helps to bring present employees into the process—in an advisory capacity. The consequences of hiring an incompatible worker in a small company can be very disruptive.

> Jody Wright learned this four years ago. The president of Motherwear, a $5 million catalog company in Northampton, Massachusetts, Wright hired a worker who was incompatible with her existing staff. After the dust had settled, she instituted a system whereby present employees help in hiring new co-workers. Having helped in the selection, they have a greater commitment to working with the new hires. Employees have interviewed and hired more than 60 percent of Motherwear's 40-member staff since then.[17]

*Preliminary Screening.* You should do some form of preliminary screening of applicants early in the selection procedure. This can be done in a formal interview or informally through reviewing a candidate's application form or letter, résumé, or other submitted material. Most firms use some form of interviewing at this point. You should look for such obvious factors as voice, physical appearance, personal grooming, educational qualifications, training, and experience. Many applicants are eliminated at this stage for reasons such as inappropriate dress, attitude, education, or experience.

> According to a study of college scouting, for example, 9 percent of college applicants were eliminated for "personal reasons" such as bad breath, dirty fingernails, and uncombed hair.[18]

It is at this stage of selection that many small business owners or managers inadvertently—or intentionally—run afoul of equal employment opportunity (EEO) laws (to be discussed in detail later). Table 13–1 presents some questions to avoid asking applicants at this stage—or at any other time before a job offer is made.

**Table 13–1** Topics to Avoid When Interviewing Applicants

Here is an up-to-date summary of 10 of the most dangerous questions or topics you might raise during an interview.

1. *Children.* Do not ask applicants whether they have children, plan to have children, or have child care.
2. *Age.* Do not ask an applicant's age.
3. *Disabilities.* Do not ask whether the candidate has a physical or mental disability that would interfere with doing the job.
4. *Physical characteristics.* Do not ask for such identifying characteristics as height or weight on an application.
5. *Citizenship.* Do not ask applicants about their citizenship. However, the Immigration Reform and Control Act does require business operators to determine that their employees have a legal right to work in the United States.
7. *Lawsuits.* Do not ask a job candidate whether he or she has ever filed a suit or a claim against a former employer.
8. *Arrest record.* Do not ask applicants about their arrest records.
9. *Smoking.* Do not ask whether a candidate smokes. While smokers are not protected under the Americans with Disabilities Act (ADA), asking applicants whether they smoke might lead to legal difficulties if an applicant is turned down because of fear that smoking would drive up the employer's health care costs.
10. *AIDS and HIV.* Never ask job candidates whether they have AIDS or are HIV-positive, as these questions violate the ADA and could violate state and federal civil rights laws.

*Source:* Adapted with permission from Janine S. Paulist, "Topics to Avoid with Applicants," *Nation's Business,* July 1992. Copyright 1992, U.S. Chamber of Commerce.

## USING TECHNOLOGY TO SUCCEED

### Revolution in Résumés

More firms are now using optical scanning devices to enter résumés into computers, then electronically searching for the ideal candidate. Many large organizations, such as the White House, Disneyland, and Ford Motor Company, have contracted with a company that uses artificial intelligence to analyze résumés, categorizing, for example, the applicant's primary work experience. Other businesses use less sophisticated technology that simply searches for keywords.

According to some human resource experts, the computer revolution changes some of the rules of résumé writing. For example, to ensure that the computer doesn't make mistakes scanning the résumé, use simple black type on white paper and don't fold or staple pages. Some experts suggest listing a keyword summary at the top and encourage using lots of nouns to match words the computer would search for.

*Source: The Wall Street Journal,* May 16, 1995, p. A1. Reprinted with permission of *The Wall Street Journal,* 

*Gathering Biographical Information.* Biographical information comes from application forms, résumés, school records, military records, credit references, and so forth. You should look for solid evidence of past performance, concrete information on which to base the decision instead of depending on opinions or assumptions. Having applicants fill out an application form in your presence—in longhand—serves as a simple performance test of their neatness and communications ability, or even simple literacy. No matter how good an applicant's record appears, don't base a decision on her or his unconfirmed statements. Unfortunately, there's a trend toward inflating résumés, so you should make it a point to verify education and employment history and check references.

> For instance, a study of 1,200 job applicants by Certified Reference Checking, of St. Louis, found that 34 percent of them had lied on their résumés.[19]

Several "red flags" may be indications of a phony résumé: gaps in dates or sequences that do not add up, such as the time between getting a degree and a job; degrees from unknown schools; vagueness; and accomplishments that don't make sense, such as years of education and experience that are greater than possible for the applicant's age. See the accompanying Using Technology to Succeed for suggestions on evaluating résumés efficiently and effectively.

*Giving Preemployment Tests.* Since 1971, when the U.S. Supreme Court ruled that preemployment tests must be job related, most small firms have minimized their use because of the cost involved and the possible legal hassles. In 1994, however, the American Management Association found that, of the companies it surveyed that had fewer than 100 employees, 37 percent tested job applicants for math skills. (Only 25 percent of the tested workers were found "lacking," as compared to 35 percent nationwide.) Reading skills were tested by 27 percent of those small companies, and 25 percent of them offered remedial training.[20]

**polygraph** is an instrument for simultaneously recording variations in several different physiological variables.

*Source: USA Today,* August 7, 1985, p. 8A. Copyright 1985, USA TODAY. Reprinted with permission.

A word of caution is needed about the use of a special test, the **polygraph,** or "lie detector." Before 1989, many companies used the polygraph. Because of conflicting results, Congress has since passed a law barring most private employers from using polygraph tests. Now, written and computerized tests for assessing employee honesty are increasingly being produced and sold.

**In-depth, preemployment,** or **diagnostic interviews** are detailed, probing, and penetrating interviews seeking to determine the applicant's character and other aspects of personality.

*Interviewing Applicants in Depth.* Applicants who have survived the procedure this far are often subjected to an **in-depth interview** at this time. Sometimes called a **preemployment** or **diagnostic interview,** its purpose is to probe the applicant's character, motivation, and other aspects of personality.

Personnel Decisions Inc. (PDI) in Minneapolis has compiled a list of 10 common mistakes an interviewer makes. The following are suggestions to overcome those mistakes:[21]

- Don't give the candidate too many clues.
- Analyze the job accurately.
- Don't ask the obvious questions.
- Don't ask legally indefensible questions.
- Try not to focus too much attention on the candidate's self-evaluation.
- Don't be afraid of probing the applicant.
- Don't be overly influenced by first impressions.
- Ask the right questions, but be sure to know how to evaluate the answers.
- Don't miss important clues.
- Don't rely too much on past credentials.

*Checking References.* References play an important role in gathering information about an applicant. The three most frequently used types of references are: personal, academic, and past employment. For applicants with any work history, the most valued references are from former employers. Using a personal visit, a telephone call, or a personal letter, you can verify work history, educational attainments, and other information the applicant has presented. By law, former employers may, if they choose, limit their responses to information about dates and title of the most recent job and total period of employment. Be sure to get the applicant's permission before contacting the present employer, who may not know the employee is job hunting.

For a more meaningful job match, applicants should also check references on the potential employer.

> This is what David Blumenthal of River Edge, New Jersey, does. He insists that serious job applicants contact *his* references—usually his customers—to get a true picture of his company, Flash Creative Management. Blumenthal has three reasons for doing this: (1) so that candidates will understand his commitment to customer service, (2) as the basis for a second round of interviews, since he then calls the references to see what they thought of the applicant, and (3) to test the applicant's willingness to take direction.[22]

Just as some applicants are not honest with their prospective employer, neither are the persons giving them a reference always entirely candid.

> For instance, a Robert Half International poll of 150 executives found that many of them admitted to erring on the favorable side when discussing an applicant. Their primary reasons for shading the truth were (1) fear of lawsuits (80 percent) and (2) bias due to friendship with the applicant.[23]

*Giving Physical Examinations.* In the past, the final step in selecting employees was some type of physical exam. Now, however, the Americans with Disabilities Act (ADA) limits the use of such exams in hiring by employers with 15 or more employees. To prevent possible discrimination against the disabled, the law prohibits asking questions about an applicant's medical history or requiring an exam *before* a preliminary job offer is made.[24]

### *Making a Job Offer*

When you have decided to hire an applicant, you should make a job offer to him or her. It should include details of working conditions, such as pay, work hours, holidays, vacations, and other employee benefits, as well as the new employee's duties and responsibilities. Given the increasing tendency for workers to sue their employers, you should put job offers in writing and get the applicant to sign, indicating his or her understanding and agreement.

### *Orienting the New Employee*

Selection also should include orienting new employees to the job. A new job is usually a difficult and frustrating experience, even for the best-qualified people. Thus, orientation should include, as a minimum, an introduction to co-workers; an explanation of the business's history, policies, procedures, and benefits; and working closely with the new employee during at least the first pay period. More employees leave a firm during that period than at any other time during their employment, as the following example shows.

> After more than 20 years as a full-time wife and mother, Elaine Reeves* accepted her first job outside the home. When she reported for work on Monday morning, Elaine was greeted by the business's owner and shown the word processor, other office machines, and the supply cabinet. Then

---

*Name disguised at her request.

she was left on her own while the owner went to call on several contractors. In these unfamiliar surroundings and with the other employees wrapped up in their own work, which made them seem unfriendly and unhelpful, she felt shaken and discouraged and was thinking of turning around and going home. The owner walked in just in time to stop her.

## Training and Developing Employees

The continued effectiveness of a business results not only from the ability of the owner but also from (1) the caliber of its employees, including their inherent abilities; (2) their development through training, education, and experience; and (3) their motivation. The first of these depends on effective recruiting and selection. The second results from personnel development. The third, motivation, which will be covered in Chapter 14, results from the manager's leadership abilities.

### Need for Training and Development

Not only must new employees be trained, but the present ones also must be retrained and upgraded if they are to adjust to rapidly changing job requirements. Some of the results of training and developing workers include (1) increased productivity, (2) reduced turnover, (3) increased earnings for employees, (4) decreased costs of materials and equipment due to errors, (5) less supervision required, and (6) improved employee satisfaction.

### Ways of Training Nonmanagerial Employees

You can use many methods to train nonmanagerial employees including (1) on-the-job training (OJT), (2) apprenticeship training, and (3) internship training.[25]

#### *On-the-Job Training.*

**On-the-job training (OJT)** or **on-the-job learning (OJL)** has the worker actually performing the work, under the supervision of a competent trainer.

The most universal form of employee development, **on-the-job training (OJT),** which is in reality **on-the-job learning (OJL),** occurs when workers perform their regular job under the supervision and guidance of the owner, a manager, or a trained worker or instructor. Thus, while learning to do the job, the worker acts as a regular employee, producing the good or service the business sells. Whether consciously planned or not, this form of training always occurs. While the methods used vary with the trainer, OJT usually involves:

- Telling workers what needs to be done.
- Telling them how to do the job.
- Showing them how it must be done.
- Letting them do the job under the trainer's guidance.
- Telling—and showing—them what they did right, what they did wrong, and how to correct the wrong activity.
- Repeating the process until the learners have mastered the job.

The main *advantages* of OJT are that it results in low out-of-pocket costs and production continues during the training. Also, there is no transition from classroom learning to actual production. Experience has repeatedly shown that OJT is a cost-effective and proven alternative to formal training programs. Also, a well-structured and well-conducted OJT program both educates *and* motivates employees.[26]

Do you remember from Chapter 7 that 40 percent of Pizza Hut managers learned their jobs as part-time crew members? And that 70 percent of McDonald's restaurant managers, and over 50 percent of its middle and senior managers, began their careers performing hourly restaurant jobs?[27]

D

On the other hand, the *disadvantages* of OJT are excessive waste caused by mistakes and the poor learning environment provided by the production area. While most OJT is done by owners and managers, they are not necessarily the best ones to do it, since their primary focus is on running the business. For this reason, another capable employee or even an outside trainer should be assigned this responsibility, if possible.

### *Apprenticeship Training*

For workers performing skilled, craft-type jobs, **apprenticeship training** blends the learning of theory with practice in the techniques of the job. If the job can best be learned by combining classroom instruction and actual learning experience on the job, this training method should be used. It usually lasts from two to seven years of both classroom learning and on-the-job training. For young people who can't—or won't—finish a high school program, an effective apprentice program can "put a good job [within] reach."[28]

**Apprenticeship training** blends OJT with learning of theory in the classroom.

### *Internship Training*

**Internship training** combines education at a school or college with on-the-job training at a cooperating business. It is usually used for students who are prospective employees for marketing, clerical, technical, and managerial positions. Co-op programs prepare students for technical positions, provide income to meet the cost of their education, and give them a chance to see if they would like to go to work for the company. This method also gives the small business owner a chance to evaluate the student as a prospective full-time employee.

**Internship training** combines OJT with learning at a cooperating school or college.

### *Cross-Training*

Q

With the shortage of skilled job applicants, some small businesses are turning to **cross-training** to make their employees more versatile—and keep them more satisfied. While specialized training tends to improve performance, it may also result in boredom and fatigue. Cross-training, which has employees learn many kinds of jobs, may reduce turnover by keeping workers more interested in their jobs.

**Cross-training** involves workers learning many job skills so they are more versatile.

> At Motor Technology, for instance, training—especially cross-training—is seen as "the prerequisite to delivering excellent customer service . . ., [helping] reduce turnover . . ., [and fostering] pride of workmanship." Thomas Ryan, president of Motor Technology, believes this type of training has helped "the family business grow as competitors had to shut down."[29]

### Outside Help with Training

Many outside programs are available to help you train your employees. For example, the National Apprenticeship Act of 1937, administered by the U.S. Labor Department's Bureau of Apprenticeship and Training, sets policies and standards for apprenticeship programs. Write to this bureau for help in conducting such a program.

Vocational-technical schools, business schools, junior colleges, and small private firms help small companies by conducting regular or special classes. Through such programs, potential employees can become qualified for skilled jobs such as machinist, lathe operator, computer operator, and legal assistant.

## Selecting and Developing Managers

Q Determining the job requirements for someone to be a manager is more difficult than filling other positions because managerial jobs differ so greatly. But one generalization usually applies: *The employee who is a good performer at the nonmanagerial level does not necessarily make a good manager, because the skills needed at the two levels differ drastically.* Adding to this difficulty is the constant change in managerial methods and terms. Many small businesses can't always be abreast of these changes. Therefore, such concepts as total quality management (TQM), reengineering, benchmarking, and rightsizing might be desirable goals, but unattainable.

### Selecting Managers

In small firms, managers are usually promoted from within, but many businesses hire college graduates for management trainee programs. We have found in developing, directing, and teaching in management development programs that the characteristics to be developed to produce good managers are creativity, productivity, innovativeness, communication skills (including oral, written, nonverbal, and telephone), self-motivation, and the drive and energy to energize others to achieve consistently large amounts of high-quality work. You can see that these tend to be the same qualities that lead to success as an entrepreneur (see Chapter 2).

### Developing Managers

Q In addition to the usual methods used to develop all employees, some special techniques are used to develop managerial personnel. These include coaching, planned progression, job rotation, and executive development programs, as shown in Figure 13–9. Also, many franchisers, such as McDonald's and Holiday Inn, have their own schools at which their franchise owners and managers learn the desired system and how to make it work.[30]

## Complying with Equal Employment Opportunity (EEO) Laws

D Federal and state laws and regulations affect almost all aspects of personnel

**Figure 13–9** Methods Used to Develop Managers

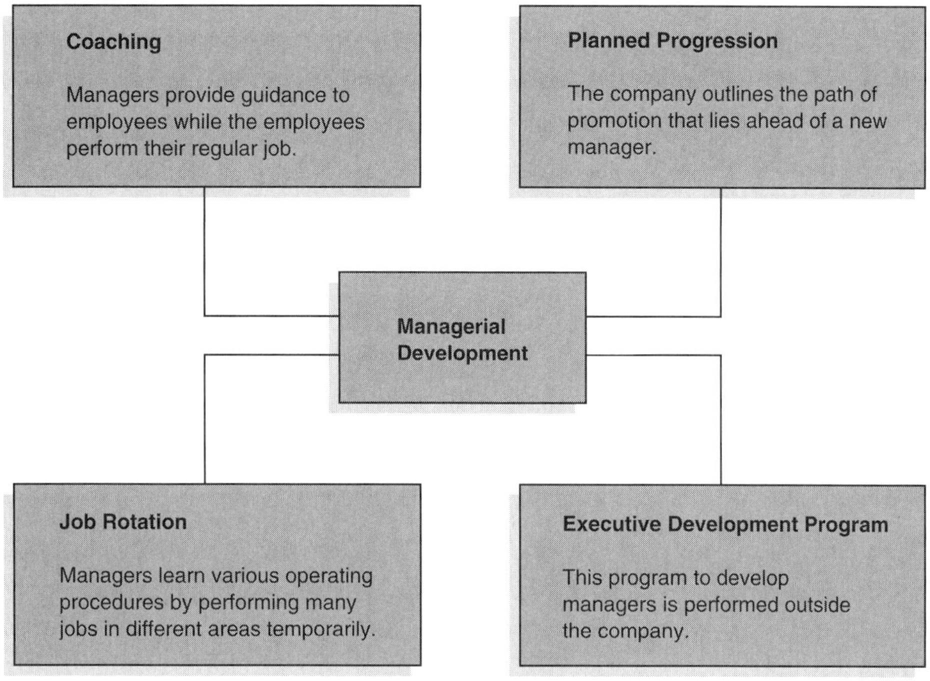


relations. Since state laws vary so widely, only the most significant federal laws affecting recruiting and selecting employees are discussed here.

Since 1963, Congress has passed various acts to create equal employment opportunity and affirmative action. Table 13–2 summarizes the most significant legislation in this area.

Special mention should be made of the **Americans with Disabilities Act (ADA)** of 1992, for it changed the way employers must deal with the 33.8 million U.S. citizens who have physical or mental disabilities. This act mandates the removal of social and physical barriers against the disabled, two-thirds of whom are unemployed. It covers disabilities such as cancer, blindness, arthritis, HIV infection, chemical dependency, speech and hearing impairment, learning disabilities, and mental retardation. The act specifically excludes sexual behavior disorders, gambling, kleptomania, and others. This act targets employers with 15 or more workers.

The **Americans with Disabilities Act (ADA)** requires the removal of many social and physical barriers to employing the disabled.

## Enforcing EEO Laws

You must remember that all employees are entitled to equality in all conditions of employment. Hiring, training, promotions and transfers, wages and benefits, and all other employment factors are covered. Posting available job openings on a bulletin board to give present employees a chance to bid on them has been found to be a good method of complying with EEO laws.

There must be no discrimination in rates of pay, including pensions or other deferred payments. Recreational activities—company sports teams, holiday parties, and the like—should be open to all employees on a nondiscriminatory basis.

**Table 13–2** Legal Influences on Equal Employment Opportunity (EEO) and Affirmative Action

| Laws | Coverage | Basic requirements | Agencies involved |
|---|---|---|---|
| Title VII of Civil Rights Act of 1964, as amended | Employers with 15 or more employees and engaged in interstate commerce; federal service workers; and state and local government workers. | Prohibits employment decisions based on race, color, religion, sex, or national origin. | Equal Employment Opportunity Commission (EEOC) |
| Executive Order 11246, as amended | Employers with federal contracts and subcontracts. | Requires contractors who underutilize women and minorities to develop affirmative action plans (AAPs), including setting goals and timetables; and to recruit, select, train, utilize, and promote more minorities and women when contracts exceed $50,000 a year. | Office of Federal Contract Compliance Programs (OFCCP) in the Labor Department |
| Age Discrimination in Employment Act of 1967 | Employers with 20 or more employees. | Prohibits employment discrimination against employees aged 40 and over, including mandatory retirement before 70, with certain exceptions. | EEOC |
| Vocational Rehabilitation Act of 1973 | Employers with federal contracts or subcontracts. | Prohibits discrimination and requires contractor to develop affirmative action programs to recruit and employ handicapped persons. Requires development of an AAP. | OFCCP |
| Vietnam-Era Veterans Readjustment Act of 1974 | Employers with federal contracts or subcontracts. | Requires contractors to develop AAPs to recruit and employ Vietnam-era veterans and to list job openings with state employment services, for priority in referrals. | OFCCP |
| Americans with Disabilities Act of 1992 (ADA) | Employers with 15 or more employees. | Prohibits discrimination based on physical or mental handicap (affirmative action required). | EEOC |
| Civil Rights Act of 1991 | Same as Title VII | Amends Title VII and ADA to allow punitive and compensatory damages in cases of intentional discrimination and permits more extensive use of jury trials. | EEOC |

*Source:* Various government and private publications.

**Figure 13–10** Principal EEOC Regulations

- Sex discrimination guidelines
- Questions and answers on pregnancy disability and reproductive hazards
- Religious discrimination guidelines
- National origin discrimination guidelines
- Interpretations of the Age Discrimination in Employment Act
- Employee selection guidelines
- Record keeping and reports
- Affirmative action guidelines
- EEO in the federal government
- Equal Pay Act interpretations
- Policy statement on maternal benefits
- Policy statement on relationship of Title VII to 1986
- Immigration Reform and Control Act
- Policy statement on reproductive and fetal hazards
- Policy statement on religious accommodation under Title VII
- Policy guidance on sexual harassment
- Disabilities discrimination guidelines

*Source: Federal Regulation of Personnel and Human Resource Management,* 2nd ed. by Ledvinka and Scarpello (Wadsworth Publishing Company). Copyright © 1992.

The **Equal Employment Opportunity Commission (EEOC)** is the federal agency primarily responsible for enforcing EEO laws.

As shown in Table 13–2, the **Equal Employment Opportunity Commission (EEOC)** is the primary enforcing agency for most EEO laws. Figure 13–10 shows some regulations it has issued to prevent discrimination such as age discrimination. For example, younger workers complain that older workers act like parents in the workplace. University of Vermont professor Barbara McIntosh identifies this practice as "intergenerational conflict."[31]

D

Another difficult issue for small—and large—businesses is how to cope with sexual harassment. The term is difficult to define because the nature of the act lies as much in the reaction of the victim as in the intentions or actions of the offender; that is, what makes a gesture, remark, or pinup photo "harassment" is that it is "unwelcome." Small employers should therefore install an effective prevention program.[32] One way to raise employees' consciousness of sexual harassment and train them to avoid it—or deal with it—is described in Using Technology to Succeed.

Language is another job-related activity that is causing problems for small businesses. The EEOC has decreed that English-only rules may violate EEO laws "unless an employer can show they are necessary for conducting business."[33]

The enforcement of these laws—as desirable as they may be—is causing problems for the EEOC. In turn, those filing charges, and those charged, are suffering long waits for decisions.

> For example, while more than 150,000 discrimination charges are filed each year, there were nearly 159,000 cases waiting to be heard in

## USING TECHNOLOGY TO SUCCEED

### Sexual Harassment Awareness

Not only is sexual harassment illegal under Title VII of the Civil Rights Act of 1961, but it is also bad for your business. Leaving aside moral and ethical considerations—which most small business owners would, of course, consider—litigation is expensive. Even if you win, your legal bills will probably be quite heavy. And if you lose, sexual harassment verdicts can result in very expensive rulings against you and your business. Perhaps of greater importance to small firms, such harassment can hurt employee morale and reduce productivity.

So how do owners recognize, prevent, and/or deal with this touchy subject? First, you should have a clear and strong anti-sexual harassment policy. Then you should train—and retrain—all employees in a supervisory capacity on how to deal with the problem. But sexual harassment—and its prevention or correction—are so intricate that small firms probably don't have the properly skilled personnel to train others.

Callahan & Associates, Inc., of Fairhope, Alabama, has developed a computer-based training program that companies can use to communicate their policy and to train employees in how to recognize the problem and avoid it—and how to respond if it does occur. The instructional software, *Sexual Harassment Awareness,* has interactive exercises, specific examples, and colorful graphics and animation to teach and reinforce your message. It also includes a "final exam" and automatically records test scores and other data to provide a convincing record of the steps taken to train your people and to prevent sexual harassment.

The four-hour package, which runs under the Windows operating system, costs $495 for a single-station license, which can be used by any number of employees on one computer. There are discounts for multiple packages.

*Source:* Based on literature provided by Callahan & Associates, Inc.; conversation with Jan Oliver of C&A; and a demonstration of the software given at a meeting of the Rotary Club of Fairhope, Alabama. For more information, call 1-800-366-1559.

mid-August 1995. The time lag between when a charge is filed and when it is resolved was "averaging 13 months to get even a meritless claim dismissed."[34]

**Affirmative action programs (AAPs)** provide guidelines to help firms eliminate discrimination against women and minorities.

The Labor Department's Office of Federal Contract Compliance Programs (OFCCP) requires employers with government contracts or subcontracts to have **affirmative action programs (AAPs)** to put the principle of equal employment opportunity into practice. The OFCCP can cancel a guilty firm's contract or prohibit it from getting future contracts if a violation is blatant.

## Terminating Employees

**Employment at will** means that employers may hire or fire workers with or without cause.

While you still have the right to terminate employees for cause, the concept of "employment at will" is losing acceptance in courts and legislatures. **Employment at will** essentially means employers may fire employees with or without cause at any time they choose. Courts and legislators are now applying instead the "good faith and fair dealing" concept, whereby terminations must be "reasonable" and not "arbitrarily" or "indiscriminately" applied. Violating this concept may lead to punitive damages in addition to actual damages that have been sustained by one of the protected employees.[35]

## WHAT YOU SHOULD HAVE LEARNED

**1.** The most important resource for any business is people. Therefore, you must determine the needed number and skills of employees and the sources from which to recruit them. This process begins with a job description and job specifications.

Employees can be recruited from either internal or external sources. When feasible, it is best to upgrade, transfer, or promote from inside the business, all of which increase employee morale and save time and money; also, employees' past performance is known. External sources include former employees, applications, friends and relatives of present employees, other businesses, social and professional organizations, schools and colleges, retirees, workers with disabilities, and part-time and temporary workers.

**2.** Employees can be recruited through advertising, employment agencies, temporary help services, networking, employee referrals, and scouting. Newspaper want ads are the most common method of recruiting.

You can evaluate prospective employees by *(a)* a preliminary screening interview or review of the candidate's application or résumé; *(b)* biographical information from the application or résumé and from school, military, and other records; and *(c)* some form of testing and verifying references, and *(d)* giving a physical examination after a preliminary job offer is made.

Ultimately, the decision of whom to employ involves your personal judgment. Once the decision has been made, a clear—preferably written—job offer should be extended. Orientation can range from a simple introduction to co-workers to a lengthy training process.

**3.** After employees are hired, they should be retrained and upgraded periodically. Training methods include *(a)* on-the-job training (OJT), *(b)* apprenticeship training, and *(c)* internship training.

**4.** In selecting managers, you should look for *managerial qualities,* which aren't the same as *nonmanagerial competence.* Techniques used for developing managers include *(a)* coaching, *(b)* planned progression, *(c)* job rotation, and *(d)* executive development programs.

**5.** You must conform to federal and state laws in your dealings with current and prospective employees. The equal employment opportunity (EEO) provisions of the Civil Rights Act and the requirements of the Americans with Disabilities Act are especially important. Legislation has been passed to prevent discrimination on the basis of race, color, sex, age, religion, disabilities, or national origin. The Equal Employment Opportunity Commission (EEOC) and the Office of Federal Contract Compliance Programs (OFCCP) enforce these laws. Age, sex, and language discrimination charges are particularly troubling to small firms.

## QUESTIONS FOR DISCUSSION

1. What does personnel planning involve in the small company?
2. What external sources are usually used by small businesses for finding new employees?

3. What are some advantages and disadvantages of filling job openings from within the company?
4. Distinguish among upgrading, promoting, and transferring employees.
5. What does the personnel selection procedure involve?
6. Describe the methods used to gather information about prospective employees.
7. Why should a physical examination be required of an applicant? Why not?
8. What are the primary methods used to train employees? Explain each.
9. What should you look for in a potential manager?
10. What methods can be used to train managers?
11. How do EEO laws affect recruiting and selecting employees?
12. What agencies enforce EEO laws? How do they enforce them?

## CASE 13

## SUPREME PLUMBING AND HEATING COMPANY: WHERE ARE THE WORKERS?

In the late 1950s, two friendly competitors formed the Supreme Plumbing and Heating Company as a partnership in a rapidly developing industrial area southwest of Houston, Texas. At first, the partners did most of the work themselves, including plumbing, heating, and wiring for both commercial and residential buildings. The business grew rapidly, and several craftsmen and other employees were added. This left the partners devoting almost all their time to managing the business rather than doing the work themselves.

Supreme competed with six other companies within a 50-mile radius both for business and for the best craftsmen. This became difficult in the 1960s when the Lyndon B. Johnson Space Center was built nearby. Most of the area's skilled workers left their jobs with the companies to work at the center for better pay and benefits, causing a great shortage of craftsmen in the area. At the same time, demand for plumbing, heating, and wiring was increasing. It would have been a good opportunity for Supreme to expand its operations—if the needed workers could have been found.

The partners decided the only way to have an adequate supply of trained craftsmen was to do their own training, so they started an apprenticeship program. The plan was to hire high school graduates or dropouts to work with some of the older craftsmen as apprentice plumbers and electricians, at the prevailing wage rate, until they learned the trade. When they finished their training, they would train others so there would be a continuous training program.

Although the program gave the young people an opportunity to learn a trade that would be valuable to them in future years, the plan didn't work.

The trainees would work for Supreme just long enough to be trained; then they would quit to take another job, go into the armed services, or go back to school. The partners had to reduce the amount of construction work they bid on because of their limited work force. To compensate for this loss of revenue, they started a wholesale plumbing, heating, and electrical supply business.

The worker shortage at Supreme continued until there were only three plumbers, three plumber's helpers, two electricians, and two electrician's helpers left. Because the craftsmen were nearing retirement age and the helpers weren't interested in learning the trade, the owners had to go on with the wholesale business, although they would have preferred to continue in construction.

*Source:* This case was prepared by Leon C. Megginson.

## QUESTIONS

1. Supreme Plumbing and Heating Company limited itself to hiring only high school graduates and even dropouts. What type of preliminary screening should there have been for this type of job, if any? Explain.
2. What types of recruiting methods could have been implemented by the two partners?
3. When the new Space Center was built nearby, what kind of actions should the partners have taken?
4. Although the apprenticeship program seemed to be the route to take, what other options were there?

# APPLICATION 13–1

Clark owns a small welding plant in a Midwestern community. For the past six years, he has been running the business quite successfully. Now, however, he is getting older and wants to retire. He wants someone else to supervise the business.

In the past, he has hired many students from the local vocational-technical school. He has also trained many of the students and tries to keep in touch with those that remain in the area. He recently promoted one of the trainees to a supervisory job and hired another trainee. The problem is that the trainee who has been promoted has no managerial experience.

## QUESTIONS

1. Do you think managerial qualities are different from nonmanagerial ones? If so, how do they differ?
2. What were Clark's other options to fill the post?
3. Do you think he made the right decisions? Explain.

# ACTIVITY 13–1

*Directions:* Use information from this chapter to solve the "management maze."

ACROSS

3 Physiological recording instrument

6 Hire or fire without cause

7 Attract applicants

8 Detailed qualifications

9 Similar to 2 Down

11 Changing job without changing pay

13 Specialized employees from another firm

15 Learning by performing

16 Retraining for complex work

DOWN

1 List duties and responsibilities

2 Blends theory with 15 Across

4 Choosing an applicant

5 Federal agency

10 Moving employee to a higher position

12 Helps eliminate discrimination

14 Removes barriers

ACROSS 3 Polygraph 6 Employment at will 7 Recruitment 8 Job specifications 9 Internship training 11 Transferring 13 Leased manpower 15 OJT 16 Upgrading
DOWN 1 Job description 2 Apprenticeship training 4 Selection 5 EEOC 10 Promoting 12 AAPS 14 ADA

CHAPTER

# 14

# Communicating With, Leading, and Motivating Employees

*The key to . . . success is superior customer service, continuing internal entrepreneurship, and a deep belief in the dignity, worth, and potential of every person in the organization.*
—Tom Peters, coauthor of *In Search of Excellence*

*The good boss selects people with demonstrated capabilities, tells them what results are expected, largely leaves them alone to decide the means by which they can be obtained, and then monitors the results.*—Sanford Jacobs, entrepreneur

## LEARNING OBJECTIVES

After studying the material in this chapter, you will be able to:

1. Explain how managerial assumptions affect human relationships with employees.
2. List some barriers to effective communication and show some ways to improve communication.
3. Explain how to improve employee motivation.
4. Tell why personnel appraisals are used.
5. Describe how to compensate employees with money and employee benefits.

*P R O F I L E*

## CATHY ANDERSON-GILES: MASTER MOTIVATOR

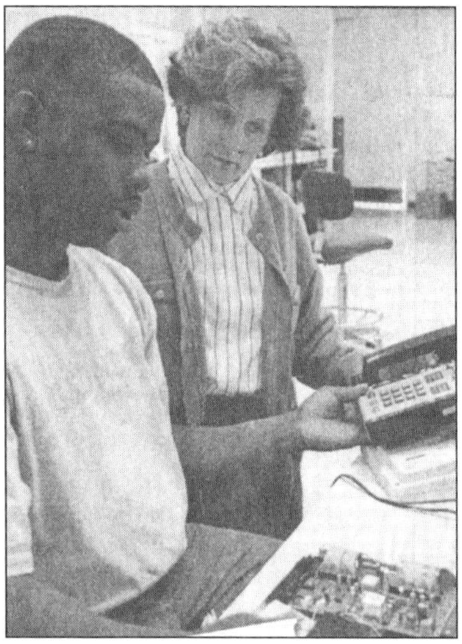

Photo by Mike Kittrell, Mobile Press Register, Inc. 

Good leadership, whether in the military, in sports, or in business, is not a one-way street in terms of communication and motivation. Effective leaders not only know how and when to speak, but they also know how and when to listen. Judging from the success of her business, Equity Technologies Inc., and the feedback from her employees, Cathy Anderson-Giles, the company's CEO, is a tremendous leader and motivator who employs a progressive management style. Her small business specializes in removing, repairing, and cleaning telecommunications equipment.

An important aspect of Anderson-Giles' leadership is having a very informal, friendly working atmosphere. Employees wear jeans and enjoy an open-door policy. One employee noted that it was Anderson-Giles' extra touches—such as using fine china at the company Christmas party, putting fresh flowers in the office, and letting employees choose the colors in their offices—that make work and the working atmosphere pleasant. "I call it employee-friendly. We're sort of a family here," remarked Reginald Croshon, repair technician coordinator. "We try not to look at it as 'I'm the boss, you're the employee.' "

Anderson-Giles' background in Vicksburg and Jackson, Mississippi, is just as nontraditional as her management style. Because her son had a disability, she originally decided to pursue a career in physical education for the handicapped. So she went back to school at Jackson State University, where she said she "was one of two white women who integrated the student body."

After a brief teaching stint, however, she realized this was not the profession for her. So she worked in the insurance industry while she attended law school at night. After receiving her law degree, she set up in private practice in her hometown of Jackson.

In 1984, her husband, who worked for AT&T, was transferred to Mobile, Alabama. At first, the couple took turns visiting each other on weekends, but they soon realized the constant travel was too much. Citing the fact that her husband had made sacrifices for her while she was preparing for her career, she says, "I made the decision [that] it was my turn to sacrifice."

In 1984, after the move to Mobile, she and her husband started their own company, Business Communication Distributors, which he continues to run. Six years later, they and two other investors started Equity Technologies Inc.

with Anderson-Giles at the helm. "It was the logical step for me," she said. "I enjoy the process of creating businesses."

Anderson-Giles' employees seem to enjoy working for her. Perhaps her most important key to success is that she listens to and actively seeks the advice of her employees. Chip McNeill, manager of information services, states: "We have a lot of input in the day-to-day operation of the company." This style of leadership not only motivates employees but also makes them feel valued.

Anderson-Giles seeks advice from her employees because she believes in them, and they believe in—and perform for—her. Another motivating factor is that the employees know performance means advancement in the company. "We know the growth's here and there are opportunities for advancement," says Darrell Coxwell, assistant manager in the auditing department.

D

LaKeshia Joiner was one of the original employees hired by Anderson-Giles. Although LaKeshia had no work experience and only a high school diploma, Anderson-Giles saw considerable potential in her and continues to encourage her. Now she has completed a degree at Southeast College of Technology, is the supervisor of the company's auditing division, and is working on a business degree. Enthusiastically, LaKeshia declares, "I haven't reached my peak yet."

Neither has Equity Technologies Inc., which has had to move four times in the past five years to expand. The company has grown from 10 to 48 employees in that time. Because of the company's excellent growth—which Anderson-Giles conservatively predicts will be 25 percent for the upcoming year—Equity Technologies recently won the Small Business Technology Award given by the Business Council of Alabama.

Anderson-Giles says that the key to her leadership and motivational skills is that she realizes "there's so much undiscovered talent in everybody." Apparently, she is quite adept at finding it.

*Source:* Prepared by William Jay Megginson from various sources, especially Sara Lamb, "Workplace Is People-Friendly," *Mobile* (Alabama) *Register,* November 12, 1995, pp. 1-F, 2-F.

The opening quotations and Profile illustrate the importance of leading and motivating people in small firms. These activities include:

- Practicing "good" human relations.
- Using enlightened leadership in dealing with employees.
- Communicating openly and truthfully with them.
- Using positive motivation.
- Compensating them fairly.
- Evaluating their performance.

## Good Human Relations Is Needed in Small Firms

Defining the term *human relations* is difficult, for it means different things to different people. Dr. Alfred Haake, lecturer for General Motors, would begin his lectures on human relations by saying, "Some people say that good human relations is treating people as if it were your last day on earth. Ah, no!" he would continue. "Good human relations is treating people as if it were *their* last day on earth." This thought is also expressed in the Golden Rule, which states: "So in everything, do to others what you would have them do to you."[1]

**Human relations** involves the interaction of people in an organization, especially in the areas of leadership, communications, and motivation. Regardless of the definition used, your success as a small business owner is based on practicing good human relations, according to the late Douglas McGregor,[2] and as the following example illustrates.

**Human relations** involves the interaction among people in an organization.

> Keith Dunn started his own restaurant because of the poor treatment he'd received from his employers. After he tried and failed at using motivational techniques, such as contests and benefits, he started including his employees in decisions affecting the business. Now that they are a vital part of the business, the annual turnover rate has dropped from 250 percent—normal for the industry—to 60 percent.[3]

Finally, good human relations occurs when both the employees and the small business owner understand organizational goals. Employees are happier and more productive when they know why their company exists, and what their roles are. There are five topics to address with employees, namely:[4]

- Reasons for being in business.
- Growth goals.
- Product goals.
- People involvement.
- Ethics statement.

## Exercising Effective Leadership

While management and leadership are similar, there are some significant differences. Leading is an important part of managing—but not the whole of it. **Leadership** is the ability of one person to influence others to strive to attain goals or objectives. Management, while requiring the use of leadership, also includes the other functions of planning, organizing, staffing, and controlling. Leadership is especially important for small business owners: Without it, they can't get workers to strive to achieve their goals or the business's objectives.

**Leadership** is the ability of one person to influence others to attain objectives.

G

According to Roderick Wilkinson, a fellow of the prestigious (U.K.) Institute of Personnel Management, a country's ability to survive depends on its ability to make things and to trade them. Wilkinson, the longtime human resource director of Caterpillar Tractor Company, Ltd., says that, while scientists may invent (or discover) new products, it is businesspeople who have "an understanding of how to motivate people, an ability to work together [in order] to earn more, to live better, and to become whole people" that make a nation great.[5]

It is tempting to say that one leadership style is better than another for small business owners. Yet experience has shown that no one style is ideal at all times. Instead, the best approach depends on the situation and the people involved. A Chinese proverb expresses this thought by saying, "Of the best leader, when he is gone, the people will say: We did it ourselves."

D

Today, effective small business owners are recognizing the role played by diversity in exercising effective leadership. In our competitive global environment, managers must realize that at work, how humans behave and interact with others is governed by their beliefs, thought patterns, and values. While these may be largely subconscious, they are often "so hard-wired into [our] brains that they generate almost reflexive behavior." And there is a growing sense among progressive owners and managers that this diversity can be managed.[6]

## Communicating with Employees and Others

**Communication** is the transfer of meaning from one person to another.

**Communication**, the process of transferring *meaning*—that is, ideas and information—from one person to another, is your number one job. A classic study showed that verbal communication takes up about 80 percent of a manager's time.[7]

G

Communication is important because people need and want to know what is going on so they can do their jobs properly. According to Andrew Grove, the Hungarian immigrant who is CEO of Intel, one of the top high-tech firms in the United States, "Good communication . . . is the lifeblood of any enterprise."[8] Owners, employees, customers, vendors, and others need to coordinate their work, so communication must be clear and complete. In addition, speaking pleasantly and persuasively makes people want to do good work, for, as a Japanese proverb says, "One kind word can warm three winter months."

### What Happens When You Communicate?

While explaining a process as complex as communication is difficult, Figure 14–1 shows that the process involves: (1) someone (the source) having an idea, thought, or impression that (2) is encoded or translated into words or symbols that (3) are transmitted, or sent as a message, to another person (the receiver), who (4) picks up the symbols and (5) decodes, or retranslates, them back into an idea and (6) sends some form of feedback to the sender. Feedback completes the process, because communication cannot be assumed to have occurred until the receiver demonstrates understanding of the message. *Since communication is an exchange of meaning (rather than words or symbols), many forms of nonverbal communication convey meaning through signals, signs, sounds (other than words), and facial expressions.*

### Barriers to Effective Communication

Despite the importance of communication and the amount of time we spend communicating, it's not always effective. One prototype study showed that up to 70 percent of all business communication fails to achieve the desired results.[9] There are many causes of this ineffectiveness, especially some barriers erected by the business itself or by the people involved.

First, because of the owner's position of authority, employees tend to believe what the owner says, regardless of whether it is true or not. In

**Figure 14–1** The Communication Process

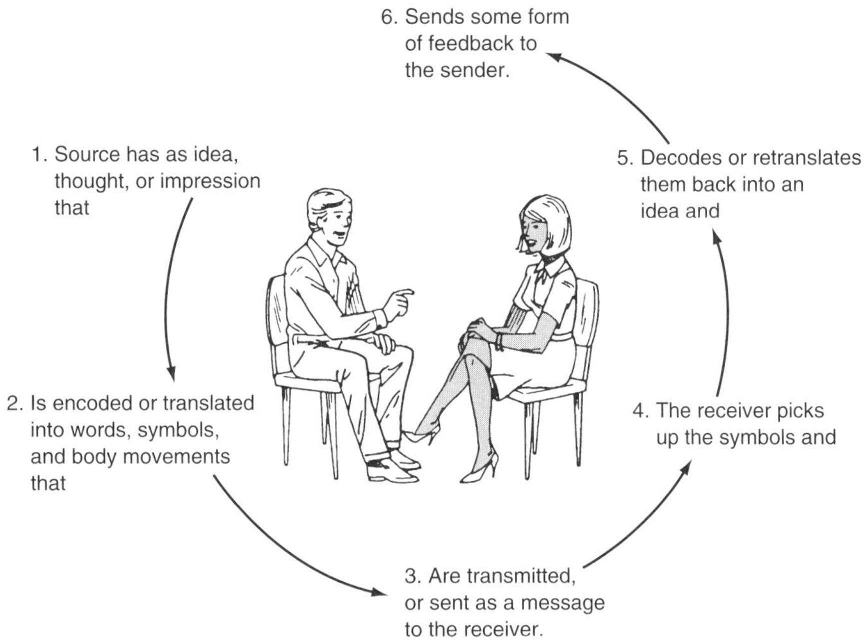
6. Sends some form of feedback to the sender.
1. Source has as idea, thought, or impression that
5. Decodes or retranslates them back into an idea and
2. Is encoded or translated into words, symbols, and body movements that
4. The receiver picks up the symbols and
3. Are transmitted, or sent as a message to the receiver.

addition, the status of the communicator either lends credibility to what is being said or detracts from it; messages of higher-status people tend to carry greater credibility than those of lower-status people.

The imprecise use of language also serves as a barrier. Have you noticed how frequently people use the expression "you know" in daily communications or adopt buzzwords (especially those from high-tech fields) without really knowing what they mean? For example, an employee being dismissed is sometimes said to be "outplaced" or "re-placed," often as a result of a "downsizing" (or "rightsizing") effort in the company.

Perhaps the greatest barriers to effective communication are simply inattention and poor listening. Small business owners, as well as managers of bigger companies, are often so preoccupied with running their business that they may not pay attention to employee feedback.

"AND DON'T YOU FORGET, JUSTIN, COMMUNICATION IS A TWO-WAY STREET!!!
"Yes, Jay"

© 1996 by Margaret P. Megginson. Used with permission.

## How to Improve Communication

You can become a more effective communicator by clarifying ideas, considering the environment in which the communication occurs, considering emotional overtones as well as the message, following up on communication, and being a good listener. As we have emphasized, communication is a two-way street. Even more important than getting your meaning across are listening to and understanding what the other person says.

**Teleconferencing**, also known as **videoconferencing**, is holding a virtual meeting using telephone, radio, closed-circuit TV, or computer communication connections.

For many small businesses—as well as larger ones—**teleconferencing** (also called **videoconferencing**) has become an effective cost- and time-saving way to communicate. As Figure 14–2 shows, teleconferencing consists of a group of people in one area using a phone, radio, closed-circuit TV, or even computers to communicate with people in another area—near or far. This technique not only saves on travel costs and time but can also increase productivity. It permits more concerned people in the business to participate in high-tech meetings, thus reducing the time supervisors spend reporting back to their people.

> For example, according to New York management consultant Karen Berg, company meetings tend to be more structured when using teleconferencing, resulting in 20 to 30 percent shorter meetings. At Hewlett-Packard, videoconferencing has hastened product development by 30 percent. And at American Greetings Corporation, decisions get made more quickly.[10]

**Figure 14–2** How Teleconferencing Operates

*Source:* "Teleconferencing," *Hello Direct: Catalog of Telephone Productivity Tools,* Spring 1996, p. 12.

## Motivating Employees

Before reading the following material, complete the exercise in Figure 14–3. This exercise helps explain why motivation is so complex and why it is so difficult to motivate some employees. You must use different incentives to motivate different people at different times in their working lives. Yet it is difficult for us to always know what a given employee wants at a given time. Understanding those needs and understanding how to use the appropriate motivation are the secrets of successful small business ownership and management.

**Figure 14–3** What Do You Want from a Job?

Rank the employment factors shown below in their order of importance to you at three points in your career. In the first column, assume that you are about to graduate and are looking for your first full-time job. In the second column, assume that you have been gainfully employed for 5 to 10 years and that you are presently employed by a reputable firm at the prevailing salary for the type of job and industry you are in. In the third column, try to assume that 25 to 30 years from now you have "found your niche in life" and have been working for a reputable employer for several years. (Rank your first choice as 1, second as 2, and so forth through 9.)

**Ranking of selected employment factors**

| Employment factor | As you seek your first full-time job | Your ranking 5–10 years later | Your ranking 25–30 years later |
|---|---|---|---|
| Fair adjustment of grievances | | | |
| Good job instruction and training | | | |
| Effective job supervision by your supervisor | | | |
| Promotion possibilities | | | |
| Recognition (praise, rewards, and so on) | | | |
| Job safety | | | |
| Job security (no threat of being dismissed or laid off) | | | |
| Good salary | | | |
| Good working conditons (nice office surroundings, good hours, and so on) | | | |

## What Is Motivation?

**Motivation** is the inner state that activates a person, including drives, desires, and/or motives.

You can use **motivation** to bring out the best in your employees by giving them reasons to perform better, but it's not easy. First, you are *always* motivating employees—either positively (to perform) or negatively (to withhold performance)—even when you're not conscious of doing so. When you give employees a reason to perform better, you create positive motivation; on the other hand, if you say or do something that annoys, frustrates, or antagonizes employees, they'll react negatively and either withhold production or actually sabotage operations.

> For example, a customer went into an ice cream shop in a college town and ordered a banana split. When it came, something was obviously wrong. There were five scoops of ice cream, double portions of fruit and nuts, and a huge serving of whipped cream, with several cherries on top. The customer asked the young employee, "What's wrong?" The young man didn't even pretend not to understand. "I'm mad at the boss," he promptly replied. A few months later, the shop went out of business.

The best way for you to succeed in business is to increase employee productivity and efficiency. While there is a limit to improvements in employee productivity, effective motivation can have a positive effect. However, *because many factors affect productivity, motivation alone is not enough.*

In general, employee performance is a product of the employee's ability to do the job and the application of positive motivation; that is,

$$\text{Performance} = \text{Ability} \times \text{Motivation}$$
$$\text{or}$$
$$P = A \times M$$

Most employees go to work for a company expecting to do a good job, receive a satisfactory income, and gain satisfaction from doing a good job. However, performance and satisfaction are dependent on the *ability* to do the job. If your employees are not performing as you would like them to, they may be unsuited for the job, inadequately trained, or unmotivated. If they are unsuited, move them to a more suitable job, and if untrained, train them. If they are both suited and trained, try harder to motivate them.

## Why Motivate Employees?

One reason managerial motivation is so difficult to use is that there are different purposes for motivating people, each of which requires different incentives. Usually managers use motivation to (1) attract potential employees, (2) improve performance, and (3) retain good employees.

### *Attracting Potential Employees*

If you want to encourage potential employees to work for you, you must find and use incentives that appeal to a person needing a job. These incentives usually include a good income, pleasant working conditions, promotional possibilities, and sometimes a signing bonus.

The exercise in Figure 14–3 has been used with junior- and senior-level business students since 1957. With very few exceptions, "good salary" has been the primary consideration in looking for a first job in over 200 surveys reviewed, while "promotion possibilities" and "good working conditions" are a close second and third. How did you rate these factors?

### *Improving Performance*

You can also use motivation to improve performance and efficiency on the part of present employees. You can do this by praising good work, giving employees more responsibility, publicly recognizing a job well done, and awarding merit salary increases. Q

> Notice in the Profile that Cathy Anderson-Giles treats her people well to bring out the best in them. She gives them personal attention and helps them with their problems.

### *Retaining Good Employees*

Motivation can also be used to retain your present employees. This is accomplished primarily through the use of employee benefits, most of which are designed to reward employees who stay with the company. However, many other incentives can help explain today's work force retention.

> For example, Cal Ripken, the shortstop for the Baltimore Orioles baseball team, had not missed playing in a scheduled game from 1982 until September 6, 1995—when he broke Lou Gehrig's record of 2,030 consecutive games played. Q
>
> There is also Elena Griffing, at Bates Medical Center, who took her last sick day in 1952. She explained her feat by saying: "Watching the healing process makes it worth going to work."
>
> Then there is Francis Longobardi, a technical analyst at Genix Group, who is motivated by the "hustle and bustle" at work. She hasn't missed a day since she was employed in 1953.[11]
>
> Vision Tek founders say that, to motivate employees to stay forever, you "let them play games." After building facilities for employees that include an indoor athletic court, a Ping-Pong table, and a weight room, the employer told employees that, if they could outplay a bigwig, they would get a free lunch with him. Friday is "challenge of the owners" day, and, as of 1995, only two playing owners are still eating alone.[12] Q

## How to Motivate Employees

The theory of motivation is relatively simple (as shown in Figure 14–4). An employee has a need or needs, and you apply some kind of incentive (or stimulus) that promises to satisfy that need. Your main problem in motivating employees is to know them well enough to know what they need and what incentives will stimulate them to perform.

## Some Practical Ways to Improve Motivation

Some tried-and-true ways of improving motivation are: (1) quality circles, (2) zero defects programs, (3) job enrichment, (4) management by objectives, and Q

**Figure 14–4** The Motivational Process

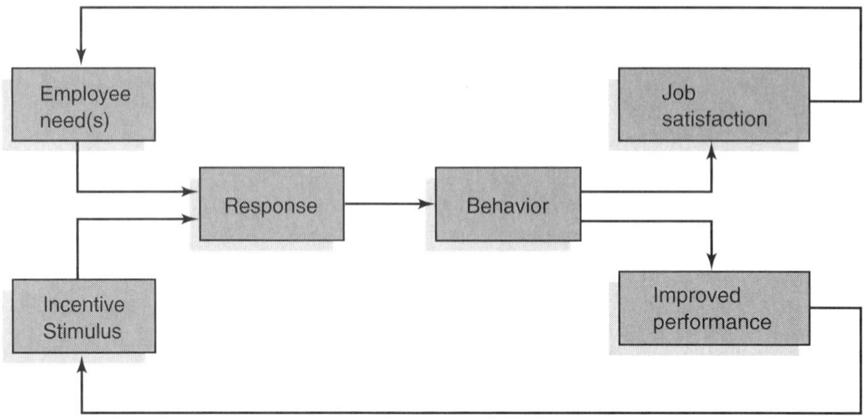


(5) variable work schedules. These techniques offer promise for motivating people, especially in small businesses.

**Quality circles (QCs)** are small employee groups that meet periodically to improve quality and output.

**Quality circles (QCs)** are small, organized work groups that meet periodically to find ways to improve quality and output. They motivate by getting employees involved and taking advantage of their creativity and innovativeness.

A **zero-defects** approach uses pride in workmanship to get workers to do their work "right the first time."

The **zero-defects** approach is based on getting workers to do their work "right the first time," thus generating pride in workmanship. It assumes that employees want to do a good job—and will do so if permitted to.

**Job enrichment** is granting workers greater responsibility and authority in their jobs.

**Job enrichment** emphasizes giving employees greater responsibility and authority over their job as the best way to motivate them. Employees are encouraged to learn new and related skills or even to trade jobs with each other as ways of making the job more interesting and therefore more productive.

**Flextime** is an arrangement under which employees may schedule their own hours, around a core time.

**Job splitting** occurs when employees divide a single job into two or more different parts, each one doing one of the parts.

**Job sharing** occurs when a single full-time job is retained, but its performance is shared by two or more employees working at different times.

Variable work schedules permit employees to work at times other than the standard workweek of five eight-hour days.[13] Such schedules are being extensively used by small firms to motivate employees. **Flextime** allows employees to schedule their own hours as long as they are present during certain required hours, called *core time*. This gives employees greater control over their time and activities. **Job splitting** is dividing a single full-time job into distinct parts and letting two (or more) employees do the different parts. In **job sharing**, a single full-time job is shared by two (or more) employees, with one worker performing all aspects of the job at one time and the other worker doing it at another time, as the following example shows.

> Cheryl Houser, burned out after selling ads for the *Seattle Weekly* for four years, wanted time to travel, do volunteer work, and eventually have a baby. Carol Cummins, a co-worker expecting a baby, also wanted to work part time. Being good salespeople, they talked their boss, Jane Levine, vice president of advertising and marketing, into letting them share one full-time job. Houser works on Mondays and Thursdays, Cummins works on Wednesdays and Fridays, and both come in on Tuesdays. In exchange for lighter work duties, since the two women each work only three days a week, the paper gets two seasoned workers for the price of one.[14]

Small business owners are faced with a dilemma when considering such motivational programs. They may believe that using one or more of the new methods will improve employee performance and hence increase profits. But they may not have the knowledge, time, money, or personnel to implement the method or methods.

### Does Money Motivate?

Some studies have concluded that money doesn't motivate and that psychological rewards may be more significant than monetary rewards.[15] But, as shown, our research indicates that most students say "good salary" is the first thing they'll be looking for in their first job. Also, several studies indicate that money does motivate. For example, one study revealed that 60 percent of women say money motivates them to achieve a better life.[16] In summary, we believe that money motivates, but so do many other factors, as indicated in the Profile.

"In the interests of a fair and equitable gratuity, your service is being evaluated."



### Motivation Is More than Mere Technique

Successful motivation of employees is based more on a managerial philosophy than on using a given technique. Thus, you should try to create an environment in your firm in which employees can apply themselves willingly and wholeheartedly to the task of increasing productivity and quality.

> This thought was expressed soon after World War II by Clarence Francis, chairman of General Foods, when he said, "You can buy a man's time; you can buy a man's physical presence at a given place; you can even buy a measured number of skilled muscular motions per hour or day; but you cannot buy enthusiasm; you cannot buy initiative; you cannot buy loyalty; you cannot buy devotion of hearts, minds, and souls. You have to earn these things."[17]

## APPRAISING EMPLOYEES' PERFORMANCE

You need an effective system of **performance appraisal** (also called *employee evaluation* or *merit rating*) to help you answer the question "How well are my people performing?" Under such a system, each employee's performance and progress are evaluated, and rewards are given for above-average performance.

**Performance appraisal** is the process of evaluating workers to see how well they're performing.

## USING TECHNOLOGY TO SUCCEED

### Employee Appraisal Software

One of the most difficult jobs managers must do is to appraise employee performance. Nothing can make the task painless, but new software packages can help to make it more rational and systematic.

*Performance Now!* by KnowledgePoint in Petaluma, California ($129), asks users to rate employees on a scale of one to five for skills ranging from "takes responsibility for own actions" to "keeps abreast of current developments in field." Then it generates descriptive text that supports the rating. It builds the review paragraph by paragraph, prompting the user to add specific examples and warning when ratings for different performance factors are inconsistent. Kent Withers, director of distribution for CKE Restaurants, the company that runs the Carl's Jr. chain, uses *Performance Now!* to write reviews for seven employees. "There is no way to tell that the finished product is computer generated," Withers says, "and writing a review takes 30 to 50 percent less time." Moreover, says Withers, *Performance Now!* has improved his reviews by making them more consistent and direct.

*Employee Appraiser,* by Austin-Hayne in Redwood, California ($129), takes a slightly different approach. Instead of using a numerical rating, it provides sample text you can adjust to be more positive or negative using a "writing tuner" function. *Employee Appraiser* also includes extensive coaching that gives managers ideas on how to improve employee performance between reviews. For example, the program suggests keeping track of writing samples and marking them with suggestions as a way of improving an employee's writing skills. One user, Ron Frederick, vice president of human resources for International Thomson Publishing, was so impressed with *Employee Appraiser* that he plans to adopt it in all of Thomson's 30 divisions.

Many software experts think programs such as *Performance Now!* and *Employee Appraiser* will be the first MBA-ware widely adopted across different industries. "Companies have a fair amount of difficulty getting people to do employee evaluations well, and this software helps them do it a whole lot better," says Jeffrey Tarter, publisher of *Softletter,* a trade publication.

*Source:* Reprinted from Alison L. Sprout, "Surprise! Software to Help You Manage," *Fortune,* April 17, 1995, p. 200. 

Often, this technique is used in determining merit salary increases, special merit raises, training decisions, layoffs, or promotions or transfers. Appraisals can also be used for disciplinary actions such as reprimands, suspensions, demotions, or discharges. Finally, the results of formal appraisals can be used to support or refute disciplinary documentation in proceedings before such bodies as the EEOC and in Unemployment Compensation Appeals hearings.

Employee appraisals are usually based on such factors as quantity and quality of work performed, cooperativeness, initiative, dependability (including attendance), job knowledge, safety, and personal habits. While appraisals are usually done by the employee's direct supervisor, they may also be done by the affected employee, his or her peers, or subordinates, or by the use of electronic devices, as you can see from Using Technology to Succeed.

Employee evaluations should be related to promotions and salary increases in addition to identifying marginal workers and designing training activities for them. They can also be used to motivate employees, if the evaluations are adequately translated into rewards.

## Compensating Employees

Another aspect of leading and rewarding employees is providing what employees consider fair pay for their activities. Their earnings should be high enough to motivate them to be good producers, yet low enough for you to maintain satisfactory profits.

### Legal Influences

There are many federal and state laws that affect how much small business owners pay their employees (see Table 14–1 for the primary federal laws involved). According to the Wage and Hour Law, 14 is the minimum working age for most nonfarm jobs. Thus, you can hire workers aged 14 and 15 for nonhazardous jobs for up to three hours on a school day and eight hours on any other day, but no more than 18 hours per week from 7:00 A.M. to 7:00 P.M. during the school term. Those aged 16 and 17 can work an unlimited time on nonhazardous jobs.

Certain retail and service companies don't have to comply if their annual sales are less than $500,000. Laundry, fabric care, dry cleaning, and some construction firms also qualify for exemptions, while those who hope to receive tips face a minimum wage of only $2.34.[18]

Since state laws vary so much from each other and from the federal law, we won't try to discuss them. You should check the laws for the state in which you operate.

### Setting Rates of Pay

In addition to legal factors, many variables influence what employees consider a fair wage. First, they think they should be paid in proportion to their physical and mental efforts on the job. The standard of living and cost of living in the area also matter. And unions help set wages in a geographic area through collective bargaining, whether the company itself is unionized or not. The economic factors of supply and demand for workers help set wages. Finally, the employer's ability to pay must be considered.

In actual practice, most small businesses pay either the minimum wage (which was set at $4.25 in 1989) or the same wages that similar businesses in the area pay. If you pay less than the prevailing wage, you will have difficulty finding employees. Conversely, you cannot afford to pay much more unless your employees are more productive. In the final analysis, you pay whatever you must to attract the people you really need—and can afford.[19]

## Using Money to Motivate

Many small businesses use some form of financial incentive to motivate their employees to use their initiative and to perform better. Some of the more popular financial incentives are (1) merit increases, (2) incentive payments, and (3) profit sharing.

Figure 14–5 shows the results of an earlier survey of 1,598 small and large manufacturing and service companies by the American Productivity

**Table 14–1** Legal Influence on Compensation and Hours of Work

| Law | Coverage | Basic requirements | Agencies involved |
|---|---|---|---|
| Public Construction Act of 1931 (Davis-Bacon Act) | Employers with federal construction contracts or subcontracts of $2,000 or more. | Employers must pay at least the prevailing wages in the area, as determined by the Secretary of Labor; overtime is to be paid at 1½ times the basic wage for all work over 8 hours per day or 40 hours per week. | Wage and Hour Division of the Labor Department |
| Public Contracts Act of 1936 (Walsh-Healy Act) | Employers with federal contracts of $1,000 or more. | Same as above. | Same as above |
| Fair Labor Standards Act of 1938 (wage and hour law) | Private employers engaged in interstate commerce; retailers having annual sales of $325,000. (Many groups are exempted from overtime requirements.) | Employers must pay a minimum of $4.25 per hour and 1½ times the basic rate for work over 40 hours per week and are limited (by jobs and school status) in employing persons under 18. | Same as above |
| Equal Pay Act of 1963 | All employers. | Men and women must receive equal pay for jobs requiring substantially the same skill, working conditions, effort, and responsibility. | Equal Employment Opportunity Commission |
| Service Contracts Act of 1965 | Employers with contracts to provide services worth $2,500 or more per year to the federal government. | Same as Davis-Bacon. | Same as Davis-Bacon |
| Family and Medical Leave Act of 1993 | Employers with 50 or more employees within a 75-mile radius; certain employees are exempted. | Employers must provide workers up to 12 weeks of unpaid leave during a 12-month period for (1) birth of a child; (2) placement of a child for adoption or foster care; (3) caring for a spouse, child, or parent with a serious health condition; and (4) a serious condition of the employee; health coverage must be continued during the leave period and same or comparable job available upon return. | Department of Labor |

*Source:* Various government and private publications.

**Figure 14–5** Incentive Pay Programs Are Popular Motivators

**Pay raises are not the only way companies reward employees. Here's the percentage of U.S. companies using nontraditional forms of compensation:**

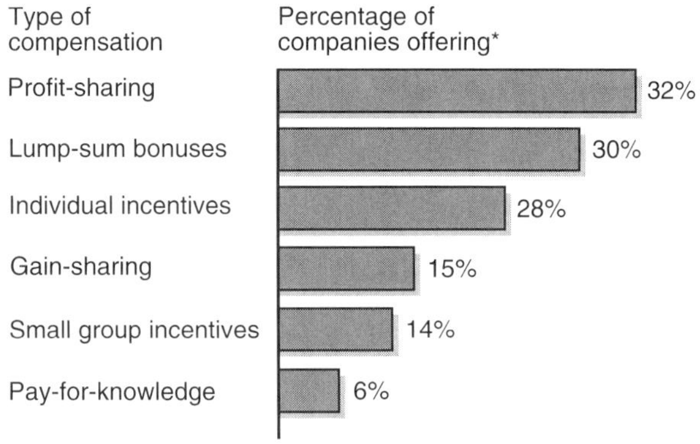


*Some companies offer more than one plan.
*Source:* "Plans Become Labor's Latest Battleground," *USA Today,* November 7, 1989, p. 1B. Copyright 1989, USA TODAY. Reprinted with permission.

and Quality Center. Notice how popular profit sharing, lump-sum bonuses, and individual incentive payments are. In 1993, a Conference Board survey of 382 companies found that around three-quarters of them provided some type of incentive pay, including bonuses for cost-saving suggestions or for learning new skills.[20]

## *Merit Increases*

**Merit increases** are based on the employee's ability and performance.

**Merit increases**, which base a person's wage or salary on ability and merit rather than on seniority or some other factor, tend to be effective motivators. Merit programs identify, appraise, and reward employees for outstanding contribution toward your company's profit. Thus, an employee's wage or salary relates directly to that person's efforts to achieve your objectives. Many companies—large as well as small—are basing employee pay on observed competence. These employers recognize that with global competition—especially since the passage of NAFTA—they can no longer pay employees whose performance does not support business strategies and organizational goals.[21]

## *Incentive Payments*

Incentive payments can be paid in the form of incentive wages, bonuses, commissions, and push money.

An **incentive wage** is the extra compensation paid for all production over a specified standard amount.

An **incentive wage**, which is the extra compensation paid for all production over a specified amount, is effective in situations where a worker can control the volume of sales or production. Piece rates, commissions, and bonuses are forms of incentive payments. Under a *piece-rate system,* an employee's earnings are based on a rate per unit times the number of units produced. But you should give some form of guaranteed base rate to ensure that the employee earns at least a minimum amount. Piece-rate systems, which are usually used in production- or operations-type activities, can be quite effective, as the following example illustrates.

> A pilot study of the use of piece rates in the corrugated shipping container industry found that 16 of 18 operations showed significantly increased productivity after use of such incentives. On the average, productivity per employee increased about 75 percent.[22]

A **commission** is incentive compensation directly related to the sales or profits achieved by a salesperson.

**Commissions**, which consist of a given amount per sale or a percentage of sales, are used extensively to reward salespeople, especially in retailing. They are particularly useful in rewarding door-to-door selling of items such as encyclopedias and magazine subscriptions, but they are also used by most department stores and similar retail outlets and are the only form of compensation for real estate agents.

A **bonus** is a reward—not specified in advance—given to employees for special efforts and accomplishments.

**Bonuses** are amounts given to employees either for exceeding their production quotas or as a reward on special occasions. Many production or sales personnel have work quotas and receive bonuses if they exceed that amount.

> For instance, W. K. Buckley, Ltd., a 75-year-old family-run Canadian cough medicine maker, still markets its original formula. In 1985, its sales were a little more than $2.5 million, and it had 22 employees. Ten years later, sales were more than $8 million—with the same number of employees. To keep employees motivated and focused on helping the firm grow, the owners pay competitive wages, provide excellent working conditions, and have a unique bonus system that "rewards everyone from the shop floor people to the highest level of management."[23]

**Push money (PM)**, or **spiff**, is a commission paid to a salesperson to push a specific item or line of goods.

Another form of incentive payment is called **push money (PM)**, or **spiff**, which is a reward given to employees for selling an item the business is making a special effort to sell—in other words, pushing.

### *Profit Sharing*

**Profit sharing** is an arrangement—announced in advance—whereby employees receive a prescribed share of the company's profits.

In **profit sharing**, employees receive a prearranged share of the company's profits. Profit sharing can be effective in motivating employees by tying rewards to company performance. Not only does it reward good performance, but a good plan can also reduce turnover, increase productivity, and reduce the amount of supervision needed.

An **employee stock ownership plan (ESOP)**, a form of profit sharing, borrows money, purchases some of the company's stock, and allocates it to the employees on the basis of salaries and/or longevity.

If you can afford to do so, you might want to use an **employee stock ownership plan (ESOP)**, which is a modification of profit sharing. In general, an ESOP borrows money, purchases a block of the company's stock, and allocates it to the employees on the basis of salaries and/or longevity. These plans are particularly attractive to small companies because they provide a source of needed capital, boost the company's cash flow, raise employee morale and productivity, and provide a very beneficial new employee benefit.

## Compensating Managerial and Professional Personnel

In general, managers of small businesses are paid on a merit basis, with their income based on the firm's earnings. Many small companies also use profit sharing, bonuses, or some other method of stimulating the interest of managerial and professional personnel, as the following example illustrates.

> In the past, managers of Radio Shack stores received a share of profits if their store's profit margin was 10 percent or more. If a given store had, say, an 11 percent profit margin, the manager would get 11 percent of those profits as a bonus; with a 15 percent profit margin, the manager would take home an extra 15 percent of profits.[24]

## Employee Benefits

**Employee benefits** (sometimes called *fringe benefits*) are the rewards and services provided to employees in addition to their regular earnings. Figure 14–6 lists some of the most popular employee benefits.

**Employee benefits** are the rewards and services provided to workers in addition to their regular earnings.

In general, these benefits increase in importance as employees' lifestyles expand and it takes more than just wages to satisfy them. But benefits are costly, as shown in Figure 14–7. And once given, they are difficult—if not impossible—to take back.

> For example, Gretchen Fields, vice president of human resources at Hanna Andersson mail order clothing company, says, "It's very difficult to take benefits away." In times of financial difficulty, benefits may become one of the first cutbacks, so *it is very important to plan benefits that you can pay not only this year, but five years from now.*[25]

Moreover, for a time their cost was rising much faster than wages. Since 1993, though, there has been a sharp drop in their growth. In 1995, for example, they grew only 2 percent—less than the 3 percent growth in wages.[26] Still, employees want and expect them, almost as much as they do their salary!

### *Legally Required Benefits*

Small employers are legally required by the Social Security Act to provide retirement, disability, survivors, and medical benefits; unemployment insurance; and workers' compensation. Also, employers with 20 or more employees must continue offering health insurance for up to 18 months for employees when they leave—either voluntarily or otherwise—and up to 36 months for widows, divorced or separated spouses, and employee dependents.

Under the **Social Security** system, you act as both taxpayer and tax collector, as you must pay a tax on employees' earnings and deduct an equal amount from their paychecks. In 1996, the tax rate was 7.65 percent (6.2 percent for Social Security and 1.45 percent for Medicare), and the taxable wage base was $62,700 for Social Security and unlimited for Medicare. Self-employed people must pay the entire cost themselves, which is twice the amount listed for employees.

**Social Security** is a federal program that provides support for the retired, widowed, disabled, and their dependents.

**Figure 14–6** Some of the Most Popular Employee Benefits

**Legally required**
Social Security/Medicare
Unemployment insurance
Workers' compensation
Family and medical leave

**Voluntary, private**

*a.* Health and accident insurance
- Eye care and eyeglasses
- Chiropractic care
- Dental and orthodontic care
- Health maintenance—diagnostic visits/physical exams
- Major medical/hospitalization
- Psychiatric and mental care
- Accident and sickness insurance

*b.* Life and disability insurance
- Accidental death and dismemberment
- Group term life insurance
- Long-term disability

*c.* Sick leave, including maternity leave

*d.* Income maintenance
- Severance pay
- Supplemental unemployment benefits (SUBs)
- Pensions

*e.* Pay for time off
- Holidays
- Personal time
- Sabbatical leaves
- Union activities
- Vacations

*f.* Employee services and others
- Alcohol and drug rehabilitation
- Auto insurance
- Child care and day care centers for other family members
- Christmas bonuses
- Clothing and uniforms
- Company car
- Credit unions
- Discount privileges on organization's products or services
- Loans and financial assistance
- Food services and cafeteria
- Group tours and charter flights
- Gymnasium and physical training center
- Legal assistance
- Liability coverage
- Matching gifts to charitable organizations or schools
- Matching payroll deductions and savings plans
- Moving and transfer allowances
- Personal counseling and financial advice
- Recreation center
- Service awards
- Stock purchase and profit-sharing plans
- Transportation and parking
- Tuition for employee and/or family members

*Source:* Various government and private publications.

**Unemployment insurance** provides some financial support to employees laid off for reasons beyond their control.

**Workers' compensation** involves payments made to employees for losses from accidents and occupational diseases.

State governments receive most of the **unemployment insurance** tax, which can be as high as 4.7 percent of a limited amount (which varies by state) of each employee's pay, while the rest goes to the U.S. government for administrative costs. If the business can lower its unemployment rate, the tax is reduced under a merit rating system. Using funds from the tax, the state pays unemployed workers a predetermined amount each week. This amount varies from state to state.

Employee losses from accidents and occupational diseases are paid for under state **workers' compensation** laws. Each employer is required to pay insurance premiums to either a state fund or a private insurance company. The accumulated funds are used to compensate victims of industrial acci-

**Figure 14–7** Benefits Costs Climb

**Employee benefits as a percentage of total compensation*:**

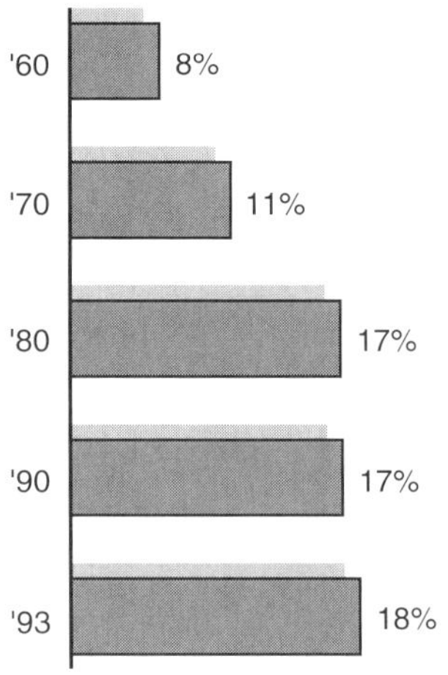


*Excludes paid leave

*Source:* Employee Benefit Research Institute, as reported in *USA Today*, May 17, 1995, p. 1B. Copyright 1995 USA TODAY. Reprinted with permission.

dents or work-related illnesses. A firm's premiums depend on the hazards involved and the effectiveness of its safety programs. The amount paid to an employee or to his or her estate is fixed according to the type and extent of injury. According to the National Council on Compensation Insurance, the costs of these programs more than doubled between 1986 and 1992, from just over $30 billion to over $60 billion, and the costs are still escalating.[27] *This trend threatens small firms, which may not be able to bear the increasing costs.*

Employers with 50 or more workers within 75 miles must guarantee workers up to 12 weeks of unpaid leave a year for births, adoptions, or the care of sick children, spouses, or parents. The **Family and Medical Leave Act**, passed February 5, 1993, covers employees on the job at least one year, but the employer can exclude the top-paid 10 percent of employees. Employees are required to give 30 days' notice when practical, such as births and adoptions, and may be required to use vacation or other leave time first. Couples employed at the same place may be restricted to 12 weeks total leave each year. Employers must continue to provide health insurance during leave and guarantee workers the same or an equivalent job on return.[28]

The **Family and Medical Leave Act** requires employers with 50 or more employees to provide up to 12 weeks of unpaid leave for births or adoptions, and to care for sick children, spouses, or parents.

## *Other Employee Benefits*

As shown in Figure 14–6, there are many voluntary benefits in addition to the legally required ones. Health, accident, life, and disability insurance are especially popular with small businesses and their employees. Yet the Bureau of Labor Statistics reports that only 71 percent of small business employees have health care provided, and only 45 percent have some type of retirement plan.[29] In trade and service businesses, discounts on the firm's goods or services are also well received. Some conscientious employers go much further.

> Employees at the Atlanta-based Chick-fil-A restaurant franchises, for instance, may be thinking about Shakespeare or physics rather than the chicken and fries you order. Chick-fil-A's founder, Truett Cathy, started a tuition program to help his employees get an education. The chain offers $1,000 in tuition assistance to all employees who have been with the company at least two years. To qualify, the employee must work 20 hours a week and maintain a C average in school. The company awarded almost $1 million in such scholarships in 1994 and has handed out more than $10 million since the program started in 1973.[30]

Pension programs were common in small firms until the passage of the Employee Retirement Income Security Act (ERISA) in 1974. Because the law proved too complex and difficult for small businesses to conform to, many of them gave up their voluntary pension programs, especially after it was amended in 1989.[31]

"Our pension plan is simple and portable. However, it does not involve much in the way of actual money."
Source: AARP Bulletin, November 1995, p. 2.

> For example, Ronald Turner, a third-generation lumber company owner in Clarksburg, West Virginia, dropped his employee pension plan, saying the changes made the benefit program too costly and complex to maintain. He gave his employees the cash due them from the fund. He said he had tried to obey the law, but quit after the required paperwork grew from 35 to 77 pages and the IRS disqualified the plan "on a technicality."[32]

**Individual retirement accounts (IRAs)** are accounts open to employees to replace pension programs; they may provide tax benefits.

A **Keogh retirement plan** permits self-employed persons and partnerships to set aside a certain amount of their earnings and deduct it from income taxes.

A **Salary Reduction Simplified Employee Pension Plan (SAR-SEP)** is a salary reduction program that allows employees to defer a portion of their compensation to an employer-sponsored retirement plan.

Many small firms have decided to let their employees establish private pension programs using **individual retirement accounts (IRAs)**. Any employee who is not covered by a qualified employer retirement plan and has a taxable income of less than $40,000 for a married couple filing jointly or $25,000 for a single taxpayer may make a deductible contribution of $2,000 annually to a qualified IRA account (plus $250 to the spouse's account).[33]

Another benefit permits self-employed persons and partnerships to set up tax-deferred retirement programs. Up to $30,000 a year—but no more than 25 percent of the person's eligible total earnings—can be put into a **Keogh retirement plan** and deducted from income taxes.[34]

Perhaps one of the most interesting plans for small businesses is the **Salary Reduction Simplified Employee Pension Plan (SAR-SEP)**. This plan is limited to organizations with 25 or fewer eligible employees. However, at least 50 percent of eligible employees must participate in the plan. Employees may contribute up to $9,240 to a SAR-SEP, and combined employee/employer contributions must not exceed $30,000 per employee per year. At payout time, these funds will be taxed as ordinary income, as is the case with the IRA.[35]

Under these two programs, employees can take their pensions with them if they leave their employers. There are, however, some restrictions.[36]

Finally, some employers have **401(k) plans**, which permit workers to place up to of $9,240 of their wages annually in tax-deferred retirement savings plans. Employers can match the employees' contributions (and often do) on a one-for-one basis, up to $22,500 for each employee and employer.[37] According to the U.S. Chamber of Commerce, more than half of all U.S. employers use this type of plan.[38]

**401(k) plans** permit workers to place up to a certain amount of their wages each year in tax-deferred retirement savings plans.

A survey of 500 small and midsize companies found that health insurance was provided by 96 percent of them; life insurance by 82 percent; tuition refunds for job-related courses, 70 percent; dental insurance, 68 percent; profit sharing, 66 percent; 401(k) plans, 52 percent; and pension/retirement plans, 34 percent.[39]

### *Flexible Approach to Benefits*

A **cafeteria-style benefit plan**, also known as **flexcomp**, can help you reduce your annual increase in benefit costs. Under this system, you tell your employees the dollar value of benefits they are entitled to receive. Each employee then tells you how to allocate the money among a variety of available programs. This system increases employee awareness of the value of the benefits and offers freedom of choice and a personalized approach. These plans are now a viable option for small firms because third-party administrators can take care of the paperwork.[40]

A **cafeteria-style benefit plan**, or **flexcomp**, allows the employer to provide all employees with the legally required benefits, plus an extra dollar amount that each employee can choose how to use.

## Need for an Integrated Approach

We would like to end this discussion of leading, communicating with, and motivating employees by returning to the ideas expressed in the Profile. As a small business owner, you need to use more than just financial rewards to get your employees to perform. You need to hire good people, train them well, communicate with them, let them make suggestions, provide them with an equitable income, and offer innovative employee benefits.

## WHAT YOU SHOULD HAVE LEARNED

**1.** To be successful, you must provide the kind of leadership and motivation that will inspire workers to perform productively. Part of the secret lies in good human relations. Leadership is the ability to inspire others to reach objectives that aren't necessarily their personal goals.

**2.** Managers spend around 80 percent of their time communicating, that is, in exchanges of meaning. Barriers to effective communication include the status of the communicator (lack of credibility), imprecise use of language, and poor listening. You can become a better communicator by identifying the audience and environment of the communication, and by being a good listener.

**3.** You can increase employee productivity and improve employee satisfaction through effective motivation. Your problem is to know your employees well enough to know what incentives will stimulate them to perform. Different incentives must be used according to the purpose of the motivation.

Some currently popular motivational techniques include quality circles, zero-defects programs, job enrichment, management by objectives (MBO), and variable work schedules. Motivation is more than mere technique, and the best motivators are based on a managerial philosophy that recognizes the worth of employees and expects the best from them.

**4.** Appraising employees' performance is an important part of your job. Merit raises and promotions should be based on such performance appraisals, and they can also point up possible training and development needs in specific areas.

**5.** Money is an important motivator, so you must pay your employees not just the minimum wage, but enough to attract and keep them. You can use merit increases, incentive payments, and profit sharing to motivate your employees.

Employee benefits, which are increasingly important to both employees and employers, are quite costly. While Social Security, Medicare, unemployment insurance, and workers' compensation are legally required, pension plans and various kinds of insurance are popular voluntary benefits. Cafeteria-style benefit plans (sometimes called flexcomp) are now feasible for small companies.

## QUESTIONS FOR DISCUSSION

1. How would you define (or explain) *good human relations?*
2. Why is communication so important in a small business? What are some barriers to effective communication? How can these barriers be overcome?
3. What is motivation? Why is it so important to a small business manager?
4. What are some practical ways to improve employee motivation?
5. How would you explain the role of money in employee motivation?
6. What is the purpose of personnel appraisals? Why are they so important?
7. What are some legal restraints that affect how much a company pays its employees?
8. What are some other factors that affect the amount and form of compensation paid to employees?
9. How can wages be used to motivate employees to perform better?
10. Explain the four legally required employee benefits. What are some other benefits frequently used by small businesses?
11. Explain what cafeteria-style benefit plans are and why they are used.

# CASE 14

## PERSONNEL POLICIES HELP INTERMATIC GROW

Photo courtesy of Intermatic, Inc.

Jim Miller, CEO of Intermatic, Inc., claims his company's personnel policies and programs have been the key to its growth, profitability, and survival. He thinks this philosophy saved the Spring Grove, Illinois, producer of timing devices and low-voltage lighting from disaster.

Several years ago, when Intermatic was on the verge of bankruptcy, Miller, a former employee, was asked to return as president. To save the company, he reduced the work force by 50 percent, closed one division, restructured the staff, consolidated positions, and instituted the employee relations policies and programs that have since assured the firm's success.

An incentive system for production workers earns them about 135 percent of their base pay, and some of the unusual employee benefits are: (1) programs that pay workers to shed pounds, (2) free eye examinations and glasses, (3) aerobics classes, (4) golf lessons, (5) an outside exercise course, (6) an indoor track, (7) tennis courts, (8) membership in arts-and-culture clubs, (9) shopping at company-subsidized stores for items such as jeans, T-shirts, and baseball caps, and (10) reimbursement of tuition for college courses.

In addition, Miller is quite open in his communications with employees, telling them what has to be done and why it must be done. He also is available to help people with their personal problems, knows them by name, and knows their family situations. The payoff? Turnover is only 3 percent, compared to over 5 percent for similar firms, and it has become such a popular place to work that there's a waiting list of people seeking employment with Intermatic.

*Source:* Correspondence with Intermatic, Inc.

## QUESTIONS

1. How do you explain the increased performance at Intermatic?
2. Would Jim Miller's methods work at all companies? Explain.
3. Do you think all the employee benefits are needed?
4. How would you like to work at Intermatic?

## APPLICATION 14–1

Joe and Ellen Walker, owners of Walker Furniture Store and several other stores in their area, have been in the furniture business for over 20 years. Their furniture prices are very competitive, as is their employees' compensation. The Walkers do not pay higher salaries than most other furniture stores, but they offer many other incentives and benefits to their employees, such as health insurance, dental insurance, a Christmas club plan (for which the Walkers provide matching funds), and a SAR-SEP plan. The credit manager drives a company-owned vehicle, and many of the employees have an expense account for travel from store to store.

The Walkers, together with the furniture manufacturers' representatives, often give away trips and prizes to their salespeople for high sales. For instance, one employee won a clock and two watches for selling the most recliners in a six-month period; another won a pair of matching lamps for selling the most refrigerators made by General Electric.

The biggest prize—a five-day, all-expense-paid trip to a five-star resort in Bermuda (sponsored by a local mattress company)—was awarded to another of the Walkers' employees who sold over $75,000 in mattresses in 12 months.

### QUESTIONS

1. Do the benefits and compensations outweigh the monetary value of higher salaries, and what do you believe is the most important?
2. What are some other ways the Walkers can compensate their employees?

## ACTIVITY 14–1

*Directions:* In the puzzle on the next page, find the following terms from this chapter: bonus, commission, communication, employee benefits, employee stock ownership plan, ESOP, flextime, human relations, incentive wage, individual retirement accounts, IRA, job enrichment, job sharing, job splitting, Keogh retirement plan, Kplans, leadership, merit increases, motivation, performance appraisals, profit sharing, quality circles, QCs, Social Security, unemployment insurance, workers' compensation, zero defects.

S M E R Q C E M P S S I O Y M E N T I V E B O N Y E E F
P T Q U A D H N R T X C E S O I R A C E S R E Z M I T L
I U N A L P T N E M E R I T E R H G O E K L L A F W B E
N S A U G M O S T W E A H K R U S M L G D Z U N O H J X
C S L B O I F H S E M L G N I R A H S T I F O R P Y O I
E E P R S C T U L N P J E I N G O N T I O N K Q S R B R
N P P E N U C M G S L U R I T O U R I T Y E X U T L E E
T L I P W K S A M V O V A N R P E R F P R C E A N E N N
I E H P S H A N T R Y W I L E A D E R S H I P L A Z R P
V C S N G B O R N N E U S M O C O M C B E M A I L C I D
E N R D Z L O E Y E E O W H A R T O N I N S D T I L C T
W R E N E M R L I T B M E C R I M C A U I D I Y J L H V
A A N T R S P A L I E J E M M P T T I A N G Q C L A M S
G N W S O L E T U L N C R R E Z F I R C Y T U I I D E E
E G O U D M M I L O E Y M N I E N P F E P B A R G E N E
Q N K N E E P O E S F L S A I T P C O S R O I C N T T U
B I C Y F C U N V R I A I T L A E E A D E N R L I S R Q
F T O T E N N S N U T T T O E C C R A G P U I E R H S O
J T T S C H U M J I S Y Z C O B K P L A N S S S A H H F
X I S B T D F H O K N P N T U Q H O I A G E C A H R A L
L L E U S V Y N C E G A I P S U I Q H F U D B A S Z W E
W P E N O Q U C O M M U N I C A T I O N R D S T B U X X
I S Y B U Q U D F R H J G E C A N O I T A V I T O M V T
N B O I C U J S O C I A L S E C U R I T Y Z Y V J X W I
S O L S K N Q F Y Y W R O L S E S A E R C N I T I R E M
U J P M O L R V O Z E S O P I X I E K U S P M O N D M E
Y D M W C E X I P S L R K C S M K C O M M I S S I O N J
U N E M P L O Y M E N T I N S U R A N C E B A I R L K I

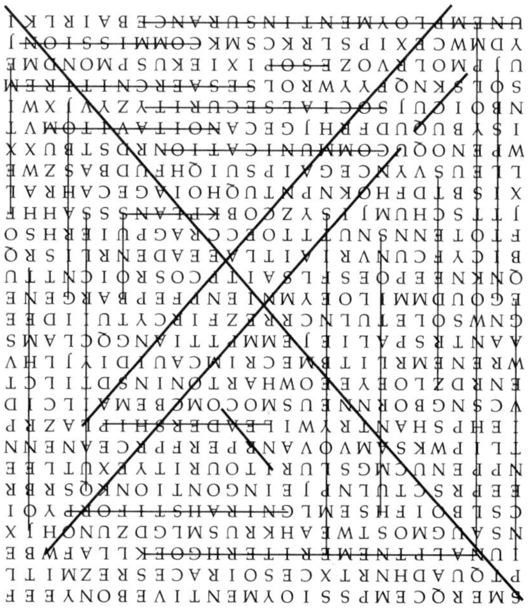

CHAPTER 15

# Maintaining Good Relationships with Employees

*The highest and best form of efficiency is the spontaneous cooperation of a free people.*
—Woodrow Wilson

*You can't manage people—you can only work with them. For your business to succeed, you must work closely with them and take exceedingly good care of them.*—Paul Hawken, *Growing a Business*

## LEARNING OBJECTIVES

After studying the material in this chapter, you will be able to:

1. Discuss some basic organizational concepts and show how small firms can use them.
2. List some factors influencing employee health and safety, and tell how to safeguard employees in small firms.
3. Define counseling and discuss some areas in which it may be needed in small firms.
4. Outline procedures for handling employee complaints and imposing discipline.
5. Discuss some complexities of dealing with unions.

## PROFILE

### JEANE BYRD PROVIDES A FANTASY ISLE

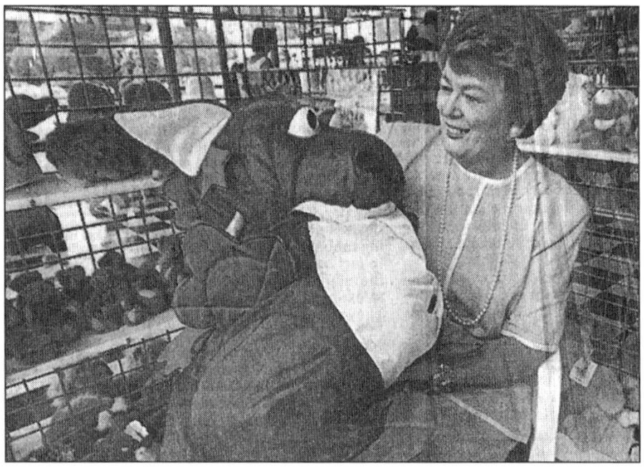

Photo by Mike Kittrell. © 1995 Mobile Press Register, Inc. All rights reserved.

Long before the likes of Toys 'Я' Us and the Baby Superstore—not to mention Wal-Mart—came to dominate the toy business, parents bought well-crafted playthings in small, independent toy stores. Reminiscent of such stores is Fantasy Island Toys in Fairhope, Alabama, which specializes in creative, educational, traditional, and out-of-the-ordinary toys. The owner, Jeane Byrd, chose as her logo a toy soldier standing inside a guardhouse, safeguarding children's fantasies. Byrd says the logo also symbolizes her business creed: "I have always marched to the beat of a different drummer. And it has worked."

When Byrd recently opened her third store, in nearby Mobile, two banks competed to finance the project—a good sign that an entrepreneur has "arrived." She is quick to point out, however, that business has not always been so easy for her, especially as a woman. In fact, 17 years ago, before she opened her first store, Byrd had to get her late husband to cosign the loan. She also recalls that, when she would take her husband to market with her, sales representatives would address their answers to him. "Things are different today when I go to market. It used to be that women got the short end of the stick. But today it's just fine."

Although Byrd has had to deal with the recent proliferation of chain and discount stores, she has held fast to her original goals. "My philosophy is: I love children. They are our most important resource. A child learns from everything he puts his hands on. But we want them to learn the right things. And we listen to the customers and see what it is they want and try to fill that want." Byrd stresses service as the key to staying competitive with the large discount stores. "Just give better service and a better environment. You've got to know your customer base and what it is they want. And above everything else, we emphasize service."

In addition to giving excellent service, Byrd says there are two very important factors in an entrepreneur's success. First, she says a business plan is an essential tool for getting started, plotting the course of the business, and measuring its progress. Second, and most important, is perseverance. "You have to be willing to work all hours, seven days a week, and you have to be willing to do it for practically nothing for a long time."

**D** Perseverance doesn't seem to be a problem for Byrd. Now 64, she says, "I kept thinking I'd retire at 60, but this is something I enjoy, and I can't imagine doing anything else." With three successful stores and the possibility of franchise looming in her future, Byrd has her hands full.

*Source:* Prepared by William Jay Megginson and adapted from various sources, including Kathy Jumper, "Toy Store Owner Guards Fantasies for Children," *Mobile* (Alabama) *Press Register,* July 21, 1993, pp. 1-E, 2-E; and Sherri Chunn and Pete Zurales, "Category Killers: Competition's Nightmare Is Consumer's Dream," *Mobile* (Alabama) *Register,* November 5, 1995, pp. 1-F, 2-F.

In previous chapters you have seen how to recruit, select, train, and motivate employees. You will now find out how to organize them, protect their health and safety, counsel them, discipline them, and deal with labor unions.

## Setting Up the Organizational Structure

**Organizing** is determining those activities that are necessary to achieve a firm's objectives, and assigning them to responsible persons.

The organizational structure of a business governs relationships between the owner, managers, and employees. **Organizing** involves determining the activities needed to achieve the firm's objectives, dividing them into small groups, and assigning each group to a manager with the necessary authority and expertise to see that they are done. A major problem for many small business owners is that they don't organize their activities properly. The following material should help you understand how best to organize a business.

### Some Basic Organizational Concepts

There are at least three basic organizational concepts that apply even to small businesses: (1) delegation, (2) span of management, and (3) specialization. While these concepts should be applied to businesses as they grow larger, they must often be adjusted when applied to mom-and-pop businesses.

#### *Delegation*

**Delegation** is assigning responsibility to subordinates for certain activities, and giving them the authority to perform those activities.

**Delegation** means assigning responsibility to subordinates for doing certain activities, giving them the authority to carry out the duties, and letting them take care of the details of how the job is done. Many owners and managers of small firms find it difficult to delegate authority. Yet you need to learn to delegate if you answer yes to most of the questions in Figure 15–1.

When you delegate work to subordinates, try to delegate sufficient authority to them to carry out their responsibilities. Otherwise, they lack the means of performing their duties.

Except in very small mom-and-pop shops, you should give employees a *job description,* which is a written statement of duties, responsibilities, authority, and relationships (see Chapter 13 for details). When you delegate authority to employees to do certain duties, you must be willing to let them do it; yet you can't relinquish your responsibility for seeing that those duties are performed.

Another important aspect of delegation is that decisions are best made by the person closest to the point of action, since he or she usually knows more about what is going on.

**Figure 15–1** How Well Do You Delegate?

- Do you do work an employee could do just as well?
- Do you think you are the only one who actually knows how the job should be done?
- Do you leave work each day loaded down with details to take care of at home?
- Do you frequently stay after hours catching up?
- Are you a perfectionist?
- Do you tell your employees how to solve problems?
- Do you seem never to be able to complete the work assigned to you?

*Source:* Adapted from Claude S. George, *Supervision in Action: The Art of Managing Others,* 4th ed., © 1985, p. 283. Reprinted by permission of Prentice Hall, Inc., Englewood Cliffs, New Jersey. And "Why Managers Fail to Delegate," in Donald C. Mosley, Paul H. Pietri, and Leon C. Megginson, *Management: Leadership in Action,* 5th ed. (New York: HarperCollins College Publishers, 1996), pp. 262–63.

### *Span of Management*

A manager's **span of management**, which is the number of employees reporting directly to him or her, should be limited. Being responsible for too many people, or for too many different types of work, will reduce the manager's ability to handle the work. In general, those with fewer activities to control can successfully manage more people, and vice versa. For example, supervisors may have 10 or more employees reporting to them because of the similarity and repetitive nature of their work. On the other hand, middle managers may have fewer subordinates, doing very dissimilar jobs. Don't try to supervise too many people personally, or the operation of the business could be severely hampered.

**Span of management** is the number of employees that report directly to a manager.

### *Specialization*

You should try to use **specialization**, whereby employees do the work they are best suited for. But, while it may lead to increased expertise, specialization can also lead to problems such as boredom, fatigue, alienation, and lack of initiative. This concept is hard to apply in very small businesses, where rigid specialization can result in some employees being idle while others are overworked. You must exercise judgment in assigning job responsibilities according to employees' talents and desires, without neglecting an equitable distribution of work.

**Specialization** is using employees to do the work that they are best suited for.

## Some Organizational Problems in Small Firms

A common problem in small firms is the owner's reluctance to delegate. This practice prevents the owner from devoting time to more pressing needs while also preventing others from developing into well-rounded workers.

> For example, the owner of a small wholesale company was chairman of the board, president, and treasurer. He handled all financial affairs; supervised accounting operations, wages, salaries, and sales commissions; and

> made recommendations to the board on the payments of dividends. Yet the company also had a vice president, sales manager, and operations manager.

This example describes an owner who does not delegate authority. Another problem is an owner who is afraid to make decisions, so the business becomes paralyzed. Then there's the owner who reverses decisions made by others. Perhaps he hasn't developed policies to cover the major repetitive situations and business functions.

The following are other indications of organizational trouble:

- Sales or production can't keep up with its workload.
- The owner holds too many meetings attended by too many people, resulting in wasted hours and excessive costs.
- Administrative expenses grow more rapidly than sales.
- The owner spends too much time following proper procedures or resolving conflicts rather than "getting production out."
- The attention of key people is not directed toward key activities of the firm and their performance.

Failure to delegate places an immense burden on you, making it impossible for you ever to be absent from the business and virtually guaranteeing its failure should you become incapacitated for a long time, because no one else has been trained to perform management tasks.

## Some Ways of Organizing a Small Business

Q

You can organize your business in many ways, but the most frequent ways are by (1) types of authority granted and (2) activities to be performed. There is now a movement in small businesses toward using teamwork to bolster effectiveness, as larger companies have been doing for some time.

### *Organizing by Types of Authority*

The organizational forms based on types of authority are (1) the line organization and (2) the line-and-staff organization. Within these types of organization is found another type—the informal organization.

In a **line organization**, the owner has a direct line of command over employees.

A **line-and-staff organization** is one that has specialists to advise and perform services for other employees.

The **informal organization** is the set of interpersonal relationships that come about as a result of friendships that develop on and off the job.

As was shown in Figure 3–6, a business may start with the owner doing all the work and then hiring a few people who do a variety of duties in producing, financing, and selling the firm's product. The owner is directly responsible for seeing that the employees do these things. This is called a **line organization**, as shown in Figure 15–2.

As the firm grows and becomes more complex, specialized workers—called staff—are hired to advise and perform services for those doing the operations, financing, and selling. Some examples are accountants (or controllers), personnel officers, and legal staff. This type of organization is called a **line-and-staff organization** (see Figure 15–3).

An **informal organization** always exists within the formal structure of a business. It involves the many interpersonal relationships that arise on and off the job. Two examples are the *informal leader* and *grapevine communication* systems. You can't fight it, so if you're wise, you'll determine who the informal leaders are and get their support for your activities.

**Figure 15–2** A Simplified Line Organization

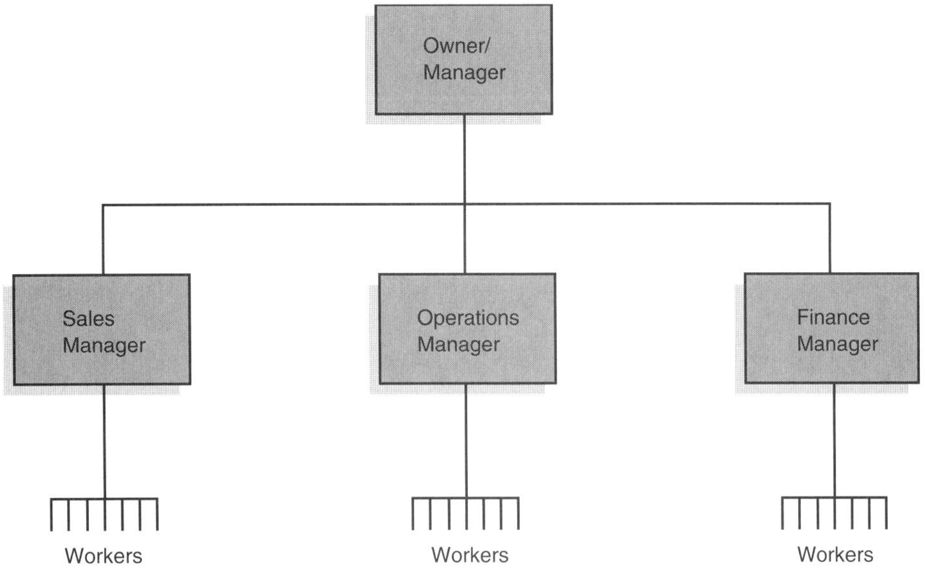


**Figure 15–3** A Simplified Line-and-Staff Organization

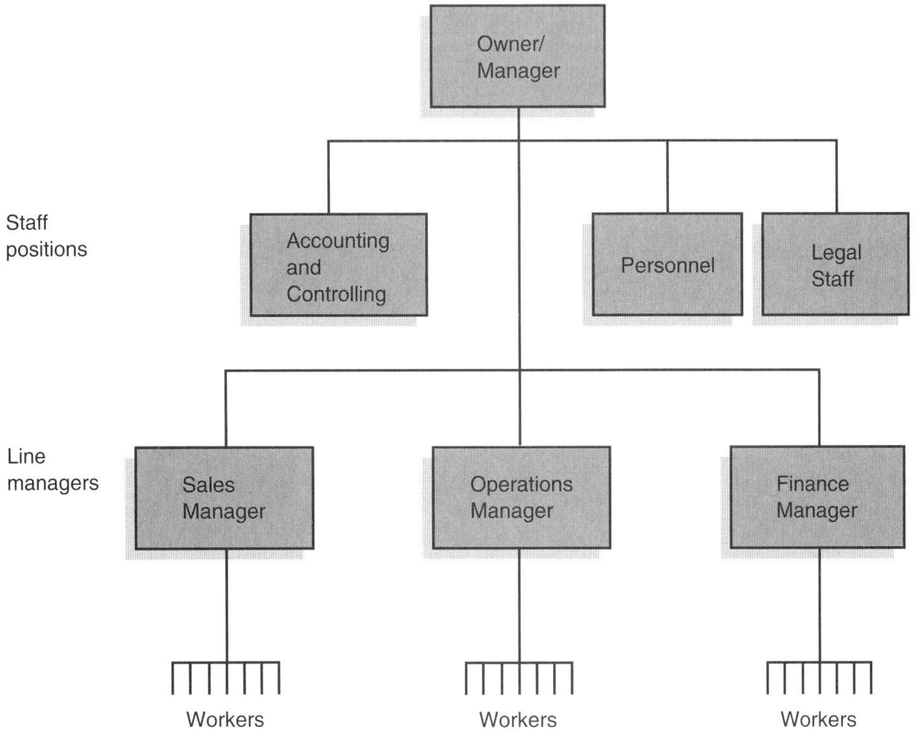

What informal organizations do you belong to? A morning coffee group? A study group? A social get-together once a week?

### *Organizing by Activities to Be Performed*

When you set up your formal organization structure, you can group the activities into small, workable groups according to:

1. *Function performed,* such as production, sales, or finance, as shown in Figure 15–2.
2. *Product sold,* such as menswear, ladies' wear, and so forth.
3. *Process used,* such as X-rays, operating room, and food service in a hospital.
4. *Area served,* such as urban, suburban, or rural.
5. *Types of customers served,* such as industrial, commercial, institutional, or governmental.
6. *Project being managed,* such as constructing a store and an apartment complex.

## Preparing an Organization Chart

There is no one structure that is best for all businesses, either large or small. However, the following discussion may help you organize your business to achieve its objectives.

An **organization chart** shows the authority and responsibility relationships that exist in a business.

Begin by setting up a series of authority and responsibility relationships expressed in a formal **organization chart**, as shown in Figure 15–2 and Figure 15–3. Even in a small business, a chart can be useful in establishing present relationships, planning future developments, and projecting personnel requirements. Therefore, a list of job titles and job specifications should accompany the chart (see Chapter 13 for details).

If the business is small and unincorporated, a tight, formal organizational structure could stifle creativity and reduce initiative. Instead, you might have a structure similar to that shown in Figure 15–4.

## Using Team Management to Improve Performance

Q

The use of team management has become an important stepping-stone in the growth of many small businesses. Of all the methods used, quality improve-

**Figure 15–4** Organization of a Small, Unincorporated Mom-and-Pop Business

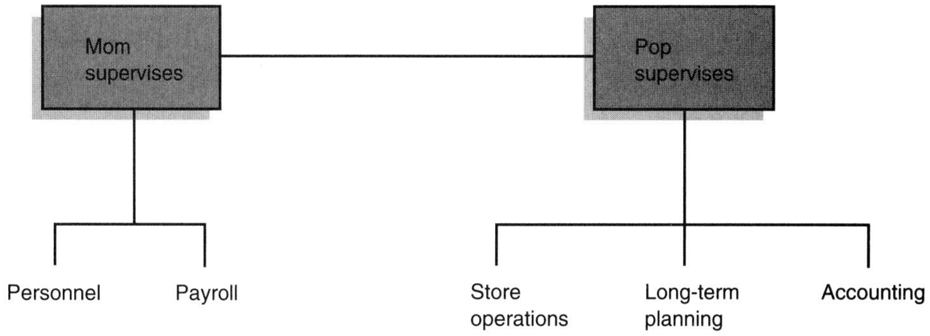

ment and teamwork may be the ones best suited to small firms. The goal of teamwork is to improve performance by involving employees in meeting customers' needs. When each member of each team fully understands the business's products and services, team members then have a better grasp of the contribution their work makes to fulfilling the company's mission. And by doing more of the work formerly done by managers, they broaden their scope in the business by acquiring new skills.

Companies can prepare employees for the use of team management by:[1]

- Setting the stage.
- Forming teams around the work.
- Providing training.

While teamwork may not be feasible for small mom-and-pop operations, several types of teams are found in larger, entrepreneurial-type small businesses. The more important types of teams are:

- **Problem-solving teams**, which meet for an hour or two a week to discuss ways to improve quality, efficiency, and the work environment.
- **Self-managing work teams**, which take over some managerial duties, such as work and vacation scheduling, hiring new members, and ordering materials.
- **Cross-functional teams**, which are formed to monitor, standardize, and improve work processes that cut across different parts of the organization, to develop products, or to otherwise address issues calling for broad representation and expertise.

**Problem-solving teams** meet on a regular basis to discuss ways to improve quality, efficiency, and the work environment.

**Self-managing work teams** take over managerial duties and produce an entire product.

**Cross-functional teams** cut across different parts of the organization to monitor, standardize, and improve work processes.

## Protecting Employees' Health and Safety

Totally safe working conditions are impossible to provide, so employee safety is a condition involving *relative* freedom from danger or injury. This section looks at how small business owners can maintain working conditions in which employees not only *are* safe but also *feel* safe. In other words, employees need to know that you care about their safety.

*"If we can't cure you, at least we'll awe you with modern medical technology."*

Reprinted from *The Wall Street Journal;* October 6, 1995 by permission of Cartoon Features Syndicate.

Unlike large firms, which employ specialists to be responsible for health and safety activities, small businesses must rely on employees with various job responsibilities to cover this area. There are, however, consulting firms that specialize in helping small businesses provide healthy and safe work environments, as the following example shows.

> Stephenson & Brook, based in Marblehead, Massachusetts, offers its services for about $150 a month to small companies—those with fewer than 50 employees. Although this firm specializes in workers' compensation issues, hot-line staffers will address other human resource topics as well.[2]

## How Serious a Problem Is Health and Safety?

According to U.S. Labor Secretary Robert Reich, about 17 people are killed at work each day.[3] And the National Safety Council reports there were 3.5 million disabling work injuries in the United States in 1994.[4] The most frequently injured body parts were the back (880,000), legs and arms (460,000 each), and thumb and finger (380,000). Of these injuries, 5,000 resulted in death. When deaths from work-related illnesses are added to those from work-related accidents, the death estimate increases to about *53,000 people each year,* OSHA officials claim.[5] Secretary Reich also estimates these deaths cost employers over $115 billion a year.[6]

Figure 15–5 shows the number of deaths by state during 1994 and the first four months of 1995. These figures are only for OSHA-inspected sites. OSHA officials say one of the primary reasons for these workplace accidents and deaths is a shortage of inspectors. State and federal officials agree that so many deaths occur because "lethal workplaces are not identified until after many serious injuries are reported."[7]

## Factors Influencing Workers' Health and Safety

There are many and varied factors affecting healthy, safe working conditions. We cover only the most significant ones: (1) organization size, (2) type of industry, (3) type of occupation, and (4) human variables.

### *Organization Size*

The smallest businesses tend to be the most unsafe places to work, according to a *Wall Street Journal* computer analysis of more than 500,000 federal and

**Figure 15–5** Workplace Deaths

**Number of deaths, by state, inspected by OSHA, January 1994–April 1995 (1,835 total)**

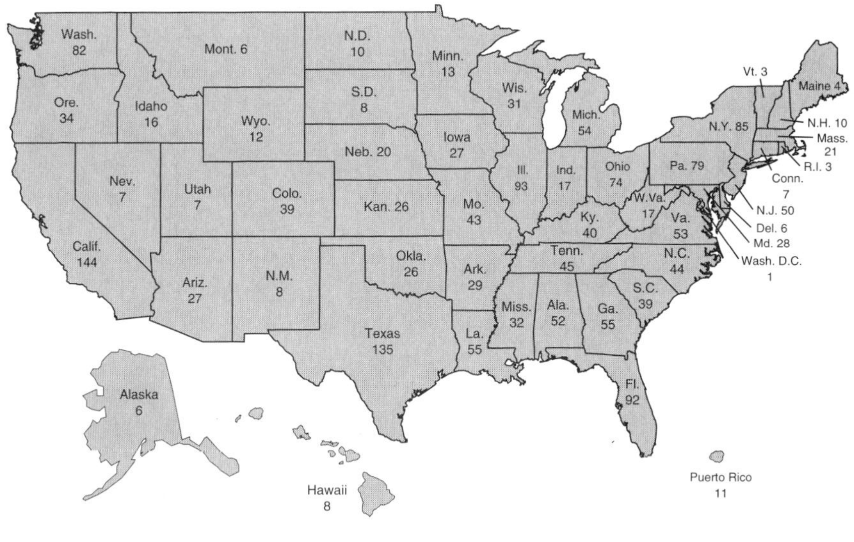


*Source:* OSHA, as reported in Bob Port and John Solomon, "OSHA Records Show Many Death Sites Not Checked," *Mobile* (Alabama) *Press Register,* September 15, 1995, p. 7-B.

state safety inspection records from 1988 through 1992. The analysis found that 4,337 workers died at inspected workplaces with fewer than 20 employees, but only 127 at those with more than 2,500 workers. There were 1.97 deaths per thousand workers at the smallest sites over the five years, compared with just 0.004 deaths per thousand at the largest workplaces.[8]

### *Type of Industry*

Although the safety records of industries change periodically, the type does affect safety. For example, the least safe industries usually include meat-packing plants, shipbuilding and repair, and metal sanitary ware.[9]

### *Type of Occupation*

The type of occupation also affects safety. Workplace dangers and injuries that once were considered likely only in construction and factories have now invaded offices and stores. For example, back injuries are quite prevalent among health care workers, who must frequently lift patients or heavy bedding, and shipbuilders. According to the Bureau of Labor Statistics, while the illness and injury rate in the entire private sector averaged 8.6 per 100 workers in 1992, it was 10.2 for health services, and 37.8 in shipbuilding.[10]

A growing health problem for small firms, especially in offices, is **repetitive-stress injuries (RSIs)**, also known as **cumulative trauma disorders (CTDs)** (one of the best known is carpal tunnel syndrome). These muscular or skeletal injuries to the hand, wrist, and other areas that bear the brunt of repeated motions have nearly doubled since 1985.[11] And the number of such injuries increased by almost 26 percent in 1992 alone.[12] They are now responsible for 56 percent of all workplace illnesses. Aetna Life & Casualty estimates that workers' compensation claims from employees such as reporters, telephone operators, data processors, and checkout clerks using scanners may soon cost as much as $20 billion a year. It has been estimated that the "average CTD workers' compensation case costs $8,500 in lost time and medical expenses."[13] And the Americans with Disabilities Act may make it easier for victims of RSIs to sue their employers.

**Repetitive stress injuries (RSIs)**, or **cumulative trauma disorders (CTDs)**, are muscular or skeletal injuries to the hand, wrist, or other areas that bear the brunt of repeated motions.

According to a recent U.S. News/CNN poll, nearly 25 percent of Americans say their work environment has recently caused them problems. The most common work-related problem for both men and women is back injuries—38 percent for women and 34 percent for men. The second for women is wrist injuries, 20 percent (as opposed to 12 percent for men, making it the third most common). Burns, cuts, and bruises are second for men (16 percent) and third for women (6 percent).[14]

### *Human Variables*

The most important human variables influencing safety are job satisfaction, personal characteristics, and management attitudes. Studies indicate a close relationship between safety and employees' satisfaction with their work. Other studies indicate that where top management actively supports safety programs, the accident frequency and severity rates are lower. Finally, research shows that most industrial injuries occur in persons 20 to 24 years old, especially males; fewer occur among the married and females.[15]

## The Occupational Safety and Health Act

The **Occupational Safety and Health Administration (OSHA)** establishes specific safety standards to assure, to the extent feasible, the safety and health of workers.

The Occupational Safety and Health Act created the **Occupational Safety and Health Administration (OSHA)** to assure—to the extent feasible—safe and healthful working conditions for U.S. employees. The law covers businesses that are engaged in interstate commerce and *have one or more employees,* except those covered by the Atomic Energy Act or the Federal Mine Safety Act.

### *Employee Rights*

If workers believe their employer's violation of job safety or health standards threatens physical harm, they may request an OSHA inspection without being discharged or discriminated against for doing so. They can participate in any resulting hearings and can protest if they think the penalty is too light. And, they can request that the Department of Health and Human Services check to see if there is any potentially toxic substance in the workplace and have safe exposure levels set for that substance.

### *Employer Obligations and Rights*

OSHA encourages increased examination and questioning of management's staffing decisions and equipment selection. Employees may claim that a crew size is unsafe or that a machine is potentially dangerous. Also, even though many accidents result from the employees' own lack of safety consciousness, employees usually don't receive citations. Instead, OSHA holds employers responsible for making employees wear safety equipment (for an example, see "The Case of Sam Sawyer" at the end of the chapter).

Employers are subject to fines for unsafe practices regardless of whether any accidents occur. Therefore, you should provide safety training for your employees, encourage and follow up on employee compliance with safety regulations and precautions, and discipline employees for noncompliance. Assistance may be obtained from OSHA and National Safety Council chapters. Also, your workers' compensation carrier may suggest ways to improve safety and employees' health. You may obtain useful information from equipment manufacturers, other employers who have had an inspection, trade associations, and the local fire department.

Also, thousands of small business owners call OSHA each year requesting a visit from one of the OSHA consultants. These inspections are free for organizations that have fewer than 250 employees and are classified as "high hazard" under the government's Standard Industrial Classification (SIC) code, but may not always be possible.

> For example, in 1994, 36,000 small businesses requested a visit from an OSHA small business consultant. Funds, however, allowed consultants to visit only 20,236 of those organizations.[16]

### *Some Generalizations about OSHA Enforcement*

Firms with fewer than eight employees don't have to maintain injury and illness records, except where a fatality occurs or an accident hospitalizes five or more persons. Also, OSHA doesn't inspect firms with 10 or fewer employ-

## USING TECHNOLOGY TO SUCCEED

### Combining Idealism with Opportunism

In the past, the computer industry has enjoyed a reputation for being environmentally clean, especially when compared to industries such as metals, paper, and petrochemicals. But groups such as the Silicon Valley Toxics Coalition have shown that computer waste products also pollute the air, soil, and groundwater. The primary problem is CFCs (chlorofluorocarbons), used as a solvent to wash the residue from printed circuit boards.

Inmos, a chip manufacturer located in the United Kingdom, has been using IPA (isopropyl alcohol) to replace CFCs. Unfortunately, it is highly flammable and is potentially dangerous, especially if used in the same quantities as CFCs.

While computers and peripherals are themselves rarely tossed into landfills, such is not true of consumables, such as batteries, disk media, paper, printer ribbons, and toner cartridges. While waste from computers makes up a small amount of municipal garbage, its proportion has grown every year since the advent of the personal computer. To prevent such waste from becoming a public relations problem, several companies have announced programs to recycle laser-printer toner cartridges. For example, Apple began its program to recycle toner cartridges in 1991. Cartridges bought in the United States include a prepaid shipping label that lets you return them when you're through with them. For every cartridge you return in the United States, Apple will donate $1 to one of two environmental organizations. Hewlett-Packard does the same.

*Source:* Adapted from Andy Reinhardt et al., "The Greening of Computers," BYTE, September 1992, pp. 147–58.

ees in "relatively safe" industries, which exempts nearly 80 percent of firms from inspections. Finally, inspectors concentrate on workplaces with unsatisfactory records.

Since 1988, small businesses have found that the paperwork burden makes it especially difficult for them to comply with OSHA's Hazard Communications Standard. It requires every employer in the country to identify hazardous substances in the workplace, list them, and train employees to use them safely. At first, the law applied only to manufacturers, but now the rule applies to all—"from accountants to zookeepers."[17]

Because the inspection program and its technical nature constantly change, you're advised to use the resources suggested previously, as well as local chambers of commerce, area planning and development commissions, and local offices of the SBA and OSHA. As indicated in Chapter 9, SBA loans may be available to help meet safety and health standards.

## Environmental Protection

Q

The Environmental Protection Agency (EPA) was created to help protect and improve the quality of the nation's environment. Its mandate includes solid-waste disposal, clean air, water resources, noise, pesticides, and atomic radiation. Environmental protection, though beneficial to society, can be hard on small firms. Many marginal plants have closed because of EPA requirements that pollution control equipment be installed. You owe it to your employees, for humanitarian reasons as well as financial ones, to protect their environment. As shown in Using Technology to Succeed, environmental protection efforts can also give your company a competitive edge.

## Counseling Troubled Employees

**Counseling** helps to provide people with an understanding of their relationships with their supervisors, fellow workers, and customers.

**Counseling** is designed to help employees do a better job by helping them understand their relationships with supervisors, fellow workers, and customers. While most small firms don't have formal counseling programs, they counsel employees on a day-to-day basis. The information in Figure 15–6 should help you do informal counseling. If you don't feel qualified to perform this activity, specialized employees may be used. Or free one-on-one counseling may be obtained from SCORE executives, who have had hands-on experience.[18]

### Areas Needing Counseling

While counseling involves all areas of employee relations, most counseling needs fall into the categories of (1) job-related activities, (2) personal problems, and (3) employee complaints.

#### *Job-Related Activities*

The activities that need counseling most are (1) performance, (2) safety, (3) retirement or termination, (4) stress, and (5) discipline, which will be treated separately.

*Performance Appraisal.* As discussed in Chapter 14, you should evaluate your employees' performance periodically, and discuss the results with them to help each see his or her strengths and weaknesses more clearly. The procedure, especially the follow-up discussion, should try to motivate workers to build on their strengths and minimize their weaknesses.

*Health and Safety.* As shown earlier, the whole area of health and safety requires considerable counseling and guidance. Because safety is largely a matter of attitude, your role is to counsel employees on the need for safe operations and to actively support all safety efforts.

**Figure 15–6** How to Approach a Troubled Employee

1. Establish the standards of job performance you expect.
2. Be specific about behavioral criteria, such as absenteeism and poor job performance.
3. Restrict criticism to job performance.
4. Be firm and consistent.
5. Be prepared to deal with resistance, defensiveness, or even hostility.
6. Point out the availability of internal or external counseling services.
7. Explain that only the employee can decide whether or not to seek assistance.
8. Discuss drinking only if it occurs on the job or the employee is obviously intoxicated.
9. Emphasize the confidentiality of the program.
10. Get a commitment from the employee to meet specific work criteria and monitor this with a plan for improvement based on work performance.

*Retirement or Termination.* Employees need considerable preparation for retirement, especially with regard to the benefits coming to them. But counseling is even more urgently needed when an employee must be terminated—with or without cause. Now that U.S. businesses are more concerned with cost saving, primarily because of foreign competition, terminations are more frequent.

Reprinted from *The Wall Street Journal;* permission Cartoon Features Syndicate.

When employees just can't produce or when the business can't afford to keep them, termination, often called *outplacement,* is sometimes the only option. But, as shown in Chapter 13, you might want to help the worker find other employment. Even with such help, though, termination is still traumatic for the worker, and counseling is needed. It has been found that 23 percent of outplaced workers must relocate, as they refuse to adapt to change.[19]

*Stress.* Stress is becoming the nasty buzzword in late 20th century workplaces. Nearly everyone feels its presence, and few can fully escape it. Stress can arise suddenly or gradually and can last for a short time or can persist for years. Whatever its nature, though, stress usually begins when individuals are placed in a work environment that's incompatible with their professional work style and/or temperament. And stress becomes aggravated when individuals find that they can exercise little control over their work environment.[20]

Contrary to popular belief, a fast-paced, chronically pressured work environment is not the primary cause of stress; instead, stress begins when individuals and environments are mismatched. Some people thrive on a fast-paced, even frenzied work atmosphere, while others prefer a slow-paced environment.

*"Well, back to the old stress buster seminars"*

Cartoon by Fred Maes. Copyright 1996 by Fred Maes.

**Job burnout** is a physical or mental depletion significantly below a person's capable level of performance.

Stress can be a killer for a small business. One study found that 75 percent of U.S. workers polled called their jobs "stressful."[21] When stress becomes great enough, it can result in **job burnout**, which is physical or mental depletion significantly below one's capable level of performance. It is a major cause of absenteeism and work site antagonisms.[22]

### *Personal Problems*

It's estimated that around a fifth of employees suffer personal problems, which reduce productivity by as much as 25 percent and result in huge dollar losses.[23] Two-thirds of those problems are drug and alcohol related, while the others tend to be emotional problems. According to Hoffman-LaRoche Inc., some problems that can result from drug abuse are:[24]

- Absenteeism.
- Accidents.
- Increases in medical expenses.
- Insubordination.
- Thefts.
- Product or service quality problems.

Employers are coping with these problems through counseling, referral to trained professionals, and employee-assistance programs (EAPs). According to the Employment Assistance Professional Association, EAPs are now serving nearly a million people—and the demand is increasing.[25]

Since 1989, small businesses with federal contracts and grants have been required to have a substance abuse policy that conforms to the Department of Defense's "Drug-Free Workforce Rules," which impose sweeping new obligations on contractors and grantees.* While the cost of such a drug-free environment is unknown, many small firms may be unable to bear the cost.

### *Employee Complaints*

Because complaints will inevitably occur, you should encourage employees to inform you when they think something is wrong and needs to be corrected. An effective procedure to do this should provide (1) assurance to employees that expressing their complaints will not jeopardize their employment, (2) a simple procedure for presenting their complaints, and (3) a minimum of red tape and time in processing complaints and determining solutions.

Unresolved complaints can lead to more problems, so you should listen patiently and deal with them promptly even if they seem to be without foundation. You should analyze the complaint carefully, gather pertinent facts, make a decision, inform the employee of it, and follow up to determine whether the cause of the problem has been corrected. Detailed, written records of all complaints (and disciplinary actions), as well as how they were resolved, should be maintained in employees' files as a defense against legal charges that may be brought against you.

---

*Contact your nearest SBA office for more information on these laws.

## IMPOSING DISCIPLINE

Employees like to work in an environment where there is **discipline**—in the sense of having a system of rules and procedures and having them enforced fairly. You can achieve such an orderly, disciplined environment by either (1) motivating employees to exercise self-discipline or (2) imposing discipline on them.

**Discipline** involves fairly enforcing a system of rules and regulations to obtain order.

### Encouraging Self-Discipline

To be effective, your employees should have confidence in their ability to perform their job, see good performance as compatible with their own interests, and know you will provide support if they run into difficulties. Therefore, you should encourage self-discipline among employees rather than rely on direct control. In this respect, the personal example of the owner is important in influencing employee discipline, as the following example illustrates.

> The owner of a small firm selling and installing metal buildings had a problem with employees taking long lunch breaks. When he asked his supervisors to correct this practice, one of them had the courage to say, "That would be easier to do if you didn't take two-hour lunches yourself."

### Using Positive Discipline

We've heard managers of small firms say that traditional discipline doesn't work for them. Instead, some are using **positive discipline** to improve morale and lower turnover. Under this approach, employees who commit some breach of conduct receive an oral "reminder," not a reprimand. Then there is a written reminder, followed by a paid day off to decide whether they really want to keep their job. If the answer is yes, the employee agrees in writing to be on his or her best behavior for a given period. The employee who doesn't perform satisfactorily after that is fired. Since the cases are fully documented, employees usually have little recourse.

**Positive discipline** deals with an employee's breach of conduct by their receiving an oral "reminder" (not a reprimand), then a written reminder, followed by a paid day off to decide if they really want to keep their job. If the answer is "yes," the employee agrees in writing to be on his/her best behavior for a given period of time.

### How to Discipline Employees

Most employees rarely cause problems. Yet if you don't deal effectively with the few who violate rules and regulations, employees' respect for you will decline. Therefore, an effective disciplinary system that meets union and legal guidelines involves:

- Setting definite rules and seeing that employees know them.
- Acting promptly on violations.
- Gathering pertinent facts about violations.
- Allowing employees an opportunity to explain their behavior.
- Setting up tentative courses of action and evaluating them.
- Deciding what action to take.
- Taking disciplinary action, while observing labor contract and EEO procedures.
- Setting up and maintaining a record of actions taken and following up on the outcome.

The **judicial due process** of discipline involves (1) establishing rules of behavior, (2) setting prescribed penalties for violating each rule, and (3) imposing the penalty(ies) only after determining the extent of guilt.

This type of discipline system follows the pattern established for **judicial due process**. The procedure should distinguish between major and minor offenses and consider extenuating circumstances, such as the employee's length of service, prior performance record, and the amount of time since the last offense.

## Dealing with Unions

The percentage of the U.S. private-sector work force belonging to unions has dropped drastically in the last four decades—from over 33 percent in 1955 to less than 11 percent in 1995.[26] Yet unions are quite powerful economically and politically, as they represent nearly 39 percent of public-sector workers,[27] so they affect small businesses in one way or another.

While union organizers have tended to concentrate their organizing efforts on larger firms, because they are easier to unionize, they're now also trying to organize smaller firms, because that's where potential new members are. Also, small business owners are more active in lobbying Congress and state legislatures, through groups such as the National Federation of Independent Business (NFIB), for laws and regulations unions oppose.[28] Therefore, you need to know something about unions and how to deal with them.

### Laws Governing Union–Management Relations

The *National Labor Relations Act (NLRA)* (also called the *Wagner Act*), as amended, requires management to bargain with the union if a majority of its employees desire unionization. (See Table 15–1 for the provisions of this and related laws.) Managers are forbidden to discriminate against employees in any way because of union activity. The *National Labor Relations Board (NLRB)* serves as the labor court. Its general counsel investigates charges of unfair labor practices, issues complaints, and prosecutes cases. The union or management can appeal a ruling of the board through a U.S. circuit court all the way up to the U.S. Supreme Court.

**Right-to-work laws** permit states to prohibit unions from requiring workers to join a union.

In some states a *union shop clause* provides that employees must join the recognized union within 30 days after being hired. But under **right-to-work laws** in effect in 21 states, the union shop is not legally permitted. Figure 15–7 shows the states with those laws in effect in 1996.

### What Happens When the Union Enters

Unions exist to bargain with the employer on behalf of their members for higher wages, fringe benefits, better working conditions, security, and other terms and conditions of employment. To do this, the union must first organize the company's employees.

The first thing you should do if your employees want to form a union is to recognize that it's because they believe they need the protection the union offers. You should therefore ask yourself such questions as: Why do my employees feel that it is necessary to have a union to represent them? Is it a lack of communication, or have I failed to respond to their needs? Am I treating them arbitrarily or unfairly? Studies of successful nonunionized companies find that management and employees participate in the business process as a team rather than as adversaries.

**Table 15–1** Some Laws Governing Union-Management Relations

| Laws | Coverage | Basic requirements | Enforcement agencies |
|---|---|---|---|
| Railway Labor Act of 1926 | Nonmanagerial employees of private railroads and airlines | Provides that employees are free to choose their own representatives for collective bargaining, and to settle disputes by mediation, arbitration, and emergency boards. | National Mediation Board; National Railroad Adjustment Board |
| National Labor Relations Act of 1935, as amended (also called the Wagner Act) | Nonmanagerial employees in nonagricultural private firms not covered by the Railway Labor Act, and postal employees | Employees have the right to form or join labor organizations (or to refuse to), to bargain collectively through their representatives, and to engage in other concerted activities such as strikes, picketing, and boycotts; there are unfair labor practices in which the employer and the union cannot engage. | National Labor Relations Board (NLRB) |
| Labor–Management Relations Act of 1947, as amended (also called the Taft–Hartley Act) | Same as above | Amended NLRA; permits states to pass laws prohibiting compulsory union membership; sets up methods to deal with strikes affecting national health and safety. | NLRB; Federal Mediation and Conciliation Service |
| Labor–Management Reporting and Discourse Act of 1959, as amended (also called the Landrum–Griffin Act) | Same as above | Amended NLRA and LMRA; guarantees individual rights of union members in dealing with their union; requires financial disclosures by unions. | U.S. Department of Labor |

*Source:* Various government and private publications.

**Figure 15–7** States with and without Right-to-Work Laws

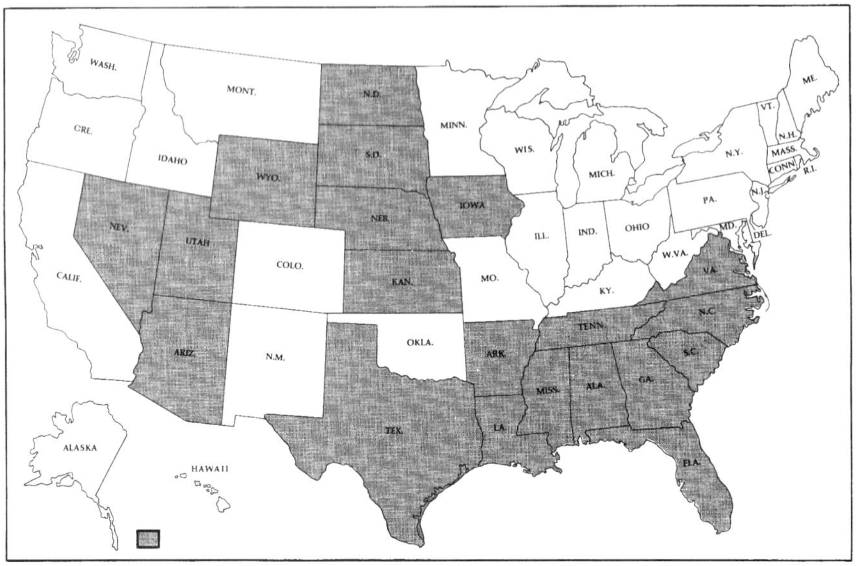


The second thing you should do is call in a competent consultant or labor lawyer. Small firms are increasingly turning to advisers to deal with unions, as the following example indicates.

> When employees tried to organize Persona Inc., a Watertown, South Dakota, manufacturing firm, its president called in Henry N. Teipel of St. Paul, Minnesota, as a consultant. He helped the personnel manager prepare for meetings with union representatives. The advice, which cost $4,000, "saved a tremendous amount of money . . . by keeping the battle short and the union out," according to the president.[29]

If your company is unionized, you should be prepared for certain changes. Your actions and statements may be reported to union officials, and the union may file unfair labor practice charges with the NLRB. Your best defense is to know your rights under the prevailing laws—and to maintain favorable relationships with employees.

## Negotiating the Agreement

Negotiating an agreement with the union requires much preparation, as well as the actual bargaining, and these require patience and understanding, so again it's advisable to consult your labor lawyer.

### *Preparing for the Bargaining*

Preparation may well be the most important step in negotiating the agreement. Obtaining facts about the issues before sitting down at the bargaining table should improve your position. You should collect information on other contracts in the industry and in the local area. Disciplinary actions, complaints, and other key matters that arose before the union's entry should be studied. Current business literature concerning business in general and the status of union–management relations in the industry can be useful. A carefully researched proposal should be developed well in advance of the first bargaining session.

### *Bargaining with the Union*

If you've prepared properly, you should be in a positive negotiating position instead of a defensive stance against the union's proposals. The "I don't want to give away any more than I have to" attitude generally leads to poor bargaining. All too frequently, however, fear seems to overcome the owner's willingness to develop in advance a proposal with attractive features that will appeal to employees, while protecting the company's position.

You should recognize the negotiation step as critical: It must be handled properly, preferably with outside assistance. Also remember that anything given away will be difficult to take back.

Be prepared to bargain over at least the following:

- Union recognition
- Wages
- Vacations and holidays
- Working conditions
- Layoffs and rehiring
- Hours of work
- Management prerogatives
- Seniority
- Arbitration
- Renewal of the agreement

Specific agreements must be reached in each of these areas, and rules established that should be obeyed by the company and the union. The **management prerogatives clause** is very important because it defines the areas in which you have the right to act freely as an employer, without interference from the union.

The **management prerogatives clause** defines the areas in which you have the right to act freely as an employer, without interference from the union.

## Living with the Agreement

Because the agreement becomes a legal document when it's signed, you must learn to live with its provisions until time for renegotiation. Your managers should be thoroughly briefed on its contents and implications. The meaning and interpretation of each clause should be reviewed and the wording clearly understood. Supervisors' questions should be answered to better prepare them to deal with labor matters.

Information and advice can be obtained from government sources, such as federal and state mediators, NLRB regional offices, state industrial relations departments, and members of SCORE. Private sources include employer groups, trade associations, labor relations attorneys, and labor relations consultants.

## WHAT YOU SHOULD HAVE LEARNED

**1.** Some important organizational concepts that apply to small firms as they grow are delegation, span of management, and specialization. Following these principles helps you delegate, tends to eliminate tensions, and eases employee frustrations.

You can organize your business by *(a)* type of authority used or *(b)* activities performed. The simplest structure is the line organization, where orders are handed down from the top to the bottom. With growth, specialized people are needed to do activities not strictly related to operations, selling, or finance, resulting in a line-and-staff structure. Informal organizations, found in all businesses, shouldn't be ignored, because their informal leaders and grapevine communications can affect your activities. Team management can also be used to improve performance.

**2.** Employee health and safety varies with the size of the organization, the type of industry, type of occupation involved, and personal and human characteristics of owners and employees. Repetitive stress injuries are becoming a serious health problem for small firms, especially in their offices. OSHA, the government agency responsible for promoting safe and healthful working conditions, concentrates on the businesses most likely to be unsafe or unhealthy.

While environmental protection is undoubtedly beneficial, the costs of required equipment and/or procedures can be a hardship for small businesses.

**3.** Counseling may involve listening to an employee gripe about some petty grievance, or it may be needed to correct a serious work problem. Counseling is needed in the job-related areas of performance appraisal, health and safety, and retirement or termination, as well as the personal areas of illness, mental and emotional problems, and substance abuse. Counseling assistance can be obtained from SCORE.

**4.** While some complaints from employees are inevitable, they can often be handled informally, but an established procedure is needed to discipline unsatisfactory employees. In the ideal work situation, employees discipline themselves, but for those who don't, a procedure should be set up to take into account the severity of the offense and the number of times it has been committed, as well as other factors and extenuating circumstances. Positive discipline, which challenges employees to discipline themselves, is being used in many small firms.

**5.** Dealing with a union is a challenge most owners and managers of small businesses don't want to face, and most will try to keep the union out. However, when a union does enter, many things change. Many laws govern labor–management relations, so hire a good consultant to help you. Negotiating an agreement with the union requires much preparation. After agreement is reached, supervisors should be briefed on the terms of the contract and instructed on how to deal with labor matters. Managers can get help in dealing with a union from many government and private sources.

## QUESTIONS FOR DISCUSSION

1. Explain some of the basic organizational concepts used in organizing a small business.
2. Describe some of the organizational problems small firms have.
3. Distinguish between organizing the business by type of authority and by grouping of activities.
4. Discuss the most significant factors that influence safe working conditions. What can a small business owner do about them, if anything?
5. Briefly discuss the Occupational Safety and Health Act and its application by OSHA.
6. Discuss the areas requiring counseling. What, if anything, can a small business manager do to improve counseling in those areas?
7. Explain the differences between self-discipline and externally imposed discipline.
8. Explain how national labor laws affect small businesses. Should you, as a small business owner, favor or oppose your employees' unionizing? Defend your answer.

## CASE 15

### THE CASE OF SAM SAWYER

Sam Sawyer was a top-rated operator in a building where a material with caustic soda was processed. The five stages were located on five separate floors. Operators moved the material in open buggies from the first stage to a chute in the floor and dumped it onto equipment on the floor below, where the next stage occured.

Because of the corrosive nature of the material, close-fitting goggles were provided. Until a year earlier, safety rules had required that goggles be worn only when removing material from equipment, because that was where the greatest possibility of injury existed. Their use at other times was up to the discretion of each operator.

At two stages in the process, though, the material was light and fluffy, and occasional backdrafts through the chutes caused it to fly. After this had resulted in three cases of eye irritations, the rules were changed, and operators were required to wear goggles whenever they were near exposed material.

Dave Watts, supervisor of operations for two years, had worked on all stages of the operation his first year out of engineering school. He had gotten along well with the men, was grateful to them for teaching him the "tricks of the trade," and might have been tempted to be lenient with them. Watts's boss, however, was very safety minded and insisted that safety rules be followed to the letter.

Sam Sawyer, who had worked on the operation for 20 years, was an outstanding operator and was looked up to by his fellow workers. His safety record was one of the best in the plant, as he had had only one minor injury in all his years of service.

When the new safety rule went into effect, Dave was bothered because everyone went along with it except Sam, who contended that it was unnecessary to wear goggles except when unloading equipment. This caused problems for Dave, because the others followed Sam's example. After much discussion, however, Sam agreed to go along with the rule.

Dave had a strong feeling that Sam was complying with the rule only while he was around. On half a dozen occasions he thought Sam had put on the goggles just as he came on the floor. Before the rule change, Sam had worn the goggles around his neck when they weren't needed, but he had recently started wearing them pushed up on his forehead.

Dave's doubts were confirmed today when he came on Sam unexpectedly and saw him bob his head to shift the goggles from his forehead to his eyes.

*Source:* Prepared by Bruce Gunn, Florida State University. Used with permission.

## QUESTIONS

1. What does the case show about the need for management emphasis on safety?
2. How can you explain the workers' lack of interest in their own safety?
3. What would you do if you were the supervisor?
4. How would you explain it to an OSHA inspector?
5. What does this case illustrate about the role of informal leaders?

# APPLICATION 15–1

Carlos, a business graduate, manages Don & Company, a small business that make dolls and markets them in local stores. The company, which has nine full-time employees, not only deals with production and sales but also purchases the raw materials from which to make the dolls.

Carlos has managed to get a contract from overseas to provide a customer with a large number of dolls. Since he now has to increase his production capacity to meet the new orders, he has included a lawyer on his staff, along with an accountant who advises him on various aspects of the business. He has also approached legal firms, accounting firms, and firms that lease manpower for counseling.

## QUESTIONS

1. What kind of organizational structure does Carlos have after expansion?
2. Do you think he made the right move? Why?

# ACTIVITY 15–1

*Directions:* Solve the clues below to fill in the puzzle using terms from this chapter.

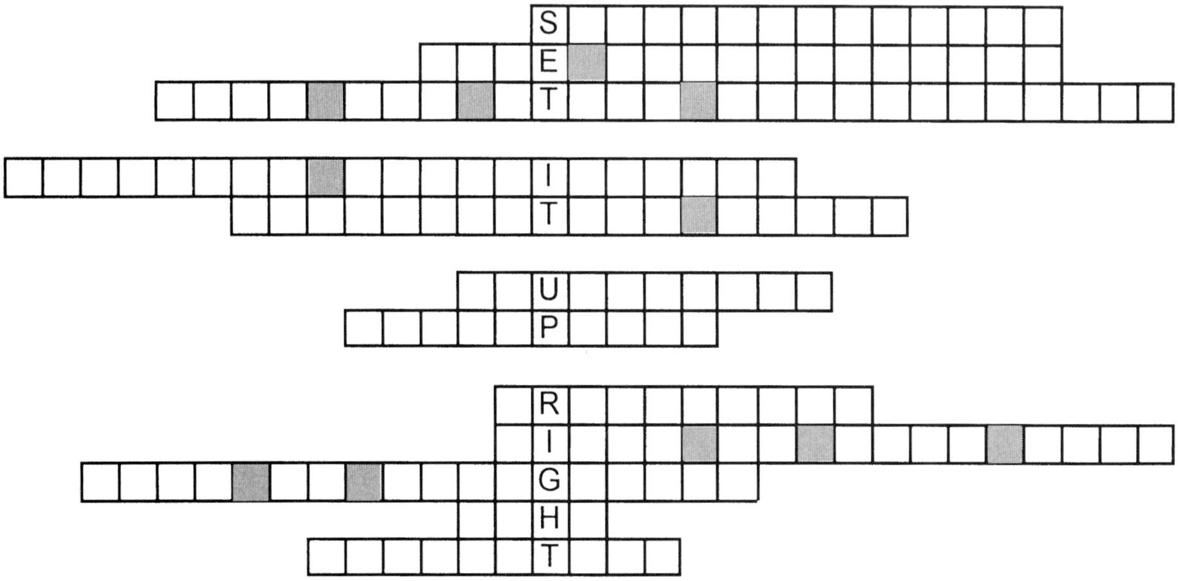


S Employees doing work for which they are best suited.

E Owner has direct command.

T Specialists advise other employees.

I Relationships result from friendships.

T Shows authority and responsibility relationships.

U Allows understanding of relations with co-workers.

P Enforcing regulations fairly.

R Determine and assign activities to achieve objectives.

I Prohibits required union membership.

G Number of employees per manager.

H Establishes worker health standards.

T Assigning responsibility and authority.

SPECIALIZATION
LINE ORGANIZATION
LINE AND STAFF ORGANIZATION

INFORMAL ORGANIZATION
ORGANIZATION CHART

COUNSELING
DISCIPLINE

ORGANIZING
RIGHT TO WORK LAWS
SPAN OF MANAGEMENT
OSHA
DELEGATION

CHAPTER 16

# Locating and Laying Out Operating Facilities

*Production is not the application of tools to materials, but logic to work.*—Peter F. Drucker

*You know your company is ready for robots when you recognize that automating is cheaper than relocating in South Korea or Taiwan.*—Bruce H. Kleiner, management professor

## LEARNING OBJECTIVES

After studying the material in this chapter, you will be able to:

1. Explain what an operating system is and how it functions.
2. Discuss how to determine the right location for a small business.
3. Describe the important factors involved in choosing a retail site.
4. Describe the most important factors involved in choosing a manufacturing site.
5. Identify the steps in planning the layout of physical facilities and show how to implement them.
6. Explain the emerging role of telecommuting in small firms.
7. Discuss some ways of improving operations.
8. Explain how to set and use performance standards.

P R O F I L E

# BOIS DES CHÊNES INN

Photo courtesy of Coerte and Marjorie Voorhies.

Located in Lafayette, Louisiana, Bois des Chênes Inn is one of the outstanding bed and breakfast (B&B) establishments in the United States. The inn, which is hosted by Coerte and Marjorie Voorhies, has been featured in *Frommer's Top 100 Bed and Breakfasts in North America.* Bois des Chênes is located in the plantation house of the historic Charles Mouton Plantation, which is listed in the National Register of Historic Places. Mouton was the son of Jean Mouton, an important figure in early Louisiana history. The house has also been owned by two mayors of Lafayette, a Louisiana lieutenant governor, and a relative of Dr. Samuel Mudd, who operated on John Wilkes Booth, President Lincoln's assassin.

D

The inn is within easy commuting distance of St. Martinville, the home of Longfellow's Cajun heroine, Evangeline, and other historic places of interest in French Louisiana. In addition to English, French and several other languages are spoken. For history lovers, this is *the* place to stay.

Three of the inn's five suites are in an 1890s Victorian carriage house located behind the plantation house, which was built around 1820. Each suite has a private entrance, a small refrigerator, and cable TV and includes a large, immaculate private bathroom. The suites are furnished in a pleasing blend of period furnishings, including queen-size tester beds. The upstairs suite, which can accommodate five guests, is furnished in country Acadian style; the two downstairs suites are done in Louisiana Empire and Victorian styles, reflecting the various periods of Cajun culture.

Photo courtesy of Coerte and Marjorie Voorhies.

The remaining two suites, in the main plantation house itself, have a sitting room and private bath; the Zouave Suite has two wood-burning fireplaces. Both are furnished with Louisiana, French Provincial, and Early American antiques. For guests who might wish to work while visiting, a conference room is available.

The price of a suite at the Bois des Chênes includes an enormous Cajun feast breakfast, which is prepared by Mrs. Voorhies. The *boudin,* a Cajun sausage, is delicious, and the French toast is proclaimed by her husband—and guests—"the best in the world." On arrival, complimentary wine is served, and the Voorhies offer a tour of the house and its furnishings in as much or as little detail as guests choose.

Mr. Voorhies is a semiretired consulting geologist who collects antique guns and samurai swords. He and his wife have remodeled and refurbished the old home and carriage house. Their sons—Kim, who recently retired from the military, and Karl, formerly the owner of Maison Bleu Bed and Breakfast—have joined them in their business efforts. Karl plans to move a Civil War–vintage Cajun cottage into the rear yard and remodel it into an antique shop.

Mr. Voorhies is a veritable encyclopedia of Cajun history, from military battles to the style of armoires. A local history expert, he helped found and organize Vermilionville, a Cajun and Creole village in Lafayette.

The Voorhies are multitalented people. In addition to helping operate their inn, Mr. Voorhies, with son Kim, also offers scenic hunting and fishing trips in season, as well as marsh and swamp boat tours of the Atchafalaya Swamp throughout the year. As a petroleum geologist, Mr. Voorhies emphasizes the geological, ornithological, floral, and faunal aspects of the area rather than just point out the alligators, birds, and snakes.

The Voorhies' enthusiasm, knowledge, and love for what they do surely are the major reasons for the success of their many business ventures. Bois des Chênes has been featured in many articles in newspapers and magazines such as the *New York Times, Saveur, Fodor's, Innsider, London Times, Le Point* of France, *Dublin Post, Toronto Star, Dallas Times Herald, Houston Chronicle, Travel & Leisure,* and *Condé Nast Traveler,* as well as on the Discovery channel's "Coast to Coast" program. The Voorhies are members of the Louisiana Bed & Breakfast Association.

*Source:* Visits, correspondence, and communication with Marjorie and Coerte Voorhies.

As the Profile illustrates, all businesses produce some product, either selling a good or providing a service. A retailer forecasts demand and then purchases merchandise and displays, sells, and delivers it to customers. A producer forecasts demand and then purchases material, processes it into products, and sells and delivers the products to customers. A service business tries to satisfy the needs of customers by providing a needed service. This is what the Voorhies are trying to do with Bois des Chênes.

This chapter examines what you must do to produce your product, how to choose the right location to produce it, how to plan and lay out physical facilities, and how to constantly improve operations.

## Developing Operating Systems

The steps required to start a business, as discussed in Chapter 5, are: (1) searching for a product, (2) studying the market for the product, (3) deciding how to get into business, (4) making strategic plans, and (5) making operational plans, including planning the many aspects of operating the business once it's started. This last step involves setting up your operating systems and providing building(s), materials, equipment, and people to produce the product.

Operating systems in different businesses are really quite similar, although the sequence of events and activities may vary as each business adjusts the system to fit its own needs. Also, support systems, such as accounting, personnel, and cash flow systems, must be integrated into the overall producing system.

Operating systems have the following productive elements: (1) a system for changing form, place, or time; (2) a sequence of steps to change the inputs into outputs; (3) special skills, tools, and/or machines to make the change; (4) instructions and goods identification; and (5) a time frame within which the work is to be done.

## What Are Operating Systems?

An **operating system** consists of inputs, processes, and outputs. The **inputs** include materials, people, money, information, machines, and other factors. The **process** involves converting these inputs into the goods or services the customers want, using the employees, machines, materials, and other factors. The **outputs** consist of the goods and services required by the customers; desired outputs also include satisfying the needs of employees and the public.

Figure 16–1 shows some examples of how inputs are processed into outputs. The processes shown are for the major operations of the company: Cloth, thread, and buttons are sewn into shirts; or a computer program is derived from customer information through design, installation, and testing. In addition, each company has processes such as accounting, maintenance, and quality control that support its main activities. All processes are designed to result in proper operating systems.

**Operating systems** consist of the inputs, processes, and outputs of a business.

**Inputs** are materials, people, money, information, machines, and other productive factors.

**Processes** convert these inputs into products customers want.

**Outputs** are the products produced and the satisfactions to employees and the public.

## How Operating Systems Work

**Operations,** or **production,** includes all the activities from obtaining raw materials through delivering the product to the customers. Thus, the word *operations* refers to those activities necessary to produce and deliver a service or good.*

All businesses usually have systems other than the production system, and as the following example shows, these systems must be coordinated for the best production.

**Operations,** or **production,** is converting inputs into outputs for customers.

> The objective of fast-food operations is to supply food quickly and with little customer effort. At Burger King, for example, there are three systems:
>
> 1. *A marketing system.* The order for a Whopper is taken from the customer and money received to pay for it.
> 2. *A production system.* The order is given to someone to prepare the hamburger and package it, while someone else prepares drinks.
> 3. *A delivery system.* The completed order is handed to the customer.

*Three activities must be performed by all businesses, regardless of their nature. They are (1) *marketing,* (2) *finance,* and (3) *operations.* In manufacturing and similar plants, operations is called *production,* but retail and service-type firms the activity is called *operations.*

**Figure 16–1** Examples of Operating Systems

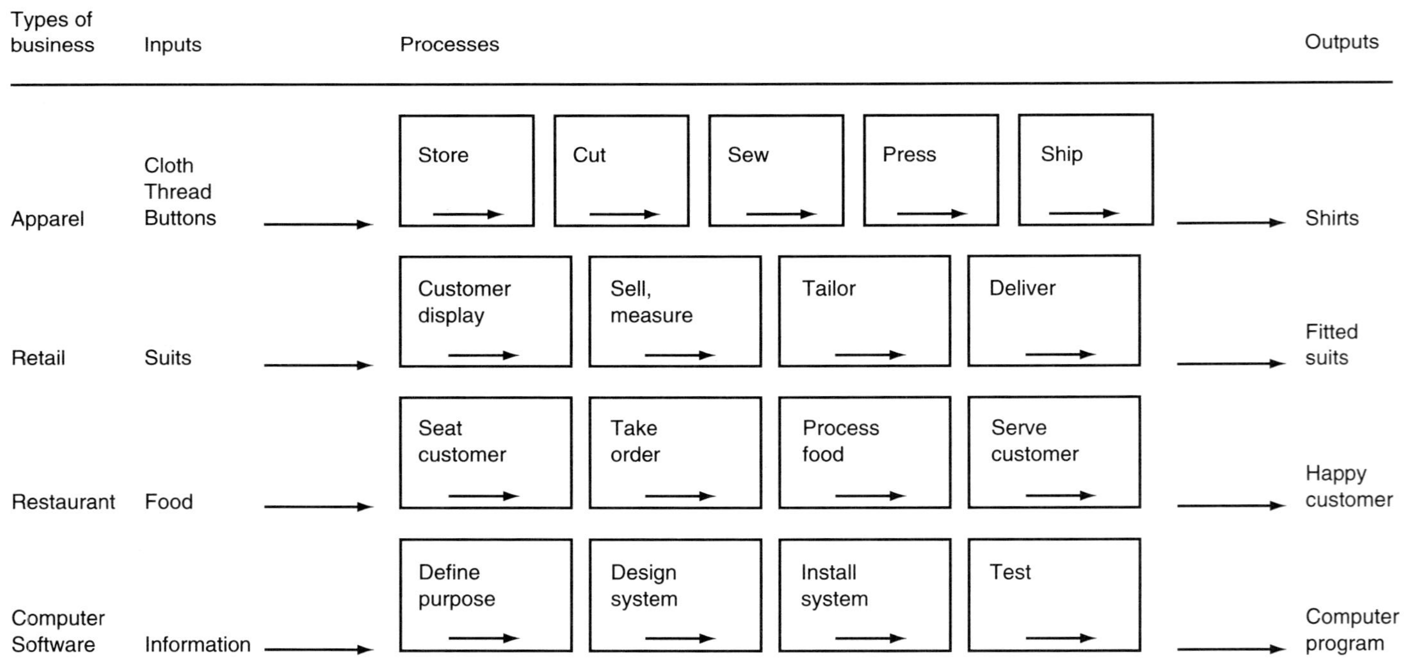

**Figure 16–2** Operations Involved in Producing a Hamburger

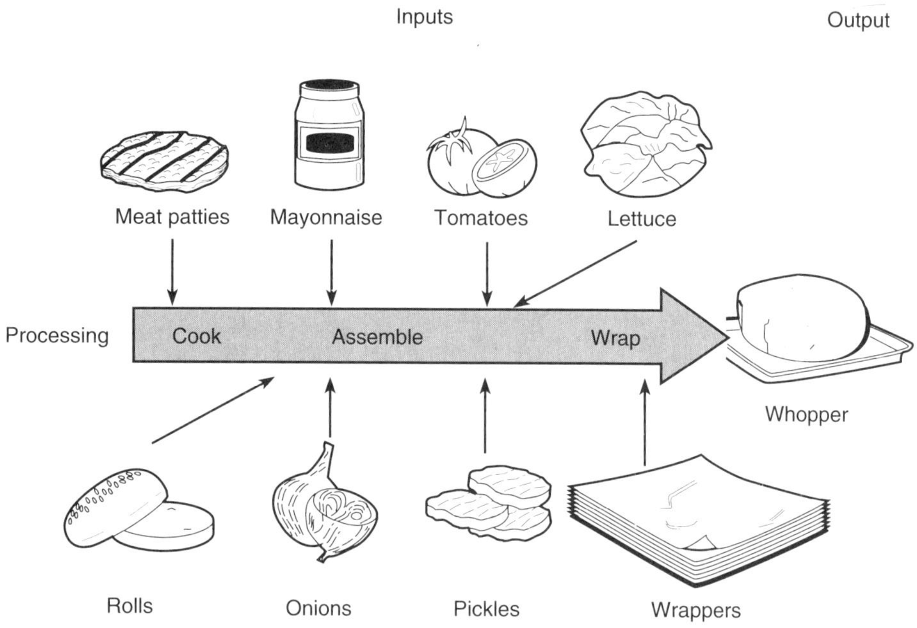


> These three systems are coordinated to provide quick service and to keep the line moving. Figure 16–2 shows how the production system operates. Notice how the inputs—such as rolls, meat patties, mayonnaise, lettuce, onions, and pickles—are processed by cooking, assembling, and wrapping into the output—a Whopper—which is then delivered to the customer.

### How to Begin Operations

After identifying the product (output), inputs, and processes, you are ready to begin operations, which involves: (1) choosing the right location, (2) planning physical facilities, (3) deciding on a layout, and (4) implementing your plans.

## Choosing the Right Location

As shown in Chapters 5, 6, and 8, you must define the character of your business and decide on your objectives and strategies before you begin to investigate available locations for your business. Since company location is a major factor in success or failure, you must ask yourself such questions as: Do I plan to have just one location or to grow regionally or nationwide? Do I intend to concentrate on one product area or expand into several? The answers to these questions will focus your search.

### Why Choosing the Right Location Is So Important

Location is one factor that can make the difference between success and failure for a small business. Sales come from customers who find it advantageous to buy from you rather than someone else. Have you, as a customer, patronized a business because it is near you? Or driven miles to obtain a special product? What factors caused you to live where you do now? Companies must consider similar factors to find suitable locations for their operations. Factors influencing the customer's choice of a business include variables such as convenience, time, cost, reliability, quality, and good service. These factors must be evaluated for each potential location before selecting the most suitable one.

When you choose a location, you usually expect to stay there for some time. Not only is it very expensive to move to another location, but also customers, who follow established patterns of activity and do not like changes, may not follow you to a new location. Employees are affected in much the same way.

## Some Important Factors Affecting Location Choice

Information on which to base a location decision can come from a variety of sources, as discussed in Chapters 5 and 12. However, you should consider at least two sets of factors when choosing a location for your business: (1) general factors that affect all types of businesses and (2) specific factors that pertain to specific types of businesses.

### *General Factors Affecting All Businesses*

The more important general factors are:[1]

1. Access to a capable, well-trained, stable work force.
2. Availability of adequate and affordable supplies and services.
3. Availability, type, use, and cost of transportation.
4. Taxes and government regulations.
5. Availability and cost of electricity, gas, water, sewerage, and other utilities.

### *Specific Factors to Consider for Various Businesses*

The type of business—retailing, producing, or service—influences most location decisions because it determines the relative importance of the general factors mentioned above. For example, location of customers may be more important to a large department store, while location of employees will be more important to a manufacturing plant. Table 16–1 shows some specific factors to be considered in making location decisions. Although the factors have been separated into retailer and producer, many of them apply equally to retailing, producing, and service organizations.

*"Mommy will take you potty as soon as she wraps up this business deal."*

**Table 16–1** Some Important Location Factors

| | Factors affecting selection of | |
|---|---|---|
| City | Area in city | Specific site |
| **Retailer** | | |
| Size of trade area | Attraction power | Traffic passing site |
| Population trends | Competitive nature | Ability to intercept traffic |
| Purchasing power | Access routes | Compatibility of adjacent stores |
| Trade potential | Zoning regulations | Adequacy of parking |
| Competition | Area expansion | Unfriendly competition |
| Shopping centers | General appearance | Cost of site |
| **Producer** | | |
| Market location | Zoning | Zoning |
| Vendor location | Industrial park | Sewer, effluent control |
| Labor availability | Transportation | Transportation |
| Transportation | | Terrain |
| Utilities | | Utilities |
| Government, taxes | | Labor availability |
| Schools, recreation | | |

*Source:* U.S. Small Business Administration, *Choosing a Retailing Location,* Management Aid No. 2.021 (Washington, DC: Government Printing Office), p. 2.

**Retailers** are concerned with people who come to, or are drawn into, the store to make a purchase. Therefore, location is concerned with people's movement, attention, attitudes, convenience, needs, and ability to buy. In other words, which location will provide sales at a reasonable profit?

**Retailers** sell goods to the ultimate consumer.

**Producers** are concerned with converting, usually in considerable volume, materials, parts, and other items into products. They emphasize selling those products through intermediaries to the ultimate consumer, as discussed in Chapter 11. Compared to retailers, producing units are often larger and fewer and sell to a smaller number of customers. The plant and customer can be located some distance apart, so other factors become more important. Still, nearness to customers and suppliers helps to keep costs down and permits more satisfactory service. Primary emphasis on locating, though, is placed on cost and service.

**Producers** convert materials to products in considerable volume for others to sell to ultimate consumers.

Service companies have some characteristics of both retailers and producers. The performance of some services—such as those provided by hair stylists, dentists and doctors, and auto service stations—usually requires customers to come to the business's location, where the service is performed. These locations, therefore, depend on convenient and economical travel.

Some other services—such as home nursing care, landscaping and gardening, and plumbing and electrical repairs—require going to the client's home. But even those who perform these services should try to locate near where customers are clustered. However, some businesses that cannot attract

**Figure 16–3** Rating Sheet for Sites

**Grade** each factor: 1 (lowest) to 10 (highest)
**Weight** each factor: 1 (least important) to 5 (most important)

| Factors | Grade | Weight |
|---|---|---|
| 1. Centrally located to reach my market. | _____ | _____ |
| 2. Raw materials readily available. | _____ | _____ |
| 3. Quantity of available labor. | _____ | _____ |
| 4. Transportation availability and rates. | _____ | _____ |
| 5. Labor rates of pay/estimated productivity. | _____ | _____ |
| 6. Adequacy of utilities (sewer, water, power, gas) | _____ | _____ |
| 7. Local business climate. | _____ | _____ |
| 8. Provision for future expansion. | _____ | _____ |
| 9. Tax burden. | _____ | _____ |
| 10. Topography of the site (slope and foundation). | _____ | _____ |
| 11. Quality of police and fire protection. | _____ | _____ |
| 12. Housing availability for workers and managers. | _____ | _____ |
| 13. Environmental factors (schools, cultural, community atmosphere) | _____ | _____ |
| 14. Estimate of quality of this site in five years. | _____ | _____ |
| 15. Estimate of this site in relation to my major competitor. | _____ | _____ |

*Note:* Copies of this *Aid* and other publications are available from the SBA for a small processing fee.
*Source:* U.S. Small Business Administration, *Locating or Relocating Your Business,* Management Aid No. 2.002, p. 6.

enough customers to a central location may take all, or a part, of their activities "on the road" to obtain more income.

For example, after grooming dogs for 27 years from a fixed location, Ronnie and Martell White, owners of On the Spot Dog Grooming, now use a grooming van. With a small office in their home, they cover an area of about 100 square miles. The van is fully loaded with an extensive unit for all aspects of dog grooming, including a built-in bathtub. On an average day, the Whites service eight dogs or more for a fee of $15 or $20 each.[2]

D

Similarly, Sue Ley, the owner of CleanDrum, Inc., a company that straightens and cleans metal oil drums, tried using a mobile unit to clean drums at customers' locations. Although she found that this was too heavy a load for her limited work force at the time, she hopes to resume the service later.*

*See IV. Sample Case: CleanDrum, Inc., in the Workbook for Developing a Successful Business Plan, at the end of this text on page 000.

Many small service businesses start and continue to operate out of the owner's home. This is a logical arrangement since the owner may be tentative about going into business and may not want to have the fixed expense of an office. Also, these owners tend to go to the clients to perform their service. Finally, as will be shown in Chapter 20, there are tax benefits.[3]

At some point, the data collected must be analyzed to provide the information necessary for a decision. A score sheet like that in Figure 16–3 can be valuable in comparing possible locations. Evaluations can sometimes be quantitative, such as number of households times median income times percentage of income spent on store items times some special factor for this store. Others are ratings, grading factors from 1 for the lowest to 10 for the highest.

Some factors are very important and should be given more weight than others. One factor in a given site might be so intolerable that the site must be eliminated from consideration.

## Locating Retail Stores

In choosing a site for a retail store, two interrelated factors are important: the type of store (i.e., the type of goods sold) and the type of location. There is a perception that market forces and the economies of scale enjoyed by big chains are relentlessly consuming small stores. A study by consultant Gary A. Wright, however, found this conclusion only partially valid. Instead, Wright found "that many small retailers who find a [specialized] niche and provide strong personal service to customers will survive and thrive into the next century."[4] In other words, *service, expertise, and location* are the dominion of small specialty retailers, as the following example illustrates.

> The 17th Street Surf Shop targets males ages 8 to 28 with specialized surf gear. The store has expanded to a nine-store operation by selling surfing gear at a ratio of 90 percent soft goods to 10 percent hard goods.

### Types of Stores

Customers view products in different ways when selecting the store from which to buy. Therefore, stores can be grouped into (1) convenience, (2) shopping, and (3) specialty stores, according to the type of goods they sell.

#### *Convenience Goods Stores.*

**Convenience goods** are usually low-priced items that are purchased often, are sold in many stores, are bought by habit, and lend themselves to self-service. Examples are candy bars, milk, bread, cigarettes, and detergents. Although the term *convenience goods* may make you think of *convenience stores* (small markets with gas pumps), convenience goods stores are better typified by the grocery and variety stores where we regularly shop for consumable items. Convenience goods stores are interested in having a high flow of customer traffic, so they try to get people to remember their needs and come in to purchase the items currently on display. The quantity of customer flow seems more important than its quality. These stores are built where the traffic flow is already heavy.

**Convenience goods** are products that customers buy often, routinely, quickly, and in any store that carries them.

For instance, our research has shown that nearly 70 percent of women patronize stores within five blocks of their residence. Store hours were also found to be very important.

### *Shopping Goods Stores*

**Shopping goods** are goods that customers buy infrequently, after shopping at only a few stores.

**Shopping goods** are usually higher-priced items, which are bought infrequently, and for which the customer compares prices. People spend much time looking for these items and talking to sales personnel. Therefore, capable salespeople with selling ability are required (see Chapter 11 for more detail). Examples of these goods are suits, automobiles, and furniture.

### *Specialty Goods Stores*

**Specialty goods** are bought infrequently, often at exclusive outlets, after special effort by the customer to drive to the store.

**Specialty goods** are high-priced shopping goods with trade names that are recognized for the exclusive nature of the clientele. By their very nature, specialty goods stores often generate their own traffic, but customer flow can be helped by similar stores in the vicinity. Some examples of specialty goods are quality dresses, precious jewelry, and expensive video and sound equipment. In essence, people do not comparison shop for specialty goods, but just buy the name on the item.

## Types of Locations

In general, the types of locations for retail businesses are (1) downtown business districts, (2) freestanding stores, and (3) community shopping centers or malls.

### *Downtown Business District*

**Downtown locations** attract business-oriented activities, as government, financial businesses, and head offices of large firms are usually located in the downtown area.

Changes in retail locations have occurred as discounters have located their stores outside the downtown area. Now, governments, financial businesses, and the head offices of large firms provide most of the business for retail stores in **downtown locations.**

A downtown location has many advantages, such as lower rents, better public transportation, and proximity to where people work. But the disadvantages often include limited shopping hours, higher crime rates, poor or inadequate traffic and parking, and deterioration of downtown areas. In some cases, one or a few downtown areas are preferred to the exclusion of others.

G

> A classic example of this trend can be seen in franchise locations in countries such as Brazil, Chile, Colombia, and Mexico. According to Enrique Gonzales Calvillo, president of the Mexican Institute of Franchisers, Mexico is suffering from the tendency of economic activity to concentrate in the center of one city. He cites limited space, arbitrary and confusing zoning laws, the persistence of out-of-date and misguided real estate practices, and overwhelming demand as among Mexico's problems. The concentration of businesses in Mexico City has made investment in small and medium-sized businesses almost prohibitive.[5]

**Freestanding stores,** found in various locations, are usually best for customers who have brand or company loyalty.

### *Freestanding Stores.*

**Freestanding stores,** found in many locations, may be the best for customers who have brand or company loyalty, or for those who identify with a given shop, where a business has a competitive edge over its competitors, where the character of customers and growth objectives blend well. Low costs, good parking, independent hours and operations, and restricted competition in these locations tend to fit the more entrepreneurial types of businesspeople. However, to attract customers, especially new ones, you may have to do considerable advertising. Moreover, acquiring a suitable building and land may be difficult.

Innovative entrepreneurs may find a lucrative location in neighborhoods formerly avoided by other businesses. But the market niche—product and clientele—must conform to the needs of the customers in the area.

**D**

Onyx Grocery, owned and operated by Albert Cooke and Rodney Tonge, is an example of such a fit. The partners opened the tiny store—about 500 square feet, or only a little larger than a two-car garage—in Fort Lauderdale, Florida, in a neighborhood where there are few cars.

Its shelves are crowded with convenience store essentials such as toiletries and cereals but also such nonessentials as hair weaves made from human hair, and the "drinks are cheap and cold."

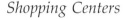

Photo courtesy of *Sun Sentinel*

The store serves a special need, for there are no other neighborhood-owned or -operated businesses in the area. And the young partners say their fledgling business is "a blueprint for achievement, a result of saving when spending was tempting—a result of preparation paying off."[6]

## *Shopping Centers*

**Shopping centers** vary in size and are designed to draw traffic according to the planned nature of the stores to be included in them.

**Shopping centers** are planned and built only after lengthy and involved studies. These centers vary in size from small neighborhood and strip centers, to community centers, to the large regional malls.

*Why Shopping Centers Are So Popular.* Shopping centers are designed to draw traffic according to the planned nature of the stores to be included in them. The design of the centers ranges from small, neighborhood convenience goods stores to giant regional centers with a wide range of goods and services, which may or may not be specialized. Shopping centers offer many services, such as specialized activities to bring in traffic, merchant association activities, parking, utilities, and combined advertising. A current trend is for large "power centers" to compete with one another to be the largest.

**Figure 16–4** An Anchor Store

Photo courtesy of William Waldorf.

Enclosed malls have eliminated weather problems for customers. Also, older and handicapped people are encouraged to use the mall to exercise in a controlled climate.

**Anchor stores** are those that generate heavy traffic in a shopping center.

The typical shopping center has two **anchor stores.** These stores, often large department stores, are usually located at the ends of the arms of the mall, where they are not only easily accessible from the parking lot but also generate heavy traffic for the small stores between them.

> Figure 16–4 shows an unusual example of an anchor store. Gayfers straddles the center of Springdale Mall in Mobile, Alabama. Because the store actually divides the mall, anyone going from one end of the mall to the other must go *through* Gayfers.

Within the malls, kiosks and carts often serve as magnets, occupying potentially prime selling spots. These small "stores" are fast growing in importance as malls increase in popularity.

D

> For example, Audrey Evans' kiosk in Gurnee Mills mall, in the Chicago suburb of Gurnee, is seen by nearly everyone who comes into the mall. Her retail stand—with its colorful rows of plastic troll figures as well as "fine collectible dolls"—occupies the center of a large corridor in the milelong mall. Evans' sales totaled $200,000 in the first 10 months of operation. She planned to add other kiosks and possibly a full-sized store.[7]

Some malls may have a theme that stores are expected to conform to. The purpose of the theme is to pull the stores together and have them handle products of similar quality. For example, the center may have regulations on shopping hours, how to use the space in front of the store (what to display and how), and so on.

*Drawbacks of Shopping Centers.* Although the above advantages are considerable, there are also disadvantages to locating in a center. Some of the most significant of these are cost, restrictions imposed by the center's theme, operating regulations, and possible changes in the center's owners and managers, which could bring policy changes.

There is now a "total rent" concept for cost that must be considered in evaluating the costs of renting space in a shopping center. These costs may include dues to the merchants' association, maintenance fees for the common areas, and the cost of special events or combined advertising. The most common rental is a basic rent, usually based on square footage, plus a percentage of gross sales (usually 5 to 7 percent). These costs tend to be high and often discourage tenants, as the following example shows.

> For several years, Kitty* operated her medium-priced women's clothing shop in a small shopping area across from one of the community's larger shopping malls. A representative of the mall tried to persuade Kitty to move to the mall. After hearing the rental terms, however, Kitty was appalled. The basic rent was $21.75 per square foot with an additional charge of 5 percent of gross sales. Later Kitty told a friend, "Do you know that just the basic rent would have cost me $2,400 a month, to which I would have had to add on 5 percent? Can you imagine what I would have had to charge for my clothes in order to make a profit after paying that kind of rent? I think I'd better stay put." Before rejecting the move to the shopping center, however, Kitty should analyze not only the costs of the move but also the potential increase in income in a higher-traffic location.

D

## Locating Manufacturing Plants

**Manufacturing** (or **production**) usually involves making, or processing, raw materials into a finished product. The materials may be those extracted from the ground, or they may be outputs of other companies (such as metal plates, silicon chips, or ground meat for hamburgers), which are changed in form or shape, or assembled into a different type of product. The location of a manufacturing plant is usually selected with the aim of serving customers properly at the lowest practical cost. Of the factors to consider in locating a manufacturing plant (see Table 16–1), the most important are nearness to customers and vendors and availability and cost of transportation.

**Manufacturing,** or **production,** usually involves making or processing materials into finished goods.

Of considerable importance to manufacturers is the time and cost of transporting finished goods to the customers and acquiring raw materials from vendors. The success of a given location can hinge on the availability and cost of the proper mode of transportation, as discussed in Chapter 12.

## Planning Physical Facilities

Once you've selected your location, you must begin planning, acquiring, and installing facilities. These **facilities,** which include the building, machines and other equipment, and furniture and fixtures, must be designed or selected to produce the desired product at the lowest practical cost.

**Facilities** are the buildings, machines and other equipment, and furniture and fixtures needed to produce and distribute a product.

These activities include five steps: (1) determine the product to be sold and the volume in which it is to be produced, (2) identify the operations and

*Name disguised.

activities required to get the product to the customer, (3) determine space requirements, (4) determine the most effective layout of the facilities, and (5) implement your plans.

## Determine Product to Be Produced

Facilities should be planned for products to be produced now, but also for changes anticipated in the foreseeable future. Projections for five years are normal, and industry standards for the space required for planned sales or production volume can be a good start in planning.

## Identify Operations and Activities to Be Performed

You will remember that operations include all the activities from buying the materials through delivering the finished product to the customer. These activities include (1) purchasing materials and parts for production or goods to sell, (2) performing operations needed to produce the product, and (3) carrying out support activities.

Sequences of operations may be fixed (e.g., producing the hamburger in Figure 16–2) or may change from order to order, as happens in retail stores or service businesses.

## Determine Space Requirements

Space is required for materials, equipment, and machines, as well as the movement of customers and employees. Space is also needed for carts and trucks, inventory, displays, waiting areas, personal facilities, maintenance and cleaning, and many other services. The number and size of all these areas depend on the volume of output planned.

Q

Determining space requirements is becoming easier—or more complicated, according to your point of view. The changing nature of production, operations, and service activities is also changing *where* people work, and therefore the amount of space needed. **Telecommuting,** which is using modern communication media—such as telephones, fax machines, computers with modems or fax/modems, and scanners—to work anywhere, has changed the concept of work.

**Telecommuting** is the use of modern communication media, such as telephones, fax machines, computers, modems and fax/modems, and scanners, to work from an office, home, or any location.

With over 9 million Americans telecommuting to work, and over 14 million others operating small businesses from their homes, *work* is no longer *a place to go to* but *something you do.* And according to June Langhoff, editor of *TeleTrends,* the official newsletter of the Telecommuting Advisory Council (TAC), use of the new technologies (see Using Technology to Succeed) permits work to be done anywhere.[8]

G

A Link Resources survey found a 120 percent increase in telecommuters from 1989 to 1992.[9] In 1995, 15 percent of U.S. workers were doing some form of telecommuting.[10] Figure 16–5 shows the rapid growth in the number of companies that allow—or are considering allowing—workers to telecommute. In a later survey, it was found that 54 percent of those who telecommute are men, while 46 percent are women.[11] There are nearly four times as many white-collar telecommuters as blue-collar ones.[12] In contrast to these professional, sales, or technical workers, however, are the many immigrants who speak little English, have no transportation, and must care for small children.[13]

## USING TECHNOLOGY TO SUCCEED:

### Office to Go

Roger Stephenson can get his work done just about anywhere. The owner of a Cassopolis, Michigan, land surveying company, Stephenson conducts business in grassy fields, lakeside boat ramps, and roadside shoulders, all from his 1993 Chevrolet Astro Mobile Office Vehicle (MO-V). Says Stephenson, "Now I can go out with my crew and get my office work done, too."

Photo courtesy of *Entrepreneur Magazine*. Reprinted with permission of *Entrepreneur Magazine*, November 1995.

Stephenson is one of a growing number of small business owners who are relying on four-wheeled offices. Auto manufacturers and van conversion companies are developing vehicles to cater to this trend.

"When people start trying to work on the road, they often find out they're ill-equipped, and they just become more inefficient," says Dayna Beal of Mobile Office Vehicles Inc., a Zeeland, Michigan, company that converts vans to MO-Vs. An ergonomic desk, swivel desk chair, cellular phone, notebook computer, portable inkjet printer, and fax machine are among the standard features of the MO-V; van conversions cost between $28,000 and $35,000.

Even if you're not such a hard-core mobile entrepreneur, take note: Some major car manufacturers are beginning to offer features for mobile businesses as well. Chrysler's line of 1996 minivans, for instance, comes standard with front electrical power outlets and removable back seats and has options for rear seats that fold flat like a table, rear power outlets, and a driver's side sliding door.

*Source:* Adapted from Heather Page, "Big Traveler: Office to Go," *Entrepreneur,* November 1995, p. 66. Reprinted with permission from *Entrepreneur Magazine,* November 1995.

**Figure 16–5** Telecommuting on the Rise

**Companies that allow or are thinking of allowing employees to work at home or on the road via computer and modem:**

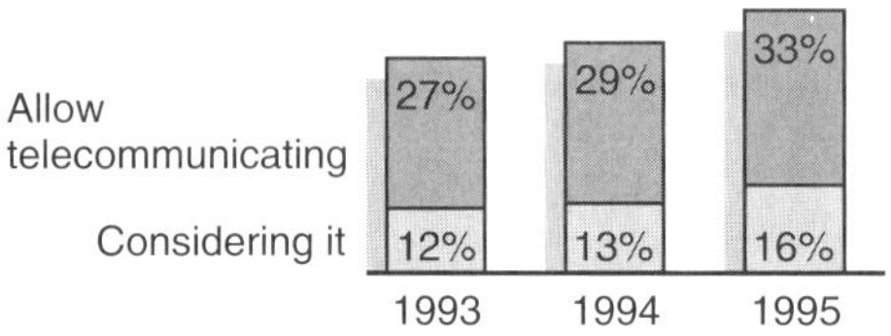


*Source:* 1995 Olsten Forum for Information Management, as reported in *USA Today,* December 15, 1995, p. 1B. © 1995, USA TODAY. Reprinted with permission.

Small businesses are particularly adaptable to telecommuting. One survey found that *59 percent of telecommuters work for a company with five or fewer employees.*[14] Finally, a recent Gallup survey found that a growing number of Americans are "buying computers to start home-based businesses."[15]

## Decide on the Best Layout

The objective in layout planning is to obtain the best placement of furniture and fixtures; tools, machines, and equipment; storage and materials handling;

**Figure 16–6** Layout of the CleanDrum, Inc., Plant*

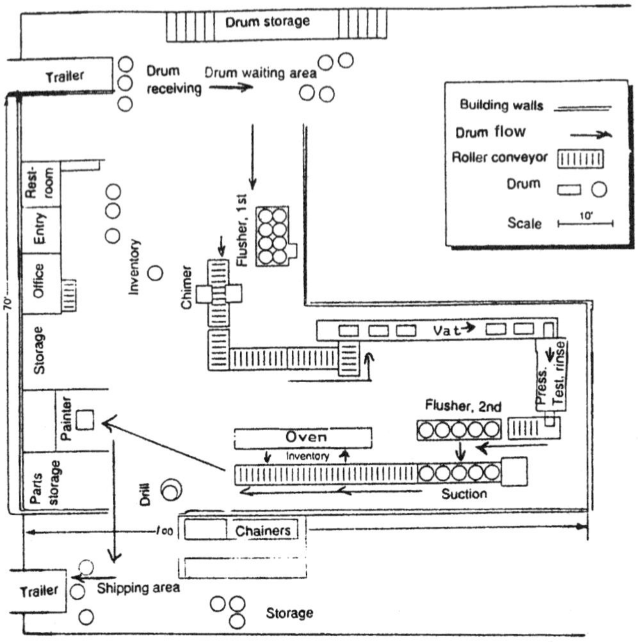


*See IV. Sample Case: CleanDrum, Inc.

service activities such as cleaning and maintenance; and places for employees and customers to sit, stand, or move about.

D

Figure 16–6 shows the layout of the previously mentioned CleanDrum, Inc., which cleans 50-gallon oil drums. Notice the movement of drums from one end of the plant to the other, the use of roller conveyors (even through machines), movement in a vat, and space for inventory, employees, and an office. Before installation, a model of the planned layout had been constructed and tested to iron out any kinks.

## *Types of Layout*

The two general types of layout are *product* and *process.* In practice, however, layouts often combine the two types.

A **product layout** has the facilities laid out according to the sequence of operations to be performed.

*Product Layout.* In a **product layout,** facilities are arranged so materials, workers, and/or customers move from one operation to another with little backtracking. That type is used in the school cafeteria shown in Figure 16–7A. The advantages of the product layout plan include specialization of workers and machines, less inventory, fewer instructions and controls, faster movement, and less space needed for aisles and storage. This arrangement tends to improve efficiency and maximize sales, especially in the automobile and fast-food industries.

**Figure 16–7** Product and Process Layout Comparison of Cafeterias

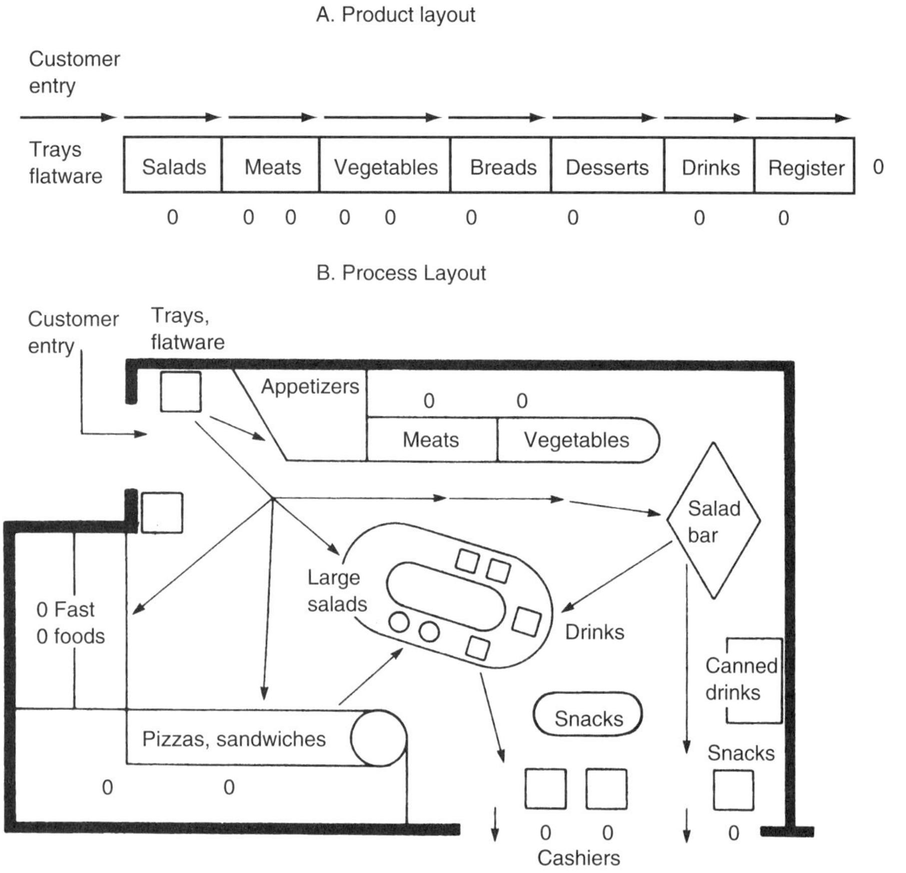


> Notice in Figure 16–2 that if you order a Whopper, its production moves forward from cooking the meat to assembling, wrapping, and delivering the Whopper to you.

*Process Layout.* The **process layout** groups machines performing the same type of work and workers with similar skills such as the cafeteria shown in Figure 16–7B.

A **process layout** groups the facilities doing the same type of work.

The process layout requires more movement of material or people, as is shown by the figure, and requires a larger inventory. But it also provides flexibility to take care of change and variety, often can use the same general-purpose machines and equipment for several steps in the operation, and permits more efficient scheduling of equipment and workers.

Few layout plans are totally product or process layouts. Instead, most layout plans combine the two to obtain the advantages of both.

## *Determining the General Layout*

The next step in the design process is determining the general layout by grouping machines, products, or departments. This helps to establish the general arrangement of the plant, store, or office before spending much time on details. Using similar layouts as an example, you can estimate the space needed. Space should also be provided, where appropriate, for maintenance, planning, and food and other needed services. Each service should be placed conveniently near the units that use it.

Entrance locations are important in the layout of retail and service establishments. Customers usually enter downtown stores from the street, parking lot, or corridors, and goods usually enter from the back. External factors to consider include entrances for employees, parking for customers, connections to utilities, governmental restrictions, and weather factors.

In manufacturing and large retail and wholesale warehouses, materials-handling devices such as conveyors, carts, hand trucks, and cranes are used to move materials. The objective is to move the items as quickly as possible, with a minimum of handling, and without increasing other costs (see Figure 16–6).

### *Determining the Final Layout*

Q

If your performance is to be efficient, the final layout must be planned in detail, so examine each operation to assure easy performance of the work. If workers spend too much time in walking, turning, twisting, or other wasted motion, the work will take longer and be more tiring. Tools and other items to be used should be located close at hand for quick service. Some specific factors to consider when doing your final layout are shown in Figure 16–8.

Since the first of these, space for movement, is particularly important, you should ask questions such as: Is there enough room if a line forms? Can shelves be restocked conveniently? Are aisles wide enough for one- or two-way traffic?

**Figure 16–8** Questions to Ask about a Production Layout

1. *Space for movement.* Are aisles wide enough for cart and truck movement? Is there enough room for lines that form at machines and checkout stations? Can material be obtained easily and shelves restocked conveniently?
2. *Utilities.* Has adequate wiring and plumbing, and provision for changes, been planned? Has provision been made for proper temperature? Does the area meet Environmental Protection Agency (EPA) standards?
3. *Safety.* Is proper fire protection provided, and are Occupational Safety and Health Administration (OSHA) standards being met? Are there proper guards on machines, in aisles, and around dangerous areas?
4. *Working conditions.* Do workers have enough working space and light? Is there provision for low noise levels, proper temperature, and elimination of objectionable odors? Are workers safe? Can they socialize and take care of personal needs?
5. *Cleanliness and maintenance.* Is the layout designed for effective housekeeping and waste disposal at low cost? Can machinery, equipment, and the building be maintained easily?
6. *Product quality.* Has provision been made to assure proper quality and to protect the product as it moves through the plant or stays in storage?
7. *Aesthetics.* Is the layout attractive to customers and employees?

> For example, grocery store aisles are designed to allow passage of two carts, but they often become blocked by special displays of new or sale items. Similarly, it may be difficult to squeeze between the display racks in department stores, and office planners often fail to allow enough space for storage of accumulated files.

The last consideration, aesthetics, is also important, so ask yourself: Are the layout and surroundings attractive to workers and customers?

> The Gloucester, Virginia, ServiStar Hardware Store, which once was patronized primarily by men, was dank, dark, and ugly. With more women becoming do-it-yourselfers and buyers of more hardware store items, ServiStar decided to change its image. It installed bright lights, chrome gridwork, and even murals. "Some of the old guys come in and kid us about being a disco," says Robert Fitchett, whose family owns the store, "but our sales are up 33 percent from last year."

### Implement Your Plans

Finally, you should test your layout plans to see if they are sound. One way to do this is to have employees, customers, or other knowledgeable people review the plans and make suggestions.

An important point to remember is that, although the layout of the interior of your facility is important, the walls and what is outside them can be equally vital to your success. Construction of a new building requires consideration of the type and method of construction, arrangements for vehicular movement and parking, provision for public transportation, if available, and landscaping.

## How to Improve Operations

Products and methods of operation are constantly changing, and competition pushes out obsolete or inefficient businesses. However, some tools are available in the disciplines of work simplification and industrial engineering to help you keep up-to-date and constantly improve your operations.

The steps used in designing and improving work are: (1) state the problem, (2) collect and record information, (3) develop and analyze alternatives, and (4) select, install, and follow up on the new work method. Computers are now used to help improve operations, particularly through the use of software that simulates operations. Be sure to record your analysis on paper, tape, or disk for review.

### State the Problem

As usual, it is best to begin by clearly stating *the problem—not a symptom of the problem.* Ask questions such as: Is the cost of the work too high? Is the quality of the service low? Is the service to customers delayed?

### Collect and Record Information

This step consists of collecting information for the *what, how, where, who, why,* and *when* of the work being done. Observing the work being performed, talking with knowledgeable people, and studying available data are methods of obtaining information.[16]

### Develop and Analyze Alternatives

Listing the available alternatives is basic to any type of analysis and a critical step in decision making. All work and services can be performed in many ways, and products can be made from many different materials.

Some questions that might be used in improving work performance include:

- Who performs the activity, what is it, and where is it being done?
- Why is the activity being performed?
- Can the activity be performed in a better way?
- Can it be combined with another activity (or activities)?
- Can the work sequence be changed to reduce the volume of work?
- Can it be simplified?

### Select, Install, and Follow Up on New Methods

Using your objectives, such as lower costs or better service, as a guide, pick the method that best suits your goals. Installing this new method includes setting up the physical equipment, gaining acceptance, and training workers. Test the method to see that it works and follow up to see that workers are familiar with it and are following procedures.

## Setting and Using Performance Standards

One of the most difficult problems you'll face in your business is measuring the performance of employees, since there are few precise tools for establishing standards against which to measure it. Instead, you must rely heavily on people's judgment. Physical work can be measured more precisely than mental work, but doing so still requires judgment.

Performance standards can be set by (1) estimates by people experienced in the work; (2) time studies, using a watch or other timing device; and (3) synthesis of the elemental times obtained from published tables. Most small business owners use the first method, using estimates of experienced people. These estimates should be recorded and given to workers for their guidance. The standards should allow for the time needed to do the work at normal speed, plus time for unavoidable delays and personal requirements. A good set of standards can be determined this way at a minimal cost.

## What You Should Have Learned

**1.** All businesses have operating systems, which process (or transform) inputs of people, money, machines, methods, and materials into outputs of goods, services, and satisfactions.

**2.** Some general factors to be considered in locating any business are access to: *(a)* the work force, *(b)* utilities, *(c)* vendors, and *(d)* transportation, as well as *(e)* the effect of taxes and government regulations.

**3.** The most important factors to consider in choosing a retail site are the type of business and the type of location. The type of business largely determines the location. Convenience goods stores are usually located where the traffic flow is high, shopping goods stores where comparison shopping can be done. Specialty goods stores often generate their own traffic but are helped by having similar stores in the vicinity.

The types of retail locations are downtown, in freestanding stores, and in shopping centers.

**4.** Among the most important factors in choosing a manufacturing site are nearness to customers and vendors and the availability and cost of transportation.

**5.** In planning physical facilities you: *(a)* determine the desired product and volume to produce, *(b)* identify the operations and activities required to process it, *(c)* estimate the space needed, and *(d)* determine the best physical arrangement and layout of those facilities. The types of layout are product and process, or a combination of both.

Physical facilities must be laid out to provide for a smooth flow of work and activities, space for movement, adequate utilities, safe operations, favorable working conditions, cleanliness and ease of maintenance, product quality, and a favorable impression.

**6.** Telecommuting is becoming more important to small business because of the convenience and flexibility it provides employees—and even some owners.

**7.** The methods used to improve operations include: *(a)* stating the problem; *(b)* collecting and recording information; *(c)* developing and analyzing alternatives; and *(d)* selecting, installing, and following up on the new methods.

**8.** Standards for measuring performance are needed.

## QUESTIONS FOR DISCUSSION

1. What are some characteristics of an operating system? What are some inputs into an operating system? What are some outputs resulting from the operating processes?
2. Explain some of the more important general factors affecting location choice.
3. Explain the two most important factors in choosing a retail site.
4. Explain the two most important factors in locating a manufacturing plant.
5. Explain the steps involved in planning facilities.
6. Explain the three different types of layout.

7. What are some characteristics of an effective layout?
8. Explain the four steps involved in improving operations.
9. Which of the two cafeteria layouts in Figure 16–7 do you think would be more effective? Why?
10. Do you remember your movements during course registration the last time? What improvements could you make in the process?
11. What is telecommuting, and why is it growing in importance for small firms?

## CASE 16–1

### TELECOMMUTING IN THE ROCKIES

Photo courtesy of Page Teahan.

In today's world of notebook computers, tiny printers, cell phones, and fax machines, many of us work at home, on the road, and at the beach. There is even a town in Colorado that bills itself as a "telecommuting town."

Located in the southwest quadrant of Colorado, Telluride has only 1,500 residents, but one-third of them now have access to the Internet. One of the advantages of having the town wired for high tech is the relief of not having to leave home to go to work (the town's average annual snowfall is 300 inches). Another advantage is the savings to one's employer—$4,000 to $6,000 a year in reduced office space alone. These advantages are the result of $130,000 provided by the State of Colorado in 1993 to bring 21st century communications into the area.

Bernie Zurbriggen of Frisco, Colorado, is an example of how telecommuting works. After a brush with death, he resigned a highly stressful job and relocated in the Rocky Mountains. There he created U.S. Trans Comm, the ultimate transportable company, through which he supplies customers, nationwide, with up-to-the-minute used car prices. In fiscal 1995, U.S. Trans Comm received 35,000 calls. As he adds new services, he predicts that call volume for 1996 will rise 43 to 71 percent. His office (home) has 10 phones—and a breathtaking view of Buffalo Mountain and the Continental Divide.

Zurbriggen uses technology (both old and new) to provide the information services needed to keep in contact with customers—and he stays at home to do it.

*Source:* Telluride Visitors Guide, Telluride Publishing Co., Winter 1995–1996; Kerry Hannon, "A Long Way from the Rat Race," *U.S. News & World Report,* October 30, 1995, pp. 86–87; Andrew Feinberg, "Frisco System," *Forbes ASAP,* October 9, 1995, p. 21; and communication and conversations with Telluride Visitor Services, November 1995.

## QUESTIONS

1. Do you think this type of arrangement and location would be beneficial to a small business? Explain.
2. Do you think your productivity—in this situation and location—would be increased, be reduced, or stay the same? Explain.

# APPLICATION 16–1

The Vermont Ladies' Club wants to have a canned food drive to stock Christmas food baskets for the poor and elderly. The club wants to take full advantage of exposure and wants to be convenient to the public.

There are several traffic signals and stop signs in town. In addition, many of the grocery stores are willing to allow the club to set up a display. One factor the ladies are considering is that the drop-off points need to be secure and located where they can be watched. However, they are having trouble finding just the right spot. Several other groups in town are also sponsoring food drives and donation checkpoints. The Ladies' Club wants to be distinct from the other clubs and also does not want to saturate the townspeople with requests for donations.

## QUESTIONS

1. What steps can the club take to assure security and achieve publicity?
2. What other locations could the ladies consider in promoting the food drive?

# ACTIVITY 16–1

Directions: Use information from this chapter to solve the "logically located" puzzle.

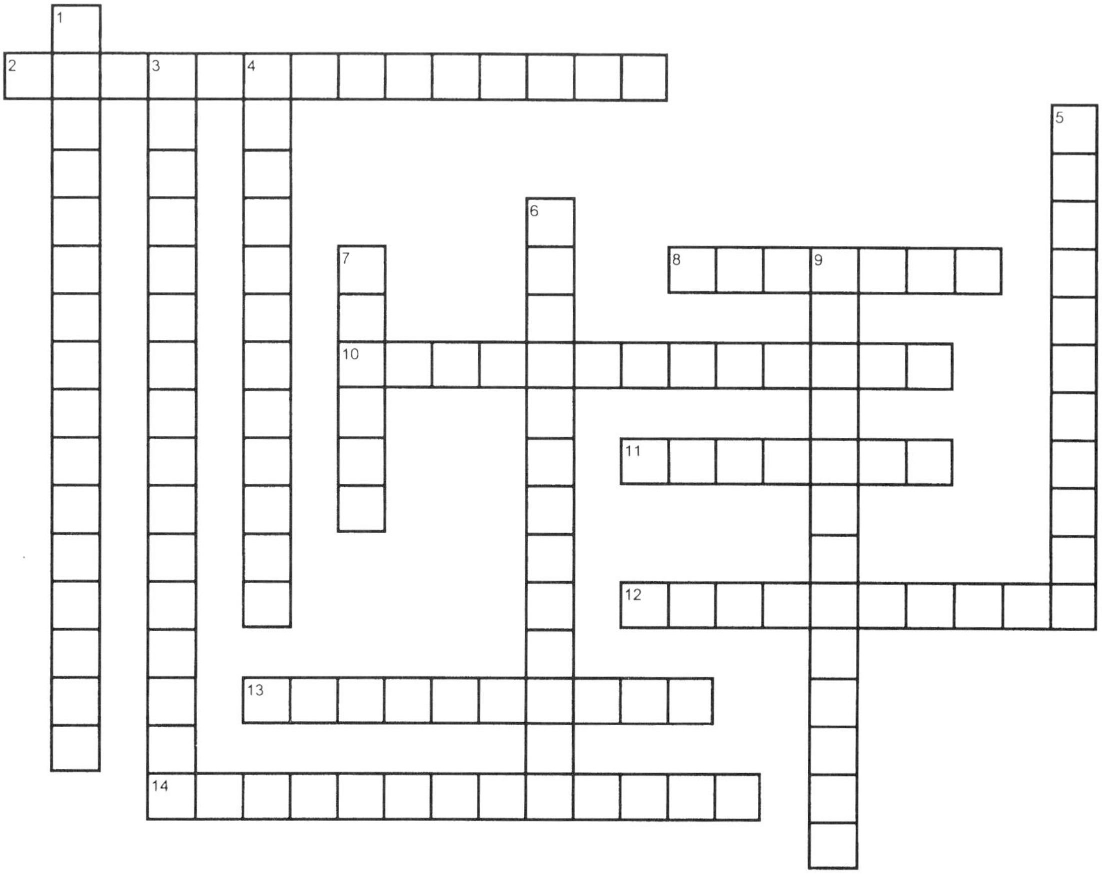


ACROSS

2 Bought infrequently

8 Satisfactions of 7 Down

10 Facilities laid out according to sequence of operations

11 Convert inputs into products customers want

12 Needed for production and distribution

13 See 5 Down

14 Customers buy infrequently after shopping at few stores

DOWN

1 Business inputs, processes, and outputs

3 Customers buy routinely

4 Generate heavy traffic

5 Converting inputs into outputs (plural)

6 Making or processing

7 Productive factors

9 Grouping together facilities doing the same type of work

ACROSS 2 Specialty goods 8 Outputs 10 Product layout 11 Process 12 Facilities 13 Operations 14 Shopping goods
DOWN 1 Operating systems 3 Convenience goods 4 Anchor stores 5 Productions 6 Manufacturing 7 Inputs
9 Process layout

CHAPTER 17

# Purchasing, Inventory, and Quality Control

*With the automation we have today, an agent can do five times the work he could do only six years ago.*—William Quartermaine, business leader, in 1885

*Resources must be employed productively and their productivity has to grow if the business is to survive.*—Peter F. Drucker

## LEARNING OBJECTIVES

After studying the material in this chapter, you will be able to:

1. Discuss the importance of purchasing.
2. Explain the need to choose suppliers carefully.
3. Describe how to establish an effective purchasing procedure.
4. Discuss how to establish and maintain effective inventory control.
5. Explain what is involved in operations planning and control.
6. Describe how to maintain quality control.

## P R O F I L E

# ANDERS BOOK STORES: DEALING WITH HUNDREDS OF SUPPLIERS

Photo © 1989, The Mobile Press Register, Inc. All rights reserved.

Bob and Kathy Summer find owning and managing Anders Book Stores (ABS) "frustrating—but fun!" They purchased the store from Jim Anders in 1982 after spending several years working for him and learning some of the ins and outs of running the business.

The Summers have divided the responsibilities so Bob specializes in college-level books and Kathy handles everything associated with textbooks and supplies for 12 private schools. After ordering and receiving the books, she groups them by grade, sells them, and returns unsold copies to publishers. In handling these activities, as well as being responsible for materials and supplies, she deals with over 1,000 suppliers each year. D

Bob handles sales to the University of South Alabama, which has its own bookstore a few blocks away, to other colleges in the area, and at the Anders branch on the University of Mobile campus, about 15 miles away. Bob receives the book orders from faculty members; buys, receives, and sells the books; reorders if necessary; and returns unsold books to publishers.

A major problem Anders faces is estimating how many copies of each text to order. Each book order has the estimated number of students in the class; so considering that some students will share a book and some won't buy a text, Bob estimates how many copies of each text to order.

Bob buys used books from students and used-book wholesalers; new textbooks come from their publishers. ABS has 1,200 publishers listed in its computer, although it regularly buys from "only" about 300 to 400 in any one year. When you consider that Kathy also buys from over 1,000 suppliers, you can understand why they say "buying and bookkeeping problems are horrendous."

About six to eight weeks before classes start, orders are sent to publishers via computer modem. Publishers then ship the books, either UPS or freight, sometimes as much as six weeks before they're needed.

Another problem is not having enough textbooks to meet student needs. Q
When this happens, Bob reorders and books are shipped UPS. The supplier usually ships the books one to seven days after the order is received. If needed immediately, a book can be shipped second-day express—at an additional charge. One year, enrollment increased so rapidly that Bob had to place over 50 reorders, for about 25 percent of the books sold.

Even worse is the problem of unsold books. Even when publishers allow returns for a refund, there is usually a restocking fee. And in the present economic climate of rapid mergers, sometimes the publisher that sold the books has been acquired by another house, so where should the books be returned? Given the already low gross profit margin of only 15 to 20 percent, returns put a severe financial strain on the business.

Poor-quality books pose another problem. In one order, some books had the first 78 pages glued together. In another, some sections came unglued and fell apart. Although the publisher replaces books, replacement is inconvenient and time-consuming.

Most of the large publishers send out an annual evaluation form for their dealers to complete. Since doing this, Bob and Kathy have noticed an improvement in service from the publishers.

*Source:* Discussions with Kathy and Bob Summer.

The Profile shows that the profitability of a small business depends largely on effective purchasing, inventory, operations, and quality control. Most small firms have many potential sources of supply for goods and services, each of which requires close study to secure the proper quality, quantity, timing, price, and service needed. This chapter emphasizes the strategies and procedures needed for effective purchasing, as well as inventory, operations, and quality control.

## The Importance of Purchasing

Q

Your business will need products provided by someone else, and the wide variety of items available requires careful study to ensure proper selection. Some items, such as electricity, come from only one supplier but even they require a careful analysis to obtain them at a favorable cost. Others, such as insurance, machines, and equipment, also require special attention because they are often expensive and are purchased infrequently. Still other items, such as paper clips and welding rods, are relatively cheap, and they're purchased routinely. Finally, materials that are part of the company's main product and have a high cost relative to revenue will take up a large amount of your time. This chapter is primarily concerned with this last group, those that are an important part of your main product.

### What Purchasing Involves

**Purchasing** determines the company's needs and finds, orders, and assures delivery of those items.

Obtaining all items, including goods and services, in the proper form, quantity, and quality, and at the proper place, time, and cost, is the main objective of **purchasing**. Purchasing identifies the needs of the company and finds, negotiates for, orders, and assures delivery of those items. Thus, you should coordinate your needs with the operations of suppliers, establish standardized procedures, and set up and maintain controls to ensure proper performance. Bob and Kathy Summer do all these things in buying for Anders Book Stores.

In retail stores, buying requires coordinating the level of stock of many items with consumer demands, which change as styles, colors, technology, and personal identification change. (And many customers may expect to buy year-round certain "standard" items that don't reflect fashion changes.) Each type of item may be handled differently, so those doing the buying must work closely with those doing the selling to satisfy these differing needs.

Purchasing for a manufacturing plant involves getting the proper materials and processing them into finished goods, while maintaining proper control of inventory and quality. Thus, those doing the purchasing must work closely with those doing the production and selling.

Purchasing by the federal government has become so complex and costly that it discourages small businesses from trying to sell to it. At the urging of the SBA, though, the Federal Acquisition Streamlining Act was passed. It urges government agencies to buy off-the-shelf goods rather than items made to its own detailed specifications. The law also permits the government to communicate with vendors on-line rather than with paperwork. These changes should make it easier for small companies to bid on small federal contracts.[1]

## Why Purchasing Is So Important

The cost of materials and other goods and services needed to produce a product is about half the revenue received for it. This means all other costs, plus profit, almost equal the cost of purchases. In many cases (Mead Pharmaceutical is one example), the cost of purchases is as much as two-thirds of sales revenues.[2]

While the price of purchases is important, other aspects can be just as critical. For example, obtaining **just-in-time (JIT)** delivery—where the materials are delivered to the user just at the time they are needed for production—can save on inventory costs. Recent statistics, for example, suggest that JIT inventory management has helped keep warehouses from overflowing. As you can see from Figure 17–1, the inventory-to-sales ratio for manufacturing has steadily declined since the early 1980s. Close coordination between you and your supplier can greatly improve efficiency by shifting inventory costs and management to the distributors. The distributor, in turn, usually discounts the price to the purchaser as a result of lower costs from

Q

**Just-in-time** delivery is having materials delivered to the user at the time needed for production.

**Figure 17–1** Shorter Shelf Life

**Just-in-time delivery management has helped keep expanding stockpiles from getting seriously out of control.**

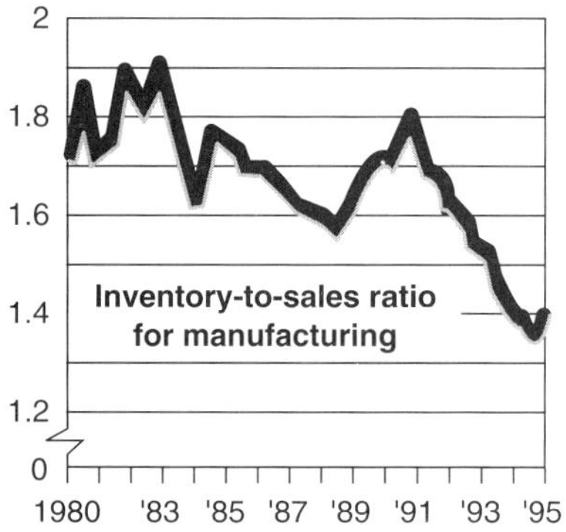


*Note:* Figures in constant dollars.
*Source:* U.S. Department of Commerce, as reported in *U.S. News & World Report.* Copyright September 18, 1995, p. 88.

increased production. These arrangements take on aspects of a partnership (as discussed in Chapter 4).

G

> For instance, Montreal-based Future Electronics is hooked up by an electronic data interchange system to Bailey Controls, an Ohio-based supplier of control systems. Every week, Bailey electronically sends Future its latest forecasts of what materials the Canadian company will need for the next six months. In this way, Future can stock up in time.[3]

**Supplier-base downsizing** means reducing the number of suppliers to concentrate purchasing.

Two current trends in purchasing that are causing considerable problems for small firms are supplier-base downsizing and fully integrated production networks. **Supplier-base downsizing**, which means reducing the number of suppliers to concentrate purchasing, is a result of corporate downsizing. This trend is especially harmful to businesses owned by women and minorities.[4]

D

> For example, AT&T Corporation's currently planned breakup "could sharply reduce its $1 billion annual expenditures on business owned by minorities and women," some of these small suppliers fear. AT&T officials claim this will not happen, as its program "is based on solid principles." According to Daniel Carroll, AT&T's vice president and chief procurement officer, its purchases from women- and minority-owned companies rose 34 percent in 1994. Also, AT&T planned to buy $1.1 billion of goods and services from about 3,000 female and minority vendors in 1995 and about $1.2 billion in 1996.[5]

G

**Fully integrated production networks** are entire geographic regions where a fully integrated supply chain, from raw materials to finished products, is built up.

The second problem, **fully integrated production networks**, is a primary problem for U.S. companies in global operations. For example, many primary competitors of U.S. firms have built up entire geographic regions where a fully integrated supply chain, from raw materials to finished products, involving hundreds of companies, is shutting out U.S. suppliers, especially smaller ones.[6] If small U.S. suppliers are to survive, they must assure that all suppliers in a supply chain achieve—and operate at—similar high standards and collectively market their skills to global competitors.

Finally, not having the appropriate stock—the right style, at the right price, at the right time, and of the proper quality—properly displayed for customers can result in added costs, lower profits, and unhappy customers.

"Sorry girls! We just didn't order enough ULTRA TOYS. Can you come back next week?"



> Chrysler had to recall the first 4,000 of its popular midsize LH cars to fix a 5-cent part. A defective washer in the steering system could disintegrate, making it harder to control the car.[7]

## Making Someone Responsible for Purchasing

While capable subordinates, such as specialty buyers, may be delegated the authority to order in their areas of expertise, in general, one person should be given the overall purchasing responsibility. But that person should ask for— and get—the help of people knowledgeable in areas such as engineering and planning.

Those doing the purchasing should be aware of trends and special situations that can affect operations and should call situations such as the following to your attention:

**Stockouts** are sales lost because an item is not in stock.

1. *Expected changes in price.* Buying later for expected decreases in price or buying increased quantities for expected inflation in price can result in savings. However, **stockouts**, which are sales lost because an item is not in stock when customers want it, and inventory costs that are too heavy should be guarded against.
2. *Expected changes in demand.* Seasonal products and high-fashion items fall into this category.
3. *Orders for specialty goods.* The quan- tity ordered should match expected demand, so no material is left over. Because demand for these items is unknown, forecasts should include estimates of losses that may occur from stockouts or old and stale inventory.
4. *Short supply of materials,* as the following example illustrates.

D

> Sally Von Werlhof started Salaminder Inc. in 1974 to design, produce, and sell only top-of-the-line American-made western apparel. Growth was steady until the 1980 movie *Urban Cowboy* caused the demand for western wear to skyrocket. Salaminder was swamped with orders and expanded its work force to 60 employees. But sales plummeted in July 1981, when the fad died—just as suddenly as it had begun.[8]

## Selecting the Right Supplier

You will be more successful in purchasing if you can find several acceptable sources of goods and services. Because reliability in delivery and quality affects nearly all operations, suppliers can be valuable sources of information for various aspects of operations, and suppliers can provide valuable service.

Q

You can find many good sources by consulting the Yellow Pages, the *Thomas Register of American Manufacturers,* the *McRae Bluebook,* newspapers, trade journals, and publications of research organizations. In addition, visits to trade shows and merchandise marts give you an opportunity to view exhibits and talk with salespeople. Internet and World Wide Web networks (to be discussed in Chapter 21) can be used to obtain information on possible sources. Many small firms are now hiring expert consultants when purchasing becomes complex.[9]

### Types of Suppliers

As discussed in Chapter 11, you can purchase from brokers, jobbers, wholesalers, producers, or others. Each provides a particular type of service. Anders Book Stores buys new books from the producers (the publishers) but buys used ones from wholesalers (used-book companies) and students. Also, supplies and other items are ordered from a variety of sources.

## Use Few or Many Suppliers?

Should you buy from one, a few, or many suppliers? A single source of supply can result in a closer and more personalized relationship so when shortages occur, you should receive better service than when many sources are used. Also, discounts may be obtained with larger-volume buying. If one seller can supply a wide assortment of the items needed, the cost of ordering is reduced. On the other hand, multiple sources provide a greater variety of goods and often better terms. Most small firms use several sources.

D As indicated earlier, many companies are trying to reduce the number of suppliers used. However, there is also a counter-trend occurring—namely, to bring minority suppliers into the vendor mainstream, as the following example illustrates.

G

> Ten years ago, 54-year-old Frank Brooks, CEO of Chicago's Economic Development Corporation, knew nothing about the food-processing business. Then a business associate told him McDonald's was looking for members of diverse groups to be vendors for its stores. So in 1985 Brooks established Brooks Sausage Company to produce and supply McDonald's midwestern outlets with pork sausages. First, however, Brooks learned the business as an apprentice—under the supervision of McDonald's—at OSI Industries.
>
> Brooks Sausage is now McDonald's "foremost minority-owned vendor," supplying several thousand restaurants. About 35 percent of Brooks' output goes to McDonald's outlets in Japan.[10]

G Sometimes it's desirable—or even necessary—to use a single source for specialized items, as the following example illustrates.

Photo by Alabama Shakespeare Festival photographer Phil Scarsbrook. Used with permission.

> Several years ago, Wynton M. and Carolyn Blount donated the land and money to build the Wynton M. Blount Cultural Park in Montgomery, Alabama, where the Alabama Shakespeare Festival is located. Because they were great admirers of Queen Elizabeth II's beautiful black swans, they inquired as to where she had found them. The answer came back from England that they'd been bought at a farm just a few miles from Montgomery—the only known source of supply of the beautiful birds.

## Investigating Potential Suppliers

Potential sources can be checked for factors such as quality of output, price, desire to serve, reliability, transportation, terms of payment, and guarantee and warranties; because all these factors affect your company's performance, a minimum standard must be set for each.

Suppliers should not be chosen on the basis of price alone, for quality and/or service may suffer if the supplier has to lower prices to obtain your order. Instead, they should be chosen to meet carefully set quality and service standards. These standards can be used to ensure acceptable quality without paying for quality higher than needed.

### Evaluating Supplier Performance

Just as you investigate potential suppliers, you should also evaluate their performance. Some services publish ratings of products. Also, while it requires some time and effort, you could develop a rating system of your own to use in selecting, evaluating, and retaining suppliers. Rating systems pick out important factors such as quality, service, and reliability, as well as price, and then use those to evaluate each supplier.

> Sharp Corporation uses a rating system of this kind in its Memphis plant to evaluate its 70 suppliers, most of which are small firms. A copy of its creed, "Practice Sincerity and Creativity," is given to each potential supplier with a statement that Sharp expects "100% quality parts," delivered precisely on schedule. Suppliers who agree to this stipulation become Sharp's suppliers and receive a periodic report card showing how they rate on satisfying quality, price, prompt delivery, and other standards.[11]

Q

## Establishing an Effective Purchasing Procedure

In addition to deciding on the suppliers to use, you must establish a purchasing procedure to ensure effective ordering and receiving of materials. While there is no one best way, Figure 17–2 presents a computer flowchart of a well-designed purchase order system. The procedure should accomplish several major objectives concerned with purchasing. The proper materials, parts, goods, and so forth needed to produce the goods or services must be obtained. The total price paid for the items purchased must be satisfactory for sale of the finished product. Moreover, the amount of resulting inventory should be in balance with customer demand to minimize total costs. Finally, a simple—yet effective—inventory control system should be established.

### Requisitioning Goods or Services

Effective small companies establish standards for various aspects of the quality of their products and/or services. These standards are usually developed with the help of professional/technical people who are knowledgeable in technical, marketing, and production areas. The derived standards are then converted into specifications to be sent with orders to suppliers (see item 1 in Figure 17–2).

The request to purchase materials or services (called a purchase requisition) can originate from many sources. If a service is needed, the request usually comes from the user of that service, as when the accounting manager requests an outside audit, the personnel manager needs to install or change an insurance program, or the marketing manager needs to place an ad with an agency. But when materials are needed, the request can originate in any of several ways, such as when: (1) someone observes that inventory is low,

**Figure 17–2** Purchase Order Process Flowchart

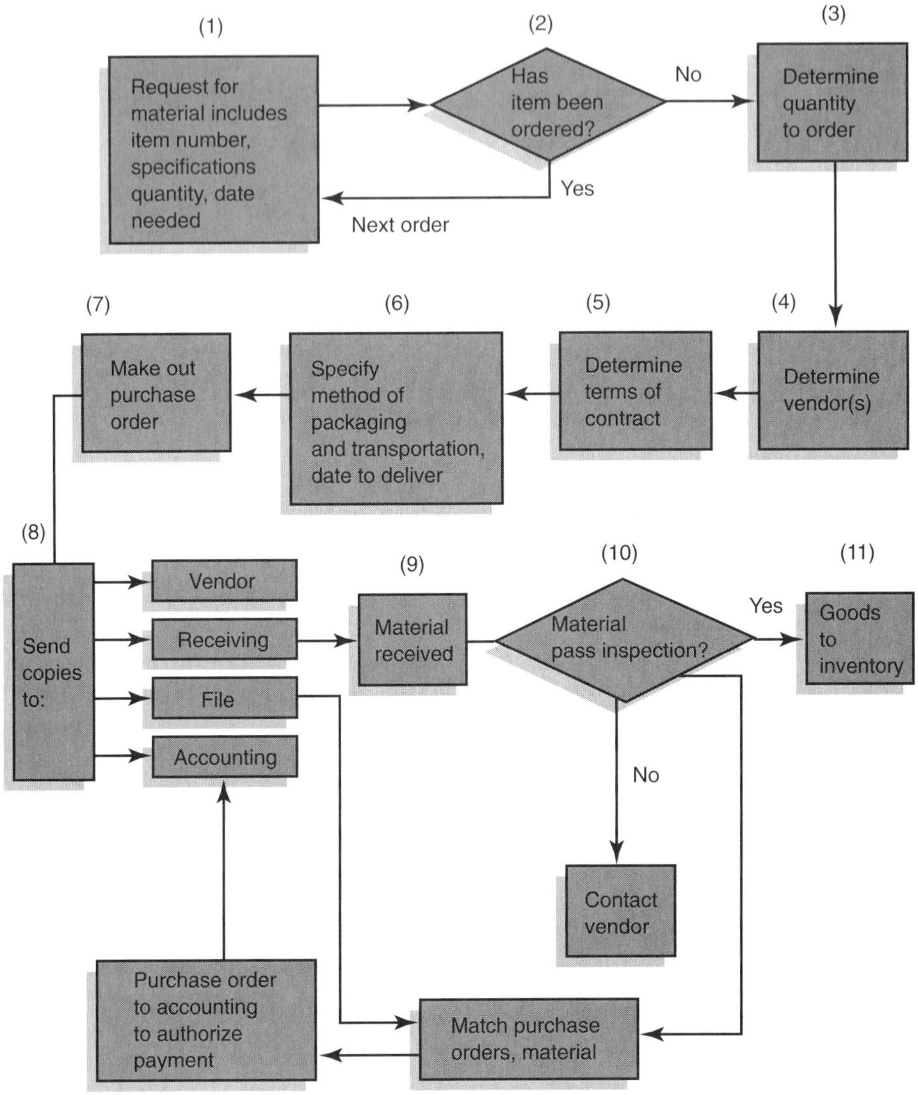


(2) the system automatically identifies the need for an item, (3) an operating manager requests it, (4) a customer requests a given item, or (5) the purchasing manager observes some special conditions that indicate the need to purchase an item.

Purchasing by retailers poses different problems from purchasing by a producer. Figure 17–3 shows a suggested schedule for a retailer to buy and sell style goods. The procedure operates as follows.

In the spring or summer of 1996, a retailer visits a trade show—or consults suppliers—and places orders based on evaluation of styles and plans. Between August—when the goods are received—and February, goods are sold, more goods are produced, and plans for the spring and summer are completed. Goods are received in time for the selling seasons; inventory and sales are checked to consider reordering. End-of-season sales late in the

**Figure 17–3** Schedule of Semiannual Production and Retail of Style Goods

| Activity | Summer 1996 | Fall 1996 | Winter 1996–97 | Spring 1997 | Summer 1997 |
|---|---|---|---|---|---|
| Retailer plans and orders | | **Plans S&S 1997 sales**<br>Selects styles and orders | Plans sales and promotion (*Reorders F&W 1996–97*) | **Plans F&W 1997–98 sales**<br>Selects styles and orders | Plans sales and promotion (*Reorders S&S 1997*) |
| Retailer receives and sells goods | Receives F&W 1996–97 goods | **Sells F&W 1996–97 goods**<br>Regular sales | Markdown sales<br>Receives S&S 1997 goods | **Sells S&S 1997 goods**<br>Regular sales | Markdown sales |
| Producer receives orders and produces goods | | Produces S&S 1997 goods | | Produces F&W 1997–98 goods | |

Legend: F&W = fall and winter; S&S = spring and summer.

winter and summer can help reduce inventory. The cycle is repeated for each selling season.

## Making and Placing the Purchase Order

There are many ways of placing orders for needed goods (item 7 in Figure 17–2), depending on your needs and the supplier's demands. Issuing **purchase orders** is very common, since they become legal records for the buyer and seller. Establishing **standing orders** with the supplier simplifies the purchasing procedure and allows for long-range planning. It involves setting schedules for delivery of goods in predetermined quantities and times and at agreed-to terms.

A **purchase order** tells the supplier to ship you a given amount of an item at a given quality and price.

**Standing orders** set predetermined times to ship given quantities of needed items, at a set price.

Technology enters the picture at this point. As indicated earlier, many big purchasers are reducing the number of vendors they deal with. In the selection process, they are "eliminating companies that are behind the curve in technology."[12] In other words, if a vendor doesn't have the appropriate technology to adequately serve a purchaser, the purchaser will look elsewhere.

For example, Aspen Press Ltd. is only two years old but already doing $1 million a year in sales. One competitive edge is its ability to receive orders and payments electronically from customers such as J. C. Penney Company and Dillard Department Stores Inc. According to Aspen's CEO, Richard Feldstein, embracing computer and network technology "levels the playing field for small business."[13]

### Paying a Satisfactory Price

The importance of the price of goods and services has been mentioned earlier in this chapter. *However, quality and price must be balanced against each other.* Customers naturally want high quality, but high quality tends to result in high production costs and a resulting high price. A low price is also attractive but generally reflects lower quality. Therefore, selection should not be made on the basis of price alone.

Prices set by suppliers are only one element of cost to be considered. There are added costs such as transportation, paperwork, reliability of the supplier, processing, and payment. Selection of a supplier should be based on total cost. Also, as discussed in Chapter 10, the possibility of discounts and allowances should be investigated.

### Receiving the Items

Receiving the ordered goods and placing them in inventory (items 9, 10, and 11 in Figure 17–2), are the last steps in the purchasing procedure. A copy of the purchase order, including the desired specifications, is sent to those receiving the goods. On arrival, the condition of the goods is checked, and they are checked against the order to make sure they are the desired items, in the correct color, material, size, quantity, and so on. Computers and proper receiving procedures help detect deviations from these standards and speed up the process.

### Using Computers to Aid Purchasing and Inventory Control

Q

The recent great advances in electronic processing of all sorts of information and the drop in costs (as will be discussed in Chapter 21) have revolutionized the purchasing and inventory operations. Small companies are increasingly using computers to keep track of inventory items, spot replenishment needs, identify sources of supply, and provide information needed for ordering and checking the accuracy of receipts. Computers now largely provide the information needed by the buyer to use in the purchasing process. For example, use of the fax (in item 8 in Figure 17–2) speeds up the transfer of information. Steps 1 through 7 can also be performed automatically with a computer and selected programs.

## Controlling Inventory

An **inventory** is a formal list of all the property of a business, or the property so listed.

An **inventory** is a formal list of property of a business, or—the way we will use the term—the property so listed. No business can operate without some kind of property, if only office supplies. Therefore, there is by definition no way to avoid carrying inventory—no matter how hard you may try—and *the best you can do is manage its movement and control its cost.*

### The Role Played by Inventory

Inventory is carried to disconnect one segment of the operating process from another so each part can operate at its optimum level. A crude example is in your home. If you didn't have a supply of food, you would have to go out, find some, buy it, bring it home, and prepare it every time you were hungry. Having surplus food in your pantry or refrigerator, however, you can buy more food at your convenience, keep it as inventory, and then process it when you get hungry.

The same holds true in a producing plant. Figure 17–4 shows what happens from the receipt of raw materials, through each of three operations, to final sale to customers. Inventories are shown at different levels at different stages of the operation, and the inventory level at a given stage depends on what activities have occurred in the operations process.

A similar situation occurs in retail stores. Retailers receive goods, store them, put them on display for sale, sell them to customers, and then order more of the goods. The level of inventory at any given time depends on the amount of goods bought—and stored in inventory—relative to the quantity sold. Thus, a retailer must have enough goods in inventory after an order is received to last until the next order is placed and received. Figure 17–5 illustrates this process. When the goods on the left are received, they're stored with similar goods as inventory. Then, after being put on display and gradually sold, they're replaced with other goods.

## Types of Inventory

Inventories exist in small firms at all times in one or more of the following forms: (1) finished items on display for sale to customers; (2) batches of goods, such as materials, parts, and subassemblies, awaiting processing or delivery; (3) repair parts awaiting use; (4) supplies for use in offices, stores, or shops, or for use in processing other goods; and (5) miscellaneous items, such as tools placed in a toolroom.

These inventories, especially the first two kinds, represent a major investment by all businesses—large ones as well as small. Many companies have failed because their inventory tied up too much money or the items in inventory became obsolete, damaged, or lost, as the following example illustrates.

> In 1985, Chris Hoelzle's Los Angeles computer repair store and computer salvage operation had 35 employees and $35 million annual revenues. Then, with the computer "bust," profits turned to losses, and Hoelzle was bankrupt—without declaring bankruptcy. He slashed staff and sold inventory—which had become "200 tons of electronic junk"—at bargain prices. Three years later, however, he had 15 employees, $3 million in annual revenues, and three times his pre-1986 profits.[14]

## Inventory Mix

According to the **80-20 rule,** approximately 80 percent of a company's income usually comes from 20 percent of its products. Companies having multiple products, parts, and services should therefore concentrate their attention on those items that have the greatest impact on costs and income. Similarly, 20 percent of the items in inventory represent 80 percent of the cost. Companies should be sure that these items are truly needed.

According to the **80 - 70 rule,** approximately 80 percent of a company's income usually comes from 20 percent of its products.

## Costs of Carrying Inventory

Having inventory on hand costs a small business much more than most people realize. The costs of carrying inventory consist of: (1) the cost of providing and maintaining storage space, (2) insurance and taxes, (3) profits lost because money is tied up in inventory (called *opportunity cost*),

**Figure 17–4** Diagram of Material Flow and Inventory

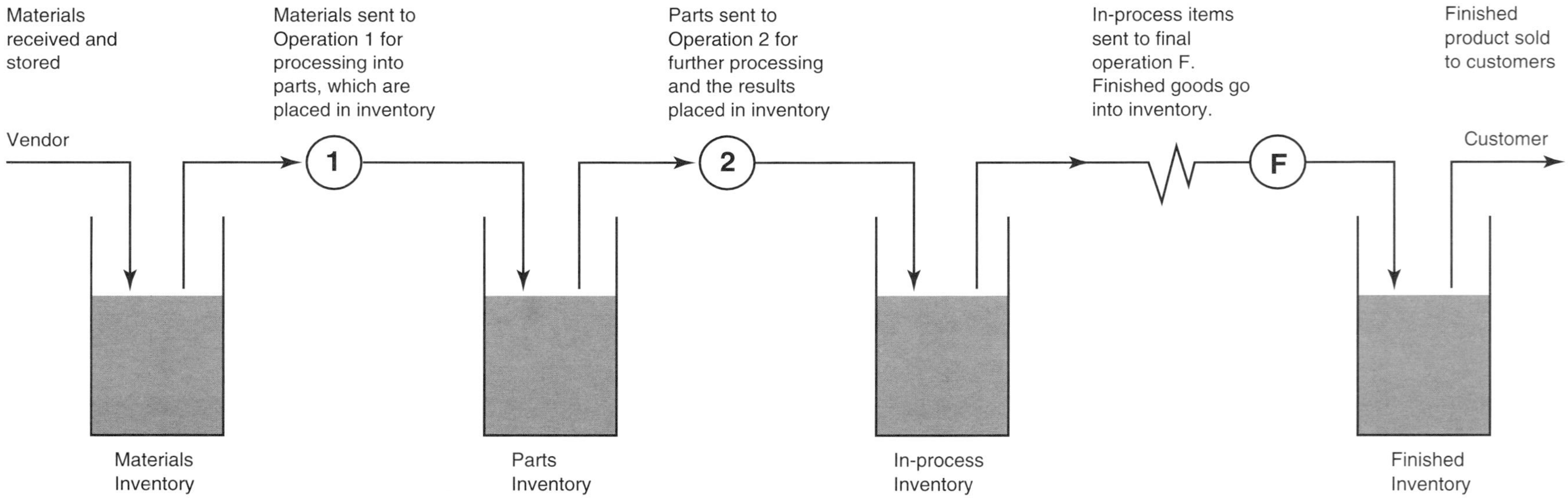

**Figure 17–5** Goods Flow and Inventory in a Retail Firm

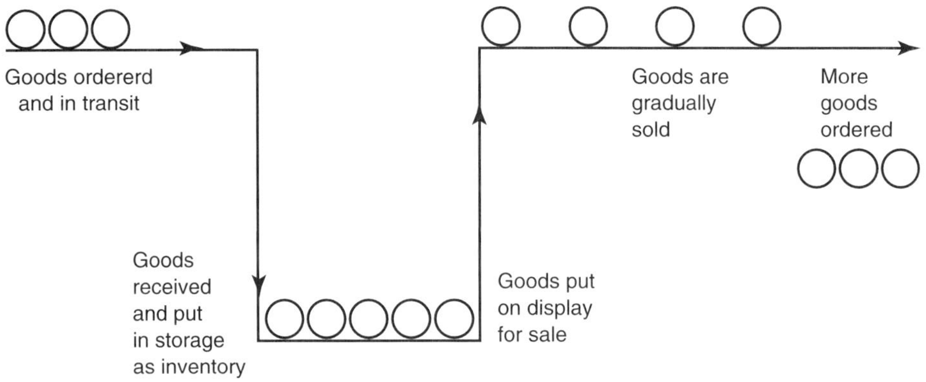


(4) theft and destruction, and (5) obsolescence and deterioration of the items. Estimates of the sum of these costs range from 15 percent to over 100 percent of their value; 20 to 25 percent is the amount most frequently mentioned.

### Determining When to Place an Order

Figure 17–4 showed the changing inventory levels as materials were ordered, processed, stored, and sold. Figure 17–5 showed how levels change as a retailer orders goods, stores them, and then sells them. The real problem in both these instances is knowing when is the most appropriate time to order needed items.

The optimum inventory level can be maintained by having items arrive just in time for sale to customers. The actual system tries to approach zero inventory, but normally balances inventory carrying costs and stockout costs. This calculation isn't easy, and you'll make mistakes, but, with rational analysis, practice, and a certain amount of intuition—and luck—you'll make it.

### Determining How Much to Order

The order quantity is determined by the level of inventory and the order interval. When orders are placed at *certain, regular intervals,* the order quantity should be set to bring the inventory level up to a predetermined amount. When *inventory level* determines the time to order, the order quantity is a fixed amount called the **economic order quantity (EOQ)**. The EOQ is determined by balancing (1) the cost of placing an order with (2) the costs of carrying the inventory.[15] Figure 17–3 shows a situation where the order size is determined by how much the company can sell during a season.

The **economic order quantity (EOQ)** is the quantity to purchase that balances the cost of placing the order with the cost of carrying the inventory.

## Operations Planning and Control

As shown in Chapter 6, operations planning and control begins when you determine what business you're going into, what product(s) you'll sell, and what resources are needed to produce the quantity you expect. If you're to have products available when demanded by customers, you must carefully forecast and plan for sales. Predicting the sales of a small company with any degree of accuracy is difficult, but even crude estimates are better than none, since considerable cost is involved in trying to serve customers if the items they seek aren't in stock.

## Handling Variations in Demand

Demand for products varies from one period to another for such reasons as changing lifestyles, economic conditions, and seasons. Most sales of goods and services have seasonal variations. Therefore, you may be constantly hiring, training, and laying off employees; not using facilities efficiently; changing levels of inventory; and facing cash flow problems and product shortages.

Several operating plans that may be used to cope at least partially with seasonal variations. The most popular such plans are these:

- Allow operations to rise and fall according to changing sales demands. This requires periodically hiring and laying off workers.
- Use self-service to reduce the number of employees and hire temporary or part-time workers during peak periods.
- Use inventory buildups (or drawdowns), to smooth out operations.
- Carry complementary products, such as winter and summer items.
- Subcontract out production during maximum demand periods.
- Lose sales by not expanding operations to meet increased demand.
- Use special inducements to stimulate sales during periods of low demand.

## Scheduling Operations

**Scheduling** is setting the times and sequences required to do work.

**Scheduling** involves setting the times and sequences needed to perform specialized activities, including when and how long it takes to do it. You are often faced with this problem of scheduling. For example, you try to schedule your classes to minimize inconvenience and for your greatest benefit. Then you have to schedule appointments with the doctor or dentist around them. Figure 17–3 showed a schedule of the steps involved in selling style items.

Q

A major entertainment event poses massive scheduling challenges, including scheduling the design and creation of clothing and costumes.

Photo © 1989. The Mobile Press Register, Inc. 

The 1989 Miss USA Pageant was such an event. The contestants' evening gowns were designed by Sherri Hill of Norman, Oklahoma (see Case 3 for more details.) Some of the other costumes were designed and produced by Los Angeles costume designer Pete Menefee. In addition, he took 12 to 14 of Hill's dress designs and made them in different fabrics. Since each contestant required a different pattern, 120 different dresses were made for the women to choose from.

The dresses, made in Los Angeles, were shipped to the contest site in Mobile, Alabama, where Menefee altered them with the help of local

## USING TECHNOLOGY TO SUCCEED

### Instant Travel Scheduling

Kari Givens and her co-workers at Springdale Travel, Vacation World, and Cruise Quarters (see Profile, Chapter 11) can schedule your business or pleasure travel with a wink and a keyboard. Thanks to a system called Worldspan, which is completely supported by Delta Airlines (software, hardware, and user support), your travel can be scheduled, reservations made, and confirmations received almost instantaneously.

Similar systems are provided by three other airlines: SABRE by American, Covia by United, and System One by Continental.

Worldspan taps into about 650 airlines, 150,000 routes, 15,000 hotels, and 19 car rental agencies. Because of the speed and quality of the system, Springdale Travel, Vacation World, and Cruise Quarters can issue your tickets on the spot. You can either pick them up or have them mailed or delivered to you by special courier. Itineraries can be faxed immediately so that you—the traveler—can see the whole picture and complete schedule of your proposed excursion.

Photo courtesy of M. Jane Byrd.

*Source:* Murray Cape, Owner, Springdale Travel Inc. See also Wendy Zellner, "Putting a Keener Edge on SABRE," *Business Week*, October 23, 1995, p. 118, for a discussion of the adverse effect the Internet and commercial online services are expected to have on SABRE's lock on the travel agency business.

seamstresses. The results are shown in the photo. In addition, he saw that each woman had the proper hosiery, shoes dyed to match, and costume jewelry to go with the gowns.[16]

Computers are now being used effectively by small businesses to perform scheduling operations. Using Technology to Succeed shows what happens when a small travel agency uses a computerized system to book a traveler.

### Controlling Operations

Even if you make the best of plans, communicate them effectively, and use the best workers and materials to perform the work effectively, controls are still needed. Without adequate control over the operations, the process will fail.

In simple systems, the comparison of planned performance with actual performance can be made informally by personal observation. Usually, though, a system of formal checks is needed. Standards are set, data on actual performance are collected, standards and actual data are compared, and exceptions are reported.

## Quality and Its Control

In recent years, American consumers have shown increasing concern about the quality of U.S. goods and services, since so often foreign companies produce and sell products of superior quality. Now, though, many U.S.

companies are taking steps to improve their products. This is particularly true of small companies, as shown in Chapter 12.

While small businesses must compete in the market with large companies, many are finding that emphasizing quality and reliability and designing output to match customer needs are better tactics than lowering prices.

Q G

> This is what is happening to the Morgan Motor Company in Malvern Link, Worcestershire, England, which has been selling its unique car since 1910. The company now produces 500 handmade cars each year to customer's individual orders. About 30 of these cars are sold to Americans. There is a long waiting list, and the wait time from ordering to final delivery is four to five years in Europe and one to two years in the United States.
>
> The company is trying to increase production to about 750 cars a year by expanding its factory operations and cutting waste. It also hopes to export more cars to the United States. But the company does not want to lose its quality advantage by increasing output beyond its staff's ability to maintain standards. An indication of the problem is the "thousands of colors, 40 different upholsteries, and four types of seats" the customer can choose from for each car.[17]

## What Is Quality?

**Quality** refers to product characteristics and/or the probability of meeting established standards.

The term **quality** can have at least two meanings. First, it refers to characteristics of products being judged. Second, it means the probability that products will meet established standards. In the discussion that follows, we will use the meanings interchangeably.

Assessment of the quality of a product is relative; it depends on the expectations of the evaluator—the customer. Customers who are used to high-quality goods and services tend to be much more critical of purchases than those accustomed to lower standards. Because small companies usually cannot cater to all quality levels, they must set their sights on the level demanded by their customers.

Quality involves many characteristics of a product: strength, color, taste, smell, content, weight, tone, look, capacity, accomplishment, creativity, and reliability, among others. Part of the quality of service are such factors as salespersons' smiles, attentiveness, friendly greetings, and willing assistance. Standards to meet the desires of customers must be established for each characteristic.

Customers tend to want high quality, but often they want to pay only a limited price for the product. Still, some qualities, such as a friendly greeting, cost little; others, such as precision jewelry settings, cost much. Quality-level analysis is thus based on the value of quality to the customer and the cost of producing that level of quality. To make the decision, you must ask the following questions: Who are my customers? What quality do they want? What quality of product can I provide, and at what cost?

How do you determine where to set the quality level? Market research, questionnaires, talking to customers, comparison with competitors' products, and trial and error are a few of the methods. Recent advances in technology have helped raise the level of quality attainable—while keeping costs low.

## Improving and Controlling Quality

There are many ways a small business can improve quality, but we will discuss only three: (1) setting up quality circles, (2) designing quality into the product and operations, and (3) installing a good quality control process.

### *Establishing Quality Circles*

Many progressive companies report good results from using quality circle programs. In **quality circles**, a small group of workers meets regularly to identify and develop ways to solve company problems, especially quality. The members, who are usually not supervisors, receive training in areas such as problem identification, communications, and problem solving. Also, as they meet, they may have access to resource people who can provide further expertise. Quality circles seem to be more successful when top management gives them unrestricted support.

**Quality circles** are small work groups meeting periodically to find ways to improve quality and performance.

### *Designing Quality into the Process*

Since quality is achieved during the production of a product, the processes must be designed to produce the desired quality. Machines must be capable of turning out the product within set tolerances, workers must be trained to produce that level of quality, and materials and goods must be purchased that meet the stated standards. In service companies, employees must be trained to understand a customer's needs and to perform the work to the customer's satisfaction. If the process or employees cannot produce the proper quality of output, no type of control can correct the situation.

### *Installing a Quality Control Process*

Quality control, or quality assurance, is the process by which a producer ensures that the finished goods or services meet the expectations of customers, as advocated by the late W. Edwards Deming, the "Quality Guru."* Deming developed his management philosophy and techniques into his "14 Points," as shown in Figure 17–6. These points stress the necessity for owners and top managers to become involved in continuous improvement processes, as the following example illustrates.

G Q

> In 1993, Mel Chambers needed a new vision and style to run his two Irvine, California, businesses—City Concrete Products Inc., a building materials firm, and Chambers Group Inc., an environmental consulting firm. "We needed a management style to survive the intense competitive challenges from foreign-held companies in the concrete industry and to encourage growth of our two companies."
>
> Chambers found his solution in one of the last seminars on quality improvement given by Dr. Deming. After two years of living with Deming's principles, the firms are showing considerable results. Cross-training, better interdepartmental communication, and improved measuring systems have helped reduce waste and improve employee attitudes. The

---

*Deming died in 1993 at the age of 93, having achieved considerable fame as a quality expert in Japan, where the country's top quality award is the Deming Medal.

Q

**Figure 17–6** Deming's 14 Points

W. Edwards Deming distilled his self-developed methods of management into 14 points. Though they have been described and elaborated on in hundreds of books, videos, and seminars, in their original form they still provide the bedrock of most Deming processes.

1. Create constancy of purpose toward improvement of product and service.
2. Adopt the new philosophy.
3. Cease dependence on mass inspection.
4. End the practice of awarding business on the basis of a price tag.
5. Improve constantly and forever the system of production and service.
6. Institute training.
7. Institute leadership.
8. Drive out fear.
9. Break down barriers between departments.
10. Eliminate slogans, exhortations, and targets for the work force.
11. Eliminate quotas.
12. Remove barriers to pride of workmanship.
13. Institute a vigorous program of education and self-improvement.
14. Take action to accomplish the transformation. It's everybody's job.

*Source:* Reprinted from Loretta Owens and Mark Henricks, "Quality Time," *Entrepreneur.* Reprinted with permission from *Entrepreneur Magazine,* October 1995, p. 161.

savings were $50,000 the first year and close to $100,000 the next. In addition, Chambers said, "Management is now a lot simpler."[18]

Q

Photo © Bob Ware, Reprinted with permission from *Entrepreneur Magaine,* October 1995, p. 156.

Regardless of what methods or techniques are used to achieve it, effective quality control involves at least the following steps:

- Setting standards for the desired quality range.
- Measuring actual performance.
- Comparing that performance with established standards.
- Making corrections when needed.

Some standards may be measured by instruments, such as rulers or gauges for length; but color, taste, and other standards must be evaluated by skilled individuals. Measurement may be made by selected people at selected spots in the process, usually on receipt of material and always before the product goes to the customer. Quality can also be controlled by feedback from customers, as shown in Figure 17–7.

**Figure 17–7** Example of Feedback Quality Control in a Restaurant

Management Encourages Your Comments

Date 5/19/96

Waiter or waitress Phyllis

Please circle meal Breakfast (Lunch) Dinner

| | Yes | No |
|---|---|---|
| 1. Were you greeted by host or hostess promptly and courteously? | ✓ | |
| 2. Was your server prompt, courteous, and attractive in appearance? | ✓ | |
| 3. Was the quality of food to your expectations? | | ✓ |
| 4. Was the table setting and condition of overall restaurant appearance pleasing and in good taste? | ✓ | |
| 5. Will you return to our restaurant? | | ✓ |
| 6. Will you recommend our restaurant to your friends and associates? | | ✓ |

Comments

Food was overcooked. Potatoes were left-overs. Meat was tough. this was my second visit and I brought a friend with me. We were both very disappointed.

Name and address
(if you desire)

Please drop this in our quality improvement box provided as you exit room

Thank you and have a good day.

## WHAT YOU SHOULD HAVE LEARNED

**1.** Purchases are a small company's largest single type of cost. Goods and services must be obtained at the proper price, quality, and time, and in the proper quantity. Someone must be responsible for the purchasing function.

**2.** Sources of supply must be found and investigated and one or more suppliers selected. Reliability in delivery and quality affect nearly all operations. You must decide whether to use one or multiple suppliers.

**3.** An effective purchasing procedure consists of *(a)* determining the items needed, in what quantity, from whom to purchase, and the terms of the contract; *(b)* sending the purchase order; *(c)* receiving the goods; *(d)* inspecting them, and *(e)* paying for them.

**4.** Inventory is carried to disconnect one part of the operating process from another so each part can operate effectively. Inventory takes many forms, from raw materials to finished products. The cost of carrying inventory consists of providing and maintaining storage space, insurance and taxes, profits lost from money tied up in it, obsolescence and deterioration, and theft and destruction. The cost of inadequate inventory is dissatisfied customers from stockouts.

**5.** Operations planning and control start with a forecast of sales from which operating plans are developed. Alternative plans for seasonal sales include: *(a)* producing to demand, *(b)* using self-service and part-time workers to help meet peak demand, *(c)* producing at a constant rate and inventorying for future demand, *(d)* carrying complementary products, *(e)* subcontracting high demand, *(f)* not meeting high demand, and *(g)* using off-season sales inducements.

Scheduling is setting the times and sequences required to do work. Control of operations is obtained by reacting to exceptions to plans.

**6.** In small firms, the emphasis should be on quality of goods and services rather than on low price. The term *quality* refers both to acceptable characteristics and to reliability of the product. Quality circles have been used by small companies to improve performance.

Quality control steps include setting standards, measuring performance, comparing actual performance with standards, and making corrections. Sampling inspections and customer feedback are used to check performance or quality.

## QUESTIONS FOR DISCUSSION

1. Discuss the advantages and disadvantages of buying locally versus buying from a distant seller.
2. What are the advantages and disadvantages of shopping at a single store rather than at several?
3. A company orders widgets in batches such as 1,000 units. The company uses a constant number each month (say 2,000) in production. Show how the inventory level changes over time between orders. What factors would cause you to change the order size up or down?
4. How would you make an economic study to determine the quantity of a food item to buy for your family on each trip to the store? How often should purchases be made?
5. In some parts of the country, building construction varies seasonally. *(a)* Is this a problem for company management? *(b)* What decisions must management make concerning these variations?

6. Many times, sales personnel do not practice good selling relations. How would you control the quality of this type of service?
7. What is quality? How can it be measured? How can it be controlled?
8. Outline instructions for installing a new quality circle.
9. In Figure 17–3, styles are changed twice a year. What changes would be required with seasonal changes of four or more styles?
10. What would you do if you received a large number of customer response forms with comments similar to those in Figure 17–7?
11. What effect on your company would the delivery of an increased percentage of defective parts have? What would you do about this?

# CASE 17

## TO MAKE, BUY, OR LEASE?

When small producers become dissatisfied with the quality, cost, or timing of purchased materials, they may be tempted to make their own. This usually requires a substantial investment in facilities to produce them. Still, when producers make their own goods, they have more control over the process and quality, there's less idle machine and personnel time, and more growth is possible in the form of new products.

> For example, Kimball International, formerly the nation's premier piano maker, now churns out regular orchestra instruments and produces office furniture as well. The latter is the largest contributor to sales and profits. Kimball's staying power is based on "making its own." It owns some hardwood forests, has its own sawmills, and produces its own lumber and plywood. It also makes plastic accessories for its products and operates a fleet of delivery trucks.

Q

Yet it's impossible for producers to make all goods and provide all services, so some must be bought. When this happens, both capital investment (in machines) and personnel costs are lower; management can specialize, devoting company time to producing its main product; and planning, directing, and controlling are less complex.

But problems may be encountered in matching inventory and production, whether one decides to "make" or "buy," so inventory control is needed to ensure a continuous, timely supply of parts and materials.

> For example, when Gillette did a superb job of promoting its new Sensor razor in early 1990, there weren't enough razors to satisfy retailers' needs. Part of the problem was that the assembly line at its South Boston plant was unable to provide enough cartridges, which contained nine parts and required microlaser welding and complex assembly.

Q

A rapidly growing trend for obtaining facilities, supplies, and services is to lease or rent them. A growing number of organizations find leasing to be an effective way to save on wear and tear—and taxes. Almost anything that can be bought can be leased, including offices; plants; stores; vehicles, such as trucks, locomotives, and cars; office machines and equipment; and even people.

> For example, Norman Hart, owner of a small Tampa print shop, hated the hassle of paperwork and bookkeeping but enjoyed building up his business. So he "fired" himself, his manager-daughter, and six other employees. The next day, Print 'n Go owners and workers were back on the job, but Miami-based Action Leasing was handling the administrative details.

*Sources:* Keith Hammonds, "It's One Sharp Ad Campaign, but Where's the Blade?" *Business Week,* March 5, 1990, p. 30; Kenneth R. Sheets, "Firms Now Lease Everything but Time," *U.S. News & World Report,* August 14, 1989, pp. 45–46; and Julianne Slovak, "Companies to Watch: Kimball International," *Fortune,* March 2, 1990, p. 90.

## QUESTIONS

Which of these methods do you think is best for each of the following, and why do you think so?

1. A small producer of high-tech equipment for sale on a long-term contract to a successful large drug company.
2. A small producer using standard parts that can be bought from many suppliers at a reasonable cost.
3. A small service firm trying to break into a new industry by selling to foreign importers.

# APPLICATION 17–1

Eddie & Company manufactures auto and truck axles for one of the large automobile companies. Because its sales have recently increased, the auto company wants to increase its production level.

This expansion would mean that Eddie & Company would need to ship many more axles to the automaker. However, Eddie & Company has already been operating at full capacity just to meet the demands of the auto giant when sales were low.

This increase in sales would mean increasing Eddie & Company's production capacity. It would also increase expenses since the company would have to either purchase or lease new manufacturing facilities.

## QUESTIONS

1. What options are available to the company?
2. What would you do if you faced the same situation?
3. Would you buy the product from your competitor to meet the contract? Explain.

# *A C T I V I T Y 17–1*

*Directions:* Use information from this chapter to unjumble the seven clues. Then use the circled letters to obtain the final answer to this puzzle.

1 G N T A I D S N D R E O S R

2 A L T U I Q Y R E C C I S L

3 S U T J N I M E I T L Y E E V D I R N

4 T U O T S K O C

5 L I D H G C U S N E

6 H R N I G S A U P C

7 R S U E C P A H O R R E D

Final solution

1. Standing orders 2. Quality circles 3. Just in time delivery 4. Stockout 5. Scheduling 6. Purchasing 7. Purchase order Final Solution: Quality controls success

CHAPTER

# 18

# Planning for Profits

*Never mind the business outlook; be on the outlook for business.*—Anonymous

*Earning a profit—staying in business—is still the No. 1 thing. Unless you can make money, you cannot do any of the other things.*—Irving Shapiro, on his retirement as chairman of Du Pont

## LEARNING OBJECTIVES

After studying the material in this chapter, you will be able to:

1. Explain the need for profit planning for a small business.
2. Discuss what causes changes in the financial position of a company.
3. Understand the financial structure of a business.
4. Learn how to plan to make a profit.
5. Plan for a profit for an actual small business.

PROFILE

## EILLEN DORSEY AND WALTER HILL, JR., USE FINANCIAL PLANNING

D

Eillen Dorsey and Walter Hill, Jr., are successful entrepreneurs today because they learned early in life the importance of personal financial planning. Eillen, the youngest of eight children, was reared in Harford County, Maryland. Her parents taught her that if she dreamed long enough—and hard enough—and was committed to a dream, she would make it become real. But that meant saving her money for college and then for investment.

Dorsey attended Catonsville and Essex Community Colleges, where she began building a network of people who worked in corporate America and in local government agencies. She developed a particularly strong relationship with Walter Hill, Jr., who had attended Morgan State University and the University of Maryland—and also knew the value of savings.

Dorsey and Hill decided to use their savings to start a business in the Baltimore, Maryland, area when they noted that almost every corporation producing machinery had to buy some type of electrical components. They also knew that many of those companies were interested in doing business with a minority firm, so they saw an opportunity to become entrepreneurs.

Dorsey had been a salesperson for Technico, an electrical component company, and was familiar with firms that wanted electrical components. Hill, who was working at Westinghouse, also knew people in the industry. So they quit their respective companies to form ECS Technologies.

Each partner contributed $5,000 to get the business started, and they secured a $35,000 loan by using their homes as equity. Their homes thus became an important investment vehicle as well. The partners had already won a contract before they applied for the loan, making it easier for the lender to grant their request. Because the partners had invested their own money and assets, the banks were willing to give them a line of credit totaling $200,000.

*Source:* Reprinted from William G. Nickels, James M. McHugh, and Susan M. McHugh, *Understanding Business*, 4th ed. (Burr Ridge, IL: Richard D. Irwin, Inc. 1996), p. 667.

Profit cannot be left to chance in small firms. Yet all too frequently it is, because small business owners tend to know little about financial planning and control.[1] Even when efforts *are* made to plan for profit, they are often inadequate, for owners tend to assume that history repeats itself—that past profits will be repeated in the future. Instead, small business managers must learn to identify all income and costs if they are to make a profit.

> For example, Wayne Hughes, "the king of self-storage," invested $50,000 in 1972, and now his fortune is estimated at $800 million. He and his family own 100 percent of Public Storage, which took very careful planning to create. Hughes locked onto two very important planning factors for the storage industry: (1) self-storage units have low cost, low maintenance, and very little cleanup between tenants, and (2) by purchasing cheap urban land, building your units, and waiting for the land to appreciate in value, you enhance your profit.[2]

## What Is Profit Planning?

**Profit planning** is a series of prescribed steps to be taken to ensure that a profit will be made.

The definition of **profit planning** may seem obvious: planning for profit. To make a profit, however, your prices must cover all costs and include a markup for planned profit. This chapter will help you (1) determine how much profit you want and how to achieve it; (2) learn how to set up an accounting system for your firm and how to read, evaluate, and interpret its accounting and financial figures;[3] and (3) evaluate, or estimate, your firm's financial position. Later in the chapter, we will outline a step-by-step process to follow to ensure that a profit results. The important thing to realize at this point is that, because it establishes targets, *profit planning must precede other activities.*

Q

A lack of accurate cost information, a recurring problem among small business owners, usually results in profits of unknown quantity—or even a loss. Also, it can foster the illusion of making a greater profit than is really earned, if any.

> The owner of Childrens' Party Caterer* illustrated this point. During the first interview with a SCORE counselor, she said she had "around $800 worth of party materials" in her pantry at home. But when asked the cost of materials used and the time involved in preparing for each party, she couldn't answer. The counselor gave her a homework assignment to determine the time she spent preparing for and giving each party, as well as the cost of materials.
>
> She was surprised to find she spent 18 to 20 hours per party, and the cost of materials ranged from $40 to $50. Also, she hadn't included the cost of transportation or the $10 to $12 baby-sitting cost for her two children. Yet she charged only about $40 to $50 for each party. To the suggestion that she raise her prices to cover these costs, plus a markup for profit, she responded, "People won't pay it." When the counselor replied, "You aren't in the charity business," her exuberant reply was, "Oh, but I enjoy doing it!"

---

*Name disguised.

## How a Business's Financial Position Changes

The operations of a small business result from decisions made by its owner and managers and the many activities they perform. As decisions are made and operations occur, the firm's financial position constantly changes. For example, cash received for sales increases the bank balance; credit sales increase accounts receivable; and purchases of material, while increasing inventory, also increase accounts payable or decrease the bank balance. At the same time, machines decrease in value, materials are processed into inventory, and utilities are used. Consequently, because the financial position of the business is constantly changing, those changes should be recorded and analyzed.

### Tracing Changes in a Company's Financial Position

Throughout its operations, the important question to small business owners is whether their business is improving its chances of reaching its primary objective—to make a profit. However, some small firms make a profit and still fail, since profits are not necessarily in the form of cash. Accounts receivable may reflect profits, but many of those accounts may not be collectible. Too much money may be tied up in other assets and not available to pay bills as they come due. In other words, focusing only on net income may be foolhardy, unless other variables are also considered.[4] The "bottom line" is not an end in itself, but it is the beginning of the more difficult process of tracking cash flow. (See Chapter 19 for more details.)

First, we should trace the changes in our own small companies. Next, we should also carefully monitor—or **benchmark**—those companies on which we depend. This would involve setting up standards (for reference), and then measuring performance against them.

**Benchmarking** is setting up standards (for reference) and then measuring performance against them.

D

> For example, Selene Wacker, a fledgling interior decorator for a small studio, was severely affected by Sears' discontinuance of catalog sales. She had been responsible for arranging the settings that were used to photograph items for the catalog. Since this work accounted for about 20 percent of its revenue, the studio lost about $400,000, and Wacker was laid off.[5]

You may have similar problems with your personal finances. Your allowance, earnings, and/or other income may be adequate to pay for food, clothing, and other operating expenses, but you may have an unexpected expense, such as replacing a worn-out car, for which you must make a cash down payment. If your funds are invested in a fixed asset, such as a loan on your car, they are not available for paying bills. The same is true of a small business. In fact, as shown in Using Technology to Succeed, you can use the same computer programs to handle both your business and your personal finances.

### Importance of Accounting

**Accounting records** are records of a firm's financial position that reflect any changes in that position.

Accounting is quite important in achieving success in any business, especially a small one. Therefore, your **accounting records** must accurately reflect the changes occurring in your firm's assets, liabilities, income, expenses, and

## USING TECHNOLOGY TO SUCCEED

### Gaining Power over Your Money

Many entrepreneurs are finding that the financial software package *Quicken* meets their accounting needs. The program, produced by Intuit Inc., is user-friendly and affordable. It can be used to budget, write checks, and keep track of expenses and investments. There is room for as many as 255 accounts. It can also generate any needed reports. Intuit provides a toll-free telephone help line.

*Source:* Dan Gutman, "Gain Power over Money: A Secret Weapon That Is Also Cheap," *Success,* April 1992, p. 14.

equity. The continued operation of your business also depends—as Irving Shapiro pointed out in the opening quotation—on maintaining the proper balance among its investments, revenues, expenses, and profit. Because profit margins are so critical to the success of a business, any decline in them should trigger an immediate search for the cause.

*"See no evil, speak no evil....I like that in an accountant, Mr. Farouche."*

Reprinted from *Management Accounting,* January 1988, p. 13.

Many small business owners don't realize their business is in trouble until it's too late, and many fail without knowing what their problem is—or even that they have a problem. All they know is that they end up with no money and can't pay their bills. Timothy O'Connell, a CPA, calls these owners "seat-of-the-pants operators" because they fail to monitor all aspects of their businesses. They often consider financial statements "a necessary evil" and think everything is fine as long as sales are increasing and there is money in the bank. "They don't realize that what they do in their businesses is reflected in the financial statements. They tend not to pay much attention to the information accountants give them."[6] One young entrepreneur found this out the hard way.

> For Richard Huttner, the hardest problem in running New York's Parenting Unlimited Inc. was doing the accounting necessary in running its new acquisition, *Baby Talk* magazine. Although *Baby Talk* had revenues of several million dollars a year, it had no financial management, accounting system, general ledger, or bank account when it was acquired. Consequently, while trying to master an ongoing business, Huttner had to spend nearly a third of his time the first three months paying bills and doing accounting. He lamented, "Stanford didn't teach me how long it takes out-of-state checks to clear. At first, that caused us constant cash flow problems."[7]

In discussing financial management in this chapter, we have used a real small business, which we have disguised as The Model Company, Inc., to illustrate the basic concepts discussed. Assume throughout the following discussion that, while the company is owned by Mr. Model, you manage it for him. Therefore, you must make the management decisions.

## What is the Financial Structure of a Business?

The assets, liabilities, and equity of a business are reflected in its financial structure. These accounts, which are interrelated and interact with each other, represent the **financial structure** of a firm, which changes constantly as business activities occur. Always keep in mind that *the total of liabilities plus owners'equity always equals the total assets of the firm.*

**Financial structure** describes the relative proportions of a firm's assets, liabilities, and owners' equity.

At regular intervals, a **balance sheet** is prepared to show the assets, liabilities, and owners' equity of the business. See Figure 18–1 for the arrangement and amounts of the accounts for our hypothetical business, The Model Company.

A **balance sheet** is a statement of a firm's assets, liabilities, and owners' equity at a given time.

Remember, you can use the balance sheet as a gauge of the financial health of your company. It not only shows how assets are being used but also provides a snapshot of the company at a given moment. To keep you from getting bogged down in your daily activities, think of the following concepts:[8]

- Remember that "cash is king"—meaning that, if the balance sheet is correct, "current assets" should be easily convertible to cash.
- Keep your assets working for you—don't keep obsolete inventory or equipment.
- Make sure your business is properly financed.
- Have a financial plan—the goals in the financial plan should match the balance sheet.

To get a realistic look at your company, you should go over the balance sheet with your accountant instead of leaving everything up to her or him. Another good source of financial support would be a trusted banker.

### Assets

**Assets**, are the things a business owns. For accounting purposes, they are divided into current and fixed assets.

**Assets** are the things a business owns.

#### *Current Assets*

**Current assets** are expected to turn over—that is, to change from one form to another—within a year. **Cash** includes the bills and coins in the cash register, deposits in a checking account, and other deposits that can be converted into cash immediately. A certain level of cash is necessary to operate a business; however, holding too much cash reduces your income because it doesn't produce revenue.[9] The question is, What is the correct level? The following example suggests a partial answer.

**Current assets** are those that are expected to change from one form to another within a year.

**Cash** includes bills, coins, deposits in a checking account, and other deposits that can be converted into cash immediately.

> Alan Goldstein, a partner in Touche Ross & Company's Enterprise Group in Boston, which helps small firms decide how much cash is needed, answers the question "When do everyday nuisances turn into disaster?" by saying, "When you're about to run out of cash."[10]

**Figure 18–1**

**THE MODEL COMPANY, INC.**
**Balance Sheet**
**December 31, 19—**

Assets

| | | | |
|---|---|---|---|
| Current assets: | | | |
| Cash | | $ 7,054 | |
| Accounts receivable | | 60,484 | |
| Inventory | | 80,042 | |
| Prepaid expenses | | 1,046 | |
| Total current assets | | | $148,626 |
| Fixed assets: | | | |
| Equipment | $100,500 | | |
| Building | 40,950 | | |
| Gross fixed assets | | 141,450 | |
| Less: accumulated depreciation | | 16,900 | |
| Net fixed assets | | | 124,550 |
| Total assets | | | $273,176 |

Liabilities and Owners' Equity

| | | | |
|---|---|---|---|
| Current liabilities: | | | |
| Accounts payable | 51,348 | | |
| Accrued payable | 3,060 | | |
| Total current liabilities | | $ 54,408 | |
| Long-term liabilities: | | | |
| Mortgage payable | | 20,708 | |
| Total liabilities | | | $ 75,116 |
| Owners' equity: | | | |
| Capital stock | | 160,000 | |
| Retained earnings | | 38,060 | |
| Total equity | | | 198,060 |
| Total liabilities and owners' equity | | | $273,176 |

**Accounts receivable** are current assets resulting from selling a product on credit.

**Accounts receivable** result from giving credit to customers for less than a year, as shown in Chapter 12. While selling on credit helps maintain a higher level of sales, care must be taken to select customers who will pay within a reasonable time.

As discussed in Chapter 17, *inventory* provides a buffer between purchase, production, and sales. Therefore, you must maintain a certain amount to serve customers adequately. But carrying an excessive amount of inventory ties up capital, which then cannot be used for income-producing assets. Thus, the amount of inventory to carry depends on a judicious balancing of income and costs.

Other current asset accounts often are called *short-term investments* and *prepaid expenses*. Usually, these make up only a small part of the current assets of a small business and need little attention (for an example, refer to Figure 18–1).

### *Fixed Assets*

Items a business expects to own for more than a year—such as buildings, machinery, store fixtures, trucks, and land—are included among its **fixed assets.** Different types of fixed assets have different lengths of *useful life,* that is, the length of time that such assets, on average, may be expected to be used. Part of their cost is written off each period as depreciation expense, with the result that the entire cost is spread over the asset's useful life.

**Fixed assets** are relatively permanent items the business needs for its continued operations.

As shown in Chapter 9, some small firms find it desirable to lease fixed assets instead of owning them. For example, a retailer may rent a store to reduce the need to make a large investment in it.

## Liabilities

As discussed in Chapter 9, a business can obtain funds by owner investment and by borrowing, which is creating an obligation to pay. The first, which is necessary, increases *owners' equity,* or the *owners' interest* in the business. The second results in a **liability** of the business to pay back the funds—plus interest. Borrowing from creditors is divided into current and long-term liabilities.

**Liabilities** are the financial obligations of a business.

### *Current Liabilities*

Obligations to be paid within a year are **current liabilities**. They include accounts payable, notes payable, and accrued items (such as payroll), which are for services performed for you but not yet paid for.

**Current liabilities** are obligations that must be paid within a year.

**Accounts payable** are obligations to pay for goods and services purchased and are usually due within 30 or 60 days, depending on the credit terms. Since any business should maintain current assets sufficient to pay these accounts, maintaining a high level of accounts payable requires a high level of current assets.[11] Thus, you should determine whether or not early payment is beneficial; some sellers offer a discount for early payment, such as 1 or 2 percent if bills are paid within 10 days. This is a good return on your money!

**Accounts payable** are obligations to pay, resulting from purchasing goods or services.

**Notes payable**, which are written obligations to pay, usually give the business a longer time than accounts payable before payment is due. An example is a 90-day note.

**Notes payable** are written obligations to pay, usually after 90 days to a year.

### *Long-Term Liabilities*

Bonds and mortgages are the usual types of **long-term liabilities**, which have terms of more than a year. A business usually incurs these liabilities when purchasing fixed assets. Long-term loans may be used to supply a reasonable amount of **working capital**, which is current assets less current liabilities. This type of borrowing requires regular payment of interest. The

**Long-term liabilities** are obligations to pay someone after one year or more.

**Working capital** is a firm's current assets minus current liabilities.

need to make these payments during slack times increases the risk of being unable to meet other obligations, so both short- and long-term strategies should be used. In general, small firms use long-term borrowing as a source of funds much less frequently than large ones do.[12]

## Owners' Equity

**Owners' equity** is the owners' share of (or **net worth** in) the business, after liabilities are subtracted from assets.

**Owners' equity** is the owners' share of (or **net worth** in) the business, after liabilities are subtracted from assets. The owners receive income from profits in the form of dividends or an increase in their share of the company through an increase in retained earnings. Owners also absorb losses, which decrease their equity. (See Chapters 9 and 20 for further details.)

As shown in Chapter 9, when owners invest in a corporation, they receive shares of stock, and the *owners' equity account*—common stock—is increased on the firm's balance sheet.

**Retained earnings** are profits kept in the business rather than distributed to owners.

**Retained earnings** are the profits kept in the business rather than being distributed to the owners. Most firms retain some profits to use in times of need or to provide for growth. Many small firms have failed because the owners paid themselves too much of the profits, thereby reducing their assets. Definite policies should be set as to what part of your earnings should be retained and what part distributed to you as income.

# Profit-Making Activities of a Business

The profit-making activities of a business influence its financial structure. These activities are reflected in the revenue and expense accounts, as shown by the following formula:

Net income (profit) = Revenue (income) – Expenses (costs)

An **income statement (profit and loss statement)** periodically shows revenues, expenses, and profits from a firm's operations.

During a given period, the business performs services for which it receives revenues. It also incurs expenses for goods and services provided to it by others. These revenues and expenses are shown in the **income statement**, also known as the **profit and loss statement** (see Figure 18–2).

## Revenue and Expenses

**Revenue (sales income)** is the value received by a firm in return for a good or service.

**Revenue** (also called **sales income**) is the value received by a business in return for services performed or goods sold. The business receives revenue in the form of cash or accounts receivable.

**Expenses** are the costs of labor, goods, and services.

**Expenses**, the costs of paying people to work for you (or for goods or services provided to you), include such items as materials, wages, insurance, utilities, transportation, depreciation, taxes, supplies, and advertising. As these costs are incurred, they are deducted from revenue.

**Fixed expenses (costs)** do not vary with changes in output.

**Variable expenses (costs)** vary directly with changes in output.

There are two types of expenses (costs): (1) fixed and (2) variable. **Fixed expenses (costs)** are those that are incurred periodically, regardless of whether operations are carried on or not. These include such items as depreciation, rent, and insurance. **Variable expenses (costs)** vary according to the level of operations. Thus, if there are no operations, there are no variable expenses. These expenses include such items as labor and material to produce and sell the product, plus sales promotion and delivery costs.

**Figure 18–2**

| THE MODEL COMPANY, INC. Income Statement January 1 through December 31, 19— | | | |
|---|---|---|---|
| Net sales | $463,148 | | |
| Less: Cost of goods sold | 291,262 | | |
| Gross income | | $171,886 | |
| Operating expenses: | | | |
| Salaries | $ 83,138 | | |
| Utilities | 6,950 | | |
| Depreciation | 10,050 | | |
| Rent | 2,000 | | |
| Building services | 4,920 | | |
| Insurance | 4,000 | | |
| Interest | 2,646 | | |
| Office and supplies | 6,550 | | |
| Sales promotion | 11,000 | | |
| Taxes and licenses | 6,480 | | |
| Maintenance | 1,610 | | |
| Delivery | 5,848 | | |
| Miscellaneous | 1,750 | | |
| Total expenses | | 146,942 | |
| Net income before taxes | | 24,944 | |
| Less: Income taxes | | 5,484 | |
| Net income after taxes | | | $19,460 |

## Profit

**Profit**, also called **income**, is the difference between revenues earned and expenses incurred. Depending on the type of expenses deducted, profit may be called *gross income, operating profit, net income before taxes*, or *net income.*

**Profit** is the difference between revenue earned and expenses incurred.

Your profit margins indicate the relationship between revenues and expenses; therefore, a decline in profit margin should trigger a search for the cause. The problem could be a rise in expenses, a per unit sales revenue decline caused by discounting or pricing errors, or changing the basic operations of the business.

## How to Plan for Profit

According to a Dun & Bradstreet report, a well-managed small business has at least the following characteristics:

Q

- It is more liquid than a badly managed company.
- The balance sheet is as important to the owner as the income statement.

- Stability is emphasized, instead of rapid growth.
- Long-range planning is important.

## Need for Profit Planning

As you study the income statement in Figure 18–2, you may interpret it as saying, "The Model Company received $463,148 in net sales, expended $291,262 for costs of goods sold, paid out $146,942 in total operating expenses, and had $24,944 left as net income (or profits) before income taxes." Under this interpretation, *profit is a "leftover," not a planned amount.* While neither you nor Mr. Model can do anything about the past, you can do something about future operations. Since one of your goals is to make a profit, you should plan the operations now to achieve your desired profit goal later. So let's see how you can do it!

## Steps in Profit Planning

To achieve your goal during the coming year, you need to take the following profit-planning steps:

1. Establish a profit goal.
2. Determine the volume of sales revenue needed to make that profit.
3. Estimate the expenses you will incur in reaching that volume of sales.
4. Determine estimated profit, based on plans resulting from steps 2 and 3
5. Compare the estimated profit with the profit goal.

If you are satisfied with the plans, you can stop at this point. However, you may want to check further to determine whether improvements can be made, particularly if you aren't happy with the results of step 5. Doing steps 6 through 10 may help you to understand better how changing some of your operations can affect profit.

6. List possible alternatives that can be used to improve profits.
7. Determine how expenses vary with changes in sales volume.
8. Determine how profits vary with changes in sales volume.
9. Analyze your alternatives from a profit standpoint.
10. Select an alternative and implement the plan.

*"If you don't consider our paper profits real—why do you consider our paper losses real?"*

Reprinted from *The Wall Street Journal;* permission Cartoon Features Syndicate.

## Need for Realism in Profit Planning

Be realistic when going through these steps, or you may be unable to reach the desired profit goal. You may feel the future is too uncertain to make such plans, but *the greater the uncertainty, the greater the need for planning.*

> For example, the president of a small firm said his forecasts were too inaccurate to be of any help in planning operations, so he had stopped forecasting. His business became so unsuccessful he had to sell out.
>
> The owner of another small business recently stated she can't forecast the next year's revenue within 20 percent of actual sales. However, she continues to forecast and plan, for she says she needs plans from which to deviate as conditions change.

## Profit Planning Applied in a Typical Small Business

This section uses the above steps to plan profits for The Model Company. As manager, you must start planning for the coming year several months in advance so you can put your plans into effect at the proper time. To present a systematic analysis, assume you are planning for the company for the first time.*

### Step 1: Establish the Profit Goal

Your **profit goal** must be a specific target value. To begin with, as you manage the business, pay yourself a reasonable salary. Also, Mr. Model should receive a return on his investment—not only his initial investment but also any earnings left in the business—for taking the risks of ownership. To do this, compare what you would receive as salary for working for someone else and the income Mr. Model would receive if the same amount of money were placed in a relatively safe investment, such as U.S. government bonds or high-grade stocks. Each of these investments provides a return with a certain degree of risk—and pleasure. If Mr. Model could invest the same amount of money at an 8 percent return, with little risk, what do you think the return on his investment in The Model Company should be?

A **profit goal** is the specific amount of profit one expects to achieve.

Mr. Model originally invested $160,000 in the company and has since left about $40,000 of his profits in the business. He made about 10 percent on his investment this past year, which he thinks is too low for the risk he is taking; he believes about a 20 percent return is reasonable. So, as step 1 in Figure 18–3, you enter his investment, desired profit, and estimate of income taxes (from the past and after consultation with his accountant). You determine that he must make $52,000 before taxes, or a 26 percent return on his investment, if he is to reach his desired profit. After you and Mr. Model have set this goal, you should determine what the profit before taxes will be from your forecast of next year's plans.

### Step 2: Determine the Planned Sales Volume

A **sales forecast** is an estimate of the amount a firm expects to sell during a given period. In preparing operating and sales budgets, these forecasts are used to estimate revenues for the next quarter, for the year, or perhaps even for three to five years. Learning how to forecast accurately can spell the

A **sales forecast** is an estimate of the amount of revenue expected from sales for a given period in the future.

---

*Actually, you should be planning for each month at least six months or a year ahead. This can be done by dropping the past month, adjusting the rest of the months in your prior plans, and adding the plans for another month. Such planning gives you time to anticipate needed changes and do something about them.

**Figure 18–3**

**THE MODEL COMPANY, INC.**
**Planning for Profit for the Year 19—**

| Step description | Analysis | Comments |
|---|---|---|
| 1. *Establish your profit goals.* | | |
| Equity invested in company | $160,000 | |
| Retained earnings | 40,000 | |
| Owners' equity | 200,000 | |
| Return desired, after income taxes | 40,000 | 20% × $200,000 |
| Estimated tax on profit | 12,000 | |
| Profit needed before income taxes | $ 52,000 | |
| 2. *Determine your planned volume of sales.* | | |
| Estimate of sales income | $530,000 | 530 units × $1,000/unit |
| 3. *Estimate your expenses for planned volume of sales.* | Estimated, 19— | Actual, last year |
| Cost of goods | $333,900 | $291,262 |
| Salaries | 88,300 | 88,138 |
| Utilities | 7,100 | 6,950 |
| Depreciation | 10,000 | 10,050 |
| Rent | 2,500 | 2,000 |
| Building services | 5,100 | 4,920 |
| Insurance | 5,000 | 4,000 |
| Interest | 3,000 | 2,646 |
| Office expenses | 6,000 | 5,550 |
| Sales promotion | 11,800 | 11,000 |
| Taxes and licenses | 6,900 | 6,480 |
| Maintenance | 1,900 | 1,610 |
| Delivery | 6,500 | 5,848 |
| Miscellaneous | 2,000 | 1,740 |
| Total | $490,000 | $442,194 |
| 4. *Determine your estimated profit, based on steps 2 and 3.* | | |
| Estimated sales income | $530,000 | |
| Estimated expenses | 490,000 | |
| Estimated net profit before taxes | $ 40,000 | |
| 5. *Compare estimated profit with profit goal.* | | |
| Estimated profit before taxes | $ 40,000 | |
| Desired profit before taxes | 52,000 | |
| Difference | –$ 12,000 | |

6. *List possible alternatives to improve profits.*
   - A. Change the planned sales income:
     - (1) Increase planned volume of units sold.
     - (2) Increase or decrease planned price of units.
     - (3) Combine (1) and (2).
   - B. Decrease planned expenses.
   - C. Add other products or services.
   - D. Subcontract work.

**Figure 18–3** *(concluded)*

| Expense item | Sales volume of 364 Fixed expenses | Sales volume of 364 Variable expenses | Sales volume of 364 Total expenses | Sales volume of 530 Variable expenses | Sales volume of 530 Total expenses | Sales volume of 700 Variable expenses | Sales volume of 700 Total expenses |
|---|---|---|---|---|---|---|---|
| *7. Determine how expenses vary with changes in sales volume.* | | | | | | | |
| Goods sold | | $229,200 | $229,200 | $333,900 | $333,900 | $440,789 | $440,789 |
| Salaries | $50,000 | 26,304 | 76,304 | 38,300 | 88,300 | 50,585 | 100,585 |
| Utilities | 6,000 | 755 | 6,755 | 1,100 | 7,100 | 1,453 | 7,453 |
| Depreciation | 10,000 | | 10,000 | | 10,000 | | 10,000 |
| Rent | 2,500 | | 2,500 | | 2,500 | | 2,500 |
| Building services | 4,000 | 755 | 4,755 | 1,100 | 5,100 | 1,453 | 5,453 |
| Insurance | 5,000 | | 5,000 | | 5,000 | | 5,000 |
| Interest | | 2,060 | 2,060 | 3,000 | 3,000 | 3,962 | 3,962 |
| Office expenses | 2,800 | 2,198 | 4,998 | 3,200 | 6,000 | 4,226 | 7,026 |
| Sales promotion | | 8,104 | 8,104 | 11,800 | 11,800 | 15,585 | 15,585 |
| Taxes and licenses | 5,000 | 1,305 | 6,305 | 1,900 | 6,900 | 2,509 | 7,509 |
| Maintenance | 800 | 755 | 1,555 | 1,100 | 1,900 | 1,453 | 2,253 |
| Delivery | | 4,464 | 4,464 | 6,500 | 6,500 | 8,585 | 8,585 |
| Miscellaneous | 2,000 | | 2,000 | | 1,000 | | 2,000 |
| Total | $88,100 | $275,900 | $364,000 | $401,900 | $490,000 | $530,600 | $618,700 |

*8. Determine how profits vary with changes in sales volume.*

| | Sales Volume of 364 | | Sales Volume of 530 | | Sales Volume of 700 | |
|---|---|---|---|---|---|---|
| Revenue @ $1,000 per unit | $364,000 | | $530,000 | | $700,000 | |
| Expenses | | | | | | |
| Fixed | | $ 88,100 | | $ 88,100 | | $ 88,100 |
| Variable | | 275,900 | | 401,900 | | 530,600 |
| Total | 364,000 | | 490,000 | | 618,700 | |
| Estimated profit before income tax | $000,000 (Break-even) | | $ 40,000 | | $ 81,300 | |

9. *Analyze alternatives from a profit standpoint.*
   Increase income by increasing price? Decreasing price?
   Increase income by increasing advertising?
   Decrease variable costs?
10. *Select and implement the plan.*

difference between growth and stagnation for your business.[13] But accurate forecasting is not always possible, especially for a product that is exploding in popularity.

> New subscribers for cellular phones grew by 51 percent in 1994, about 44 percent in 1995, and will probably grow 32 percent in 1996. The decreasing growth in demand is attributed to the prevailing high charges per

G

minute of use. Analysts believe the market is taking a wait-and-see attitude, holding out for lower prices, and that competition will effectively bring them about.

Scandinavia will probably be the role leader in this movement, for competition is fierce there, and the phones' penetration is 30 percent as compared to 12 percent in the United States. This is the kind of information the entrepreneur must have as a basis for profit planning.[14]

Different parts of the business use these forecasts for planning and controlling their parts of the operations. Thus, the forecasts influence decisions about purchasing materials, scheduling production, securing financial resources, purchasing plant or equipment, hiring and paying personnel, scheduling vacations, and planning inventory levels.

In our example, you would probably forecast sales for the coming year on estimates of several factors, such as market conditions, level of sales promotion, estimate of competitors' activities, and inflation. Or you could use forecasts appearing in specialized business and government publications. Also, your trade associations, banker, customers, vendors, and others can provide valuable information. Using all this information—and assuming 6 percent inflation for the coming year—you estimate that sales will increase about 8 percent, to $530,000 ($1,000 per unit × 530 units), which you enter as step 2 in Figure 18–3.

### Step 3: Estimate Expenses for Planned Sales Volume

To estimate expenses for the coming year, you record last year's figures as part of step 3. You should then adjust them for changes in economic conditions (including inflation), changes in expenses needed to attain the planned sales, improved methods of production, and a reasonable salary for the services of the owner.

You then compute that about 63 percent of your revenue is to pay for materials and labor used directly to produce the goods you will sell. Using this figure—adjusted 6 percent for inflation—you enter the result, $333,900, as "cost of goods." You then estimate the amount of each of the other expenses, recognizing that some expenses vary directly with volume changes, while others change little, if at all. Enter each expense figure in the appropriate place. The total of all expected expenses is $490,000.

### Step 4: Determine the Estimated Profit

In this step, you first deduct the figure for estimated expenses from the estimated sales income; then add the total of any other income, such as interest. You calculate this amount and find that profit before taxes is estimated to be $40,000 ($530,000 – $490,000), which is higher than the $24,944 made last year.

### Step 5: Compare Estimated Profit with Profit Goal

Next, you compare the estimated profit ($40,000) with your profit goal ($52,000). Because estimated profit is $12,000 less than you would wish, you decide to continue with steps 6 through 10.

## Step 6: List Possible Alternatives to Improve Profits

As shown in step 6 of Figure 18–3, you have many alternatives for improving profits. Some of these are as follows:

A. Change the planned sales income by:
   1. Increasing planned volume of units sold by increasing sales promotion, improving the quality of the product, making it more available, or finding new uses for it.
   2. Increasing or decreasing the planned price of the units. The best price may not be the one you're using.
   3. Combining (1) and (2). On occasion, some small business owners become too concerned with selling on the basis of price alone. Instead, price for profit and sell quality, better service, reliability, and integrity.

> For example, in 1984, Bert Olson stopped using pesticides on his 450-acre farm for two reasons. One was concern for the environment. The other consideration was cost: he was going broke as a conventional farmer. He now sees not just profits, but *increasing* profits as consumers' demand for organically grown foods increases.[15]

Q

B. Decrease planned expenses by:
   1. Establishing a better control system. Spotting areas where losses occur and establishing controls may reduce expenses.
   2. Increasing productivity of people and machines through improving methods, developing proper motivators, and improving the types and use of machinery.
   3. Redesigning the product by developing new materials, machines, and/or methods for improving products and reducing costs.

C. Reduce costs per unit or add other products or services by:
   1. Adding a summer product to a winter line of products.
   2. Using idle capacity innovatively.
   3. Making some parts that are customarily purchased from the outside.
   4. Using the Japanese concept of **kaizen costing**, which sets in advance cost targets in all aspects of product design, development, and production. Kaizen costing requires each department—or cost center—to set specific cost reduction plans for each accounting period.[16]

D. Subcontract work.

G

**Kaizen costing** sets costs targets for all phases of design, development, and production of a product for each accounting period.

Having listed possible alternatives, you must evaluate each of them and concentrate on the best one or ones.

## Step 7: Determine How Expenses Vary with Changes in Sales Volume

Although you have estimated your planned sales volume at 530 units (at $1,000 per unit), you will probably want to see what happens to expenses if you sell fewer or more units. This can be done by reviewing your expected expenses in step 3 and varying them up and down, remembering that some are fixed and some vary with level of sales. We've done this in step 7 at three

**Figure 18–4** Car Phone Bills Grow—Phone bills now account for about a quarter of expenses for cars used for business.

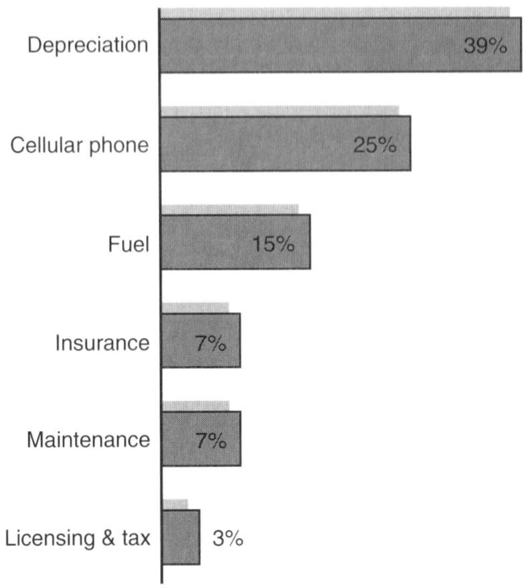


*Source:* PHH Vehicle Management Service survey of 400,000 autos in business use, as reported in *USA Today*, August 2, 1995. © 1995 USA TODAY. Reprinted with permission.

levels: 364, 530, and 700 units. Notice that total expenses increase from $364,000 at 364 units, to $490,000 at 530 units, and to $618,700 at 700 units.

While an analysis of past costs is helpful in projecting future expenses, be aware that:

1. The relationships exist only within limited changes in sales volume. Very high sales volumes may be obtained by extraordinary and costly efforts; low volumes result in extra costs from idle capacity, lost volume discounts, and so forth.
2. Past relationships may not continue in the future. Inflation or deflation, changing location of customers, new products, and other factors can cause changes in the unit costs.

Q

For example, Figure 18–4 illustrates that the high cost of cellular phones can represent a significant proportion of the expense of maintaining company vehicles. Also remember that almost all such phone providers charge for usage time in addition to a flat monthly rate.

## Step 8: Determine How Profits Vary with Changes in Sales Volume

As you notice in step 8 of Figure 18–3, profit (or loss) can be estimated for different levels of sales. We've done that for the three levels—364, 530, and 700 units—using fixed expenses, variable expenses, and the resulting profit before income taxes.

The **break-even point** is that volume of sales where total revenue and expenses are equal, so there is neither profit nor loss.

These figures were then incorporated into a chart (Figure 18–5) to show what sales volume would result in The Model Company's neither making nor losing money on its operations. This figure, called the **break-even point**, was 364 units, where sales revenues and total expenses were $364,000.

**Figure 18–5** Break-Even Chart for the Model Company

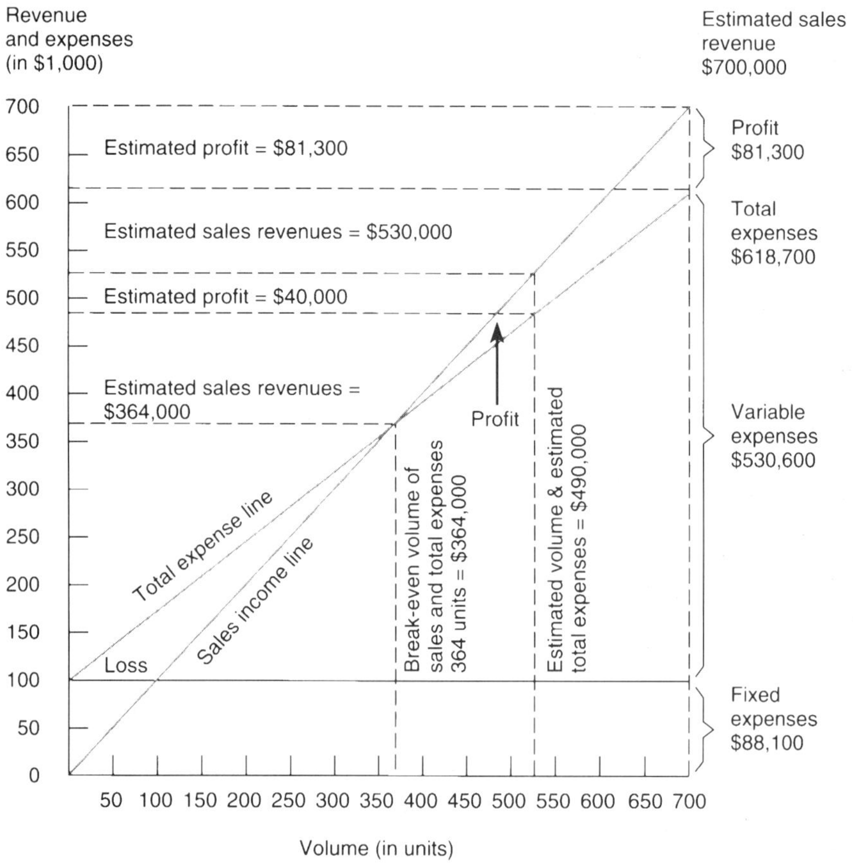


## Step 9: Analyze Alternatives from a Profit Standpoint

Using the information you've generated so far, especially from steps 6, 7, and 8, can lead you to consider alternatives such as the following to increase profits:

- Change sales price.
- Change media—and/or amount budgeted—for advertising.
- Reduce variable costs.
- Change quality of products.
- Stop producing and selling low-margin products.

Other alternatives can be evaluated in much the same manner. Then, having made these economic analyses, you will be ready to make your final plan for action.

## Step 10: Select and Implement the Plan

The selection of the plan for action depends on your judgment as to what will most benefit the business.[17] The results of the analyses made in the prior steps provide the economic inputs. These must be evaluated along with other goals. Cost reduction may result in laying off employees or in reducing service to customers.

**Figure 18–6**

**THE MODEL COMPANY, INC.**
**Income Statement for the Year 19—**

| | | | |
|---|---|---|---|
| Sales income | | $530,000 | |
| Less: | | | |
| Cost of goods sold | $327,200 | | |
| Other expenses | 156,100 | | |
| Total expenses | | 483,300 | |
| Net profit before taxes | | | $46,700 |
| Pretax return on equity | | | 23.4% |
| Pretax profit margin | | | 8.8% |

Mr. Model has just read this text and has been studying other management literature. After hearing you present the above analyses to him, he believes the company can reduce the cost of goods sold by about 2 percent. Figure 18–6 shows a simplified statement of the planned income and outgo for the next year, based on the work you and he have done. How does it look to you?

## WHAT YOU SHOULD HAVE LEARNED

**1.** Not only do small business owners often fail to plan for a profit, but they also sometimes don't even know whether or not they are making a profit. Because healthy sales income doesn't guarantee a profit, it's important to determine the true cost of a product to set a fair price and budget and plan accordingly.

**2.** A business's financial position is not static. Every time a product is sold, money comes in, inventory is bought, or credit is given, assets and liabilities fluctuate. Rapid growth and "paper profits" can be the downfall of small business owners who don't keep accurate records and don't listen to the conclusions accountants draw from the figures.

**3.** A company's financial structure consists of its assets, liabilities, and owners' equity. Assets are the things a company owns. Current assets, which turn over within a year, include cash, accounts receivable, and inventory, as well as short-term investments and prepaid expenses. Fixed assets—such as buildings, machinery, store fixtures, trucks, and land—are things the company expects to own for a longer time. Part of their cost is written off each year as depreciation expense.

Liabilities are obligations created by borrowing or buying something on credit. Current liabilities, payable within one year, include accounts payable, notes payable, and accrued expenses. Long-term liabilities, with terms of a year or longer, should be used to pay for fixed assets and to acquire working capital.

Owners' equity is the owners' share of a business after liabilities are subtracted from assets. Profits may be distributed to owners as cash or dividends, or accumulated in the business in the form of retained earnings.

**4.** A company's profit (net income) is what is retained after expenses—the costs of doing business—are subtracted from revenues—the proceeds from sales. When sales increase, not only does sales income rise, but variable costs change as well, and it may sometimes be necessary to increase fixed costs.

To plan for a profit, you must have a profit target, which is your reason for being in business. Detailed profit planning includes at least the first 5 of the following 10 steps: (1) establish the profit goal, (2) determine the planned volume of sales, (3) estimate the expenses for the planned sales volume, (4) determine estimated profit for the planned sales volume, and (5) compare the estimated profit with the profit goal. If the results of (5) are unsatisfactory, (6) list possible alternatives that can be used to improve the profit position, (7) determine how costs vary with changes in sales volume, (8) determine how profits vary with changes in sales volume, (9) analyze alternatives from a profit standpoint, and (10) select an alternative and implement the plan.

**5.** The chapter concluded by illustrating these steps for a hypothetical company.

## QUESTIONS FOR DISCUSSION

1. Why is planning for profit so important to a small business?
2. In analyzing the changing financial position of a small business, what things should you look for?
3. "If a small firm is making a profit, there's no danger of its failing." Do you agree? Why or why not?
4. What is a firm's financial structure? What are the components of this structure?
5. Explain each of the following: *(a)* assets, *(b)* current assets, *(c)* fixed assets, *(d)* liabilities, *(e)* current liabilities, *(f)* long-term liabilities, *(g)* owners' equity, *(h)* retained earnings, *(i)* income (profit and loss) statement, *(j)* balance sheet, and *(k)* profit.
6. What steps are needed in profit planning?
7. How do you establish a profit goal?
8. *(a)* How do you determine planned volume of sales? *(b)* How does profit change with volume of product sold?
9. How do you determine planned expenses? Variable? Fixed?
10. What are some alternatives that could improve planned profits? Explain each.

# CASE 18

## WHAT IS PROFIT?

The Powell Company* was started in a small metal building in Louisiana two years ago to sell and service small boats. The company needed to hire some experienced personnel from an established competitor. Phil Powell, the owner, approached several of these people and offered them the same wages they were earning from their current employers. Because there were no immediate benefits from changing jobs, they were told of the advantages of getting in on the ground floor of the newer, though smaller, business. They were told that as the firm grew and sales and profits increased, it would be management's policy to pay a higher basic wage and also larger employee benefits. Several of these employees joined Powell.

During the first year, sales didn't come up to expectations. Powell decided that to increase sales he should move to a more desirable location, where modern equipment and facilities could improve production. The search for a new location was begun, and the employees were excited at the prospect of being located in a newer building with expanded facilities and the latest tools and equipment.

While the new facilities were being readied, morale was high and employee performance was superior. When the facilities were occupied, morale improved even further. During the first few months, more orders were obtained by the sales force than the firm was able to fill, but production quotas were met and surpassed. It appeared to all concerned that the company was well on its way to becoming a leader in its field.

With the new and expanded facilities, though, came new and unexpected problems. For example, overhead greatly expanded and there was a larger tax burden. Also, costs incurred for insurance, utilities, and personnel increased, which significantly increased expenses. So, while revenues were obviously increasing, expenses were increasing faster, and the business wasn't even breaking even, much less making a profit.

Powell felt he couldn't keep his promise to increase wages and add more employee benefits. He told the employees they would have to wait until the financial position improved before receiving what he had promised them. He said the increases wouldn't be given until the company's sales were sufficiently higher than expenses to provide a profit.

Bob Benjamin, the production manager, agreed with Powell that wages couldn't be raised at that time, but he believed that unless the employees were shown a detailed report of expenses, they would continue to believe the firm was making a substantial profit and had gone back on its word.

Powell, realized this was true. He also felt the employees had no justification for looking into the company's financial situation. In view of this, he knew the only alternative was the one he had previously outlined.

*Source:* Prepared by Gayle M. Ross, Ross Publishing Company.

---

*Name disguised at the request of the owner.

## QUESTIONS

1. What does this case show about the relationships among income, expenses, and profits (losses)?
2. What did the move to new facilities do to the firm's break-even point?
3. Should the owner show the books to the employees? Why or why not?
4. What would you do now if you were the owner?

## APPLICATION 18–1

A small firm in Wichita, Kansas, specialized in the sale and installation of swimming pools. The company was profitable, but the owners devoted very little attention to the management of working capital. For example, the company had never prepared a cash budget.

To be sure that money was available for payments as needed, the owner of the firm kept a minimum of $25,000 in a checking account. At times, this account grew larger, until at one time it totaled $43,000. The owner felt that this practice of cash management worked well for a small company because it eliminated all the paperwork associated with cash budgeting. Moreover, it had enabled the firm to always pay its bills in a timely manner.

## QUESTIONS

1. What are the advantages and weaknesses of the minimum-cash-balance practice?
2. There is a saying, "If it ain't broke, don't fix it." In view of the firm's present success in paying bills promptly, should it be encouraged to use a cash budget? Defend your answer.

# ACTIVITY 18–1

*Directions:* Use information from this chapter to solve the puzzle below.

ACROSS

1 Difference between revenue earned and expenses

4 Obligations after a year

5 Financial obligations

6 Statement of equity

7 Varies directly with changes in output

11 Equity after liabilities

14 Estimate of expected revenue

15 Resulting from selling a good on credit

18 Profits kept in the business

19 Bills and coins

20 Obligations to pay

21 Costs of labor, goods, and services

22 Total revenue and expenses are equal

23 Written obligations to pay

DOWN

1 Income statement

2 Things a business owns

3 Relatively permanent

8 Expected to change within a year

9 Must be paid within a year

10 Describes relative proportions of assets

12 Current assets minus current liabilities

13 Tangible goods expected to sell

16 Do not vary with changes in output

17 Sales income

ACROSS 1 Profit 4 Long-term liabilities 5 Liabilities 6 Balance sheet 7 Variable expenses 11 Net worth 14 Sales forecast 15 Account receivable 18 Retained earnings 19 Cash 20 Accounts payable 21 Expenses 22 Breakeven point 23 Notes payable
DOWN 1 Profit and loss statement 2 Assets 3 Fixed assets 8 Current assets 9 Current liabilities 10 Financial structure 12 Working capital 13 Inventory 16 Fixed expenses 17 Revenue

CHAPTER 19

# Budgeting and Controlling Operations

*If you think your business can fly without a budget, you may be in for a crash landing.*—Bob Weinstein

*Double-entry bookkeeping is one of the most beautiful discoveries of the human spirit . . . Without too much difficulty, we can recognize in double-entry bookkeeping the ideas of gravitation, or the circulation of the blood, and of the conservation of matter.*—Johann Wolfgang von Goethe, 1796

## LEARNING OBJECTIVES

After studying the material in this chapter, you will be able to:

1. Explain how managers exercise control in a small business.
2. Describe the characteristics of control systems.
3. Tell what a budget is, explain the different types, and tell how they are prepared and used.
4. Describe how budgetary control operates.
5. Discuss how information on actual performance can be obtained and used.
6. Explain how ratios can be used to evaluate a firm's financial condition.

# PROFILE

## M & I FORD: "WE DON'T HAVE A BUDGET"

Photo courtesy of Leon C. Megginson.

In the spring of 1980, James M. Wooten purchased M & I Ford, Inc., which was then primarily a distributor of Ford industrial engines. With Wooten serving as president, M & I Ford grew very rapidly and in 1986 moved from its inner-city location to a rural setting in Baldwin County, Alabama. After moving into this new 21,000-square-foot building, M & I added Ford tractors and farm equipment to its product line.

Expanding into new businesses while sticking with the basic blue of the Ford Power Products and Farm Equipment has been a way of life for James Wooten. He has been associated with Ford for over 40 years, beginning as a manager of a Power Products distributorship.

By the end of 1995, this rapidly growing company had a total inventory of about $1.8 million, with over $600,000 in parts, over $500,000 in engines, and over $550,000 in tractor inventory. The size of this inventory and the service necessary to support this line of equipment has proved to be a financial challenge to the relatively new and small business. However, it has developed a reputation for supplying reliable products and quick, dependable service in the south Alabama and northwest Florida areas.

Providing the engines for various types of logging equipment and forklifts is still a large part of M & I's business, even after moving to the more rural, farming environment. The reliability of the products and the stability of the company helped M & I enter the business of supplying engines to a local producer of aircraft de-icers. M & I has shown a 500 percent increase in sales and service over its short history. Wooten has learned during his long association with Ford and the tractor and equipment business that inventory control is very important.

When he was asked about the budgetary controls of M & I Ford, Wooten's first answer was, "We don't have a budget." Under further examination it was discovered that, while M & I does not have a formal full-year budget, it does use a form of rolling budget. A projection for the year ahead is made each month, based on the performance of that same month the previous year. Then Wooten and his partner, Bill Estes, adjust this projection based on local conditions facing area farmers and current economic conditions.

Wooten is proud that, even though he is involved in a very seasonal business, the firm has never had to lay off an employee. This is due to sound financial planning based on what to expect in the near future. Q

*Source:* Prepared by Dr. Walter Hollingsworth, University of Mobile.

The Profile illustrates what this text has stressed throughout—especially in the previous chapter—namely, the importance of controlling your firm's operations. In this chapter, we emphasize the nature, objectives, and methods of control, along with the design and use of budgets and the importance of budgetary control.

## What Is Involved in Control?

Profit planning alone is not enough! After developing plans for making a profit, you must design an operating system to implement those plans. As you will see, that system, in turn, must be controlled to see that plans are carried out and objectives, such as profit and customer satisfaction, are reached.

### The Role of Control

**Control** is the process of assuring that organizational goals are achieved.

We continually exercise **control** over our activities and are, in turn, subject to controls. We control the speed of the car we drive; signal lights control the traffic flow. We control our homes' thermostats, which keep the temperature within an acceptable range. Ropes in an airport terminal guide passengers to the next available clerk. Controls that have been established to help accomplish certain objectives are found everywhere.

As shown in Chapter 5, planning provides the guides and standards used in performing the activities necessary to achieve company goals. Then, a system of controls is installed to ensure that performance conforms to the organization's plans. Any deviation from these plans should point to a need for change—usually in performance, but sometimes in the plans themselves, as the following example shows.

G

> A Calgary, Alberta, machine-shop owner developed a special machine to produce wooden display stands for art objects. He arranged to display the machine at a trade show for art dealers in Vancouver. This new equipment was well received, and he received orders—but no down payments—for 10 machines. Returning home, he spent a year raising capital, setting up production, and producing the machines. By that time, his orders had evaporated, and he had 10 unsold machines and $27,500 (Canadian) of materials inventory. A system of controls to align delivery with customer needs and to obtain advance payments would have prevented the problem.

### Steps in Control

Q

The control process consists of five steps:

1. Setting up standards of performance.
2. Measuring actual performance.
3. Comparing actual performance with planned performance standards.
4. Deciding whether any deviations are excessive.
5. Determining the appropriate corrective action needed to equalize planned and actual performance.

These steps are performed in all control systems, even though the systems may be quite different. Later in this chapter, these five steps are covered in detail, but the first step should be strongly emphasized at this point.

### Setting Performance Standards

**Performance standards** tell employees—in advance—what level of performance is expected of them. They also measure how well employees meet expectations. Performance standards are usually stated in terms of (1) units consumed or produced or (2) price paid or charged. Some examples are *standard hours per unit* to produce a good or service, *miles per gallon* of gasoline used, and *price per unit* for purchased goods. There are many ways of developing these standards, such as intuition, past performance, careful measurement of activities, and comparison with other standards or averages.

**Performance standards** set—in advance—acceptable levels to which employee achievement should conform.

Once standards of performance are set, they should be communicated by means of written policies, rules, procedures, and/or statements of standards to the people responsible for performance. Standards are valuable for stimulating good performance, as well as in locating sources of inefficiencies.

## Characteristics of Effective Control Systems

Effective control systems should be: (1) timely, (2) cost-effective, (3) accurate, (4) quantifiable and measurable, and they should (5) indicate cause-and-effect relationships, (6) be the responsibility of one individual, and (7) be generally acceptable to those involved with them.[1]

### Timely

To keep control systems timely, checks should be made frequently and as quickly as feasible. You can't wait until the end of the year to find out whether sales meet expectations. Computer technology has speeded up the collection, flow, and use of information for control purposes.

### Cost-Effective

Any control system requires the time of a person or equipment, both costly. But the cost of a control system should be balanced against its value. Some systems are simple; others are more complex and costly. While you should try to reduce the time and paperwork needed to collect information, the system must do what it's supposed to do—control. A simple inspection of shelf stock may give enough information for inventory control without having a clerk provide a tabulated summary, but there are times when the extra cost of the tabulated summary may be justified.

### Accurate

If controls are to be useful, they must be reliable; to be reliable, they must be accurate. Thus, a basic tenet of any control system or procedure is to obtain accurate data and then use them correctly.

### Quantifiable and Measurable

Although quality must sometimes be judged subjectively, it's much easier to measure and control things that can be expressed in quantitative terms. (Estimates can also be useful.) The choice of measuring unit for control is vital. Sales can be measured in dollars, pounds, tons, barrels, gallons, grams, kilograms, meters, or other units.

### Indicative of Cause-and-Effect Relationships—When Possible

A report of increasing costs of a product may indicate the actual situation but not tell *why* costs increased. On the other hand, a report showing that the cost per unit of raw materials is higher than planned because a supplier raised prices not only pinpoints the problem but also identifies its cause.

*"I know we don't have an office in Alaska. That's why I'm transferring you there."*
Reprinted from *The Wall Street Journal* with permission of Cartoon Features Syndicate.

### The Responsibility of One Individual

Because you won't have time to control all activities yourself, you'll need to delegate the authority for some aspects of control to subordinates. As shown in Chapter 15, you should give those people authority, provide the necessary resources, and then hold them responsible for achieving the desired control.

### Acceptable to Those Involved with Them

People tend to resent controls, especially those they consider unnecessary, unreasonable, unfair, or excessive. They show their resentment by rebelling, that is, by finding a way to "beat the system." Therefore, if controls are to be accepted, it is important for those involved to clearly understand the purpose of the controls and believe they have an important stake in them.

## Using Budgets to Communicate Standards

A **budget** is a detailed statement of financial results expected for a given future period.

Performance standards serve as building blocks for the preparation of the **budget**, which is a detailed statement of financial results expected for a given future period. The time period may be a month, a quarter, or a year. The budget is expressed in monetary terms but may also include other measurements, such as number of units expected to be sold, units of inventory used, and labor hours worked. The budget should be based on realistic and attainable goals and should be applied to items needing control. In essence, budgets are the communication devices used to tell people responsible for performing tasks what is expected of them. This is especially true if one stops to consider that budgets are not only a financial tool but also a management tool. Instead of forcing a fit with your budget, ask employees for their input and recommendations. By including those employees directly involved, you will probably achieve both greater accuracy and increased motivation—employee empowerment.

## Types of Budgets

The three most important types of budgets are (1) capital budgets, (2) operating budgets, and (3) cash flow budgets.

**Q**

The **capital budget** reflects a business's plans for obtaining, expanding, and replacing physical facilities. It requires that management preplan the use of its limited financial resources for needed buildings, tools, equipment, and other facilities.

A **capital budget** plans expenditures for obtaining, expanding, and replacing physical facilities.

The **operating budget** is based on profit plans for the budget period (as shown in Chapter 18). It contains a forecast of the amounts and sources of sales income and the materials, labor, and other expenses that will be needed to achieve the sales forecast. Business experts do not always agree on the need for a specific management technique, but there is one thing they do agree on: the importance of a budget.[2]

An **operating budget** forecasts sales and allocates expenses for achieving them.

> For example, Ron Christy, associate director of the Center for Entrepreneurship at Wichita State University, advises start-up entrepreneurs that "a budget is an integral part of a company's planning process, the heart and soul [of it] being an accurate sales forecast."[3]

The **cash flow budget** is a forecast of expected cash receipts and necessary cash payments. It shows whether sufficient cash will be available for timely payment of budgeted expenses, capital equipment purchases, and other cash requirements. It also tells whether arrangements need to be made for external sources of cash, such as borrowing or owner investments. The lack of ready cash resources is the primary reason firms are forced into liquidation. Thus, effective forecasting is essential.[4]

A **cash flow budget** forecasts the amount of cash receipts and cash needed to pay expenses and make other purchases.

Neil Churchill, professor of entrepreneurship at Babson College, thinks the biggest crisis for small business is lack of cash. Therefore, dealing quickly with cash flow problems can mean the difference between success and failure. His tips on how small firms can cope with this problem are given in the case at the end of this chapter. Also, the SBA has a form called "Monthly Cash Flow Projection," with instructions for its use, which should be of help to you.

## Preparing the Operating Budget

The objective of the operating budget is to plan and control revenue and expenses to obtain desired profits. Therefore, the *sales budget* is planned first, giving consideration to the production and personnel functions. The *production budget* is then set to meet the sales budget plans. This budget includes production, purchasing, and personnel schedules and inventory levels. It includes units such as amount of materials and personnel time, as well as their costs. Next, a *personnel budget* is developed for the number of people needed to produce the product, any costs of training them, their pay and benefits, and other factors needed. The amount of detail in each of these budgets depends on its value to the company.

The sales budget is the most basic consideration. As you saw in Figure 18–3, step 2, the sales budget must be prepared before you can plan your production and personnel budgets. Because it was discussed in detail there, we'll not discuss it further in this chapter.

## Preparing the Cash Flow Budget

It surprises some small business owners that their businesses may be making profits and yet fail because they don't have the cash to pay current expenses. Therefore, provision must be made for adequate cash to pay bills when they are due and payable. This cash planning takes two forms: (1) the daily and weekly cash requirements for the normal operation of the business and (2) the maintenance of the proper balance for longer-term requirements.

### *Planning Daily and Weekly Cash Needs*

The first type of planning tends to be routine and is done on a daily or weekly basis.[5] For example, you may have a fairly constant income and outgo, which you can predict. Thus, you can establish policies for the amount of cash to maintain and set up procedures to control that level of cash. These routine demands represent a small part of the needed cash on hand, and they tend to remain fairly constant.

### *Planning Monthly Cash Needs*

The second type of planning requires a budget for, say, each month of the year. Payments for rent, payroll, purchases, and services require a regular outflow of cash. Insurance and taxes may require large payments a number of times each year. A special purchase, such as a truck, will place a heavy demand on cash. So, it takes planning to have the *right* amount of cash available when needed.

## Procedure for Planning Cash Needs

Figure 19–1 shows the form used by The Model Company to budget its cash for three months ahead. Each month is completed before the next month is shown. Items 1 through 4 give estimates of cash to be received. For example, The Model Company expects to receive 20 percent of its monthly sales in cash (item 1). A check of its accounts receivable budget can provide an estimate of the cash to be received in January (item 2). Other income (item 3) might come from interest on investments or the sale of surplus equipment. Item 4 shows the expected total cash to be received.

Expected cash payments, items 5 through 18, show the items The Model Company might list in its planned budget (see step 3 in Figure 18–3). Cash is often paid in the month during or after which the goods are received or the service is performed. Examples include payments for electricity and for material purchases. Some cash payments can be made at any one of several times. For example, payments on a new insurance policy can be set up to come due when other cash demands are low.

As shown in Figure 19–1, the cash budget shows when payments are to be made. For example, the cash balance on the first of January (item 20), plus the month's receipts (item 4), less the month's cash payments (item 19), provide an expected cash balance at the end of January as follows:

$$\begin{matrix}\text{Balance at}\\ \text{beginning of month}\end{matrix} + \begin{matrix}\text{Total cash}\\ \text{receipts}\end{matrix} - \begin{matrix}\text{Total cash}\\ \text{payment}\end{matrix} = \begin{matrix}\text{Balance at}\\ \text{end of month}\end{matrix}$$

## Figure 19–1

| THE MODEL COMPANY<br>Cash Budget<br>For Three Months Ending March 31, 19__ | | | | | | |
|---|---|---|---|---|---|---|
| | January | | February | | March | |
| Items that change cash level | Budget | Actual | Budget | Actual | Budget | Actual |
| **Expected cash receipts**<br>1. Cash sales | | | | | | |
| 2. Collections—accounts receivable | | | | | | |
| 3, Other income | | | | | | |
| 4. Total cash receipts | | | | | | |
| **Expected cash payments**<br>5. Goods purchases | | | | | | |
| 6. Salaries | | | | | | |
| 7. Utilities | | | | | | |
| 8. Depreciation | | | | | | |
| 9. Rent | | | | | | |
| 10. Building services | | | | | | |
| 11. Insurance | | | | | | |
| 12. Interest | | | | | | |
| 13. Office expenses | | | | | | |
| 14. Sales promotion | | | | | | |
| 15. Taxes and licenses | | | | | | |
| 16. Maintenance | | | | | | |
| 17. Delivery | | | | | | |
| 18. Miscellaneous | | | | | | |
| 19. Total cash payments | | | | | | |
| **Cash balance**<br>20. Cash balance—beginning of month | | | | | | |
| 21. Change—item 4 minus item 19 | | | | | | |
| 22. Cash balance—end of month | | | | | | |
| 23. Desired cash balance | | | | | | |
| 24. Short-term loans needed | | | | | | |
| 25. Cash available—end of month | | | | | | |
| **Cash for capital investments**<br>26. Cash available—line 25 | | | | | | |
| 27. Desired capital cash | | | | | | |
| 28. Long-term loans needed | | | | | | |

A negative balance will require an increase in cash receipts, a decrease in payments, or the floating of a short-term loan. A company should have a certain amount of cash to take care of contingencies. Item 23 shows the desired amount of cash needed as a minimum balance.

A three-month projection is probably the optimum time estimate for a cash budget. If sales are seasonal or you expect heavy demands on the cash balance, longer periods may be necessary.

### *Rationale for Cash Flow Budgeting*

The cash flow budget controls the flow of cash into your business so you can make needed payments and not maintain too high a cash balance. Many small business people, though, don't realize the importance of moving money through their systems as quickly and effectively as possible. Everything else being equal, the faster you can move your money and turn it over in sales and income, the greater the profits and the less the interest payments should be.

The use of electronic banking in small business has many advantages, as well as drawbacks.[6] Because the name of the game is using money most effectively to make more money, many small and medium-sized companies don't use electronic transfer of funds to pay their bills. Instead, they prefer to take maximum advantage of *float time,* which is the time it takes for a check to go to the receiver, be deposited, and clear the banks. Robert Anton of Sages Electric Supply Company in Hingham, Massachusetts, explains it this way: "We write checks one or two days before they are due. Then we have two days until the check clears the bank. With electronic transfer, we'd lose those two days of float."[7]

## Using Budgetary Control

**Budgetary control** is the system of budgets used to control a company's financial activities.

By itself, a budget is only a collection of figures or estimates that indicate plans. But when a system of budgets is used for control purposes, it becomes **budgetary control**. This process involves careful planning and control of all the company's financial activities. It includes frequent and close controls in the areas where poor performance most affects a company. Other areas may be controlled less often. For example, the cost of goods sold by The Model Company is planned for 63 percent of the sales dollar, and utilities are 1.34 percent of sales (see steps 2 and 3 in Figure 18–3). Cost of goods sold may be divided into material and labor and checked weekly, while utilities might be checked monthly.

### Controlling Credit, Collections, and Accounts Receivable

As shown in Chapter 12, extending credit increases the potential for sales—and losses from bad debts. You may have found that the amount of accounts receivable for The Model Company was large relative to its credit sales (see Figures 18–1 and 18–2). Waiting until the end of the year to find this out is potentially dangerous, since the average retailer loses more from slow accounts than from bad debts. Checks should be made often enough to identify customers who are slow in paying and to determine the reason for it.

In general, the longer an account goes unpaid, the less the chance of collection. A rule of thumb: You can expect to collect only a quarter of accounts over two years old, and none after five years.

The best control of bad-debt losses starts with investigating the customer's ability and willingness to pay and by providing clear statements of terms. Then, proctor past-due accounts each month so that each slow account is followed up promptly.

You may decide to write off some accounts as a bad-debt expense, while providing some incentive for earlier payment by slow-paying customers. Uncollectible accounts receivable create a misstatement of income and therefore an unjustified increase in business income tax liability. Unless there exists a reasonable expectation of collecting the account, a good rule is to *write off all accounts receivable over six months old at tax time.*

## Other Types of Budgetary Control

Many other types of budgetary control can be used to restrain a company's activities and investments. Any expense can increase gradually without the change being recognized. Have you noticed how fast the cash in your pockets disappears? You know you must control this, but it's very hard to do. Some call it being "nickeled and dimed to death." A small business has similar problems. Contributing to this creeping increase in the firm's costs may be such diverse situations as a clerk added to process increased paperwork, a solicitor asking for donations, a big customer requesting special delivery, an employee or union demand for additional services, rising energy costs, and inflation-increased costs. These costs must be controlled if the firm is to survive.

## Using Audits to Control the Budget

An **audit** of a company consists of a formalized, methodical study, examination, and/or review of its financial records, with the intent of verifying, analyzing, informing, and/or discovering opportunities for improvement.[8] There are three main types of audits: (1) financial, (2) internal, and (3) operations audits.

An **audit** is a formalized examination and/or review of a company's financial records.

In *financial auditing,* an outside certified public accountant (CPA) examines the records and provides financial statements of a company once a year. This audit furnishes the owner(s) with information on the company's financial status and operations and provides authenticity for anyone using the financial statements.

> CD-ROMs are now used to store information to send to auditors. The primary advantages are reduced storage space and ease of finding citations when doing research. The main disadvantages are that indexing of audit materials is time-consuming, and to keep current, new discs must be sent to auditors as frequently as every three months.[9]

*Internal auditing* is an independent appraisal of accounting, financial, and/or operations activities with the intention of measuring and evaluating the effectiveness of controls. Such audits function primarily as a service to management for the improvement of its financial controls.

An *operations audit* studies the basic operations of a company to identify problem areas. It may include studies of functional areas (marketing, finance, production, organization structure, personnel, and planning). Closely related to internal auditing, operations auditing emphasizes operations more than financial activities.

In summary, a company should be audited annually to ensure continued proper financial reporting. Bankers often require financial statements audited by a CPA before they will loan money. If any questions arise as to proper controls, inefficient operations, or lost opportunities, some form of internal or operations audit should also be considered.

## Obtaining and Using Performance Information

**Feedback** is the response a receiver gives through further communication with the sender of the message or some other person.

Information on actual performance comes through some form of **feedback**: observation, oral reports, written memos or reports, and/or other methods.

### Obtaining the Information

*Observation* will probably be most satisfying because you are at the scene of action and have direct control over the situation. However, this method is time-consuming, and you can't be in all places at one time. But you can justify using this method if your knowledge is needed, your presence may improve the work, or you are present for other purposes.

*Oral reports,* the most prevalent type of control used in small firms, are also time-consuming, but they provide two-way communication. Rumors are an informal form of feedback and can be useful so long as one can "separate the wheat from the chaff."

*Written memos or reports* are prepared when a record is needed or when many facts must be assembled. This type of feedback is costly unless the reports are the original records. A good record system, as will be discussed in Chapter 21, is a valuable aid, and it should be designed to be a ready source of reports. Using Technology to Succeed tells how to use portable computers to minimize this task.

### Comparing Actual Performance with Standards

The ability to keep costs low is a primary advantage of small businesses. To do this, an effective cost accounting system and cost-sensitive controls are vital. Information about actual performance, obtained through feedback, can be compared with predetermined standards to see if any changes are needed.

Simple, informal controls can usually be used by small firms. Performance measures are carried in the owner's head; comparisons are made as feedback is received, and decisions are made accordingly. This type of control follows the same steps as the more formal types of control needed when delegating authority. Examples of the use of standards were discussed in Chapter 17 and follow the same pattern as control through the use of budgets.

### Determining Causes of Poor Performance

Poor performance can result from many factors, both internal and external, including the following:

## USING TECHNOLOGY TO SUCCEED

### The Painless Way to Prepare Expense Reports

Dread returning from a business trip because you hate filling out expense reports? Just load *QuickXpense for Windows* software onto your portable computer—and handle it all on the road.

With Portable Software's program, you can store frequently used account numbers, airlines, hotels, and restaurants, then enter your expenses on the checkbook-style screen in any order. *QuickXpense* will separate food, lodging, and telephone expenses with the touch of a button, do all the math for you, and even notify you if you are reaching your credit card limit.

For the base price of $99.95, you can choose from 15 industry- and occupation-specific forms. Or have Portable Software create a custom version of your company's form for an additional $99.95.

*Source:* "Happy Trails," *Entrepreneur,* March 1995, p. 111. Reprinted with permission from *Entrepreneur Magazine* March 1995.

- Having the wrong objectives.
- Customers not buying the company's product.
- Poor scheduling of production or purchases.
- Theft and/or spoilage of products.
- Too many employees for the work being performed.
- Opportunities lost.
- Too many free services or donations.

*"Never mind the dramatics, Snodgrass-just read the treasurer's report!"*

Reprinted from *The Savant* (a SCORE publication), March 1989.

Once management isolates the true causes of the firm's poor performance, remedies can probably be found, as the following example shows.

> A small company oriented toward research and development (R&D) was providing customers with special R&D service without reimbursement for the thousands of dollars spent in this manner. After the policy was changed, the company's profits improved.

## Evaluating the Firm's Financial Condition

Having considered the financial structure and operations of a company, we now consider the methods of evaluating its financial condition. Look at Figures 18–1 and 18–2 (pages 444 and 447), which show the financial statements of The Model Company. Is the company in a good financial position? How can you tell? You can do so by establishing and analyzing **ratios**, which are relationships between two or more variables. For example, the amount of current assets needed depends on other conditions of a company, such as the size of its current liabilities. So the **current ratio**—current assets divided by current liabilities—shows how easily a company can pay its current obligations.

**Ratios** are relationships between two or more variables.

The **current ratio** is the amount of current assets divided by the amount of current liabilities.

Unfortunately, no standard figures have been determined for successes or failures, but reasonable evaluations are possible. Two sets of values can be used for evaluation purposes: (1) a comparison of the current value of your firm's operations with those of the past and (2) a comparison of your operations with those of similar businesses.

### Comparing Your Company's Current and Past Performance

A change in the value of selected ratios for a business indicates a change in its financial position. For example, suppose the current ratio for The Model Company has moved gradually from a value of 1:1 to its present value of 2.73:1 (which is $148,626 ÷ $54,408 in Figure 18–1). In the past, a ratio of 2:1 has been used as a rule of thumb for the current ratio. However, no one value of a ratio is favorable for all companies. For example, The Model Company is now better able to pay its current bills; but it has relatively fewer assets generating income. Careful analysis is needed to plan a course of action.

### Comparing Your Company with Similar Companies

Average values and ranges of values for the ratios are published for a variety of small to large companies. These provide a guide to what your competitors are doing. Suppose the current ratio for companies with assets of $300,000 or less is found to be 1.3:1, while The Model Company has a ratio of 2.73:1. Again, the company's ratio looks good, but it may be losing income by maintaining too many nonproductive assets in a period of high interest rates.

Another controlling indicator is individual line items—for example, individual salaries. In many cases, the owner of a small business is also the chairman, CEO, and president. Therefore, analysts should be careful to consider this fact when comparing industry averages to those of a small business. Small businesses do not necessarily contribute enough overhead dollars to be able to pay their CEO a huge salary.

Q

> For instance, a recent survey of CEO salaries found that small business CEOs make—on the average—less than 40 percent of the amount their counterparts in large organizations command. The study also indicated that small and midsized concerns use various means to tie salary to company performance, more often than do larger firms.[10]

## Some Important Ratios and Their Meanings

Some of the more important ratios, and the ways to compute them, are shown in Table 19–1. Spaces are provided for computing the ratios for The Model Company, using the data provided in Figures 18–1 and 18–2. Comparable figures for the industry are provided for comparative purposes.

These ratios will help you answer such questions as the following: (1) Are profits satisfactory? (2) Are assets productive? (3) Can the business pay its debts? (4) How good are the business's assets? and (5) Is your equity in the business satisfactory?

**Table 19–1** Financial Ratios

| Ratio | Formula | The model company | Industry average* |
|---|---|---|---|
| 1. Net profit to owner's equity | Net profit before taxes / Owners' equity | = ______ | 18.4% |
| 2. Net profit to net sales | Net profit before taxes / Net sales | = ______ | 3.1 |
| 3. Net sales to fixed assets | Net sales / Fixed assets | = ______ | 5.8 |
| 4. Net sales to owners' equity | Net sales / Owners' equity | = ______ | 7.5 |
| 5. Current ratio | Current assets / Current liabilities | = ______ | 1.3 |
| 6. Acid test (quick ratio) | Current assets − Inventory / Current liabilities | = ______ | 1.0 |
| 7. Receivables to working capital† | Accounts receivable / Working capital | = ______ | 1.2 |
| 8. Inventory to working capital | Inventory / Working capital | = ______ | 0.4 |
| 9. Collection period | Accounts receivable / Average daily credit sales‡ | = ______ | 43.0 days |
| 10. Net sales to inventory | Net sales / Inventory | = ______ | 22.0 |
| 11. Net sales to working capital | Net sales / Working capital | = ______ | 10.0 |
| 12. Long-term liabilities to working capital | Long-term liabilities / Working capital | = ______ | 0.7 |
| 13. Debt to owners' equity | Total liabilities / Owners' equity | = ______ | 1.6 |
| 14. Current liabilities to owners' equity | Current liabilities / Owners' equity | = ______ | 1.1 |
| 15. Fixed assets to owners' equity | Fixed assets / Owners' equity | = ______ | 1.2 |

*Times unless otherwise specified.
†Working capital = Current assets − Current liabilities.
‡If 80 percent of sales are on credit, average daily credit sales are: Annual sales ÷ 365 × 0.80 = ________.

## Are Profits Satisfactory?

Is the owner of The Model Company getting an adequate or reasonable return on investment? The ratio of *net profit (income) to owners' equity* (Ratio 1 in Table 19–1)—often called **return on equity (ROE)**—is used to evaluate this, but several other ratios should be considered in profit planning and decision making.

**Return on equity (ROE)** is the percentage of net profit your equity earns, before taxes.

How much return does your company make on its sales dollar? The ratio of *net profit (income) to net sales* (Ratio 2) provides this information. Suppose The Model Company now makes 4.3 cents profit (after taxes) per dollar of sales. Is the trend up or down? How does it compare with the experience of similar companies? If it is dropping, why? Costs may be increasing without an increase in price; competitors may be keeping their prices lower than The Model Company; it may be trying to obtain a large sales volume at the expense of profit. An increase in sales volume with the same investment and net profit per dollar of sales will increase ROE; a decrease will reduce ROE.

## Are Assets Productive?

Does your company obtain enough sales from its producing assets? The answer is reflected in the ratio of *net sales to fixed assets* (Ratio 3)—fixed assets representing the producing units of the company. So many variables exist (such as leasing instead of owning fixed assets) that this ratio can change with changes in policy.

Does your company have enough sales for the amount of investment? The ratio of *net sales to owners' equity* (Ratio 4) provides an answer. This ratio can be combined with the *net profit to net sales* ratio (Ratio 2) to obtain the *return on equity (ROE)* ratio (Ratio 1).

## Can the Business Pay Its Debts?

The **acid test (quick) ratio** is the ratio of current assets, less inventory, to current liabilities.

**Working capital** is the amount of current assets less current liabilities.

Can your business pay its current obligations? A number of ratios can help answer this question. As mentioned earlier, the best known is the *current ratio* (Ratio 5), which is the ratio of current assets to current liabilities. You may be making a good profit but not be able to pay your debts, for cash doesn't necessarily increase when you make a profit. The **acid test (quick) ratio** (Ratio 6), which is the ratio of current assets minus inventory to current liabilities, is an even more rigorous test of the ability to pay debts quickly.

Another check is obtained by using **working capital**, or current assets less current liabilities, as a basis.[11] Working capital is the margin of safety a company has in paying its current liabilities. The ratios of *accounts receivable to working capital* (Ratio 7) and *inventory to working capital* (8) provide an insight into the riskiness of the company's ability to make current payments.

## How Good Are the Business's Assets?

How good are your assets? Cash in hand is the best asset, but it doesn't produce any revenue. *Accounts receivable* represent what you will receive in cash from customers sometime in the future. However, as indicated earlier, the older an account, the greater the chance of loss. So the *collection period* ratio (Ratio 9), accounts receivable to average daily credit sales, provides a guide to their quality.

*Inventories* can be evaluated in about the same way as accounts receivable. Because goods in inventory become obsolete if not sold within a reasonable time, they should be turned over at least once during the year. The turnover rate is expressed by the ratio of *net sales to inventory* (Ratio 10). If your company turns its inventory over too slowly, you may be keeping obsolete or deteriorating goods. Too high a ratio may result from an inventory so low that it hurts production or from not providing satisfactory service to customers.

For example, Bayview Fabrics had a "going-out-of-business" sale recently; some of the inventory had been in the store 10 years or longer.

To get an idea of the support that you receive from your current assets, compute the ratio of *net sales to working capital* (Ratio 11). Accounts receivable and inventory should increase with an increase in sales, but not out of proportion. Increases in payroll and other expenses require a higher level of cash outflow. On the other hand, too low a ratio indicates available surplus working capital to service sales.

### Is Your Equity in the Business Satisfactory?

How much equity should you have in your company? Assets are financed either by equity investments or by the creation of debt—a liability. Thus, any retained earnings, which are part of your equity, can be used to increase your assets or decrease your liabilities. You can maintain a high level of equity, with a relatively low level of risk, or a relatively high level of liabilities with a higher expected return on equity, but greater risk.

Most small companies don't like to maintain a large amount of long-term debt, since the risk is too great. The ratios commonly used to check the company's source-of-funds relationships are *long-term liabilities to working capital* (Ratio 12), *debt to owners' equity* (Ratio 13), *current liabilities to owners' equity* (Ratio 14), and *fixed assets to owners' equity* (Ratio 15). An extremely high value for any of these puts your company in a risky situation. While a bad year will probably decrease your income, the obligation to pay continues. On the other hand, a very good year results in large returns to you.

### Ratios Are Interrelated

While each ratio indicates only part of the firm's position, the ratios overlap because a company is a complex system, and a change in the size of one of the accounts, such as cash, affects other values.

The financial ratios for the items on the profit and loss statement can be expressed in percentages of sales. This information is usually hard to obtain from competing small firms. High cost of goods sold as a percentage of sales income may indicate a poor choice of vendors, inefficient use of material or labor, or too low a price. A high percentage of salaries may indicate overstaffing of the company.

## WHAT YOU SHOULD HAVE LEARNED

**1.** After planning is done, a control system should be established to aid in carrying out the plans. The control process is composed of: (1) setting standards, (2) measuring, (3) comparing, (4) deciding, and (5) acting.

**2.** Controls should be timely, cost-effective, accurate, quantifiable and measurable, show cause-and-effect relationships, be administered by one individual, and be acceptable to those involved in their use. Before controls can be used, standards of performance must be set and communicated to those responsible for meeting them.

**3.** Budgets are used to communicate planned income and expenses during a given period in the future to people responsible for control. Small businesses need at least control of investments in fixed assets, of operations leading to profit, and of cash flow to meet current needs.

**4.** The budgetary control system is designed and used for control of financial affairs. Items in the financial statements should be checked frequently, with emphasis on where poor performance most affects the company.

An audit, which is a formalized, methodical examination of the company's financial records, can be used to control financial condition. Outside CPA firms usually perform financial audits, but internal audits can also be used to measure and evaluate the effectiveness of controls. A financial audit is needed at least once a year.

**5.** Information on actual performance can be obtained by observation or from oral or written reports. Actual performance can be compared to standards to determine the causes of poor performance.

**6.** Various ratios can be used to compare the company's current and past performance, as well as its performance relative to competitors. They can help determine whether profits are satisfactory, whether assets are productive, how able the company is to pay its debts, how good its assets are, and how much equity the owners have.

## QUESTIONS FOR DISCUSSION

1. What is control? List the steps in an effective control process.
2. What are some characteristics of effective control systems?
3. What are performance standards? Why are they used? List some examples.
4. What are some benefits of using a well-planned budget? Discuss the different types of budgets.
5. What is budgetary control? How can it be used by a small business?
6. How can auditing be used to control the budget of a small firm?
7. How can information about actual performance be obtained in a small firm?
8. Compute the ratios listed in Table 19–1 for The Model Company, using the data in Figures 18–1 and 18–2.
9. Evaluate the financial condition of The Model Company.
10. Evaluate your personal financial situation and operations, using material developed in this chapter.
11. Develop a budget for yourself for the coming year.

# CASE 19–1

## THEME RESTAURANTS

Photo courtesy of Gerald Byrd.

The latest craze in restaurants is *theme restaurants,* and they are booming everywhere from Boston to Bangkok to Berlin. The craze is believed to have started with the introduction of the Hard Rock Cafe in London, England; Hard Rock Cafes are now found in many of the major cities of the world, and the name is a much imitated and hotly defended trademark. Other theme restaurants include Planet Hollywood, the Harley-Davidson Cafe, and the Rainforest Cafe.

The success of these restaurants can be attributed to a perfect balance between novelty and food. Many of the theme restaurants such as the Hard Rock Cafe and Planet Hollywood look to celebrities to bring in the crowds. Both of these restaurants feature artifacts from past and present celebrities. And celebrities often visit the restaurant, making a diner's experience even more enjoyable. Planet Hollywood restaurants are designed to fit the culture and customs of the region. The Harley-Davidson Cafe attracts customers with vintage motorcycles, while the Rainforest Cafe mimics a peaceful outdoor setting.

But novelty alone is not enough. According to one restaurant owner, theme restaurants draw their initial crowd with the "wow," but if the food isn't good, they won't come back. To attract repeat customers, theme restaurants try to create menus that follow the image portrayed by the theme. The Rainforest Cafe, for example, offers food seasoned with spices from South America. The Harley-Davidson Cafe, on the other hand, has a general line of American fare with specialty drinks such as the Shock Absorber and Wheelie, while Planet Hollywood looks to its signature Chicken Crunch to bring people back.

To successfully provide the appropriate food, excellent service, and requested products to the customer, the manager must have specific guidelines for control. One area of need is found in the budgeting process. Many operations use a food cost percentage (FCP) as a guideline for quality control. FCP is the comparison of the sales price to the cost of the materials necessary for production. For instance, if the FCP is too low, it could indicate unacceptable ingredients; on the other hand, if the FCP is too high it might indicate inventory shrinkage (employee theft), purchasing fraud, and lack of appropriations skills, or indicate a need to raise prices. The individual operations can also compare these data to the industry average or to competitors' data to establish a yardstick by which to measure and compare. For example, according to the National Restaurant Association, in 1995 the average FCP was 29 and was expected to increase 0.8 percent in 1996.[12]

FCP is only one aspect of the budgeting process. Budgets should be realistic, flexible, and prepared for various time frames. For example, the capital budget that outlines major expansions and acquisitions may project five to seven years into the future, while the operating budget outlines the operating or fiscal cycle for one year.

How long will the theme cafe craze last? No one can say for sure, but Standard and Poor's Industry Surveys indicate that midscale sit-down restaurants are expected to benefit from increased demand.[13] U.S. customers spent about $215 million in bars and restaurants in 1995—or more than $400,000 every day on eateries. For a restaurant chain there are basically three ways to grow: build sales at existing sites, open new units, and make acquisitions.

Can these restaurants be successful over a long time? That is still to be seen, but getting people to come back is what separates successful theme restaurants from the nice ideas that won't turn heads or profits.

## QUESTIONS

1. Do you think theme restaurants are a permanent part of the restaurant industry? Why?
2. What suggestions would you make to improve the attraction of these restaurants?
3. Would you like to own and operate a theme restaurant? Why?

## CASE 19–2

## HOW TO DEAL WITH CASH FLOW PROBLEMS

Financial experts can suggest many ways to deal with cash flow problems. You, the small business owner, must remember to always make finances your number one priority. Constant monitoring is the best way to identify problems at the earliest possible stage. Many small business operators, and those who have at one time or another been involved with small business, will tell you that you can never spend too much effort or time on the financing aspect of operations. Key areas to watch include:

- Cash balances
- Accounts receivable turnover

- Accounts payable balance
- Interest payments and percentages
- Worker productivity
- Unnecessary expenses or excesses
- Obsolete assets and inventory
- Make sure that the people handling your cash are capable and honest.

## QUESTIONS

1. Which of the above can you quantify?
2. Which of the above do you think is the most important point? Why?
3. Which of the above can be compared to a budget? Which budget?
4. What other suggestions do you have? Explain.

## APPLICATION 19–1

Scott owns a small contracting business in a New England community. He has been experiencing a cash flow problem recently. To stop the cash drain, Scott decided to offer discounts to increase his business and improve cash flow.

Scott also noticed that his financial ratios are declining compared to those of his competitors. For example, his return on assets has declined, which adversely affected many aspects of his performance.

## QUESTIONS

1. Do you think offering discounts will increase cash flow? Why or why not?
2. What can Scott do to improve his performance?
3. What could be the reasons for the decline in his return on assets?
4. How can he improve his return on assets?

# ACTIVITY 19–1

*Direction:* Use information from this chapter to solve the puzzle below.

ACROSS

5 Acceptable performance levels

6 Formalized examination

7 Current assets less current liabilities

8 Planned expenditures for physical facilities

10 See 13 down

11 Process of assuring organizational goal achievement

12 Response

14 Quick ratio

DOWN

1 Allocates expenses

2 Forecast cash receipts and cash needed

3 Planning and control of financial activities

4 Relationships

8 Current assets divided by current expectations

9 Detailed statement of financial expectations

13 Percent of net profit equity before taxes

ACROSS 5 Performance standards 6 Audit 7 Working capital 8 Capital budget 10 Return on equity 11 Control 12 Feedback 14 Acid test ratio
DOWN 1 Operating budget 2 Cash flow budget 3 Budgetary control 4 Ratios 8 Current ratio 9 Budget 13 ROE

CHAPTER

# 20

# Taxes, Estate Planning, and Record Keeping

*Noah must have taken two taxes into the ark—and they have been multiplying ever since!*
—Will Rogers

*Our Constitution is in actual operation; everything appears to promise that it will last; but in this world nothing can be said to be certain but death and taxes.*—Benjamin Franklin

## LEARNING OBJECTIVES

After studying the material in this chapter, you will be able to:

1. Explain how the U.S. tax system operates.
2. Name and describe the taxes imposed on the small business itself.
3. Name and describe employment-related taxes.
4. Explain how the ownership of the business results in direct taxation of the owner.
5. Show how taxes may be reduced by careful estate planning.
6. Understand the importance of record keeping and tax reporting.

## PROFILE

# HAZEL MAH: "REPAYING DEBTS IS PART OF ASIAN CULTURE"

Photo courtesy of Owen Egan. Used by permission. 

In the highly volatile world of restaurants—where today's trendy eating place is tomorrow's leftovers—Hazel Mah stands out for her many achievements. Born in Taipei, Taiwan, she helped her mother raise four siblings after her father died when she was five years old.

As a young woman, she studied commerce at the university in Taiwan, working from 9 P.M. to 5 A.M. as a "coat check girl" in a hotel. She sent her paychecks to her mother.

After serving as a hostess at the Chinese pavilion at Montreal's Expo '67, she returned to Canada to live and worked for Montreal-based International Civil Aviation Authority

Following the birth of her two sons, she went to Concordia University, where she earned her second commerce degree. She then joined a Montreal laser-boat maker as comptroller. Later she became an accountant at the Montreal unit of a pharmaceuticals giant, American Home Products Corporation. She subsequently rose to the position of chief operating officer, which required much traveling.

Because she and her husband saw little of each other, she quit her job to go into business for herself. Her first attempt was a tiny restaurant in downtown Montreal. Discouraged by cockroaches and rats, she gave it up after nine months, but she used the experience she gained there to open Le Piment Rouge, which was immediately and exceedingly successful. She served Szechuan and Hunan cuisine to the rich and famous, including Mick Jagger and Liza Minelli.

Her success led her to open more restaurants in Montreal and Toronto, some of which met with less success. During the past five years, she has closed two of the Montreal restaurants, for a $1.4 million loss. Instead of declaring bankruptcy, however, she sold assets, drew on family money, and "repaid every penny . . . Repaying debts is very much a part of the Asian culture," she declared.

After 16 years in the restaurant business, Mah is thinking of winding down. She plans to sell a portion of Le Piment Rouge, which is partly owned by her husband, to members of the staff.

*Source:* Adapted from Ann Gibbon, "The Entrepreneurs: More Than a Hint of Red Pepper," *The Globe and Mail,* July 24, 1995, p. 1F.

**Taxes** are charges levied by a government on persons and groups subject to its jurisdiction.

The Profile dramatizes small business owners' need to lower their **expenses**, which include charges levied by a government on persons and groups subject to its jurisdiction. Therefore, we'll try to explain how the U.S. tax system affects small business.

## The U.S. Tax System

The U.S. tax system includes all the federal, state, and local tax systems, each of which has at least two parts. The first part is the system for determining what the taxes will be and who will pay them. The second part is the system for collecting the taxes.

### Who Pays the Taxes?

**Indirect taxes** are not paid by a person or firm, but by someone else.

**Direct taxes** are those paid directly to a taxing authority by the person or business against which they are levied.

Taxes can be either indirect or direct. **Indirect taxes** are paid not by the person or firm against which they're levied but by someone else. Since indirect taxes are part of the cost of doing business, they must either be added to the price of the firm's product or shifted backward to the persons who produced the product.

**Direct taxes** are paid directly to the taxing authority by the person or business against which they're levied.

> For example, the owner of a building containing a retail shop pays the property tax (direct) to the tax collector, but the amount of the tax is included in the rent paid by the retailer to the owner (indirect). In turn, the retailer includes this tax in the price a customer pays for the goods or services being sold (indirect).
>
> Also, as will be shown later, you pay tax on your income (direct) even though your employer may withhold it and send it to the tax collector for you.

Table 20–1 gives an overview of some selected taxes on small businesses. It shows the kind of tax, the taxpayer, the point of collection, and the governmental unit collecting the tax.

### How Taxes Affect Small Businesses

Taxes affect almost every aspect of operating a small business. First, there is the direct taxation of business income, whether in the form of sales taxes levied as a tax on business receipts or as an income tax on corporate profits.

Second, employers must withhold—and often match—a variety of employment-related taxes levied on their employees, such as federal and state taxes on personal wage and salary incomes, and federal taxes levied to fund the Social Security/Medicare system.

Third, owners must pay personal taxes on their salaries and other ownership-related income they withdraw from the business. And, if part of their wealth is invested outside the business, they face taxes on the investment income they receive.

Fourth, taxes are levied on the transfer of ownership of the business, so the owner must do careful estate planning to minimize the tax bite on an inheritance and as will be discussed later.

**Table 20–1** Selected Direct Taxes Paid by Small Firms

| Kind of tax | Taxpayer | Point of collection | Collecting agency |
|---|---|---|---|
| Corporate income tax | Corporations | Tax collectors | Internal Revenue Service<br>State revenue departments<br>City tax collectors |
| Corporate franchise tax (on capital stock) | Corporations | Tax collectors | States |
| Undistributed profits tax | Corporations | District IRS office | Internal Revenue Service |
| Customs duties | Corporations | Customs agents | U.S. Customs Service |
| Excise taxes | Businesses<br>Customers | Utility companies<br>Wholesale distributors<br>Tax collectors | Internal Revenue Service<br>State revenue departments |
| Motor fuel taxes | Businesses | Wholesale distributors | Internal Revenue Service<br>State revenue departments |
| Highway use tax | Motor transport businesses | Interstate Commerce Commission | Interstate Commerce Commission |
| Unemployment compensation | Employers | Internal Revenue Service | Internal Revenue Service |
| Licenses, permits | Businesses | Tax collectors | City tax collectors<br>State revenue departments<br>CAB, ICC, FCC, etc. |
| Old Age, Survivors, Disability, and Hospital Insurance (OASDHI) | Employers<br>Employees | Businesses | Internal Revenue Service |
| Sales and use taxes | Customers | Businesses | City and state revenue departments |
| Property tax | Businesses | Local tax collectors | City and county tax collectors |
| Inventory or floor tax | Businesses | Local and state tax collectors | City and county tax collectors |
| Public utility taxes | Utility companies | City, county, and state tax collectors | City, county, and state tax collectors |

*Note:* This table applies to direct taxes only; the shifting of taxes from the point of collection backward or forward is not considered.

Fifth, taxes also affect business decisions on other levels as well. For example, as shown in Chapter 4, the choice of the best form of business largely depends on the profitability of the business and the tax status of the owner(s).

Finally, the administrative cost of being a tax collector for the government is becoming burdensome. As shown in Table 20–1, it's the responsibility of the business owner to collect several taxes for the government by withholding sums from employees' paychecks or by adding the tax (such as sales or use taxes) to the price of products sold to customers. These administrative costs become very expensive in terms of personnel, time, and money.

## Get Professional Help!

Q

The purposes of this chapter are to make you aware of the current tax environment in which you will operate and to raise some basic tax issues important to every business owner. *It is very important for someone in every small firm to understand the tax system in order to take advantage of the opportunities available for deductions, credits, and tax savings.* Therefore, it is wise to hire a competent adviser on tax and other important financial matters. Table 20–2 shows the outside sources small business owners and managers most often turn to for advice.

While the U.S. Internal Revenue Service, as well as state and local agencies, will willingly help you determine whether you owe additional taxes, *they accept no responsibility for the accuracy of their advice.* The responsibility is yours, so get professional help! Also, you should familiarize yourself with the *Tax Guide for Small Business,*[1] which covers income, excise, and employment taxes for individuals, partnerships, and corporations. Remember, *the final responsibility for determining and paying your taxes rests with you.*

## Types of Taxes

Since it is impossible to discuss all the taxes you will have to pay, we've grouped them into four categories: (1) taxes imposed on the business itself, (2) employment-related taxes, (3) personal taxes that owners pay, and (4) estate taxes.

# Taxes Imposed on the Business

Numerous taxes are imposed on the small firm as a condition of its doing business. We've grouped these together as (1) taxes and fees paid for the "right" to operate the business; (2) excise and intangible property taxes; (3)

**Table 20–2** Sources of Outside Assistance for Small Businesses

| Source | Percentage using source | Importance rank of source |
|---|---|---|
| Accountant | 78% | 1 |
| Other business owners | 77 | 3 |
| Friends/relatives | 76 | 5 |
| Bankers | 72 | 2 |
| Lawyers | 63 | 6 |
| Books/manuals | 62 | 7 |
| Suppliers | 59 | 4 |
| Trade organizations | 47 | 9 |
| Seminars | 41 | 8 |
| Government sources | 33 | 10 |

*Source:* William G. Nickels, James M. McHugh, and Susan M. McHugh, *Understanding Business,* 4th ed. (Burr Ridge, IL: Richard D. Irwin Inc., 1996), p. 195.

state and local taxes on business receipts; and (4) federal, state, and local income taxes.

## Taxes and Fees Paid to Operate the Business

Some license fees, incorporation taxes, and the cost of permits must be paid before the business begins operating. Figure 20–1 lists some of the most important of these. These fees and permits are often intertwined with taxes, insurance, capital requirements, and the nature and scope of the business itself.

## Excise and Intangible Property Taxes

The federal government places an **excise tax** on many items such as tires for automobiles and other moving vehicles, cigars and cigarettes, and alcoholic beverages. Many states also apply such taxes. Taxes on intangibles such as copyrights, patents, and trademarks are another source of income for many states. Some states even have a tax on inventories in stock.

An **excise tax** is an additional tax on certain items imposed by the federal government.

**Figure 20–1** Selected Licenses, Permits, and Registrations Required of Small Firms

- *Business license (city, county, state).* Generally, you must apply for one or more business licenses. Often a tax identification number will be printed on your business license, and you'll use the number when filing various tax returns. Your state department of revenue can assist you in defining your reporting requirements.
- *Employer's federal ID number (SS–4)(federal).* A federal ID number is needed to identify an employer on all federal tax filings. Some local jurisdictions also require the federal ID number on various filings. The SS–4 form is available from the IRS.
- *Incorporation or partnership registration (state).* You should plan on using an attorney to assist with registering your company as a corporation or partnership. If it is a corporation, you'll also need articles of incorporation, bylaws, stock certificates, a corporate seal, and other items.
- *Trade name registration (state).* You'll need to register any trade names used in your business (e.g., if your legal incorporated name is Superior Semiconductors of California, Ltd., but you generally go by the name "Superior," you'll need to register your alternative name).
- *Zoning permits (city or county).* If your business constitutes an "alternative use" or other special case, you'll need appropriate zoning permits.
- *Building permits (city or county).* If you are doing any remodeling, construction, or related work, be sure you have the appropriate permits.
- *Mailing permits (federal).* Check with your post office about any bulk, presorted first class, business reply mail, or other mailing permits.
- *Professional registrations (state).* Generally, these are employee specific, such as registered engineer, notary public, and so forth. You may, however, wish to reimburse employees for any job-related expenses.

*Source: Building the High Technology Business: Positioning for Growth, Profitability, and Success* (New York: Peat Marwick Main & Co., 1988), p. 59.

## State and Local Sales and Use Taxes

A **use tax** is a tax on the use, consumption, or storage of goods within a taxing jurisdiction.

A **sales tax** is a tax added to the gross amount of the sale for goods sold within the taxing jurisdiction.

Many states and localities have sales and use taxes, which generate large sums. **Use taxes** are usually imposed on the use, consumption, or storage of goods within the taxing jurisdiction. This type of tax is often applied to automobiles and other moving vehicles that are purchased outside the jurisdiction and brought in for future use.

**Sales taxes** are usually based on the gross amount of the sale for goods sold within the taxing jurisdiction. A new trend is to tax sales in other locations as well, so you will need to check for your liability for sales taxes in those locations. Exemptions from sales taxes are often provided for goods to be resold and for machinery or equipment used exclusively in processing or assembling other goods. Service businesses are often totally exempt, as are drugs, unprepared foods, and agricultural products in certain states. For example, in Maryland, not only are drugs and food items in grocery stores exempt but also prepared foods under $1 (such as concession sales and restaurant orders such as a cup of coffee).

*One word of caution: Even if you do not collect these taxes from your customers or clients, you will probably be held liable for the full amount of the uncollected taxes.*

## Federal, State, and Local Income Taxes

Almost everyone, businesses and individuals alike, is concerned about income taxes—those presently in effect and those that may result from proposed changes. Because of the variation and complexities of the state and local laws, we'll discuss only the federal law.

From the very beginning of your business, you should have a qualified accountant to provide you with information and help you make important decisions, compile facts for accurate tax returns, and protect you from costly errors. There are three major decisions involving these taxes that you must make at the start, namely: (1) the method of handling your income and expenses, (2) the time period for paying taxes, and (3) the form of business to use.

## Accounting Method and Tax Period

Choosing the appropriate accounting method and the period of your business "year" can save your company unnecessary future tax liabilities.

The **accrual method** of accounting permits income and expenses to be charged during the period in which they occur.

As discussed in Chapter 21, using the **accrual method** of accounting, income and expenses are charged to the period in which they occur, regardless of whether the money has been received or paid. Thus, if you sell goods on credit and they have not been paid for, you still record them as income during the period when they were sold.

The accrual method *is required* for inventories that are significant in amount and for corporations and partnerships with annual gross receipts of more than $5 million.

Tax returns for your business may be prepared on a calendar- or fiscal-year basis. If the tax liability is calculated on a calendar-year basis, the tax return must be filed with the IRS no later than April 15 each year. However, to pick a more favorable filing month, many firms use a fiscal-year basis.

## How the Form of a Business Affects Its Taxes

As discussed in Chapter 4, the amount and methods of handling income taxes affect the choice of business form. Thus, you may choose a partnership or proprietorship rather than pay higher taxes on corporate income and then pay additional individual taxes on dividends.

U.S. tax laws permit some corporations to seek S corporation status. S corporation shareholders (individuals, estates, and certain trusts) are taxed at individual rates, which are lower than corporate rates; yet they still enjoy the legal protection that comes with corporate status.[2] But remember: S corporations do have disadvantages, such as restrictions on benefit plans and a limit of 35 shareholders.

Finally, as shown in Chapter 9, the use of employee stock ownership plans (ESOPs) can lead to tax advantages as well as cash flow advantages.

## Treatment of Federal Corporate Income Taxes

There are three questions small corporations need to answer when handling their federal income taxes:

1. What tax rate applies to the business?
2. What is taxable income?
3. What are deductible expenses?

### *What Tax Rate Applies*

As shown in Table 20–3, your tax rate will depend on the level of your taxable income. As you can see, the rate varies from 15 percent up to 38 percent.

### *What Is Taxable Income*

For income tax purposes, **taxable income** is defined as total revenues minus deductible expenses. While this definition sounds simple, problems arise in measuring both income and expenses. While the government has set the rules for calculating income for tax purposes, the firm may have discretion in reporting income to its stockholders.[3]

**Taxable income** is total revenues minus deductible expenses.

**Table 20–3** Federal Income Tax Rates for Corporations, 1995

| **If taxable income is:** | | **Tax is:** | |
|---|---|---|---|
| Over— | But not over— | | Of the amount over— |
| $0 | $50,000 | 15% | $0 |
| 50,000 | 75,000 | $7,500 + 25% | 50,000 |
| 75,000 | 100,000 | 13,750 + 34% | 75,000 |
| 100,000 | 335,000 | 22,250 + 39% | 100,000 |
| 335,000 | 10,000,000 | 113,900 + 34% | 335,000 |
| 10,000,000 | 15,000,000 | 3,400,000 + 35% | 10,000,000 |
| 15,000,000 | 18,333,333 | 5,150,000 + 38% | 15,000,000 |
| 18,333,333 | ....... | 35% | 0 |

*Source:* Excerpted from Hoffman, Raabe, Smith, and Maloney, *West's Federal Taxation: Corporations, Partnerships, Estates & Trusts*, 1996 edition (St. Paul, MN: West Publishing, 1996), inside front cover.

**Table 20–4** Major Categories of Tax-Exempt Organizations

| Type | Number |
|---|---|
| Religious, charitable | 599,745 |
| Social welfare | 140,143 |
| Fraternal beneficiary societies | 92,284 |
| Business leagues | 74,273 |
| Labor, agriculture | 68,144 |
| Social and recreation clubs | 65,273 |
| War veterans | 30,292 |

*Source:* Internal Revenue Service, as reported in John R. Emshwiller, "More Small Firms Complain about Tax-Exempt Rivals," *The Wall Street Journal,* August 8, 1995, p. B1. Reprinted with permission of THE WALL STREET JOURNAL, © 1995 Dow Jones & Company, Inc. All Rights Reserved Worldwide.

D

Many not-for-profit businesses generally pay little or no tax. Table 20–4 lists the number of each type of tax-exempt organization according to the Internal Revenue Service (IRS). The growing trend toward non-taxpaying competitors has become a source of concern, frustration, and anger on the part of some small business owners.

> There have been many lawsuits alleging misuse and/or abuse of not-for-profit status. No one seems to know how many of these abusers there are, but Congress was investigating the question as we went to press.[4]

## *What Expenses Are Deductible?*

Normally, deductions from income are classified as *cost of goods sold, selling expenses,* and *administrative expenses.* The following are the expenses most frequently deducted from revenue to determine net income: (1) administrative expenses; (2) depreciation; (3) inventory valuation; (4) interest payments; (5) business lunches, entertainment, and travel; and (6) automobile, home, and computer expenses.

*Administrative Expenses.* Administrative expenses are those needed to run a business office, such as rent, accounting and legal expenses, telephone and other utilities, dues and subscriptions to business publications, and professional services.

*Depreciation.* The determination of the amount of depreciation to be deducted from income tax each year is an example of the effect that different accounting procedures can have on income. For example, you can use cash-value depreciation or tax-related depreciation.[5]

*Cash value depreciation* is based on the difference between the cost of a piece of equipment and its fair market value at the end of a given time period. *Tax-related depreciation,* on the other hand, can be used to maximize the allowable deduction permitted by tax laws in figuring your net taxable income.

*Inventory Valuation.* Another accounting decision you must make is how to value inventory that is used during the year. The problem is particularly acute when prices are changing and/or when a firm holds inventory for long periods. The three methods of computing inventory used in production are (1) the *first-in, first-out (FIFO) method,* (2) the *last-in, first-out (LIFO) method,* and (3) the *average-cost method.* In general, when prices are rising, small firms tend to use the LIFO method to save taxes. For example, by switching to LIFO, the Chicago Heights Steel Company lowered its income taxes by 5 to 10 percent. The company still had a LIFO reserve at the end of 1995.[6]

*Interest Payments.* The U.S. Revenue Code favors the use of debt by small firms, since interest on debt is deductible while dividends paid to stockholders are not. The total amount of interest paid is deducted from revenue to find taxable income.

*Business Lunches, Entertainment, and Travel.* Meals are 100 percent deductible if business is discussed before, during, or after the meal. Otherwise, only 80 percent of the cost of business meals and entertainment expenses is deductible. To deduct any meals and entertainment expenses, you must keep records of: (1) whom you entertained, (2) the purpose of the meeting, (3) the amount spent, and (4) when and where it occurred.

Travel, food, and lodging expenses for out-of-town business travel are deductible if you stay overnight. Such costs as air, bus, or auto transportation; hotel cost; meals; taxes; and tips are deductible. The cost of seminars, conferences, and conventions is also deductible.

*Automobile, Home, and Computer Expenses.* Many small business owners operate out of their home, and certain expenses—such as automobile, utilities, repairs and maintenance, computer operations and maintenance, and home insurance and taxes—can be deducted from income taxes if they are business related. The deductions are quite beneficial to the owner, but there are restrictions, which are enforced. For an automobile, you can either deduct the actual cost of running your car or truck, or take a standard mileage rate. You must use actual costs if you use more than one vehicle in your business. In 1995, the standard mileage rate was 30 cents, in addition to parking fees and tolls.[7]

When you work out of your home, you can claim *actual business-related expenses,* such as telephone charges, business equipment and supplies, postage, photocopying, computer paper and magnetic media, and clerical and professional costs.[8] A deduction is also allowable for any portion of your home used "exclusively" and "regularly" as your principal place of business. For example, you can deduct expenses for taxes, insurance, and depreciation on that portion of your home that is used exclusively as your office. The IRS rule is this: The home must be the principal place of business for your trade or business, or a place of business used by clients, patients, or customers.[9]

The Deficit Reduction Act of 1984 limits the conditions under which computers used in the home can be deducted as business expenses. The simple test is this: If you use a home computer for business purposes over 50 percent of the time, it qualifies for the appropriate credits or deductions.

## Employment-Related Taxes

As shown in Chapter 14, employers are legally required to provide their employees with Social Security/Medicare, unemployment compensation insurance, and industrial insurance (commonly called workers' compensation). In addition, the employer must withhold taxes from employees for city, county, state, and federal income taxes. Also, since 1986, the Employee Retirement Income Security Act (ERISA) has required employers with 20 or more employees to continue health insurance programs for limited periods for employees who are terminated and for widows, divorced spouses, and dependents of employees.

### Income Tax Withholding

The IRS and certain states, counties, and localities require you to withhold the appropriate amount of income tax from each employee's earnings during each pay period. The amount of this pay-as-you-go tax depends on each employee's total wages, number of exemptions claimed on his or her withholding exemption certificate, marital status, and length of pay period. Each employee must complete and sign a W–4 form for your files.[10] See Figure 20–2 for the important employee-related forms needed by small firms.

The amount withheld from all employees must be submitted to the IRS, along with Form 941, on a quarterly basis. However, if $3,000 or more has been withheld from employees during the month, that deposit must be made within three banking days following the end of the month.

**Figure 20–2** Selected Employee-Related Tax Forms Needed by Small Firms

**Federal tax forms**

For companies with paid employees:

- Form SS–4, Application for Employer Identification Number
- Form W–2, Wage and Tax Statement
- Form W–2P, Statement for Recipients of Periodic Annuities, Pensions, Retired Pay, or IRA Payments
- Form W–3, Transmittal of Income and Tax Statements
- Form W–4, Employee's Withholding Allowance Certificate, for each employee
- Form 940, Employer's Annual Federal Unemployment (FUTA) Tax Return
- Form 941, Employer's Quarterly Federal Tax Return
- Form 1099–MISC, Statement for Recipients of Nonemployee Compensation

Income tax forms and schedules, which vary depending on your organizational status, type of income/losses, selection of various elections, etc.

ERISA Form 5500 series, depending on your status under the Employee Retirement Income Security Act

**State and local forms**

Income and/or business and occupation taxes

Industrial insurance ("workers' compensation")

Unemployment compensation insurance

Form W–2, Wage and Tax Statement, must be completed and mailed to each employee by January 31 immediately following the taxable year. Employers submitting 250 or more W–2 or W–2P forms must transmit those forms to the IRS by magnetic media.

### Social Security/Medicare Taxes

As shown in Chapter 14, the Social Security program requires employers to act as both tax collectors and taxpayers. Therefore, not only do you have to withhold a certain percentage of each employee's income, but you must also match it with a payment of your own. These taxes are technically for the Federal Insurance Contributions Act (FICA) but are usually referred to as the Social Security and Medicare taxes. In 1995, the employer had to collect 6.2 percent of an employee's total earnings—up to a maximum of $61,200—and then match that amount out of business revenues. Another 1.45 percent of the employee's total earnings must be collected for Medicare. These taxes are sent to the IRS each quarter, along with Federal Form 941, Employer's Quarterly Federal Tax Return. Self-employed people must pay the combined employee's and employer's amount of taxes, which amounted to 15.3 percent in 1996.

### Unemployment Compensation Insurance

Unemployment compensation insurance has two parts. First, a small basic amount is paid to the U.S. government as a **federal unemployment tax** to administer the program. A second part, which is determined by the states, builds up a fund from which employees are paid in case they are laid off. Federal Form 940, Employer's Annual Federal Unemployment (FUTA) Tax Return, must be filed annually. However, you may be liable for periodic tax deposits during the year.

The **federal unemployment tax** is a tax paid to the federal government to administer the unemployment insurance program.

### Workers' Compensation

Employers are required to provide industrial insurance for employees who are harmed or killed on the job. These payments are usually funded through an insurance program, with higher rates for higher-risk employees.

## Personal Taxes Paid by Owners

There are several ways of withdrawing cash from the business for your own use. Some of these are taxable to you, and some are taxable to the firm.

### Taxes on Amounts Withdrawn from the Business

First, salaries and bonuses received from the business are an expense to the business. But individual income taxes are also paid on those sums, at the rate

**Table 20–5** Federal Income Tax Rates for Individuals, 1995

**Single—Schedule X**

| If taxable income is: Over— | But not over— | The tax is: | Of the amount over— |
|---|---|---|---|
| $0 | $23,350 | 15% | $0 |
| 23,350 | 56,550 | $3,502.50 + 28% | 23,350 |
| 56,550 | 117,950 | 12,798.50 + 31% | 56,550 |
| 117,950 | 256,500 | 31,832.50 + 36% | 117,950 |
| 256,500 | ......... | 81,710.50 + 39.6% | 256,500 |

**Married filing separately—Schedule Y–2**

| If taxable income is: Over— | But not over— | The tax is: | Of the amount over— |
|---|---|---|---|
| $0 | $19,500 | 15% | $0 |
| 19,500 | 47,125 | $2,925.00 + 28% | 19,500 |
| 47,125 | 71,800 | 10,660.00 + 31% | 47,125 |
| 71,800 | 128,250 | 18,309.25 + 36% | 71,800 |
| 128,250 | ........ | 38,631.25 + 39.6% | 128,250 |

**Married filing jointly or qualifying widow(er)—Schedule Y–1**

| If taxable income is: Over— | But not over— | The tax is: | Of the amount over— |
|---|---|---|---|
| $0 | $39,000 | 15% | $0 |
| 39,000 | 94,250 | $5,850.00 + 28% | 39,000 |
| 94,250 | 143,600 | 12,798.50 + 31% | 94,250 |
| 143,600 | 256,500 | 31,832.50 + 36% | 143,600 |
| 256,500 | ........ | 81,710.50 + 39.6% | 256,500 |

*Source:* Hoffman, Smith, and Willis, *West's Federal Taxation: Individual Income Taxes,* 1996 edition (St. Paul, MN: West Publishing, 1996), inside back cover.

shown in Table 20–5. You can also withdraw cash from a proprietorship or partnership, and these sums are also taxable to you as an individual.

When owners receive a dividend from a corporation, it is taxed twice. The corporation pays taxes on it but gets no tax deduction, and owners must pay taxes at their individual rates.

Employees can also receive tax-free benefits from the business, which are deductible by the firm. These include such non-cash items as medical and legal reimbursements, tuition assistance, and other fringe benefits, as well as travel and entertainment expense reimbursements.

Finally, there are many pension and profit-sharing plans, the payment of which is deductible by the business. Payments from the plans are not taxable to the recipients until they are received.

### Taxes on Amounts Received from Sale of the Business

Usually, when entrepreneurs sell their companies, the contracts contain the following important provisions: (1) a noncompeting clause from the seller, (2) warranties and representations by the seller about the debt and liabilities of the company being sold, and (3) the purchase price—whether it is paid in cash, with a promissory note, in stock in the acquiring company, or with some combination.

Under the Tax Reform Act of 1986, most sales of assets are subject to double taxation, both corporate and personal, as shown earlier, so many transactions now involve the exchange of stock. Therefore, the form in which the proceeds are to be received can be as critical as the price and should be included in negotiations between buyer and seller, as the following example illustrates.

> Jan and Al Williams started Bio Clinic Co. in their garage in Southern California in the early 1960s. By 1985, it was so successful that Sunrise Medical Inc., a Torrance, California, company, offered $7.2 million for it. The Williamses, who were in the process of divorcing at the time, wanted different things when they negotiated the terms of sale. Jan wanted stock, since she expected the stock of Sunrise to grow in value. Al, on the other hand, wanted as much cash as possible. The parties worked out a compromise—$2 million in stock, and $5.2 million in cash.[11]

D

In summary, the tax consequences from the sale of a business are that either (1) you pay an immediate capital gains tax on cash payments from the sale, or (2) if you receive part of the payment in stock, you may be able to defer some taxes to a later period.

## Estate Planning to Minimize Taxes

No one wants to pay more taxes than necessary, especially when you're trying to pass the benefits of the estate you've built up over the years to your family. You want to reduce taxes to the minimum so they will get the maximum.

Since the owners frequently do not have the financial skills needed for estate planning, they should rely on a Certified Financial Planner (CFP). Figure 20–3 shows an ad sponsored by the Institute of Financial Planners, which emphasizes their qualifications and professionalism.

D Q

### Estate Planning Issues

For entrepreneurs, several issues are involved in estate planning. The most important of these are (1) trying to minimize taxes, (2) retaining control of the business, and (3) maintaining flexibility of operations.

**Figure 20–3**

*Source:* Institute of Certified Financial Planners, Denver, Colorado.

## Estate Planning Techniques

While it is impossible to avoid all estate taxes, the following can be used to minimize them: (1) family gifts, (2) family partnerships, (3) stock sales to family members, and (4) living trusts.

### *Make Gifts to Family*

One way to reduce taxes on your estate is to start giving parts of it to your family as soon as feasible. The rules are:

1. The gifts must be of "present interest," such as a direct cash gift, rather than a "future interest," such as gifts of cash that go into a trust fund for later distribution.
2. The first $10,000 in gifts made by each spouse to each person during the year is tax free.
3. Lifetime gifts of up to $300,000 by a single person, or $600,000 from a couple, are essentially tax free, so you can exhaust this privilege in 30 years.
4. The gifts, which are based on the fair market value of the property, can be cash, bonds, real estate, the family business, interest in a partnership, and so forth.[12]

### Establish Family Partnerships

You can form a family partnership to take money out of your company at lower tax rates. It must be a passive partnership that owns some type of property but does not operate the business. For example, a business owner may elect to set up a family limited partnership, retaining at least 2 percent of the stock as a general partner and giving the balance to the children as limited partners and subject only to gift tax. Because this type of tax shelter is very complex, don't try to do it by yourself; get professional help.

### Sell Stock to Children

You can also sell all or a part of your business to your children, but, like establishing a family partnership, this is complicated. First, your children will need a source of income to make nondeductible payments to you for the stock. And second, you must pay capital gains tax on the stock you sell. You may want to combine this method with gifts to the family. If the value of your business is greater than the amount you can give as gifts during your lifetime, you may want to give up to the maximum and sell stock for the rest of the business.

### Establish a Living Trust

A **living trust** resembles a will but, in addition to providing for distributing personal assets on the maker's death, it also contains instructions for managing those assets should the person become disabled.

A **living trust** is a legal document that provides for distributing and managing personal assets on the maker's death or disability.

Living trusts are more difficult to contest than wills. Also, the firm's assets can be immediately and privately distributed to the beneficiaries. Finally, a living trust can save on estate taxes.[13] For example, if you have a will for an estate valued at more than $600,000, federal estate taxes must be paid at your death, at a rate beginning at 37 percent. A living trust, on the other hand, lets you and your spouse pass on up to $1.2 million to your beneficiaries tax free. When one of you dies, the trust is divided into two separate trusts, each with a $600,000 estate tax exemption.

But there are some disadvantages of a living trust. First, when you establish such a trust, you must also change the title on all real estate, securities, and other assets to the name of your trust. From a legal point of view, you no longer own these properties, so there is nothing to probate when it becomes time to distribute your assets. You (and your spouse) may find it advantageous to become joint trustees in order to bypass the probate process. Finally, if you need to refinance your home or other assets, some lenders may refuse to refinance it if it is in a trust.

To avoid the many pitfalls of this device, hire an experienced trust attorney and select a capable and trustworthy trustee. Also, carefully weigh the benefits against the time and effort required.[14]

## Record Keeping and Tax Reporting

The importance of record keeping has been emphasized throughout this text. There are essentially two reasons for keeping business records. First, tax and

## USING TECHNOLOGY TO SUCCEED

### Computerized Record Keeping for Small Businesses

In the '90s most small businesses—especially start-ups—already use computers in one way or another. Probably the most universal application is for record keeping. Sole proprietors often start with a home computer, and many of them use personal finance software, such as Intuit's *Quicken*, Microsoft *Money*, or *Managing Your Money* from Block Financial Software, to keep business records. As a business grows, however, such programs may not be adequate.

"If you currently run your business using a personal finance program, you're not alone," says Theresa W. Carey, founder of Alta Business Solutions in Palo Alto, California. "Many small business owners gravitated to the friendlier interface of products such as Intuit's *Quicken*. But these products lack accounting basics such as invoices, accounts payable, and accounts receivable. And if you run your business from your home, you'll earn brownie points from the IRS by using a program that's completely separate from your personal finance program."

A wealth of small business accounting programs (in both Mac and PC formats) is available at a cost any business can afford (street prices range from about $50 to less than $200). These include *Peachtree Accounting*, *Peachtree First Accounting* (a starter program selling for less than $50), and *Peachtree Complete Accounting*, all from Peachtree Software; BestWare's *M.Y.O.B. Accounting; DacEasy* (from DacEasy, Inc); Automatic Software's *Big Business;* 4Home Productions' *Simply Accounting;* and numerous others. Business owners who are already using *Quicken* for their personal financial record keeping may find it especially easy to migrate to Intuit's *Quickbooks* and *Quickbooks Pro*. These programs also have the added advantage that they can easily import data from *Quicken* and export data to the popular *TurboTax* and *MacInTax* income tax software programs.

When it comes time to do those tax returns, many personal tax programs are available that are adequate to handle small sole proprietorships. These include Block Financial Software's *TaxCut* and 4Home Productions' *Simply Tax*. Street prices for these programs (which must be purchased annually) range from $25 to $50. Intuit's *TurboTax* is also available in a *"Business 1040"* CD-ROM version (for about $70) that includes an on-screen *Tax Savvy for Small Business* tax guide, small business–specific tax advice, planning, and help; and all major business IRS publications on-screen.

*Source:* Adapted from Theresa W. Carey, "Bean Counting Made Easy," *PC World*, September 1995, pp. 165–78; and various mail-order software catalogs. Reprinted with the permission of *PC World Communications, Inc.*

other records are required by law; second, they help you manage your business better. While the IRS allows some flexibility in records systems, it does require that records be kept, be complete, and be separate for each individual business.

### Maintaining Tax Records

When you start your business, as shown in Chapter 5, you should set up the kind of records system most suitable for your particular operations. Also, keep in mind that the records should be readily available to compute, record, and pay taxes as they become due and payable. As shown in Using Technology to Succeed, a variety of accounting software is available to help small businesses maintain the necessary records.

**Table 20–6** List of Selected Tax-Reporting Periods

| Tax | Reporting period |
|---|---|
| Estimated income tax deposits | Quarterly |
| Income tax withholding deposits | Quarterly |
| FICA tax deposits | Quarterly |
| FUTA tax deposits | Quarterly |
| Income tax | Annually |
| Income tax withholding | Annually |
| Self-employment tax | Annually |
| FICA (Social Security) tax | Annually |
| FUTA (unemployment) tax | Annually |

*Note:* Even though tax deposits are made quarterly, a return (which reports income and the bases for calculating the tax due) is filed only annually. Reporting periods and payment dates differ. Please consult Circular E, *Employers' Tax Guide,* for instructions.

The IRS requires that tax records be retained for up to three years after a tax return is filed. If there's reason to suspect fraud, it may look at your tax records for longer periods. Fraud may be suspected when deductions seem excessive or appear to have been claimed with the intent to defraud the government out of tax revenues, or when income seems unnaturally low. While the IRS has up to three years to look at your records, you also have up to three years from the date of filing to straighten out tax matters as the circumstances demand. If changes are needed, you may file a one-page amended return on Form 1040X.

## Reporting Your Taxes

All federal, state, and local governments having jurisdiction over your business require that you submit a written monthly, quarterly, or annual report on income. Since the requirements vary so much for state and local agencies, we will list only the federal reporting requirements, which are shown in Table 20–6.

## WHAT YOU SHOULD HAVE LEARNED

**1.** The U.S. tax system is very complex. Federal, state, and local governments impose taxes directly on individuals and businesses and require them to collect taxes from others. The four types of business taxes are *(a)* those imposed on the business itself, *(b)* employment-related taxes, *(c)* personal taxes paid by the owners, and *(d)* estate taxes.

**2.** Taxes imposed on the business itself include *(a)* taxes paid for the right to operate the business, *(b)* excise and property taxes, *(c)* taxes on business receipts, and *(d)* income taxes.

Taxes paid to operate the business include fees paid for a business permit or license, state incorporation or partnership registration, zoning variances, building permits, mailing permits, occupational or professional registration, and other such licenses.

Excise and intangible property taxes are paid on such items as tires; cigars, cigarettes, and alcoholic beverages; and intangibles such as copyrights, patents, and trademarks. Sales and use taxes are imposed on the purchase, use, consumption, or storage of goods. Exceptions are often made for service businesses, drugs, and industrial goods. The three important questions regarding the federal corporate income tax are *(a)* What tax rates apply to your business? *(b)* What is income? and *(c)* What are deductible expenses?

**3.** You are required to provide Social Security, Medicare, unemployment insurance, and workers' compensation for your employees, and to withhold taxes from them. Each employee must complete a W–4 form. The withheld amounts must be submitted to the IRS periodically. A Form W–2 must be mailed to each employee by January 31 of the following year. Unemployment insurance payments build up a fund from which a state can pay employees if they are laid off.

**4.** The owners must also pay taxes on funds withdrawn from the business by *(a)* receiving salaries or bonuses, *(b)* withdrawing sums from a proprietorship or partnership, *(c)* receiving dividends from a corporation, *(d)* receiving tax-free benefits from the business, and *(e)* receiving pension and profit-sharing benefits. When you sell the business, you must pay taxes on the capital gain received.

**5.** Estate planning can be used to minimize taxes by *(a)* giving gifts from the business to the family, *(b)* forming family partnerships, *(c)* selling stock to family members, and *(d)* setting up a living trust. All have advantages and disadvantages, so get professional help in using them.

**6.** From the time you begin your business, you should maintain complete and accurate tax records. For tax purposes, records must be retained up to three years after the date of filing the return. If for any reason the IRS suspects fraud, there is no time limitation.

## QUESTIONS FOR DISCUSSION

1. What is included in the U.S. tax system?
2. Name the three main types of taxes a small firm must pay.
3. Name and explain at least five taxes a firm must pay for the right to do business.

4. How does the form of a business affect its taxes?
5. Name and explain the three types of employment-related taxes.
6. How can funds be withdrawn from a small business, and how are they treated for tax purposes?
7. What are the three main issues in estate planning? What are the ways a small business owner can reduce estate taxes?
8. Why are records so important for tax purposes?

# CASE 20–1

## HOW TO REDUCE YOUR BUSINESS TAX BURDENS

A business can make several strategic moves at year-end to reduce its tax burden. The first consideration is choosing the right form for the business. Many small firms use the S corporation form because it can be taxed similarly to a proprietorship or partnership. For an S corporation, the business income or loss is reported directly by the shareholders, not by the business. Also, the business is not subject to the personal holding company or accumulated earnings penalty taxes that apply to regular corporations. An existing corporation can elect S corporation status; however, it may have to pay tax on income reported in the 10-year period following the conversion if the income is attributable to a "built-in gain."

Next, there are several year-end tax-saving moves that involve income shifting. Perhaps the most time-honored year-end planning strategy involves shifting income and expenses between years. If it appears that your income will be high this year, shift some of your income to future years or prepay some expenses for future years.

Another way to reduce the business tax burden is to keep it in the family. Having your business employ and make salary payments to your children shifts income from you to them, where it is subject to little or no income tax. Of course, services must actually be performed by the children, and their salaries must be reasonable and well documented.

## QUESTIONS

1. What do you think of these methods?
2. Which one would you favor?
3. Can you think of others?

# APPLICATION 20–1

Jack Howell and his wife own and operate a small business, Howell's Roofing, out of the spare bedroom of their home. Jack spends most of his day doing roofing work on the job site, while his wife answers phone calls—when she is at home. The Howells deduct their spare bedroom and Jack's personal vehicle as business expenses on their income tax.

Jack's business setup has worked well for him so far, but he is ready to expand the business outside of their home. He feels comfortable with the market demand for his services. Jack realizes he will incur more expenses in the beginning. However, if he can attract more customers with a more professional image, the added revenue should cover the added cost.

## QUESTIONS

1. What are some expenses Jack might incur that he doesn't have now?
2. What are some things Jack may have to do to become profitable?

# ACTIVITY 20–1

Directions: Solve the clues below to fill in the puzzle using terms from this chapter.

T Added to the gross amount of a sale

I Paid by someone else

E Total revenues minus deductible expenses

U Placed on use, consumption, or storage

P Paid to administer unemployment insurance program

T Used in case of death or disability

A Permits income and expenses to be charged

X Levied by government on subjects in its jurisdiction

E Paid directly

S Additional tax imposed by federal government

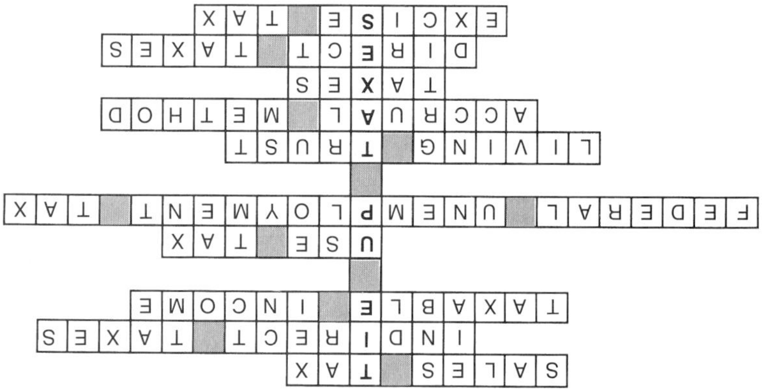

CHAPTER 21

# Using Computer Technology and Management Information Systems*

*Technology* enables *me to change, and technology* forces *me to change.*—David H. Freeman

*Farms, factories, even tiny one-person businesses are reaping the benefits—and surviving the frustrations—of computerization.*—Jared Taylor, business consultant

## LEARNING OBJECTIVES

After studying the material in this chapter, you will be able to:

1. Explain the importance of information to a small business, and state what information is needed.
2. Discuss the need for—and how to choose—management information systems (MISs) for a small business.
3. Describe the growing role of computers in business.
4. Explain how the microcomputer (PC) has affected small business.
5. Discuss the origin, growth, and uses of the Internet.
6. Explain some potential problems with computer technology in small business.
7. Discuss how accounting is part of a small business's management information system.

*The authors thank Dr. Charles E. Scott of Loyola College (Baltimore, Maryland) for his original contributions to this chapter and Dr. Walter H. Hollingsworth of the University of Mobile for his revision of it.

## PROFILE

# TOM WILLIAMS IS OFF TO A HEADY START IN COMPUTERS

Imagine that you have a house by a lake, own a thriving business in the hot new world of technology, and work with recording artists such as Eric Clapton. Yet you still have time to hang out with friends, become one of Blockbuster's favorite customers, read a lot, and play the cello. Does this sound to you like the ideal life? And imagine having all that by the time you're only 16!

Photo by John Makely.

Tom Williams, as the owner of White Sands Software and as marketing/technical consultant for *Head Tripp*, has it all—and he *is* only 16. He produced an Enhanced CD—music plus multimedia—featuring 10 artists from Polydor/A&M Records, which recently premiered in Tower Records stores in New York, Los Angeles, Seattle, Chicago, Boston, and Austin, Texas.

D

The Enhanced CD, being demonstrated at in-store Macintosh computer kiosks, features audio and video from Clapton, the Velvet Underground, and such new artists as Gene, Fig Dish, Sensor, Shed Seven, and 8 Story Window. Q

The *Head Tripp* promotion is also on the World Wide Web (http://www.polydor-atlas.com/polydor)and America Online (the key word is "Tower") and via Apple (on the Web at http://quicktime.apple.com). A downloadable screen saver will be available on the Polydor site.

This is pretty heady stuff for a promotion launched by a youth too young to drive. Williams, who has the poise and presence of a corporate vice president, explains his success by saying, "My first introduction to the multimedia business was at age 11, when my family got a computer at home. I was looking for the games. All I could find was a word processor and a thing called Hypercard, a basic programming environment. As the summer progressed, I started to teach myself Hypercard and make simple games for myself."

When he entered the seventh grade that fall, Williams discovered that his new school had a color Macintosh with a music keyboard, a scanner, and other hardware that enabled him and his friends to create more elaborate games. "It was not like the nerdy thing to do," he hastens to add. "We were all on the sports teams as well."

While Williams admits that the games they created were "rip-offs of TV shows and whatever" the entrepreneurial bug had bitten him. His classmates bought floppy disks and labels from a local store and began selling their games "like we were selling drugs." Total gross sales for the first venture were $100, "which in grade seven was so much money." The games improved as the skill level of the programming increased. So Williams founded White Sands Software in 1993.

Then, in July 1994, Williams, who had himself legally declared an adult, moved from his British Columbia home to Cupertino, California. There he began working as an intern for a San Francisco multimedia company to learn the business ropes. In November, Apple asked if he'd be a consultant in its interactive music development, which led him to the *Head Tripp* assignment.

"From an early age, even to be associated with Apple was a dream come true," he says. His youth was a plus, for he fit into a large demographic group that Apple was wooing. "They could get a feel [from me] for what makes a 'cool' Enhanced CD, what tools were needed."

Although he consults for Apple, Williams is still developing White Sands, where his mother is chairman of the board. He is in the process of creating screen savers, Web sites, and Enhanced CDs. The company has also been "talking to Capitol Records about potential work, [and] we have a lot of corporate clients."

He's also developing an edutainment CD-ROM, titled *When Mother Nature Is Missing.* It's based on a concept learned at the dinner table when he was two years old. His mother would mix food he didn't like with food he did like, so he couldn't tell the difference. "If you take that same concept to edutainment, [kids will have] so much fun they [won't] realize they're learning."

While an advanced placement test got him out of high school, he doesn't rule out college. He says he will "have to get a new set of goals, because a lot of them I have already accomplished. I consider myself very fortunate that I wake up every morning and I like what I do."

*Source:* Adapted from Bruce Haring, "Teen Off to a Heady Start in Computer Business," *USA Today,* October 31, 1995, p. 8D. 

The Profile illustrates the explosive nature of computers and related technologies. It also shows the great diversity now being found in small businesses. The computer industry may have been started by more mature individuals, such as J. Presper Eckert, Jr., and John Mauchly (developers of the first commercially successful electronic computer—the Univac), but it is bright, brash, and adventurous young people who are developing today's advancing technology. Yet older entrepreneurs and workers are learning to cope.

This chapter is designed to show how computers and related technologies are revolutionizing small business operations. However, other systems—such as accounting, financial, and management information systems—are still needed for successful operations.

## Importance of Information

Have you ever considered how many records you keep or generate? You probably have in your possession at least a driver's license, credit card(s), student ID, Social Security card, and checkbook. Without these items, you would find it difficult to transact much of your daily business. Also, whenever you use one of these items, records (or entries in the records) are generated.

*"I suppose you're just going to sit there and let this computer craze sweep right by you?"*

> When you use a credit card, it generates a sales or credit slip, a monthly statement, and a record of payment. You use the statement to write a check and to deduct the amount from your bank balance. All the while, you keep some information (such as your Social Security number) in your head to save time in filling out forms.

As you can see, information is a most important resource for a small business, as well as for a person. It should help provide answers to such questions as: Is the product selling properly? Will the cash flow be adequate? Are the employees paid the correct amounts and on time, and are the employment taxes handled properly?

Obviously, these questions cannot be answered without the appropriate data. Just as your personal records provide data for your personal decisions, your company must also collect data for its operations.

Efficient accounting and information systems are needed by small firms—as well as large ones—to convert data to information so management can use it to operate successfully. And, as you will see, many of these information systems are now computerized—even in many small businesses.

## Elements of a Management Information System

As shown in Chapter 16, all types of systems involve the same basic elements: inputs, processes, and outputs. A **management information system (MIS)** is designed to collect, record, process, report, and/or convert data into a form suitable for management's use. For example, as will be shown later, an accounting system records and processes data and produces reports. A system may be entirely manual or, at the other extreme, almost entirely machine or computer operated.

A **management information system (MIS)** collects, records, processes, reports, and/or converts data into a usable form.

All these systems start with inputs, process them, and furnish outputs. Whether or not computers are used, an organized MIS is necessary for the efficient operation of any business. Figure 21–1 diagrams a system that can be manually or computer operated or can use some combination of both. Defining the needs of each part of a business for information and its processing and use is the first step in designing an information system.

## What Information Is Needed?

Everyone in the small firm should consider the questions "What do I need to know to do my job better?" and "What information do I have that will help others do their jobs better?" The accumulation of these pieces of information, with analysis of what data are reasonably available, is the initial step in forming an information system. Emphasis should be on developing a system adapted to present needs—yet flexible enough to accommodate future changes. An obvious but often overlooked bit of advice: *Even the best information system is of no value if it is not used—and used properly.*

### *Purposes for Which Information Is Used*

In determining what information is needed, you should ask yourself why you want it. The usual answers are:

- *To plan a course of action,* such as deciding the number of items to purchase, the number of salespeople to hire, and/or the amount of accounts receivable to expect.
- *To meet obligations,* such as repaying borrowed money.
- *To control activities,* such as assuring that ordered materials have arrived.
- *To satisfy government regulations,* such as conforming to safety, employment, and ethical standards.
- *To evaluate performance.*

In addition to determining the information needed, you must know how to use it. This involves classifying it into a usable form and establishing systems and procedures to assure the availability of critical information.

### *Examples of Needed Information*

The kinds of information you might need are too numerous to discuss, but the most important are (1) records of service provided to customers and (2) records of services performed for the business.

*Services to customers* provide revenue in the form of cash, checks, or promises to pay. Figure 21–1 shows a diagram of a system for recording sales of goods or services. Both real-time and delayed transactions occur in this system. For example, when products are sold, sales slips are made out to give to customers. Later, the slips are used as daily summaries of sales, sales taxes, and so forth, which are then recorded in journals. Unlike direct sales, rental of items requires additional transactions.

*Services performed for the business* must also be recorded. Goods sold to, or services performed for, a firm are its expenses of doing business, and payments must be made for them. In addition, payments are made to increase assets and reduce obligations.

**Figure 21–1** Accounting for Sales

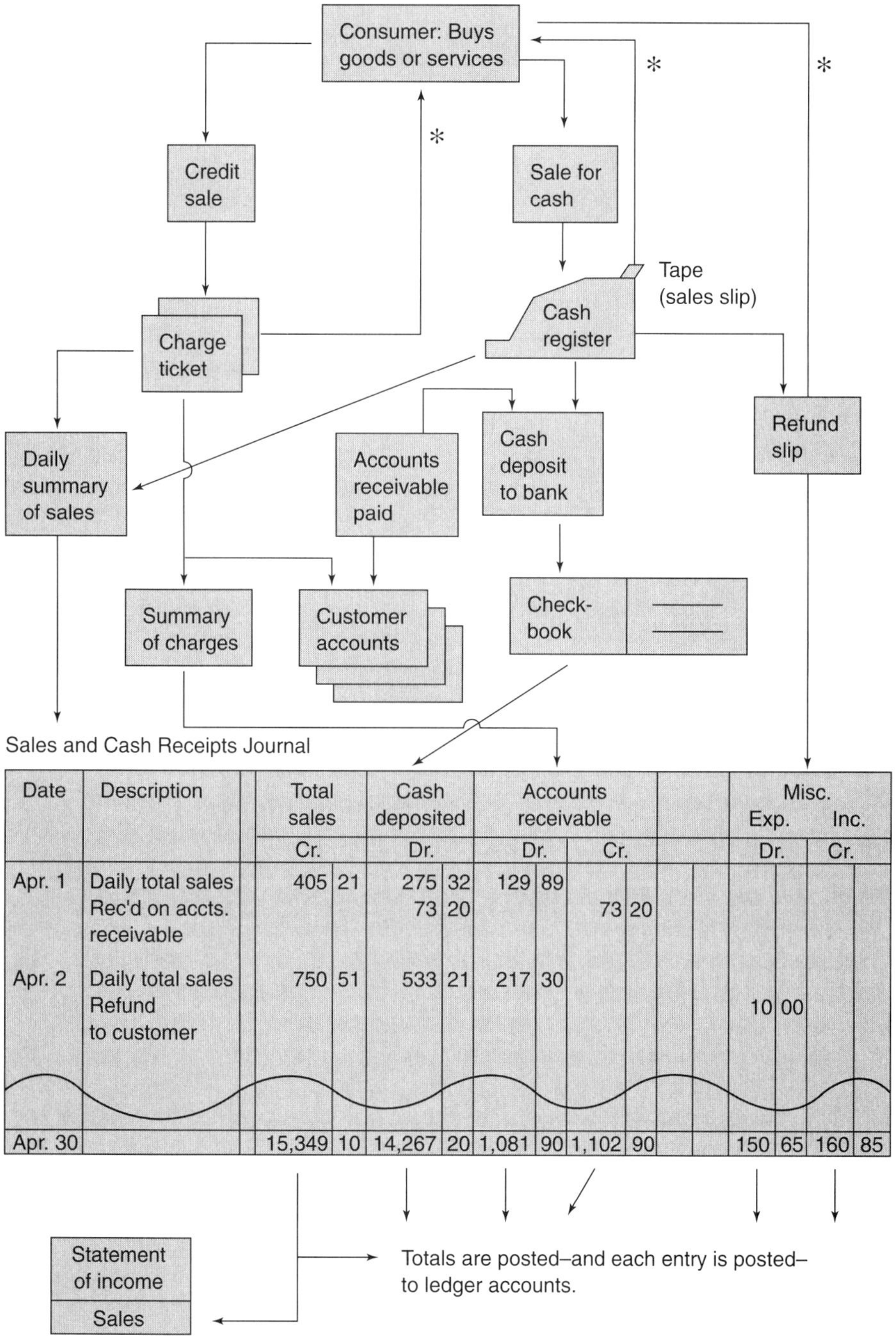


| Date | Description | Total sales Cr. | Cash deposited Dr. | Accounts receivable Dr. | Accounts receivable Cr. | | Misc. Exp. Dr. | Misc. Inc. Cr. |
|---|---|---|---|---|---|---|---|---|
| Apr. 1 | Daily total sales | 405 21 | 275 32 | 129 89 | | | | |
| | Rec'd on accts. receivable | | 73 20 | | 73 20 | | | |
| Apr. 2 | Daily total sales | 750 51 | 533 21 | 217 30 | | | | |
| | Refund to customer | | | | | | 10 00 | |
| Apr. 30 | | 15,349 10 | 14,267 20 | 1,081 90 | 1,102 90 | | 150 65 | 160 85 |

*Copy to customer

Even very small businesses need formal systems for keeping records. In the past, very simple record-keeping systems such as manila folders, shoe boxes, and entries in a checkbook have been used. These methods are simple and easy to understand but in many cases do not meet the demands of today's competitive marketplace.

## Timing of Information Flows

Data from activities may be needed (1) at the time of transaction (real-time processing) or (2) after transactions accumulate (batch processing). For example, as shown in Figure 21–1, a customer is given a sales slip on completion of the sale, which is *real-time processing*. An MIS can be designed to take care of such immediate feedback. For example, portable computers, modems, mobile phones, electronic wands or scanners, and radios can be used to collect and provide information quickly, as in the following example.

> Ernest Gore, an architect, visited Jean Soor, who was interested in building a house. During the discussion, Ernest opened his laptop computer and laid out the house plan as Jean described her ideas. Several times, they discussed "what ifs," and he made the changes to show their effects. He left with the plans well developed. Ernest attributes a great deal of his success in making the sale and satisfying the customer to this type of rapid feedback.

*Batch processing* is done after more than one transaction has occurred, such as at the end of an hour or at the end of the day, as shown in Figure 21–1, when the daily sales are summarized. Slower turnaround may meet the requirements of the system and be less expensive, so you should balance the speed and convenience of real-time processing with the economy of batch processing, as the following example illustrates.

> A chef in a restaurant is usually a highly skilled individual who schedules, cooks, and assembles meals. The server is a less skilled person who uses an information system to transmit information from the customer to the producer. Many restaurants use turnstiles for placing orders. First, the orders are written. Then the slips are clipped to a turnstile that the chef can turn to read the order. The slips on the turnstile serve to schedule orders in sequence, and they may also become the customer's bill. The turnstile causes a brief delay in the MIS but is simple and effective. Also, being impersonal, it does not make the higher-status chef seem to be taking orders from the lower-status servers.

Now, though, many restaurants, especially fast-food chains, are using computers to convey orders from servers or front-counter order takers to the kitchen staff. In addition to eliminating bottlenecks in taking orders, these systems can also reduce waste and labor costs in food preparation and even serve as a marketing tool by tracking customers and their eating habits.

> For example, the assistant manager of a Boston Market Restaurant in San Francisco uses a computer program to track sales of every menu item hour by hour and to set cooking schedules. By consulting a computer printout, he can determine how much chicken to cook, when to put it in the rotisserie, and what time to serve it.[1]

Companies that apply computer technology effectively, as in the above example, stand a good chance of achieving a competitive edge. Unfortunately, there is no universal set of rules for bringing technology into a small business.[2]

### Choosing an MIS

Figure 21–2 presents a checklist you can use to define your company and the types and volume of information it needs. Completion of this checklist should help you form a better idea of the system to install.

## The Role Of Computers in Business

As their capabilities mushroom and costs decline, computers are rapidly taking over the roles of record keepers, clerks, and analysts. Through the use of computers, data can be quickly received, collected, processed, and reported. As a business grows, computers become more essential because of the increased volume of relevant information.

### The Development of Computers for Business Use

A modern computer information system consists of hardware, software, and people. The **hardware** consists of a central processing unit CPU, a monitor, a keyboard, and other parts that you can see, feel, and touch. (The CPU is the part of the computer hardware that controls all other parts of the system.)

**Hardware** consists of the CPU, monitor, keyboard, and other parts that you can see and touch.

**Software** is the programs, manuals, and procedures that cause the hardware to operate in a manner desired by the problem solver. Neither of these components is of any use without the people to use and operate them.

**Software** is the programs, manuals, and procedures that cause the hardware to operate in a desired manner.

### Early Business Use of Computers

The first computer used for a business application was the Univac, a giant mainframe installed by Sperry-Rand Univac at GE's Louisville, Kentucky, plant in 1954. While such computers were too big and expensive for small business use, they did dominate until the 1960s, as you can see from Figure 21–3.

Digital Equipment Corporation (DEC) produced the next development, the minicomputer. DEC marketed its first model in 1960 and, with a few other companies, dominated the market in the 1970s.

It was the microcomputer, however, that finally made computer technology feasible for small business use. Because of the abundance of inexpensive microcomputer hardware and software available to small firms (see Using Technology to Succeed), we will limit our discussion of computers to this type.

### The Microcomputer—The Small Business Computer

The terms *microcomputer, personal computer,* and *desktop computer* are used interchangeably to refer to computers based on the **microprocessor,** which is a miniaturized computer processor designed and based on a silicon chip.

A **microprocessor** is a miniaturized computer processor designed and based on a silicon chip.

The first mass-produced microcomputer was the Radio Shack TRS-80, introduced in the early 1970s, which was soon followed by the Commodore Pet 2000. Then, in 1976, Steven Jobs and Stephen Wozniak opened a makeshift production line in Jobs' garage to produce the Apple, a small, easy-to-use computer to help families and small businesses.*

---

*To raise the $1,500 needed for the start-up, Jobs sold his VW microbus, and Wozniak sold his Hewlett-Packard scientific calculator.

**Figure 21–2** Defining What a Company Needs in An MIS

**Type of Business**
Retail ___ Wholesale ___ Mfg. ___ Professional services ___
Real estate ___ Agriculture ___ Nonprofit ___ Other ___

**Business Size**
Gross income ___ Net profit as percentage of gross income ___

**Types of Information Needed**
Numerical ___ Textual ___ Graphics ___ Communications ___

**Location(s)**
Single ___ Dispersed ___ Franchise ___ Subsidiary ___

**Transaction Volume**
Invoices/month ___Average accounts receivable ___ Average inventory ___
Inventory turnover ___ Number of inventory items ___
Number of customers ___ Number of employees ___

**Current Information System** (Describe.)

______________________________________________

______________________________________________

**Trouble Areas** (Rank each according to importance and number of people involved. Use more paper if needed. Be as complete as possible.)

______________________________________________

______________________________________________

______________________________________________

**Potential Future Needs** (Include all possible needs, as they may be economically feasible in any system designed.)

______________________________________________

______________________________________________

**Applications**

**Business Areas to Be Addressed** (Number in order of priority.)
Accounting ___ Financial reporting ___ Inventory management ___
Cash flow planning ___ Market and sales analysis ___ Decision support ___
Billing ___ Scheduling ___ Quality control ___ Payroll ___
Employee benefits ___ Commissions ___ Customer tracking ___
Portfolio management ___ Legal defense ___ Long-term planning ___
Tax reporting ___ Word processing ___ Other (be specific)

______________________________________________

**Computer Skills Available in Company**

______________________________________________

**Proposed Budget for MIS**
$ __________ Maximum __________

**Time Frame**
Desired start ________ Latest allowed start ________

**Figure 21–3** How Computer Use by Business Has Changed in the Past Four Decades

1960s – Mainframes
Big, expensive, centralized computers.
Dominant companies: The BUNCH (Burroughs, Univac, NCR, Control Data, Honeywell) and IBM.
AP
IBM: The company's San Jose, Calif., offices were state of the art in the 1960s.
1970s – Minicomputers
Smaller, less-expensive, centralized computers.
Dominant companies: Digital Equipment and others on Boston's Route 128.
DEC: Co-founder Kenneth Olsen's company has been a minicomputer leader.
1980s – PCs
Inexpensive but isolated desktop computers.
Dominant companies: Microsoft, Intel, Apple, Compaq.
By Rick Browne, Picture Group
APPLE: Former chairman John Sculley with co-founders Steve Jobs, l; Steve Wozniak, r.
1990s – Networks
The Internet connecting computers.
Dominant companies: To be determined.
By John Makely, AP
NETSCAPE: Co-founder Marc Andreessen could become a leader of next computer age.

*Source: USA Today,* November 10, 1995, p. 1B. Copyright 1995, USA TODAY. Reprinted with permission.

The development of the microprocessor made the development of the microcomputer possible. All of the so-called personal computers (PCs) have used these "computers on a chip" as the heart of their system. Continuing improvement of the microprocessor chip has made possible more and more powerful computers in smaller and smaller boxes.

Apple and Commodore based their computers on a chip made by Motorola, rather than the one made by Intel® Corporation that was used in the TRS-80. This chip required different software, since the computers were not compatible, and programs that would run on the Apple would not run on the TRS-80 and vice versa.

Because of the ease of entry into the computer market, the number of companies mushroomed. Machines made by the emerging new companies were hardware compatible with the TRS-80 or Apple but not software compatible with either machine. Figure 21–4 shows how dramatically software for PCs has changed over the past two decades.

In 1981, IBM introduced its Personal Computer (IBM® PC), which soon became the standard of the industry. The IBM PC used the Intel 8088 chip, which was similar to the older chips already in use, except by Apple, so it was compatible with existing technology.

The introduction of the IBM PC gave instantaneous credibility to the personal computer market. While Apple and some others continued to use the Motorola chip, most of the other producers followed IBM's lead, using Intel® chips and operating systems created by Microsoft under the designation *MS-DOS®* or *PC-DOS®*. In rapid succession, 8088 computers were followed by

# USING TECHNOLOGY TO SUCCEED

## Software That Helps Entrepreneurs Do More with Less

Entrepreneurial companies spent an average of about $2,000 on software during 1994. But this lucrative market is still largely untapped by most small businesses. Few off-the-shelf programs meet the typical needs of small firms, which do not have big computer staffs. Consequently, software producers such as Microsoft are developing products aimed at companies that have few employees.

One of the first applications tailed for small businesses was general-ledge accounting. Intuit, which produces *Quicken,*® the leading personal finance package, also makes the popular *Quickbooks*® accounting program (mentioned in Using Technology to Succeed in Chapter 20). The company followed that program with a payroll package and a subscription to current tax tables. Intuit planned to offer more specialized programs during 1995 that would focus on different segments of the small business market. General contractors and other project-based firms were to be prime targets.

Microsoft is taking a different approach. It is adding tools for small business use to its popular *Office*® suite, which contains a word processing program called *Word,*® the *Excel*® spreadsheet, the *PowerPoint*® presentation package, *Schedule+*® calendar/contact management software, and (in some versions) the *Access* database management program. Microsoft's *Office Assistant,*® a $99 set of templates including invoices and press releases, is aimed at the nearly 25 percent of *Office*® users with fewer than 100 employees.

*Source:* Box shot reprinted with permission from Microsoft Corporation.

Like Microsoft, Claris is developing add-ons to its low-end *ClarisWorks* suite for small businesses, which make up a third of the software maker's customers. The *Small Business Solutions Pack* from Claris (priced between $20 and $30) provides templates such as business plans, invoices, and time sheets. What's next from Claris? Products to help small companies drum up more business.

*Source:* Adapted from Mary K. Fleet "Small Business," US News' & World Report, June 19, 1995, pp. 51–52.

**Figure 21–4** Key Dates in PC Software History

Here's a recap of how software for personal computers has changed since 1975.

| | |
|---|---|
| **1975** | Bill Gates and Paul Allen adapt BASIC for microprocessors, the first language for programmers to develop PC applications software. |
| **1979** | *VisiCalc,* the first spreadsheet, unveiled for the Apple II. |
| **1980** | 2.3 million PCs in use in the United States. |
| **1981–82** | IBM offers a PC using DOS, a Microsoft operating system, IBM licenses the system from Microsoft; Microsoft then licenses DOS to others. |
| **1983** | *Lotus 1-2-3,* the first heavy-duty business program, a detailed spreadsheet, introduced. As a result, IBM PCs are propelled into the office. Novell offers *NetWare* to link PCs on networks. |
| **1984** | The Apple Macintosh, the first popular computer with a user-friendly screen and mouse, makes its debut. |
| **1985** | First version of Microsoft's Windows, an operating system that uses on-screen icons and a mouse, introduced. |
| **1990** | Windows 3.0 introduced.<br>More than 50 million PCs in use in the United States. |
| **1992** | Windows 3.1, an improved version of Windows 3.0, reaches the market. |
| **1995** | Windows® 95 debuts.<br>90 million PCs in use in the United States. |

*Source:* William J. Cook, "Software Struggle," *U.S. News & World Report,* June 19, 1995, pp. 48–49. Adapted with permission.

Q

those based on the 8086, 80286, 80386, and 80486 chips. The 80586—marketed under the trade name Pentium®—was introduced in early 1993.

Changes in computer and related technologies are so swift and innovative that small business owners might consider leasing, rather than buying, computer hardware. While the new hardware is **backward compatible,** which allows existing programs to run on the new hardware, the latest software is written to take advantage of the most recent technological advances in hardware. These new programs, in many cases, will not run on computers based on the older microprocessors.

**Backward compatible** hardware will run existing programs designed for older equipment.

Q

If the user wishes to use the latest software, and thereby gain a possible competitive advantage, it is necessary to use the most recent and advanced hardware. As the stated goal of Intel® Corporation is to double computing power every 18 months, it will probably be necessary to upgrade hardware every 18 to 24 months to stay abreast of the newest and best information-processing technology. Intel's goal is not unrealistic in view of what has been happening in the past few years.

> For example, the speed of computers *increased 55 percent per year from 1987 to 1994.* Today's top-of-the-line PC is 171 times faster than the original IBM PC produced in 1981. And it has 256 times more random-access memory (RAM).[3]

Q

Cartoon by Fred Maes. Copyright 1996 by Fred Maes.

**Random-access memory (RAM)** is the amount of usable memory (volatile storage) within the computer.

**Read-only memory (ROM)** is unchangeable memory in the computer or on a disk that can be used for specialized applications.

**A laptop, notebook,** or **subnotebook** computer is a small, battery-powered package that can be used anywhere.

Most advances in computer technology have made the machines faster and more powerful, with more **RAM (random access memory)**, larger disk storage, and a variety of efficient peripherals, including printers, modems, fax machines, and Internet access.

One recent development being marketed with some success for business use is the "multimedia" computer, which includes, at a minimum, a sound card and a CD-ROM drive. **ROM (read-only memory)** disks, which resemble audio CDs, can store whole encyclopedias of print information, plus pictures and sound—even moving pictures and animation.

## The Laptop, or Notebook, Computer

Photo courtesy of M. Jane Byrd.

One innovation that is accelerating computer usage is the **laptop** (or **notebook** or **subnotebook**) **computer**.[4] Although still comparatively expensive for their power, these notebook-sized—and smaller—devices, in a battery-operated package, can be taken anywhere. For sales representatives on the road, engineers in the field, or employees taking inventory, they are ideal. While records or computations can be made on the spot, they can also be stored for later transfer to other computers either directly or by modem. They are also ideal for introducing students to the computers.

## Strengths and Weaknesses of Computers for Small Firms

The key to whether a computer is an asset or a liability in a small firm is the use made of it. The computer itself is not likely to be a limiting factor. The primary limitation is the availability of software that can economically accomplish the desired tasks. Figure 21–5 lists the activities for which a computer is especially well suited and for which software is currently available.

**Figure 21–5** What Computers Do Best—and Worst

The computer is most helpful in the following applications, for which software is readily available:

- Repetitive, data-oriented operations, such as accounting, record keeping, or mailing lists.
- Organizing data into information, such as financial reporting.
- Codifying and monitoring procedures, such as technical manuals and production control.
- Calculations, such as financial ratios and tax analyses.
- Forecasting, such as trend projection and materials requirements planning.

The computer is less valuable, and may even be a liability, in operations of the following types:

- Solving unstructured problems or those that are not clearly defined, as in invention or innovation.
- Defining and/or establishing true authority in a company, such as leadership roles.
- Identifying new markets or products. The computer can be a major asset here, but only as a tool to assist human workers.
- Interpersonal relations, such as contract negotiations or establishing corporate culture.
- Defining the corporate mission.

The areas in which computer technology can be *most useful* are *repetitive, high-volume, quantitative tasks.* By contrast, the areas where this technology is less useful are the unstructured, open-ended activities where human creativity or judgment is required. While the latter are more innovation- or people-oriented activities, the former are the boring, detail-oriented jobs once performed by lower-paid employees. Smart business owners will delegate these activities to the computer, freeing competent staff to handle the more interesting, long-term problems.

> For example, four advertising veterans founded Rossin Greenberg Seronick & Hill, an advertising agency in Boston. Neal Hill, as CEO, was responsible for creating an organization to support the others so they could be creative. He soon found that most of the people's time involved moving information around, leaving little time to create ads.
>
> Hill computerized the noncreative work, but the employees resisted the change. Then Hill got top managers to use word processors. According to one partner, who used one only reluctantly, "My capacity to do the paperwork quadrupled." After that, the partners were able to motivate all the employees to use computers.
>
> In a year and a half, billings doubled, while personnel increased only 25 percent![5]

As shown in Figure 21–6, most U.S. executives indicate they use computers in their job. Conversely, nearly half of Japanese executives do not. G

**Figure 21–6** How Executives View Computers

G

**Japanese executives are less likely than their U.S. counterparts to use computers. How executives describe their computer usage:**

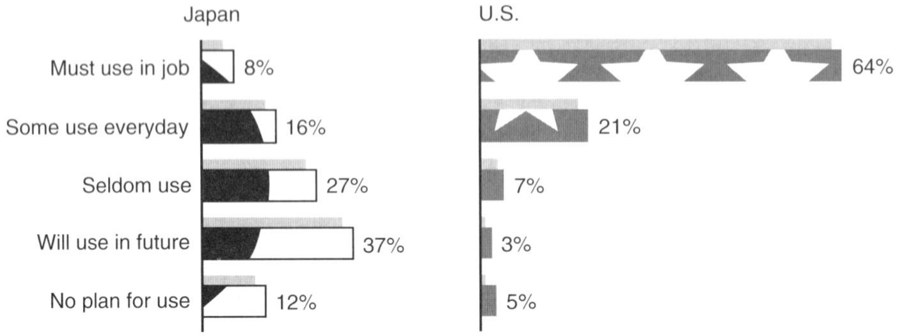


*Source:* Fuld & Co./Fujitsu Research Institute, as reported in *USA Today,* July 12, 1995, p. 1B. Copyright 1995, USA TODAY. Reprinted wtih permission.

As you saw in Figure 21–3, the PC dominated business during the 1980s. But now it's the 1990s, and the Internet has arrived!

## And Now—the Internet!

What is the Internet? Who owns the Internet? Who controls the Internet? These and other questions regarding the Internet are difficult, if not impossible, to answer. One fact is true, though: the Internet is here and will have a tremendous effect on our lives for many years. A whole new business arena has grown up in and around the Internet.

### *What Is the Internet*

The **Internet** is a collection of computers and computer networks linked together to receive and distribute information around the world.

The **Internet** is a collection of computers and computer networks linked to receive and distribute information around the world. Most colleges and universities, along with public schools, government agencies, businesses, and individuals, are connected to "the 'Net."

The Internet began as a means of communication between researchers, the military, and some parts of industry. In the early 1960s, scientists needed an efficient way to communicate the various aspects of their research efforts. Computers could process and print text very effectively. By networking computers (wiring them together so that each computer could communicate directly with the others), information could be shared very quickly and efficiently. Because the military needed a robust and secure computer network, the Department of Defense appointed the Advanced Research Projects Agency to design such a network. The result was the ARPANET, which was put in use in the late 1960s.

Academicians who wished to use the same type of networking technology did not have the same need for security as the military. Therefore, the academic community developed a network using the same basic development theory as the military but backed and primarily financed by the National Science Foundation (NSF). Eventually the military and academic networks, along with some others, were interconnected and became the Internet.

## *How to Use the Internet*

We will now attempt to answer the questions put forth above as best defined by current technology. The Internet collection of computer networks is ever changing. Each day hundreds, or even thousands, of new computers and networks come on line. There is no central control (although bills are currently pending in Congress to establish it) or ownership of the Internet. Corporations, educational institutions, government agencies, and individuals around the world join, use, and leave the 'Net in any way they wish every day. At the end of 1995, an estimated 30 million people were connected to it worldwide.[6]

Every unit on the 'Net is free to use its own operating system and methods, but there is general agreement (protocols) as to how to ship information over the Internet. To use it, however, you must have a service provider. There are many commercial providers, such as America Online®, Prodigy®, Genie®, CompuServe®, Sprint®, MCI®, local phone companies, bulletin boards, and others. There are also Freenets (free or nearly free service provided by a local government agency) and colleges and universities that provide Internet access service. The Internet itself is free, but you may have to pay a fee to your service provider.

## *The World Wide Web*

The World Wide Web (WWW) is rapidly becoming the preferred method of navigating the Internet. The Web is a very powerful, yet easy-to-use interface to the many sites on the Internet. If the user has the proper computer hardware and software, the Web is capable of communicating not only text but also sounds, graphics, videos, and more. Many individuals, educational institutions, government agencies, and businesses have "home pages" on the Web. This allows the user to employ the mouse to "point and click" to move about a site on the 'Net or even between Web sites. But there must be some organized way of finding information on the 'Net. So some entrepreneurs have developed ways to do this. One of the most popular of these systems is Yahoo (http://www.yahoo.com/) (see Figure 21–7).

## *Entrepreneurship on the 'Net*

Yahoo is a prime example of new and successful businesses that have grown directly from a relationship with the Internet. Yahoo was started by two graduate students at Stanford University, Jerry Yang and David Filo, who started indexing sites on the World Wide Web while working on their electrical engineering dissertations. At the time they began their endeavor, the Web was starting a rapid growth from what had been only a dozen or so sites in 1990 to the myriad of worldwide sites available today. Yang and Filo were soon working almost full time adding Web sites to their index. Soon Yahoo was being accessed by thousands of people each day. What had started as a hobby (dare one say an obsession?) now had strong commercial possibilities.

The two young entrepreneurs were joined by Marc Andreesen, who, while a graduate student at the University of Illinois, had written the Web browser "Mosaic," which brought simple point-and-click commands and colorful graphics to the 'Net. With financing from Sequoia Capital, Yahoo has grown to a search engine with over 4 million hits per day. With this number

**Figure 21–7** Yahoo Home Page

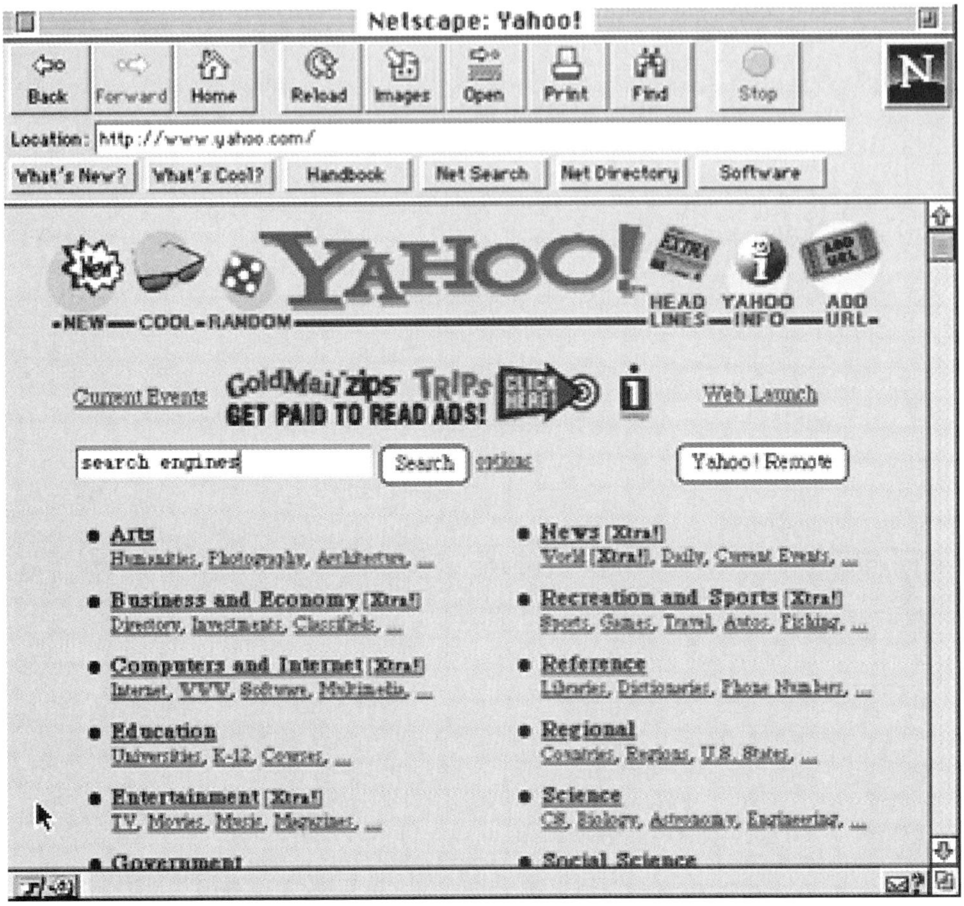


*Source:* Box shot reprinted with permission from Netscape.

of users, Yahoo is able to generate considerable income from advertising clients on its home page.

Marc Andreesen has also been successful with his ventures based on the ever-growing Internet. He is the co-founder of Netscape Navigator, one of the most popular Web browsers. Netscape Communications reported revenues of $40.6 million in the last quarter of 1995, up from $1.2 million for the same period in 1994. The company's stock, which sold for $28 a share when it went public in August 1995, hit a high of $171 per share in December of that year. It has since fallen to around $160.[7]

Figure 21–8 shows the uses made by small company CEOs of on-line services.

## Potential Problems with Computer Technology

There are many advantages and disadvantages to using computer technology. Therefore, careful planning is needed to assure accuracy, acceptability, and adaptability. Errors or inadequacies that develop in the system are much easier to detect and correct if the system is carefully designed and if employees are supportive and motivated to make it work. But even when errors and malfunctions are detected, they may not be easy to correct.

**Figure 21–8** Why Bosses Go On Line

**What CEOs of small companies (median annual revenue of $10 million) say they use on-line services for:**

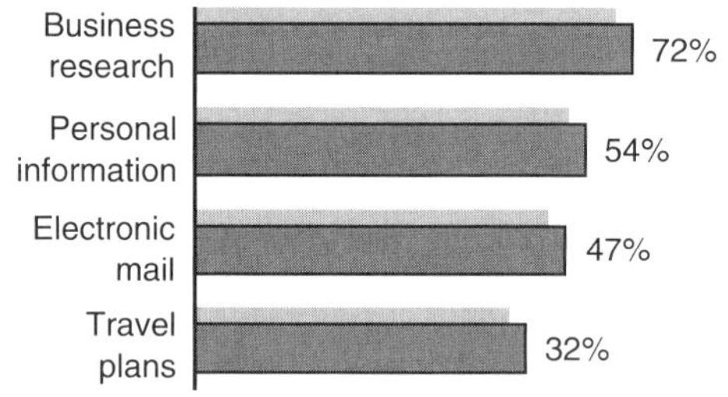


*Note:* Respondents could choose more than one.
*Source: Inc.* magazine, as reported in *USA Today,* February 16, 1995, p. 1B. Copyright 1995, USA TODAY. Reprinted with permission.

> According to Betty Shaffer, of Richardson, Texas, doing freelance bookkeeping in her home was "driving me insane." So she bought an IBM PC and an accounting program. Even after she learned to run the program—by reading the instruction manual—the system would not copy data from one magnetic disk to another. Naturally, it had all worked fine at the outlet where she had bought it.
>
> After several painful months nursing the sick computer, Shaffer persuaded the store manager to make a house call. He found that the machine worked well when the display monitor was moved from the top of the drive unit and put on a table. He suspected the screen must have been mistakenly given a magnetic coating.
>
> With her computer "cured," Shaffer's business took off. Because the computer does the calculations and prints the reports, she can do three times as much work—for three times more income.[8]

Another problem caused by the introduction of computerized operations is the need to upgrade your and your employees' skills. If this seems overwhelming to you, please take note. Help is available through other small companies specially set up to help you revamp or even get started in the computer world. One example is the Internet Business Center, which helps small businesses navigate the Internet (as discussed earlier in the chapter).[9]

## Computers Require Added Security

Computers are used for generating and storing important—often confidential—records, which makes controlling access an important issue. In addition, as more people have access to information, it becomes more important to set up procedures to ensure that data are accurately entered and protected from being accidentally (or intentionally) destroyed or altered. This suggests that an important part of a computerized MIS is the procedures set up for entry, updating, and control. Steps to provide security include:

- Physical control of facilities, such as guards and emergency power.
- Access control, such as identification of users and specifying who has the authority to use the equipment.
- Backups, such as appropriate saving of data.

Just as important as the security of the information you are storing is the integrity of that information. "Hackers" (computer programmers who experiment to see what they can do) have created computer viruses that can destroy your data and programs. These programs hide in other programs and are transmitted from one computer to another through exchange of disks or by downloading files from a remote computer or network. *To protect your system, you need to get antiviral programs along with the system and minimize the use of programs and/or disks of unfamiliar origin.* Your antiviral program should be of the type that can be updated frequently.

## The "01-01-00 Syndrome"

**Q** There is a technical problem facing users of most existing computers. With the end of the 20th century just a few years away, it is time to start thinking about how your computer will react to the 21st century. During the 1960s, to save what was then extremely valuable memory, programmers lopped off the first two digits of the year. Most existing computers won't know what to do at midnight, December 31, 1999. Experts see two scenarios for computer users. First, the computer resets to 01-01-00 but assumes it's January 1, 1900. Second, the system may crash!

> According to Bill Goodwin, whose consulting firm is called "2000 AD," and who publishes the newsletter *Tick, Tick, Tick,* "This is going to be the biggest maintenance job ever." While many manufacturers now ship computers with systems to handle the problem, others will require software that is now available, but very costly.[10]

## Reluctance of Some Owners to Use Computer Technology

In case we have led you to believe that most small businesses use computer technology, that isn't necessarily so! According to the Business Research Group Inc., of Newton, Massachusetts, only about a third of mom-and-pop operations use PCs. And only 57 percent of companies with up to 100 employees use them.[11]

**D** Also, many middle-aged and older entrepreneurs have resisted computerizing their small businesses. While part of their reluctance is due to the cost involved, anxiety over having to learn a new skill has been a major hangup.

> Ben Satterfield, age 55, overcame his fear of computers only three years ago. That's when he realized he could no longer manage the bills and orders overwhelming his business, Mug-A-Bug Pest Control, Inc., of Lawrenceville, Georgia. While the move was tough, it was worthwhile. "The savings .... I generated the first year paid for my computer and program."[12]
>
> On the other hand, Earl B. Christy, the 72-year-old president of Christy Company in Fremont, Ohio, still resists the efforts of his children and 15 grandchildren to get him to computerize his 104-year-old pocketknife-manufacturing business. Ironically, in the late 1940s Christy "wangled his father into buying an adding machine to help with the bookkeeping." Now, however, Christy fears losing his independence. "I can run any of the equipment in the factory," he says, "but I would need to hire someone computer literate to operate the computer."

## USING TECHNOLOGY TO SUCCEED

### The Hawthorne Hotel: 19th Century Hotel, 20th Century Technology

The Hawthorne Hotel, a stylish 89-room inn located in Salem, Massachusetts—where the 17th century witch hunts took place—has spent over $2 million restoring its appearance to what it must have been in the 19th century. The hotel's manager, Kenneth Boyles, says the beauty of his hotel is its history, charm and grace.

To reap the benefits of 20th century technology, Boyles bought an Apple® computer. Initially purchased for bookkeeping, its workload has steadily increased. Boyles added financial projections using income statements and balance sheets; later, he began controlling the food and beverage inventory. Recently, Boyles added an IBM® PC to the inn's system to be used as part of a new reservation system and for night audits. He also integrated the dining room into the system.

Boyles credits his success to two things: a step-by-step implementation of the computer and help from Tod Riedel, president of First Micro Group Inc. of Boston. Riedel believes that starting small is the best approach for small companies: "It gets technology in the door."

The Hawthorne Hotel circa 1920. Photo courtesy of Hawthorne Hotel.

> While he "cheerfully tests computers at the local computer store with games of solitaire," his children and grandchildren "are eager to give him computer lessons."[13]

## Choosing Software, Hardware, and Employee Training

The primary software applications likely to be needed by a small business include word processing, spreadsheet analysis, account processing, file management, and electronic mail/messaging. It is easy to assume that your business is unique and requires a specially designed system to match your needs. Be wary of this approach, however, because there are many off-the-shelf programs (already designed and available) that, while they may not satisfy all your needs, will likely provide a cost-effective solution to most of them.

Having defined your computer needs and the software desired, you must then choose the hardware. A wide range is available, from simple, inexpensive micros to complicated, expensive mainframes. Most small companies need a system somewhere in the middle—one that is not too costly but does the work satisfactorily (see Using Technology to Succeed). We suggest you

**Figure 21–9** Sources of Information about Computer Hardware, Software, and Training

The following sources can be used to obtain information to help in choosing hardware, software, and training.

- *Computer stores and consultants.* These can provide need-specific advice, packaged systems, and ongoing support, but they may be more oriented toward their sale than to your needs. The quality of advice may vary. Future availability of recommended systems is critical.
- *Friends or peers, user groups, bulletin boards, and seminars or workshops.* These can give more specialized advice, though it may not match your needs. Since hands-on experience is often possible, you may gain a better understanding of your needs, if not a specific answer. These are good sources of answers to technical questions, but beware of sales pitches.
- *Magazines, books, and libraries.* Although these are good sources of background information and comparative evaluations of hardware and software, the volume and technical nature of the information may create information overload, and the information is usually not tailored to your needs.
- *Computer company promotional material and mail order.* This is more oriented to specific hardware and software than to your needs, but it permits comparison of detailed technical specifications. Some mail-order firms offer ongoing support, but be sure to check, because this is important.
- *Industry associations.* These may have systems already fully designed to handle your specific problems and data that could be useful to you, but they may include a membership cost or licensing fee.
- *Government publications and SCORE/SBA.* These are inexpensive sources of information, data services, consultant referrals, and possibly even funding, but the quality may vary and may not include the most recent technology.

focus primarily on PCs because their speed and capacity make them capable of handling most of the needs of a small business. Figure 21–9 lists selected sources of information to help you choose hardware, software, and employee training. Appendix A at the end of the chapter provides some information to help you select a PC.

## The Accounting System as an MIS

There are many parts to the MIS of a small business. Some of the more important of these are:

- Forecasting.
- Reporting to tax authorities, management, and workers.
- Inventory control.
- Human resources records.

These require collecting, storing, and analyzing data. One major MIS is the accounting system, which, because of its highly quantitative nature, has historically been the first system to be computerized even in very small companies.

The rest of this chapter traces the flow of data for selected transactions in the accounting system. The discussion is based on the flow shown in Figure 21–1. Note the level of detail needed to design systems and how the logical flow of data tends to lead to computerization. An expert may be needed to help on the more complex transactions.

## Sales

Profits result from the sale of goods or the performance of a service, for which a record must be kept. Figure 21–1 showed how a record of sales and cash receipts can be made and accounted for.

The sale of a product generates a sales slip, on which the number and type of items, unit price, and total price are entered. When cash registers are used, cash sales can be recorded on a tape to be used as the sales slip. Cash registers and computers can record and total sales variables including types of product, salesperson, and department.

Information on the sales forms is used to accumulate the sales income, to reduce inventory, to make analyses, and—in the case of a credit sale—to enter in the accounts receivable a record for the customer. A computer is particularly useful in keeping records and warning of late-paying customers.

Daily summaries of sales, sales on account, cash received (including charges to bank credit cards), sales by department, and other vital data can be recorded on multicolumnar or computer paper. Then, periodically, the total is entered in the ledger account. An analysis of this sheet can provide valuable information on the sales trends, where the major volume is, or who is selling the most.

## Cash Income and Outgo

Recorded sales totals must equal the total of recorded cash, credits, and other values if your accounts are to balance. Since cash is highly negotiable, the system for recording it should be designed and established with care to minimize mishandling and consequent losses. For cash sales, goods sold and cash received should be recorded independently of each other—if possible—for control purposes.

> For example, a waitress makes out the bill for a customer at a restaurant, and a cashier receives the money. The cash register, placed in view of customers paying their bill, allows them to check the cash recording.

Also, to maintain control, only certain people should be allowed to handle the cash and then only on an individual basis: Each person starts with a standard amount for change, and the cash balance is reconciled each day, or more often if feasible. The reconciliation assures that cash on hand equals the beginning cash on hand, plus cash sales, less cash returns.

At the end of each day, businesses usually deposit in the bank the cash received that day, less the change needed for the next day's operations. The deposited amount is added to the checkbook stub. The business then makes payments by check. Each check is entered in the cash journal to identify the account to which it is charged.

## Accounts Receivable

When customers buy goods using open accounts or a store's credit card, each sale is entered on a customer account record, as shown in Figure 21–1. At the end of each period, usually a month, customers' accounts are totaled and bills sent requesting payment. As payments are received, the amount is posted to each customer's account and totaled for entry in the sales and cash receipts journal. Sales to customers using outside credit cards are treated as cash sales and processed as cash through the bank.

## Accounts Payable

A business incurs many obligations for materials purchased, utilities, wages, and taxes. The bills and invoices for these are entered in the purchases or expense journal or computer and may be filed by date to be paid. The journals can be multicolumnar to show how the money is spent. Columns are for categories with many similar items, such as materials purchases, and the miscellaneous column is for categories, such as insurance, that require few entries. Individual files keep track of whom to pay, when to pay, and how much to pay. After payment, the bills are filed for future reference. The paid bill amount is entered on the check stub and in the purchases and cash disbursements journal.

## Inventory

Among the most troublesome records to keep are those dealing with inventory. While the physical planning and control of inventory were discussed in Chapter 17, we will discuss here the accounting aspects of inventory.

When materials are received, their costs are recorded as materials inventory and paid for with cash, as shown in 1(a) in Figure 21–10. Inventory increases by $100, and cash decreases by $100. As the materials are used, it's recorded as an expense of $80, leaving an inventory balance of $20 at the end of the month. In another method, often used by high-volume purchasers, purchases are charged to expense as they are received, and then, at the end of the month, the unused portion is moved to inventory.

A business selling a high volume of many items—a grocery store, for example—depends on periodic visual inspection of the items on the shelves. Holograph scanners or bar code readers, connected to a computer, are often used to read the product number, comparing the amount in inventory with expected needs and entering the amount that needs to be ordered. The introduction of computers and point-of-sale scanners has made the use of *perpetual inventory records,* for timely control, more feasible.

## Expenses

A business purchases services and goods from other businesses, and these become expenses. Material is transformed and sold, electricity is used, machines decrease in value, and insurance protection lapses. The payment interval for these costs of doing business varies from one day to several years. To determine true profit—say for the month of March—income and expenses must be determined for that month. This can be done on a cash or accrual basis.

**Figure 21–10** Examples of Recording and Adjusting Transactions

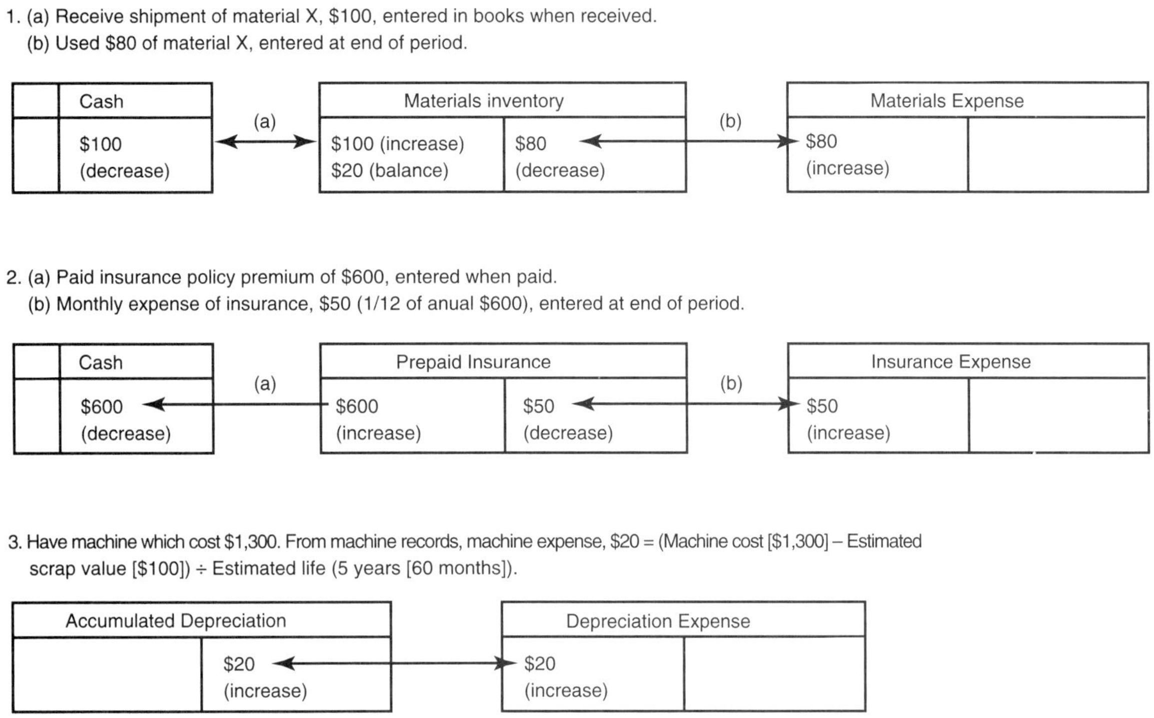


Many small businesses compute their profit on the cash rather than accrual basis because the cash basis is simpler. The **cash basis** assumes that payments and use occur in the same time period. But payment is not always received (or made) in the same period in which services are performed—as in the case of credit sales, for example. The **accrual basis** makes adjustments to reflect the actual expense of a service and the income received for it in a given time period, not past expenses or anticipated income. In deciding which method to use, *balance the value of accuracy against the cost of each method.*

The **cash basis** assumes payments and use occur in the same time period.

The **accrual basis** makes adjustments to income and expenses to reflect actual expenses incurred and income earned during the period.

To calculate expenses by the accrual method, (1) obtain the values of all assets, payments, and obligations; (2) determine how much of each has been used during the period; and (3) transfer the used portion to expense and reduce the asset or increase the obligation. Items 2 and 3 in Figure 21–10 are examples of the accrual method.

Insurance may be paid monthly, quarterly, or annually. Usually, annual payments reduce the cost and are prorated as shown in Figure 21–10, example 2. In the illustration, $600 is charged to prepaid insurance (an asset) when it is paid by the small firm, with 1/2, or $50, charged to expenses each month.

Machinery, equipment, and buildings are used over a number of years, so their value is only gradually used up. To assign a part of their expense to each period, an accounting method must reflect their **depreciation**, which is the amount of value a facility loses over a period of time. The most common method, *straight-line depreciation,* depreciates a machine at a constant rate

**Depreciation** is the gradual loss of value to a facility.

over its useful life. The amount to be charged for each month may be determined by the following formula:

$$\frac{\text{Cost of machine} - \text{Disposal value (sell or scrap) at the end of expected life}}{\text{Expected life (in months)}}$$

The amount that has already been charged to *depreciation expenses* is called *accumulated depreciation*. Figure 21–10, example 3, shows the adjustment of the two depreciation accounts by the amount thus arrived at. Many other items of expense and income need the same types of adjustment just discussed.

### Financial Statements

As shown in Chapter 18, financial statements, prepared from accounting records discussed in this chapter, aid you in making these analyses. They are usually the balance sheet and income statement. Income statements should be prepared monthly, while the balance sheets can be prepared less often. Tax reports are completed for the various government divisions many times during the year. These include reports for income, sales, Social Security, and excise tax.

## WHAT YOU SHOULD HAVE LEARNED

**1.** Information is an important resource for small businesses as well as for people. Companies collect and process data, make decisions, act on those decisions, and start the cycle anew.

**2.** A management information system (MIS) collects, processes, records, reports, and/or converts data into a usable form for management. Data can be processed in real time, with instantaneous feedback, or batch processed later at a lower cost.

**3.** Computers are increasingly important in business because they can process data so quickly. A computer—hardware—is physical equipment used for storing, processing, and presenting large quantities of data. Programs—software—direct the computer to process the data. Much of the value of a computer system comes from the software.

**4.** The microcomputer (PC) has made it feasible for a small business to process data related to such areas as accounting, employees, forecasting, and operations. Most systems involve both manual and computer operations, and the choice of the appropriate system depends on output, cost, and the situation in the business. In choosing a computer system, analyze the present situation in terms of available software, hardware, and employee training.

**5.** The Internet is a collection of computers and computer networks linked together to receive and distribute information around the world. There is no central control or ownership, but companies, educational institutions, government agencies, and individuals around the world (some 30 million) can join, use, and leave the 'Net at will. It helps small firms do research, send and receive electronic mail, and order materials.

**6.** A potential problem with computer technology is that the possibility of errors and inaccurate information being turned out is magnified. Also, the owner and employees need to continually upgrade their skills. Greater security of the equipment and information is required. Some middle-aged and older owners are reluctant to install the technology for various reasons. Finally, some older computers will have to be reprogrammed, at considerable expense, to enter the 21st century.

**7.** Accounting systems are part of a firm's MIS. The sale of goods starts a series of accounting entries using sales slips; cash register receipts; credit card receipts; multicolumnar paper (or computer files); and ledgers to record changes in cash, sales, and accounts receivable. Computers can facilitate this process and enhance its value. Secure systems must be designed to handle cash because stolen cash is not traceable.

When a sale is made on credit, the amount of the sale is entered into accounts receivable, and the customer is billed later.

Bills for purchases and other items used are recorded in suppliers' accounts for proper payment. Monthly, the amount used during the month is moved to an expense account. Keeping track of inventory can be one of the greatest challenges for any business. Expenses can be recorded on either the cash or the accrual basis. The simpler cash basis charges items as they are actually paid. The accrual basis assigns the amount of revenue and expenses to the period in which they occur.

## QUESTIONS FOR DISCUSSION

1. What are some management decisions owners of small businesses must make?
2. What types of information do they need to make those decisions?
3. What are some sources of the needed information?
4. Explain how the use of computers by business has grown.
5. Explain how the microcomputer (PC) has affected small business.
6. What effect(s) do you think the Internet will have on small business?
7. What are some problems with computer technology for small firms?
8. Distinguish between the cash and accrual methods of handling expenses.

# CASE 1

## HERMAN VALENTINE: CUSTOMIZING COMPUTERS FOR MILITARY USE

Photo courtesy of Systems Management American Corporation.

Herman Valentine, chairman and president of Systems Management American (SMA) Corporation, remembers the time years ago when he shined shoes on the corner of Monticello and Market streets in downtown Norfolk, Virginia. His best customers were executives working in the 4-story department store and the 16-story Maritime Towers office building across the street. He now owns the entire block, including the store—which serves as headquarters for his company—and the office building.

SMA is a computer systems integrator serving the government and private industry. Its capabilities include manufacturing, installation, integrated logistics support, software/hardware development, configuration management, command and control, image processing, and data conversion services.

SMA has grown from a one-man operation in 1970 into a national corporation with a staff of 430. Not realizing how difficult it was going to be, Valentine "put in long hours, borrowed often from banks, and spent a lot of time on proposals for contracts he did not get." SMA is now one of the largest black-owned businesses in the United States.

An outstanding high school basketball player, Valentine wanted to play in college and the NBA, but he wanted a car more! So he took part-time jobs to buy one, finished high school, went into the Army, married, and at age 23 returned to Norfolk. After earning a bachelor's degree from Norfolk State University in three years (paid for by more part-time jobs), he became an executive officer for the U.S. Department of Agriculture and later business manager for Norfolk State.

In 1970, he opened Systems Management Associates, a consulting firm for black businesses, with $5,000 he had saved. With an answering service, a post office box, and a part-time secretary, Valentine sold administrative and financial advice to black entrepreneurs and performed data processing and programming for them. Two years later, with 12 employees (mostly part-timers), he began bidding on—and winning—small government data processing jobs.

But his business really took off in 1981, when he snagged a contract to design, install, and maintain sophisticated record-keeping computers aboard Navy ships. The Navy thought the job was too big for him, but he persuaded it to send an evaluation team, which found no reason he couldn't do the job. Revenues skyrocketed for a while, and they have been as high as $60 million. Valentine has pared down his operations somewhat, but SMA continues to bid on—and be awarded—government contracts.

Valentine is concentrating on more contract diversification—which includes the government—as well as the private sector, as military budget cuts begin to affect the computer industry. After closing three small offices around the country and cutting $4 million out of overhead, he and his staff are "lean and competitive."

He trains his employees, many of whom are unskilled workers, to be computer technicians and high-tech specialists. He also encourages other minorities to become entrepreneurs.

*Source:* Correspondence with Systems Management American Corporation.

## QUESTIONS

1. How do you explain Valentine's success?
2. To what extent do you think his diversification plan will work? Explain.
3. What suggestions would you make to him for adjusting to the changing economic environment?

## APPLICATION 21–1

Cassady's, a fast-food business, has been computerizing its ordering process. Customers can now order by using touch-screen computers, and the information is instantaneously relayed to the kitchen. Cassady's is doing this to be competitive in the market and is trying to prepare itself for the labor crisis in the near future, as predicted by some economists. These computer systems are expensive, but Cassady's has experienced a gain in sales in the stores where these computers are installed.

## QUESTIONS

1. What factors should Cassady's consider before implementing this program nationwide?
2. Do you think Cassady's will get a competitive edge over other fast-food businesses by implementing this program?
3. Do you think you would order more if you were entering your order through a computer?

# ACTIVITY 21–1

*Directions:* Use information from this chapter to unjumble the six clues. Then use the circled letters to obtain the final answer to this puzzle.

1 T R A O W S E F

2 L A A C U C R I S S B A

3 E N E G T A M M A N T N O F A I I R N O M

T E S S Y M

4 P I E N O C E A D T I R

5 W E R H A A D R

6 H C S A A I B A S

Final Solution

?

1. Software 2. Accrual basis 3. Management information system 4. Depreciation 5. Hardware 6. Cash basis
Final solution: The computer is down Are we?

## APPENDIX A PC Buyer's Checklist

| | Model: | Model: | Model: | Model |
|---|---|---|---|---|
| **VENDOR** | | | | |
| Type (mail order, independent dealer, francise dealer, superstore) | | | | |
| Phone number | | | | |
| Address | | | | |
| Salesperson | | | | |
| **COST** | | | | |
| System price (as configured) | $ | $ | $ | $ |
| Shipping charges | $ | $ | $ | $ |
| Taxes | $ | $ | $ | $ |
| Other charges | $ | $ | $ | $ |
| **TOTAL CHARGES** | $ | $ | $ | $ |
| **CASE, BAYS, SLOTS, AND PORTS** | | | | |
| Case style (desktop, tower, minitower) | | | | |
| Power switch location (front, back, left, right) | | | | |
| Free externally accessible 3½-inch/5¼-inch drive bays | 3½ ___ 5¼ ___ | 3½ ___ 5¼ ___ | 3½ ___ 5¼ ___ | 3½ ___ 5¼ ___ |
| Free internal 3½-inch/5¼-inch drive bays | 3½ ___ 5¼ ___ | 3½ ___ 5¼ ___ | 3½ ___ 5¼ ___ | 3½ ___ 5¼ ___ |
| Free expansion slots (32-bit EISA/16-bit ISA/8-bit ISA) | 32-bit ___ 16-bit ___ 8-bit ___ | 32-bit ___ 16-bit ___ 8-bit ___ | 32-bit ___ 16-bit ___ 8-bit ___ | 32-bit ___ 16-bit ___ 8-bit ___ |
| Free local bus slots | PCI ___ VL ___ | PCI ___ VL ___ | PCI ___ VL ___ | PCI ___ VL ___ |
| Serial/parallel ports | / | / | / | / |
| **MOTHERBOARD** | | | | |
| CPU manufacturer (Intel, AMD, Cyrix, IBM) | | | | |
| CPU model/clock speed (MHz) | / | / | / | / |
| CPU upgrade method (OverDrive for SX or DX, Pentium OverDrive, plug-in card) | | | | |
| Zero-insertion force socket | Yes ___ No ___ | Yes ___ No ___ | Yes ___ No ___ | Yes ___ No ___ |
| BIOS developer (AMI, Award, Phoenix)/date | / | / | / | / |
| Flash/Plug and Play BIOS | Flash ___ PnP ___ | Flash ___ PnP ___ | Flash ___ PnP ___ | Flash ___ PnP ___ |
| Secondary cache installed/maximum (K) | / | / | / | / |
| **MEMORY** | | | | |
| RAM installed/maximum (MB) | / | / | / | / |
| Type of SIMMs supported (512K, 1MB, 2MB, 4MB, 8MB, 16MB) | | | | |
| Number of SIMM pins | 30-pin ___ 72-pin ___ | 30-pin ___ 72-pin ___ | 30-pin ___ 72-pin ___ | 30-pin ___ 72-pin ___ |
| SIMM sockets/number free | / | / | / | / |

*Source:* "PC Buyer's Checklist," Instant Reference Card #52, *PC World,* March 1995, pp. 211–12.

## APPENDIX A *continued*

| STORAGE | Model: | Model: | Model: | Model: |
|---|---|---|---|---|
| Hard disk manufacturer and model | | | | |
| Size (MB) | | | | |
| Interface (IDE, SCSI) | | | | |
| Adapter manufacturer | | | | |
| Average access time (ms) | | | | |
| Transfer rate (MB/sec) | | | | |
| Floppy drive (1.2MB, 1.44MB, 2.88MB, combo) | | | | |
| **GRAPHICS** | | | | |
| Monitor manufacturer and model | | | | |
| Size (diagonal inches)/dot or stripe pitch (mm) | / | / | / | / |
| Intended resolution (640 × 480, 800 × 600, 1024 × 768, 1280 × 1024) | | | | |
| Refresh rate at intended resolution (Hz) | | | | |
| Front-mounted controls | Yes ___ No ___ | Yes ___ No ___ | Yes ___ No ___ | Yes ___ No ___ |
| Graphics adapter manufacturer and model | | | | |
| Installed VRAM/DRAM WRAM (MB) | / | / | / | / |
| Adapter form (integrated, plug-in card) | | | | |
| Local bus adapter | Yes ___ No ___ | Yes ___ No ___ | Yes ___ No ___ | Yes ___ No ___ |
| **KEYBOARD AND MOUSE** | | | | |
| Keyboard manufacturer and model | | | | |
| Number of keys | | | | |
| Mouse/trackball manufacturer and model | | | | |
| Number of buttons | | | | |
| **FAX MODEM** | | | | |
| Fax modem manufacturer and model | | | | |
| Price | $ | $ | $ | $ |
| Fax speed/modem speed (kbps) | / | / | / | / |
| Error correction (MNP4, MNP10, V.42) | | | | |
| Data compression (MNP5, MNP7, V.42bis) | | | | |
| Fax program | | | | |
| **CD-ROM DRIVE AND SOUND CARD** | | | | |
| CD-ROM drive manufacturer and model | | | | |
| Price | $ | $ | $ | $ |
| Interface type (IDE, SCSI, proprietary) | | | | |
| Speed factor (1X, 2X, 3X, 4X, 6X, 8X) | | | | |

## APPENDIX A *concluded*

| | Model: | Model: | Model: | Model: |
|---|---|---|---|---|
| Access time (ms)/transfer rate (K/sec) | / | / | / | / |
| Sound card manufacturer and model | | | | |
| Price | $ | $ | $ | $ |
| Speakers and headphones | Yes ___ No ___ | Yes ___ No ___ | Yes ___ No ___ | Yes ___ No ___ |
| **INCLUDED OR DISCOUNTED SOFTWARE** | | | | |
| **SERVICE AND SUPPORT** | | | | |
| Warranty (years) | | | | |
| Money-back guarantee (days) | | | | |
| On-site service price/restocking fee | $ /$ | $ /$ | $ /$ | $ /$ |
| Service center turnaround (days) | | | | |
| Toll-free support | Yes ___ No ___ | Yes ___ No ___ | Yes ___ No ___ | Yes ___ No ___ |
| Weekday support hours | ___ a.m. to ___ p.m. | ___ a.m. to ___ p.m. | ___ a.m. to ___ p.m. | ___ a.m. to ___ p.m. |
| Weekend support hours | ___ a.m. to ___ p.m. | ___ a.m. to ___ p.m. | ___ a.m. to ___ p.m. | ___ a.m. to ___ p.m. |
| BBS support and fax support | Yes ___ No ___ | Yes ___ No ___ | Yes ___ No ___ | Yes ___ No ___ |

*Source:* "PC Buyer's Checklist," Instant Reference Card #52, *PC World,* March 1995, pp. 211–12. Reprinted with the permission of PC WORLD *Communications,* Inc. To subscribe please call (800) 234-3498 and mention special order code 3AGA6.

CHAPTER

# 22

# Risk Management, Insurance, and Crime Prevention

*Everything is sweetened by risk.*—Alexander Smith

*Carrying liability insurance these days is almost a liability in itself. . . . Premiums are rising at a fantastic rate . . . [and] in some cases insurance coverage has become impossible to obtain—at any cost.*—Charles W. Patchen, CPA and writer

## LEARNING OBJECTIVES

After studying the material in this chapter, you will be able to:

1. Define risk and explain some ways of coping with it.
2. Explain what insurance is and show how it can be used to minimize loss due to risk.
3. Discuss some guides to be used in choosing an insurer.
4. Show how crime prevention can reduce risk and protect people and assets.
5. Describe how to safeguard employees with preventive measures.

P R O F I L E

## DR. JEFFREY F. VAN PETTEN: A UNIQUE ENTREPRENEUR

Q

Jeff Van Petten's veterinary practice includes much more than traditional family pets and traditional pet care. When asked to describe his activities, he explained, "My practice is rapidly becoming an alternative medicine animal hospital that utilizes acupuncture, chiropractic, and homeopathy forms of treatment. As a professional, I like to look past the normal for better answers to problems."

Photo courtesy of Joyce Allen Baker and Jeffrey Van Petten.

Van Petten's interests and research have led to video productions, such as those dealing with "barrel horse wellness." His films identify ways to diagnose musculoskeletal problems in horses and ways to prevent them.

Growing up in a rural environment gave Van Petten his love of animals and desire to keep them healthy. He is active in many associations that help him stay current on the latest discoveries and techniques in veterinary medicine. He is a member of the International Veterinary Acupuncture Society, was certified by the society in 1991, and serves on its Member Education Committee. Van Petten is also involved with the American Veterinary Chiropractic Association, the American Association of Equine Practitioners, the Kansas Veterinary Medical Association (in which he served on the Public Relations Committee), and the American Veterinary Medical Association.

In addition to his many professional affiliations, Van Petten is very active in many local organizations. He is a member of the local school board, the Jefferson County (Kansas) Health Board, the Jefferson County Extension Council, and the board of Jefferson County Rural Water District Number One. Yet he still has time for hobbies such as hunting, fishing, roping, and riding horses.

When asked what motivates him to continue his practice, besides a love of animals, he will tell you that the pay is good. While there are approximately 66,000 veterinarians in the United States, most veterinary practices generate less than $500,000 in annual revenue.[1]

Van Petten's veterinary practice is an S corporation, employing an office staff as well as a second veterinarian, Dr. Tanner. Van Petten purchased his practice a few years ago with 100 percent borrowed capital. The previous owner held a contract on the building, and a local bank financed equipment and start-up funds. The location was very attractive to the purchaser, being located on a highway, in a growing area, and near family and friends.

D Being near family is important because, like many small businesses, Van Petten's practice is a family enterprise. Van Petten's wife, Jackie, daughter, Jolie, and son, Jerek, are supportive in many ways. Besides encouraging his involvement in professional activities and research—and tolerating the hours involved—they also pitch in as needed to help with client relations, clean cages, exercise animals, or perform any other needed support services.

The operation of veterinary medicine involves many liabilities. Some examples are zoning, health department regulations, regulations on the size of and space available in the facilities, runoff animal waste, and handling of needles and prescription drugs. Regulations for prescription drugs for veterinary use are much the same as those for medical doctors and pharmacists.

Since there is an inherent danger in handling animals, the State of Kansas has passed the Kansas Livestock Liability Act, which was designed to create relief for both animal owners and handlers. Briefly described, it protects against liability for injury to people. This law has not been tested, so, to be on the safe side, veterinarians obtain a written release. Veterinarians also carry malpractice, professional liability, and errors and omissions insurance—in addition to the usual fire, theft, and similar coverage. Some of Van Petten's insurance is a form of self-insurance handled by the AVMA.

*Source:* Correspondence and conversations with Joyce Allen Baker and Jeffrey and Jackie Baker Van Petten.

We will discuss in this chapter some of the most prevalent risks facing you as a small business owner, such as the liability and omissions risks mentioned in the Profile, and we will show how you can cope with them.

The first part of the chapter deals with risk and its management; the second part, with using insurance to minimize loss due to risk; the third part discusses crime prevention; and the last part explains how security systems can protect the assets of a small business.

## Risk and Its Management

Small business losses of money and property occur as a result of such things as fire, severe weather, theft, lawsuits, bankruptcy, and politics, as well as the death, disability, or defection of key personnel. For example, a physical peril like a hurricane, fire, or tornado may destroy your property outright. Or remodeling, street repairs, or flooding may temporarily close your business and reduce income. Goods may be stolen, damaged, destroyed, or spoiled in transit, for which the common carrier isn't liable. Banks may either call in, or refuse to renew, loans. Customers may be unable to pay accounts receivable. The government may cut back on military spending. A competitor may hire one of your key employees. Given this rogues' gallery of lurking perils, what's a small business to do?

The answer is to use **risk management**, which is the process of conserving a firm's earning power and assets by minimizing the financial shocks of accidental losses. It lets a firm regain its financial balance and operating effectiveness after suffering an unexpected loss.

**Risk management** is the process of conserving earning power and assets by minimizing the shock from losses.

## Types of Risk

There are two primary types of risk you will face as a small business owner. A **pure risk** is uncertainty as to whether some unpredictable event that can result in loss will occur. Pure risk always exists when the possibility of a loss is present but the possible extent of the loss is unknown. For example, the consequences of a fire, the death of a key employee, or a liability judgment against you cannot be predicted with any degree of certainty. Many of these risks, however, can be analyzed statistically and are therefore insurable.

**Pure risk** is the uncertainty that some unpredictable event will result in a loss.

On the other hand, a **speculative risk** is uncertainty as to whether a voluntarily undertaken activity will result in a gain or a loss. Production risks, such as building a plant that turns out to have the wrong capacity or keeping an inventory level that turns out to be too high or too low, are speculative risks. Speculative risk is the name of the game in business.

**Speculative risk** is the uncertainty that a voluntarily undertaken risk will result in a loss.

> For example, Levi Strauss tried to sell its jeans through mass merchandisers such as Sears and Penney's, only to have department stores turn to Lee jeans.

Some business risks are insurable and others uninsurable. And, as you know, the greatest risk facing any small business—the possibility that it will be unprofitable—is uninsurable. Other uninsurable risks are associated with the development of new products, changes in customers' preferences, price fluctuations, and changes in laws. In this chapter we deal only with insurable risks.

## Ways of Coping with Risk

There are many ways you can cope with risk. The most common of these are:

- Risk avoidance
- Risk prevention, or loss control
- Risk transfer
- Risk assumption

**Risk avoidance** is refusing to undertake, or abandoning, an activity in which the risk seems too costly.

**Risk avoidance** is refusing to undertake an activity where the risk seems too costly.

> For instance, a New York bank experimented with having depositors of less than $5,000 either pay a fee to see a teller or use an automatic teller machine. When customers rebelled, the project was dropped as too risky.[2]

**Risk prevention**, or **loss control**, consists of using various methods to reduce the probability that a given event will occur. The primary control technique is prevention, including safety and protective procedures. For example, if your business is large enough, you might try to control losses by providing first-aid offices, driver training, and work safety rules, not to

**Risk prevention (loss control)** is using various methods to reduce the possibility of a loss occurring.

mention security guards to prevent pilferage, shoplifting, and other forms of theft, as the following example illustrates.

Q

> Many malls are now using uniformed security guards to replace plainclothes officers. For example, New Orleans' Plaza Mall has moved its security station to a glass-enclosed room in the center of the mall. Passersby can see the officers monitoring closed-circuit TV sets. Some shopping centers are even having uniformed officers patrol their parking lots on horses or bicycles.[3]

Photo by Jeff Reinking Photography.

**Risk transfer** means shifting the consequences of a risk to persons or organizations outside your business. The best-known form of risk transfer is **insurance**, which is the process by which an insurance company agrees, for a fee (a premium), to pay an individual or organization an agreed-upon sum of money for a given loss. But, because of escalating health care costs, many companies are shifting part of the risk to their employees, who must pay higher deductibles and a larger percentage of nonreimbursed expenses.[4]

**Risk assumption** usually takes the form of **self-insurance**, whereby a business sets aside a certain amount of its own funds to meet losses that are uncertain in size and frequency.[5] This method is usually impractical for very small firms because they do not have the large cash reserves needed to make it feasible.

**Risk transfer** is shifting a risk to someone outside your company.

**Insurance** is provided by another company that agrees, for a fee, to reimburse your company for part of a loss.

**Risk assumption** or **self-insurance** is setting aside funds to meet losses that are uncertain in size and frequency.

Generally, more than one method of handling risks is used at the same time. For example, a firm may use self-insurance for automobile damage, which costs relatively little, while using commercial insurance against liability claims, which may be prohibitively great.

## Using Insurance to Minimize Loss Due to Risk

The principal value of insurance lies in its reduction of your risks from doing business. In buying insurance, you trade a potentially large but uncertain loss for a small but certain one (the cost of the premium). In other words, you trade uncertainty for certainty. But, if the insurance premium is a substantial proportion of the value of the property, don't buy the insurance.

A well-designed insurance program not only compensates for losses but also provides other values, including reduction of worry, freeing funds for investment, suggestions for loss prevention techniques, and easing of credit.

In deciding what to do about business risks, you should ask yourself questions such as those shown in Figure 22–1. Often, when such disasters occur in small companies with inadequate or no insurance protection at all, either the owners are forced out of business or operations are severely restricted.

**Figure 22–1** How to Determine Whether You Need Insurance

To determine how to handle business risks, ask yourself, What will happen if:

- I die or suddenly become incapacitated?
- A fire destroys my firm's building(s), machines, tools and equipment, and/or inventories?
- There is theft by an outsider, a customer, or an employee, or an employee embezzles company funds?
- My business is robbed?
- A customer is awarded a sizable settlement after bringing a product or accident liability suit against me?
- Someone, inside or outside the business, obtains unauthorized information from my computer?

## Types of Insurance Coverage

Because there are so many types of insurance, we will discuss only those you will need most as a small business owner.

The basic *fire insurance policy* insures only for losses from fire and lightning and those due to temporary removal of goods from the premises because of fire. In most instances, this policy should be supplemented by an *extended-coverage endorsement* that insures against loss from windstorm, hail, explosion, riot, aircraft, vehicle, and smoke damage.

To ensure reimbursement for the full amount of covered losses, most property insurance contracts have a **coinsurance** provision. It requires policyholders to buy insurance in an amount equal to a specified percentage of the property value—say, 80 percent.

**Coinsurance** is having the business buy insurance equal to a specific percentage of property value.

*Business interruption coverage* should also be provided through endorsement, because such indirect losses are frequently more severe in their eventual cost than are direct losses. For example, while rebuilding after a fire, the business must continue to pay fixed expenses such as salaries of key employees and such expenses as utilities, interest, and taxes. You also need this type of insurance for other types of business interruption.

G

> For example, Ali Kamber, executive vice president for Ferromin International, a metals and minerals trading company with four employees, said his company lost $100,000 during the week following the bombing of the World Trade Center in early 1993. The company "lacked insurance for business interruptions," he said.[6]

*Casualty insurance* consists of automobile insurance (both collision and public liability) plus burglary, theft, robbery, plate glass, and health and accident insurance. Automobile liability and physical-damage insurance are necessary because firms may be legally liable for vehicles used on their behalf, even those they do not own. For example, when employees use their own cars on company business, the employer is liable in case of an accident.

**Product/service liability insurance** protects a business against losses resulting from the use of its product. It is particularly important for small firms because in conducting business, companies are subject to common and

**Product/service liability insurance** protects a business from losses resulting from the use of its product.

statutory laws governing negligence to customers, employees, and anyone else with whom they do business. One liability judgment, without adequate insurance, can easily result in the liquidation of a business. As a result, premiums for liability coverage are becoming almost prohibitive. In fact, the crisis has reached such proportions that some companies are dropping products rather than face the danger of bankruptcy.

> After spending more than $100 million defending itself against charges that Bendectin, an antinausea drug used by millions of pregnant women for decades, caused birth defects, its only producer quit making it in 1983.[7]

According to the Consumer Federation of America, product liability insurance costs "only 26 cents per $100 of product sale."[8] That estimate appears to be low, however, as U.S. companies paid $2.2 billion for product liability insurance in 1993.[9] The problem has escalated since courts began interpreting "liability" so broadly.

> For example, Jeanine Pelletier was awarded $40,000 by the Maine Supreme Court when she sued the Fort Kent Golf Club of Portland for nose and facial injuries. Her injuries resulted when her own golf ball ricocheted off railroad tracks that run through the course and hit her in the nose.[10]

Another growing problem for small firms is what to do about liability when sponsoring athletic teams or some potentially dangerous activities. Employers are facing the problem in two ways. Some are trying to get reasonably priced insurance coverage. When this isn't feasible, many small firms are abandoning the practice.

Workers' compensation policies typically provide for medical care, lump sums for death and dismemberment, and income payments for disabled workers or their dependents.

The workers' comp problem is rapidly getting out of control because of "unrestrained medical costs, excessive legal disputes in what is supposed to be a no-fault system, broadening definitions of what are job-related injuries, and rampant fraud and abuse."[11] This is now *the biggest insurance expense* for American businesses.

Q

There are some things owners and managers of small companies can do to improve safety. These actions, which should also help reduce premiums, are:[12]

- Involve employees in safety matters.
- Establish an open, two-way communication system.
- Make participation companywide.
- Make a big deal of the safety awards that are given, and be sure awards have a reasonable value.
- Keep the program exciting.
- Be especially watchful during high-risk periods.

Group health and life insurance for employees are also important in small firms. Life insurance provides protection for an employee's estate when he or she dies while still in the income-producing years, or lives beyond that time but has little or no income. Health insurance provides protection against the risk of medical expenses, including doctor and hospital bills and prescription expenses.

Health insurance is one of the most important benefits offered by small firms, but it's also one of the costliest. A major cause of low coverage by small firms is the cost. Health insurance costs have increased at more than twice the inflation rate for over a decade, and some small firms have experienced 25 to 50 percent annual increases. Widely recognized as an acute problem for the entire country, this is critical for small businesses.[13]

In 1994, small companies' average health care costs increased 6.2 percent to $3,308. However, it is not unusual for a company to save 10 to 15 percent by switching to a managed care plan, as the following example illustrates.

> Dixon Ticonderoga Company, a pencil maker, has noted that the company's health care claims costs dropped about 20 percent after it entered a managed care plan. About 600 of the company's 1,000 employees participate in the plan.[14]

Finally, insurance companies treat large and small businesses differently. If a big company has a bad year, with a high total health bill, the insurer regards it as a natural occurrence and assumes that costs will decline the following year. But it's common for rates at a very small business—one with 10 to 20 people covered—to skyrocket if just one employee racks up huge health claims during the year.

Business owner's insurance is another important protection you need. It consists of (1) protection of owner or dependents against loss from premature death, disability, or medical expenses and (2) provision for the continuation of a business following the death of an owner. Also, business continuation life insurance is used in closely held corporations to provide cash on the death of an owner. The cash can be used to retire the interest of a partner or, in case of death, to repurchase the stock of a closely held corporation.

Insurers issue fidelity and surety bonds to guarantee that employees and others with whom the company transacts business are honest and will fulfill their contractual obligations. Fidelity bonds are purchased for employees occupying positions that involve the handling of company funds. Surety bonds provide protection against the failure of a contractor to fulfill contractual obligations. Problems with bonding restrict the growth of many small contractors.

> For example, in a poll of 150 contractors in New York and New Jersey, more than three-fourths of them said that difficulty in getting bonded limited their access to jobs, especially the bigger and more profitable ones.[15]

## Guides to Choosing an Insurer

In choosing an insurer, consider the financial characteristics of the insurer, the insurer's flexibility in meeting your requirements, and the services rendered by the agent. While insurance companies have agents representing them, independent agents represent more than one company. These independent agents use the following logo:

## Some Red Flags to Look For

As in any industry, there are some black sheep or shady operators to look out for in choosing an insurer. To make sure you are being provided the coverage you have paid for, be on the lookout for the following red flags:[16]

- An agent who delays giving answers, fails to hand over a policy, or neglects to provide proof of endorsements.
- Routine answers such as: "Don't worry about it, it's a computer glitch."
- A delayed premium refund.
- A hand-delivered policy instead of one sent directly from the company.
- An adjuster who says it will cost you more to process the claim than the amount of your deductible.
- Delay tactics to encourage you into a lower settlement.
- Attempts to minimize your damages to save the company from having to pay on the claim.
- Request by the adjuster to keep the claim or proposed settlement a secret.
- An offer of a new policy to replace one that is flawed.

## Financial Characteristics and Flexibility of Insurer

The major types of insurers are stock companies, mutual companies, reciprocals, and Lloyd's groups. While mutuals and reciprocals are cooperatively organized and sell insurance "at cost," in practice their premiums may be no lower than those of profit-making companies. In comparing different types of insurers, you should use the following criteria:

- Financial stability and safety.
- Specialization in your type of business.
- Ability to tailor its policy to meet your needs.
- Cost of protection.

Valid comparisons of insurance coverage and its costs are difficult to make, but your insurance brokers, independent insurance advisers, or agents can assist you. In addition, the following are a few things you can do to ease the pain when your insurance comes up for renewal:

- Consult your agent for methods of minimizing your premium.
- Consider boosting your policy deductibles to keep premium costs within manageable limits.
- Before renewal time arrives, shop around among several agents for coverage.
- Find out if your professional organization offers lower-cost coverage for its members.
- Check out the special-risk pools.
- Consider alternatives to insurance coverage, such as self-insurance or coinsurance.

### Services Rendered by the Agent

Decide which qualifications of agents are most important, and then inquire about agents among business friends and others who have had experience with them. In comparing agents, look for contacts among insurers, professionalism, degree of individual attention, quality of service, and help in time of loss. Choose an agent who is willing and able to: (1) devote enough time to your individual problems to justify the commission, (2) survey exposure to loss, (3) recommend adequate insurance and loss prevention programs, and (4) offer alternative methods of insurance.

## Crime Prevention to Protect People and Assets

Small business owners need to practice crime prevention to reduce risks and protect their assets. Not only do you need to prevent major crimes, such as armed robbery, theft, and white-collar crimes, but you also need protection from trespassing, vandalism, and harassment.

An awareness of the potential dangers helps to minimize the risks involved and reduces losses from crime. It's impossible to have a security program that will prevent all criminal acts, so you can only hope to minimize their occurrence and severity.

A recent study conducted by America's Research Group, Inc., revealed that more than a third of American customers have changed their shopping habits because of safety concerns. The study found that 42 percent of shoppers no longer shop after dark, 25 percent keep car doors locked, 15 percent refuse to shop alone, and 60 percent are very uneasy about carrying large amounts of money. And businesses are suffering as a consequence.

> For instance, almost 40 percent of the respondents to another survey believed it was the responsibility of individual store owners to make shopping safer. Similarly, 31 percent felt shopping centers should be responsible, while 30 percent looked to local government for safety.[17]

Law enforcement agencies and the business community are learning to identify areas particularly susceptible to crime. Crimes appear to fall into patterns. Armed robbery may occur frequently in one type of neighborhood, theft in another, and both in a third. A prospective business owner needs to evaluate a potential site with this problem in mind. Examples of sites that appear to be particularly vulnerable to criminal acts are public housing projects, low-rent neighborhoods, areas of high unemployment, and areas with a high incidence of illiteracy.

Criminal acts have forced not only small but even large businesses into insolvency. Armed robbery, theft, and white-collar crimes are the major crimes affecting small firms.

## Armed Robbery

In recent years, the number of armed robberies has increased significantly. An armed person enters the premises with the intent of obtaining cash or valuable merchandise and leaves as quickly as possible to minimize the risk of identification or apprehension. Since time is critical in such circumstances, locations that afford easy access and relatively secure escape routes seem most vulnerable. This type of criminal usually wants to be in and out of the location in three minutes or less, and the pressure of the situation tends to make the robber more dangerous.

Several measures can be taken to reduce the chances of being robbed. They include modifying the store's layout, securing entrances, using security dogs, controlling the handling of cash, and redesigning the surrounding area.

### *Modifying Store Layout*

Location of the cash register and high visibility inside and from outside the store are important in preventing armed robbery. If robbers cannot dash in, scoop up the cash, and dash out again within a short time, they aren't as likely to attempt the robbery, as the following example shows.

> One convenience food chain removed from the windows all material that would obstruct the view into the store. In addition, it encouraged crowds at all hours with various gimmicks and attracted police officers by giving them free coffee. The average annual robbery rate dropped markedly.

*"The salesman said it was the most effective home security system on the market."*

Reprinted from *The Wall Street Journal*, permission Cartoon Features Syndicate.

### *Securing Entrances*

The security of entrances and exits is extremely important in preventing robbery. Windows and rear doors should be kept locked and barred. In high-crime neighborhoods, many businesses use tough, shock-resistant transparent materials in their windows instead of glass.

### *Using Security Dogs*

Security dogs are trained to be vicious on command. Businesspeople have found these animals to be effective deterrents against armed robbers. For example, when 589 convicted criminals were asked how best to foil burglars, the largest number—15.8 percent—said, "Have a dog."[18] However, health and sanitation regulations in some jurisdictions may prevent the use of dogs.

### *Controlling the Handling of Cash*

Making daily cash deposits and varying the deposit time from day to day are highly recommended. Some cash registers signal "too much cash" and will not operate until an employee has removed the excess to a safe and reset the register with a key. Banks and other businesses rigidly enforce minimum-cash-on-hand rules for cash drawers to reduce losses in the event of an armed robbery.

Many businesses hide safes in unobtrusive hiding places and limit knowledge of their combinations to only one or two people. It is not uncommon for a sign to be posted on the safe, or near it, advising that the person on duty does not have access to the combination or saying, "Notice: Cash in drawer does not exceed $50." Other stores, such as gas stations, use locked cash boxes and accept only correct change, credit cards, and/or payment through secured windows during certain hours.

### *Redesigning the Surroundings*

Well-lighted parking lots help deter robbers. If possible, try to keep vehicles from parking too near the entrance to your business. Armed robbery can be reduced by making access less convenient. For example, many convenience food store parking lots have precast concrete bumper blocks distributed so as to deter fast entry into and exit from the lot. Also, some businesses use silent alarms, video cameras to photograph crime in action, or video cameras tied to TV monitors in a security office.

The National Crime Prevention Council's Bureau of Justice Statistics has suggested a number of ways to make your workplace safer (including those mentioned above). The suggestions are shown in Figure 22–2.

## Theft

Theft has become a serious problem for businesses for numerous reasons: drug use, inflation, and unemployment, for example, as well as the challenge theft offers. Because of the extent of the problem, many national merchandising businesses add 2 to 3 percent to their prices to cover the cost of theft, but even this may not be enough to compensate for the total loss.

### *Types of Theft*

The two major types of theft are (1) that done by outsiders, usually known as shoplifting, and (2) that done by employees, as shown in Figure 22–3. Retailers sometimes refer to losses from both kinds of theft as *shrinkage.*

*Shoplifting.* Shoplifting is a major problem for retail establishments. While some losses are due to amateurs and kleptomaniacs, professional shoplifters cause the greatest prevention problems for businesses. The amateur may be a thrill seeker who takes an item or two to see whether or not he or she can get away with it. (This is often the case with children and teenagers.) The *kleptomaniac* has an uncontrollable urge to take things, whether they are

**Figure 22–2** How to Make Your Workplace Safe

Q

Tips for protecting yourself against robbery or assault at your place of business:

- Protect all openings and roof areas with burglar bars, steel mesh wires, or an alarm system.
- Consider installing a surveillance camera.
- Keep your purse or wallet in a locked drawer or closet at all times.
- Be extra cautious when using stairwells or restrooms that are open to the public.
- Get identification from delivery or repair people who want to enter a restricted area or take equipment.
- Check the identification of strangers who ask for confidential information.
- Call security or the police if you notice anyone suspicious.
- Keep emergency numbers for security, police, and fire assistance posted near phones.
- Never write down a safe or vault combination or a computer password.
- If you're working late, try to arrange your schedule so you'll be working with another employee.
- Ask the security guard or a co-worker to escort you to the parking lot or a cab.

*Source:* National Crime Council, Bureau of Justice Statistics; research by Pat Carr, *Long Beach Press-Telegram,* as reported in the *Mobile* (Alabama) *Register,* August 29, 1994, p. 1-D. Reprinted by permission: Tribune Media Services.

**Figure 22–3** Look Who's Stealing

Sources of inventory loss in the retail industry

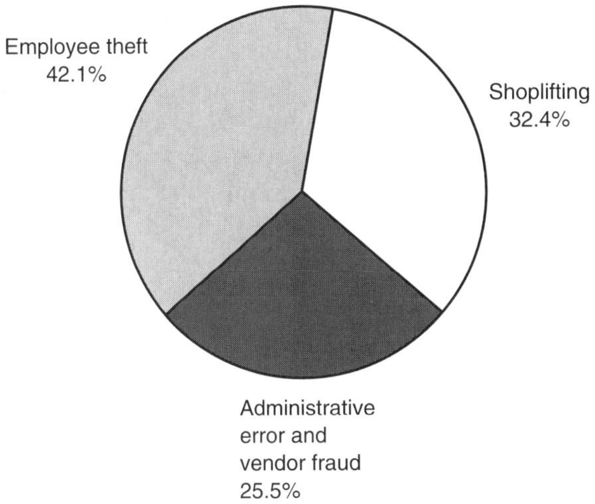


*Source:* Adapted from Harrison Donnelly, "Store Security: The Retail Impact," *Stores,* November 1994, pp. 57–58. Dr. Bart Weitz.

needed or not. Kleptomaniacs are more easily detected than the professional shoplifter, who may wear specially prepared or large garments, carry a large handbag, or ask for an empty box to conceal stolen merchandise. Business owners and managers are often shocked by the various techniques people use to remove merchandise from their premises, as the following example illustrates.

> A well-known matron was at the checkout counter. Upon inspection, her large purse was found to contain several prepackaged steaks and packages of luncheon meat. The store owner observed, "I thought she was one of our best customers. She has been coming here for years. I wonder how much she has taken."

Retailers are now striking back at shoplifters by means of a new tactic called *civil recovery,* or *civil restitution,* whereby they send letters to shoplifters or their parents demanding payment for the items taken. Some states permit not only recovery of the amount stolen but also damage awards for additional costs of crime prevention, damage to displays, or injuries resulting from the act. Civil Demand Associates, of Sherman Oaks, California, which specializes in this type of recovery, has clients nationwide.[19]

*Employee Theft.* As shown in Figure 22–3, employee theft is the major source of inventory loss in the retail industry. It may range from the simple act of an individual who takes only small items (such as pens or paper clips) to raids by groups that remove truckloads of merchandise. Surveys have found as many as 50 percent of employees admit stealing from their employer.[20]

Also, employees sometimes conspire with outsiders to steal from their employer. They may do this in various ways—for example, by charging the outsiders a lower price or by placing additional merchandise in their packages.

How serious is employee theft? It has been estimated that it costs all businesses around $40 billion annually.[21]

### Who Steals?

Research has shown that employees who think their income is too low, or stagnating, steal more often and in greater amounts than other employees. For example, an earlier study showed that those who steal tend to be young, full-time employees operating alone, and they steal merchandise more often than cash.[22]

### Techniques for Preventing Theft

Retail establishments have found the use of some of the following measures effective in reducing theft:

- Wide-angle and one-way mirrors to observe employee or customer behavior.
- TV cameras, tied to monitors, to observe a large area of the store.
- Electronic noise activators—some visible, some not—to warn of unprocessed merchandise leaving the store.

- Using paper-and-pencil tests of a potential employee's honesty.
- Security guards, if economically feasible.
- Security audits, such as the following:
    - Unannounced spot checks of critical activity areas, such as cash registers, employees' packages, car trunks, lunch pails, and waste disposal holding areas.
    - Visible security surveillance of work activities.
    - Weekly, monthly, or quarterly physical inventory checks.

In addition to using dogs and security guards (discussed earlier), construction contractors have found the following measures effective:

- Scheduling operations and purchasing materials for just-in-time delivery.
- Scheduling lower inventory levels on weekends.
- Fencing and lighting storage yards and clearing the area adjacent to the fence.
- Using locking systems that are difficult to jimmy.
- Unannounced rotation of the person responsible for receiving materials.
- Assigning a trusted employee the responsibility for checking materials into the job site, to prevent problems such as that in the following example.

> A contractor purchased a mobile concrete mixer and sent it to the site of one of his jobs. Those responsible for the mixer left it outside the fenced-in area that night, and it was stolen. Later, the contractor found that a subordinate had failed to record it for insurance coverage.

## White-Collar Crime

Another category of serious abuse against business is white-collar crimes. Like other types of crime, these have been rising rapidly.

### *Types of White-Collar Crimes*

**White-collar crimes** are those committed by managerial, professional, and technical employees.

**White-collar crimes** are committed by managerial, professional, and technical employees. They include the falsification of accounts; fraudulent accessing and manipulating of the computer; bribery of purchasing agents and other officials; collusion that results in unrecorded transactions; sale of proprietary information; and sabotage of new technology, new or old products, or customer relations. According to a recent survey, white-collar crime adds 15 to 20 percent to the price of everything we buy.[23]

Computer security is becoming a real problem for small firms. The two main problems are fraudulent use and intentional destruction of data. Not only has the number of such crimes increased, but so has their magnitude.

A survey of 73,000 on-line users by Yahoo! and Jupiter Communications found them averaging 9.7 hours a week "surfing the 'Net." Figure 22–4 shows their reasons for using it. Look at the last three figures to see how much of that was not related to work.

**Figure 22–4** Internet's Time Toll

**Reasons for on-line usage**

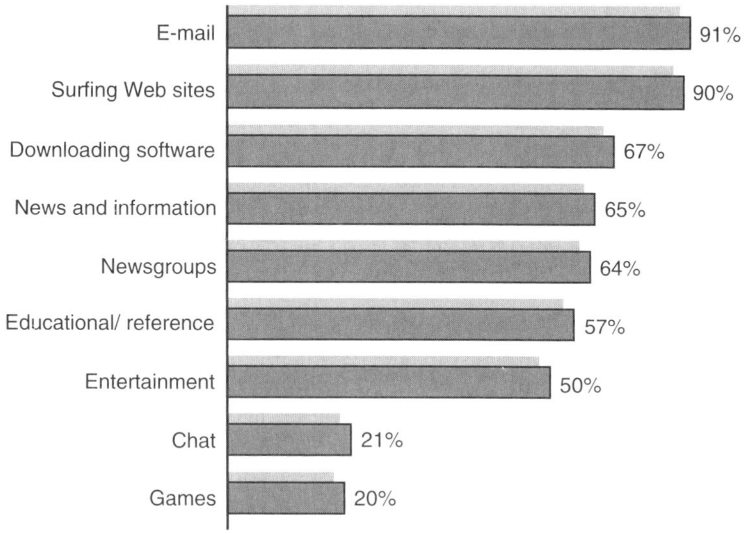

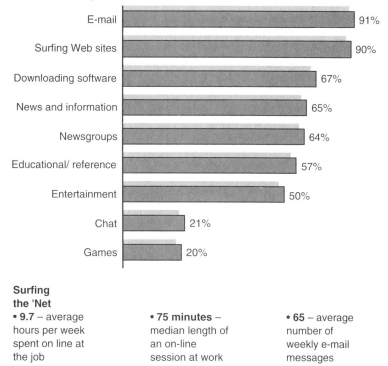

**Surfing the 'Net**

- **9.7** – average hours per week spent on line at the job
- **75 minutes** – median length of an on-line session at work
- **65** – average number of weekly e-mail messages

*Source:* Yahoo! and Jupiter Communications survey of 73,000 on-line users, as reported in *USA Today,* December 8, 1995, p. 1A. Copyright 1995, USA TODAY. Reprinted with permission.

Other surveys indicate that time lost due to leisure computer usage on the job amounts to about 1½ hours per employee per day.[24] Thus, 25 employees could cost a small organization about $37,500 per year in unnecessary on-line charges.

> For example, the Playboy Web site gets 90,000 to 200,000 "visits" daily, mostly for pictorials. Not surprisingly, the peak usage happens during business hours.[25]

Another problem area is pirating software and computer disks. Figure 22–5 shows the magnitude of this problem. Using Technology to Succeed explores another dimension of the issue.

Another form of white-collar crime is often committed against potential entrepreneurs. Scam artists, working with telephones and a "suckers list," tend to target individuals out of work as a result of corporate downsizing. These swindlers, pushing bogus get-rich-quick schemes, have cheated many inexperienced entrepreneurs out of several hundred million dollars. "The victims are not greedy rich people but distressed middle Americans," says Deborah Bortner of the Washington State Securities Division.[26]

> For example, investors lost an average of $20,000 buying popcorn vending machines sold by Worldwide Marketing and Distribution. The FTA said the machines randomly dispensed "popcorn cups and half-cooked kernels."

## USING TECHNOLOGY TO SUCCEED

### Is That Disk Genuine?

Once regarded as an "offshore" issue affecting primarily Southeast Asia and Eastern Europe, software piracy, especially in the form of counterfeit CD-ROMs, has now become a serious concern in the United States. With the cost of CD-ROM duplicators down to as little as $999, counterfeiting has become an easy investment.

Because street prices of software vary widely, purchasers might not question even a suspiciously reasonable price, but caution is needed because counterfeit CDs are turning up everywhere. Companies reporting counterfeiting include Broderbund, Intuit, Microsoft, and Novell, and they warn that "among the possible pitfalls of winding up with a counterfeit CD-ROM [are] poor performance, bugs, incomplete or nonexistent documentation, no technical support or upgrade deals, and the risk that a virus will infect your computer." Not to mention that it's a crime!

It's not always easy to tell a legitimate copy from a counterfeit one, but here are some clues:

- Poor print quality on the package or on the disc.
- Smudged letters or misspellings in the package's text.
- Documentation that's incomplete or missing.
- Blurred or off-center artwork on the box or jewel case.
- No holographic seal on the spine of the packaging.
- No certificate of authenticity (Microsoft ships one with every copy of DOS and Windows).

Another precaution is to limit where you buy software. Microsoft corporate attorney Anne M. Murphy says that well over half the software titles and CD-ROMs sold at computer fairs and flea markets are counterfeit. "You might find a reseller selling overstock of legitimate products," she concedes, "but the overwhelming majority of the goods are counterfeit." As for retail stores, most industry experts agree that consumers are fairly safe buying from large national chains, but they say the chances of getting an illegal copy increase when you buy from mom-and-pop stores. "They're more vulnerable to the economic pressures," says Bob Kruger, director of enforcement for the Business Software Alliance (BSA). Kruger is quick to point out, however, that retailers may not know they're selling counterfeit goods, particularly when the CDs are in one of the popular 10-packs that include legitimate disks from many leading publishers.

In an effort to curb the distribution of illegal software, the BSA planned to launch a campaign in early 1996 to authorize software resellers as BSA Approved Software Dealers. It will take time before a significant number of dealers are on board, but those who are will have posters and other materials to let customers know of their participation in the program.

In the meantime, even though counterfeit goods might show up more frequently at small, single-location stores, consumers shouldn't stop shopping at those establishments. What they should do is keep a wary eye out for deals that seem to be too good to be true.

*Source:* Roberta Furger, "Counterfeiting Comes to CD-ROMs," *PC World,* March 1996, pp. 292–93. Reprinted with the permission of PC WORLD Communications, Inc.

### *Ways to Minimize White-Collar Crime*

Special measures must be taken to minimize crimes by white-collar personnel. Some deterrents you can use include audits, being aware of employee work habits, identification, and bonding. Also, as mentioned above, small firms that use computers may need the services of a firm with computer security expertise.

**Figure 22–5** Hard Time for Software

**Worldwide, software companies lost more money to piracy than McDonald's made in 1993.**

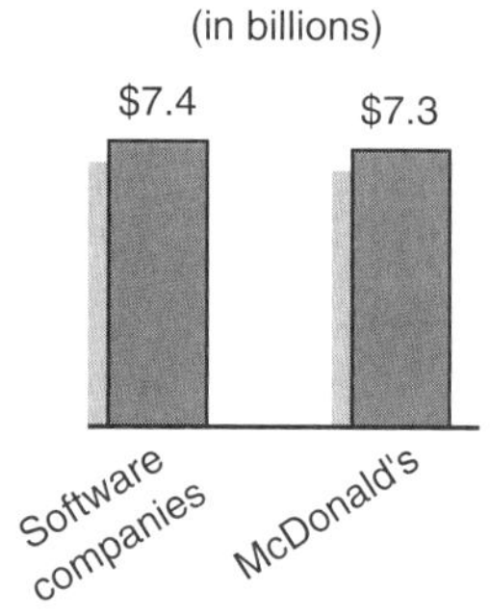


*Source:* Software Publishers Association, as reported in *USA Today,* September 1, 1994, p. 1A. Copyright 1994, USA TODAY. Reprinted with permission.

Audits of data such as past sales transactions, inventory levels, purchase prices, and accounts receivable may uncover undesirable activities.

You should be aware of your white-collar employees' work habits. They may all be open and aboveboard, but they should be checked. You should ask such questions as: Do they work nights regularly? Do they never take a day off? Do they forgo their usual vacation? Standards of living, dress, car, housing, entertainment, and travel that seem to cost more than an employee should be able to afford often signal economic misconduct.

Proper identification, along with a device that takes pictures of a check and the person cashing it, tends to discourage bad-check artists. Although this practice may be too expensive for your small firm, your bank may assist in developing effective identification procedures. Many states have passed bad-check laws, which permit a business that receives a bad check to collect not only its face value but also double to triple damages in small claims court. This financial penalty helps to reduce loss.

Since credit cards are frequently stolen, additional identification should be required. Be sure the signature corresponds to the one on the card. Also, you should be sure to ascertain the validity of trade documents, such as invoices and securities. Each year, millions of dollars are lost by businesspeople through carelessness that allows others to palm off bogus documents.

Fidelity bonding helps insure against employee fraud or theft. The employer pays a premium to an insurance company, which then assumes the risk and reimburses the company for any loss.

## Document Security

Our personal experience in working with small businesses, as well as press releases in recent years, has made us aware of the importance of document security. As shown in Chapter 21, *information is a vital factor in managing and controlling business activities,* and its management and maintenance help to assure the continuation of the business. The life of your business depends on the appropriate recording of information, its transmission to the appropriate person, and its security. Records with confidential information should be stored in bank lockboxes, safes, or restricted areas, and only authorized persons should have access to them. And all records should be protected by backups.

## USING TECHNOLOGY TO SUCCEED

### Accustomed to Your Face

We as a society spend an inordinate amount of time, energy, and money safeguarding our belongings. Think about it: We purchase expensive alarm systems for our cars and homes; our ATM cards have personal identification numbers; our long-distance calling cards have access numbers; high-end professional software systems have access codes and passwords—you can't even check your credit card balance over the telephone without first giving your Social Security number. Whether it's a simple deadbolt or a long series of access codes to a software system, for the most part, the security measures of today are fairly easy to circumvent. In other words, "where there's a will, there's a way" to break even the most complicated codes and passwords.

Identification Technologies International (ITI) has a solution to this dilemma. The company has come up with a high-tech computer program that does away with keys, PINs, secret codes, and passwords. Instead, it uses a set of defining features so individual that your identical twin couldn't even imitate it—your face.

ITI calls its product the "one-on-one" facial imaging system. It records a person's facial characteristics, sets up a digitized facial map, and transfers the data to a microchip that is embedded in a credit-card-sized access card. When a person tries to gain access to a building or a program, the access card is inserted into a computer reader. A camera then photographs the person; the system digitizes the photograph and compares it to the image saved on the access card. If the images match, access is granted.

The system has been thoroughly tested and has shown uncanny accuracy—even in distinguishing identical twins. Only changing one's appearance will disrupt the system. For example, a new mustache or beard or unusually heavy makeup will alter a person's image so the system will not grant access.

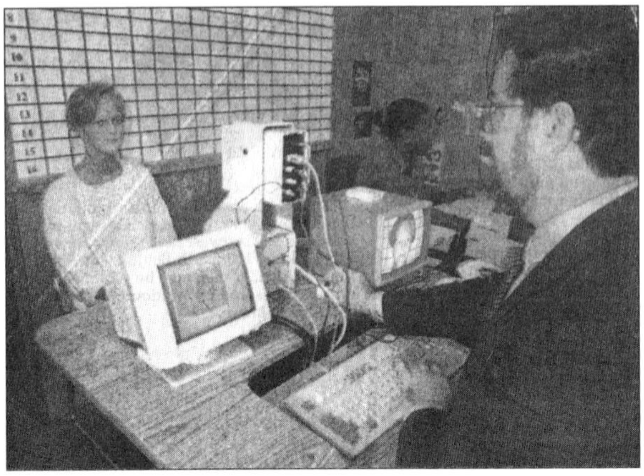

AP/Wide World Photos.

For obvious reasons, credit card companies, banks, hospitals, universities, and the government have shown interest in the system. A prototype at the University of Miami College of Engineering computer lab has proven to be more than up to the task of guarding hundreds of thousands of dollars worth of equipment and programs.

ITI planned on marketing the system during the summer of 1996. Although the cost of the system had not been determined, the company says prices will depend on variables such as how much equipment is needed, the degree of security desired, and the number of people who will use the system. The prototype at the University of Miami cost around $2,000.

*Source:* Adapted by William Jay Megginson from Evan Perez, "This Company Never Forgets a Face," *Mobile* (Alabama) *Press Register,* January 7, 1996, pp. 1-F, 2-F. Used with permission of Associated Press.

The proprietary nature of confidential business records and various documents makes it essential that you protect them from unauthorized eyes and hands, as shown in Using Technology to Succeed. The trade secrets and competitive advantage of your business may be lost if this information passes into the wrong hands. Therefore, a list of authorized personnel should be prepared and provided to those responsible for document security.

An unbending rule should be that under no circumstance is it permissible to remove confidential material from the restricted area or from the business premises. Some business owners think they can save on personnel costs by permitting material to be carried to an employee's residence where the employee works on the firm's records after hours. The chance of loss, the opportunity for access by unauthorized persons, and the risk of a claim for adequate compensation make this practice inadvisable.

## Safeguarding Employees with Preventive Measures

Within a business, various types of accidents and health problems occur, causing potential losses. The use of insurance to eliminate or minimize disastrous financial losses in a company was discussed earlier in this chapter. In addition, safeguards can be instituted to reduce human suffering as well as costs to a company and employees.

Employees are a valuable resource that you should protect through proper safety procedures as shown in Chapter 15. These procedures should be preventive in nature. Not only should you provide a safe place for workers, but, in addition, they must work safely, since most accidents occur because of human error, such as driving an automobile carelessly or handling equipment improperly.

Guards over moving tools, devices to keep hands away or stop machines, employee protective gear, warnings of unsafe conditions, and medical treatment are some safeguards used to protect employees from accidents and health problems and to prevent lawsuits.

## What You Should Have Learned

**1.** One of the greatest challenges for small businesses is dealing with risk. Risk management minimizes financial shocks. While pure risk is uncertain, it is often measurable and insurable. Speculative risk occurs with voluntary decisions. Risk may be avoided, prevented, assumed, or transferred.

**2.** Insurance can be used to minimize losses due to risks. Small businesses usually need insurance for: (*a*) fire, (*b*) casualty, (*c*) product/service liability, (*d*) workers' compensation, (*e*) employee life and health, and (*f*) business continuation, as well as (*g*) fidelity and surety bonds.

**3.** In choosing an insurer, consider its financial characteristics, flexibility in meeting your requirements, and the services it renders. An insurance company can be judged on financial stability, specialization in types of coverage, ability to tailor policies to meet your needs, and cost of protection.

**4.** Although businesses should be insured against losses, they should also take steps to prevent crimes, such as armed robbery, theft, and white-collar crime, especially computer crimes. Measures that can reduce the chances of being robbed include modifying the store's layout, securing entrances, using security dogs, controlling the handling of cash, and redesigning the surrounding area.

Theft includes shoplifting by outsiders and employee theft. Security measures to reduce theft include wide-angle and one-way mirrors, TV cameras, electronic noise activators on merchandise, screening of prospective employees, security guards, and security audits.

White-collar crime includes removal of cash; falsification of accounts; fraudulent computer access and manipulation; bribery; collusion resulting in unrecorded transactions; sale of proprietary information; and sabotage of new technology, products, or customer relations. Ways to minimize white-collar crime include auditing of records, observing employees' work habits, requiring proper identification with checks and credit cards, and fidelity bonding. Confidential documents should be stored in bank lockboxes, safes, or restricted areas.

**5.** A small firm has a special responsibility to protect employees, to provide a safe workplace, and to encourage employees to maintain safe work habits.

## QUESTIONS FOR DISCUSSION

1. What is meant by risk management?
2. Distinguish between pure risk and speculative risk as they apply to small businesses.
3. Discuss four ways small firms can cope with risk.
4. What are some considerations in determining a small business's need for insurance?
5. What types of insurance are commonly carried by small businesses? Describe each type of coverage.
6. What criteria should you use in choosing an insurer?
7. Discuss some methods a small business can use to reduce the chances of being robbed.
8. What is meant by white-collar crime? What are some ways to minimize it?
9. What are some methods used to safeguard employees?

## *CASE 22*

### BEWARE OF "SOFTLIFTING"

These days, even the smallest of businesses are using computers. As mentioned in Chapter 21, the microcomputer has replaced the file cabinet, resulting in a great need for computer security. When we think about computer security we generally think in terms of protecting the equipment or the data on the hard disk. However, there is another aspect of computer security that business owners must be aware of and guard against, namely, "softlifting." A business owner who has more than one computer may be tempted to buy one copy of the needed software and install it on all the computers to save money. *DON'T DO IT!*

This is softlifting and it's a very common problem. According to the Software Publishers Association (SPA), one in five personal computer programs in use today is an illegal copy. Software bootlegging costs U.S. software publishers $1.2 billion each year, on sales of only $6 to $7 billion. This is why "Software Police" are cracking down hard and the penalties are harsh. Softlifting recently became a felony with penalties of up to $250,000 and five years in jail.

The University of Oregon Continuation Center in Eugene, Oregon, thought it would "save a few bucks" by softlifting. But it got caught and had to pay a $130,000 fine and hold a national conference on copyright laws and software use.

Parametrix Inc. of Seattle also learned the hard way. It was raided by the "Software Police," who had a search warrant and were accompanied by a U.S. marshall. The raid turned up dozens of bootlegged copies of software programs. Parametrix agreed to pay fines totaling $350,000. How does the SPA find out about these abuses? The tipoff usually comes from a call to the SPA's toll-free piracy hotline. Often the caller is an ex-employee or a disgruntled employee who is seeking revenge. Regardless, more and more companies are getting caught. Obviously, thousands don't get caught, but since 1984 the SPA has conducted 75 raids and filed more than 300 lawsuits.

The best advice is: *Stay legal!* Don't risk losing the business you've worked so hard to build just to save a few bucks, because according to the SPA, if you're softlifting you are definitely living on borrowed time.

*Source:* "Companies, Beware of 'Software Police,' " Associated Press release, in *Mobile* (Alabama) *Press Register,* November 16, 1992, p. 5B. Used with permission of Associated Press.

## QUESTIONS

1. How severe do you perceive this problem to be? Why or why not?
2. Are you aware of any organizations that have participated in "softlifting"? If so, do they deserve to be caught and punished, in your opinion?
3. How can a small business owner prevent employees from making bootlegged copies of software programs for themselves?
4. You have a small business with five computers. Your old software is obsolete and must be replaced, but your business is struggling financially. Would you risk buying one copy of the software and installing it on all five machines? Explain why or why not.

## APPLICATION 22-1

Jeff Thomas, manager of a clothing store in Dallas, Texas, observed that over the last several months, inventory and sales were not equaling. When he began to compare evening to daytime sales, he noticed that sales were staying the same, but the inventory count was lower in the evening than in the morning. Most of his 20 employees are on alternate schedules from daytime to evening. In an effort to curb possible stealing, Jeff began taking inventory more frequently and keeping a tighter control over the employees he placed over the inventory counting and control.

## QUESTIONS

1. What are some ways Jeff can improve security?
2. How can Jeff detect whether an employee is stealing?

## ACTIVITY 22–1

*Directions:* Use information from this chapter to solve the puzzle below.

ACROSS

1 Risk prevention

3 Refusal to undertake risky activity

4 Managerial crime

6 Provided at fee to reimburse loss

8 Conserve earning power by minimizing shock from losses

9 Insurance equal to percentage of property value

11 Risk assumption

12 Uncertainty that unpredictable event will result in loss

13 Another word for the answer to 11 Across

DOWN

2 Protects a business from losses resulting from its service

5 Uncertainty that voluntary risk will result in loss

7 Shifting risk to someone outside

10 Result of calculated risk

ACROSS 1 Loss control 3 Risk avoidance 4 White collar crimes 6 Insurance 8 Risk management 9 Coinsurance 11 Self insurance 12 Pure risk 13 Risk assumption
DOWN 2 Service liability insurance 5 Speculative risk 7 Risk transfer 10 Success

CHAPTER

# 23

# Business-Government Relations and Business Ethics

*No man shall be judged except by the legal judgment of his peers or the law of the land.*
—Magna Carta (1215)

*Business has a soul, and management has social responsibilities as a major partner in the community, alongside capital and labour.*—Oliver Sheldon, *The Philosophy of Management* (1923)

*The dominant issues are the small-business person's access to capital; and, second, the burden of regulation.*—Philip Lader, SBA

## LEARNING OBJECTIVES

After studying the material in this chapter, you will be able to:

1. Understand the legal system in which small businesses operate, and explain some basic business laws affecting them.
2. Discuss the role played by government assistance.
3. Describe some burdensome aspects of government regulations and paperwork.
4. Explain how to choose a lawyer.
5. Describe what is ethical and socially responsible behavior.

# P R O F I L E

## EVANGELINE OAK OF CARENCRO

Photo by Leon C. Megginson.

Evangeline Oak, located in Carencro, Louisiana, is a modern 152-bed nursing home, with 48 more beds being added. It is, in reality, a miniversion of a hospital. Unlike an impersonal hospital, however, with patients checking in and checking out, Evangeline Oak provides a home away from home for its *residents*—the term always used for those in its care.

There is a nurses' station in each of the facility's two wings. One wing houses 68 tube-fed or bed-bound patients, while 84 to 85 residents who are fully ambulatory and self-sufficient occupy the other wing.

The home, which is a Louisiana-chartered corporation, is owned by some 20 shareholders, but a majority interest is held by Mr. and Mrs. Frankie LaFleur, who also own and operate several group homes for the mentally impaired. Mr. LaFleur, who retired from active management of Evangeline Oak in 1991, is only indirectly involved in its day-to-day operation, but Mrs. LaFleur still prepares and handles payroll for all their employees. Mr. LaFleur, together with his children, is actively involved in the operation of the group homes.



Ruth R. Stelly, administrator, has been a licensed nursing home administrator for 20 years and has worked at Evangeline for four. She has a degree in nursing home administration from the University of Southwestern Louisiana in nearby Lafayette.

Photo by Leon C. Megginson.

Stelly has a good relationship with the residents. She knows them all by name and knows their families on a personal, yet professional basis. "There are times when the residents need someone to talk to and confide in," she says, "and I try to be available to talk to the residents and encourage them to do for themselves." The residents know who she is and appear to appreciate the attention she gives them. Stelly also said she must be very careful to treat all the residents alike and give each of them equal attention.

Evangeline Oak, which has been operating for 12 years, has 127 full-time and part-time employees, all of whom are paid minimum wage or above. The full-time salaried employees are the administrator, a director of nursing, and an assistant director of nursing. Other employees, paid on an hourly basis, include registered nurses (RNs) aides, and orderlies. There is an RN on duty at all times to comply with the State of Louisiana regulations for nursing homes with over 100 beds. Resident food service is provided every day of the week by a dietary manager, an assistant dietary manager, and other employees. There are also activity directors, a social service director, a beautician three days a week, a barber once a month, two maintenance men, quality assurance aides who are in charge of the nurses' aides, and employees to provide laundry and housekeeping services. All employee wages conform to federal wage and hour guidelines, and employees receive Social Security and Medicare benefits and are eligible to receive workers' compensation and unemployment insurance. They are also covered by the Family and Medical Leave Act of 1993.

Because the home must comply with the Occupational Safety and Health Act of 1970, there is a full-time OSHA coordinator. The home is in full compliance with the Americans with Disabilities Act (ADA) of 1990, providing ramps and other facilities to aid the impaired.

The employees make every effort to maximize the residents' health and quality of care. All residents are encouraged to bring personal belongings with them. Each room is personalized with the occupant's curtains, knickknacks, books, pictures—familiar things to make them feel at home and impress on them the fact that they belong there.

Evangeline Oak provides many activities for residents. They are frequently taken on group outings in the community—to the zoo, out dancing, to restaurants, and so on. At the home, residents are encouraged to participate in games and other activities that promote interaction with one another, creating a feeling of involvement and belonging.

*Source:* Meetings, communication, and correspondence with Ruth Stelly.

Your small business will operate in a legal and governmental environment that sets rules and regulations for activities from starting the business to going out of business. Throughout the book, we've talked about the operation of a small business within the framework of government assistance and regulation. Now we would like to go into greater detail about this environment. We will look at some of the most important government laws and regulations affecting small firms, as well as show how governments provide assistance and control. Then we will discuss how to choose a lawyer and how to maintain ethical and socially responsible behavior.

## Understanding the Legal Environment

Because it is so important to know and obey government laws and regulations, we will give you an overview of the subject. For further coverage, you

**Table 23–1** Selected Basic Legal Terminology

| | |
|---|---|
| **Common law** | Unwritten law derived from judicial decisions based on customs and usages accepted by the people. |
| **Statutory law** | Body of laws passed by federal, state, and local governments. |
| **Interstate commerce clause** | Gives Congress the right to "regulate commerce with foreign nations, and among the several states." |
| **Police power** | States' right to regulate business, including the right to use the force of the state to promote the general welfare of citizens. All laws must be based on the federal or a state constitution. |
| **Due process** | Implies that everyone is entitled to a day in court, and all processes must be equal and fair. |
| **Legislative branch of government** | The U.S. Congress, state legislature, county/city council, or any other body that passes laws. |
| **Executive branch of government** | President, governor, mayor, or any other who enforces the laws through regulatory agencies and decrees. |
| **Judicial branch of government** | The court system, or those who interpret the laws and supervise enforcement. |
| **Public law** | Deals with the rights and powers of the government. |
| **Criminal law** | Deals with punishing those who commit illegal acts. |
| **Private law** | Is administered between two or more citizens. |
| **Civil law** | Deals with violations against another person who has been harmed in some way. |

should obtain competent legal assistance from someone familiar with local business conditions.

You're already familiar with some of the most basic legal principles, such as *Everyone is equal under the law, Everyone is entitled to his or her day in court,* and *A person is presumed innocent until proven guilty.* Table 23–1 provides a closer look at some basic legal principles and terminology.

All laws affecting small businesses are based on the federal or a state constitution. However, the making, administering, and interpreting of laws are separated into three distinct branches of government: legislative, executive, and judicial. Moreover, laws are made at all levels of our government, including federal, state, county, and municipal levels. These levels are generally referred to as *multiple levels of government,* and each level administers its own laws. Occasionally some of these laws are contradictory, so be prepared to retain competent legal representation.

## Basic Business Laws

The most important laws, as far as small firms are concerned, are those dealing with (1) contracts; (2) sales; (3) property; (4) patents, copyrights, and trademarks; (5) agency; (6) negotiable instruments; (7) torts; and (8) bankruptcy. Influencing all of these—and, in turn, influenced by them—is the Uniform Commercial Code (UCC).

## The Uniform Commercial Code (UCC)

The **Uniform Commercial Code (UCC)** is a set of uniform model statutes to govern business and commercial transactions in all states.

Since laws affecting business vary greatly from state to state, an effort was made to draft a set of uniform model statutes to govern business and commercial transactions in all 50 states.[1] The result was the **Uniform Commercial Code (UCC)**, consisting of the following 10 parts: (1) general provisions, (2) sales, (3) commercial paper, (4) bank deposits and collections, (5) letters of credit, (6) bulk transfers, (7) documents of title, (8) investment securities, (9) secured transactions, and (10) effective date and repealer.

The code has been adopted by all 50 states, the U.S. Virgin Islands, and the District of Columbia, with minor exceptions. For example, Louisiana, which still has many laws based on the Code Napoléon, the French Civil Code that has been in effect there since the Louisiana Purchase, has adopted only Articles 1, 3, 4, and 5 of the UCC.

Instead of trying to describe the entire UCC, we will look at the most important of the business laws.

## Contracts

A **contract** is an agreement between two individuals or groups that is enforced by law.

The law of contracts deals with legal business relationships resulting from agreements between two or more individuals or businesses. A **contract** is an agreement between two individuals or groups that is enforced by law. A contract may be valid and enforceable whether it is oral or written. Without contracts there would be no business as we know it, for contract law affects almost all business operations.

For a contract to be legal in the United States, the following conditions must be met:

1. Both parties must be legally competent to act. This means not only being of sound mind but also being the authorized representative of a group or corporation.
2. The agreement must not involve illegal actions or promises.
3. A valid offer to enter into an agreement must be made by one party, in a serious manner, not in jest. The offer may be explicit—an automobile salesperson may offer to sell you the Super Deluxe Whizbang for "only $15,000 plus your old car." Or it may be implicit—a retailer marks a VCR on display "$299.99."
4. The second party must voluntarily accept this offer, equally seriously, without duress (physical force or other compulsion) or "undue influence."
5. Each party must promise the other something of value, such as money, services, goods, or the surrender of some legal right.
6. The contract must be in a legal form, even if oral, but may be quite simple (as Figure 23-1 illustrates). It must contain at least four elements to be a valid contract—the identity of the two parties, an offer, consideration, and acceptance—but little else is needed.

Notice in the sample contract that (1) both Pete Roe, the leader of the band, and Sheri Doe, elected by the residents of Georgia Avenue, were authorized representatives; (2) the dance was legal; (3) there was a valid offer—to provide music for the dance—which (4) was accepted; and (5)

**Figure 23–1** A Simple Contract

CONTRACT

The band called the "Music Masters," composed of six musicians, agrees to play for the South Georgia Avenue Street Dance on Saturday, October 26, 199_ , from 3:30 to 6:30 P.M., with two 20-minute intermissions. The band will be paid a total of $600 ($100 on acceptance of the contract and the balance in cash on completion of the performance).

Signed on July 1, 199_ , at 168 S. Georgia Avenue, Mobile, Alabama.

*Sheri Doe*
Sheri Doe, Dance Chairman
and
*Pete Roe*
Pete Roe, Leader of the "Music Masters"

there was something of value offered by each party—a payment of $600 in return for three hours of music.

Remember, a contract is a legally binding document, and ignorance is no excuse. So take to heart the message in Figure 23–2.

## Sales

Laws affecting the sale of products are really part of contract law. When we pay the stated price for a product without negotiation, we don't usually realize we are entering into an **implied contract**, which can be inferred from the actions of the parties involved. If two parties negotiate and reach an agreement, an **express contract** is formed, even if nothing is written down.

An **implied contract** is an unwritten contract that results from the actions of the parties involved.

An **express contract** results when two parties negotiate and reach an agreement.

**Figure 23–2**

*Source:* Courtesy of Schieffelin & Somerset Co.

For example, if you go to a physician, state your symptoms, and receive treatment, a valid implied contract can be inferred. If a prospective buyer makes an offer on a house and it is accepted by the seller, an express contract exists.

## Warranties

A **warranty** is a representation made by the seller to the buyer regarding the quality and performance of a product.

A **warranty**, which is a representation made by the seller to the buyer regarding the quality and performance of a product, may be express or implied. Express warranties, which are specific representations made by the seller regarding the product, often come in the form of warranty cards to be completed and returned by the buyer. Implied warranties are those legally imposed on the seller. For example, the FDA defines what is meant by "cheese" as opposed to "pasteurized process cheese food"; a seller who labels a product with one of those names implies that the buyer has a right to expect that it will be as defined. Unless implied warranties are disclaimed before the sale, in writing, by the seller, they are automatically applied. The law of warranties for sales transactions is set forth in the UCC.

## Product Liability

As shown in Chapter 22, a serious problem you face these days is product liability. An ever-present question facing a small business is: How safe *should* the product be? Much attention is now being focused on the design of products and quality control to ensure product safety. But if all possible safety precautions were built into all products and their production, they'd be prohibitively expensive—and sometimes impossible to use. Thus, the degree of safety required depends on the product. While a defective compact disc may present only a minor inconvenience, the proper functioning of a heart pacemaker is a matter of life and death, so each pacemaker must be perfect.

For example, Cordis Corporation, a medical equipment manufacturer, pleaded guilty in 1989 to charges of selling thousands of defective pacemakers and batteries prone to corrode. Cordis agreed to pay $564,000 in claims and penalties.[2]

## Property

Property law involves the rights and duties resulting from the ownership or use of personal or real property. Contract, sales, and other types of law also apply to the transfer of such property. Table 23–2 presents some selected aspects of property law.

## Patents, Copyrights, and Trademarks

The legal protection of personal property also includes protecting patents, copyrights, and trademarks.

A **patent** is a grant giving the inventor of a product the exclusive right to make, use, or sell it in the United States.

A **patent** is a grant from the U.S. Patent and Trademark Office giving the inventor of a product the exclusive right to make, use, or sell the invention in the United States for 17 years from the date it is issued. After that time, the patent expires and cannot be renewed. To be patented, a device must be new,

**Table 23–2** Selected Components of Property Law

| | |
|---|---|
| **Real property** | Land or anything permanently attached to it. |
| **Personal property** | Anything of value that can be individually owned, other than land. |
| **Deed** | Transfer of ownership of real property. |
| **Lease** | Allows limited use of a property granted by the owner in writing. |
| **Tangible property** | Material good or product that can be touched, seen, and felt. |
| **Intangible property** | Represents ownership; examples are a stock certificate and a bank deposit book. |
| **Title** | Proof of ownership that may be conveyed. |

useful, and not obvious to a person in the related field of ordinary skill or knowledge. Inventors can enhance their chances of getting a patent by following the basic steps suggested by the Patent and Trademark Office.[3]

The number of patent applications per year has soared during the last 12 years. From about 60,000 applications in 1983, the number escalated to around 118,000 in 1995. The number of software-related applications was less than 1,000 in 1983 but skyrocketed from around 2,500 in 1993 to around 6,000 in 1995. This increase reflects a healthy growth in computer operations in recent years.[4]

A **copyright** is the exclusive right that protects creators of "original works of authorship" such as artistic, literary, dramatic, and musical works. It protects only the form in which the idea is expressed, not the idea itself. While you can copyright something merely by claiming the right to do so, *Form TX must be filed with the Copyright Office of the Library of Congress to register the copyright.* A valid copyright lasts for the life of the creator plus 50 years. When a copyright expires, the work becomes public property and can be used by anyone, free of charge. The internationally recognized symbol © is used to designate a copyrighted work.

A **copyright** is the exclusive right that protects creators of "original" artistic, literary, dramatic, and musical works.

A **trademark** is any distinctive name, term, word, design, symbol, or device used to identify the origin of a product or to distinguish it from other products on the market. Registration of a trademark prevents others from employing a similar mark to identify their products. In the United States, a trademark cannot be reserved in advance of its use. Instead, the owner must establish the right to a trademark by actually using it. (Until it is registered, it can be distinguished by the symbol ™.)

A **trademark** is a distinctive name, term, word, design, symbol, or device used to identify a product or to distinguish it from other products.

A registered trademark (denoted by the symbol ®) cannot keep anyone else from producing the same item or from selling it under a different trademark. It merely prevents others from using the same or a confusingly similar trademark for the same or a similar product.

To register a trademark, the applicant must prove it is distinctive. As long as a producer continues to use a trademark, no one can legally infringe on it. But an owner may lose the exclusive right to a trademark if it loses its unique character and becomes a generic name. *Aspirin, cellophane, thermos,* and *shredded wheat* were once enforceable trademarks but, because of common usage, can no longer be licensed as a company's trademark. On the other hand, Velcro®, Kelly Girl®, Xerox®, Kleenex®, and Rollerblade® are still valid trademarks fiercely protected by their owners.

## Agency

The **principal** is one who wants to do something but is unable or unwilling to do it personally.

The **agent** is the person or company engaged to act on behalf of the principal.

The term *agency* describes the legal relationship between a principal and an agent. The **principal** is the person who wants to do something but is unable or unwilling to do it personally. The **agent** is the person or company engaged to act on behalf of the principal. All types of business transactions, and many personal ones, involve agency.

## Negotiable Instruments

A **negotiable instrument** is a financial document that is transferable from one party to another.

Special laws are needed to deal with buying, owning, and selling negotiable instruments. A **negotiable instrument** is some form of financial document, such as a check, bank draft, or certificate of deposit, that is transferable from one party to another. The law requires that negotiable instruments be written, not oral; signed by the maker; good for the promise of a specified sum of money; and payable when endorsed by the payee.

## Torts

A **tort** is a wrongful act by one party, not covered by criminal law, that results in injury to a second party's person, property, or reputation, for which the first party is liable.

A **tort** is a wrongful act by one party, not covered by criminal law, that results in injury to a second party's person, property, or reputation, for which the first party is liable. Laws dealing with torts provide for the performance of duties and compensation for the physical, mental, or economic injuries resulting from faulty products or actions of employees. This usually involves some form of economic restitution (monetary payment) for damages or losses incurred.

> For example, Kenneth T. Kaltman was recently charged with harassment, larceny, and 20 counts of computer crime. Kaltman worked for National Regulatory Services of Salisbury, Connecticut, until he was fired in May 1995. He then went to work for Securities Consultants, Inc., of Boca Raton, Florida.
>
> According to state police, Kaltman tapped into his former employer's voice mail, listened to business calls, deleted messages, and intercepted clients. After noticing irregularities in its voice mail system—and getting irate calls from clients whose previous calls had not been returned—National Regulatory's president contacted authorities. The FBI ran a "sting" operation by setting up a phone with a planted message from one of National Regulatory's legitimate customers. Kaltman allegedly retrieved the message, deleted it from National's system, and called the client to solicit business. Kaltman was held on $510,000 bail.[5]

**Bankruptcy** is a formal legal condition of inability to repay debts. People or businesses can petition the courts to be relieved of this financial obligation.

## Bankruptcy

Under **bankruptcy** law, people or businesses can petition the courts to be relieved of the obligation to pay debts they can't repay. There are two types of bankruptcy, voluntary and involuntary. *Voluntary bankruptcy* occurs when a debtor files an application with a court claiming that debts exceed assets and asks to be declared bankrupt. When one or more creditors file the bankruptcy petition against the debtor, it's called *involuntary bankruptcy*. The Bankruptcy Reform Act of 1978 provides for quick and efficient handling of both types.

**Chapter 11** of this act contains a provision for reorganizing the bankrupt business, whether the bankruptcy petition is filed voluntarily or involuntarily. Thus, the firm can continue to operate while its debts are being repaid. If the business is so far gone that it can't keep operating, it must be liquidated.

**Chapter 11** provides for reorganizing a bankrupt business, whether the bankruptcy petition is filed voluntarily or involuntarily.

You should consult a lawyer as soon as possible if your business is ever faced with a bankruptcy situation. See "Choosing and Using a Lawyer" later in this chapter for more details.

## Government Help for Small Businesses

Many examples of assistance to small businesses have been given throughout this text. Because most such help is provided by the SBA and the U.S. Department of Commerce, their assistance will be summarized.

### Small Business Administration (SBA)

As shown in Chapter 9, the SBA provides many types of direct and guaranteed loans for small firms.

D

> The SBA has created a program to simplify approval of SBA-guaranteed loans of less than $100,000. This program is called "LowDoc" and accounted for over half of the loans made in 1995. One study indicated that about 33 percent of these loans are to minority-owned businesses.[6]
>
> In addition to the LowDoc program, limitations are set on SBA loans. For instance, on January 1, 1995, the SBA set a limit of $500,000 on most of the loans it guarantees.[7]

The SBA's publications, such as its series of Management Aids; local workshops; small business development centers; and small business institutes provide help for small firms. Also, information on overseas marketing is provided. As shown in Figure 23–3, the SBA now has an "SBA Answer Desk" with a toll-free number.

**Figure 23–3**

SBA Answer Desk
1-800-U-ASK-SBA (800-827-5722)

The toll-free telephone number listed above is for the small business information and referral service being offered by the U.S. Small Business Administration. Call for information on starting a new business or for sources of technical and financial assistance for an already existing business.

*Source: Journal of Small Business Management* 32 (October 1994): 27.

**Figure 23–4** President Bill Clinton Presenting Awards at White House Ceremonies for 1995 Small Business Week

Photo courtesy of Kathy Mitcham, at the SBA.

In addition, the SBA sponsors the Service Corps of Retired Executives (SCORE). SCORE's 750 chapters and satellites nationwide comprise 13,000 volunteer members who specialize in helping people develop their business ideas. As shown in Case 23–1, SCORE can match one or more of these counselors to a specific business. It can also call on its extensive roster of public relations experts, bankers, lawyers, and the like to answer the important and detailed questions you might have about setting up a business. Now they'll even work with you as long as you need after you start your business. Some clients consult with SCORE counselors for several years.

Another way the SBA helps is by encouraging small business owners to try to perform more effectively. It does this by making state and national awards for the "Small Business Persons of the Year." Figure 23–4 shows President Bill Clinton announcing the 1995 awards at the White House.

## U.S. Department of Commerce

As indicated in earlier chapters, the U.S. Department of Commerce offers assistance through its International Trade Administration (ITA), its U.S. and Foreign Commercial Service Agency (USFCSA), and its Minority Business Development Agency (MBDA). Finally, the department's Census Bureau furnishes much demographic information. For small firms in a hurry, data may be obtained electronically.

## Other Government Agencies

Among the other agencies helping small business are the U.S. Department of Agriculture, which provides assistance through the Cooperative Extension Service, the Federal Land Bank Association, the Production Credit Association, and the Farmers Home Administration, and the IRS. In addition, a wide range of state and local agencies provide help when contacted.

## HANDLING GOVERNMENT REGULATIONS AND PAPERWORK

As we mentioned in Chapter 1, if you want to see a small business person become incensed, mention government regulations and paperwork, which are a growing problem. At one time, smaller firms were exempt from many federal regulations and even some state and local ones. Today, though, these firms tend to be regulated the same as their larger competitors. While most small business owners are willing to comply with government regulations, compliance is often complex, costly, and time-consuming, and regulations are often confusing or contradictory, as the following example illustrates.

> According to Ron Smith, Colorado director of the National Federation of Independent Business, his state recently repealed laws requiring retail stores to get special licenses to sell ice or foil packages of aspirin. Still on the books, though, is a regulation saying hospitals will be fined if they don't present their annual budgets to the Colorado Hospital. The only problem is, the hospital was abolished several years ago.[8]

### Dealing with Regulatory Agencies

In theory, a regulatory agency is more flexible and sensitive to the needs of society than Congress can be, since less time is needed for an agency to develop and issue new regulations than for Congress to enact new legislation. Experience, however, doesn't seem to support this theory. Many small business managers believe, for example, that on occasion an agency's findings may be arbitrary or may protect its own security or that of the industry it's supposed to regulate.

*"Sparky's found a way to get a bite back out of the government."*

© 1996 Margaret P. Megginson. Reprinted with permission.

### Benefits of Government Regulation

Do the benefits of government regulation outweigh the costs? Since there's no profit mechanism to measure this, as there is in private business, and since both costs and benefits are hard to determine, estimates must be made. Even with these measurement limitations, though, it's been shown that some regulations are truly cost-effective.

> For example, air pollution requirements have provided economic benefits that far outweigh the costs of complying with them, according to the White House Council on Environmental Quality.[9]

When regulations are imposed on one industry or business they often generate opportunities for other small entrepreneurs.

> For example, when the EPA announced standards for replacements for automobile catalytic converters a few years ago, it created a market for replacement models that could be made more cheaply because they didn't have to last as long. Perfection Automotive Products Corp. of Livonia, Michigan, broadened its product line to make them. It added nearly 100 employees, doubling its previous work force, to serve the market.[10]

## Problems with Government Regulation

There are at least four areas of concern that small firms have with government regulations. The first problem is *the difficulty of understanding some of the regulations.* Many of them are often confusing and of a very restrictive nature, as the following example illustrates.

D

> The jobs at Koch Poultry Company in Chicago involve carving out the breasts of cold, raw chicken and flipping them onto a conveyor belt, which carries them to other workers who weigh, pack, and freeze them. While the pay is low—$4.50 an hour for beginners, up to a top of $6.75—the jobs require no education and few skills.
>
> According to Mark Kaminsky, chief financial officer, more than 90 percent of the 300 employees are Hispanic. It wasn't planned that way—it just happened, as the company uses employee referrals as the main recruiting method. It simplifies hiring, as there is no advertising cost or large human resource department.
>
> To the employees of the Chicago office of the EEOC, however, "Koch Poultry is a villain because it has too many Hispanics." Also, "hiring through 'word-of-mouth' was inherently discriminatory." Instead of letting Koch correct the problem by simply hiring more non-Hispanics, the EEOC worked up a formula based on (1) the number of workers, (2) how much they are paid, and (3) how many non-Hispanics Koch didn't hire. It then proposed to fine the company a sum based on this formula—at first $5.2 million (which was more than the company was worth), later $1.5 million, then $800,000.
>
> Next, Koch was to take out newspaper ads seeking people "who didn't work for Koch, but might have if they knew the jobs were available."
>
> After "some angry exchanges between the bureaucrats and Koch's lawyers," the company decided it would be better off "going to court and spending $100,000 in lawyers' fees," according to Kaminsky.[11] (It had cost Koch about $250,000 by early 1995.)[12]

A second problem is *the enormous amount of paperwork involved in preparing and handling the reports needed to comply with government regulations and in maintaining the records needed to satisfy the regulators.*

A third problem is *the difficulty and cost of complying with the regulations.* According to Jack Faris, president and CEO of the National Federation of Independent Business, "The avalanche of federal regulations robs employers

**Figure 23–5** Growth in Federal Regulatory Agencies

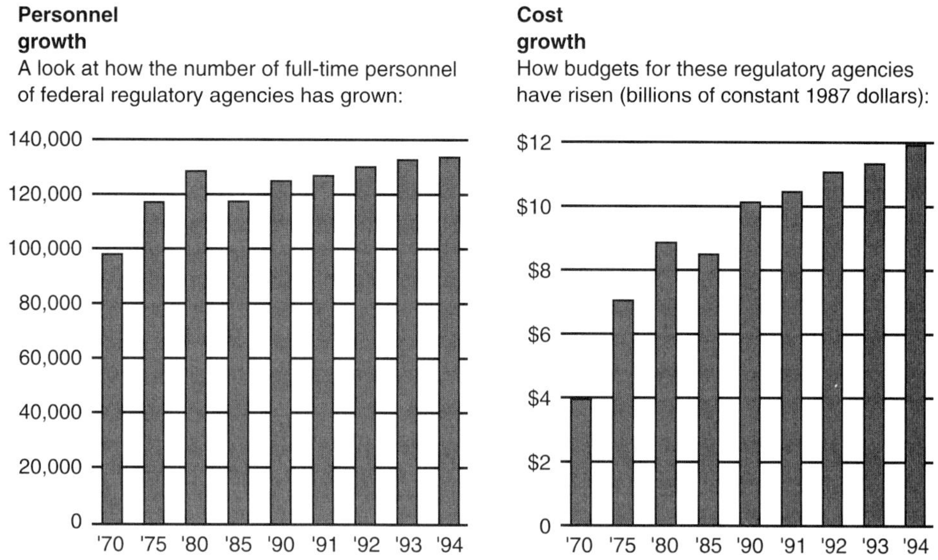


*Source:* Center for the Study of American Business, as reported in *USA Today,* December 19, 1994, p. 11A. Copyright 1994, USA TODAY. Reprinted with permission.

of 1 billion hours of productive time wasted filling out government paperwork."[13] The costs are greater than just the administrative expenses; bringing actual operations into compliance with the regulations is also expensive.

> For instance, Murray Wiedenbaum and Melinda Warren, economists at the Center for the Study of American Business, suggest that "industry-specific rules limiting entry or price . . . almost invariably cost the nation more than the benefits derived by the group these rules are designed to protect." They estimate that "regulations cost the economy $500 billion to $600 billion a year, or more than $2,000 per person." The two scholars stress that these regulations "save their greatest punishment for small businesses and low-income customers."[14]

Figure 23–5 shows the Center's estimates of how the number of employees—and costs—of federal regulatory agencies grew from 1970 through 1994.

Finally, a fourth problem is that *regulations tend to discourage small firms from hiring more workers as their employment approaches the cutoffs set by federal laws and regulations.* The following laws apply to small companies with the number of employees shown:

| | |
|---|---|
| • Occupational Safety and Health Act | 10 |
| • Federal civil rights laws | 15 or more |
| • Americans with Disabilities Act | 25 |
| • Family and Medical Leave Act | 50 |
| • Worker Adjustment and Retraining Act | 100 |

According to Wiedenbaum and Warren, these thresholds serve as a barrier to **discouraged employers** who tend not to hire new people if it brings them

**Discouraged employers** tend not to hire new people if it would make them subject to certain federal laws and regulations.

under one of these regulations. They report that "businesses with a work force of 49 report that they avoid hiring the [50th] person in order to avoid falling under the Family and Medical Leave Act regulations."[15]

## How Small Firms Can Cope with Government Regulations

What can small business managers do about burdensome government regulations and paperwork? There are several approaches to consider.

1. Learn as much as you can about the law, particularly if it is possible that a law can help you.

> For example, over the years, the Alta Group, a titanium refiner in Fombell, Pennsylvania, has formed a partnership with OSHA to develop a comprehensive safety program. The OSHA Consultation Service, which is independent of OSHA's enforcement branch, provides free workplace safety reviews for small businesses—usually those with 250 or fewer employees at a work site.[16]

2. Challenge detrimental or harmful laws, perhaps by joining organizations such as the National Federation of Independent Business, the National Small Business Association, or National Small Business United. At the very least, you can get your message across to your elected representatives. For businesspeople too busy to write to officials, there are other entrepreneurs who will do it for them—for a price.

D

> For instance, in 1994, Diane and Karl Woods, of Silver Spring, Maryland, launched a service for harried citizens who have something to say to their elected officials but are squeezed for time to say it. For $11.95, they will compose letters reflecting your feelings on a local or national issue, let you read and sign them, then send them off in your name to your governor, congressman, senator, or the White House. Woods Enterprises wants to "put the power back where it belongs—in the hands of the people—by acting as a private secretary to [its] clients."[17]

3. Become involved in the legal–political system to elect officials of your choosing who will help change the laws.

> Close to 40 members of the National Federation of Independent Business ran for Congress in 1992, with the encouragement of the Small Business Legislative Council.[18] And nine months before the 1996 elections, about 60 business owners had declared their candidacy for congressional seats.[19]

4. Find a better legal environment, if possible, even if it means moving to a different city, county, or state.

> Sam Chapman, an aquaculture specialist, has been breeding an exceptionally rare bright-blue lobster. Now the research facility wants to use his space for other activities. This opens an opportunity for Chapman to start a small business based on 10 years of expensive research and to sell the crustaceans for $200 each as rare pets. The state of Maine, however, has

## USING TECHNOLOGY TO SUCCEED

### Ready, Set, Go!

The recently formed Go Communications—with 11 employees—is a fledgling company that has yet to receive any revenues. Yet AT&T, MCI Communications, Sprint, and several Baby Bells can't wait to do business with Go! The reason? Go Communications will soon bid for the federal licenses set aside for start-ups and new companies. It appears that these licenses are much easier for a small business to get than for large ones.

Why all the interest? The big companies want a better chance for a license and can get it through a small firm. One Baby Bell, SBC Communications, has offered "up-front money" in exchange for a 10-year lease on a piece of Go's personal communications services (PCS) spectrum.

As the estimated cost to set up a PCS network is $25 million, some critics believe small firms will be unable to afford the costs of new PCS networks. They will therefore have to cave in to large interests and eventually sell out.

*Source:* Gautam Naik, "Wireless License Makes the Large Woo the Small," *The Wall Street Journal,* December 5, 1994, pp. B1, B6. Reprinted by permission of *The Wall Street Journal,* 

> strict rules about possessing lobsters smaller than the state's legal eating size. Chapman's rare lobsters fall below this allowed size.
>
> He is now trying to find a more conducive legal climate.[20]

5. Learn to live with the laws and regulations. As you can see from Using Technology to Succeed, this might mean forming an alliance with a larger company.

### Dealing with Private Regulators

Governments are not alone in posing a problem for small firms: Many professional organizations also establish standards of practice for their members. The guidelines are created to ensure professional conduct in various areas. Some of these areas include ethics, technical knowledge, competence, and compliance.

> For example, Gerald Byrd (see Profile, Chapter 10) serves on the committee that specifies minimum technical standards for the Alabama Society of Professional Land Surveyors.

History indicates that government regulations are legislated when the business world neglects to regulate itself. However, sometimes the private regulators need to be regulated, as the following incident illustrates.

> A major professional society issued a "guideline" discouraging manufacturers from using a given product. As it turned out, a major supplier of a competing product was a member of the society.[21]

## Choosing and Using a Lawyer

You can see from the previous discussion that, from a legal point of view, it isn't easy to start and operate a small business. Therefore, one of the first things you should do when forming a business is to retain a competent lawyer. Actually, your attorney should be retained at the time you are developing your business plan, as well as when you are obtaining financing—not when you get in trouble.

## Choosing the Lawyer

You should choose a lawyer as you would a consultant, an accountant, or anyone else who provides services. Comparison shop! Check the credentials of different attorneys! Discuss fees with them candidly! And, whatever you do, don't forget to talk with them about the wisdom of retaining legal counsel. For example, does it make sense to spend $500 in legal fees and court costs to recover a $300 bad debt?

### *Where to Look*

How do you look for a lawyer? The first and most obvious step is to define the nature of your legal problem. Once you have defined the problem, there are a number of ways to find a lawyer to help you with it. The American Bar Association recommends four sources:[22]

1. *Personal referral* from someone whose opinion you value, such as your banker, your minister, a relative, or another lawyer.
2. The *Martindale-Hubbell Law Directory,* which is the most nearly complete roster—as up-to-date as possible—of the members of the bar in the United States and Canada.
3. *Lawyer Referral and Information Services (LRS),* which are provided by most bar associations in larger cities.
4. *Advertising,* since lawyers can now advertise certain information in newspapers and the Yellow Pages and on radio and television.

### *What to Look For*

First, look for appropriate experience with your type of small business. While you may not necessarily rely on the lawyer for business advice, the one chosen should at least have sufficient background and information about the particulars of your business and its problems to represent you effectively.[23]

Second, since there should be compatibility between lawyer and client, observe the lawyer's demeanor, the style and atmosphere of his or her office, and any clients—if possible (Does the lawyer represent a competitor?)—before making your choice.

Third, does the lawyer have time for you and your business? If you have difficulty getting an appointment or are repeatedly kept waiting on the phone, you should probably look elsewhere.

Finally, since cost is an important consideration, do not hesitate to discuss fees with the prospective attorney, for performance must be balanced against the cost of the service provided. Lawyers' time is expensive!

## Maintaining Relationships with Your Attorney

Lawyers usually have three basic ways of charging for their services. First, a flat fee may be charged for a specific assignment. Thus, the cost of the service is known, and funds can be allocated for it. Second, the lawyer may charge an

**Figure 23–6** A Sample Contract for a Lawyer's Services

I, John Doe, hereby agree to employ the law firm of Ruth Roe to represent me and act on my behalf and in my best interest in presenting a claim for any and all damages, including my personal injury, resulting from an accident which occurred on or about June 29, 1993, near Bethesda, Maryland.

I agree to pay to said firm an amount equal to 30 percent of any and all sums collected by way of settlement or from legal action. In the event of trial (as determined as of the time a jury is impaneled), I agree to pay said firm an amount equal to 50 percent of any amounts received.

Be it further understood that no settlement will be made without consent of client. It is understood that if nothing is obtained on client's behalf, then client owes nothing to said law firm, except for the expenses associated with handling this case.

Said law firm agrees to act on client's behalf with all due diligence and in client's best interest at all times in prosecuting said claims.

DATED this ______ day of ________________, 19___
Ruth Roe
By: ________________________

hourly fee based on the type of activities to be performed and the amount of staff assistance required. Third, a contingency fee may be set. If the stakes are really high, and if time and risks are involved, the attorney may charge a percentage (say 30 percent) of the negotiated settlement, or even more if the amount is obtained through a trial (as high as 50 percent), as shown in the sample contract in Figure 23–6.

Also, the lawyer will expect to be reimbursed for expenses. In long, involved cases, the lawyer should provide periodic reports, including a statement of expenses.

## Socially and Ethically Responsible Behavior

While most small business people have long accepted—and practiced—social responsibility and ethical behavior, considerable external emphasis is now being placed on these topics.

Sometimes, however, small businesses are put at a disadvantage when they try to capitalize on being socially responsible.

> For example, a group called Business for Social Responsibility (BSR) was formed when many entrepreneurs took a media beating because a few journalists took a jaundiced view of the social responsibility movement. Immediately, responsible organizations were charged with the need to reach an unreachable set of standards, approaching perfection. BSR is a group of those targeted entrepreneurs who now fight for credibility in the eyes of the media.[24]

Q

## Social Responsibility

**Social responsibility** is a business's obligation to follow desirable courses of action in terms of society's values and objectives.

**Social responsibility** is a business's obligation to set policies, make decisions, and follow actions that are desirable in terms of the values and objectives of society. Whether that term is used or not, it means the business acts with the best interests of society in mind, as well as those of the business.

Social responsibility as practiced by small firms usually takes the form of: (1) consumerism, (2) employee relations, (3) environmental protection, and (4) community relations.

### *Consumerism*

**Consumerism** is the organized efforts of independent, government, and business groups to protect consumers from undesirable effects of poorly designed and produced products.

**Consumerism** is the organized efforts of independent, government, and business groups to protect consumers from undesirable effects of poorly designed and poorly produced products. As shown in Part III, the consumerism movement became popular during the 1960s and 1970s. The Child Protection and Toy Safety Act set up the Consumer Product Safety Commission (CPSC) to set safety standards, require warning labels on potentially unsafe products, and require recall of products found to be harmful.

### *Employee Relations*

Enlightened **employee relations** is showing interest in and concern for employees' rights.

Enlightened **employee relations** involves a concern for employee rights, especially as to meaningful employment; training, development, and promotions; pay; and health and safety. As shown in Part IV, there is now a greater effort to hire qualified persons without regard to race, sex, religion, color, creed, age, or disabilities. While much is still to be done, small firms have made tremendous strides in this area.

### *Environmental Protection*

**Environmental protection** tries to maintain a healthy balance between people and their environment.

**Pollution control** is the effort to prevent the contamination or destruction of the natural environment.

**Environmental protection** is trying to maintain a healthy balance between people and their environment. It takes two forms: (1) controlling pollution, and (2) conserving natural resources.

**Pollution control** is trying to prevent the contamination or destruction of the natural environment. It is one of the most difficult problems facing not only small business but also all aspects of society. While efforts are being made to prevent—or control—air, land, noise, and water pollution, the problem is very complex. It involves balancing our current use of natural resources and also conserving them for future use. The real problem—from a small business perspective—is balancing environmental needs with economic ones. This is becoming increasingly difficult; for example, recent court rulings have held banks liable when their customers pollute, so banks started demanding an environmental audit and proof that they'd never polluted.[25]

> In 1980, the Bank of Montana—Butte lent $275,000 to a local firm that coated telephone poles with PCP and other chemicals to protect against bugs and rot. The firm left behind a heavily contaminated site when it failed in 1984. Projected cost of the cleanup was $10 to $15 million, which regulators tried to obtain from former owners—including the bank, whose total capital was $2.4 million.[26]

**Figure 23–7** Recycling Savings

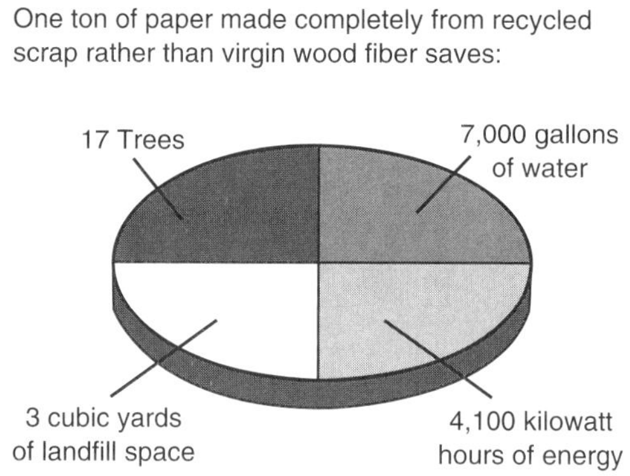


*Source:* Carolina Pad, as reported in *USA Today,* March 9, 1995, p. 1A. Copyright 1995, USA TODAY. Reprinted with permission.

**Conservation** means practicing the most effective use of resources, while considering society's current and future needs. One form of conservation is **recycling**, which is reprocessing used items for future use.

**Conservation** means practicing the most effective use of resources, while considering society's current and future needs.

**Recycling** is reprocessing used items for future use.

> For example, the aluminum industry cuts its energy by 95 percent when it recycles instead of making aluminum from ore. In 1994, 65 percent of aluminum cans were recycled.[27]
>
> According to the National Soft Drink Association, 94 percent of soft drink containers—cans, glass, and plastic—were recycled in 1994.[28]
>
> One of the most popular—and successful—conservation programs is recycling paper. Figure 23–7 shows the savings from this practice.

## *Community Relations*

There are several other areas of social responsibility in which small firms participate: (1) educational and medical assistance, (2) urban development and renewal, and (3) the arts, culture, and recreation.

Entrepreneurs and small business owners are very active in providing assistance to educational and medical institutions.

> Truett Cathy, founder and CEO of Atlanta-based Chick-Fil-A, Inc., offers $1,000 college scholarships to all restaurant employees who have worked at least 20 hours per week for two consecutive years. Another unique feature of Chick-Fil-A is Cathy's refusal to open on Sundays. His "never on Sunday" policy gives him an edge in attracting and retaining a high-quality staff.[29]

D

Small business owners are particularly interested in urban development and renewal. First, it helps improve the environment in which they operate. Second, it helps provide them with a higher purpose.

> For example, Johnson & Higgins, an insurance broker in New York, celebrated its 150th anniversary in 1995 by shutting down all 120 offices around the world to let employees do volunteer work with children. It donated 50,000 work hours, building benches for a Harlem school, helping orphaned Japanese children, and planting trees by the Great Wall of China.[30]

G

D

Most companies—from mom-and-pop stores to large corporations—contribute in some way to hometown arts, cultural, and recreational activities. These efforts include such activities as art workshops for children, civic orchestras or ballet or opera companies, and youth sports teams.

Q

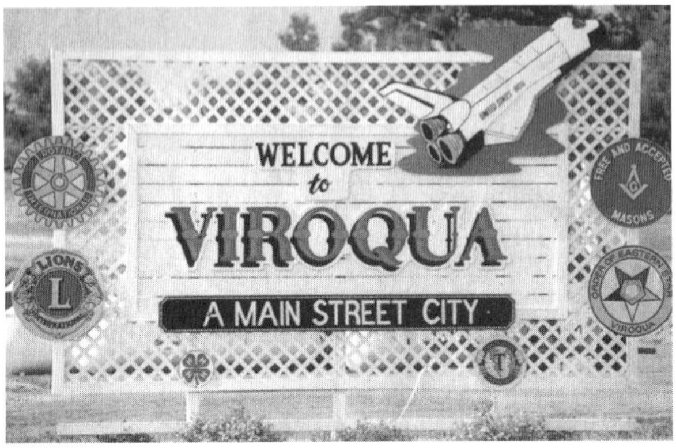


Photo by Michael Melford, from *Smithsonian,* October 1992, p. 47. Used by permission of Michael Melford.

For instance, when small merchants in Viroqua, Wisconsin, heard that Wal-Mart was building a 40,000-square-foot "Discount City" two miles north of town on the main highway, they decided to fight back. Trygve Overbo of Overbo's Shoe Inn worked out a strategy to cope with the "WE SELL FOR LESS" giant. He offered discounts on sneakers to high school athletes and cheerleaders.

In addition, the merchants banded together to renovate and modernize the town. The efforts resulted in so much pride that a welcoming sign was posted billing the town as "A Main Street City."[31]

## Business Ethics

**Business ethics** are the standards used to judge the rightness or wrongness of a business's relations to others.

**Business ethics** are the standards used to judge the rightness or wrongness of a business's relations to others. Small business people are expected to deal ethically with employees, customers, competitors, and others. For example, ethical behavior is expected in decisions concerning bribery, industrial theft and espionage, collusion, tax evasion, false and/or misleading advertising, and conflicts of interest, as well as in personal conduct, such as loyalty, confidentiality, respecting others' privacy, and truthfulness.[32]

Many large and small companies are embracing business ethics to be socially responsible, while others do it to enhance profits. Do social responsibility and ethical behavior affect profits? While the final answer isn't in yet, the answer for now appears to be "maybe."

For example, one study found that many companies are discovering that doing good ethically and doing well financially go hand in hand.[33] Another study did not find a positive relationship between ethical behavior and profits, but such behavior did result in good public relations.[34]

In general, if you launch a business ethics program solely to enhance profits—*or* only to be socially responsible—the program will fail at the first sign of trouble.[35] Instead, socially responsible behavior and profits are both needed.

What course are you to follow, then? As a minimum, the public expects small business owners and managers to obey both the letter and the spirit of laws affecting their operations. Finally, they should go beyond laws and social responsibility to behavior based on ethical considerations. Sometimes,

**Figure 23–8** High Grade for Small Business Owners

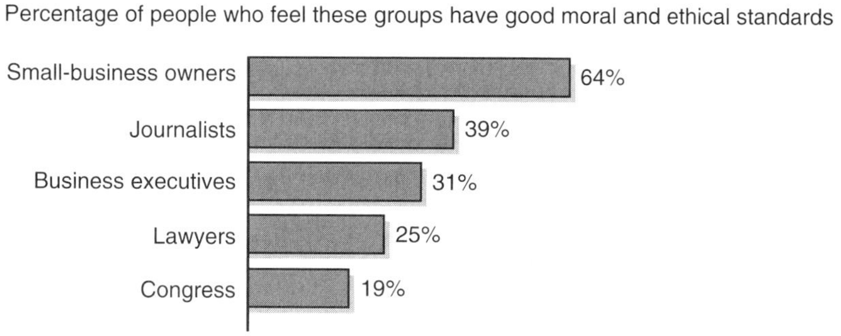


*Source:* Harris Poll of 1,256 adults, as reported in Grant Yifusa, "Who Do We Trust?" *Reader's Digest,* January 1993, p. 109. Adapted with permission.

though, it is difficult for the small business to act ethically and still satisfy the customer. Apparently, as shown in Figure 23–8, small businesses are succeeding better than big business executives, lawyers, Congress, and others.

Perhaps your best test of ethical behavior is Rotary International's "The Four-Way Test" of the things we think, say, or do:

1. Is it the TRUTH?
2. Is it FAIR to ALL concerned?
3. Will it build GOODWILL and Better Friendships?
4. Will it be BENEFICIAL to ALL concerned?

The great entrepreneur James Cash Penney, who became a Rotarian in 1942, tried a practical application of this test—even before Rotary was founded in 1905. In 1902, he opened his first Golden Rule Store—later known as J. C. Penney Company—to provide top-quality customer service, treat his employees fairly, and apply ethical standards of the golden rule to business.

Photo courtesy of J. C. Penney Archives & Historical Museum.

In 1913, he formalized his beliefs into the "The Penney Idea," which are:[36]

- "To serve the public, as nearly as we can, to its complete satisfaction."
- "To expect for the service we render a fair remuneration and not all the profit the traffic will bear."
- "To do all in our power to pack the customer's dollar full of value, quality and satisfaction."
- "To continue to train ourselves and our associates so that the service we give will be more and more intelligently performed."
- "To improve constantly the human factor in our business."
- "To reward men and women in our organization through participation in what the business produces."
- "To test our every policy, method, and act in this wise: 'Does it square with what is right and just?'"

## WHAT YOU SHOULD HAVE LEARNED

**1.** The U.S. legal system is based on many principles, including: *(a)* everyone is equal under the law, *(b)* everyone is entitled to a day in court, *(c)* a person is presumed innocent until proven guilty, and *(d)* there are multiple levels of government and laws. The most important areas of business laws for small firms are *(a)* contracts; *(b)* sales; *(c)* property; *(d)* patents, copyrights, and trademarks; *(e)* agency; *(f)* negotiable instruments; *(g)* torts; and *(h)* bankruptcy. Many of these laws, which differ in the various states, have been codified into the Uniform Commercial Code.

**2.** Both the federal and local governments provide considerable assistance for small businesses. The SBA, U.S. Department of Commerce, U.S. Department of Agriculture, Internal Revenue Service, and other agencies provide assistance.

**3.** There is considerable regulation and paperwork from government agencies, which causes problems for small firms, including *(a)* difficulty of understanding some of the regulations, which may be confusing and even contradictory; *(b)* enormous amounts of paperwork needed to comply with them; and *(c)* the difficulty and cost of complying with the regulations; and *(d)* that regulations tend to discourage small firms from hiring more workers as they near the cutoffs set by laws and regulations.

Small firms can cope with regulation by *(a)* learning about the laws and using them for their benefit; *(b)* challenging detrimental or harmful laws and trying to get them modified or repealed; *(c)* becoming involved in the legal–political system; *(d)* finding a better legal environment, if possible; and *(e)* learning to live with the laws.

**4.** In choosing a lawyer, look for one who's familiar with small business activities, as well as with the problems you are facing. You can use the local lawyer referral service, talk to friends, or use word of mouth in searching for a competent lawyer. Some criteria for choosing a lawyer are to be sure that *(a)* the lawyer is knowledgeable about your type of business, *(b)* you and the lawyer are compatible, *(c)* the lawyer has time to deal with you and your business, and *(d)* the costs are not prohibitive.

**5.** Small businesses are expected to act in an ethical and socially responsible manner in dealing with employees, customers, and the public, and to consider not only the owners but also others in making decisions that affect them. Most small businesses have always acted ethically and responsibly—and continue to do so. As a minimum, small business owners are expected to obey both the letter and the spirit of laws affecting them.

## QUESTIONS FOR DISCUSSION

1. What is the Uniform Commercial Code?
2. What is a contract? What are the elements necessary to make a contract legal?
3. What is a warranty? Distinguish between *express* and *implied* warranties.

4. What are a patent, a copyright, and a trademark? How are these protected under U.S. law?
5. Distinguish between voluntary bankruptcy, involuntary bankruptcy, and Chapter 11 bankruptcy.
6. Describe some of the assistance available to small firms from government agencies.
7. Explain the five ways in which small firms can cope with regulations.
8. Describe the characteristics you should look for in a lawyer. How would you find such a lawyer? How are lawyers compensated for their services?
9. What is social responsibility? Why is it important to small firms?
10. What are business ethics, and why are they so important?

# CASE 23

## GEORGIO CHERUBINI: SCORE SCORES A HIT!

Photo courtesy of the late Marcel Sutton.

Georgio Cherubini, an Italian immigrant living in Minneapolis, Minnesota, had long dreamed of owning his own restaurant. But since he needed the security of a steady income, the restaurant had to wait while he earned a living. However, his security was shattered when economic conditions forced cutbacks at his company and he was laid off. Fortunately, with the help of Marcel Sutton, a SCORE counselor, he was able to turn misfortune into opportunity and use his vision and motivation to enter the restaurant business.

Cherubini's success was not based on luck, although that did come into play, as you will see. He was also well prepared, since he had received his training as a cook and in restaurant operation in his native Florence. After immigrating to the United States, he worked as an engineer until 1985, when he lost his job. He took a job as a waiter at the Rosewood Room, one of Minneapolis's finer dining spots.

On December 5, 1985, Cherubini contacted SCORE for counseling. His case was turned over to Marcel Sutton, who counseled Cherubini at the SCORE office a week later. After that, Sutton worked with Cherubini several times, including telephone discussions.

Cherubini's proposed 60-table restaurant, specializing in regional Tuscan cooking, would require about $300,000 for leasehold improvements, equipment, decor, and other start-up needs. Because Cherubini had only $10,000 available for investment, Sutton tried to get him an SBA-guaranteed bank loan, but it couldn't be negotiated because of the lack of required capital investment and collateral needed for a $300,000 loan.

However, there was one possible way Cherubini could open such a restaurant with his limited capital. First, he had to find a suitable location where a previous restaurant had gone into bankruptcy; then, he had to lease the location with all the existing equipment as part of the lease. Thus, the $10,000 would be enough for his initial operating capital. After a year and a half, he found such a restaurant in a good downtown location.

Hosteria Fiorentina opened in May 1987 and succeeded immediately. It showed a profit by the end of its second week of operation. By September, it had received the *Minneapolis Star-Tribune*'s coveted three-star rating, and Cherubini had to turn customers away on weekends.

*Source:* Correspondence and discussions with the late Marcel Sutton, and others.

## QUESTIONS

1. Evaluate the role played by SCORE.
2. To what primary factors do you attribute Georgio's success?
3. What future do you predict for Georgio and the Hosteria Fiorentina?

## APPLICATION 23–1

Matt Snipes has been with the Turner Foods grocery store chain for one year. During that time he has gone from assistant manager to manager of his own store in five months. The company is now promoting Matt to a store twice as big that does twice as much sales. Matt is 26 years old, married, and has one son. This company has been good to Matt and feels that he has a promising career with the company. Matt is hoping to move into the corporate office once he has his degree, which he is working on at night.

Bob Lindsey is the manager of another Turner Foods store in the district. Matt and Bob have become friends, and their families get together as often as their schedules permit. Bob may not be as good a manager as Matt, but he tries. Bob and his wife have two children, with another on the way. They want to buy a bigger house and feel that, if they cut back and budget, they can afford an increase in house payments. Bob has worked with this company for seven years and doesn't have a lot of career options.

While visiting with the district manager, Matt was told that Bob was probably going to be demoted back to assistant manager. Matt feels that because Bob is his friend he should warn him. If Matt does this, however, he could lose his job.

## QUESTIONS

1. What is Matt's appropriate action?
2. Should Matt have been privy to such information?
3. What responsibility does Matt have to Bob?

# ACTIVITY 23-1

## RECIPROCAL RELATIONS

*Directions:* Use information from this chapter to solve the puzzle below.

ACROSS

5 UCC
6 Unwritten agreement
9 Acts on behalf of principal
10 Exclusive right of product
13 Exclusive creative rights
14 Distinctive symbol
15 Agreement enforced by law
17 Obligation to follow desirable courses of action
18 See 5 Across
19 Organized efforts to protect consumers

DOWN

1 Balance between people and environment
2 Interest in employees' rights
3 Wants to do something but not personally
4 Transferable financial document
7 Deals with bankruptcy
8 Regarding quality and performance of a product
11 Petition courts for debt relief
12 Two parties reach an agreement
16 Wrongful act

ACROSS 5 Uniform Commercial Code 6 Implied contract 9 Agent 10 Patent 13 Copyright 14 Trademark 15 Contract 17 Social responsibility 18 UCC 19 Consumerism

DOWN 1 Environmental protection 2 Employee relations 3 Principal 4 Negotiable instrument 7 Chapter Eleven 8 Warranty 11 Bankruptcy law 12 Express contract 16 Tort

CHAPTER

# 24

# Planning for the Future

*Time present and time past*
*Are perhaps both contained in time future,*
*And time future contained in time past.*—T. S. Eliot

*And 'tis a shameful sight,*
*When children of one family*
*Fall out, and chide, and fight.*—Isaac Watts

## LEARNING OBJECTIVES

After studying the material in this chapter, you will be able to:

1. Discuss some problems involved in organizing and operating small family-owned businesses.
2. Explain how family relationships can affect the business.
3. Discuss the importance and method of preparing for management succession.
4. Describe the activities needed to prepare the next generation to enter the firm.
5. Discuss the need for tax and estate planning in small companies.

*P R O F I L E*

# BLOOMIN' LOLLIOPS, INC.—ALL IN THE FAMILY

D

In 1989, Dot and Jiggs Martin, along with their married daughters, Michele Statkewicz and Renee Thompson, started a small business—named Bloomin' Lollipops, Inc.—to supplement their retirement income and provide future income for their children—and grandchildren, one of whom worked in the business. They specialized in making chocolate flowers, hard candy lollipops, candy animals, a caramel-chocolate-pecan-dipped gourmet apple "drizzled" with white chocolate, and eight varieties of gourmet popcorn. These were arranged in gift baskets, mugs, vases, and other containers. Their unique arrangements were sold in the store and also delivered by van within a 15-mile radius and shipped beyond that range by UPS. The owners advertised on local radio and TV and in local upscale magazines.

Photographs © 1990 Mobile Press Register. All rights reserved.

The aspiring entrepreneurs did extensive research for about six months before opening their store. The family members worked closely together on all aspects of organizing, promoting, opening, and operating the store. They searched for and tried many recipes for candy, then developed their own by combining the best aspects of the ones they liked. Although each person specialized in one particular job—such as making candy, arranging items creatively in containers, serving customers and answering the phone, or delivering the wrapped items—each one helped in all the activities as demand dictated.

The organizers also studied what form of ownership would be best. They wanted to form an S corporation but for technical reasons decided on a C corporation with the Martins holding 50 percent of the stock (25 percent each), Michelle 30 percent, and Renee 20 percent. There was a buyout clause in the charter, which permitted the other stockholders to buy the stock of anyone leaving the business. This occurred in 1993 when Renee left to return to her "first love," being a dental technician.

The business grew so rapidly that the stockholders have opened a satellite location, which was immediately successful, and expanded into wholesaling on a limited basis. Even with the normal growing pains, the family not only did an outstanding job of running the business but also enjoyed social interaction with each other and the employees, many of whom were friends or relatives.

By early 1995, however, the volume of business and the resulting record keeping were so great that something had to be done. The family realized they would either have to sell out or hire more people, build a separate "kitchen" to make the products, and expand the wholesaling activities. Because she had a growing family, Michele had little time to give to the business, and Jiggs and Dot didn't look forward to at least five more years of "working around the clock" before Michele could return to full-time employment. For these and other reasons, they sold the business in the summer of 1995.

While Dot is enjoying the role of grandmother to her many grandchildren, Jiggs and Michele have started another small business. They provide a select group of high-volume service stations with car-washing machinery, sophisticated automobile vacuum cleaners, and coin-operated pneumatic tire pumps. Michele and Jiggs buy the equipment and provide it to their clients under a lease, profit-sharing, or financing arrangement.

Q

As a result of the Martin family's vision, enterprise, and hard work, Bloomin' Lollipops has continued to expand and prosper. Its new owners have a kiosk in one of the city's shopping malls and have expanded their wholesaling operation to include major retailers in New York and other large cities. Their new production facility was completed and in full operation in December 1995.

*Source:* Conversations with the original owners, and various newspaper and magazine articles, including "Bloomin' Has an Apple for the Gourmet," *Mobile* (Alabama) *Press Register,* October 4–5, 1995, p. 1-E.

This Profile is a good illustration of how a small family business is started and grows. It also shows the decision the owners must make when business escalates to the point where family members can no longer cope with its increasing demands.

Many small business owners are not as fortunate as the Martins. Instead of selling the company or providing for their business to continue operating effectively, they put off selecting a successor until it is too late. Many family business executives, facing possible retirement, feel that finding a successor can be done quickly. But the odds are against them. It has been estimated that fewer than one-third of U.S. family businesses pass successfully from the first to the second generation.[1] Moreover, according to a poll of 614 family business owners by Massachusetts Mutual Life Insurance Company of Springfield, Massachusetts, *a mere 8 percent make it to the third generation or beyond.*[2] The study found that *the median age of all U.S. firms is about 12 years.* By contrast, Asian family businesses tend to be longer lived.

G

> For example, the Mogi family has made Kikkoman Soy Sauce since 1630. The Mogis have handed down basic business and family values from generation to generation, including the following precepts:[3]

- Family members must be polite to one another.
- Business depends on people.
- Don't make decisions about important matters by yourself.
- Don't fall carelessly into debt.
- All members must desire peace.

Over 80 percent of all U.S. businesses—large, medium, and small—are family owned, and they account for 50 percent of our gross national product, as well as half of our work force.[4] Yet, as indicated, only about 1 out of 12 of them makes it to the third generation, often because of unwillingness or inability to deal with the challenges that are unique to family-run enterprises.

But most small business owners don't like to talk about the question of succession. According to the American Family Survey 1995, 40 percent of the companies surveyed had not appointed a successor. Yet within those companies their CEOs were expected to retire or go into semiretirement within the next 10 years.[5] Perhaps this reluctance to select a successor reflects a denial of their own mortality, the same instinct that makes people reluctant to make a will.

However, to be realistic in assuring the continuation of your business, or in providing an ongoing concern for family members to operate, you must look at this question analytically. We do that in this chapter.

## Role of Family-Owned Businesses

While family-owned businesses provide a living and personal satisfaction for many people, they must be managed just like any other small firm if they are to succeed. Family businesses are the backbone of America, but they can also be a source of unresolved family tensions and conflicts, which can create obstacles to achieving even the most basic business goals. When close relatives work together, emotions often interfere with business decisions. Also, unique problems, such as the departure of the founder-owner, develop in family-owned firms. When more than one family member is involved, emotions and differing value systems can cause conflicts between members.

### The Family and the Business

We usually think of family businesses as being started, owned, and operated by the parents, with children helping out and later taking over. This has been the normal pattern, as many examples in the text have shown. Now, though, two contrary trends are developing. First, many young people are going into business for themselves—and tapping their parents for funds to finance their ventures. In return, the children often give one or both parents an executive position in the company, including a seat on the company's board. Also, many retirees want to work part time for the children's businesses, without assuming a lot of responsibility.

For example, the two brothers who run the Levy Organization in Chicago employ their mother as a hostess at one of their restaurants. They even named a deli after her and use her recipes. According to Mark Levy, the company's vice chairman, "My mom is a very integral part of our business."[6]

D

**Figure 24–1** Making It in Business with Your Spouse

Following are some tips for spouses to follow in running a jointly owned business:

- Don't be blinded by romance; follow all the rules.
- Define each person's role and accentuate each other's talents.
- Don't ignore business conflicts in an attempt to spare a personal relationship.
- Agree to disagree—set the ground rules.
- Be clear and specific about your expectations of each other.
- Set aside family time, and stick to it.
- Set up a system for recognizing and rewarding hard work done by family members.

*Source:* Adapted from Paula Ancona, "Define Partners' Role in Family-Run Business," *Mobile* (Alabama) *Register,* June 6, 1993, p. 4-F.

Another trend is the large number of spouses doing business together. We used to think of married couples running a small neighborhood store, toiling long hours for a modest living. Now, though, a new breed of husband-and-wife entrepreneurs has emerged. They typically run a service enterprise out of their home and use computers, modems, and phone lines as the tools of their trade. As shown in Chapter 2, the number of such firms nearly doubled in the 1980s, and this is the fastest-growing category of new businesses during the 1990s. Figure 24–1 offers some tips on how to get along with your spouse in business.

Although ownership of a small firm is usually controlled by one or a few family members, many others in the larger family are often involved. The spouse and children are vitally interested because the business is the source of their livelihood. In addition, some relatives may be employed by the firm, some may have investments in it, and some may perform various services for it.

The founder-owner may set any one or more of a variety of goals, such as adequate income and perpetuation of the business, high sales, service to the community, support of family, and production of an unusual product, just to name a few. This variety of goals exists in all companies, but in family firms strong family ties can improve the chances of consensus and support, while dissensions can lead to disagreement and/or disruption of activities.

## Family Interactions

Usually the founder—or a close descendant—is the head of a small business. Relatives may be placed in high positions in the company, while other positions are filled by nonfamily members. In some cases, it is expected that the next head of the firm will be a family member and other members will move up through the ranks, according to their position in the family.

G Q

Asplundh Tree Expert Company is such a business. Asplundh defines itself as "a bunch of tree cutters." That may be true, but this bunch now operates in all 50 states and eight foreign countries. Outsourcing has enabled Asplundh to remain a family business since 1928. There are 65

> members in the fourth generation, and a few will work in the company and help carry on the family work. When asked why they do not go public, Chris Asplundh replied, "Then we'd just have money—that isn't what this family is about."[7]

Family members' sense of "ownership" can be a strong, positive motivator in building the business and leading to greater cooperation, as happened with Bloomin' Lollipops in the Profile. The opposite can also be true, however. Conflicts can occur because each relative looks at the business from a different perspective. Relatives who are silent partners, stockholders, or directors may see only dollar signs when judging capital expenditures, growth, and other important matters. On the other hand, relatives involved in daily operations may judge those matters from the viewpoint of marketing, operations, and personnel necessary to make the firm successful.

## *How to Deal with Incompetent Family Members*

A related problem can be the inability of family members to make objective decisions about one another's skills and abilities. Unfortunately, their quarrels and ill feelings may spread to include nonfamily employees. One possible solution is to convince family members, as well as nonfamily employees, that their interests are best served by a profitable firm with strong leadership, as the following example illustrates.

> The Chapman House grew into a profitable chain of restaurants, motels, and textile industries. In time, the second generation took over many activities from the matriarch, and the third generation began its entry into the business. This resulted in an overexpansion of activities, an increase in internal conflicts, and a decrease in profitability. The death of the matriarch was followed by 90 days of internal strife.
>
> Then a third-generation family member with an M.B.A. and previous employment experience in a major industrial corporation developed some centralized objectives and an organizational structure appropriate to reaching the objectives. After that, most family members recognized that they should keep the business intact and expand only in those areas offering the best return on investment.

Some members want to become the head of the business but do not have the talents or training needed. Others may have the talents, but because of their youth or inexperience, these talents may not be recognized.

Family members with little ability to contribute to the firm can be placed in jobs where they do not disturb other employees. Sometimes, though, relatives can demoralize the business by their dealings with other employees or customers or by loafing on the job, avoiding unpleasant tasks, or taking special privileges. They may be responsible for the high turnover rate of top-notch nonfamily managers and employees. Such relatives should be assigned to jobs allowing minimal contact with other employees. In some cases, attitudes may be changed by formal or informal education.

### *How to Compensate Family Members*

Compensating family members and dividing profits among them can also be difficult because some of them may feel they contribute more to the success of the firm than others. Compensation should be based on job performance, not family position. Fringe benefits can be useful as financial rewards, but they must conform to those given to nonfamily employees. Stock can be established as part of the compensation plan. Deferred profit-sharing plans, pension plans, insurance programs, and stock purchase programs can all be effective in placating disgruntled family members, as can a managerial title.

D

> When success leads a company into the second generation, titles start to matter to the children and younger relatives. A title is perceived as a confirmation of a job well done and also tends to serve as a motivator. Some warn, however, that this technique must be used carefully to avoid counterproductive behavior in the future.[8]

## Family Limitations

Entrepreneurs tend to be specialists in an activity such as marketing, production, or finance, so they aren't usually good general managers. While managerial skills can be developed through training and/or experience, the skill of sometimes saying no to family members wanting to enter the business may still be missing.

Another problem is that family managers may feel it is necessary to clear routine matters with the top family member. Also, bottlenecks that work against efficient operations can be caused by personality clashes and emotional reactions. Therefore, lines of authority and responsibility in the company must be clear and separated from those in the family. This is an important distinction because a person's age often determines the lines of authority in a family, while ability must be the primary guide in a business.

The number of competent family members from whom to choose the managers of the company is usually limited. Some members do not want to join—or are not capable of joining—the company in any position; some are capable of filling only lower-level jobs; and some are not willing to take the time or expend the effort to prepare themselves for a management position. So it's amazing that so many family businesses have such good leadership—family and nonfamily. But, as the leader grows older, he or she must keep up with the times and guard against letting past successes lead to trying to maintain the status quo.

> For example, the five stockholders of Donald & Asby, engineers, established a policy of encouraging growth. One of the younger stockholders suggested using media advertising to obtain new business. But Mr. Donald, who had helped found the firm 30 years earlier, said this would produce an undesirable type of growth. He suggested that they continue

to depend on the company's reputation to expand requests for job proposals. How do you think the stockholders decided? Why?

Some families form their businesses into corporations and hire professional managers to run them when no members are in positions to manage or no agreement can be reached on who should run the company. This solution has the advantages of using professional management, freeing family time for other purposes, reducing friction, and having employees treated more fairly. However, the disadvantages are loss of a personal touch, reduced family employment, lower income, concentration of power in small cliques, and difficulties in finding and keeping a good management team.

## Family Resources

The amount of capital available within the family may limit expansion. While family resources and contacts may be adequate for a small business, as the company grows, the borrowing power is limited by the amount of family assets. Then, family members may disagree about such issues as the following: Should money be obtained by borrowing, issuing stock, selling assets, or other financial techniques? Should planning be for the short or long run? Because of the diversity of opinion, even the choice of a consultant can be controversial.

## Preparing the Next Generation

D

It might be assumed that children (or grandchildren) automatically want to enter the family business. But this isn't always true. A growing problem facing many small family businesses today is apathy on the part of offspring. Often, children who are reared in a small business become bored or uninterested, or simply lack the drive and desire to succeed that their parents displayed. They may feel that since the business has supported them in the past, it will continue to do so in the future.

What leads children to follow in their parent's footsteps? In a significant early study, Nancy Bowman-Upton of Baylor University found that the two primary reasons were money and liking the business. Figure 24–2 shows the importance of these and other reasons for joining the family business.

**Figure 24–2** Reasons Children Join Family Businesses*

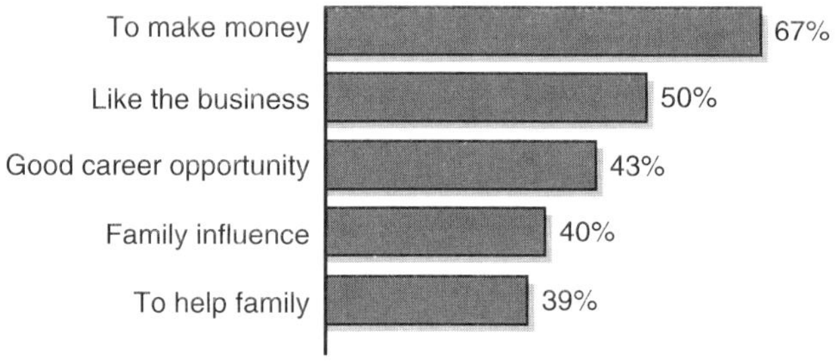


*Respondents could give more than one answer.
*Source:* Survey by Nancy Bowman-Upton, Baylor University, as reported in *The Wall Street Journal*, May 19, 1989, p. B1. Reprinted by permission of THE WALL STREET JOURNAL, © 1989 Dow Jones & Company, Inc. All Rights Reserved Worldwide.

### *Start at Part-Time or Full-Time Jobs?*

One way to prepare children to take over the family business is to let them work on simple jobs, or on a part-time basis, which provides insights that may influence them into—or away from—the business. The experience often encourages them to finish their education to be better prepared when it's their turn to run the business.

Another form of preparation is working for another company to broaden their training and background. Such experience helps justify moving a family member into the family business at a higher level.

> For example, a groundbreaking study by the Los Angeles accounting firm of Laventhal & Horwath found that the vast majority of owners of family firms thought children should have outside experience, either as their own boss or working for someone else, before joining the family business. As you can see from Figure 24–3, 65 percent of respondents felt this way.

### *Start at Entry-Level or Higher-Level Positions?*

Should a family member start in an entry-level job to learn the business from the ground up? There is some disagreement on this point, but none about the need for knowing the business, regardless of how it's done. The following are some techniques that have worked for others:[9]

- Never allow a son or daughter to work in senior management until he or she has worked for someone else for at least two years.
- Rotate the person in varying positions.
- Give promotions only as they are earned.
- Devote at least half an hour each day to face-to-face teaching and training.
- Don't take business matters home.

If the newcomer is really to learn the business, true responsibility must be given. Otherwise, the person cannot learn to manage the business, as the following example shows.

**Figure 24–3** When Should Children Join Family Businesses?

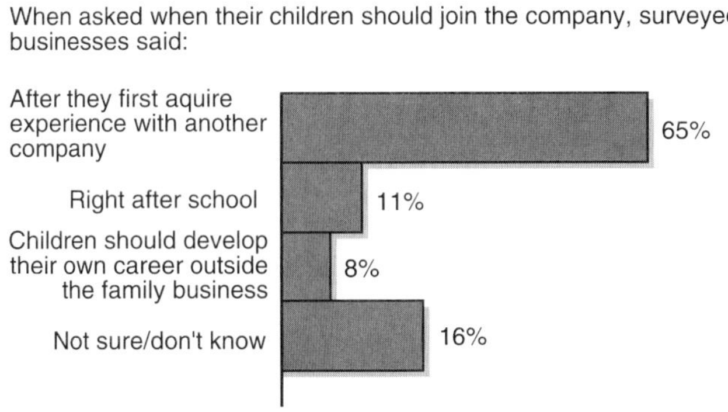


*Source:* Laventhal & Horwath, as reported in *The Wall Street Journal,* December 19, 1989, p. 25. Reprinted by permission of THE WALL STREET JOURNAL, © 1988 Dow Jones & Company, Inc. All Rights Reserved Worldwide.

> A son who took over his father's business said, "My father had difficulty trusting me. It's not what you might think. He just didn't want to see me fail. When he saw that something I was doing might not pan out, he would step in and take over. I never had a chance to fail."
>
> Thus, when he took over the business, making it work was very difficult, but he finally succeeded.[10]

## Preparing for Management Succession

Any business must be ready for changes in its top management. It's not enough to select a person to step into the top job when it becomes vacant. That key job requires much training and experience, because the decisions the person makes can vitally affect the company and its future. Thus, every transfer of ownership and power is an invitation to disaster. To prevent that from happening, the owner should do two things: *Plan early and carefully, and groom a successor!*

### Why Succession Is a Problem

When preparing someone for management succession, many small business owners have some grave concerns about passing the business on to their children. In the previously mentioned survey by Nancy Bowman-Upton, it was found that the main concern was treating all children fairly. Of the entrepreneurs surveyed, 31 percent gave this as their main concern. Another 22 percent were concerned about the reaction of nonfamily employees. And 20 percent gave family communication, conflict, and estate taxes as concerns.[11]

Another trend is having two or more children succeed the parent in running the business. A survey of family-owned business owners with two or more children working for the company was conducted by John Ward, a professor at Loyola University's Graduate School of Business. He found the owners planned to resolve the issue of who would take over when the owners step aside as follows:[12]

- 35 percent plan to groom one child from an early age to take over. **D**
- 25 percent plan to let children compete and to choose one or more successors with help from the board of directors.
- 15 percent plan to let the children compete and choose one or more successors without input from a third party.
- 15 percent plan to form an "executive committee" of two or more children.
- 10 percent plan to let the children choose their own leader or leaders.

In essence, over half the respondents wanted to include two or more children in future ownership and management. The following example illustrates how this can be done.

> When Somer Obernauer retired, his daughter Lorie and her brother, Somer, Jr., split ownership and management of the firm. She became executive vice president, in charge of sales, while he became president, in **D**

charge of accounting. They were already essentially running the Keystone Ribbon & Floral Supply Company, according to Lorie: "I was in charge out front, and he was in charge in back. We each had our own territory."[13]

If family members are going to be used to run the business, rather than bring in outsiders, ongoing training should begin early. One or more replacements should be started early on the path toward taking over the reins of the firm. This process sometimes does not work, as the case at the end of the chapter illustrates. But, as shown in the following example, sometimes it can work well.

D

The O'Reilly family with sample wares: (from left) David, Charlie, Chub, Rosalie, and Larry.

Photo courtesy of Eli Reichman, photographer. © 1995.

Charles O'Reilly began selling auto parts in 1914. In 1957, he and his son "Chub" opened their own store. And, even though many family businesses are ripped apart by the third generation, this one still thrives.

Chub's children started working and learning the business at an early age. They worked after school and on weekends. Early on, each of them was recognized for his or her own unique talents. At age 60, Chub began turning his business over to his well-trained children, and major decisions were made only after careful consultation with them.

Now David, Charlie, Rosalie, and Larry are training the fourth generation of O'Reillys "to run this—or their own—business." The key to successful succession, they say, is to "get the inheritors to think like a team, rather than as sibling rivals."[14]

When the choice of replacements is limited, the owner may consider reorganizing the present assignments and using present managers more effectively. The job specifications for a new manager may be written more broadly to widen the range of choices. All present managers—family and nonfamily—should participate in this planning so they feel they have contributed to the decision.

## An Overlooked Problem

In most firms, the development of managerial personnel and the provision for management succession are greatly neglected, often until it is too late to do anything about it. According to one expert, research studies indicate that most entrepreneurs simply don't want to face the inevitable.

> For example, in interviews a few years ago with 400 owners of small companies across the United States, Peter Collins, head of Buckingham Associates, a New York consulting firm, found that 85 percent *had no formal plan* to leave their business. Moreover, 31 percent had "no idea at all how they would exit their business."[15]

But this trend is changing. A growing number of entrepreneurs are turning to formal succession plans to save their heirs endless squabbles, according to Massachusetts Mutual Life Insurance Company. Its annual survey of more than 1,000 family business owners found that, in 1995, 44 percent of them had written plans to guide the next generation's succession to control. That figure was up from 28 percent in 1994 and 21 percent in 1993.[16] Q

## PLAN AHEAD!

Management succession occurs when the family leader: (1) dies, (2) becomes incapacitated, (3) leaves the company—voluntarily or otherwise—or (4) retires. To avoid family succession problems, entrepreneurs should start planning for their replacements as much as 10 to 15 years ahead of the actual passing of power, according to John Schoen of Baylor University's Institute for Family Business in Waco, Texas.[17] Such a comprehensive succession plan involves more than just laying out the role of the younger generation in the business and ownership of the business. Instead, operating authority must pass from one generation to the next. These plans should be flexible enough to include (1) a sudden departure or (2) a planned one.

### Sudden Departure

A successful business must continue to operate even when the owner/manager leaves, for whatever reason. Plans can easily be made for vacations because they are of short duration, they require a limited number of decisions, and the vacationer is available if needed. When the owner takes a vacation, a form of on-the-job training is provided for those left in charge. Those persons can take over temporarily under those circumstances.

But the sudden death or incapacity of the owner can be very disruptive if not adequately provided for. If the owner has left no will or instructions on what to do, family members will probably have conflicting opinions about what should be done. For this reason, an owner should make a will and keep it current, including instructions about what should be done in—or with—the business.

As shown in Chapter 22, the firm can take out life insurance on the owners, the proceeds from which will go to the company in case of death. This money can be used to help the business operate until it recovers from the loss of its owner-manager.

### Planned Departure

When owners plan to leave or retire, they have a number of options, as shown in Figure 24–4. If the company is a corporation, there will probably be less controversy, because the replacement top officer should be known by the time the owner departs, and the transition should go smoothly. The board of directors can select a family or nonfamily employee, or an outsider, for the

**Figure 24–4** Options for Replacing Family Management

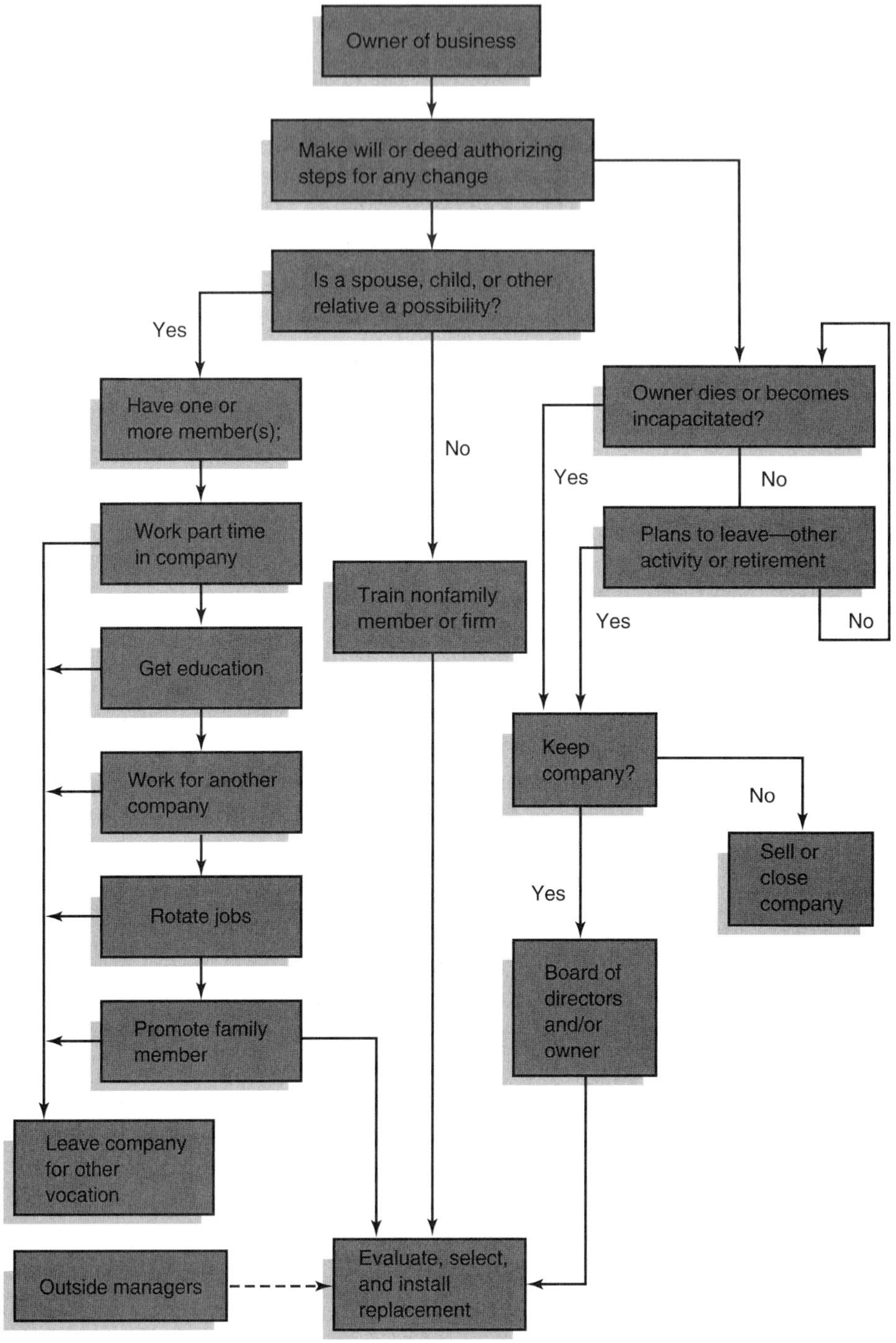

top job. The handling of the stock can be delayed, but stock retention may give the new key executive the feeling that the departed one is still looking over his or her shoulder.

The entire family tends to become involved in the replacement decision in proprietorships and partnerships. Therefore, in planning for departure, the owner should look for someone in the family able and willing to take over. This persons may already be recognized as the "heir apparent."

> In the Keystone Ribbon & Floral Supply Company example, both the daughter (Lorie) and the son (Somer, Jr.) were designated "heirs apparent."

## Selling to Family Members

If the transition is to be complete, the business should be sold to the offspring so that full responsibility is handed over to them. The advantages of this type of change for the original owner are as follows:

- The business stays in the family.
- It provides a source of employment for family members.
- The family's stature is maintained.
- The former owner is free to relax or travel.
- There is pleasure when the successor is successful.
- It can strengthen family bonds rather than produce additional family friction.

Sometimes, however, the business is sold to outsiders and later repurchased by one or more family members. This may occur when the owner wants to retire and the children are too young or lack interest, skills, or the funds needed to purchase the company. D

> For example, Charles Alfieri sold his hair replacement business to a Japanese company with a long-term employment contract. After disagreements with management, he retired from the firm. G
>
> Nine years later, the company was preparing to close, and Charles's cousin Andy (who had stayed on at the firm) bought the operation. Now Andy Alfieri is at the helm of the organization where he worked and learned from his cousin Charles while still in high school.[18]

## Selling to Outsiders

If no relative will assume responsibility for the running of the business, the owner can sell out to a partner or an outsider, or can even close the business. Many small businesses are now being sold and moved offshore. Sometimes companies will see an opportunity for expansion in other countries, open businesses there, and later sell the established fledglings to locals. Mexico, where American interests grew by 33 percent in 1994, is a good example.[19] G

### *Reasons for Selling to Outsiders*

There are many advantages to turning the reins over to an outsider. Among these are the following:

- Assured income.
- Lack of worry about what subsequently happens.

- Possible opportunity to consult.
- Release of family tension.
- Relief from further responsibility.

Selling to someone outside the family can mean loss of family identification and resulting sadness, since it marks the end of years of effort and the loss of something the founder built. Still, selling to outsiders can have a beneficial effect on family relationships, as the following example illustrates.

D

> When a troubled family business was sold, the reaction of one child was: "A number of financially enmeshed families were liberated to pursue individual courses. A company had shed its burdensome past and could look forward to a renewal under new leadership. Ray, Joyce, and I are no longer wrangling siblings polarized in an ugly triad. We are free to be friends."[20]

### *Helpful Hints on Selling Your Business*

Deciding to sell the business is the easy part. The difficult part is going through with it. It can take a year or longer to negotiate a trouble-free transfer of ownership—so start planning early!

Q

Ric Zigmond, head of the small business practice at Laventhal & Horwath, a Los Angeles tax accounting firm, lists the following as the most important basic considerations:[21]

Q

- Decide on your goal. If you plan to retire immediately, this may reduce the firm's attractiveness, because some buyers want to keep the founder around during the transition.
- Set a price, with specialized help in evaluating assets.[22] (See Using Technology to Succeed.)
- Shift some assets to your heirs, to lower or spread out taxes.
- Build up profits, to make the company more attractive to buyers.
- Update financial records to truly reflect your firm's worth.
- Consider what you'll lose by selling—such as pension, health insurance, company car, and club dues—and set the selling price accordingly.
- Check tax considerations such as the state sales tax on assets, or transfer taxes, as well as state and federal income taxes.

## Making the Transition Easier

What preparations should you make when you plan to turn the business over to someone else? Too often, a small firm suffers under these circumstances, and sales may decrease or production lag.

### *For the Owner*

To make transitions easier for themselves, owners need to broaden their focus. The narrower the owners' experience and skills, the more difficult it will be to make a smooth transition to other activities after leaving their business. Owners should also begin to devote more time to hobbies and outside group activities, which should help develop a sense of worth apart from the business.

## USING TECHNOLOGY TO SUCCEED
### Let Your Computer Value Your Business

One of the most difficult problems in deciding to sell your business is determining a price that is acceptable to you and the buyer. While there are many methods of doing this, Valuesource, a San Diego software company, has developed a highly specialized spreadsheet designed specifically to calculate the cash value of a business. Its simplified version, called *ValueExpress,* sells for $195 and is very popular with buyers, estate planners, and even divorce lawyers, among others.

Valuesource has developed a more sophisticated version of the package for the IRS that's linked to databases that contain information on businesses with comparable values.

*Source:* William M. Bulkeley, "With New Planning Software, Entrepreneurs Act Like M.B.A.s," *The Wall Street Journal,* June 2, 1992, p. B1. Reprinted with permission of *The Wall Street Journal,* © 1992 Dow Jones & Company, Inc. All Rights Reserved Worldwide.

Finally, the transition can be made in phases, by gradually turning part of the business over to the successors.

#### *For the New Owner or Manager*

To minimize the problems for the new owner or manager, be prepared to have him or her pick up where you leave off. The key is to make available to the successor the specialized knowledge you have accumulated over the years. To accomplish this, an inventory of the various kinds of information can be developed, including your goals and objectives, facts about the general management of the company, data concerning the firm's finances, and information about operational and technical aspects. This type of inventory should also help in estimating the value of the firm at any time and in making projections of cash flow and profit or loss.

### The Moment of Truth

Ultimately, the moment arrives when you must turn over to someone else the business you have created by your own ambition, initiative, and character. Built well, it will survive as a testament to that creativity. A successful changeover requires advance preparation and transition, yet a recent Yankelovich Partners survey found that most small business owners are not usually ready. It found that, although 87 percent of respondents think they will have enough money to retire comfortably, only 29 percent had actually started setting aside the needed funds.[23]

## Tax and Estate Planning

As shown in Chapter 20, in projecting the future of your business, planning is needed to minimize estate taxes. A business and its assets may appreciate in value much more than the owners are aware, and inheritance taxes can be devastating. Therefore, estate plans should be reviewed frequently, along with possible estate tax liability and the provisions for paying such taxes.

### Tax Planning

In planning your firm's future activities, consider the influence taxes will have on profits and the business's capital structure. Since tax laws and regulations change frequently, stay current in the knowledge of these matters. As the following example illustrates, you should probably have annual planning conferences with a CPA well versed in business tax matters.

> When entrepreneur Ray Ford died in 1988 at the age of 100, his executors estimated that his Omaha, Nebraska, moving and storage business was worth $994,000. After a seven-year legal battle, the U.S. Tax Court agreed with the IRS that it was worth more than $2 million. The $500,000 tax bill was expected to put the firm "in serious jeopardy."[24]

## Estate Planning

**Estate planning** is preparing for the orderly transfer of the owner's equity in the business when death occurs.

**Estate planning** is preparing for the orderly transfer of the owner's equity when death occurs. The major concerns are usually the perpetuation of a family business and maintaining liquidity. Without sufficient cash to pay estate taxes, heirs have little choice but to siphon cash from the business or even sell it.[25]

Tax rates on estates are now such that the assets bequeathed to beneficiaries may be needed to pay taxes, resulting in removal of equity from a business. By planning for the transition, this problem can be minimized.

From the small firm's standpoint, estate planning can: (1) reduce the need for beneficiaries to withdraw funds, (2) help maintain beneficiaries' interest in keeping funds in the firm, and (3) provide for a smooth transition. As discussed in Chapter 20, estate planning for the above objectives can be in the form of: (1) gifts to children, (2) stock sales to family members, (3) living trusts, and (4) **family limited partnerships**. This type of partnership allows business owners to pass assets to heirs with a minimum of income and estate tax costs—while retaining control of the assets during their lifetime.[26]

A **family limited partnership** allows business owners to pass assets to heirs with a minimum of income and estate tax costs while retaining control of assets during their lifetime.

In carrying out those planning steps, appropriate steps should be taken to assure compliance with IRS regulations, especially the valuation of the business. Three methods for determining the true value of a business are: (1) determining the value of a comparable business that is publicly traded, (2) ascertaining the business's value by capitalizing its earnings, and (3) estimating the business's value by determining its book value.

Certain actions are possible to assure that the IRS is bound by a predetermined agreement. One way of accomplishing this is to use a predetermined shareholder **buy/sell agreement**, whereby the corporation agrees to buy back the stock or sell it for the shareholder. Such an agreement becomes binding on the IRS. In addition, a properly prepared buy/sell agreement assures a market for the stock. It also provides protection for the minority stockholder. If such a stockholder is terminated without such an agreement, he or she may be placed at a serious disadvantage, as the following example illustrates.

A **buy/sell agreement** provides for the corporation to buy back a shareholder's stock when he or she leaves the company.

> A young woman held 28 percent of the stock in her employer's corporation; a majority of her personal assets were tied up in the stock. Without warning, she lost her job, and her unsympathetic ex-employer was unwilling to redeem the stock.

A number of references may be used to aid in estate and tax planning, but we recommend using the services of a lawyer, accountant, and/or professional tax planner as well. If you wish to do your own planning, *LegalPoint* is a new software package from Teneron Corporation that can be of assistance.[27]

## WHAT YOU SHOULD HAVE LEARNED

**1.** This chapter shows that members of family-owned firms have different viewpoints depending on their relationships in the family and the business. Founders expect that some family members, especially their children, will follow them into the firm.

**2.** To the extent feasible, ownership and management should be separated from family affairs in order to be fair to nonfamily employees and to reduce friction. Accepted upward movement of family and other employees in the business can generate positive motivation, but evaluation of family members' skills is often difficult. Disruptive members should be isolated, delegation should be practiced, and compensation should be based on job performance—not personal or family relationships—if possible.

**3.** Family businesses are usually limited in the number and caliber of people from whom to choose managers, and in the money available for such purposes. Age may hamper the progress of younger family members and may lead to disagree- ments on money matters. Forming a corporation tends to lessen family stress within the company. Ongoing training, including early employment in the business and personal contact with the owner, is recommended for developing younger members.

**4.** Start planning for succession early in the game to help smooth any sudden transition. If the new CEO is known early, planning has been good; if not, selection may have to be made under adverse conditions. Transfer of the firm to other family members has many advantages, including continuity and family support.

**5.** Planning for the future should also include estate planning to minimize the tax burden of the business owner's heirs. Strategies to reduce beneficiaries' need to withdraw funds, maintain their interest in leaving funds in the firm, and provide for a smooth transition include gifts to children, selling stock to family members, setting up a living trust, and setting up a family limited partnership. In all such planning, owners are advised to consult professionals such as lawyers, accountants, or professional tax planners, and to assure that IRS regulations are met.

## QUESTIONS FOR DISCUSSION

1. Why is management succession so important an issue for any small firm? For a family firm?
2. Why is it often difficult to make reasonable decisions in a family business? What problems are caused by a family organization structure?
3. What problems face a company when a key officer leaves suddenly?
4. If you start a business when you are in your 20s or 30s, should you do anything about your replacement? Explain.
5. Suppose you have a successful business now but decide you want to leave it. What might be some reasons for leaving it? What alternatives do you have for the business?
6. How important is estate planning? How can you do it?

# CASE 24–1

## THE SON-IN-LAW

Fred Clayton, a college graduate with a degree in sociology, was inducted as a commissioned officer in the U.S. Navy. While in the service, he married the daughter (and only child) of Art Carroll, a prosperous manufacturers' agent in the electronics industry.

When Fred completed his military service, he accepted a sales position in his father-in-law's organization, the Carroll Sales Company. Carroll had high hopes that Fred would take an interest in the business and eventually relieve him of some managerial responsibilities. Fred was trained for a short while in the home office and was assigned a territory in which to make sales calls and to promote the products offered by his company. A new car and a liberal expense account were provided. He presented a pleasing personal appearance to the customers. However, it was soon evident to Carroll that Fred did not possess the necessary characteristics to become a good salesman.

For a number of years, Fred continued to receive a share of the available business in his area with little sales effort. This condition was primarily due to the tremendous demand for electronic equipment, which far exceeded the supply at that time.

Carroll was concerned about the fact that Fred was not spending sufficient time in his territory. He would frequently leave town on Tuesday and return on Thursday of the same week after attempting to cover an area that, to be properly serviced, would normally take from Monday through Friday. Fred's expenses were extremely high for the time he spent in the field. On occasion, Carroll would discuss Fred's progress with him. Carroll requested that his son-in-law, as a future officer in the company, set an example for the other sales personnel by putting in more time in his territory and by cutting down on his weekly expenses. After these talks, Fred would improve, but within a short time he would return to his original routine.

The company continued to prosper and expand as a result of a good sales effort from most of the sales force and because of the continued demand for their products. Five years ago, the company covered a sales area comprising nine states. At that time, the son-in-law was appointed district sales manager of a two-state territory and was responsible for the supervision of a warehouse and five salespeople. Fred did not work closely with any of his sales personnel, but he took time to scrutinize all expense accounts and often returned them with items marked "not approved." The salespeople felt he was very petty about this and were frequently infuriated by his actions. He also controlled all their correspondence and information flowing to and from the territory. The other sales districts within the company had more liberal expense accounts, and salespeople could make decisions on their own. The district under the supervision of Fred Clayton never led the company in sales, although it had the greatest potential of all the districts.

Carroll was quite disappointed in the lack of sales progress in Fred's division. He was also very concerned over the results of a survey indicating that Fred's district had an unusually high turnover of sales personnel.

About a year ago, Carroll took his son-in-law out of sales. He still hoped that there might be some position in the firm where the younger man would be a real asset. With this thought in mind, he placed Fred in charge of operations to supervise and regulate the operation of the warehouses. Fred was to control inventories. He continued to have problems with personnel, causing so much unrest among employees that a number of key employees talked of leaving.

A year later, Carroll realized that the situation was critical. He asked himself, "Why, after 16 years with the company, is Fred unhappy? Is he completely unmotivated to succeed because he thinks he doesn't have to? Doesn't he feel at least a moral obligation to try to get along with his associates? How have I failed to give his best abilities an opportunity? How far must I go in trying to fit him into the situation?"

*Source:* Prepared by Gayle M. Ross of Ross Printing Company.

## QUESTIONS

1. Comment on Fred's capabilities for managing a small business.
2. What could Carroll do to help Fred become a better manager?
3. Who was responsible for developing Fred into a capable executive? Has Fred or Carroll succeeded or failed? Explain the success or failure of each.
4. How would you answer each of Carroll's questions?
5. What does the case show about the problem of management succession in a small family-owned business?

# CASE 24–2

## PARKVIEW DRUG: A TUSCALOOSA TRADITION

For 36 years, Bert and Barbara English have owned and operated Parkview Drug Store in Tuscaloosa, Alabama. Although not as high profile as Tuscaloosa's two main institutions—University of Alabama football and Dreamland Ribs—Parkview Drug Store is an institution. **D**

The Englishes believe it is the "personal touch" that keeps customers coming back. "Big business has its place, but this is still the place for the personal touch," says Bert.

"We really thrive on the people and the relationships with families we've made throughout the years. Most people who come here know us on a first-name basis," adds Barbara.

Their "personal touch" philosophy definitely does not ring hollow like the marketing ploys and ad campaigns of many big businesses. Bert and Barbara truly foster a family atmosphere, and the effects of this approach are readily evident in their long-term relationship with customers. For example, the great-grandchildren of some of their original customers still patronize the

© 1996 *Tuscaloosa News*. Used with permission.

store. Remarkably, five generations of one family have been—and still are—customers of the Englishes.

The bond between the owners and their customers is so strong, in fact, that over the years many customers have joined the Parkview family as employees. "Several of our customers' children have come back to work for us," says Barbara. "One time we had a grandmother and her three grandchildren working here at the same time."

One aspect of the Englishes' business and personal philosophy of establishing relationships with customers is their policy of never turning away a college student who needs medicine. "There's nothing worse than being in an unfamiliar place, sick, and alone," says Bert. "We decided a long time ago that we would not turn away any student who needed medicine. If a student can't pay for a prescription or over-the-counter medicine, we set up an account and bill the parents. We've been doing that for 35 years, and we've never been burned."

The Englishes were recently awarded a Community Service Award by the family pharmacy division of Amerisource Health Corporation.

Fittingly, Bert and Barbara met at Brown's Drug Store in Selma, Alabama, in 1959, when he was the young pharmacist, and she was a college student who worked on weekends and during the summers. Bert says it was a whirlwind courtship. "We met that winter, I gave her a ring on Mother's Day, and married her in July. She didn't get a chance to think about it."

In September of that year, J. W. Brown, the store owner, made Bert an offer he couldn't refuse: Brown would buy Parkview Drug Store in Tuscaloosa if Bert would operate it. "I didn't have any money," Bert explains, "but I had the sweat. He had a lot of faith in me; I was so young and inexperienced." So the young couple was off, and the rest is history.

No success story, though, is complete without a recounting of "the hard times." Those came for the Englishes only two years after they moved to Tuscaloosa. For an entire year, the street facing Parkview Drug was closed to widen it to four lanes. "It was very difficult for anyone to get to us," Bert recalls. "We'd sit here a couple of hours and no one would come in the store." Things got so bad that friends began encouraging the young couple to declare bankruptcy and cut their losses. But Bert says they enjoyed what they were doing. "I figured we were young, our life was before us, and we had a great future mapped out for ourselves. We didn't want to give it up. We just tightened our belts and did a lot of praying and refinancing." Soon "the hard times" were over—they had made it through.

At 59, Bert says he is more than up to the challenges that face a small pharmacy in today's market, namely, insurance policies that require participants to purchase medicine by mail and large chain stores with in-house pharmacies. Because Bert and Barbara are not ready to retire just yet, their son recently suggested that they hire another pharmacist to help out. True to his "personal touch" business approach, Bert responded, "I don't want another pharmacist. I want to deal with my customers myself."

Bert sums up their success: "You treat people the way you want to be treated, and they'll remember you."

*Source:* Prepared by William Jay Megginson, with heavy reliance on Gilbert Nicholson, "Down-Home Atmosphere," *Tuscaloosa* (Alabama) *News*, January 7, 1996, pp. 1E–2E.

## QUESTIONS

1. Do you think the "personal touch" is still feasible in today's mass-merchandising climate? Explain.
2. What are your thoughts on hiring customers? What are the strengths and weaknesses of this practice?
3. Is the policy of letting students without funds have medicine a practical one?
4. How do you explain the owners' success in using the Golden Rule as an operating philosophy?

## APPLICATION 24–1

John and Barbara Smith have operated a farming business for over 30 years. Now, after great success, it is time to turn the business over to one of their three children. The business is now operating as a brokerage firm for wholesale produce and has a strong customer base. The Smiths have built the company up over the years, but they feel that new management would increase profits.

All three of the Smith children have been working in the business. Tim, the oldest, with a degree in business administration, has handled the paperwork and administrative duties.

Sarah, who has a degree in sales, recently came to work for her parents. She was one of the top five salespeople with her previous company but decided to quit because the paperwork was becoming too much. Her previous employer expected her to supervise a new sales force.

The third son, Bert, has some college but primarily has worked with his parents. Bert has more knowledge about produce than the other two, as his primary job has been to buy the produce for the business from the other farmers. Bert is not a very good salesperson or administrator, but he has a great deal of knowledge about the product and the growers.

All three have agreed to stay on with the company because they are perfectly willing to abide by their parents' decision; they only want what is best for the company and the family.

## QUESTIONS

1. How should the Smiths choose their replacement in managing their business?
2. What qualifications do you think are the most important in choosing the successor? Why?

## ACTIVITY 24–1

*Directions:* In the puzzle below, find the following terms from throughout the book: AAP, accrual method, advertising, agents, audit, bond, budget, business ethics, business plan, buy/sell agreement, cash, cash flow, commission, consumerism, cooperative, depreciation, discipline, distribution, diversification, EEOC, environmental protection, equity, ESOPs, exporting, facilities, failure, flextime, franchise, franchisee, franchiser, hardware, importing, inputs, insurance, IRAs, lease, living trust, LLC, loss control, markup, MBO, MIS, objectives, OJT, operations, organizing, OSHA, partnership, policies, polygraph, profit, publicity, purchasing, pure risk, QC, ratios, recruitment, revenue, right-to-work laws, ROE, SBICs, scheduling, SCORE, small business, software, stockouts, taxes, trust, UCC, upgrading, warranty.

```
M O N E C A S H L I S
K E R U L I A F B L E A S E R
Y L T T S E I T I L I C A F P C I S T
Z E H S S E F V T E L B A I R U E S O P S
G S E A R N L L I B U C W O P E R A T I O N S
E N V I R O N M E N T A L P R O T E C T I O N L U
H A X P E D P U P X G G R O R S O F R A N C H I S E E
Q I S O F T W A R E T T A E I O A C C I P R T I O D S A V
R N U O O U A K M T I R N E N F P I N S U R A N C E I W E
N P P D C L R R U I H M U I O G I E C I K S G M S O P H A Q A
J T U G E C A E P S I E S Z C C T T R S M E D T C M R C R U D
I J T R D I S T R I B U T I O N N W E A N L O K W M E N R D V W
L T H S E C A S H F L O W X D P E A I S T S C I A H I C A A I E X
M O N X S S H B U C R O E O R M A C S S G K T R A A S I R N T R A
B U S T R O P A S B I L O T E N I R K C O A B C P R S A F T O T I
O E G H S C I B S J T A X E S L K L T U H M I F D T I T M Y E I L
F C O O P E R A T I V E R Q O R S V T N U E T P O O O I S N N S U
G N I Z I N A G R O N G M P W X M S L Y E Z D A C N N O I B I I L
U P G R A D I N G G A G H A D A A E I O J R K U L F E N R D L N O
A P S A C C R U A L M E T H O D R V T S R U S R L Q O N E M P G E
B U D G E T D C L R B S C O R E K I A H A T Z H Y I U X M W I W S
B E H R E V E N U E F G Q C I U T H A T T N K I L N M U N C O Y
S S E N I S U B L L A M S A U P C P V I T S O R P Q G S P S Q
C X A C Y D E H O J T G I U Z J E A K O L F B C Y U M N W I P
D C U E X P O R T I N G D P S J R T S Y A T U S R Q O N D
B U S I N E S S E T H I C S B G T I I L K O O S I C V O
E X A R T E V I T T S T N E O Y T I U Q E D I T O W N
B U S I N E S S P L A N Y T L G N I T R O P M I L
F N N A R U D S W A L K R O W O T T H G I R M
R E C R U I T M E N T Z P U B L I C I T Y
G T L L D I V E R S I F I C A T I O N
H I W A R R E S I H C N A R F
J K I R A S B O N D L
```

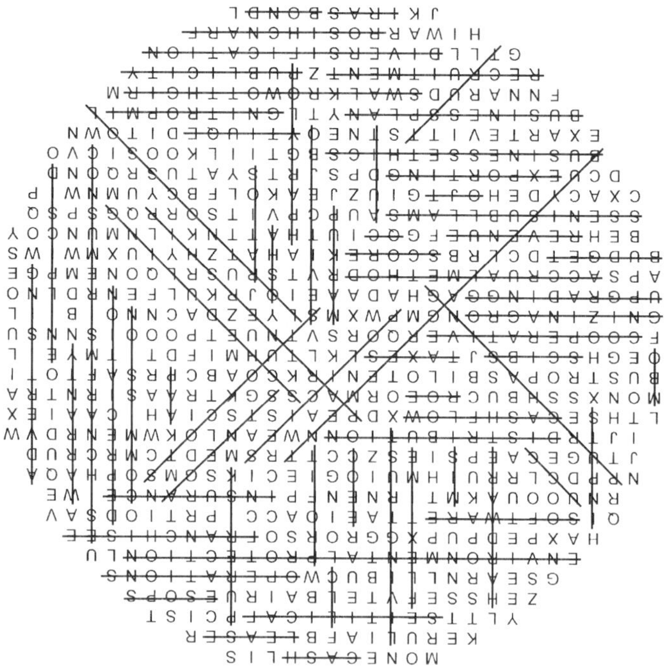

# Workbook for Developing a Successful Business Plan

## I. Introduction

### A. What Is a Business Plan?

The business plan is probably the most useful and important document you, as a present or prospective small business owner, will ever put together. It is a written statement setting forth the business's mission and objectives, its operational and financial details, its ownership and management structure, and how it hopes to achieve its objectives.

### B. What Is the Purpose of a Business Plan?

A well-developed and well-presented business plan can provide you with a "road map to riches"—or at least a pathway to a satisfactory profit. There are at least five reasons for preparing a business plan, which include the following:

1. It provides a blueprint, or plan, to follow in developing and operating the business. It helps keep your creativity on target and helps you concentrate on taking the actions that are needed to achieve your goals and objectives.
2. It can serve as a powerful money-raising tool.
3. It can be an effective communication tool for attracting and dealing with personnel, suppliers, customers, providers of capital, and others. It helps them understand your goals and operations.
4. It can help you develop as a manager, because it provides practice in studying competitive conditions, promotional opportunities, and situations that can be advantageous to your business. Thus, it can help you operate your business more effectively.
5. It provides an effective basis for controlling operations so you can see if your actions are following your plans.

In summary, the plan performs three important functions: (1) being an effective communication tool to convey ideas, research findings, and proposed plans to others, especially financiers; (2) serving as a blueprint for organizing and managing the new venture; and (3) providing a measuring device, or yardstick, by which to gauge progress and evaluate needed changes.

### C. What Is Included in a Business Plan?

Regardless of the specific format used, an effective plan *should include at least* the following:

1. Cover sheet.
2. Executive summary.

3. Table of contents.
4. History of the (proposed) business.
5. Description of the business.
6. Description of the market.
7. Description of the product(s).
8. Ownership and management structure.
9. Objectives and goals.
10. Financial analysis.
11. Appendixes.

## II. How to Prepare a Business Plan

You should start by considering your business's background, origins, philosophy, mission, and objectives. Then, you should determine the means for fulfilling the mission and obtaining the objectives. A sound approach is to (1) determine where the business is at present (if an ongoing business) or what is needed to get the business going, (2) decide where you would like the business to be at some point in the future, and (3) determine how to get there; in other words, determine the best strategies for accomplishing the objectives in order to achieve your mission.

The following is one feasible approach you can use in preparing a business plan:

1. Survey consumer demands for your product(s) and decide how to satisfy those demands.
2. Ask questions that cover everything from your firm's target market to its long-run competitive prospects.
3. Establish a long-range strategic plan for the entire business and its various parts.
4. Develop short-term detailed plans for every aspect of the business, involving the owner(s), managers, and key employees, if feasible.
5. Plan for every facet of the business's structure, including finances, operations, sales, distribution, personnel, and general and administrative activities.
6. Prepare a business plan that will use your time and that of your personnel most effectively.

## III. How to Use This Business Plan Workbook

This workbook is a detailed, practical, how-to approach to researching and preparing an actual business plan. It is designed so that you can answer the questions that are asked or find the information that is called for, record it in the spaces provided, and prepare the final plan.

### A. Sources of Information

There are several possible sources of information you can use in preparing this workbook. First, we have included a case study of an actual business (the name has been disguised at the request of the owner) that contains most of the information—except the location—that you will need to complete the workbook. A second source is a business with which you trade, the business of a friend or relative, or some other business that will be willing to provide the information.

Finally, you may want to come up with a possible business to start on your own. In that case, you would start from scratch, gathering the information you need to complete the workbook.

## B. Completing the Workbook

The workbook should be completed essentially in two stages. The first stage is to gather the information beginning with Item 4, History of the Business, and going through Item 11, Appendixes.

After this information is gathered and recorded, come back and complete Item 1, Cover Sheet; Item 2, Executive Summary; and Item 3, Table of Contents.

Finally, type (or word process) the information from the worksheet into a final form (such as the example at the end of Chapter 8).

### *Item 1, Cover Sheet*

On the cover sheet you should include identifying information so that readers will immediately know the business name, address, and phone number; the names and titles of the principals; and the date the plan was prepared.

1. Cover Sheet
   Business name, address, and phone number:

   ________________________________________

   ________________________________________

   ________________________________________

   Principals:

   ________________________________________

   ________________________________________

   ________________________________________

   Date: ____________________________________

### *Item 2, Executive Summary*

The executive summary should be a succinct statement of the purpose of the plan. Thus, it should be designed to motivate the reader to go on to the other sections of the plan. It should convey a sense of excitement, challenge, plausibility, credibility, and integrity. Even though the summary is the second item in the plan, *it should be written last, after the rest of the plan has been developed.* Remember, *the executive summary is just that—a summary—so keep it short!*

2. Executive Summary

   Brief summary of plan

   ________________________________________

   ________________________________________

   ________________________________________

   ________________________________________

   ________________________________________

   ________________________________________

   ________________________________________

   ________________________________________

Major objectives

Description of product(s)

Marketing strategy

Financial projections

*Item 3, Table of Contents*

Because the table of contents provides the reader an overview of what is contained in the plan itself, it should be written and presented concisely, in outline form, using numerical and alphabetical designations for headings and subheadings.

3. Table of Contents (each section listed, with subheads)

## *Item 4, History of the (Proposed) Business*

The history of the (proposed) business should include a discussion of how the idea for the business, or product, originated and what has been done to develop the idea up to this point. If the owners or managers have been in business before, and their experience is pertinent to the success of the business, include that information. Other relevant background information on the persons, products, capitalization, source(s), funds, and anything else of potential interest to the readers should also be included.

4. History of the Business

Background of the principals, and/or company origins

Background of the product(s)

Corporate structure

Capitalization, or source of funds

Brief outline of company successes or experiences, if any

### *Item 5, Description of the Business*

Item 5 is the place to define your business, as you see it. Therefore, you should essentially answer such questions as: What business am I in? What services do I provide? This item should include more than just a statement of plans and a listing of activities. It should tell readers what customer needs the business intends to meet. In writing this component, try to put yourself in the position of the reader and include information that potential investors, customers, employees, and community members in general might need to assess your plan.

5. Description of the Business

### *Item 6, Description of the Market*

The description of the market is one of the most important—but most difficult—items of the plan for you to develop. In it, you should try to answer such questions as: Who will buy my product? Where is my market? What is my sales strategy? What marketing strategy(ies) will I use? Who buys what, when, where, and why? What are my customers like? Who constitutes my target market (or what special niche am I aiming for)? You should also look at your competition and appraise it carefully, showing any weaknesses it has that you are able to, and plan to, exploit.

6. Description of the Market

   Target market: Who? How many?

   Market penetration projections and strategies

   Analysis of competition: How many? Strengths and weaknesses?

*Item 7, Description of the Product(s)*

Item 7 should describe all of your existing or planned products, including services to be performed as well as goods to be produced. You should also look at any research-and-development activities and new plans to improve or redevelop the product, along with any patents, trademarks, and copyrights you hold—or that are pending.

7. Description of the Product(s)

What is to be developed or sold?

Status of research and development

Patents, trademarks, copyrights

### *Item 8, Ownership and Management Structure*

Item 8 is the place to describe the owner(s), including those you identified by name and title in Item 1. Here you would want to give more detail about their experience and expertise. Also, you should describe your management team, along with their abilities, training and development, and experience. Then, designate who will carry out the plan once it is enacted. Finally, something should be included about organizational structure, including employee policies and procedures.

8. Ownership and Management Structure

Owners and their expertise

Managers and their abilities, training and development, and experience

Organizational structure

*Item 9, Objectives and Goals*

In essence, your objectives and goals outline what you plan to accomplish in your business, as well as showing how it will be done. Include such items as sales and revenue forecasts; marketing plans, including how sales are to be made and what advertising, sales promotion, and publicity will be used; manufacturing plans, including provisions for quality assurance and control; and financial plans (but not the specific financial data, ratios, or analyses, which are in the next item).

9. Objectives and Goals

Revenue forecasts

Marketing plans

How sales are to be made

Advertising and sales promotion

Manufacturing plans

Quality assurance plans

Financial plans

### *Item 10, Financial Analyses*

Since one purpose of the plan is to attract prospective investors or lenders, Item 10 is the place in the plan where you can indicate the expected financial results of your operations. It should show prospective investors or lenders *why* they should provide funds, *when* they can realistically expect a return, and *what* the expected return on their money *should* be. While you must make assumptions—or educated guesses—at this point, you should at least try to include projected income statements and balance sheets for up to three years, as well as projected cash flow analyses for the first year by months. There should be an analysis of costs/volume/profits, where appropriate. Finally, you should provide projected statements of changes in financial position that you anticipate. If practical, you might want to provide some financial ratios.

10. Financial Data

Projected income statements (three years)

Projected balance sheets (three years)

Projected cash flow analyses (first year, by months)

Cost/volume/profit analyses, where appropriate

Projected statements of changes in financial position

Financial ratios, if practical

## *Item 11, Appendixes*

In the appendixes you can include pertinent information about yourself and your business that is not included elsewhere in the plan. Some possible details to include are (1) narrative history of firm; (2) organizational structure (if not done in Item 8), including management structure, organization chart(s), and résumés of key people; (3) major assumptions you have made in preparing the plan; (4) brochures or other published information describing the product(s) and services you provide; (5) letters of recommendation or endorsement; (6) historical financial information, for the past three years (if not done in Item 10); (7) details of objectives and goals; and (8) catalog sheets, photographs, or technical information.

11. Appendixes

Use separate sheet(s) of paper to write this information.

## IV. Sample Case: Cleandrum, Inc.

For nine years, Sue Ley served as a forklift truck operator for a local oil company.* Then she drove a tractor-trailer for the company for four more years. Tiring of this type of work, and thinking she'd like to get into selling, she applied to participate in the company's education program, which pays tuition for employees taking college courses, and was accepted.

Sue enrolled in the marketing program at the local university. While continuing to drive the truck, she completed her marketing course work in three years and graduated with a bachelor's degree in business administration. But, when she applied for a transfer to the marketing department, she was told that it would be "four or five years" before there'd be an opening for her.

Sue's uncle, who had taken over her grandfather's steel oil drum cleaning business, suggested that she start a similar business. Assuring her that she could make around $100,000 per year ($300,000 by the third year) if she founded a business of this sort, he offered to help her get the business started. She could not see any future with the oil company in marketing and did not want to drive trucks the rest of her life. Having saved $25,000 that she could put into the business, she decided to take a chance and start her own company.

### History of the Business

Sue approached the local Small Business Development Center (SBDC) to find out if there was a large enough market for such a company in her area. The Center's survey of 200 firms confirmed that a sufficient market existed for a "quality operation." While other firms were performing a similar service, their quality was not high enough to be considered true competition.

*See Case 1 for more details about the start of the business.

In 1990, using information provided by her uncle, Sue had an accounting firm prepare projected balance sheets, income statements, and changes in cash for five years. Sales projections were for 31,000 units in 1990 and up to 50,000 in 1995. Sales were estimated to be $367,000 in 1990, up to $558,000 in 1995, and net income was estimated to increase from $9,000 to $62,000.

Armed with these projections, and at the request of her banker, Sue approached potential customers and obtained letters indicating their willingness to do business with her "if high quality, good service, and competitive prices were offered."

Sue then prepared a business plan. On the basis of the plan, the SBDC report, financial projections, the letters, a personal history, and interviews with the loan officer, the bank approved a $60,000 loan. Adding her $25,000 as equity, Sue had a lawyer draw up incorporation papers for CleanDrum, Inc (CDI). Sue was ready to enter the business of buying, straightening, cleaning, painting, and selling used 55-gallon steel drums; and buying, cleaning, and selling used plastic drums for transporting and storing oil, chemicals, and similar products.

She started by renting a building. Her uncle then arranged for purchase of the necessary machinery (at a "special" price of $59,000). (She later learned that he had bankrupted her grandfather's business and that the quality of the equipment he had purchased was "suspect.")

When the machinery arrived, her uncle failed to come to supervise its installation. It took Sue three months to hire mechanics, plumbers, and electricians to set up and connect the equipment, and to hire and train six laborers to operate the machinery. She studied her uncle's plant for two weeks to learn enough to enable her to run CDI. All these extra activities delayed her start-up and drained much of her cash.

Sue sold only 500 drums during the first month of operation, which did not provide sufficient income to cover her direct labor costs. In the first four months, she drove a truck during the daytime hours four days a week, and ran the drum-cleaning operations until 11 P.M. each night. The rest of the time, she was on the road selling CDI's drum-cleaning services.

So she concentrated her sales activities on the people that had responded positively to the SBDC survey.

CDI's losses continued. She had expected her uncle to help her sell, but he didn't. Her banker insisted that she quit driving trucks and devote her full energies to her business or close it.

At the end of 1990, CDI had cleaned and sold about 18,000 drums, but it was still $30,000 in the hole. The bank loaned her another $12,000, and she mortgaged her home to obtain additional funds.

## Management, Ownership, and Personnel

Early the next year, the financial situation was the lowest point. At that time, a friend, Edie, invested $32,000 in CDI in return for 50 percent ownership.

Shortly thereafter, Edie expressed concern about the firm's losses and felt that labor costs should be reduced and a supervisor hired. Sue argued, however, that despite already low wages, the employees were efficiently producing a quality product. She said, "In the past, when I came to work, I often found a breakdown, a lack of materials, or that an employee hadn't shown up for work. Now, however, after their training, they have become productive."

By the eighth year, the number of workers had grown from six to eight, and the pay scale had grown from minimum wage to a range from minimum for recently hired employees to $8 per hour for the group leader. Social Security, workers compensation, and unemployment insurance were the only employee benefits provided.

Sue had discussed with her SCORE advisers the possibility of giving the workers a bonus to recognize and encourage good work. "But," she added, "how do we pay for it?" She said that she was considering using temporary workers in order to avoid the problems of handling fringe benefits.

## Product Line and Production Process

CDI performs two types of service. First, it buys steel and plastic drums with the intention of processing and selling them. This requires finding, pricing, purchasing, transporting, and selling drums. It then owns the drums until they are cleaned and sold.

Second, it has an ongoing drum exchange service, whereby it delivers processed drums and picks up old drums to be processed. CDI does not own those drums during that time. Sales are about evenly split between the two types of service, and steel drums make up about 85 percent of those handled.

The company rents a 5,000-square-foot building, where operations are conducted. (See Exhibit 1 for its layout.) Sue estimated that the machinery could process about 5,000 drums a month and that current production averaged about 4,000 drums per month. Machines are not fastened to the floor, but have electrical and pipe connections. The operations and their sequence for processing steel drums are shown in Exhibit 2.

**Exhibit 1** Layout of CleanDrum Plant

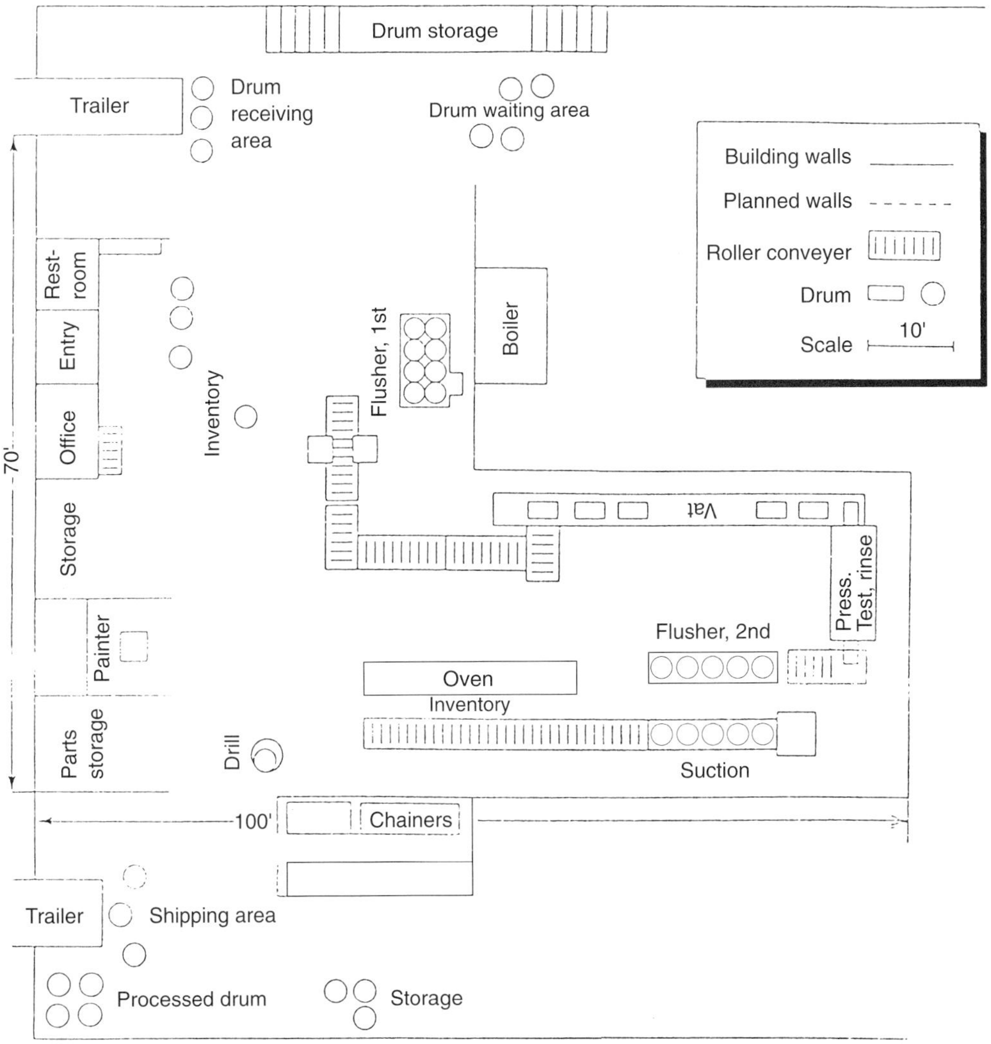

**Exhibit 2** Sequence of Operations at CleanDrum

**Operations**

| Steel drums | Plastic drums | Machines | Time in drum |
|---|---|---|---|
| 1. Receive | 1. Receive | Trailer | |
| 2. First flush | 2. First flush | Flusher | 3 minutes |
| 3. Inspect for rust; | | Visual | 3 minutes |
| if so, clean with chain | | Chainer* | 15 minutes |
| 4. Straighten | | Chimer | 1 minute |
| 5. Clean | | Vat | 10 minutes |
| 6. Outside rinse | | Rinser | 3 minutes |
| 7. Pressure test; | | Forced air | 20 seconds |
| if not passed, cut out top | | Hand cutter | 10 minutes |
| | 3. Pressure test | Hand tester | 2 minutes |
| 8. Last flush | 4. Flush | Flusher | 4 minutes |
| | 5. Wash outside | Hand washer | 3 minutes |
| 9. Dry | | Suction/Oven | 2 minutes |
| 10. Inspect for rust; | | Visual | 2 minutes |
| if not passed, cut 9″ hole | | Drill press | 10 minutes |
| 11. Paint (90%) | | Pain booth | 4 minutes |
| 12. Ship | | Truck | |

*About 5 percent

The drums are brought to the plant in trailers, pulled by CDI's only tractor (267 drums make up a trailer load). The company has two trailers so that two can stay at the plant to be unloaded and loaded while the other is delivering clean drums to customers. CDI tries to move drums in full trailer loads which sometimes requires several stops. However, CDI has learned that orders for fewer than 50 drums are not profitable, so it does not accept them—unless the customer pays the transportation costs. The production process involves the following steps—in the order shown:

1. Drums are received and unloaded over a period of several days. The bungs (stoppers screwed in the tops of the drums) are removed and the drums checked for quality. The drums are stacked, moved to a waiting area, or moved to first flush. About 300 drums are in each of the receiving and shipping areas.
2. Each drum is upended on a pipe and flushed with steam and a chemical.
3. Each drum is righted, and a light is lowered into it so the drum can be inspected for rust. Rusty drums are rolled to a separate room where the rust is removed. They are then returned for further processing.
4. Drums needing straightening are run through the chimer.
5. Drums are placed on a conveyor, and rolled into a vat for cleaning. Six drums can be cleaned at the same time.
6. Drums are mechanically lifted, turned, and rolled into the outside rinser.
7. Drums are pressure tested. Those not meeting the pressure test are removed from the operation for further processing or discarding.

**Exhibit 3** The CleanDrum Flushing and Drying Operation

8. Drums roll down the conveyor where a worker lifts and upends each onto a steam pipe for final flushing.
9. Each drum is righted and placed on the floor where a suction pipe is inserted to dry the inside (see Exhibit 3).
10. Final inspection for rust is made.
11. Drums are rolled to the paint booth for individual spray painting while being turned. A label is affixed to signify that the drum has gone through the entire cleaning process and conforms to established standards.
12. Drums are put into a waiting trailer for delivery or are moved to storage.

Freight can be a prime factor in the cost of some jobs. First, the distance that a tractor-trailer travels is a cost variable. And second, it is critical to keep empty or partial truckloads to a minimum. Therefore, *scheduling is very important.*

Plastic drums follow a separate path which "causes some confusion." After the first flush, they are manually pressure tested, flushed again, and washed on a mobile cradle.

At times, space around the machines is crowded with drums (some stacked) awaiting the next operation. During the summer, the plant is extremely hot even with the draft through the open ends of the building. So, to help reduce the heat, a six-foot-diameter fan is placed in the wall by the vat. In rainy weather, workers in receiving and shipping wear raincoats or other protective wear.

Sue has considerably enlarged the production facilities since starting the company. She now feels that she needs to reduce the handling of the drums and, in the process, increase production capacity. She has found a larger first flusher, a larger chainer, a delivery trailer, and some roller conveyers at used-equipment prices that will give production the efficiency and capacity desired. Also, she needs a cutter-beader to get into the open top drum market. To rearrange the layout and reduce congestion, the plant needs to be enlarged to 70 feet by 100 feet.

Quality inspection of drums was recently combined with receiving drums to better tie the price to their condition. Sue feels that the changes are showing up in profits. They may also result in moving the chaining (rust removal) nearer the receiving area.

Recently, an outside firm made an environmental health and safety audit of the company. This audit included fire protection, human protection and movement, management policies, signs, and guards. Sue also explained that steps were being taken to make corrections that should avoid problems when OSHA inspectors come again. The $400 cost of the study should probably save from $1,500 to $2,000 in OSHA penalties.

## Marketing and Sales Promotion

Since starting the company, Sue has spent part of her time on the road selling CDI's services. Currently, she spends two to three days each week on the road making contact with customers. Although she also makes many phone calls to her clients, Sue believes that these can't replace face-to-face contacts. She plans her itinerary to stay within a 200-mile radius in order to minimize travel time and mileage costs.

The 200-mile radius is considered the extent of CDI's market. This area is served by five companies, and total market demand is estimated to be 13,000 drums a month. Currently, CDI's sales volume places it in the lower middle of the group.

Sue estimates that she has over 100 customers, including about 50 percent of the companies that originally indicated a need for her services. About 75 percent of the sales have been drawn from competitors' customers.

Oil and chemical companies are CDI's major customers. Some call in to alert CDI to their need for its product. For example, one of the major customers calls to say, "We have 100 drums ready to be cleaned, and will have 200 by the end of next week." Several companies order twice a month, while some order once every six months.

Sue has been selling about 3,500 to 4,000 drums a month, but her eye is set on sales of 5,000 per month. She explains that the goal is attainable for several reasons. First, the number of customers has steadily increased since CDI opened. Second, a competing company recently went bankrupt, and Sue picked up most of its customers. Finally, as will soon be discussed, several customers and sales reps from other noncompeting companies have "boosted" CDI to their customers.

Presently, Sue feels that quality and service should be her main selling emphasis. Even though CDI has chosen to compete on these points, however, it must also compete with price cutting by some competitors. Pricing practices vary. Sue has heard reports that one competitor quotes a high price for the purchase of good drums and then finds enough wrong with them to drive the purchase price down so it can sell the processed drums for lower prices.

But Sue estimates the market for CDI drum cleaning is mainly among quality processors. She also believes that the market is restricted by freight costs, is expanding in the local market, and is stable, because several national companies need CDI's services.

Sue says she has seen delivered drums, processed by others, that have been carelessly processed, while others have not been pressure tested. Early on, CDI "almost lost a good customer because a part-time worker left some refuse in some drums."* Sue also cited a customer that was lost because somebody tampered with some of CDI's delivered drums. She hopes to convince potential customers who are currently buying substandard processing that it's in their best interest to obtain quality service.

CDI, which does only limited advertising and sales promotion, distributes magnetic calling cards and is the only company listed under "Barrels & Drums—Equipment & Supplies" in the Yellow Pages of the local telephone directory. Sue does not know of any other publication in which it would be worthwhile to advertise.

Some companies, having received poorly processed used drums, now use only new drums. Sue has approached some of these companies asking for a chance to demonstrate the quality of CDI's delivered drums. Although she hasn't had much success, she says she plans to continue trying this sales pitch. Also, her satisfied customers and others are referring other companies to CDI.

---

*Sue has consistently emphasized to the authors how important the workers' performance is to the company.

## Financial Affairs

During the early years of the company, Sue used her checkbook to do the accounting. When cash was received, she entered it in the checkbook; when she paid a bill, she paid it by check. She used sales and shipping slips to keep track of sales and invoices received. At the end of the year, she took all the slips, invoices, and checks to the firm's accountant and received in return a financial package, plus completed tax forms.

Several years ago, however, a multicolumn income/expense form was introduced. Each column was designed for an item of income or expense and each sheet represented a month of

**Exhibit 4**

CLEANDRUM, INC.
Balance Sheet
December 31, 1995
($000s)

| | 1993 | 1994 | 1995 |
|---|---|---|---|
| **Assets** | | | |
| Current assets: | | | |
| Cash in bank | $ 6.7 | $ -- | $ 4.0 |
| Accounts receivable | 12.8 | 19.8 | 21.4 |
| Inventory | 7.7 | 27.6 | 35.5 |
| Prepaid items | -- | -- | 23.0 |
| Total current assets: | 27.2 | 47.4 | 73.9 |
| Property and equipment | | | |
| Equipment | 156.6 | 178.8 | 203.7 |
| Leasehold improvements | 5.5 | -- | 53.0 |
| Less: accumulated depreciation | -102.2 | -123.0 | -146.1 |
| Net property and equipment | 59.9 | 55.8 | 110.6 |
| **Total assets** | $ 87.1 | $ 103.2 | $ 184.5 |
| **Liabilities and Stockholder Equity** | | | |
| Current liabilities: | | | |
| Accounts payable | $ 38.9 | $ 50.5 | $ 51.0 |
| Current long-term debt | 16.4 | 15.0 | 50.7 |
| Notes payable | 59.0 | 15.3 | 1.6 |
| Accruals | 11.8 | 6.9 | 14.4 |
| Total current liabilities | 126.1 | 87.7 | 117.7 |
| Long-term debt | 96.5 | 78.7 | 128.1 |
| **Total liabilities** | 222.6 | 166.4 | 245.8 |
| Stockholders equity | | | |
| Common stock | 1.0 | 1.0 | 1.0 |
| Added paid-in capital | 16.7 | 108.3 | 108.3 |
| Accumulated deficit | (153.2) | (172.9) | (165.1) |
| Total stockholders' equity | (135.5) | (63.6) | (55.8) |
| Total liabilities and stockholders' equity | $ 87.1 | $ 102.8 | $ 190.0 |

**Exhibit 5**

CLEANDRUM, INC.
Profit and Loss Statements
($000s)

| Item | 1993 | 1994 | 1995 |
|---|---|---|---|
| Sales | $320.4 | $436.2 | $490.1 |
| Cost of sales: | | | |
| Materials | 99.1 | 175.4 | 183.9 |
| Labor | 74.6 | 87.3 | 104.9 |
| Freight | 42.0 | 11.3 | 23.3 |
| Total cost of sales | 215.7 | 274.0 | 312.1 |
| Gross profit | $104.7 | 262.2 | $178.0 |
| Operating, administrative, and selling costs: | | | |
| Depreciation | 16.7 | 24.3 | 23.1 |
| Repair and maintenance | 14.5 | 19.0 | 17.2 |
| Rent | 7.2 | 11.9 | 13.6 |
| Utilities | 18.0 | 19.0 | 24.9 |
| Salary | 20.9 | 25.0 | 25.0 |
| Insurance | 14.5 | 17.0 | 10.7 |
| Office expense | 3.6 | 2.6 | 3.8 |
| General tax, legal, accounting | .5 | 14.2 | 13.6 |
| Selling, travel, auto | 10.4 | 10.3 | 14.6 |
| Telephone | 7.6 | 9.3 | 6.0 |
| Miscellaneous | 0.5 | 0.2 | 0.0 |
| Total operating, administrative, and selling costs | $114.4 | $152.8 | $152.5 |
| Operating profit | (9.7) | 9.4 | 25.5 |
| Income-legal | 10.1 | -- | -- |
| Interest expense | 19.9 | 11.7 | 17.9 |
| Net Income | $ (19.5) | $ (2.3) | $ 7.6 |

activities. The form was summarized each month in order to obtain accounting information for management to use in decision making.

A computer has been installed and accounting programs are used for storage and processing data throughout the company. Costing and pricing have been simplified as well as the printing of statements, such as those shown in Exhibits 4 and 5.

During the early years, when annual sales were below $350,000, CDI incurred losses which accumulated and are now shown as a negative value in the equity section of the balance sheet. This negative value has been of grave concern to Sue and she has discussed CDI's pricing policy many times with the SCORE counsellors. Some counselors have suggested reducing the price to gain sales, while others have suggested raising prices to increase profit margins. Sue says, however, she cannot raise prices because of the competition.

CDI's pricing procedure is basically as follows: Used drums are purchased from various sources for about $4 each, depending on their condition. Those needing straightening and/or rust removal can be purchased at lower prices. After processing, a cleaned and painted drum is sold for about $12 to $13.

Customers' drums are processed and returned to them for about $7 a drum—again depending on the condition before processing. Drums sold for waste and parts storage are sold for about $5 each. Sue feels that CDI's pricing is in line with its competitors'. (One competitor sells drums at a lower price, but he doesn't pressure test them and appears to obtain dirty drums at lower prices than CDI.)

Recently, CDI obtained a contract to clean (only) a new type of drum that Sue feels will be profitable. Also, she sees a new market opening up for drums with removable tops, but this will require an investment in a cutter/beader. A year ago, CDI had a mobile cleaning unit made to service cleaning at drums' source. Sue feels there is a future in this business, but not now. The unit is only used as backup equipment.

While Sue has enlarged the production facilities in the past, she now feels they need to be expanded further—as noted earlier. Her plans would cost about $40,000, including machines and rearrangements. Rent would increase about $500 per month.

Sue has often spoken of CDI's difficulty with its cash flow. She is gathering information to use in a business plan to approach an investor or loan agent. As she has had difficulty in the past, Sue knows that she must present the most favorable impression of the company.

But, Sue is optimistic, as she sees an expanding market, and 1995 showed that the company has a bright future. Also, she has found some sources of money where entrepreneurial women such as she are favored.

# ENDNOTES

## Chapter 1


1. Brent Schlender, "How We Did It," *Fortune,* October 2, 1995, p. 69.
2. Joseph Nebesky, "There's No Business Like Your Own Business," *Perspective on Aging,* July–October 1992, p. 17.
3. Robert Moore, "Mr. Clinton, Please Check the Label," *The Wall Street Journal,* March 22, 1993, p. A14.
4. *USA Today,* October 25, 1985, p. 1A.
5. Steve Bass, "Big Help for Small Business," *PC World,* October 1993, p. 348.
6. "Small Talk," *The Wall Street Journal,* July 6, 1995, p. B2.
7. "Millions of New Jobs to Be Created in '86, Survey Shows," *Mobile* (Alabama) *Register,* March 31, 1986, p. 3A.
8. *Your Business and the SBA* (Washington, DC: U.S. Small Business Administration, September 1990), p. 2.
9. Udayan Gupta, "New Business Incorporations Reached Record in 1994," *The Wall Street Journal,* June 6, 1995, p. B2.
10. "Business Beat: Brighter Days," *Entrepreneur,* July 1995, p. 16.
11. Ibid.
12. "A Surprising Finding on New-Business Mortality Rates," *Business Week,* June 14, 1993, p. 22.
13. "Now Hiring: Small Business; But Labor Costs Stay Subdued," *Business Week,* August 21, 1995, p. 20.
14. R. Wendell Moore, "The Smaller They Are the Better They Grow," *USA Today,* March 20, 1992, p. A13; and Constance J. Pritchard, "Forget the Fortune 500," *The Wall Street Journal,* "Managing Your Career," Fall 1992, p. 12.
15. "Pay Bonus: Small Firms Actually Improve the U.S. Wage Picture," *The Wall Street Journal,* May 4, 1993, p. A1.
16. "Profits Hot, Jobs Not at *Forbes'* 500," *USA Today,* April 11, 1994, p. 2B.
17. Linda Chavez, "Cut the Feds Down to Size," *USA Today,* January 11, 1995, p. 11A.
18. Robert L. Bartley, "On Clinton's Recipe for Growth," *The Wall Street Journal,* July 16, 1992, p. A10.
19. "Odds and Ends," *The Wall Street Journal,* July 17, 1992, p. B1.
20. Stephanie N. Mehta, "Entrepreneurial Spirit Enters High School," *The Wall Street Journal,* November 29, 1994, p. B2.
21. "The American Dream: Your Own Business," *Nation's Business,* November 1988, pp. 10–11.
22. "Building a Better Entrepreneur," *New York Times Magazine,* March 22, 1992, p. 6A.
23. Amy Salzman, "Big Firm, Dead-End Career?" *U.S. News & World Report,* March 27, 1995, p. 62.
24. Suzanne Alexander, "Student Entrepreneurs Find Road to Riches on Campus," *The Wall Street Journal,* June 23, 1989, P. B1.
25. Mehta, "Entrepreneurial Spirit Enters High School."
26. Ibid.
27. Brian O'Reilly, "The New Face of Small Business," *Fortune,* May 2, 1994, pp. 82–88.
28. Stephanie N. Mehta, "Young Entrepreneurs Turn Age to Advantage," *The Wall Street Journal,* September 1, 1995, pp. B1, B2.
29. As told to Dr. M. Jane Byrd by Megan Crump.
30. *ABC Evening News,* November 14, 1989.
31. Susan E. Kuhn, "Retire Today: Find a New Job Tomorrow," *Fortune,* July 24, 1995, p. 104.
32. "Entrepreneurship First Option for Those Over 40," *Working Age* (AARP), July/August 1994, p. 7.
33. Stephanie N. Mehta, "Retirees Starting Business Trip Over Stumbling Blocks," *The Wall Street Journal,* February 14, 1995, p. B1.
34. From *Meeting the Special Problems of Small Businesses* (New York: committee for Economic Development, 1974), p. 14.
35. W. B. Barnes, *First Semi-Annual Report of the Small Business Administration* (Washington, DC: Small Business Administration, January 31, 1954), p. 7.
36. G. Russell Merz, Patricia B. Weber, and Virginia B. Laetz, "Linking Small Business Management with Entrepreneurial Growth," *Journal of Small Business Management,* October 1944, p. 48.
37. Peter Nultz, "Serial Entrepreneur: Tips from a Man Who Started 28 Businesses," *Fortune,* July 10, 1995, p. 182.
38. Communication and correspondence with Digital Network Inc.
39. U.S. Bureau of the Census, *Statistical Abstract of the United States,* 1991, 111th ed. (Washington, DC: U.S. Government Printing Office, 1991), Table 861, p. 525.
40. Cited in *USA Today,* March 13, 1987, p. 13.
41. Bill Saporito, "What Sam Walton Taught America," *Fortune,* May 4, 1992, p. 104.
42. John Hillkirk, "Challenging Status Quo Now in Vogue," *USA Today,* November 9, 1993, pp. 1B, 2B.
43. Sue Shellenbarger, "In Re-Engineering, What Really Matters Are Workers' Lives," *The Wall Street Journal,* March 1, 1995, p. B1.
44. See Warren Cohen, "Exporting Know-How," *U.S. News & World Report,* September 6, 1993, p. 53; and James E. Ellis, "Why Overseas? Because That's Where the Sales Are," *Business Week,* January 10, 1994, pp. 62–63

## Chapter 2


1. "Happiness Is Looking in the Mirror—and Seeing Yourself," *Business Week,* July 12, 1993, p. 22.
2. Kathy Jumper, "Couple Gets Balloon Company Off Ground," *Mobile* (Alabama) *Press,* July 14, 1993, pp. 1-E, 2-E.
3. Tait Trussel, "The Untypical Typical Millionaire," *Nation's Business,* November 1988, p. 62.
4. Nelson A. Aldrich, Jr., "Private Lives: Staubach Co.," *Inc.,* December 1985, pp. 66–68.
5. Kathy Chen, "Rags to Riches Story: How Rebiya Kader Made Her Fortune," *The Wall Street Journal,* September 21, 1994, pp. A-1, A-6.
6. *The State of Small Businesses: A Report to the President* (Washington, DC: Government Printing Office, March 1983), p. 54.
7. Maggie Jackson, "Death's Sting: Families Opt for More Economical Funerals," *Mobile* (Alabama) *Register,* October 8, 1995, p. 54.
8. Hal B. Pickle and Brian S. Rungeling, "Empirical Investigation of Entrepreneurial Goals and Customer Satisfaction," *Journal of Business,* April 1973, pp. 268–73.
9. Stephanie N. Mehta, "Entrepreneurial Spirit Enters High School," *The Wall Street Journal,* November 29, 1994, p. B2.
10. Nancy Madlin, "The Venture Survey: Probing the Entrepreneurial Psyche," *Venture,* May 1985, p. 24.
11. Micheline Maynard, "Executives Claim Niche, Top Jobs," *USA Today,* September 20, 1994, p. 1B.
12. Scott Boeck and Marcy E. Mullins, "How Often Does Your Family Eat Dinner Together?" *USA Today,* October 23, 1995, p. 1D.
13. John H. Johnson with Lerone Bennett, Jr., *Succeeding Against the Odds* (New York: Warner Books, 1989).
14. Lynn Langway, "Like Fathers, Like Daughters," *Newsweek,* January 16, 1984, pp. 78–80.
15. Donald C. Mosley, Paul H. Pietri, and Leon C. Megginson, *Management: Leadership in Action,* 5th ed. (New York: HarperCollins College Publishers, 1996), p. 542.
16. Ibid.
17. Hal Lancaster, "Life Lessons: There May Be a Job That You Were Born to Do," *The Wall Street Journal,* July 11, 1995, p. B1.
18. Based on material provided by Levi Strauss & Co.
19. "Personality Traits Distinguish Employees from Entrepreneurs," *Mobile* (Alabama) *Press Register,* September 27, 1992, p. E-4.
20. Janice Castro, "Big vs. Small," *Time,* September 5, 1988, pp. 48–50.
21. Eric Morganthaler, "Snuggling Business Booms as Babes in Pouches Proliferate," *The Wall Street Journal,* April 23, 1982, pp. 1, 29.
22. Mark Robichaux, "Fledgling Honeybee Learns to Fly with the Big Guys," *The Wall Street Journal,* May 12, 1989, p. D2; and Tom Waters, "The Robot's Reach," *Discover,* October 1990, pp. 68–74.
23. See Mark Robichaux, "Business First, Family Second," *The Wall Street Journal,* May 12, 1989, p. B1.
24. As reported in Carrie Dolan, "Entrepreneurs Often Fail as Managers," *The Wall Street Journal,* May 15, 1989, p. B1.


## Chapter 3


1. James Aley, "Where the Jobs Are," *Fortune,* September 18, 1995, pp. 53–54, 56.
2. Ibid.
3. David Gumpert, "Entrepreneurial Edge: 10 Hot Businesses to Start in the '90s," *Working Woman,* June 1991, pp. 55–56, 96.
4. Rusty Brown, "Women Entrepreneurs Dominate '80s," *Mobile* (Alabama) *Press Register,* January 18, 1986, p. 4-A.
5. Steve Kaufman, "Female Entrepreneurs Still Face Walls," *Mobile* (Alabama) *Register,* May 21, 1995, p. 4-F.
6. Arthur L. Dolinsky, Richard K. Caputo, and Kishore Pasumartz, "Long-Term Entrepreneurship Patterns: A National Study of Black and White Female Entry and Stayer Status Differences," *Journal of Small Business Management* 32 (January 1994), p. 18.
7. "Women Business Owners: 'Breaking the Boundaries,' " *Working Age,* July/August 1995, p. 3.
8. "The Checkoff," *The Wall Street Journal,* October 31, 1995, p. A1.
9. "Entrepreneurs and Ethnicity," *Fortune,* October 3, 1994, p. 29.
10. Maria Mallory, "From the Ground Up," *U.S. News & World Report,* February 19, 1996, p. 69.
11. Susan Rook, "Beyond the Glass Ceiling," Special CNN Report, November 15, 1992.
12. "A Woman's Work," *Fortune,* August 24, 1992, p. 59.
13. Janean Chun, "Hear Them Roar," *Entrepreneur,* June 1995, pp. 10–11.
14. "Small Business: How Women Are Changing the Landscape," *Business Week,* April 18, 1994, p. 107.
15. Barbara Marsh, "States Face Pressures to Rule 'No Room at the Inn,' " *The Wall Street Journal,* November 17, 1994, p. B2.
16. Mark Robichaux, "Business First, Family Second," *The Wall Street Journal,* May 12, 1989, p. B1.
17. "New Task Force to Meet to Help Businesswomen," *The Wall Street Journal,* February 24, 1995, p. B2.
18. Lisa Green, "Businesswoman Overcame the Odds," *USA Today,* June 23, 1995, p. 5B.
19. Carol Hymowitz, "World's Poorest Women Advance by Entrepreneurship," *The Wall Street Journal,* September 5, 1995, p. B1.
20. "She's the Boss," *USA Today,* June 21, 1989, p. 1A.
21. "The Immigrants," *Business Week,* July 13, 1992, pp. 114–21.
22. Andrew S. Grove, "Immigration Pays," *The Wall Street Journal,* January 8, 1996, p. A18.

23. Stephanie N. Mehta, "Big Companies Heighten Their Pitch to Minority Firms," *The Wall Street Journal,* October 23, 1994, p. B2.
24. James Overstreet, "Minority Businesses Riding a Wave of Success," *USA Today,* October 25, 1994, p. 4B.
25. *Fortune,* October 3, 1994, p. 29.
26. Melissa Lee, "Diversity Training Brings Unity to Small Companies," *The Wall Street Journal,* September 2, 1993, p. B2.
27. Randolph E. Schmid, "Black-Owned Firms Show Greatest Rise," *Mobile* (Alabama) *Press Register,* December 12, 1995, p. 7-B.
28. Ibid.
29. "Sales Up for Black-Owned Companies," *Mobile* (Alabama) *Register,* May 12, 1994, p. 9-B.
30. John Emshwiller, "Former TV Actor Stars as Entrepreneur," *The Wall Street Journal,* July 10, 1992, p. B1.
31. Stephanie N. Mehta, "Black Entrepreneurs Benefit," *The Wall Street Journal,* October 19, 1995, pp. B1, B2.
32. Nan Fairley, "Summit to Urge Unity among Black Entrepreneurs," *Mobile* (Alabama) *Register,* October 9, 1994, pp. 1-F, 2-F.
33. Elizabeth Lesley and Maria Mallory, "Inside the Black Business Network," *Business Week,* November 29, 1993, p. 70ff.
34. Kevin Johnson, "McDonald's Recruits Duo to Make Its McCroutons," *USA Today,* January 27, 1989, p. 7.
35. Ani Hadjian, "He Wants You to Eat Fish Tacos," *Fortune,* May 20, 1995, p. 31.
36. As reported in Andrea Stone, "Asian Growth: 105% in 10 Years," *USA Today,* February 27, 1991, p. 11A.
37. Nancy Archuleta, "Stand-In," *Inc.,* February 1995, p. 21.
38. Andrea Gerlin, "Radio Stations Gain by Going after Hispanics," *The Wall Street Journal,* July 14, 1993, p. B1.
39. "US Asian and Pacific Islander Population," *The Christian Science Monitor,* July 27, 1993, p. 10.
40. As reported in Margaret L. Usdansky, "Asian Businesses Big Winners in '80s," *USA Today,* August 2, 1991, p. 1A.
41. Nathan Glazer, "Race, Not Class," *The Wall Street Journal,* April 5, 1995, p. A12.
42. Mortimer B. Zuckerman, "Beyond Proposition 187," *U.S. News & World Report,* December 12, 1994, p. 123.
43. Robert Lewis, "Asian Immigrants Find Large Profits in Small Stores," *Mobile* (Alabama) *Press Register,* March 5, 1989, p. G-1.
44. "Asian Entrepreneurs: Success Isn't Cultural," *The Wall Street Journal,* April 3, 1989, p. B1.
45. Timothy L. O'Brien, "Tribes Use Loans to Small Businesses to Create Jobs," *The Wall Street Journal,* August 27, 1993, p. B2.
46. Ibid.
47. Ibid.
48. Todd Logan, "Trapped," *Inc.,* January 1995, pp. 21–22.

## Chapter 4

1. Correspondence with Charlene Mitchell of Mel Farr Enterprises; and others, including Blair S. Walker, "Group: Ford Unfair to Minority Dealers," *USA Today,* November 23, 1992, p. 1B.
2. Lee Berton and Joann S. Lublin, "Seeking Shelter: Partnership Structure Is Called in Question as Liability Rises," *The Wall Street Journal,* June 10, 1992, pp. A1, A9.
3. Frances A. McMorris and Michael Siconolfi, "Prudential's Limited-Partnership Woes Seem Near End as Legal Pact Advances," *The Wall Street Journal,* February 6, 1995, p. A12.
4. Harry Edelson, "Dispatch from the Boardroom Trenches," *The Wall Street Journal,* February 6, 1995, p. A12.
5. "Corporate Structure: Protecting Subchapter S Status," *Inc.,* January 1992, pp. 107–8.
6. David Warner, "S-Corporation Reform Outlook," *Nation's Business,* September 1995, p. 8.
7. Wayne Wells, "Limited Liability Companies: Something New, Something Different," *Journal of Small Business Management* 32 (January 1994), pp. 78–82.
8. George Livanos, "LLCs: The Entity of the Future," *CIA Journal* 65 (March 1995), pp. 166–67.
9. Barbara L. Bryniarski, "Structuring for Limited Liability," *Nation's Business,* April 1992, pp. 46–48.
10. Adrian Ladbury, "KPMG May Give Up Partnership," *Business Insurance,* July 11, 1994, p. 17.
11. John R. Emshwiller, "SEC Sets Sights on Certain Limited Liability Companies," *The Wall Street Journal,* March 31, 1994, p. B2.
12. Correspondence with Carolyn Ann Sledge, assistant director of marketing for Delta Pride.
13. David R. Evanson, "Found Money," *Entrepreneur,* April 1995, pp. 112–13.
14. Leo Paul Dana, "Small Firms in International Joint Ventures in China: The New Zealand Experience," *Journal of Small Business Management* 32 (April 1994): 88–102.
15. David Knott, "How a Small Producer Survives in Russia, *Oil and Gas Journal,* February 27, 1995, p. 24.

## Chapter 5

1. This section is based on F. J. Roussel and Rose Epplin, *Thinking About Going into Business?* (U. S. Small Business Administration Management Aid No. 2.025). This and other publications are available for a small processing fee.
2. An excellent guide to use is the SBA's *Checklist for Going into Business,* Management Aid No. 2.016. To obtain this aid, contact your nearest SBA office.
3. Keith H. Hammonds, "What B-School Doesn't Teach You about Start-ups," *Business Week,* July 24, 1989, p. 208.

4. *Forbes*, October 20, 1989, p. 208.
5. Adrienne Gusoff, "Invention Makes Abbey Queen of Bacon," *React*, October 16, 1995, p. 5.
6. Bruce Sims, "Phone Call Initiates Idea for Business," *Baldwin* (County, Alabama) *Press Register*, February 27, 1995, p. 3.
7. Hammonds, "What B-School Doesn't Teach You," p. 41.
8. Janean Chun, "Back in the Saddle," *Entrepreneur*, October 1995, p. 110.
9. "Retirees Give Free Business Advice," *Mobile* (Alabama) *Press Register*, June 22, 1994, pp. 1-E, 2-E.
10. Joseph Nebesky, "There's No Business Like Your Own Business," *Perspective on Aging*, July–October 1992, pp. 17–19.
11. Michael Treacy, "Face to Face," *Inc.*, April 1995, pp. 27–28.
12. Otto Friedrich, "Seven Who Succeeded," *Time*, January 7, 1985, pp. 40–44.
13. Guy Kawasaki, "How to Drive Your Competitors Crazy," *The Wall Street Journal*, July 17, 1995, p. A10.
14. "Franchising: The Take-Out Recipe for Success," *Small Business Success* 11 (1989): 28.


## Chapter 6


1. Ming-Jer Chen and Donald C. Hambrick, "Speed, Stealth, and Selective Attack: How Small Firms Differ from Large Firms in Competitive Behavior," *Academy of Management Journal* 38 (June 1995): 453.
2. *The Wall Street Journal*, October 31, 1986, p. 37.
3. Jacqueline L. Babicky, Larry Field, and C. Norman Pricher, "Focus On: Small," *Journal of Accountancy* 177 (May 1994): 41.
4. Gordon W. Couterier and Jack Munyan, "Client/Server Conversion: A Case Study," *Information Strategy: The Executive's Journal* 11 (Winter 1995): 53–57.
5. "An Exterior View May Be What Some Companies Need in Their Strategic Plans," *The Wall Street Journal*, December 14, 1995, p. A1.
6. James T. McKenna, "Majors Retreat Boasts Prospects for Regionals," *Aviation Week & Space Technology*, March 13, 1995, pp. 71–74.
7. Hal Lancaster, "Fear of Flying Solo? Some Takeoff Tips from Two Consultants," *The Wall Street Journal*, February 28, 1995, p. B1.
8. Guy Kawasaki, "How to Drive Your Competitors Crazy," *The Wall Street Journal*, July 17, 1995, p. A10.
9. Theodore B. Kinni, "Process Improvement, Part II," *Industry Week*, February 20, 1995, pp. 45–50.
10. See *Keeping Records in Small Business*, Management Aid No. 1.017, which can be obtained free from the Small Business Administration, P.O. Box 15434, Fort Worth, TX 76119.
11. Lynn Asinof, "Considering Self-Employment? Think about This," *The Wall Street Journal*, October 13, 1995, p. C1.
12. As reported in "Dig Deep to Open Business," *USA Today*, August 26, 1994, p. 1B.
13. Udayan Gupta, "Public Investors Are Keen on Venture-Backed Start-Ups," *The Wall Street Journal*, October 24, 1995, p. B2.
14. David Tortorano, "Small Firms Have Access to Trade Loans," *Mobile* (Alabama) *Register*, October 16, 1994, p. 1-F.


## Chapter 7


1. Arthur G. Sharp, "Enfranchising Europe," *TWA Ambassador*, January 1991, p. 52.
2. U.S. Department of Commerce, *Franchising in the Economy, 1988–1990* (Washington, DC: Government Printing Office), p. 4.
3. Sharp, "Enfranchising Europe."
4. Robert S. Bond and Christopher E. Bond, *Franchising Opportunities, 1991–1992 Edition* (Homewood, IL: Richard D. Irwin, 1992), p. 3.
5. U.S. Department of Commerce, *Franchising in the Economy, 1989–1992*, p. 115.
6. See Earle Eldridge, "New Options Drive Hard Deal for Middle Man," *USA Today*, December 13, 1995, pp. 1B, 2B; and "Revolution in the Showroom," *Business Week*, February 19, 1996, pp. 70–72 for more details.
7. Barbara Marsh, "Franchisees Frolic but Focus on Deals at Annual Meeting," *The Wall Street Journal*, February 9, 1989, p. B2. For other estimates, see Jeffrey A. Tannenbaum, "Dispute Grows over True Rate of Franchisee Failures," *The Wall Street Journal*, July 3, 1992, p. B2.
8. Kevin Maney, "Fast Food's Country Roots," *USA Today*, October 1, 1993, p. 2B.
9. *Franchising Opportunities* (Babylon, NY: Pilot Industries, 1992), p. 76.
10. "So You Want to Make It on Your Own," *Franchising World*, April 1989, pp. 10–15.
11. Nancy Kennedy, "Should You Franchise Your Business?" *Income Opportunities—The No. 1 Source of Affordable Money-Making Ideas*, February 1995, pp. 42–52.
12. See Leon C. Megginson, Charles R. Scott, and William L. Megginson, *Successful Small Business Management*, 6th ed. (Homewood, IL: Richard D. Irwin, 1991), pp. 113–15, for further details.
13. Jeffrey A. Tannenbaum, "Right to Retake Subway Shops Spurs Outcry," *The Wall Street Journal*, February 2, 1995, pp. B1, B2.
14. Jeffrey A. Tannenbaum, "Franchisees Balk at High Prices for Supplies from Franchisers," *The Wall Street Journal*, July 5, 1995, pp. B1, B2.
15. Jeffrey A. Tannenbaum, "To Pacify Irate Franchisees, Franchisers Extend Services," *The Wall Street Journal*, February 24, 1995, pp. B1, B2.
16. Jeffrey A. Tannenbaum, "Once Red-Hot PIP Faces Legal Assault by Franchisees," *The Wall Street Journal*, April 8, 1993, p. B2.

17. Jeffrey A. Tannenbaum, "Re-Emerging Risk? FTC Says Franchisers Fed Clients a Line and Failed to Deliver," *The Wall Street Journal*, May 16, 1994, p. A1.
18. Jeffrey A. Tannenbaum, "Focus on Franchising: A Federal Agency," *The Wall Street Journal*, January 23, 1995, p. B2.
19. Don L. Boroughs, "Serving Up Hot Profits," *U.S. News & World Report*, November 28, 1994, pp. 83–86.
20. "Lube Shops on Corner Stations," *Mobile* (Alabama) *Register*, October 4, 1992, p. 8-E.
21. Audrey Genrich, "Small Businesses Drive Need for Support Services," *Franchising World*, November/December 1994, p. 24.
22. Jeffrey A. Tannenbaum, "Fowler Finds Franchising More Fun Than Retirement," *The Wall Street Journal*, March 23, 1994, p. B2.
23. Jeffrey A. Tannenbaum, "Mergers Between Strong Franchisees Begin to Catch On," *The Wall Street Journal*, May 4, 1995, p. B2.
24. Lynn Beresford, "Seeing Double," *Entrepreneur*, October 1995, pp. 164–67.
25. Jeffrey A. Tannenbaum, "Small Business: Getting Started: Part of the Plan," *The Wall Street Journal*, October 14, 1994, p. B12.
26. Jeffrey A. Tannenbaum, "More Franchisers Try Alternatives to Stand-Alone Sites," *The Wall Street Journal*, November 10, 1994, p. B2.
27. "Flying Arches May Be Next as McDonald's Prepares to Take to the Skies," *The Wall Street Journal*, October 5, 1995, p. A1.
28. Sharp, "Enfranchising Europe," p. 48.
29. Carol Steinberg, "Franchising: A Global Concept," *USA Today*, April 9, 1992, p. 5B.
30. "Bright Spot: Franchising Again Stands Out in the Trade-Balance Picture," *The Wall Street Journal*, November 9, 1995, p. B2.
31. "All the World's a McStage," *Business Week*, May 8, 1995, p. 8.
32. Correspondence with Richard Detwiler, director, public affairs, KFC International.
33. Richard W. Stevenson, "Pepsi to Show Ad in Russian," *New York Times*, January 20, 1989, p. C5.
34. "Non-Kosher McDonald's Causes Jerusalem Stir," *Mobile* (Alabama) *Press Register*, June 10, 1995, p. E-2.
35. "All the World's a McStage."
36. Joyce Barnathan, "The Gloves Are Coming Off in China," *Business Week*, May 15, 1995, p. 61.
37. Jeffrey A. Tannenbaum, "Burger King Franchisees in Europe Are Growing Restive," *The Wall Street Journal*, October 3, 1995, p. B2.
38. Emory Thomas, Jr., "Chick-fil-A to Announce Expansion into Africa," *The Wall Street Journal*, September 27, 1995, p. S2.
39. "South Africa Draws More Franchisers, but Some Remain Skittish," *The Wall Street Journal*, December 8, 1993, p. B2.
40. "Moving South of the Border," *USA Today*, April 9, 1992, p. 7B; and Tannenbaum, "More Franchisers Try Alternatives to Stand-Alone Sites."
41. Sharp, "Enfranchising Europe," p. 52.
42. *Franchising in the Economy, 1989–1992*, p. 19.
43. As reported in Carol Steinberg, "Minority Recruitment Efforts Underway," *USA Today*, June 25, 1992, p. 4B.
44. The actual term used by Walter Mondale in the early 1980s—and a few years later by Secretary of Labor Robert Reich in a lecture at Harvard—was "McDonald's jobs, burger flipper jobs." See Amith Shlaes, "About Those McDonald's Jobs . . . ," *The Wall Street Journal*, August 15, 1995, p. A17, for more details.
45. Ibid.
46. These examples are from the same source.

## Chapter 8

1. "Behind Success: Ordinary Ideas," *USA Today*, May 30, 1989, p. 7B.
2. Oscar Suris, "It's a Bumpy Road, but the Kid Drives Himself, So He'll Go Far," *The Wall Street Journal*, February 1, 1995, p. B1.
3. See "Our Hero Restaurant (B)," in Leon C. Megginson, Charles R. Scott, and William L. Megginson, *Successful Small Business Management*, 6th ed. (Homewood, IL: Richard D. Irwin, 1991), pp. 251–54, for further details.
4. Timothy Aeppel, "From License Plates to Fashion Plates," *The Wall Street Journal*, September 21, 1994, pp. B1, B2.
5. Jay Wasserman, "In the Market for Tips?" *Business Mexico*, September 1994, pp. 14–15.
6. The SBA has several free publications to help you in preparing a plan. For example, SBA Management Aid No. 2.007 is a *Business Plan for Small Manufacturers*.
7. William G. Nickels, James M. McHugh, and Susan M. McHugh, *Understanding Business*, 5th ed. (Burr Ridge, IL: Richard D. Irwin, 1996), p. 189.
8. John G. Burch, *Entrepreneurship* (New York: John Wiley & Sons, 1986), pp. 377–82.
9. David R. Evanson, "Make No Mistake," *Entrepreneur*, September 1995, pp. 50–53.

## Chapter 9

1. Julie Candler, "Leasing's Link to Efficiency," *Nation's Business*, May 1995, pp. 30–34. See also Dean D. Baker, "Lease vs. Buy: Avoid Excess Costs," *Management Accounting*, July 1995, pp. 38–39, for some pitfalls to avoid when leasing.
2. "NBC Nightly News," December 18, 1995.
3. David R. Evanson, "SCORing Points," *Entrepreneur*, June 1995, pp. 38–41. In 1995, only Connecticut, Georgia, Illinois, Maryland, New Jersey, New York, and Washington did not accept SCOR.

4. Udayan Gupta, "Seed Capital for Early-Stage Companies Grows Strongly," *The Wall Street Journal,* August 29, 1995.
5. Kathleen Devlin, "Disbursements Hit 10-Year Low," *Venture Capital Journal,* June 1992, p. 29; and Gregg Wirth, "Industry Resources Edge Down," *Venture Capital Journal,* July 1995, p. 38.
6. Udayan Gupta, "Venture Capitalists' Protégés Fetch Less from IPOs," *The Wall Street Journal,* January 10, 1995, p. B2.
7. Udayan Gupta, "Small Venture-Capital Firms Fill Void Left by Big Ones," *The Wall Street Journal,* July 13, 1995, pp. B1, B2.
8. Correspondence with the Vancouver Stock Exchange. Also see Cynthia E. Griffin, "Northern Exposure," *Entrepreneur,* May 1995, p. 15.
9. Udayan Gupta, "Financing Small Business: A Foundation," *The Wall Street Journal,* March 10, 1995, p. B2.
10. John Freear, Jeffrey E. Sohl, and William E. Welzel, Jr., "Angels and Non-Angels: Are There Differences?" *Journal of Business Venturing* 9 (March 1994): 109–23.
11. Ellie Winninghoff, "The Trouble with Angels," *Working Woman,* March 1992, p. 37.
12. "Pension-Fund Money Goes to Small Business," *The Wall Street Journal,* August 25, 1989, p. B1.
13. Carolyn M. Brown, "Park Your Company Here," *Black Enterprise,* November 1995, pp. 84–90.
14. Correspondence with June Lavelle.
15. Udayan Gupta, "Business Incubators Devise New Ways to Make Ends Meet," *The Wall Street Journal,* June 8, 1995, p. B2.
16. Jill A. Fraser, "How Swap Deals Pay Off," *Inc.,* April 1994, p. 116; Susan Groenwald, "Creative Trends in Trade," *Small Business Reports,* October 1994, pp. 9–13; and Kim Cleland, "Bartering Improves Its Image with Firms," *Advertising Age's Business Marketing,* December 1994, pp. 3, 32.
17. T. Carter Hagaman, "Why Can't Small Business Borrow?" *Managerial Accounting,* March 1995, p. 14.
18. Udayan Gupta, "Seed Capital for Early-Stage Companies Grows Strongly," *The Wall Street Journal,* August 29, 1995, p. B2.
19. Michael Selz and Udayan Gupta, "Lending Woes Stunt Growth of Small Firms," *The Wall Street Journal,* November 16, 1994, p. B1.
20. Ibid.
21. "Small Business Break," *U.S. News & World Report,* February 27, 1995, p. 76; and "A Loan at Last," *Entrepreneur,* June 1995, p. 115. For more information, call the SBA at (800) 827-5722.
22. Except where otherwise noted, this discussion is based on the SBA publications *Lending the SBA Way* and *Your Business & the SBA.* Since Congress periodically passes new legislation that determines the kind of assistance the SBA provides, contact the nearest SBA district office to ascertain what types of assistance are currently available to you.
23. Philip Lader, "To the Rescue," *Entrepreneur,* December 1995, p. 92.
24. Michael Selz, "Venture Capitalists Fear the U.S. May Renege on SBICs," *The Wall Street Journal,* February 3, 1995, p. B2.
25. John Carey, "Teaching Old Crops New Tricks," *Business Week,* June 13, 1994, p. 48.
26. Paul M. Barrett, "SBA Minority Program Is Under Attack in GAO Report," *The Wall Street Journal,* October 6, 1995, p. B2.
27. "Minority Contracts Aid White Areas," Associated Press, *Mobile* (Alabama) *Press Register,* April 11, 1994, p. 5-B.
28. Andrew Tobias, "You Can Still Make a Million Dollars," *Parade Magazine,* October 29, 1995, pp. 14–15.

## Chapter 10

1. "Secrets from the Market Pros," *Small Business Reports,* January 1994, p. 27.
2. Linda Lee Small, "Surviving the Superstore Steamroll," *Working Woman,* July 1994, pp. 62–64.
3. Yumiko Ono, "Going Door to Door with Palazzo Pants," *The Wall Street Journal,* September 8, 1995, p. B1.
4. Bob Levy, "The Prime Offender: Business Itself," *Washington Post,* May 12, 1988, p. D20.
5. Suzanne Alexander, "Tiny Ryka Seeks a Foothold with Sneakers for Women," *The Wall Street Journal,* July 31, 1989, p. B2.
6. Reported in *USA Today,* November 28, 1989, p. 1A.
7. Sara Olkon, "For Deals, Don't Be Shy about Your Age," *The Wall Street Journal,* October 13, 1995, p. B7.
8. Faye Rice, "Making Generational Marketing Come of Age," *Fortune,* June 26, 1995, p. 110.
9. *The Wall Street Journal,* October 14, 1982, p. 1; and "Targeting You by ZIP," *USA Today,* March 16, 1989, p. B1.
10. Joseph Spiers, "Where Americans Are Moving," *Fortune,* August 21, 1995, p. 38.
11. "17,000 Ideas Can't Be All Bad," *USA Today,* December 21, 1992, p. 3B.
12. Tom Shales, "It Came, It Thawed, It Conquered," *Washington Post,* April 16, 1987, pp. C1, C6.
13. Meera Somasundaram, "Red Symbols Tend to Lure Shoppers Like Capes Being Flourished at Bulls," *The Wall Street Journal,* September 18, 1995, p. B10a.
14. Eleena de Lisser, "Pepsi Puts Spotlight on New Packaging," *The Wall Street Journal,* August 11, 1993, p. B1.
15. " 'Just Enough Packaging' and Right-Size Packages Carry Clout," *The Wall Street Journal,* September 7, 1995, p. A1.
16. Seth Lubove, "Salad in a Bag," *Forbes,* October 23, 1995, pp. 201–3.
17. Anne B. Lowery, "The Four Cs of Pricing: A Pricing Primer for Small Business," *TSU Business and Economic Review,* April 1994, p. 10.

18. "ProServ Inc.," *New York Times,* February 21, 1989, p. C8.
19. Cathy Hainer, "Tea Time Is Surviving Nicely," *USA Today,* August 25, 1995, p. 9D.
20. Allanna Sullivan, "Mobil Bets Drivers Pick Cappuccino Over Low Prices," *The Wall Street Journal,* January 30, 1995, pp. B1, B8.
21. Discussion and correspondence with Ms. Brown; and Susan French Cone, "Business Circle: Their Housework Not Just Routine; They Find No Two Days the Same," *Baldwin* (County, Alabama) *Press Register,* July 10, 1989, p. 5.
22. Bruce Horowitz, "Boston Chicken Goes to Market, Beefs Up Menu," *USA Today,* February 17, 1995, p. 10B.

## Chapter 11

1. Lloyd Gite and Harriet C. Johnson, "Pair Cooks Up Success in Potato Chip Business," *USA Today,* June 20, 1986, p. 4B.
2. Kathy Kelly, "Pest Repeller Is QVC's Entrepreneurial Best," *USA Today,* December 18, 1995, p. 3D. Copyright 1995, USA TODAY. Adapted with permission.
3. Letter from Virginia Scoggins to Suzanne Barnhill, May 1987.
4. Correspondence with Professor Russell Eustice, Husson College, Bangor, Maine.
5. William M. Bulkeley, "Finding Targets on CD-ROM Phone Lists," *The Wall Street Journal,* March 22, 1995, p. B1.
6. Walter Kiechell, "How to Manage Sales People," *Fortune,* March 14, 1988, pp. 179–80.
7. Published by Career Press.
8. Distributed by Nightingale-Conant Corporation.
9. Correspondence with Sue Willis of Wendy's International, Inc.; and Guy Boulton, "Wendy's Keeps Eye on Basics," *Mobile* (Alabama) *Register,* December 6, 1992, p. 16-E.
10. Marj Charlier, "Upstart Ski Maker Plows Money into Ads amid Slump," *The Wall Street Journal,* November 25, 1991, p. B2.
11. Peter Pae, "Low-Power TV Expands, Fed by New Programming," *The Wall Street Journal,* May 30, 1989, p. B1.
12. Louis S. Richman, "Pioneers of a New Way to Sell," *Fortune,* October 31, 1994, p. 248.
13. Ibid.
14. Mark Henricks, "Waste Not," *Entrepreneur,* March 1995, p. 62.
15. David D. Jefferson, "Travel Concern Keeps Dreams Alive Despite Recession," *The Wall Street Journal,* April 3, 1992, p. B2.
16. William F. Allman, "Science 1, Advertisers 0," *U.S. News & World Report,* May 1, 1989, p. 60.
17. Thomas Petzinger, Jr., "Druggist's Simple Rx: Speak the Language of Your Customers," *The Wall Street Journal,* June 16, 1995, p. B1.
18. "William Wrigley and Family," *Forbes 400,* October 16, 1995, p. 136.
19. Leon E. Wynter, "Reaching Hispanics Across a Racial and Cultural Divide," *The Wall Street Journal,* February 15, 1995, p. B1.
20. Joanne Lipman, "Nielsen to Track Hispanic TV Ratings," *The Wall Street Journal,* July 24, 1989, p. B4.
21. Alfredo Corchado, "Demand for Hispanic Ads Outstrips Specialists in Field," *The Wall Street Journal,* June 29, 1989, p. B1.

## Chapter 12

1. "Japan Globalizes: A Company Profile—NEC," *Business Week,* July 31, 1995, p. 28.
2. Ken Wells, "Trade Irony: Many African Nations Now View South Africa as an Economic Hope," *The Wall Street Journal,* January 30, 1995, p. A1.
3. Andrew S. Grove, "A High-Tech CEO Updates His Views on Managing and Careers," *Fortune,* September 18, 1995, pp. 229–30.
4. Here are the answers to the questions in Figure 12–1:
   **Made in China**
   - Alarm clocks
   - Sneakers—50 percent of all athletic shoes sold in the United States
   - Cordless telephones—38.8 percent of imports from China
   - Christmas ornaments
   - Aladdin, the action figure

   **Made in the USA**
   - Sheets and blankets—79 percent of cotton sheets sold here
   - Vacuum cleaners—88.5 percent sold in the USA
   - Miracle Bra
   - Office machinery
   - *Aladdin,* the video

   *Source:* Ellen Neuborne, "A 'Made in China' Day in the USA," *USA Today,* February 24, 1995, p. 1A.
5. "VCRs Cause Failure of Firm," *Mobile* (Alabama) *Register,* July 31, 1989, p. 2-A.
6. Robyn Meredith and Tammi Wark, "Does 'Made in USA' Label Fit?" *USA Today,* July 14, 1995, p. 4B.
7. Reported in William J. Holstein and Kevin Kelley, "Little Companies, Big Exports," *Business Week,* April 13, 1992, p. 70.
8. "Terminator Not," *U.S. News & World Report,* July 31, 1995, p. 18.
9. Patrick Oster, Vince Gagetta, and Rob Hoff, "10,000 New EC Rules," *Business Week,* September 7, 1992, pp. 48, 50.
10. Mark Hendricks, "Another Day, Another Dollar," *Entrepreneur,* October 1995, pp. 150, 155.
11. "Protocol Primer," *Entrepreneur,* March 1995, p. 72.
12. AP bulletin, "McDonald's Bags Draw Complaints from Muslims," *Mobile* (Alabama) *Press Register,* June 8, 1995.
13. "The Forbes Four Hundred Over $1,000,000," *Forbes 400,* October 16, 1995, p. 138.

14. Edwardo Lachica, "China Risks Losing Assistance for Electronics Industries," *The Wall Street Journal*, February 17, 1995, p. A5C.
15. Erika Kotite, "The Hot Zones," *Entrepreneur*, May 1995, p. 78.
16. Albert Warson, "Tapping Canadian Markets," *Inc.*, March 1993, pp. 90–91.
17. Holstein and Kelley, "Little Companies, Big Exports."
18. Catherine Funkhouser, "SBA Upgrades Its Financial Assistance for Small Business Exporters," *Business America*, February 1995, pp. 10–15.
19. Its hotline can be reached at 800-872-8723.
20. "Markets You May Have Missed," *Inc.*, November 1985, p. 162.
21. David Tortorano, "Small Firms Have Access to Trade Loans," *Mobile* (Alabama) *Register*, October 16, 1994, p. 1-F. Anyone interested in this program can reach the Ex-Im Bank's Business Development Group at 800-565-EXIM.
22. Funkhouser, "SBA Upgrades Its Financial Assistance," pp. 10–15.
23. "Edsel and Friends: Ten World-Class Flops," *Business Week*, August 16, 1993, p. 80.
24. Magrid Abraham, "Getting the Most out of Advertising and Promotion," *Harvard Business Review* 68 (May/June 1990): 50–52.
25. Jacquelyn Lynn, "Survey Says . . . ," *Entrepreneur*, May 1995, pp. 60, 61.
26. AP bulletin, "Caller I.D. Aids Businesses," *Mobile* (Alabama) *Press Register*, January 30, 1995, p. 7-B.
27. Daniel Machalaba, "Intermodal Shipping Is Brightening Earnings Outlook for Major Railroads," *The Wall Street Journal*, November 29, 1993, p. A5B.

## Chapter 13

1. Barbara Marsh, "Small Firms' Disadvantage in Hiring Likely to Grow," *The Wall Street Journal*, November 27, 1989, p. B1.
2. As reported in *The Aging of the Work Force* (Washington, DC: American Association of Retired Persons, n.d.), p. 7, Figure 1.
3. Michael Selz, "Small-Business Owners Find New Worries," *The Wall Street Journal*, December 6, 1994, p. B2.
4. "The Big Picture: The Worried Rich," *Business Week*, December 5, 1994, p. 8.
5. Mortimer B. Zuckerman, "Editorial: Who Does Feel Your Pain?" *U.S. News & World Report*, January 2, 1995, p. 126.
6. Raju Narisette, "Manufacturers Decry a Shortage of Workers While Rejecting Many," *The Wall Street Journal*, September 8, 1995, pp. A1, A4.
7. "When Temps Become Permanent," *Inc.*, October 1995, p. 112.
8. Udayan Gupta and Jeffrey A. Tannenbaum, "Labor Shortages Force Changes at Small Firms," *The Wall Street Journal*, May 22, 1989, p. 1B.
9. Rael Jean Isaac, "Invite the Guest Workers Back," *The Wall Street Journal*, November 9, 1995, p. A23.
10. Robert Lewis, "Escaping from the Jobless Maze," *AARP Bulletin*, October 1994, p. 2.
11. Carrie Beth Marston, "Temporary Insanity," *Office Systems95*, May 1995, p. 30.
12. Marsh, "Small Firms' Disadvantage," p. B2.
13. James Aley, "The Temp Biz Boom: Why It's Good," *Fortune*, October 16, 1995, pp. 53, 55.
14. "The Boom in the Temporary-Help Business Might Slow, but Not by Much," *The Wall Street Journal*, April 11, 1995, p. A1.
15. Timothy D. Schellhart, "Temporary-Help Rebound May Prove Permanent," *The Wall Street Journal*, July 28, 1992, p. B4.
16. Larry A. DiMatteo and Rene Sacasas, "Employee Leasing: No Panacea," *Business and Economic Review* 41 (July–September 1995): 16–20.
17. Donna Fenn, "Hiring: Employees Take Charge," *Inc.*, October 1995, p. 111.
18. "Taking Advantage," Chicago TV station WGN, February 9, 1984.
19. Marlene Brown, "Checking the Facts on a Résumé," *Personnel Journal* Supplement, January 1993, p. 6.
20. "Basic Skills Testing," *Small Business Reports*, November 1994, p. 63.
21. "When You Are Face to Face," *Personnel* 67 (October 1990): 6.
22. Donna Fenn, "Hiring? Check My References—Please," *Inc.*, April 1995, p. 111.
23. "References Not Always Honest," *USA Today*, June 6, 1994, p. 1B.
24. See Michael A. Verespej, "How Will You Know Whom to Hire? No More Questions about Medical History," *Industry Week*, September 17, 1990, p. 70; and Julia Lawlor, "Disabilities No Longer a Job Barrier," *USA Today*, June 22, 1993, pp. 1A, 1B, for more information about this subject.
25. For an excellent approach to training, see Iris Randall, "10 Ways to Train Your Staff on a Tight Budget," *Black Enterprise*, February 1991, pp. 165–68.
26. Ellen Gragg, "Teach Your Employees Well," *Office Systems94*, September 1994, pp. 68, 70; and Jerry McLain, "Practice Makes Perfect," *Office Systems 95*, April 1995, pp. 74, 75, 77.
27. Amity Shlaes, "About Those McDonald's Jobs . . . ," *The Wall Street Journal*, August 15, 1995, p. A17.
28. Kerry Hannon, "No Bachelor's Degree Needed," *U.S. News & World Report*, November 1, 1993, p. 99.
29. Roberta Maynard, "Helping Employees Hone Their Skills," *Nation's Business*," July 1995, p. 12.
30. See, for example, Lynn Beresford, "McSchool Days," *Entrepreneur*, August 1995, pp. 200–202.
31. "Older Workers Continue Their Battle to Win Respect at Work," *The Wall Street Journal*, November 29, 1994, p. A1.

32. Equal Employment Opportunity Commission, *Guidelines on Discrimination Because of Sex,* 29 C.F.R., Section 1604.11 (July 1, 1992).
33. "English-Only Rules Become a Growing Problem in the Workplace," *the Wall Street Journal,* April 4, 1995, p. A1.
34. Peter Eisler, "Complaints Now Sit for at Least a Year," *USA Today,* August 15, 1995, p. 1A.
35. Amy Dockser, "Wrongful-Firing Case in Montana May Prompt Laws in Other States," *The Wall Street Journal,* July 3, 1989, p. 11.

## Chapter 14

1. Matthew 7:12 (NIV).
2. Douglas McGregor, *The Human Side of Enterprise* (New York: McGraw-Hill, 1960).
3. Joshua Hyatt, "The Odyssey of an Excellent Man," *Inc.,* February 1989, pp. 63–69.
4. "Share Company's Goals with Workers," *Mobile* (Alabama) *Press Register,* April 4, 1993, p. E-1.
5. Roderick Wilkinson, "We Need Leadership, Not Just 'Brains,' " *The Rotarian,* October 1994, p. 4.
6. Jay Stuller, "The Edge of Diversity," *Kiwanis,* November/December 1994, pp. 36–38, 62.
7. For more information on this topic, see Rosemary Stewart, *Managers and Their Jobs* (New York: Macmillan, 1967); and Henry Mintzberg, *The Nature of Managerial Work* (New York: Harper & Row, 1973), p. 38.
8. Andrew Grove, *High Output Management* (New York: Random House, 1983), p. 103.
9. Ralph W. Weber and Gloria E. Perry, *Behavioral Insights for Supervisors* (Englewood Cliffs, NJ: Prentice-Hall, 1975), p. 138.
10. "Lights, Camera, Meeting: Teleconferencing Becomes a Time-Saving Tool," *The Wall Street Journal,* February 21, 1995, p. A1.
11. "These Workers Would Make Cal Proud," *USA Today,* September 1, 1995, p. 2B.
12. "Ping Pong Pangs," *Inc. 500,* 1995, p. 119.
13. *The Wall Street Journal,* February 18, 1992, p. B1.
14. Amy Saltzmann, "One Job, Two Contented Workers," *U.S. News & World Report,* November 14, 1988, pp. 74, 76.
15. Alfie Kahn, "Why Incentive Plans Cannot Work," *Harvard Business Review* 71 (September–October 1993): 55.
16. *U.S. News & World Report,* October 28, 1991, p. 16.
17. Clarence Francis, "Management Methods," speech given in 1952; reprinted in *Management Methods Magazine,* 1952.
18. *The Wall Street Journal,* August 7, 1992, p. A14.
19. See Stephen Barlas, "Bottom Dollar," *Entrepreneur,* June 1995, p. 174, for more details on the minimum wage.
20. Peter Nulty, "Incentive Pay Can Be Crippling," *Fortune,* November 13, 1995, p. 235.
21. E. Vogelly and L. Schaeffer, "Link Employee Pay to Competencies and Objectives," *HRMagazine,* October 1995, p. 75.
22. Donald L. McManis and William G. Dick, "Monetary Incentives in Today's Industrial Setting," *Personnel Journal* 52 (May 1973): 387–89.
23. Frank Buckley and John Meehan, "Keeping Bad Taste in the Family," *Business Quarterly* 59 (Spring 1995): 22–29.
24. Margaret Magnus, "Personnel Policies in Partnership with Profit," *Personnel Journal* 66 (September 1987): 102–9.
25. Robert McGarvey, "Something Extra," *Entrepreneur,* May 1995, pp. 70, 72–73.
26. "Lumped Together," *Business Week,* November 13, 1995, p. 40.
27. As reported in *Business Week,* February 3, 1991, p. 72.
28. See Julia Lawler, "Landmark Act Leaves Some Businesses Fuming," *USA Today,* February 8, 1993, p. 4B, for an excellent analysis of the law.
29. McGarvey, "Something Extra," p. 70.
30. Charles Bartels, "Tuition Assistance Faces Uncertain Future," *Tuscaloosa* (Alabama) *News,* November 5, 1995, p. 1E.
31. Bryna Brennan, "Small Firms Dropping Pension Plans; Laws Too Complex," *Birmingham* (Alabama) *News,* December 17, 1989, p. 2D.
32. Ibid.
33. Since the requirements are complex and change frequently, check with your accountant before setting up an IRA or any other type of retirement plan.
34. See "Retirement," *U.S. News & World Report,* November 18, 1985, p. 55, for a fuller explanation of IRAs and Keogh plans.
35. Dean Witter Trust Company, "Salary Reduction Simplified Employee Pension (SAR-SEP)," *DWT Retirement: Choosing a Retirement Plan for Your Business,* April 1994, p. 4.
36. Carol Lee Morgan, "You *Can* Take It with You," *Parade Magazine,* May 7, 1989, pp. 22–23.
37. Ibid.
38. *Nation's Business,* February 1992, p. 43.
39. "Beyond the Pay Envelope," *Inc.,* December 1991, p. 158.
40. See Jeffrey S. Hornsby, Donald F. Kuratko, and Douglas W. Naffziger, "Flexible Employee Benefit Plans for Small Businesses," *Small Business Forum* 11 (Spring 1993): 35–43, for more information and examples.

## Chapter 15

1. See J. H. Zenger et al., *Leading Teams: Mastering the New Role* (Homewood, IL: Business One Irwin, 1994), for more details.
2. Rabina A. Gangemi, "FMLA? ADA? OSHA? HELP!" *Inc.,* April 1995, p. 112.

3. "Workplace Safety," *USA Today,* January 28, 1994, p. 1B; and Bob Port and John Solomon, "OSHA Records Show Many Death Sites Not Checked," *Mobile* (Alabama) *Press Register,* September 5, 1995, p. 7-B.
4. "Body Parts Hurt at Work," *USA Today,* January 16, 1995, p. 1A.
5. "OSHA Crackdown: Agency Focuses More on Flagrant Workplace Hazards," *The Wall Street Journal,* October 31, 1995, p. A1.
6. "Workplace Safety," p. 1B.
7. Port and Solomon, "OSHA Records Show Many Death Sites Not Checked."
8. Barbara Marsh, "Workers at Risk: Chance of Getting Hurt Is Generally Far Higher at Smaller Companies," *The Wall Street Journal,* February 3, 1994, p. A1.
9. U.S. Bureau of the Census, *Statistical Abstract of the United States,* 1994, 114th ed. (Washington, DC: Government Printing Office, 1994), p. 437.
10. Ibid., Tables 679 and 680.
11. Michele Galen et al., "Repetitive Stress: The Pain Has Just Begun," *Business Week,* July 13, 1992, p. 142. OSHA is preparing ergonomics standards, but they won't be ready for years. These standards would require employers to provide appropriate furniture and equipment (such as chairs and keyboards) to help prevent or relieve problems such as RSI.
12. Bob Bettendorf, "Health and Safety in the Office," *Office Systems94,* June 1994, p. 11.
13. Ibid., p. 13.
14. "Sore Workers," *U.S. News & World Report,* April 24, 1995, p. 70.
15. See Leon C. Megginson, Geralyn M. Franklin, and M. Jane Byrd, *Human Resource Management* (Houston: Dame Publications, 1995), p. 346, for more details.
16. Stephen Barlas, "Safety Last?" *Entrepreneur,* October 1995, p. 100.
17. Sanford L. Jacobs, "Small Business Slowly Wakes to OSHA Hazard Rule," *The Wall Street Journal,* November 22, 1988, p. B1.
18. Melissa Campanelli, "Getting Good Advice," *Sales & Marketing Management,* March 1995, p. 42.
19. James Aley, "Where the Laid-Off Workers Go," *Fortune,* October 30, 1995, pp. 45–47.
20. Richard G. Ensman, Jr., "Stress Test," *Office Systems95,* August 1995, p. 46.
21. Robert McGarvey, "On the Edge," *Entrepreneur,* August 1995, pp. 76–79.
22. Megginson, Franklin, and Byrd, *Human Resource Management,* p. 344.
23. Stuart Elliott, "Workers' Woes Give Firms Financial Fits," *USA Today,* June 13, 1989, p. 1B.
24. As reported in *USA Today,* December 7, 1989, p. 1A.
25. R. Higby, "Helping Hand to Employees," *Management Today,* June 1995, p. 16.
26. "NBC Nightly News," November 20, 1995; Susan Dentzer, "Anti-Union, but Not Anti-Unity," *U.S. News & World Report,* July 17, 1995, p. 47; and "Uncle Sam Gompers" *The Wall Street Journal,* October 25, 1995, p. A14.
27. "Uncle Sam Gompers."
28. Albert R. Karr, "Small Business Scores Big in Congressional Lobbying," *The Wall Street Journal,* October 3, 1988, pp. B1, B2.
29. Jeffrey A. Tannenbaum, "Consultants, Small Business Come to Need One Another," *The Wall Street Journal,* September 28, 1989, p. B1.


## Chapter 16


1. See Mark Bautz, "The 20 Top Spots for Entrepreneurs," *Money,* November 1994, pp. 126–34, for other factors to consider.
2. Jeffrey Theodore, "They Groom Dogs 'On the Spot,' " *Baldwin* (County, Alabama) *Press Register,* June 12, 1989, p. 4.
3. See Karen Levine, "Making Money from Home," *Parent's,* November 1991, pp. 89–92, for more details.
4. Paul W. Cockerham, "The Little Fish Survive," *Stores,* November 1994, pp. 64–65.
5. Justin Bicknell, "Where to Set Your Sites: On Location with Firms," *Business Mexico,* September 1994, pp. 6–7.
6. " 'Afrocentric Mind-Set' Part of Business," *Mobile* (Alabama) *Register,* July 31, 1994, p. 4-F.
7. Barbara Marsh, "Kiosks and Carts Can Often Serve as Mall Magnets," *The Wall Street Journal,* November 23, 1992, p. B1.
8. June Langhoff, "Telecommute America: Get Ready for Business in the Fast Lane," Special Advertising Section, *Fortune,* October 30, 1995, p. 229.
9. Reported in *USA Today,* August 12, 1992, p. 1A.
10. "Unfinished Homework," *The Wall Street Journal,* January 6, 1993, p. A1.
11. "Who Works from Home," *USA Today,* September 21, 1994, p. 1B.
12. "Employees Who Prefer to Work at Home," *Personnel Journal* 71 (November 1992): 27.
13. "Unfinished Homework," p. A1.
14. "Employees Who Prefer to Work at Home," p. 27.
15. Udayan Gupta, "Home-Based Entrepreneurs Expand Computer Use Sharply, Study Shows," *The Wall Street Journal,* October 13, 1995, p. B2.
16. Consult any basic industrial engineering or production/operations management text for a more detailed discussion of this process. There will probably be some sample forms you can use.


## Chapter 17


1. Laura M. Litvan, "Selling to Uncle Sam: New Easier Rules," *Nation's Business,* March 1995, pp. 46–48.
2. Leon C. Megginson, Donald C. Mosley, and Paul H. Pietri, Jr., *Management: Concepts and Applications,* 4th ed. (New York: HarperCollins, 1992), p. 662.

3. Myron Magnet, "The New Golden Rule of Business," *Fortune,* February 21, 1994, pp. 60–61.
4. "Minority Supplier Development, Part 3: Why Aren't Minority Supplier Programs More Successful?" *Purchasing,* February 16, 1995, pp. 97–100.
5. Udayan Gupta, "Firms Owned by Women, Minorities Fear AT&T Split," *The Wall Street Journal,* October 12, 1995, p. B2.
6. David Friedman, "The Enemy Within," *Inc.,* October 1995, pp. 47–52.
7. Micheline Maynard, "5-Cent Part Defect Forces LH Recall," *USA Today,* September 4, 1992, p. 1B.
8. Donna Fenn, "Growing by Design," *Inc.,* August 1985, p. 86.
9. "Consultants: For a Complex Purchase, an Outside Expert May Be Just What You Need," *Inc.,* October 1991, pp. OG 65–OG 66.
10. Dale D. Buss, "Supply-Side Economics," *Income Opportunities,* January 1995, pp. 18–24.
11. Conversation with Alan Lowe, Department of Product Planning and Development, Sharp Corporation.
12. Gary McWilliams, "Mom and Pop Go High Tech," *Business Week,* November 21, 1994, p. 82.
13. Ibid.
14. David E. Gumpert, "Lighten Load, Trim Sails to Ride Out the Storm," *USA Today,* May 8, 1989, p. 10E.
15. See any current marketing or production management text for formulas you can use to compute this quantity.
16. Kathy Jumper, "Menefee Wants His Clients to Be Happy, Look Good," *Mobile* (Alabama) *Register,* February 20, 1989, p. 1-B.
17. Ken Cross, "A Chat with Charles Morgan," *Fortune,* October 2, 1995, p. 27.
18. Loretta Owens and Mark Henricks, "Quality Time," *Entrepreneur,* October 1995, pp. 156, 158–62.

## Chapter 18

1. Mary Rowland, "Why Small Businesses Are Failing," *The New York Times,* August 11, 1991, sec. 3, p. 16.
2. Howard Rudnitsky, "The King of Self-Storage," *Forbes,* October 23, 1995, pp. 126–27.
3. Gus Gordon, *Understanding Financial Statements* (Cincinnati: South-Western, 1992).
4. Jeffrey M. Lademman, "Earnings, Shmernings—Look at the Cash," *Business Week,* July 24, 1989, pp. 56–57.
5. Judith Valente and Christina Duff, "Demise of the Catalog Hurts Small Businesses That Counted on Sears," *The Wall Street Journal,* March 2, 1993, p. A1.
6. Sanford L. Jacobs, "Watch the Numbers to Learn If the Business Is Doing Well," *The Wall Street Journal,* August 26, 1985, p. 19.
7. Roger Ricklefs and Udayan Gupta, "Traumas of a New Entrepreneur," *The Wall Street Journal,* May 10, 1989, p. B1.
8. Bob Weinstein, "Balancing Act," *Entrepreneur,* March 1995, pp. 56–61.
9. Roberta Maynard, "Smart Ways to Manage Cash," *Nation's Business,* August 1992, pp. 43–44.
10. David M. Gumpert, "Don't Let Optimism Block Out Trouble Signposts," *USA Today,* May 8, 1989, p. 10E.
11. "Strategies That Pay Off," *Inc.,* March 1991, p. 74.
12. M. K. Kolay, "Managing Working Capital Crises: A System Dynamics Approach," *Management Decisions* 29 (September 1991): 46–52.
13. Jill A. Fraser, "On Target," *Inc.,* April 1991, pp. 113–14.
14. Julie Schmit, "High Charges Stunt Growth of Cellular Phones," *USA Today,* September 16, 1995, p. B1.
15. Phillip Piña, "Organic Can Mean Profits for Farmers," *USA Today,* September 19, 1995, p. B1.
16. Yasuhiro Monden and John Lee, "How a Japanese Auto Maker Reduces Cost," *Management Accounting,* August 1993, pp. 22–26.
17. See Michelle L. Singletary, "Trimming the Fat," *Black Enterprise,* June 1991, pp. 246–49, for some helpful suggestions as to how to do this.

## Chapter 19

1. See "The Five Cardinal Rules of Financial Control," *Inc.,* May 1992, p. 156, for a different set of characteristics.
2. Bob Weinstein, "Let's Get Fiscal," *Entrepreneur,* June 1995, p. 68.
3. Ibid.
4. See Alan Wilson, "Effective Cash and Profit Forecasting," *The Accountant's Magazine,* August 1990, pp. 45–47, for some techniques you can use.
5. Teri Lammers, "The Weekly Cash-Flow Planner," *Inc.,* June 1992, pp. 99–102.
6. See Ripley Hotch, "Not Just the Numbers," *Nation's Business,* January 1992, pp. 42–44; and William F. Zachmann, "Beware the Shrink-Wrap Fallacy," *PC Magazine,* September 15, 1992, p. 105, for some of these.
7. "Financial Tactics: The Check Is in the Mail," *Inc.,* June 1985, p. 123.
8. For some suggestions on how you can best use auditors, see John E. McEldowney, Thomas L. Barton, and Edward J. Todd, "The Audit of a Small Business: War Stories and Dreams," *The CPA Journal,* November 1990, pp. 32–36.
9. G. Paschal Zachary, "CDs to Store Data Are Music to Auditors' Ears," *The Wall Street Journal,* August 4, 1989, p. B1.
10. Stephanie Mehta, "Pay Increases Get Bigger for CEOs of Smaller Firms," *The Wall Street Journal,* August 25, 1995, p. B2.
11. Dean Planeaux, "Factoring Guarantees Cash Flow for Diaper Startup," *Corporate Cashflow Magazine,* August 1991, p. 42.
12. "Challenges and Opportunities in the Greying '90s," *Industry Surveys,* April 6, 1995, p. 51.

13. "Modest Growth in Consumer Spending in 1995," *Industry Surveys,* April 6, 1995, p. 15.

## Chapter 20

1. U.S. Department of the Treasury, Internal Revenue Service, *Tax Guide for Small Business,* Publication 334 (Washington, DC: Government Printing Office, 1992).
2. See U.S. Department of the Treasury, Internal Revenue Service, *Tax Information on S. Corporations,* Publication 589 (Washington, DC: Government Printing Office, 1991), for more details.
3. Gordon Alexander and William F. Sharpe, *Fundamentals of Investments* (Englewood Cliffs, NJ: Prentice-Hall, 1987), pp. 72–73.
4. John R. Emshwiller, "More Small Firms Complain about Tax-Exempt Rivals," *The Wall Street Journal,* August 8, 1995, p. B1.
5. Eugene Willis et al., *West's Federal Taxation: Comprehensive Volume, 1993 Edition* (St. Paul, MN: West, 1992), p. A10.
6. Conversation with Rich Gollner on December 12, 1995.
7. U.S. Department of the Treasury, Internal Revenue Service, "Schedule C: Profit or Loss from Business, 1995, Form 1040," *Forms and Instructions,* p. 3C.
8. See U.S. Department of the Treasury, Internal Revenue Service, *1992 Forms and Instructions, 1040* (Washington, DC: Government Printing Office, 1992).
9. Willis, *West's Federal Taxation,* pp. 9–26.
10. For more information, see U.S. Department of the Treasury, Internal Revenue Service, *1991 Federal Employment Tax Forms,* Publication 393 (Rancho Cordova, CA: IRS, 1991).
11. Sandra Salmans, "Cutting the Deal," *Venture,* January 19, 1988, pp. 32, 34.
12. Hoffman, Raabe, Smith, and Maloney, *West's Federal Taxation: Corporations, Partnerships, Estates & Trusts, 1996 Edition* (St. Paul, MN: West, 1995) pp. 17–9, 17–17.
13. Louis Austin, Vickie Schumaker, and Jim Schumacher, "Living Trusts Replace Wills as Estate Planning Tools," *Small Business Reports,* March 1989, p. 93.
14. Diane Weber, "A Living Trust Can be Great If You Dodge These Pitfalls," *Medical Economics,* August 20, 1992, pp. 90–95.

## Chapter 21

1. G. Pascal Zachary, "Restaurant Computers Speed Up Soup to Nuts," *The Wall Street Journal,* October 25, 1995, p. B1.
2. David H. Friedman, "Plenty of Challenges, No Rules," *Inc. Technology,* Summer 1995, p. 9.
3. "Computer Power," *U.S. News & World Report,* December 26, 1994, p. 108.
4. See M. S. Mossberg, "Computer Notebooks Get Smaller, Lighter, and Costlier," *The Wall Street Journal,* February 2, 1995, p. B1, for further details.
5. Tom Richman, "Break It to Me Gently," *Inc.,* July 1989, pp. 108–10.
6. Jonathan Newcomb, "Stealing on the 'Net," *USA Today,* December 20, 1995, p. 11A.
7. James Kim, "Netscape Earnings Beat Expectations," *USA Today,* February 1, 1996, p. 1B.
8. Jared Taylor, "Keeping Up with the Computers," *The Wall Street Journal,* Special Report, May 20, 1985, p. 84C.
9. Stephanie N. Mehta, "Centers Spring Up to Help Firms Profit from Internet," *The Wall Street Journal,* August 1, 1995, p. B2.
10. Tim Carvell, "Mainframe Time Bomb: 01-01-00," *Fortune,* March 6, p. 24.
11. "Mom and Pop, Unplugged," *The Wall Street Journal,* April 13, 1995, p. A1.
12. Stephanie Mehta, "Older Business Owners Ponder the New Technology," *The Wall Street Journal,* May 27, 1994, p. B2.
13. Ibid.

## Chapter 22

1. U.S. Bureau of the Census, *Statistical Abstract of the United States, 1994* (114th ed.), (Washington, DC: Government Printing Office, 1994), pp. 254, 415; and Margaret Isa, "Pet Practice's Coming IPO May Not Have Much Bite," *The Wall Street Journal,* July 31, 1995, p. C1.
2. "Citibank's Test of Paying to See Tellers Doesn't Pay," *The Wall Street Journal,* May 26, 1983, p. 6.
3. Adapted from Shelly Reese and Ellen Neuborne, "Malls Sell Shoppers on Security," *USA Today,* December 20, 1994, p. 2B.
4. "Making Insurance Cost Shifting Less Painful," *Inc.,* March 1992, p. 104.
5. David Scott, "How Much Risk Can Your Company Stand?" *Risk Management,* June 1991, pp. 85–88.
6. Rob Wells, "Trade Center Firms Struggle to Resume Business Activity," AP bulletin to *Mobile* (Alabama) *Register,* March 2, 1993, p. 6-A.
7. Linda Chavez, "Suits Are Big Problem," *USA Today,* September 10, 1992, p. 14A.
8. Sean F. Mooney, "Hunter Off the Mark on Product Liability," *National Underwriter,* March 27, 1995, pp. 25–26.
9. Joseph McCafferty, "Reform and Insurance Rates," *CFO: The Magazine for Senior Financial Managers,* April 1995, p. 72.
10. "Hooking a Tort," *The Wall Street Journal,* July 20, 1995, p. A12; and "Only in America," *Fortune,* September 4, 1995, p. 127.
11. Roger Thompson, "Workers' Comp Costs: Out of Control," *Nation's Business,* July 1992, pp. 22–30.
12. "Play It Safe," *Entrepreneur,* June 1995, pp. 58–59.
13. Various sources, but especially Roger Thompson, "How to Buy Health Insurance," *Nation's Business,* October 1992, pp. 16–22.

14. Stephanie N. Mehta, "Small Businesses Follow Big Companies on Health Care," *The Wall Street Journal,* August 26, 1994, p. B2.
15. Udayan Gupta, "Enterprise," *The Wall Street Journal,* April 21, 1992, p. B2.
16. Jane Easter Bahls, "Inside Jobs," *Entrepreneur,* June 1995, pp. 72–75.
17. Janean Huber, "Never Fear," *Entrepreneur,* May 1995, p. 14.
18. "To Stop a Thief," *U.S. News & World Report,* May 1, 1989, p. 76.
19. Conversation with Frank Luciano, December 12, 1995.
20. John R. Emshwiller, "Employers Lose Billions of Dollars to Employee Theft," *The Wall Street Journal,* October 5, 1992, p. B2.
21. Haidee Allerton, "Working Life Rock Bottom," *Training and Development,* September 1993, p. 87.
22. *Security Management* magazine, as reported in *The Wall Street Journal,* November 11, 1986, p. 39.
23. Allerton, "Working Life Rock Bottom."
24. Del Jones, "On-line Surfing Costs Firms Time and Money," *USA Today,* December 8, 1995, pp. A1, A2.
25. Ibid.
26. David Lynch, "Entrepreneurs Lose in Get-Rich Schemes," *USA Today,* July 19, 1995, p. 1B.

## Chapter 23

1. For some selected sections from the UCC, see Douglas Whitman et al., *Law and Business* (New York: Random House, 1987), pp. 781–855.
2. "Selling Faulty Pacemakers Costs Firm Plenty," *Mobile* (Alabama) *Register,* March 29, 1989, p. 2-A.
3. For more details on how to get a patent, call the U.S. Patent Office at (703) 557-3158. To register a trademark, write the U.S. Trademark Association at 6 East 45th Street, New York, NY 10017.
4. Neil Gross, "New Patent Office Pending," *Business Week,* October 23, 1995, p. 130.
5. "FBI: Salesman Stole Clients from Competitor's Voice Mail," *Mobile* (Alabama) *Register,* February 10, 1996, p. 8-A.
6. Michael Selz, "Study Suggests SBA Loan Program Chiefly Aids Nonminority Companies," *The Wall Street Journal,* August 8, 1995, p. B2.
7. Michael Selz, "Small Business Agency Is Likely to Face Severe Budget Cutbacks in Congress," *The Wall Street Journal,* February 7, 1995, p. B2.
8. Brent Bowers, "The Doozies: Seven Scary Tales of Wild Bureaucracy," *The Wall Street Journal,* June 19, 1992, p. B2.
9. U.S. Department of Commerce, *Survey of Current Business* (Washington, DC: Government Printing Office, August 1983), p. 24.
10. Jeffrey A. Tannenbaum, "Government Red Tape Puts Entrepreneurs in the Black," *The Wall Street Journal,* June 12, 1992, p. B2.
11. Mike Royko, "U.S. Trying to Pluck a Chicken Company," *Mobile* (Alabama) *Press Register,* June 23, 1994, p. 13-A.
12. James Bovard, "The Latest EEOC Quota Madness," *The Wall Street Journal,* April 27, 1995, p. A14.
13. Jack Faris, "Give Small Biz a Break," *USA Today,* June 13, 1995, p. 11A.
14. Tony Snow, "Curtain Finally May Ring Down on Regulatory Follies," *USA Today,* December 19, 1994, p. 11A.
15. Ibid.
16. Laura M. Litvan, "A Low-Stress OSHA Review," *Nation's Business,* January 1995, p. 37.
17. From *The Wall Street Journal,* as reported in "Couple Forms Letter-Writing Business," *Mobile* (Alabama) *Press Register,* February 19, 1995, p. 4-F.
18. Jeanne Saddler, "Small Business Owners Increase Their Political Activity," *The Wall Street Journal,* April 2, 1992, p. B2.
19. Michael Selz, "Dozens of Entrepreneurs Campaign for Seats in Congress," *The Wall Street Journal,* January 23, 1996, p. B2.
20. William M. Bulkeley, "If Someone Breeds a Purple Cow, They'll Have a Crazy Surf 'n' Turf," *The Wall Street Journal,* March 15, 1993, p. B1.
21. Thomas Petzinger, Jr., "The Front Lines: He Ran Up Against Latest Business Foe: Private Regulations," *The Wall Street Journal,* September 22, 1995, p. B1.
22. *How to Choose and Use a Lawyer* (Chicago: American Bar Association, 1990). For information, contact the ABA at 750 N. Lake Shore Drive, Chicago, IL 60611.
23. Jeffrey A. Tannenbaum, "Small-Business Owners Must Pick a Lawyer Judiciously," *The Wall Street Journal,* February 15, 1989, p. B2.
24. "Good for Nothing," *Entrepreneur,* June 1995, p. 16.
25. Gary Hector, "A New Reason You Can't Get a Loan," *Fortune,* September 21, 1992, pp. 107–12.
26. Ibid.
27. The Aluminum Association, as reported in "Recycling: Earth Day Legacy," *USA Today,* April 21, 1995, p. 1B.
28. As reported in "Soft Drink Turnaround," *USA Today,* August 23, 1995, p. 1A.
29. From various sources, including a conversation with a Chick-fil-A manager and "A Helping Hand," *Sports Spectrum,* January 1994, p. 27.
30. "Good Deed of the Week," *The Wall Street Journal,* May 5, 1995, p. A1.
31. Donald D. Jackson, "It's Wake-Up Time for Main Street When Wal-Mart Comes to Town," *Smithsonian,* October 1992, pp. 36–42, 46–47.
32. The Annenberg/CPB Project has an audio and video series entitled "Ethics in Business." A preview can be arranged by writing The Annenberg/CPB Project, c/o Intellimation, P.O. Box 4069, Santa Barbara, CA 93140, or calling 1-800-LEARNER.
33. Don L. Boroughs, "The Bottom Line on Ethics," *U.S. News & World Report,* March 20, 1995, pp. 61–66.

34. Kenneth Labich, "The New Crisis in Business Ethics," *Fortune*, April 20, 1992, p. 172.
35. W. Michael Hoffman and Edward S. Petry, Jr., "Abusing Business Ethics," *Phi Kappa Journal*, Winter 1992, pp. 10–13.
36. Thomas M. Goodsite, "The 'Golden-Rule' Rotarian," *The Rotarian*, October 1994, pp. 38–39.


## Chapter 24


1. Hank Gilman, "The Last Generation," *The Wall Street Journal*, May 20, 1985, p. 29C; and Terence Pare, "Passing On the Family Business," *Fortune*, May 7, 1990, pp. 81–82.
2. Shu Shu Costa, "100 Years and Counting," *Small Business Reports*, September 1994, pp. 24–32.
3. Ibid.
4. Wendy C. Handler, "Key Interpersonal Relationships of Next-Generation Family Members in Family Firms," *Journal of Small Business Management* 29 (July 1991): 21.
5. Amy F. Bischoff, "Arthur Andersen Survey—Latest Insights from Family Business," *Succeeding Generations* 1 (1995): 4.
6. "The New Business: Smith & Parents," *The Wall Street Journal*, December 8, 1988, p. B1.
7. Randall Lane, "Let Asplundh Do It," *Forbes 400*, October 16, 1995, pp. 56–64.
8. Patricia Schiff Estess, "What's in a Name?" *Entrepreneur*, April 1995, p. 80.
9. David L. Epstein, "Prepare Your Heir," *Restaurant Business*, January 20, 1988, p. 70.
10. "So You're Going to Take Over the Family Business," *Agency Sales Magazine*, July 1988, p. 34.
11. John R. Emshwiller, "Handing Down the Business," *The Wall Street Journal*, May 19, 1989, p. B1.
12. John Ward, as reported in Buck Brown, "Succession Strategies for Family Firms," *The Wall Street Journal*, August 4, 1988, p. 23.
13. Sharon Donovan, "Boss's Daughter, Son Get Down to Business," *USA Today*, May 8, 1989, p. 10E.
14. Terzah, Ewing, "Highly Effective Management Team," *Forbes*, October 23, 1995, pp. 312–14.
15. "Entrepreneurs Neglect One Type of Planning," *The Wall Street Journal*, April 8, 1992, p. B1.
16. Michael Selz, "More Family-Owned Firms Make Plans for Succession by the Next Generation," *The Wall Street Journal*, September 8, 1995, p. B2.
17. "Planning Ahead Can Ease Succession," *The Wall Street Journal*, May 19, 1989, p. B1.
18. Patricia Schiff Estess, "Good Buy?" *Entrepreneur*, May 1995, pp. 74, 76.
19. Michael Selz, "Mexico's Appeal to Small Businesses Continues to Grow," *The Wall Street Journal*, October 4, 1994, p. B2.
20. Jean K. Mason, "Selling Father's Painful Legacy," *Nation's Business*, September 1988, p. 30.
21. Harriet C. Johnson, "Ready to Sell? Helpful Tips from Experts," *USA Today*, May 9, 1988, p. 11E. See also Paul Sperry and Beatrice Mitchell, *The Complete Guide to Selling Your Business* (Dover, NH: Upstart, 1992), for a comprehensive step-by-step guide through the process of selling your firm, from deciding to sell through negotiating the final terms.
22. Richard K. Berkowitz and Joseph A. Blanco, "Putting a Price Tag on Your Company," *Nation's Business*, January 1992, pp. 29–31.
23. Anne Field, "Enrich Your Own Retirement," *Money*, March 1995, pp. 90–95.
24. Michael Selz, "More Owners of Small Businesses Face Unexpectedly High Estate-Tax Bills," *The Wall Street Journal*, September 19, 1995, p. B2.
25. David Roehr, "Keep It Flowing," *Small Business Reports*, February 1994, pp. 49–53.
26. See Dianne S. Cauble, "Making Partners of Your Heirs," *Small Business Reports*, October 1994, pp. 54–57; and Mary Rowland, "Keeping It in the Family," *Nation's Business*, January 1995, pp. 63–64, for further details.
27. See Rhonda Reynolds, "Protecting Your Own Business," *Black Enterprise*, January 1995, p. 44, for more details.

# INDEX